OXFORD PAPERBACK REFERENCE

The Oxford Dictionary of

Literary Quotations

Peter Kemp has long been involved with the literary world as an academic, critic, and journalist. He is Fiction Editor of the *Sunday Times* and a Visiting Fellow of Kellogg College, Oxford. His previous publications include *Muriel Spark* (1974) and *H. G. Wells and the Culminating Ape* (1982, revised 1996). He reviews and broadcasts widely, and is a regular contributor to BBC Radio 4's *Front Row* and BBC Radio 3's *Night Waves*. He was a Booker Prize judge in 1995.

The Oxford Dictionary of

Literary Quotations

Edited by

PETER KEMP

Oxford New York

OXFORD UNIVERSITY PRESS

1999

OXFORD
UNIVERSITY PRESS

Oxford University Press, Great Clarendon Street, Oxford OX2 6DP

Oxford New York
Athens Auckland Bangkok Bogota Bombay
Buenos Aires Calcutta Cape Town Dar es Salaam
Delhi Florence Hong Kong Istanbul Karachi
Kuala Lumpur Madras Madrid Melbourne
Mexico City Nairobi Paris Singapore
Taipei Tokyo Toronto Warsaw

and associated companies in
Berlin Ibadan

Oxford is a trade mark of Oxford University Press

Published in the United States by
Oxford University Press Inc., New York

First published by Oxford University Press 1997
First issued as an Oxford University Press paperback 1999

British Library Cataloguing in Publication Data
Data available

Library of Congress Cataloging in Publication Data
Data available

ISBN 0 19-280090 6

10 9 8 7 6 5 4 3 2 1

Designed by Jane Stevenson

Typeset in Monotype Photina and Meta
by Interactive Sciences Ltd, Gloucester

Printed in Great Britain by
Cox & Wyman Ltd,
Reading, Berkshire

Contents

Project Team

Managing Editor	Elizabeth Knowles
Index Editors	Susan Ratcliffe Christina Malkowska Zaba
Library Research	Ralph Bates Marie G. Diaz
Reading Programme	Charlotte Graves Taylor Jean Harker Helen McCurdy Verity Mason Penelope Newsom
Proof-reading	Fabia Claris Penny Trumble

We are grateful to Gerald Blick for additional research.

Introduction

Fossils, mantras, jokes, boasts, grumbles, aphorisms, outbursts, insights, insults, epigrams, epitaphs: literary quotations can be many things. What they have in common is a shared concern with a phenomenon unique to our species—the ability to provoke thought, stir emotion, excite the imagination, and give different kinds of pleasure by means of words.

This book brings together more than 4,000 observations about this activity by outstanding practitioners of it and a host of other commentators. Chronologically, the quotations extend from Ancient Egypt to the present-day world of the Internet and multiculturalism via Belshazzar's Feast, Periclean Athens, Imperial Rome, early Christian monasteries, a medieval Japanese court, a twelfth-century Persian library, the Mermaid Tavern in Elizabethan England, eighteenth-century coffee houses, Victorian publishers' offices, and numerous other literary enclaves. Remarks about the life of letters are to be found ranging from A (the captain of twenty-four lead soldiers in an old French conundrum about print) to Z (a 'whoreson . . . unnecessary letter', according to Kent in *King Lear*). Authors comment on all aspects of their craft from inspiration to last words (a particularly resonant term in this context).

One theme that looms with especial insistence is the motivation for writing. What possesses people to devote time and energy—sometimes the bulk of their lives—to making marks on paper (or papyrus or parchment) that they hope will make marks on other people's minds and sensibilities? Answers vary widely. For some authors, literature, which temporarily endows life with shape and significance, constitutes a substitute for things actuality lacks: a kind of aesthetic comfort blanket. Others, such as Muriel Spark, see their books ('glimpses that seem like a microcosm of reality') as reflections of a deity's larger-scale devices and designs. Amusedly mocking the notion of art as 'uplift', Julian Barnes puts in a good word for it as a survival-mechanism: 'Art is not a *brassière*. At least, not in the English sense. But do not forget that *brassière* is the French for life-jacket'. There are writers who consider it their vocation to jolt readers into viewing the familiar world afresh, writers who offer escapist retreat from the world, writers whose aim is to change the world.

Many authors acknowledge a craving for attention. Others unabashedly admit to being in the business for the money—a motive voiced with brisk frankness by Frances Hodgson Burnett when she submitted her first story to a magazine in the 1860s: 'My object is remuneration.' D. H. Lawrence's miner father may have gasped with outraged amazement at his son's earnings from his novel, *The White Peacock*, 'Fifty pounds! An' tha's niver done a day's hard work in thy life.' But, elsewhere, authors regularly chafe about the inadequacy of their increments. According to Samuel Johnson, 'No man but a blockhead ever wrote except for money.' Despite this, writers are actuated by all kinds of incentives: indignation (Juvenal), rancour (D. H. Lawrence: 'I like to write when I feel spiteful; it's like having a good sneeze'), loneliness (Henry James), fun (Robert Burns), boredom (Graham Greene), nosiness (Margaret Atwood). These miscellaneous motives typify the diversity of authors' reactions to most aspects of their profession. Notably, just one theme unites them in near-unanimity: the iniquity of publishers. Harold Macmillan's demurral, 'Publishers should not have the Garter', proves the least of reservations on this subject. The Canadian novelist Robertson Davies attempts a case for the defence: 'Very harsh things have been said about publishers, but there can be nothing but good in the heart of a man who regales an author with figgy pudding.' Eliza Acton's *Modern Cookery* (1845), however, gives a more traditional view of a publisher's desserts. Her recipe, 'Poor Author's Pudding', is a meagre mix of not much more than milk and bread; 'The Publisher's Pudding'—baked in a '*thickly* buttered basin' covered with 'a sheet of buttered writing paper'—drips with cream, egg yolks, almonds, nutmeg, cherries, 'best Muscatel raisins', and 'best cognac'.

The impulsion to write is something numerous writers compare to a painful involuntary seizure: the Muse as malady. Metaphors of illness and dementia are rife. For Juvenal, in the Rome of the Emperor Domitian, writing is an 'incurable disease'. Almost two millennia later, George Orwell likens literary composition to 'a long bout of some painful illness'. As usual, voices can be heard putting the opposite case. With characteristic paradox, G. K. Chesterton maintains that making things up is a prophylactic against losing a grip on reality: while the rigidly logical go mad, the imaginative stay sane. In an image of wonderfully vivid virulence, Ibsen suggests that writing constitutes a therapeutic purge:

> I kept a scorpion in an empty beer bottle on my table. Now and then the animal was sick; then I used to throw it a piece of soft fruit, which it hurled itself on with fury and into which it poured out its poison; then it became healthy again.
>
> Is there not something similar in us poets? The laws of Nature hold for the intellectual field as well.

Some authors—most famously, Flaubert—speak of literature as a kind of *cordon sanitaire*: the Ivory Tower as a gated community amid the unruly wasteland of life. 'The only way not to be unhappy', Flaubert asserts, 'is to shut yourself up in Art.' His bulletins from his writing-desk hardly bear this out, though. 'Stylistic abscesses' and sentences that 'keep itching without coming to a head' plague him. When not irritated by this authorial eczema, he is afflicted by even more alarming symptoms. As he describes a military assault on Carthage in his historical novel, *Salammbô*, muscular arches and pains rack his arms. As he pens the scene in which Emma Bovary dies from arsenic-poisoning, he vomits his dinner into his chamber-pot.

Though usually less drastic than this, the strains of composition are generally agreed to be severe. 'What a heavy thing is a pen!' Zola groans. Plying his, Balzac likens himself to a galley-slave. Other authors compare themselves to an ox heaving a plough (Martial), a bricklayer (H. L. Mencken), a carpenter (William Golding), and an old woman sprawled on the hearth trying to blow a few pitiful sticks of firewood into a blaze (Samuel Richardson). For Joseph Conrad, completing *Nostromo* is as stressful as sailing round Cape Horn in the face of terrible winter storms. Edna Ferber regards writing as 'a combination of ditch-digging, mountain-climbing, treadmill and childbirth'. For Patrick White, it's equivalent to self-evisceration.

The long line of tribulations by which authors are bedevilled begins with writer's block. Veteran battlers against this such as Conrad or George Gissing feelingly testify to its tortures. Paul Scott alludes with a shudder to the 'implacable, blank sheet of white paper'. For Graham Greene, agonizing over 'the dreaded essential opening sentences', even that blank sheet of paper isn't empty of tormenting suggestion: the term 'foolscap' takes on cruelly mocking implications; the ruled lines start to resemble prison bars. To overcome writer's block, authors favour different remedies. Zola informs Edmond de Goncourt that he finds a bout of copulation handy for dislodging it. H. G. Wells concurs. Dreams can kick-start Greene's imagination. Erskine Caldwell recommends penning limericks as a warm-up exercise. More widely, drink and drugs are much advocated, and much relished, as stimulants. 'No verse can give pleasure for long, nor last, that is written by drinkers of water', Horace affirmed in the last century BC. Throughout twenty succeeding centuries, authors have agreed, and held up their chosen inspirational tipple: Canary wine (Ben Jonson), brandy (Samuel Johnson), whisky (Burns), claret (Keats), gin-and-water (Byron). Opium is advocated (by De Quincey and Baudelaire) as a turner of 'the keys of Paradise'. W. H. Auden experiments with LSD. Barbara Pym thinks there's something to be said for Camp coffee essence.

Pym is perhaps the most poignant contributor to another category of authorial woes: rejection. 'The letter I wrote to *The Author* about not being published was never published', she informs Philip Larkin, a fellow rueful connoisseur of literary chagrins (which continue to take new forms: in his 2nd January entry in his 1997 journal, Alan Bennett reports with glum glee, 'Sent a complimentary (sic) copy of Waterstone's Literary Diary which records the birthdays of various contemporary figures. Here is Dennis Potter on 17 May, Michael Frayn on 8 September, Edna O'Brien on 15 December, so naturally I turn to my own birthday. May 9 is blank except for the note: first British Launderette is opened on Queensway, London 1949'). Some manuscripts never make it into print for other reasons—among them, accidental incineration. Isaac Newton's dog reportedly knocks over a candle and sets fire to 'the almost finished labours of some years'. John Stuart Mill's housemaid burns the first version of Carlyle's *The French Revolution*. Conrad achieves an acme of lucklessness when an oil-lamp explodes on his study table and destroys in a blaze the much-toiled-over manuscript of his story, 'The End of the Tether'.

More sinister than the chance singeing of scripts is the deliberate burning of books. Ideological arson is a menace authors have always had to be conscious of, as has its grim companion, ideological homicide. George Bernard Shaw's chilly quip, 'Assassination is the extreme form of censorship', takes on contemporary configurations with the fatwa levelled at Salman Rushdie—declaring that he and his publishers are '*madhur el dam* (those whose blood must be shed)'—and the hanging of the writer, Ken Saro-Wiwa, in Nigeria.

Less lethal modes of censorship—from prudish bowdlerization to political correctness—still constitute an impediment of which authors are uncomfortably aware. Trying to express himself under the constraints of Tsarist Russia, Chekhov feels as though there's a bone stuck in his throat. Editorial interference with texts, such as the 'damned cutting and slashing' that Byron berates John

Murray for perpetrating on his work, irks others. A vexation that can occur after manuscripts achieve publication is the risible misprint: Henry James finds that a scene he admired as full of 'idle vistas and melancholy nooks' becomes populated by 'idle sisters and melancholy monks'.

Apprehension at the idea of being written about often agitates those who write. It's an anxiety that peers nervously in three directions. First, there's edginess about reviewers and critics, figures who—from Grub Street hacks to jargon-clad deconstructionists—get a predictably bad press here. Newspapers and the publicity-machine are another bugbear (while authors before the rise of interviews, 'profiles', and PR wistfully covet renown, some of their modern counterparts shrink from celebrity—'a mask that eats into the face', John Updike observes with typically elegant sageness). Even posthumously, authors wincingly recognize, they can be brought to book by biography. Over the last three centuries, this can be seen swelling into an increasing source of dread: 'one of the new terrors of death' (John Arbuthnot), 'exhumation' and 'Cannibalism' (Rudyard Kipling). Gladstone may have deplored J. W. Cross's *Life of George Eliot* as 'a Reticence, in three volumes', but reticence is something likely subjects of literary biography usually can't say enough in favour of.

The formidable array of harassments authors document themselves as enduring leaves you curious to discover what compensations for all this are on offer. One considerable reward, it emerges, is the sense of having—in some way and for some time at least—thwarted extinction. 'I shall not altogether die', Horace tells us across a span of 2,000 years. A quotation surviving from Pharaonic Egypt has a scribe, more than three millennia ago, expressing his faith that 'The scroll is better than the carved stone' for durability. Horace considers his poetry 'a monument more lasting than bronze'. Showing the long shelf-life of that image, Shakespeare trusts his own verses will outlive marble and gilded monuments. In a more ambivalent but still celebratory metaphor, Longfellow speaks of leaving 'footprints on the sands of time'.

Closer-to-hand gratifications are available too, of course. Whether Graham Greene's *Brighton Rock* will prove more lasting than bronze remains to be seen, but, in the meantime, its author notes in a letter, 'a new shade for knickers and nightdresses' from Peter Jones department store has been named after it. The fillip of seeing people enjoying your work is savoured by Martial in the first century AD:

> All Rome is mad about my book:
> It's praised, they hum the lines, shops stock it,
> It peeps from every hand and pocket.

Nearly two thousand years later, J. M. Barrie appealingly confesses to the Critics' Circle in London, 'For several days after my first book was published I carried it about in my pocket, and took surreptitious peeps at it to make sure that the ink had not faded.' Enthusiasm for the book as object and concept—'the greatest interactive medium of all time', in the recent words of the head of Penguin Books—glows through authors' comments across the centuries.

Some writers plume themselves on the power of the pen (a potency that alluringly glints even from Saint Augustine's malediction on poetry as 'devil's wine'). In his scathing lines on the Soviet invasion of Czechoslovakia in August 1968, Auden simultaneously proclaims and exemplifies articulacy's telling strengths:

> But one prize is beyond his reach,
> The Ogre cannot master Speech.
> About a subjugated plain,
> Among its desperate and slain,
> The Ogre stalks with hands on hips,
> While drivel gushes from his lips.

It's nicely in accord with this that Czechoslovakia's President after the country regained independence should be a playwright, Vàclav Havel.

As well as the outer world, the inner one has its distinctive satisfactions for authors. A taking motif—especially evident in the nineteenth century—is a writer's enthralled involvement with his or her characters. Jane Austen declares her affection for Elizabeth Bennet and her belief that no one tolerable could dislike her. There are haunting glimpses of what it feels like, on finishing a novel, to see your creations now fading away. In his preface to *David Copperfield*, Charles Dickens registers a novelist's pangs of regret at the spectacle of 'a crowd of the creatures of his brain . . . going from him for ever'. Conrad, completing *Almayer's Folly* on 24th April 1894, watches as, after the final scratch of his pen, the 'band of phantoms' he has co-existed with for several years 'dissolve' and 'are made pallid and indistinct by the sunlight of this brilliant and sombre day'.

Literature, Zola stresses, is 'a human secretion'. One of the fascinations in collecting quotations about it lies in the reminders this brings of the extraordinarily diverse personalities that have exuded this imaginative by-product, and the remarkably changing circumstances under which they have done so. The urge to produce literature persists but the tools of the writer's trade alter. Papyrus and parchment are replaced by paper. Quills give way to print. Henry James can be observed 'trying to make use of an accursed "fountain" pen' and, later, apologizing voluminously for recourse to the 'typewriting machine'. Under Seamus Heaney's gaze, 'the dead-pan cloudiness of a word processor' takes on oracular promise.

Another authorial accessory—a dictionary—is described by one writer here as 'a frozen pantomime'. A dictionary of literary quotations is, among other things, a frozen cavalcade. Open it anywhere and vignettes of literary life in different eras flicker into view: a Roman poet near the Forum passing a bookshop whose doorposts are plastered with advertisements; a medieval scribe noting down the affinities between his mental processes and the concentration-and-pounce of his mousing cat; Lady Murasaki, at the Japanese court around 1000 AD, casting a caustic eye over a rival's accomplishments ('She thought herself so clever and littered her writings with Chinese characters . . .'); Shakespeare commenting on the scenic deficiencies of the Globe; Edward Gibbon receiving inspiration for his *Decline and Fall of the Roman Empire* as he sits 'musing amidst the ruins of the Capitol, while the barefoot friars were singing vespers in the Temple of Jupiter' on the fifteenth of October 1764; Jane Austen joking as to whether the copyright of *Sense and Sensibility* 'should ever be of any value'; a Victorian magazine editor warning an author, 'You have left your hero and heroine tied up in a cavern under the Thames for a week, and they are not married'; Arnold Bennett, at dinner chez H. G. Wells, fretting at Shaw's garrulity and longing to have a verbal 'scrap' with Virginia Woolf; Philip Larkin almost meeting a fatal accident as he listens to the Immortality Ode on his car radio while speeding down the M1; the adapter of *Middlemarch* for television grousing that his task was 'like getting an elephant into a suitcase'.

While this dictionary's miscellany of quotations exhibits the variety and individuality of literary achievement, it also displays the multiple filaments—allusion, homage, sequels, parodies, quotations, titles borrowed from others' lines—that weave authors together into a web of imaginative interconnectedness. Genres can be seen evolving, mutating, and splitting apart into new forms. Christopher Frayling remarks on the way four classic horror stories—*Frankenstein*, *Dracula*, *The Hound of the Baskervilles*, and *Dr Jekyll and Mr Hyde*—have spawned swarming progeny in twentieth-century popular culture. Other boom-areas within that culture—best-sellers, romantic fiction, crime writing—also give rise to clusters of comment, including tribute from more recognizedly 'literary' fellow-authors. Arnold Bennett deplores the prejudice of assuming that the work of a writer who enjoys 'immense circulation . . . merits only indifference and disdain'. Robert Graves applauds Agatha Christie's detective novels, in 1944, as first-rate specimens of 'the most characteristic pleasure-writing of this epoch'. The most consequential development throughout recent centuries of writing makes itself eloquently heard too. Despite misogynist bigotry—male strictures such as Voltaire's claim, 'the composition of tragedy requires *testicles*', and Hawthorne's recommendation that the faces of female authors should be 'deeply scarified with an oyster shell'—women growingly establish literature as every bit as much their province as men's.

Irrepressibly expansive and exploratory, literature, for Margaret Atwood, is 'a revelation of the full range of our human response to the world'. Fullness is something a work on the scale of this volume would be foolhardy to lay claim to, but its selection of soundings from over 3,000 years of writing does aim to give a sense of the range of human response to literature. Throughout the putting-together of this dictionary, one quotation included in it nagged uncomfortably: the author of Ecclesiastes's sigh that 'Of making many books there is no end'. Hammond Innes's disclosure that he has felt impelled to plant trees to replace 'some of the timber used up by my books' gave pause too.

Ultimately, the justification for this venture must be that it hopes to cast light—both for the hunter of references and the interested browser—on a phenomenon without which human existence would be inconceivably poorer. 'If writing did not exist, what terrible depressions we should suffer from', wrote Sei Shōnagon, an attendant at the imperial Japanese court a thousand years ago. This book is for all who agree with her—and who are intrigued by the patterns and diversities the forms and practices of literature have taken over the centuries.

Inevitably, in a work that conforms to Dr Johnson's directive—

> He used to say that no man read long together with a folio on his table: —Books, said he, that you may carry to the fire, and hold readily in your hand, are the most useful after all

—pressures of selectivity have been tight. The Tools of the Trade section, for instance, could have been extended almost indefinitely to incorporate all the idiosyncratic paraphernalia writers have relied on, and should perhaps have included some literary furniture—such as that of Balzac who, Arnold Bennett admiringly noted, 'literally wore out four chairs'. Also inevitably, some quotations—several cited in this introduction—turned up too late for inclusion in the body of the text.

Credit for the text, whose basis came from the files of the Oxford University Press, is very much due to the editorial staff and researchers of the OUP's Dictionary Department: their knowledge, scholarship, and keen expertise have been exemplary. In addition, a large debt of gratitude is owed to the generosity and acumen of friends who have supplied choice quotations. Particular thanks must go to A. S. Byatt, David Grylls, Rhoda Koenig, Laurence Lerner, and Ruth Rendell, all of whom have added considerably to the scope and quality of this book.

PETER KEMP

January 1997

How to Use the Dictionary

The text falls into two divisions, **The Writer's World**, containing themes covering all aspects of literary life, and **Writers and their Works**, in which quotations primarily about specific writers are grouped under the writer's name.

In **The Writer's World**, the sequence of entries is by alphabetical order of themes, from **Adaptation and Screenwriting** and **Admiration and Praise** to **Writer's Block** and **Writing**. Theme titles range from broad general categories such as **Art, Death,** and **Morality**, to more specific categories such as **Characters, Description, The Power of the Pen, Punctuation, Tools of the Trade**, and **Words**. Literary genres have their own themes, from **Ballads** through **Horror and the Gothic** to **Science Fiction** and **Travel Writing**. Related topics may be covered by a single theme. Where helpful, this is made explicit in the title, as in **Grammar and Usage, Humour and Comedy**, and **Newspapers and Magazines**. A cross-reference from the second element of the pair appears in its appropriate place in the alphabetic sequence both in the main text and in the **List of Themes**, so that '**Mystery** *see Crime and Mystery*' follows **Movements and Trends** and precedes **Names**.

Where themes are closely related, 'see also' references are given immediately following the theme title. The heading **Fame** is thus followed by the direction 'see also **Reputation and Achievement**', and **Humour and Comedy** by 'see also **Irony, Wit and Satire**'.

Quotations are arranged in chronological order. Where possible, quotations are precisely dated, as by the composition date of a letter or diary, or the publication of a book published in the author's lifetime, or by external circumstances, as a contemporary comment on a specific event. When the date is uncertain or unknown, and the quotation cannot be related to a particular event, the author's date of death has been used to date the quotation.

Contextual information regarded as essential to a full appreciation of the quotation precedes the text in an italicized note; information seen as providing useful amplification follows in an italicized note.

Each quotation is accompanied by the name of the author to whom it is attributed; dates of birth and death (where known) are also given. In general, the authors' names are given in the form by which they are best known, so that we have H. G. Wells (rather than Herbert George Wells) and Rebecca West (rather than Cicily Isabel Fairfield). Bibliographical information as to the source from which the quotation is taken follows the author's name; titles and dates of publication are given, but full finding references are not. Where a quotation cannot be traced to a citable source, 'attributed' is used to indicate that the attribution is generally accepted, but that a specific reference has not been traced.

The division **Writers and their Works** consists of quotations dealing primarily with a named author; these categories are arranged alphabetically by the names of the authors covered, and the headings consist of the authors' names and dates.

Cross-references are made within themes and to specific items within other themes in either division. In each case the reference is to the page number followed by the unique quotation number on the page. So **45:2** indicates the second quotation on page 45. The use of 'see' indicates that following up the cross-reference will supply essential information; 'cf.' is used to indicate information that amplifies what is already given. Authors who have their own entries in the **Writers and their Works** division are typographically distinguished by the use of bold (of **Balzac**, by **Chaucer**) in context or source notes.

Indexes

There is an author index for tracing quotations by named authors (and collections with authorial status, such as **The Bible**), and a keyword index for tracing individual quotations. Both the keywords and the entries following each keyword, including those in foreign languages, are in strict alphabetical order. Singular and plural nouns (with their possessive forms) are grouped separately.

References are to the page number, followed by the unique quotation number on the page, as **53:2**.

List of Themes

The Writer's World

Academe *see Scholarship and Academe*
Achievement *see Reputation and Achievement*
Adaptation and Screenwriting
Admiration and Praise
Age
Agents
Allusion *see Quotation and Allusion*
Art
Audience
Autobiography

Bad Writing *see Good and Bad Writing*
Ballads
Beginning and Ending
Best-sellers
The Bible
Biography
Books
Borrowed Titles
Borrowing Books
Brevity

Censorship
Characters
Children's Literature
Choice of Words
Closing Lines
Comedy *see Humour and Comedy*
Conversation *see Dialogue and Conversation*
Creativity *see Inspiration and Creativity*
Crime and Mystery
Criticism
Critics

Death
Dedications
Description
Dialogue and Conversation
Diaries
Dictionaries
Drama
Drink and Drugs

Earning a Living
Editors and Editing
Effort
Ending *see Beginning and Ending*
Erotic Writing and Pornography
Essays

Fables and Fairy Stories
Fame
Family and Friends
Fantasy
Feeling
Fiction
Figures of Speech
Food
Friends *see Family and Friends*

Genius and Talent
Ghost Stories
Good and Bad Writing
The Gothic *see Horror and the Gothic*
Grammar and Usage

Historical Fiction
Historical Writing
Horror and the Gothic
The Human Race
Humour and Comedy

Imagination
Inspiration and Creativity
Intelligence *see Knowledge and Intelligence*
Irony
Journalism

Writers and their Works

Joseph Addison
Kingsley Amis
Martin Amis
Maya Angelou
Matthew Arnold
W. H. Auden
Jane Austen

Francis Bacon
Honoré de Balzac
J. M. Barrie
Charles Baudelaire
Simone de Beauvoir
Samuel Beckett
Max Beerbohm
Hilaire Belloc
Saul Bellow
Alan Bennett
Arnold Bennett
John Betjeman
William Blake
Jorge Luis Borges
James Boswell
Elizabeth Bowen
Marjorie Bowen
Bertolt Brecht
Charlotte Brontë
Emily Brontë
Rupert Brooke
Elizabeth Barrett Browning
Robert Browning
Arthur Bryant
John Buchan
John Bunyan
Edmund Burke
Frances Hodgson Burnett
Robert Burns
Lord Byron

Jane Welsh Carlyle
Thomas Carlyle
Catullus
Raymond Chandler
Thomas Chatterton
Geoffrey Chaucer
Anton Chekhov
G. K. Chesterton
Agatha Christie
Samuel Taylor Coleridge
Joan Collins
Ivy Compton-Burnett
William Congreve
Cyril Connolly
Joseph Conrad
James Fenimore Cooper
Noël Coward
Abraham Cowley

Dante Alighieri
Charles Dickens
Emily Dickinson
John Donne
Fedor Dostoevsky
John Dryden
Gerald Durrell
Lawrence Durrell

George Eliot
T. S. Eliot
Ralph Waldo Emerson
Gavin Ewart

Henry Fielding
F. Scott Fitzgerald
Gustave Flaubert
Ford Madox Ford
E. M. Forster

John Galsworthy
Elizabeth Gaskell
John Gay
Edward Gibbon
André Gide
Elinor Glyn
Johann Wolfgang von Goethe
Oliver Goldsmith
Maxim Gorky
Robert Graves
Thomas Gray
Graham Greene
Thomas Hardy
Nathaniel Hawthorne
William Hazlitt
Joseph Heller
Lilian Hellman
Ernest Hemingway
George Herbert
Robert Herrick
James Hogg
Homer
Horace
A. E. Housman
Ted Hughes
Victor Hugo
Aldous Huxley

Henrik Ibsen
Christopher Isherwood

Henry James
Samuel Johnson
Ben Jonson
James Joyce

Franz Kafka
Molly Keane
John Keats
James Kelman
Rudyard Kipling
Thomas Kyd

Charles Lamb
Philip Larkin
D. H. Lawrence
Edward Lear
F. R. Leavis
Mikhail Lermontov
Henry Wadsworth Longfellow

Lord Macaulay
Roger McGough

The Writer's World

Academe see Scholarship and Academe

Achievement see Reputation and Achievement

Adaptation and Screenwriting

1 All things considered, I prefer cinema to stage. The movie is just a silly stunt for silly people—but the theatre is more compromising since it is capable of falsifying the very soul of one's work both on the imaginative and on the intellectual side—besides having some sort of inferior poetics of its own which is bound to play havoc with that imponderable quality of creative literary expression which depends on one's originality.
on adaptations

Joseph Conrad 1857–1924: letter, 18–23 August 1920

2 The trouble, Mr Goldwyn, is that you are only interested in art and I am only interested in money.
telegraphed version of the outcome of a conversation between ***Shaw*** *and Sam Goldwyn*

George Bernard Shaw 1856–1950: Alva Johnson *The Great Goldwyn* (1937)

3 The challenge of screenwriting is to say much in little and then take half of that little out and still preserve an effect of leisure and movement.

Raymond Chandler 1888–1959: in *Atlantic Monthly* November 1945

4 They don't want you until you have made a name, and by the time you have made a name, you have developed some kind of talent they can't use. All they will do is spoil it, if you let them.

Raymond Chandler 1888–1959: letter, to Dale Warren, 7 November 1951

5 Radio and television . . . have succeeded in lifting the manufacture of banality out of the sphere of handicraft and placed it in that of a major industry.

Nathalie Sarraute 1902– : in *Times Literary Supplement* 10 June 1960

6 Take the money and run.

Ernest Hemingway 1899–1961: attributed; W. Goldman *Adventures in the Screen Trade* (1984)

7 Book—what they make a movie out of for television.

Leonard Louis Levinson 1904– : Laurence J. Peter (ed.) *Quotations for our Time* (1977)

8 Words are cheap. The biggest thing you can say is 'elephant'.
on the universality of silent films

Charlie Chaplin 1889–1977: B. Norman *The Movie Greats* (1981)

9 Schmucks with Underwoods.
describing writers

Jack Warner 1892–1978: attributed

10 For me it is impossible to write a film play without first writing a story.

Graham Greene 1904–91: *Ways of Escape* (1980)

11 The writer, in the eyes of many film producers, still seems to occupy a position of importance somewhere between the wardrobe lady and the tea boy, with this difference: it's often quite difficult to replace the wardrobe lady.

John Mortimer 1923– : *Clinging to the Wreckage* (1982)

1 The secret of being a successful screenwriter is that you have to write very, very badly, *but you also have to write as well as you possibly can.*

Christopher Hampton 1946– : *Tales from Hollywood* (1985)

2 The less it resembled my book, the better I felt.
on the film of his novel, The Witches of Eastwick

John Updike 1932– : letter to his agent, 10 July 1987

3 A good film script should be able to do completely without dialogue.

David Mamet 1947– : in *Independent* 11 November 1988

4 It's not so much that I write well—I just don't write badly very often, and that passes for good on television.

Andy Rooney 1919– : in *Spectator* 3 March 1990

5 I had a great deal of say . . . but the producer didn't have a great deal of listen.
on the adaptation for television of The Hitch-Hiker's Guide to the Galaxy

Douglas Adams 1952– : Stan Nicholls (ed.) *Wordsmiths of Wonder* (1993)

6 The difference between writing for stage and for television is almost an optical one. Language on the stage has to be slightly larger than life because it is being heard in a much larger space. Plot counts for less on the television screen because one is seeing the characters at closer quarters than in the theatre.

Alan Bennett 1934– : *Writing Home* (1994)

7 Film is drama at its most impatient, 'What happens next?' the perpetual nag. One can never hang about, thinks the writer, petulantly.

Alan Bennett 1934– : in *Independent on Sunday* 12 February 1995 'Overheard'

8 Andrew Davies said adapting *Middlemarch* was like getting an elephant into a suitcase; Jane Austen is much easier. In *Pride and Prejudice* the plot works like a Swiss clock.
a producer's view on adapting to television

Sue Birtwistle 1945– : in *Guardian* 13 October 1995

Admiration and Praise see also **Rivalry**

9 How far thou didst our Lyly outshine,
Or sporting Kyd, or Marlowe's mighty line.

Ben Jonson *c.*1573–1637: 'To the Memory of My Beloved, the Author, Mr William Shakespeare' (1623); cf. **312:3**

10 The praise of ancient authors proceeds not from the reverence of the dead, but from the competition, and mutual envy of the living.

Thomas Hobbes 1588–1679: *Leviathan* (1651) 'A Review and Conclusion'

11 The reciprocal civility of authors is one of the most risible scenes in the farce of life.

Samuel Johnson 1709–84: preface to *Christian Morals* (1756)

12 Biographers, translators, editors,—all, in short, who employ themselves in illustrating the lives or the writings of others, are peculiarly exposed to the *Lues Boswellianae*, or disease of admiration.

Lord Macaulay 1800–59: in *Edinburgh Review* January 1834

13 You are as unyielding as marble and as penetrating as an English fog.
to ***Baudelaire***

Gustave Flaubert 1821–80: letter, 13 July 1857

14 What a man! . . . He crushes the entire century.
of ***Balzac***

Émile Zola 1840–1902: letter, 1867

1 It is not until the pack has yelled itself hoarse that the level voice of justice is heard in praise.

Max Beerbohm 1872–1956: letter, May 1894

2 You reduce me to mere gelatinous grovel.
to H. G. ***Wells***

Henry James 1843–1916: letter, 20 November 1899

3 I live for your agglomerated lucubrations.
to H. G. ***Wells***

Henry James 1843–1916: letter, 18 November 1902

4 People ask you for criticism, but they only want praise.

W. Somerset Maugham 1874–1965: *Of Human Bondage* (1915)

5 The worst tragedy for a poet is to be admired through being misunderstood.

Jean Cocteau 1889–1963: *Le Rappel à l'ordre* (1926) 'Le Coq et l'Arlequin' p. 20

6 My literary success puzzled and embarrassed my old friends far more than it impressed them, and in my own family it created a kind of constraint which increased with the years. None of my relations ever spoke to me of my books, either to praise or blame—they simply ignored them.

Edith Wharton 1862–1937: *A Backward Glance* (1934)

7 Every genius needs praise.

Gertrude Stein 1874–1946: Edmund White *The Burning Library* (1994)

8 Oh Marianne, all my congratulations. It seems to me so intricately impressive, with a kind of grinding caterpillar tread that is almost too upsetting.
on the poem 'In Distrust of Merits'

Elizabeth Bishop 1911–79: letter to Marianne Moore, 29 June 1943

9 With each book you write you should lose the admirers you gained with the previous one.

André Gide 1869–1951: Edmund White *The Burning Library* (1994)

10 It would be nice if sometimes the kind things I say were considered worthy of quotation. It isn't difficult, you know, to be witty or amusing when one has something to say that is destructive, but damned hard to be clever and quotable when you are singing someone's praises.

Noël Coward 1899–1973: William Marchant *The Pleasure of His Company* (1981)

Age

11 *Quand vous serez bien vieille, au soir, à la chandelle,*
Assise auprès du feu, dévidant et filant,
Direz, chantant mes vers, en vous émerveillant,
Ronsard me célébrait du temps que j'étais belle.

When you are very old, and sit in the candlelight at evening spinning by the fire, you will say, as you murmur my verses, a wonder in your eyes, 'Ronsard sang of me in the days when I was fair.'

Pierre de Ronsard 1524–85: *Sonnets pour Hélène* (1578)

12 But years hath done this wrong,
To make me write too much, and live too long.

Samuel Daniel 1563–1619: *Philotas* (1605) 'To the Prince'; dedication

1 Amidst the mortifying circumstances attendant upon growing old, it is something to have seen the *School for Scandal* in its glory.

Charles Lamb 1775–1834: *Elia* (1823)

2 In youth men are apt to write more wisely than they really know or feel; and the remainder of life may be not idly spent in realizing and convincing themselves of the wisdom which they uttered long ago.

Nathaniel Hawthorne 1804–64: preface to *The Snow Image* (1852)

3 I am past thirty, and three parts iced over.

Matthew Arnold 1822–88: letter, to Arthur Hugh Clough, 12 February 1853

4 It had taken too much of his life to produce too little of his art.

Henry James 1843–1916: 'The Middle Years' (1893)

5 When you are old and grey and full of sleep,
And nodding by the fire, take down this book
And slowly read and dream of the soft look
Your eyes had once, and of their shadows deep.

W. B. Yeats 1865–1939: 'When You Are Old' (1893)

6 I've been dissecting for forty years. Let me dream a little in my waning days.
to Octave Mirabeau, on his review of Zola's final novel Fécondité

Émile Zola 1840–1902: letter, 29 November 1899

7 Byron!—he would be all forgotten today if he had lived to be a florid old gentleman with iron-grey whiskers, writing very long, very able letters to *The Times* about the Repeal of the Corn Laws.

Max Beerbohm 1872–1956: *Zuleika Dobson* (1911)

8 Here I am, an old man in a dry month
Being read to by a boy, waiting for rain.

T. S. Eliot 1888–1965: 'Gerontion' (1920)

9 A young man when the old men are done talking
Will say to an old man, 'Tell me of that lady
The poet stubborn with his passion sang us
When age might have chilled his blood.'

W. B. Yeats 1865–1939: 'Broken Dreams' (1914)

10 You think it horrible that lust and rage
Should dance attention upon my old age;
They were not such a plague when I was young;
What else have I to spur me into song?

W. B. Yeats 1865–1939: 'The Spur' (1939)

11 Oh yes, between 50 and 60 I think I shall write out some very singular books if I live.

Virginia Woolf 1882–1941: attributed

a final letter to a young correspondent:

12 Dear Elise,
Seek younger friends; I am extinct.

George Bernard Shaw 1856–1950: letter, 1949

13 With sixty staring me in the face, I have developed inflammation of the sentence structure and a definite hardening of the paragraphs.

James Thurber 1894–1961: in *New York Post* 30 June 1955

14 Each year brings new problems of Form and Content,
new foes to tug with: at Twenty I tried to
vex my elders, past Sixty it's the young whom
I hope to bother.

W. H. Auden 1907–73: 'Shorts I' (1969)

1 My father, who had derived such happiness from his childhood, found in me the companion with whom he could return there . . . When I was three he was three. When I was six he was six. We grew up side by side and as we grew so the books were written . . . I—as I have already mentioned—needed him. He no less but for a different reason needed me. He needed me to escape from being fifty.

Christopher Milne 1920–96: *The Enchanted Places* (1974)

2 A writer's old age can be very strange. Sometimes it's like his books: Evelyn Waugh, who made such fun of Apthorpe's 'thunder-box', died in the w.c. Zola, like the miners in *Germinal*, was suffocated by charcoal fumes.

Graham Greene 1904–91: Marie-Françoise Allain *The Other Man, Conversations with Graham Greene* (1983)

3 I am getting progressively less fond of poems about old age as I near the Pearly Gates.

Philip Larkin 1922–85: letter, 30 January 1984

4 I'm apt to forget my age. The other day I saw Kingsley Amis and asked how well he knew D. H. Lawrence. His eyes bulged and his face grew purple.

Peter Quennell 1905–93: in *Observer* 25 September 1988 'Sayings of the Week'

Agents

5 The author's agent fosters in authors the greed for an immediate money return . . . at the cost of all dignity and repose.

William Heinemann 1863–1920: in *The Author* c.1890; George Greenfield *Scribblers for Bread* (1989)

6 Mrs Morland very wittily defined an agent as someone whom you pay to make bad blood between yourself and your publisher.

Angela Thirkell 1890–1961: *Pomfret Towers* (1938)

7 Agents have not changed much since I first became dependent upon them. To be dependent on an agent is like entrusting your most precious future to your mother-in-law or your bookmaker.

John Osborne 1929–94: *Almost a Gentleman* (1991)

8 It's the old Catch-22; you can never get an agent unless you're published, and when you most need one, you can't have one.

C. J. Cherryh 1942– : Stan Nicholls (ed.) *Wordsmiths of Wonder* (1993)

Allusion see Quotation and Allusion

Art

9 Life is short, the art long.
often quoted 'Ars longa, vita brevis' *after Seneca* De Brevitate Vitae, *and translated 'That lyf so short, the craft so long to lerne' by* ***Chaucer***

Hippocrates c.460–357 BC: *Aphorisms*; cf. **124:8**

10 The value and rank of every art is in proportion to the mental labour employed in it, or the mental pleasure produced by it.

Joshua Reynolds 1723–92: *Discourses on Art* 10 December 1771

1 In art the best is good enough.

Johann Wolfgang von Goethe 1749–1832: *Italienische Reise* (1816–17) 3 March 1787

2 Art for art's sake, with no purpose, for any purpose perverts art. But art achieves a purpose which is not its own.

describing a conversation with Crabb Robinson about the latter's work on Kant's aesthetics

Benjamin Constant 1767–1834: diary, 11 February 1804

3 The only time a human being is free is when he or she makes a work of art.

Friedrich von Schiller 1759–1805: Edmund White *The Burning Library* (1994)

4 The excellence of every art is its intensity, capable of making all disagreeables evaporate, from their being in close relationship with beauty and truth.

John Keats 1795–1821: letter to George and Thomas Keats, 21 December 1817

5 The arts babblative and scribblative.

Robert Southey 1774–1843: *Colloquies on the Progress and Prospects of Society* (1829)

6 The only way not to be unhappy is to shut yourself up in Art and count all the rest as nothing.

Gustave Flaubert 1821–80: letter, 13 May 1845

7 If art does not enlarge men's sympathies, it does nothing morally.

George Eliot 1819–80: letter to Charles Bray, 5 July 1859

8 Art is a jealous mistress.

Ralph Waldo Emerson 1803–82: *The Conduct of Life* (1860)

9 Art requires, about all things, a suppression of one's self.

Henry James 1843–1916: 'Mr Walt Whitman' (1865)

10 Art is a human product, a human secretion; it is our body that sweats the beauty of our works.

Émile Zola 1840–1902: 'Le Moment artistique' (1868)

11 It appears to me that no one can ever have made a seriously artistic attempt without becoming conscious of an immense increase—a kind of revelation of freedom. One perceives . . . in that case . . . that the province of art is all life, all feeling, all observation, all vision—it is all experience.

Henry James 1843–1916: 'The Art of Fiction' (1888)

12 All art is immoral.

Oscar Wilde 1854–1900: *Intentions* (1891) 'The Critic as Artist'

13 Art finds her own perfection within, and not outside of herself. She is not to be judged by any external standard of resemblance. She is a veil, rather than a mirror.

Oscar Wilde 1854–1900: *Intentions* (1891) 'The Decay of Lying'

14 We know that the tail must wag the dog, for the horse is
drawn by the cart;
But the Devil whoops, as he whooped of old: 'It's clever,
but is it Art?'

Rudyard Kipling 1865–1936: 'The Conundrum of the Workshops' (1892)

1 To evoke in oneself a feeling one has once experienced and having evoked it in oneself then by means of movements, lines, colours, sounds, or forms expressed in words, so to transmit that feeling—this is the activity of art.

Art is a human activity consisting in this, that one man consciously by means of certain external signs, hands on to others feelings he has lived through, and that others are infected by these feelings and also experience them.

Leo Tolstoy 1828–1910: *What is Art?* (1898)

2 Art must be parochial in the beginning to become cosmopolitan in the end.

George Moore 1852–1933: *Hail and Farewell: Ave* (1911)

3 Art and Religion are, then, two roads by which men escape from circumstance to ecstasy. Between aesthetic and religious rapture there is a family alliance. Art and Religion are means to similar states of mind.

Clive Bell 1881–1964: *Art* (1914)

4 It is art that *makes* life, makes interest . . . and I know of no substitute whatever for the force and beauty of its process.

Henry James 1843–1916: letter to H. G. Wells, 10 July 1915

5 Art exists that one may recover the sensation of life; it exists to make one feel things, to make the stone *stony*. The purpose of art is to impart the sensation of things as they are perceived and not as they are known. The technique of art is to make objects '*unfamiliar*', to make forms difficult, to increase the difficulty and length of perception because the process of perception is an aesthetic end in itself and must be prolonged. *Art is a way of experiencing the artfullness of an object; the object is not important.*

Victor Shklovsky 1893–1984: 'Art as Technique' (1917)

6 The rhetorician would deceive his neighbours,
The sentimentalist himself; while art
Is but a vision of reality.

W. B. Yeats 1865–1939: 'Ego Dominus Tuus' (1917)

7 Art is vice. You don't marry it legitimately, you rape it.

Edgar Degas 1834–1917: Paul Lafond *Degas* (1918)

8 The lower one's vitality, the more sensitive one is to great art.

Max Beerbohm 1872–1956: *Seven Men* (1919)

9 A work of art has an author and yet, when it is perfect, it has something which is anonymous about it.

Simone Weil 1909–43: *Gravity and Grace* (1927)

10 Art is significant deformity.

Roger Fry 1866–1934: Virginia Woolf *Roger Fry* (1940)

11 Art is not life and cannot be
A midwife to society.

W. H. Auden 1907–73: *New Year Letter* (1941)

12 Art is not Magic, i.e., a means by which the artist communicates or arouses his feelings in others, but a mirror in which they may become conscious of what their own feelings really are: its proper effect, in fact, is disenchanting.

W. H. Auden 1907–73: 'The Poet of the Encirclement' (1943)

13 Art is the imposing of a pattern on experience, and our aesthetic enjoyment is recognition of the pattern.

Alfred North Whitehead 1861–1947: *Dialogues* (1954) 10 June 1943

1 I suppose art is the only thing that can go on mattering once it has stopped hurting.

Elizabeth Bowen 1899–1973: *The Heat of the Day* (1949)

2 Life is very nice, but it has no shape. The object of art is actually to give it some and to do it by every artifice possible—truer than the truth.

Jean Anouilh 1910–87: *La Répétition* (1950)

3 *L'art est un anti-destin.*

Art is a revolt against fate.

André Malraux 1901–76: *Les Voix du silence* (1951)

4 Art is born of humiliation.

W. H. Auden 1907–73: Stephen Spender *World Within World* (1951)

5 Art is the objectification of feeling, and the subjectification of nature.

Susanne Langer 1895–1985: in *Mind* (1967)

6 Art has its roots in social realities; when you see an Aztec statue you don't doubt that it had an essential social function. People believed in that god and made sacrifices to it. I don't know why literature should be any different.

Margaret Atwood 1939– : in an interview, March/April 1976; Earl G. Ingersoll (ed.) *Margaret Atwood: Conversations* (1990)

7 *Beauty plus pity*—that is the closest we can get to a definition of art.

*on **Kafka**'s* Metamorphosis

Vladimir Nabokov 1899–1977: *Lectures on Literature* (1980)

8 In the eyes of God, Who cuts through appearances and goes beyond them, there is no novel, no art, for art thrives on appearances.

Jean-Paul Sartre 1905–80: Edmund White *The Burning Library* (1994)

9 Do not imagine that Art is something which is designed to give gentle uplift and self-confidence. Art is not a *brassière*. At least, not in the English sense. But do not forget that *brassière* is the French for life-jacket.

Julian Barnes 1946– : *Flaubert's Parrot* (1984)

10 A revelation of the full range of our human response to the world—that is, what it means to be human on earth. That seems to be what 'hope' is about in relation to art. Nothing so simple as 'happy endings'.

Margaret Atwood 1939– : in an interview, December 1986; Earl G. Ingersoll (ed.) *Margaret Atwood: Conversations* (1990)

11 If you want art to be like ovaltine, then clearly some art is not for you.

Peter Reading 1946– : in *Critics' Forum*, Radio 3, 22 November 1986; attributed

12 Art comes out of art; it begins with imitation, often in the form of parody.

Alan Bennett 1934– : *Writing Home* (1994)

Audience

13 *Pro captu lectoris habent sua fata libelli.*

The reader's fancy makes the fate of books.

Terentianus Marcus fl. late 2nd cent. AD: *De Litteris Syllabis*

14 Authors have established it as a kind of rule, that a man ought to be dull sometimes; as the most severe reader makes allowances for many rests and nodding places in a voluminous writer.

Joseph Addison 1672–1719: *The Spectator* 23 July 1711

1 'Till authors hear at length, one gen'ral cry,
Tickle and entertain us, or we die.
The loud demand from year to year the same,
Beggars invention and makes fancy lame.

William Cowper 1731–1800: 'Retirement' (1782)

2 I propose to myself to imitate, and as far as possible, to adopt the very language of men . . . I wish to keep my reader in the company of flesh and blood.

William Wordsworth 1770–1850: preface to *Lyrical Ballads* (1800)

3 Until you understand a writer's ignorance, presume yourself ignorant of his understanding.

Samuel Taylor Coleridge 1772–1834: *Biographia Literaria* (1817)

4 The book . . . requires to be read in the clear, brown, twilight atmosphere in which it was written; if opened in the sunshine, it is apt to look exceedingly like a volume of blank pages.

Nathaniel Hawthorne 1804–64: preface to *Twice-Told Tales* (1851)

5 *—Hypocrite lecteur,—mon semblable,—mon frère!*
Hypocritical reader, my fellow-man and brother!

Charles Baudelaire 1821–67: 'Au Lecteur' (1855)

6 Do not fire too much over the heads of your readers.

Anthony Trollope 1815–82: letter to George Eliot, 1862

7 Read my little fable:
He that runs may read.
Most can raise the flowers now,
For all have got the seed.
And some are pretty enough,
And some are poor indeed;
And now again the people
Call it but a weed.

Alfred, Lord Tennyson 1809–92: 'The Flower' (1864)

8 Every book is, in an intimate sense, a circular letter to the friends of him who writes it. They alone take his meaning; they find private messages, assurances of love, and expressions of gratitude, dropped at every corner. The public is but a generous patron who defrays the postage.

Robert Louis Stevenson 1850–94: dedicatory letter to *Travels with a Donkey* (1879)

9 Camerado, this is no book,
Who touches this touches a man,
(Is it night? Are we here together alone?)
It is I you hold and who holds you.
I spring from the pages into your arms—decease calls me
forth.

Walt Whitman 1819–92: 'So Long!' (1881)

10 It is perhaps hardly too much to say that the future of English fiction may rest with this Unknown Public—a reading public of three millions which lies right out of the pale of true literary civilization—which is now waiting to be taught the difference between a good book and a bad.

Wilkie Collins 1824–89: Q. D. Leavis *Fiction and the Reading Public* (1932)

11 What kind of talent is required to please this mighty public? That was my first question, and was soon amended with the words, 'if any'.

Robert Louis Stevenson 1850–94: *Essays Literary and Critical* (1923) 'Popular Authors'

1 One writes only half the book; the other half is with the reader.

Joseph Conrad 1857–1924: letter to Cunninghame Graham, 1897

2 I should so much have loved to be popular!

Henry James 1843–1916: Alfred Sutro *Celebrities and Simple Souls* (1933)

3 Writing in English is the most ingenious torture ever devised for sins committed in previous lives. The English reading public explains the reason why.

James Joyce 1882–1941: letter, 5 September 1918

4 An author ought to write for the youth of his own generation, the critics of the next, and the schoolmasters of ever afterward.

F. Scott Fitzgerald 1896–1940: letter, April 1920

5 When a man writes a letter to himself, it is a pity to post it to somebody else. Perhaps the same is true of a book.

D. H. Lawrence 1885–1930: *Aaron's Rod* (1922)

6 That ideal reader suffering from an ideal insomnia.

James Joyce 1882–1941: *Finnegans Wake* (1939)

7 The play was consumed in wholesome fashion by large masses in places of public resort; the novel was self-administered in private.

Flann O'Brien 1911–66: *At Swim-Two-Birds* (1939)

8 The demand that I make of my reader is that he should devote his whole LIFE to reading my works.

James Joyce 1882–1941: Richard Ellmann *James Joyce* (1982)

9 Let us invent a character, a nice respectable, middle-class, middle-aged, maiden lady, with time on her hands and the money to help her pass it. She enjoys pictures, books, music, and the theatre and though to none of these arts (or rather, for consistency's sake, to none of these three arts and the one craft) does she bring much knowledge or discernment, at least, as she is apt to tell her cronies, she 'does know what she likes'. Let us call her Aunt Edna . . . Aunt Edna is universal, and to those who may feel that all the problems of the modern theatre might be solved by her liquidation, let me add that I have no doubt at all that she is also immortal.

Terence Rattigan 1911–77: *Collected Plays* (1953) vol. 2, preface

10 Where are the clerisy? . . . They are people who like to read books . . . the clerisy are those who read for pleasure, but not for idleness; who read for pastime but not to kill time; who love books, but do not live by books.

Robertson Davies 1913–95: *A Voice from the Attic* (1960)

11 A work of art has no importance whatever to society. It is only important to the individual, and only the individual reader is important to me.

Vladimir Nabokov 1899–1977: *Strong Opinions* (1973)

12 The ideal reader of my novels is a lapsed Catholic and a failed musician, short-sighted, colour-blind, auditorily biased, who has read the books that I have read. He should also be about my age.

Anthony Burgess 1917–93: George Plimpton (ed.) *Writers at Work* 4th Series (1977)

13 The Ideal Reader is the reader who reads what you write according to the text, just what's on the page, is conscious of everything that you are doing in a literary way,

Margaret Atwood 1939– : in an interview, November 1983; Earl G. Ingersoll (ed.) *Margaret Atwood: Conversations* (1990)

responds on an emotional level at the right places, laughs at the jokes, doesn't mistake irony for straight comment, gets the puns: all those things the Ideal Reader does. The Ideal Reader for me is somebody who reads the book on the first read-through to see what happens.

1 Novelists who write for a public are, in my opinion, no good; they've discovered who their readers are and, in submitting to their judgement, they're dishing things up like short-order cooks.

Graham Greene 1904–91: Marie-Françoise Allain *The Other Man, Conversations with Graham Greene* (1983)

2 It's the job of the novelist to provide the information through which the book is read. You can't really expect the reader to bring anything other than their interest.

Salman Rushdie 1947– : interview in *Independent* 10 September 1988

3 I occasionally have an anti-Roth reader in mind. I think, 'How he is going to hate this!' That can be just the encouragement I need.

Philip Roth 1933– : George Plimpton (ed.) *The Writer's Chapbook* (1989)

4 There are readings—of the same text—that are dutiful, readings that map and dissect, readings that hear a rustling of unheard sounds, that count grey little pronouns for pleasure and instruction . . . There are personal readings, that snatch for personal meanings, I am full of love, or disgust, or fear, I scan for love, or disgust, or fear. There are—believe it—impersonal readings—where the mind's eye sees the lines move onwards and the mind's ear hears them sing and sing.

Now and then there are readings which make the hairs on the neck, the non-existent pelt, stand on end and tremble, when every word burns and shines hard and clear and infinite and exact, like stones of fire, like points of stars in the dark—readings when the knowledge that we *shall know* the writing differently or better or satisfactorily, runs ahead of any capacity to say what we know, or how.

A. S. Byatt 1936– : *Possession* (1990)

5 I've gotten the readers I want.

Anne Rice 1941– : Michael Riley *Interview with Anne Rice* (1996)

Autobiography see also Biography

6 I am commencing an undertaking, hitherto without precedent, and which will never find an imitator. I desire to set before my fellows the likeness of a man in all the truth of nature, and that man myself.

Myself alone! I know the feeling of my heart, and I know men. I am not made like any of those I have seen; I venture to believe that I am not made like any of those in existence.

Jean-Jacques Rousseau 1712–78: *Confessions* (1782)

refusing an offer to write his memoirs:

7 I should be trading on the blood of my men.

Robert E. Lee 1807–70: attributed, perhaps apocryphal

disclaiming any intention of recording his inner (or even family) life:

1 No man ever did so truly, and no man ever will.

Anthony Trollope 1815–82: *Autobiography* (1883)

2 I write no memoirs. I'm a gentleman. I cannot bring myself to write nastily about persons whose hospitality I have enjoyed.

John Pentland Mahaffy 1839–1919: W. B. Stanford and R. B. McDowell *Mahaffy* (1971)

3 If you do not want to explore an egoism you should not read autobiography.

H. G. Wells 1866–1946: *Experiment in Autobiography* (1934)

4 Reformers are always finally neglected, while the memoirs of the frivolous will always eagerly be read.

Henry 'Chips' Channon 1897–1958: diary, 7 July 1936

5 If I write anything of an autobiographical nature, as I have sometimes idly thought of doing, I shall send it to the British Museum to be kept under lock and key for fifty years. There is no biography of Matthew Arnold . . . in accordance with his own advice; so there certainly need be none of me.

A. E. Housman 1859–1936: letter, 14 December 1933

6 To write one's memoirs is to speak ill of everybody except oneself.

Henri Philippe Pétain 1856–1951: in *Observer* 26 May 1946

7 Autobiographies ought to begin with Chapter Two.

Ellery Sedgwick 1872–1962: *The Happy Profession* (1948)

8 Every autobiography . . . becomes an absorbing work of fiction, with something of the charm of a cryptogram.

H. L. Mencken 1880–1956: *Minority Report* (1956)

9 He made the books and he died.
his own 'sum and history of my life'

William Faulkner 1897–1962: letter to Malcolm Cowley, 11 February 1949

10 Only when one has lost all curiosity about the future has one reached the age to write an autobiography.

Evelyn Waugh 1903–66: *A Little Learning* (1964)

11 Autobiography is now as common as adultery and hardly less reprehensible.

John Grigg 1924– : Leon Harris *The Fine Art of Political Wit* (1965)

12 My problem is that I am not frightfully interested in anything, except myself. And of all forms of fiction autobiography is the most gratuitous.

Tom Stoppard 1937– : *Lord Malquist and Mr Moon* (1966)

13 It is an awkward thing about autobiography; you can't write it in advance.

Bertrand Russell 1872–1970: attributed, 1967

14 An autobiography is an obituary in serial form with the last instalment missing.

Quentin Crisp 1908– : *The Naked Civil Servant* (1968)

15 Next to the writer of real estate advertisements, the autobiographer is the most suspect of prose artists.

Donal Henahan : in *New York Times* 1977

16 Because I am too imaginative.
on being asked why she had refused to write an autobiography

Sylvia Townsend Warner 1893–1978: Claire Harman (ed.) *Diaries of Sylvia Townsend Warner* (1994)

1 I regard that [autobiography] as the height of egotism.

Roald Dahl 1916–90: on 16 May 1983; Jeremy Treglown *Roald Dahl* (1994)

2 Interviews are an art form in themselves. As such, they're fictional and arranged. The illusion that what you're getting is the straight truth from the writer and accurate in every detail is false.

Margaret Atwood 1939– : in an interview, December 1986; Earl G. Ingersoll (ed.) *Margaret Atwood: Conversations* (1990)

3 I shall never write a formal memoir (I have never been my own subject, a sign of truly sickening narcissism).

Gore Vidal 1925– : *Armageddon* (1987)

4 Autobiographies tell more lies than all but the most self-indulgent fiction.

A. S. Byatt 1936– : *Sugar* (1988)

5 There's no such thing as autobiography. There's only art and lies.

Jeanette Winterson 1959– : in *Guardian* 5 July 1994

6 Top politicians generally have an arm's-length acquaintance with their own language: they only truly mean what other people help them say.
on Margaret Thatcher's memoirs

Julian Barnes 1946– : *Letters from London* (1995)

7 Autobiography is an awkward form . . . It's difficult to be honest, not because you're hiding something but because you start self-dramatizing.

David Malouf 1934– : in *Daily Telegraph* 7 September 1996

Bad Writing see Good and Bad Writing

Ballads

8 Certainly I must confess mine own barbarousness, I never heard the old song of Percy and Douglas, that I found not my heart moved more than with a trumpet.

Philip Sidney 1554–86: *The Defence of Poetry* (1595)

9 About six or seven o'clock, I walk out into a common that lies hard by the house, where a great many young wenches keep sheep and cows and sit in the shade singing of ballads . . . I talk to them, and find they want nothing to make them the happiest people in the world, but the knowledge that they are so.

Dorothy Osborne 1627–95: letter, 2 June 1653

10 I knew a very wise man so much of Sir Chr—'s sentiment, that he believed if a man were permitted to make all the ballads, he need not care who should make the laws of a nation.

Andrew Fletcher of Saltoun 1655–1716: 'An Account of a Conversation concerning a Right Regulation of Government for the Good of Mankind. In a Letter to the Marquis of Montrose' (1704)

11 The farmer's daughter hath soft brown hair;
(*Butter and eggs and a pound of cheese*)
And I met with a ballad, I can't say where,
Which wholly consisted of lines like these.

C. S. Calverley 1831–84: 'Ballad' (1872)

1 The true ballads touch a depth and breadth of life, a seriousness and summary finality, that belongs to the species rather than to individuals, and which shuts instantly against the author who separates himself, by name or by rôle or by motive, from the general dumb chorus of human evidence.

Ted Hughes 1930–98: in *Guardian* 14 May 1965

2 The steel and bite of the ballads, so remorseless and yet so lyrical, entered my literary bloodstream, never to depart.

Muriel Spark 1918– : *Curriculum Vitae* (1992)

Beginning and Ending

3 *Semper ad eventum festinat et in medias res*
Non secus ac notas auditorem rapit.

He always hurries to the main event and whisks his audience into the middle of things as though they knew already.

Horace 65–8 BC: *Ars Poetica*; cf. **16:13**

4 Whoa, little book! Slow up! Easy there! Steady!
We've reached the finishing post, yet you're still ready
To gallop uncontrollably on, to run
Past the last page, as if your job weren't done.

Martial AD *c.*40–*c.*104: *Epigrammata*, tr. James Michie

5 Thus endeth the story of the Sangreal, that was briefly drawn out of French into English, the which is a story chronicled for one of the truest and the holiest that is in this world.

Thomas Malory d. 1471: *Le Morte D'Arthur* (1485)

6 Be of good cheer, my weary readers, for I have espied land, as Diogenes said to his weary scholars when he had read to a waste leaf.

waste *in the sense of 'blank'*

Thomas Nashe 1567–1601: *Nashes Lenten Stuffe* (1599)

7 The last thing one knows in constructing a work is what to put first.

Blaise Pascal 1623–62: *Pensées* (1670)

8 I would not give a groat for that man's knowledge in pen-craft, who does not understand this—That the best plain narrative in the world, tacked very close to the last spirited apostrophe to my uncle Toby—would have felt both cold and vapid upon the reader's palate;—therefore I forthwith put an end to the chapter, though I was in the middle of my story.

Laurence Sterne 1713–68: *Tristram Shandy* (1759–67)

on his completion of The Decline and Fall of the Roman Empire*:*

9 I will not dissemble the first emotions of joy on the recovery of my freedom, and, perhaps, the establishment of my fame. But my pride was soon humbled, and a sober melancholy was spread over my mind, by the idea that I had taken an everlasting leave of an old and agreeable companion.

Edward Gibbon 1737–94: *Memoirs of My Life* (1796)

10 The futility of all prefaces I long ago realized; for the more a writer strives to make his views clear, the more confusion he creates.

Johann Wolfgang von Goethe 1749–1832: *Poetry and Truth* (1814)

1 Readers . . . will see in the tell-tale compression of the pages before them, that we are all hastening together to perfect felicity.

Jane Austen 1775–1817: *Northanger Abbey* (1818)

2 My way is to begin with the beginning.

Lord Byron 1788–1824: *Don Juan* (1819–24) canto 1, st. 7

3 All tragedies are finished by a death,
All comedies are ended by a marriage;
The future states of both are left to faith.

Lord Byron 1788–1824: *Don Juan* (1819–24)

4 I want to leave everybody dissatisfied and unhappy at the end of the story—we ought all to be with our own and all other stories.

William Makepeace Thackeray 1811–63: letter, 3 September 1848

5 It would concern the reader little, perhaps, to know, how sorrowfully the pen is laid down at the close of a two-years' imaginative task; or how an author feels as if he were dismissing some portion of himself into the shadowy world, when a crowd of the creatures of his brain are going from him for ever.

Charles Dickens 1812–70: preface to *David Copperfield* (1850)

6 I am finding it very hard to get my novel started. I suffer from stylistic abscesses; and sentences keep itching without coming to a head.
on beginning Madame Bovary

Gustave Flaubert 1821–80: letter, 23 October 1851; cf. **298:8**, **299:2**

7 Conclusions are the weak point of most authors, but some of the fault lies in the very nature of a conclusion, which is at best a negation.

George Eliot 1819–80: letter to John Blackwood, 1 May 1857

8 The end of a novel, like the end of a children's dinner-party, must be made up of sweetmeats and sugar-plums.

Anthony Trollope 1815–82: *Barchester Towers* (1857)

9 Beginnings are always troublesome . . . Even Macaulay's few pages of introduction to his 'Introduction' in the English History are the worst bit of writing in the book.

George Eliot 1819–80: letter to Sara Hennell, 15 August 1859

10 'Where shall I begin, please your Majesty?' he asked. 'Begin at the beginning,' the King said, gravely, 'and go on till you come to the end: then stop.'

Lewis Carroll 1832–98: *Alice's Adventures in Wonderland* (1865)

11 I *do* incline to melancholy endings.

Henry James 1843–1916: letter, 30 October 1878

12 Great is the art of beginning, but greater the art is of
ending;
Many a poem is marred by a superfluous verse.

Henry Wadsworth Longfellow 1807–82: 'Elegiac Verse' (1880)

13 Perhaps the method of rushing at once 'in medias res' is, of all the ways of beginning a story . . . the least objectionable. The reader is made to think the gold lies so near the surface that he will be required to take very little trouble in digging for it.

Anthony Trollope 1815–82: *The Duke's Children* (1880); cf. **15:3**

14 When I sit down to write a novel I do not at all know, and I do not very much care, how it is to end.

Anthony Trollope 1815–82: *Autobiography* (1883)

15 A 'happy ending' . . . a distribution at the last of prizes, pensions, husbands, wives, babies, millions, appended paragraphs, and cheerful remarks.

Henry James 1843–1916: 'The Art of Fiction' (1888)

1 It is just as well that it came to an end. The endless cohabitation with these imaginary people had begun to make me not a little nervous.
on finishing Hedda Gabler

Henrik Ibsen 1828–1906: letter, 1890

2 There is no difficulty in beginning; the trouble is to leave off!

Henry James 1843–1916: in 1891; Leon Edel (ed.) *The Diary of Alice James* (1965)

3 If you are going to make a book end badly, it must end badly from the beginning.

Robert Louis Stevenson 1850–94: letter to J. M. Barrie, November 1892

4 It's finished! A scratching of the pen writing the final word, and suddenly this entire company of people who have spoken into my ear, gesticulated before my eyes, lived with me for so many years, becomes a band of phantoms who retreat, fade, and dissolve—are made pallid and indistinct by the sunlight of this brilliant and sombre day.
on finishing Almayer's Folly

Joseph Conrad 1857–1924: letter, 24 April 1894

5 The time-honoured bread-sauce of the happy ending.

Henry James 1843–1916: *Theatricals* (1894) 2nd series

6 A poem is never finished; it's always an accident that puts a stop to it—that is to say, gives it to the public.

Paul Valéry 1871–1945: *Littérature* (1930)

7 My last page is always latent in my first; but the intervening windings of the way become clear only as I write.

Edith Wharton 1862–1937: *A Backward Glance* (1934)

8 I have three more chapters and an epilogue to do, and then I shall spend about two months putting on the twiddly bits.
of Keep the Aspidistra Flying

George Orwell 1903–50: letter to Rayner Heppenstall, September 1935

9 I find it only too easy to write opening chapters—and at the moment the story is not unfolding. I squandered so much on the original 'Hobbit' (which was not meant to have a sequel) that it is difficult to find anything new in that world.
of the genesis of The Lord of the Rings

J. R. R. Tolkien 1892–1973: letter to Stanley Unwin, February 1938; Humphrey Carpenter *J. R. R. Tolkien* (1977)

10 The beginning of a book holds more apprehensions for the novelist than the ending. After living with a book for a year or two, he has come to terms with his unconsciousness—the end will be imposed. But if a book is started in the wrong way, it may never be finished.

Graham Greene 1904–91: *In Search of a Character* (1961)

11 The dreaded essential opening sentences.

Graham Greene 1904–91: *In Search of a Character* (1961)

12 The important thing is not what the author, or any artist, had in mind to begin with but at what point he decided to stop.

D. W. Harding 1906– : *Experience into Words* (1963)

13 Ends always give me trouble. Characters run away with you, and so won't fit on to what is coming.

E. M. Forster 1879–1970: George Plimpton (ed.) *The Writer's Chapbook* (1989)

1 A good beginning means a good book.

John Braine 1922–86: *Writing a Novel* (1974)

2 Such a sentence makes you hear the sound of books slapping shut all over the library.
of the opening sentence of Ivanhoe

Joan Aiken 1924– : *The Way to Write for Children* (1982)

3 I . . . have an entire cemetery of abandoned books, or rather, of fragments.

Graham Greene 1904–91: Marie-Françoise Allain *The Other Man, Conversations with Graham Greene* (1983)

4 I always wanted to write a book that ended with the word *mayonnaise.*

Richard Brautigan 1935–84: attributed

5 When I have finished a novel, I am usually exhausted. I have exhausted my fiction energy, and there comes a period during which I don't write much.

Margaret Atwood 1939– : in an interview, February 1985; Earl G. Ingersoll (ed.) *Margaret Atwood: Conversations* (1990)

6 The first sentence of every novel should be: 'Trust me, this will take time but there is order here, very faint, very human.'

Michael Ondaatje 1943– : *In the Skin of a Lion* (1987)

7 One of the most difficult things is the first paragraph. I have spent many months on a first paragraph and once I get it, the rest comes out very easily. In the first paragraph you solve most of the problems with your book. The theme is defined, the style, the tone.

Gabriel García Márquez 1928– : George Plimpton (ed.) *The Writer's Chapbook* (1989)

8 I always start a novel by writing its first page and its last page, which seem to survive almost intact through all the following drafts and changes.

Jerzy Kosinski 1933–91: George Plimpton (ed.) *The Writer's Chapbook* (1989)

9 If you read twenty or thirty pages by a writer, and want to continue, you are in his sea and swimming in that sea. He can write quite badly after that. Because by that time, you're in his sea, and you're moving forward.

Brian Moore 1921– : Rosemary Hartill *Writers Revealed* (1989)

10 It's pure instinct. The curtain comes down when the rhythm seems right—when the action calls for a finish. I'm very fond of curtain lines, of doing them properly.

Harold Pinter 1930– : George Plimpton (ed.) *The Writer's Chapbook* (1989)

11 I'm always aware, when I've 'finished' a piece, of being utterly defeated and excluded—as if I'd been shoved aside by somebody I do not like one bit. Yet it seems to be the only way I can do it.

Ted Hughes 1930–98: letter to William Scammell, 23 November 1990

12 You don't say, 'I've done it!' You come, with a kind of horrible desperation, to realize that this will do.

Anthony Burgess 1917–93: Clare Boylan (ed.) *The Agony and the Ego* (1993)

Best-sellers see also **Popular Fiction**

13 All Rome is mad about my book:
It's praised, they hum the lines, shops stock it,
It peeps from every hand and pocket.

Martial AD *c.*40–*c.*104: *Epigrammata* tr. James Michie

1 Kansas City's literary tone is improving. The six best sellers here last week were 'Fools of Nature' [etc.].
OED's earliest citation for the term 'best-seller'

Anonymous: in *Kansas Times & Star* 25 April 1889

2 I attribute my good fortune to the simple fact that I have always tried to write straight from my own heart to the hearts of others.
on the success of her first novel, The Romance of Two Worlds, *in 1886*

Marie Corelli 1855–1924: Jerome K. Jerome (ed.) *My First Book* (1894)

3 If *Hamlet* and *Oedipus* were published now, they wouldn't sell more than 100 copies, unless they were pushed.

D. H. Lawrence 1885–1930: letter to Edward Garnett, 1913

4 Nearly all bookish people are snobs, and especially the more enlightened among them. They are apt to assume that if a writer has immense circulation, if he is enjoyed by plain persons, and if he can fill several theatres at once, he cannot possibly be worth reading and merits only indifference and disdain.

Arnold Bennett 1867–1931: in *Evening Standard* 19 July 1928

5 I don't know about selling the pass, but he has sold twenty thousand copies.
to the comment that in suppressing all footnotes to his biography of Elizabeth I in order not to discourage the general reader, Neale had 'sold the pass'

Eileen Power 1889–1940: John Neale in *Nature* 24 August 1963 'History in a Scientific Age'

6 A best-seller is the gilded tomb of a mediocre talent.

Logan Pearsall Smith 1865–1946: *Afterthoughts* (1931)

7 Even the most critical reader who brings only an ironical appreciation of their work cannot avoid noticing a certain power, the secret of their success with the majority. Bad writing, false sentiment, sheer silliness, and a preposterous narrative are all carried along by the magnificent vitality of their author.

Q. D. Leavis 1906–81: *Fiction and the Reading Public* (1932)

8 My brother took to the trade without a moment's reluctance. He wrote a best-seller before he was eighteen.
Alec Waugh (1898–1981) published The Loom of Youth *in 1917*

Evelyn Waugh 1903–66: in *Nash's Pall Mall Magazine* March 1937

9 The principle of procrastinated rape is said to be the ruling one in all the great best-sellers.

V. S. Pritchett 1900–97: *The Living Novel* (1946) 'Clarissa'

10 A best-seller was a book which somehow sold well simply because it was selling well.

Daniel J. Boorstin 1914– : *Images* (1961)

11 Only a person with a Best-Seller mind can write Best-Sellers.

Aldous Huxley 1894–1963: attributed

12 Best-sellers are about murder, money, revenge, ambition, and sex, sex, sex. So are literary novels. But best-selling authors give you more per page: there are five murders, three world financial crises, two bankruptcies and a civil war in *A Dangerous Fortune*. There is more drama in it than a literary author will deal with in a lifetime of work.

Ken Follett 1949– : Barry Turner *The Writer's Companion* (1996)

13 I was tired of writing a lot of serious stuff that didn't pay the bills. I wanted to create a best-seller.
of writing The Godfather

Mario Puzo 1920– : in *Daily Telegraph* 19 October 1996

The Bible

1 Hooly writ is the scripture of puples, for it is maad, that alle puplis schulden knowe it.

St Jerome c. AD 342–420: attributed, in J. Forshall and F. Madden (eds.) *The Holy Bible . . . in the Earliest English Versions* (1850) vol. 1 'The Prologue' [probably by John Purvey, c.1353–c.1428]

2 The devil can cite Scripture for his purpose.

William Shakespeare 1564–1616: *The Merchant of Venice* (1596–8)

3 I walk many times into the pleasant fields of the Holy Scriptures, where I pluck up the goodly green herbs of sentences, eat them by reading, chew them up musing, and lay them up at length in the seat of memory . . . so I may the less perceive the bitterness of this miserable life.

Elizabeth I 1533–1603: Adam Fox (ed) *A Book of Devotions* (1970)

4 The pencil of the Holy Ghost hath laboured more in describing the afflictions of Job than the felicities of Solomon.

Francis Bacon 1561–1626: *Essays* (1625) 'Of Adversity'

5 You cannot name any example in any heathen author but I will better it in Scripture.

James I 1566–1625: Thomas Overbury 'Crumms Fal'n From King James's Table'

6 Blessed Lord, who hast caused all holy Scriptures to be written for our learning; Grant that we may in such wise hear them, read, mark, learn, and inwardly digest them, that by patience, and comfort of thy holy Word, we may embrace, and ever hold fast the blessed hope of everlasting life.

The Book of Common Prayer 1662: *Collects*; collect for the second Sunday in Advent

7 I have not for these things fished in other men's waters; my Bible and my Concordance are my only library in my writing.

John Bunyan 1628–88: 'Solomon's Temple Spiritualized' (1688); preface

Samuel ***Johnson*** *noticed that* ***Collins****'s only literary possession was a testament:*

8 I have but one book, but that is the best.

William Collins 1721–59: in *Dictionary of National Biography*

9 These books (OT), beginning with Genesis and ending with Revelation (which by the **** is a book of riddles that requires a revelation to understand it), are, we are told, the word of God.

Thomas Paine 1737–1809: *The Age of Reason* (1793) pt 1

10 The English Bible, a book which, if everything else in our language should perish, would alone suffice to show the whole extent of its beauty and power.

Lord Macaulay 1800–59: T. F. Ellis (ed.) *Miscellaneous Writings of Lord Macaulay* (1860) 'John Dryden' (1828)

11 There's a great text in Galatians,
Once you trip on it, entails
Twenty-nine distinct damnations,
One sure, if another fails.

Robert Browning 1812–89: 'Soliloquy of the Spanish Cloister' (1842)

1 He [the translator] will find one English book and one only, where, as in the *Iliad* itself, perfect plainness of speech is allied with perfect nobleness; and that book is the Bible.

Matthew Arnold 1822–88: *On Translating Homer* (1861)

2 Never forget, gentlemen, never forget that this is *not* the Bible. This, gentlemen, is only a *translation* of the Bible.
to a meeting of his diocesan clergy, as he held up a copy of the 'Authorized Version'

Richard Whately 1787–1863: H. Solly *These Eighty Years* (1893)

3 We have used the Bible as if it was a constable's handbook—an opium-dose for keeping beasts of burden patient while they are being overloaded.

Charles Kingsley 1819–75: *Letters to the Chartists*

4 LORD ILLINGWORTH: The Book of Life begins with a man and a woman in a garden.
MRS ALLONBY: It ends with Revelations.

Oscar Wilde 1854–1900: *A Woman of No Importance* (1893)

5 The New Testament, and to a very large extent the Old, *is* the soul of man. You cannot criticize it. It criticizes you.

John Jay Chapman 1862–1933: letter, 26 March 1898

of reading the Bible daily with his mother:
6 The one essential part of all my education.

John Ruskin 1819–1900: in *Dictionary of National Biography*

7 An apology for the Devil: It must be remembered that we have only heard one side of the case. God has written all the books.

Samuel Butler 1835–1902: *Notebooks* (1912)

8 I read the book of Job last night. I don't think God comes well out of it.

Virginia Woolf 1882–1941: letter to Lady Robert Cecil, 12 November 1922

9 Those who talk of the Bible as a 'monument of English prose' are merely admiring it as a monument over the grave of Christianity.

T. S. Eliot 1888–1965: *Religion and Literature* (1935)

10 The Bible . . . is a lesson in how not to write for the movies.

Raymond Chandler 1888–1959: letter to Edgar Carter, 28 March 1947

11 The number one book of the ages was written by a committee, and it was called the Bible.

Louis B. Mayer 1885–1957: attributed

12 I know of no book which has been a source of brutality and sadistic conduct, both public and private, that can compare with the Bible.

Reginald Paget 1908–90: in *Observer* 28 June 1964

13 It's just called 'The Bible' now. We dropped the word 'Holy' to give it a more mass-market appeal.
a publisher's view

Judith Young: attributed, 1989

Biography see also **Autobiography**

14 Many brave men lived before Agamemnon's time; but they are all, unmourned and unknown, covered by the long night, because they lack their sacred poet.

Horace 65–8 BC: *Odes*

1 Our Grubstreet biographers watch for the death of a great man, like so many undertakers, on purpose to make a penny of him.

Joseph Addison 1672–1719: *Freeholder* (1715–6)

2 Curll (who is one of the new terrors of Death) has been writing letters to everybody for memoirs of his life.

John Arbuthnot 1667–1735: letter to Jonathan Swift, 13 January 1733; cf. **22:12, 23:8**

3 There has rarely passed a life of which a judicious and faithful narrative would not be useful.

Samuel Johnson 1709–84: 'Dignity and Uses of Biography' (1750)

4 Nobody can write the life of a man, but those who have eat and drunk and lived in social intercourse with him.

Samuel Johnson 1709–84: James Boswell *Life of Samuel Johnson* (1791) 31 March 1772

5 If a man is to write *A Panegyric* he may keep vices out of sight; but if he professes to write *A Life*, he must represent it as it really was.

Samuel Johnson 1709–84: James Boswell *Life of Samuel Johnson* (1791) 1777

6 A funeral oration rather than a history.
of Thomas Sprat's Life of Cowley *(1668)*

Samuel Johnson 1709–84: in *Dictionary of National Biography*

7 This new-fashioned biography seems to value itself upon perpetuating every thing that is injurious and detracting.

Hannah More 1745–1833: letter, 1786

8 Many of the greatest men that ever lived have written biography. Boswell was one of the smallest men that ever lived, and he has beaten them all.

Lord Macaulay 1800–59: in *Edinburgh Review* 1831

9 Lives of great men all remind us
We can make our lives sublime,
And, departing, leave behind us
Footprints on the sands of time.

Henry Wadsworth Longfellow 1807–82: 'A Psalm of Life' (1838)

10 A well-written Life is almost as rare as a well-spent one.

Thomas Carlyle 1795–1881: *Critical and Miscellaneous Essays* (1838) 'Jean Paul Friedrich Richter'

11 There is no life of a man, faithfully recorded, but is a heroic poem of its sort, rhymed or unrhymed.

Thomas Carlyle 1795–1881: *Critical and Miscellaneous Essays* (1838) 'Sir Walter Scott'

12 Then there is my noble and biographical friend who has added a new terror to death.
on Lord Campbell's Lives of the Lord Chancellors *being written without the consent of heirs or executors*

Charles Wetherell 1770–1846: Lord St Leonards *Misrepresentations in Campbell's Lives of Lyndhurst and Brougham* (1869); also attributed to Lord Lyndhurst (1772–1863); cf. **22:2, 247:6**

13 No quailing, Mrs Gaskell! no drawing back!
apropos her undertaking to write the life of Charlotte ***Brontë***

Patrick Brontë 1777–1861: letter from Mrs Gaskell to Ellen Nussey, 24 July 1855

14 I never *did* write a biography, and I don't exactly know how to set about it; you see I have to be accurate and keep to facts; a most difficult thing for a writer of fiction.
while writing her Life of Charlotte Brontë

Elizabeth Gaskell 1810–65: letter to Harriet Anderson, 15 March 1856

15 Mind, no biography!
injunction to his daughters

William Makepeace Thackeray 1811–63: John Sutherland *Is Heathcliff a Murderer?* (1996)

1 It would not suffice . . . to scrape together a few facts, to indulge in some fiction, to tell a few anecdotes, and then to call his book a biography.

Anthony Trollope 1815–82: *Ralph the Heir* (1871)

2 Biographers are generally a disease of English literature.

George Eliot 1819–80: Michael Holroyd 'How I Fell into Biography' (1988)

3 A biography written with a single eye to giving all the information presumably desirable by an intelligent reader may be not only useful, but intensely interesting, and even a model of literary art.

Leslie Stephen 1832–1904: in *Athenaeum* 23 December 1882

4 Every great man nowadays has his disciples, and it is always Judas who writes the biography.

Oscar Wilde 1854–1900: *Intentions* (1891) 'The Critic as Artist'

5 Collect all the facts that can be collected about the life of Racine and you will never learn from them the art of his verse.

Paul Valéry 1871–1945: *Introduction to the Method of Leonardo da Vinci* (1895)

6 It is not a Life at all. It is a Reticence, in three volumes.
on J. W. Cross's Life of George Eliot

W. E. Gladstone 1809–98: E. F. Benson *As We Were* (1930)

7 The Art of Biography
Is different from Geography.
Geography is about Maps,
But Biography is about Chaps.

Edmund Clerihew Bentley 1875–1956: *Biography for Beginners* (1905)

8 It occurred to him that, in a world governed by the law of mortality, men might be handsomely entertained on one another's remains . . . He had learned the wisdom of the grave-digger in *Hamlet*, and knew that there are many rotten corpses nowadays, that will scarce hold the laying in. So he seized on them before they were cold, and commemorated them in batches . . . His books commanded a large sale, and modern biography was established.
on the bookseller and publisher Edmund Curll (1675–1747)

Walter Raleigh 1861–1922: *Six Essays on Johnson* (1910); cf. **22:2**

9 My sole wish is to frustrate as utterly as possible the post-mortem exploiter . . . I have long thought of launching, by a provision in my will, a curse not less explicit than Shakespeare's own on any such as try to move my bones.

Henry James 1843–1916: letter, 7 April 1914

on hearing that Arthur Benson was to write the life of Rossetti:
10 No, no, no, it won't do. *Dear* Arthur, we know just what he can, so beautifully, do, but no, oh no, this is to have the story of a purple man written by a white, or at the most, a pale green man.

Henry James 1843–1916: George Lyttelton, letter to Rupert Hart-Davis, 28 February 1957

11 Discretion is not the better part of biography.

Lytton Strachey 1880–1932: Michael Holroyd *Lytton Strachey* vol. 1 (1967)

12 How far we are going to read a poet when we can read about a poet is a problem to lay before biographers.

Virginia Woolf 1882–1941: *The Common Reader* (2nd series, 1932)

1 I wonder how people can write the lives of poets, since the poets themselves could not write their own lives. There are too many mysteries, too many true lies, too many entanglements.

Jean Cocteau 1889–1963: *Opium* (1933)

2 A biography should be a dissection and demonstration of how a particular human being was made and worked.

H. G. Wells 1866–1946: *Experiment in Autobiography* (1934)

3 A shilling life will give you all the facts.

W. H. Auden 1907–73: 'A Shilling Life' (1936)

4 Do not send me your manuscript. Worse than the practice of writing books about living men is the conduct of living men in supervising such books.

A. E. Housman 1859–1936: letter to his would-be biographer Houston Martin, 22 March 1936

5 If I have given you delight
By aught that I have done,
Let me lie quiet in that night
Which shall be yours anon:
And for the little, little span
The dead are borne in mind,
Seek not to question other than
The books I leave behind.

Rudyard Kipling 1865–1936: 'The Appeal' (1940)

6 The 'Higher Cannibalism' in biography . . . The exhumation of scarcely cold notorieties, defenceless females for choice, and tricking them out with sprightly inferences and 'sex' deductions to suit the mood of the market.

Rudyard Kipling 1865–1936: *Something of Myself* (1937)

7 Anyone turning biographer commits himself to lies, to concealment, to hypocrisy, to flattery, and even to hiding his own lack of understanding, for biographical truth is not to be had, and even if it were it couldn't be used.
in a letter to Arnold Zweig who had suggested being his biographer

Sigmund Freud 1856–1939: Paul Roazen *Freud and his Followers* (1971)

8 There never was a good biography of a good novelist. There couldn't be. He is too many people, if he's any good.

F. Scott Fitzgerald 1896–1940: Edmund Wilson (ed.) *The Crack-Up* (1945)

9 Almost any biographer, if he respects facts, can give us much more than another fact to add to our collection. He can give us the creative fact; the fertile fact; the fact that suggests and engenders.

Virginia Woolf 1882–1941: *The Death of the Moth* (1942) 'The Art of Biography'

10 And kept his heart a secret to the end
From all the picklocks of biographers.
of Robert E. Lee

Stephen Vincent Benét 1898–1943: *John Brown's Body* (1928)

11 Just how difficult it is to write biography can be reckoned by anybody who sits down and considers just how many people know the truth about his or her love affairs.

Rebecca West 1892–1983: in *Vogue* 1 November 1952

12 A biographer has an overriding duty: he is the servant of the reading public, not of a family. If faced with a ban, he can decline to write the book. At the very least, he must state that evidence exists which he has not been able to use fully.

A. J. P. Taylor 1906–90: in *Observer* 1 November 1964

1 One of my strongest opinions is that investigation of an author's biography is an entirely vain and false approach to his works.

J. R. R. Tolkien 1892–1973: Humphrey Carpenter *J. R. R. Tolkien* (1977)

2 The past exudes legend: one can't make pure clay of time's mud. There is no life that can be recaptured wholly; as it was. Which is to say that all biography is ultimately fiction.

Bernard Malamud 1914–86: *Dubin's Lives* (1979)

3 What novelist, given the choice, wouldn't prefer you to reread one of his novels rather than read his biography?

Julian Barnes 1946– : *Flaubert's Parrot* (1984)

4 I can take some credit for having achieved the opposite of what biographers usually do. I wrote about someone famous and succeeded in plunging him into public obscurity.

her assessment of the effect of her biography of Patrick Pearse

Ruth Dudley Edwards 1944– : 'Confessions of an Irish Revisionist' (1988)

5 The Meals-on-Wheels service of the book world.

a definition of literary biography

Sheridan Morley 1941– : Hilary Spurling 'Neither Morbid nor Ordinary' (1988)

6 There are plenty of biographies that are excellent, really wonderful, and out of print. They'd rather commission a new one by some dolt than reprint the great ones.

A. S. Byatt 1936– : in *Observer* 31 March 1991 'Sayings of the Week'

7 To make a life intelligible, it must first become coherent.

Peter Ackroyd 1949– : in a review, 1991; John Haffenden in *Times Literary Supplement* 23 February 1996

8 I read biographies backwards, beginning with the death. If that takes my fancy I go through the rest. Childhood seldom interests me at all.

Alan Bennett 1934– : *Writing Home* (1994)

9 It's an excellent life of somebody else. But I've really lived inside myself, and she can't get in there.

on a biography of himself

Robertson Davies 1913–95: interview, in *The Times* 4 April 1995

10 A burglar at the subject's keyhole, shamelessly marketing voyeuristic delights.

on biographers

Janet Malcolm : in *London Review of Books* 19 October 1995

11 The shadow in the garden.

describing his biographer James Atlas

Saul Bellow 1915– : in *New Yorker* 26 June 1995

12 Biographies are likely to be either acts of worship or acts of destruction. And the best ones have elements of both.

Humphrey Carpenter 1946– : in conversation with Lyndall Gordon; John Batchelor (ed.) *The Art of Literary Biography* (1995)

13 Biographers know nothing about the intimate sex lives of their own wives, but they think they know all about Stendhal's or Faulkner's.

Milan Kundera 1929– : *Testaments Betrayed* (1995)

when asked about the difference in his practice between writing novels and biographies:

14 Fiction requires truth-telling, whereas in a biography one can make things up.

Peter Ackroyd 1949– : John Haffenden in *Times Literary Supplement* 23 February 1996

1 The facts of life are to the biographer what the text of a novel is to the critic.

Victoria Glendinning 1937– : John Haffenden in *Times Literary Supplement* 23 February 1996

2 To be more interested in the writer than the writing is just eternal human vulgarity.

Martin Amis 1949– : on BBC2 *Bookmark*, 9 March 1996

3 For the English, biography is a wonderful way out of having to think—the more somebody is biographed, the less he or she is read.

Germaine Greer 1939– : on BBC2 *Bookmark*, 9 March 1996

4 Along comes this little petty bourgeois biographer who has a totally uninteresting life herself or himself and who tries to measure this giant by their own pygmy standards. Biography is a form by which little people take revenge on big people.

Edmund White 1940– : on BBC2 *Bookmark*, 9 March 1996

5 The problem with biographies of writers is that the early parts of their lives are very interesting—what's laid out is all the material they're eventually going to use—but after a certain point the most significant thing a writer does is—write books. All the interest is in the work.

David Malouf 1934– : in *Daily Telegraph* 7 September 1996

6 I have done my best to die before this book is published. It now seems possible that I may not succeed . . . I shall try to keep my sense of humour and the perspective of eternity.

to his biographer, Humphrey Carpenter, shortly before publication

Robert Runcie 1921– : postscript to the biography; in *The Times* 7 September 1996

7 I could not pin him down to a conventional biographical text like a dead insect.

of his biography of Robert Runcie

Humphrey Carpenter 1946– : in *Sunday Telegraph* 15 September 1996

Books see also Reading

8 A large book is like great evil.

proverbially contracted 'Great book, great evil'

Callimachus *c.*305–*c.*240 BC: fragment 465

9 *Cui dono lepidum novum libellum*
Arido modo pumice expolitum?

To whom shall I give my nice new little book polished dry with pumice?

Catullus *c.*84–*c.*54 BC: *Carmina* no. 1

10 Homer on parchment pages!
The *Iliad* and all the adventures
Of Ulysses, foe of Priam's kingdom!
All locked within a piece of skin
Folded into several little sheets!

Martial AD *c.*40–*c.*104: *Epigrammata* tr. W. C. A. Ker

11 The reason why there is no table or index added hereunto, is, that every page in this work is so full of signal remarks, that were they couched in an index, it would make a volume as big as the book, and so make the postern gate bear no proportion with the building.

James Howell 1594?–1666: *Proedria Basilike* (1664)

1 An empty book is like an infant's soul, in which anything may be written. It is capable of all things, but containeth nothing.

Thomas Traherne *c.*1637–74: *Centuries of Meditations*

2 Their books of stature small they took in hand,
Which with pellucid horn securèd are,
To save from finger wet the letter fair.

William Shenstone 1714–63: *The Schoolmistress* (1742)

3 I hate books; they only teach us to talk about things we know nothing about.

Jean-Jacques Rousseau 1712–78: *Émile* (1762)

4 He used to say, that no man read long together with a folio on his table:—Books, said he, that you may carry to the fire, and hold readily in your hand, are the most useful after all.

Samuel Johnson 1709–84: John Hawkins *Works of Samuel Johnson* (1787) vol. 11

5 A book reads the better which is our own, and has been so long known to us, that we know the topography of its blots, and dog's ears, and can trace the dirt in it to having read it at tea with buttered muffins.

Charles Lamb 1775–1834: *Last Essays of Elia* (1833)

6 Books think for me.

Charles Lamb 1775–1834: *Last Essays of Elia* (1833) 'Detached Thoughts on Books and Reading'

7 A good book is the best of friends, the same to-day and for ever.

Martin Tupper 1810–89: *Proverbial Philosophy* Series I (1838) 'Of Reading'

8 A good book is the purest essence of a human soul.

Thomas Carlyle 1795–1881: speech in support of the London Library, 24 June 1840

9 No furniture so charming as books.

Sydney Smith 1771–1845: Lady Holland *Memoir* (1855); cf. **28:6**

10 Bessie asked if I would have a book: the word *book* acted as a transient stimulus, and I begged her to fetch 'Gulliver's Travels' from the library.

Charlotte Brontë 1816–55: *Jane Eyre* (1847)

11 'Rasselas' looked dull to my trifling taste; I saw nothing about fairies, nothing about genii; no bright variety seemed spread over the closely-printed pages.

Charlotte Brontë 1816–55: *Jane Eyre* (1847)

12 Books are made not like children but like pyramids . . . and they're just as useless! and they stay in the desert! . . . Jackals piss at their foot and the bourgeois climb up on them.

Gustave Flaubert 1821–80: letter to Ernest Feydeau, November/December 1857

13 'What is the use of a book', thought Alice, 'without pictures or conversations?'

Lewis Carroll 1832–98: *Alice's Adventures in Wonderland* (1865)

14 All books are divisible into two classes, the books of the hour, and the books of all time.

John Ruskin 1819–1900: *Sesame and Lilies* (1865)

15 I am afraid I can think of no suggestions for plates for my 'English Vignettes'—and to tell the truth the somewhat impracticable purpose of these few lines is to express my grief at my would-be-delicate and to-be-read-on-its-own-account prose being served up in that manner. The thought is painful to me.

Henry James 1843–1916: letter, 29 July 1878

1 There is no Frigate like a Book
To take us Lands away
Nor any Coursers like a Page
Of prancing Poetry.

Emily Dickinson 1830–86: *Complete Poems* (1955) 'A Book (2)'

2 Child! do not throw this book about;
Refrain from the unholy pleasure
Of cutting all the pictures out!
Preserve it as your chiefest treasure.

Hilaire Belloc 1870–1953: *A Bad Child's Book of Beasts* (1896) dedication

3 I have known her pass the whole evening without mentioning a single book, or *in fact anything unpleasant*, at all.

Henry Reed 1914–86: *A Very Great Man Indeed* (1953 radio play)

4 The possession of a book becomes a substitute for reading it.

Anthony Burgess 1917–93: in *New York Times Book Review* 4 December 1966

5 It is a mistake to think that books have come to stay. The human race did without them for thousands of years and may decide to do without them again.

E. M. Forster 1879–1970: attributed

6 Books do furnish a room.

Anthony Powell 1905– : title of novel (1971); cf. **27:9**

7 Books are a refuge and a reservoir of power. The mills of books grind slowly but they grind exceedingly small.

Arthur Bryant 1899–1985: at a Foyle's lunch June 1981; Andrew Roberts *Eminent Churchillians* (1994)

8 The good of a book lies in its being read.

Umberto Eco 1932– : *The Name of the Rose* (1981)

9 It's certainly difficult to think of a better symbol of civilization.
of books

Philip Larkin 1922–85: *Required Writing* (1983)

10 After all, human beings come and go, while books remain forever.

Amos Oz 1939– : in *New Yorker* 25 December 1995 'Chekhov in Hebrew'

11 The book is the greatest interactive medium of all time. You can underline it, write in the margins, fold down a page, skip ahead. And you can take it anywhere.
on taking over as head of Penguin Books

Michael Lynton : in *Daily Telegraph* 19 August 1996

12 You can't tell a book by its cover.

Anonymous: proverb

Borrowed Titles

13 Antic hay (1923).

Aldous Huxley 1894–1963

My men, like satyrs grazing on the lawns,
Shall with their goat feet dance an antic hay.

Christopher Marlowe 1564–93: *Edward II* (1593)

1 Arms and the man (1898). — **George Bernard Shaw** 1856–1950

Arma virumque cano, Troiae qui primus ab oris
Italiam fato profugus Laviniaque venit
Litora, multum ille et terris iactatus et alto
Vi superum, saevae memorem Iunonis ob iram.

I sing of arms and the man who first from the shores of Troy came destined an exile to Italy and the Lavinian beaches, a man much buffeted on land and on the deep by force of the gods because of fierce Juno's never-forgetting anger.

Virgil 70–19 BC: *Aeneid*

2 Blithe spirit (1942). — **Noël Coward** 1899–1973

Hail to thee, blithe Spirit!
Bird thou never wert,
That from Heaven, or near it,
Pourest thy full heart.

Percy Bysshe Shelley 1792–1822: 'To a Skylark' (1819)

3 Blue remembered hills (1984). — **Dennis Potter** 1935–94

What are those blue remembered hills,
What spires, what farms are those?

A. E. Housman 1859–1936: *A Shropshire Lad* (1896)

4 Brave new world (1932). — **Aldous Huxley** 1894–1963

How beauteous mankind is! O brave new world,
That has such people in't.

William Shakespeare 1564–1616: *The Tempest* (1611)

5 Cakes and ale (1930) — **W. Somerset Maugham** 1874–1965

Dost thou think, because thou art virtuous, there shall be no more cakes and ale?

William Shakespeare 1564–1616: *Twelfth Night* (1601)

6 Darkness visible (1979). — **William Golding** 1911–93

No light, but rather darkness visible
Served only to discover sights of woe.

John Milton 1608–74: *Paradise Lost* (1667)

7 The darling buds of May (1958). — **H. E. Bates** 1905–74

Rough winds do shake the darling buds of May,
And summer's lease hath all too short a date.

William Shakespeare 1564–1616: sonnet 18

8 Devices and desires (1989). — **P. D. James** 1920–

We have followed too much the devices and desires of our own hearts.

The Book of Common Prayer 1662: *Morning Prayer* General Confession

9 The dogs of war (1974). — **Frederick Forsyth** 1938–

Cry, 'Havoc!' and let slip the dogs of war.

William Shakespeare 1564–1616: *Julius Caesar* (1599)

10 Fame is the spur (1940). — **Howard Spring** 1889–1965

Fame is the spur that the clear spirit doth raise
(That last infirmity of noble mind)
To scorn delights, and live laborious days.

John Milton 1608–74: 'Lycidas' (1638)

1 Far from the madding crowd (1874). — **Thomas Hardy** 1840–1928

Far from the madding crowd's ignoble strife,
Their sober wishes never learned to stray.

Thomas Gray 1716–71: *Elegy Written in a Country Churchyard* (1751)

2 For whom the bell tolls (1940). — **Ernest Hemingway** 1899–1961

Any man's death diminishes me, because I am involved in Mankind; And therefore never send to know for whom the bell tolls; it tolls for thee.

John Donne 1572–1631: *Devotions upon Emergent Occasions* (1624)

3 Gone with the wind (1936). — **Margaret Mitchell** 1900–49

I have forgot much, Cynara! gone with the wind,
Flung roses, roses, riotously, with the throng,
Dancing, to put thy pale, lost lilies out of mind.

Ernest Dowson 1867–1900: 'Non Sum Qualis Eram' (1896)

4 The grapes of wrath (1939). — **John Steinbeck** 1902–68

He is trampling out the vintage where the grapes of
wrath are stored.

Julia Ward Howe 1819–1910: 'Battle Hymn of the Republic' (1862)

5 The heart is a lonely hunter (1940). — **Carson McCullers** 1917–67

My heart is a lonely hunter that hunts on a lonely hill.

Fiona McLeod 1855–1905: 'The Lonely Hunter' (1896)

6 Many inventions (1893). — **Rudyard Kipling** 1865–1936

God hath made man upright; but they have sought out many inventions.

Bible: Ecclesiastes

7 Remembrance of things past (1913–27, translation by C. K. Scott-Moncrieff and S. Hudson of *À la recherche du temps perdu*). — **Marcel Proust** 1871–1922

When to the sessions of sweet silent thought
I summon up remembrance of things past.

William Shakespeare 1564–1616: sonnet 30

8 Rewards and fairies (1910). — **Rudyard Kipling** 1865–1936

Farewell, rewards and fairies,
Good housewives now may say,
For now foul sluts in dairies
Do fare as well as they.

Richard Corbet 1582–1635: 'The Fairies' Farewell'

9 The seven pillars of wisdom (1926). — **T. E. Lawrence** 1888–1935

Wisdom hath builded her house, she hath hewn out her seven pillars.

Bible: Proverbs

10 The sound and the fury (1929). — **William Faulkner** 1897–1962

It is a tale
Told by an idiot, full of sound and fury,
Signifying nothing.

William Shakespeare 1564–1616: *Macbeth* (1606)

1 A summer birdcage (1963).

Margaret Drabble 1939–

'Tis just like a summer birdcage in a garden; the birds that are without despair to get in, and the birds that are within despair, and are in a consumption, for fear they shall never get out.

John Webster c.1580–c.1625: *The White Devil* (1612)

2 Tender is the night (1934).

F. Scott Fitzgerald 1896–1940

Already with thee! tender is the night.

John Keats 1795–1821: 'Ode to a Nightingale' (1820)

3 An unofficial rose (1962)

Iris Murdoch 1919–

Unkempt about those hedges blows
An English unofficial rose.

Rupert Brooke 1887–1915: 'The Old Vicarage, Grantchester' (1915)

4 Where angels fear to tread (1905).

E. M. Forster 1879–1970

For fools rush in where angels fear to tread.

Alexander Pope 1688–1744: *An Essay on Criticism* (1711)

Borrowing Books see also **Libraries**

5 Your *borrowers of books*—those mutilators of collections, spoilers of the symmetry of shelves, and creators of odd volumes.

Charles Lamb 1775–1834: *Essays of Elia* (1823) 'The Two Races of Men'

6 Please return this book; I find that though many of my friends are poor arithmeticians, they are nearly all good bookkeepers.

Sir Walter Scott 1771–1832: attributed, perhaps apocryphal

7 Never lend books, for no one ever returns them; the only books I have in my library are those that other people have lent me.

Anatole France 1844–1924: *La Vie littéraire* (1888)

8 I opened it at page 96—the secret page on which I write my name to catch out borrowers and book-sharks.

Flann O'Brien 1911–66: *Myles Away from Dublin* (1990)

9 Yes, the collection of a lifetime and I guard it well. I never lend! Only fools lend books. All the books on this shelf once belonged to fools.

Anonymous: 'a man [who] is proudly displaying his library to an envious visitor', quoted by Bertrand Russell to C. Williams-Ellis *Architect Errant* (1971)

Brevity

10 It is a foolish thing to make a long prologue, and to be short in the story itself.

Bible: II Maccabees

11 I strive to be brief, and I become obscure.

Horace 65–8 BC: *Ars Poetica*

12 Ek gret effect men write in place lite;
Th' entente is al, and nat the lettres space.

Geoffrey Chaucer c.1343–1400: *Troilus and Criseyde*

13 Words are like leaves; and where they most abound,
Much fruit of sense beneath is rarely found.

Alexander Pope 1688–1744: *An Essay on Criticism* (1711)

1 In all pointed sentences, some degree of accuracy must be sacrificed to conciseness.

Samuel Johnson 1709–84: 'The Bravery of the English Common Soldier' in *The British Magazine* January 1760

2 Was there ever yet anything written by mere man that was wished longer by its readers, excepting *Don Quixote*, *Robinson Crusoe*, and the *Pilgrim's Progress*?

Samuel Johnson 1709–84: Hester Lynch Piozzi *Anecdotes of . . . Johnson* (1786)

3 And, on the label of the stuff,
He wrote this verse;
Which one would think was clear enough,
And terse:—
When taken,
To be well shaken.

George Colman, the Younger 1762–1836: 'The Newcastle Apothecary' (1797)

4 Another damned, thick, square book! Always scribble, scribble, scribble! Eh! Mr Gibbon?

William Henry, 1st Duke of Gloucester 1743–1805: Henry Best *Personal and Literary Memorials* (1829); also attributed to the Duke of Cumberland and King George III; D. M. Low *Edward Gibbon* (1937)

Laman Blanchard, a young poet, had submitted some verses entitled 'Orient Pearls at Random Strung' to Household Words*:*

5 Dear Blanchard, too much string—Yours. C.D.

Charles Dickens 1812–70: Frederick Locker-Lampson *My Confidences* (1896)

6 If there is anywhere a thing said in two sentences that could have been as clearly and as engagingly said in one, then it's amateur work.

Robert Louis Stevenson 1850–94: letter to William Archer, February 1888

7 Brevity is the sister of talent.

Anton Chekhov 1860–1904: letter to Alexander Chekhov, 11 April 1889; L. S. Friedland (ed.) *Anton Chekhov: Letters on the Short Story . . .* (1964)

8 No flowers, by request.
summarizing the principle of conciseness for contributors to the Dictionary of National Biography

Alfred Ainger 1837–1904: speech to contributors, 8 July 1897; cf. **235:1**

9 I summed up all systems in a phrase, and all existence in an epigram.

Oscar Wilde 1854–1900: letter, from Reading Prison, to Lord Alfred Douglas, January–March 1897

10 The covers of this book are too far apart.

Ambrose Bierce 1842–*c.*1914: attributed

explaining why he wrote opinions while standing:

11 Nothing conduces to brevity like a caving in of the knees.

Oliver Wendell Holmes Jr. 1841–1935: Catherine Drinker Bowen *Yankee from Olympus* (1944); attributed

1 The realistic artist ought, if he is to be logical, to use several volumes to describe characters and settings, still without managing to exhaust all the details. Realism is indefinite enumeration. This shows that its ambition is the conquest not of the unity but of the totality of the real world.

Albert Camus 1913–60: *The Rebel* (1951)

2 I have never believed that arithmetic is important for the appreciation of literature. I have been criticized for writing too concisely, but I find that Babel's style is even more concise than mine . . . It shows what can be done. Even when you've got all the water out of them, you can still clot the curds a little more.

Ernest Hemingway 1899–1961: remark made to Ilya Ehrenburg and quoted by him in a speech on Isaac Babel, Moscow, 11 November 1964

3 Long books, when read, are usually overpraised, because the reader wishes to convince others and himself that he has not wasted his time.

E. M. Forster 1879–1970: note from commonplace book, in O. Stallybrass (ed.) *Aspects of the Novel and Related Writings* (1974)

4 Windbags can be right. Aphorists can be wrong. It is a tough world.

James Fenton 1949– : in *The Times* 21 February 1985

Censorship

5 *'Pictoribus atque poetis*
Quidlibet audendi semper fuit aequa potestas.'
Scimus, et hanc veniam petimusque damusque vicissim.

'Painters and poets alike have always had licence to dare anything.' We know that, and we both claim and permit others this indulgence.

Horace 65–8 BC: *Ars Poetica*

6 Tell it not in Gath, publish it not in the streets of Askelon; lest the daughters of the Philistines rejoice.

Bible: II Samuel

7 I beg you, read my verses with the same
Face as you watch Latinus on the stage
Or Thymele the dancer. Harmless wit
You may, as Censor, reasonably permit:
My life is strict, however lax my page.

Martial AD *c.*40–*c.*104: *Epigrammata* tr. James Michie

8 As good almost kill a man as kill a good book: who kills a man kills a reasonable creature, God's image; but he who destroys a good book, kills reason itself, kills the image of God, as it were in the eye.

John Milton 1608–74: *Areopagitica* (1644)

9 If we think to regulate printing, thereby to rectify manners, we must regulate all recreations and pastimes, all that is delightful to man . . . And who shall silence all the airs and madrigals, that whisper softness in chambers?

John Milton 1608–74: *Areopagitica* (1644)

10 For Sir Ph—p well knows
That innuendos
Will serve him no longer in verse or in prose,
Since twelve honest men have decided the cause,

William Pulteney, Lord Bath 1684–1764: 'The Honest Jury' (1729)

And were judges of fact, tho' not judges of laws.
on Sir Philip Yorke's unsuccessful prosecution of The Craftsman *for seditious libel*

1 I disapprove of what you say, but I will defend to the death your right to say it.
his attitude towards Helvétius following the burning of the latter's De l'esprit *in 1759*

Voltaire 1694–1778: attributed to Voltaire, the words are in fact S. G. Tallentyre's summary; *The Friends of Voltaire* (1907)

2 What a fuss about an omelette!
what Voltaire apparently *said on the burning of* De l'esprit

Voltaire 1694–1778: James Parton *Life of Voltaire* (1881)

3 No government ought to be without censors: and where the press is free, no one ever will.

Thomas Jefferson 1743–1826: letter to George Washington, 9 September 1792

4 Wherever books will be burned, men also, in the end, are burned.

Heinrich Heine 1797–1856: *Almansor* (1823)

5 Neither Bowdler's, Chambers's, Brandram's, nor Cundell's 'Boudoir' Shakespeare, seems to me to meet the want: they are not sufficiently 'expurgated'. Bowdler's is the most extraordinary of all: looking through it, I am filled with a deep sense of wonder, considering what he has left in, that he should have cut *anything* out.

Lewis Carroll 1832–98: preface to *Sylvie and Bruno* (1889); cf. **77:3**

6 It takes away any desire you have to express yourself freely; whenever you write, you get a feeling there's a bone stuck in your throat.
on Russian censorship

Anton Chekhov 1860–1904: letter, 19 January 1895

7 Imagine the future historian writing in wonderment of the absurd reticence with which our novelists treat sexual subjects, and comparing this with their licence to describe in detail the most hideous of murders.

George Gissing 1857–1903: *Commonplace Book* (1962)

8 Assassination is the extreme form of censorship.

George Bernard Shaw 1856–1950: *The Showing-Up of Blanco Posnet* (1911)

9 Writers often achieve a power of concentration which political liberty or literary anarchy would have allowed them to escape, when they are constrained by the tyranny of a monarch or of a poetic, by the strictness of prosodic rules or of the official religion.

Marcel Proust 1871–1922: *Guermantes Way* (1921)

10 I think you can leave the arts, superior or inferior, to the general conscience of mankind.
on the censorship of films

W. B. Yeats 1865–1939: speech in the Irish Senate, 1923

11 God forbid that any book should be banned. The practice is as indefensible as infanticide.

Rebecca West 1892–1983: *The Strange Necessity* (1928)

12 If we can't stamp out literature in the country, we can at least stop its being brought in from outside.
a Customs officer's view

Evelyn Waugh 1903–66: *Vile Bodies* (1930)

13 *All* fiction . . . is censored in the interests of the ruling class.

George Orwell 1903–50: in *Horizon* March 1940

14 Wherever there is an enforced orthodoxy—or even two orthodoxies, as often happens—good writing stops.

George Orwell 1903–50: 'The Prevention of Literature' (1946)

1 The crime of book purging is that it involves a rejection of the word. For the word is never an absolute truth, but only man's frail and human effort to approach the truth. To reject the word is to reject the human search.

Max Lerner 1902– : 'The Vigilantes and the Chain of Fear' in *New York Post* 24 June 1953

2 Free speech is not to be regulated like diseased cattle and impure butter. The audience . . . that hissed yesterday may applaud today, even for the same performance.

William O. Douglas 1898–1980: dissenting opinion in *Kingsley Books, Inc. v. Brown* 1957

3 It's red hot, mate. I hate to think of this sort of book getting into the wrong hands. As soon as I've finished this, I shall recommend they ban it.

words spoken by Tony Hancock

Ray Galton 1929– and **Alan Simpson** 1930– : 'The Missing Page', *Hancock's Half Hour* (BBC) 26 February 1960

4 Freedom of the press is guaranteed only to those who own one.

A. J. Liebling 1904–63: 'The Wayward Press: Do you belong in Journalism?' (1960)

5 If decade after decade the truth cannot be told, each person's mind begins to roam irretrievably. One's fellow countrymen become harder to understand than Martians.

Alexander Solzhenitsyn 1918– : *Cancer Ward* (1968)

6 I'm all in favour of free expression provided it's kept rigidly under control.

Alan Bennett 1934– : *Forty Years On* (1969)

7 Anybody who stands up and says total freedom may not be a good thing is immediately swamped with appreciative letters from old ladies whose twin hobbies are prize cucumbers and the castration of sex offenders.

Alan Bennett 1934– : *Getting On* (1972)

8 Woe to that nation whose literature is cut short by the intrusion of force. This is not merely interference with freedom of the press but the sealing up of a nation's heart, the excision of its memory.

Alexander Solzhenitsyn 1918– : in *Time* 25 February 1974

9 I dislike censorship. Like an appendix it is useless when inert and dangerous when active.

Maurice Edelman 1911–75: attributed, 1982

10 Censorship, like charity, should begin at home, but, unlike charity, it should end there.

Clare Boothe Luce 1903–87: attributed, 1982

11 A censor is a man who knows more than he thinks you ought to.

Laurence J. Peter 1919– : attributed, 1982

12 I suppose that writers should, in a way, feel flattered by the censorship laws. They show a primitive fear and dread at the fearful magic of print.

John Mortimer 1923– : *Clinging to the Wreckage* (1982)

13 Literature is one of the few areas left where black and white feel some identity of purpose; we all struggle under censorship.

Nadine Gordimer 1923– : in *Writers and Work* (6th series, 1984)

14 I would like to inform all the intrepid Muslims in the world that the author of the book entitled *The Satanic Verses*, which has been compiled, printed and published in opposition to Islam, the Prophet and the Qur'an, as well as those publishers who were aware of its contents, have

Ruhollah Khomeini 1900–89: issued 14 February 1989; Malise Ruthven *A Satanic Affair* (1990); cf. **36:1, 188:7, 323:1**

been declared *madhur el dam* [those whose blood must be shed]. I call on all zealous Muslims to execute them quickly, wherever they find them, so that no-one will dare to insult Islam again. Whoever is killed in this path will be regarded as a martyr.
fatwa against Salman **Rushdie**

1 The Khomeini cry for the execution of Rushdie is an infantile cry. From the beginning of time we have seen that. To murder the thinker does not murder the thought.
Arnold Wesker 1932– : in *Weekend Guardian* 3 June 1989; cf. **35:14**

2 What is freedom of expression? Without the freedom to offend, it ceases to exist.
Salman Rushdie 1947– : in *Weekend Guardian* 10 February 1990

3 The people who have control of your stories, control of your voice, also have control of your destiny, your culture.
Lenore Keeshig-Tobias: Hartmut Lutz *Contemporary Challenges: Conversations with Canadian Native Authors* (1991)

4 It's very, very easy not to be offended by a book. You just have to shut it.
Salman Rushdie 1947– : in *Daily Telegraph* 8 October 1994 'They Said It'

5 I believe that political correctness can be a form of linguistic fascism, and it sends shivers down the spine of my generation who went to war against fascism.
P. D. James 1920– : in *Paris Review* 1995

Characters

6 I must confess that I think her as delightful a creature as ever appeared in print, and how I shall be able to tolerate those who do not like *her* at least I do not know.
of 'Elizabeth Bennet'
Jane Austen 1775–1817: letter, 29 January 1813

7 I am going to take a heroine whom no-one but myself will much like.
on starting Emma
Jane Austen 1775–1817: J. E. Austen-Leigh *A Memoir of Jane Austen* (1926 ed.)

8 I draw from life—but I always pulp my acquaintance before serving them up. You would never recognize a pig in a sausage.
Frances Trollope 1780–1863: remark, *c.*1848; S. Baring-Gould *Early Reminiscences 1834-1864* (1923)

9 You are not to suppose any of the characters in *Shirley* intended as literal portraits . . . We only suffer reality to *suggest*, never to *dictate*.
Charlotte Brontë 1816–55: letter to Ellen Nussey, 16 November 1849

10 My poor Bovary, without a doubt, is suffering and weeping at this very hour in twenty villages in France.
Gustave Flaubert 1821–80: letter, 14 August 1853

11 If she had been faultless, she could not have been the heroine of this story; for I think some wise man of old remarked, that the perfect women were those who left no histories behind them.
Mary Elizabeth Braddon 1837–1915: *Aurora Floyd* (1863)

1 I have lived with my characters, and thençe has come whatever success I have attained.

Anthony Trollope 1815–82: *Autobiography* (1883)

2 We can only vary our characters by altering the age, the sex, the social position, and all the circumstances of life, of that *ego* which nature has in fact enclosed in an insurmountable barrier of organs of sense. Skill consists in not betraying this *ego* to the reader, under the various masks which we employ to cover it.

Guy de Maupassant 1850–93: preface to *Pierre et Jean* (1887)

3 What is character but the determination of incident? What is incident but the illustration of character?

Henry James 1843–1916: 'The Art of Fiction' (1888)

4 My souls (or characters) are conglomerates, made up of past and present stages of civilization, scraps of humanity, torn-off pieces of Sunday clothing turned into rags—all patched together as is the human soul itself.

Johan August Strindberg 1849–1912: preface to *Miss Julie* (1888)

5 When you think of Tolstoy's Anna Karenina, all Turgenev's gentlewomen with their seductive shoulders vanish into thin air.

Anton Chekhov 1860–1904: letter, 24 February 1893

6 In every first novel the hero is the author as Christ or Faust.

Oscar Wilde 1854–1900: attributed

7 Six characters in search of an author.

Luigi Pirandello 1867–1936: title of play (1921)

8 When the characters are alive, really alive before their author, the latter merely follows them in the words and actions which they in fact suggest to him.

Luigi Pirandello 1867–1936: *Six Characters in Search of an Author* (1921)

9 Things were easier for the old novelists who saw people all of a piece. Speaking generally, their heroes were good through and through, their villains wholly bad.

W. Somerset Maugham 1874–1965: *A Writer's Notebook* (1949) written in 1922

10 We may divide [fictional] characters into flat and round . . . The test of a round character is whether it is capable of surprising in a convincing way. If it never surprises, it is flat. If it does not convince, it is flat pretending to be round.

E. M. Forster 1879–1970: *Aspects of the Novel* (1927)

11 When writing a novel a writer should create living people; people not characters. A *character* is a caricature.

Ernest Hemingway 1899–1961: *Death in the Afternoon* (1932)

12 I have just got a letter asking me why I don't give Bloom a rest. The writer of it wants more Stephen. But Stephen no longer interests me to the same extent. He has a shape that can't be changed.

James Joyce 1882–1941: Frank Budgen *James Joyce and the Making of Ulysses* (1934)

13 True writers encounter their characters only *after* they've created them.

Elias Canetti 1905–94: *The Human Province* (1973) notebook 1946

14 People in life hardly seem definite enough to appear in print.

Ivy Compton-Burnett 1884–1969: attributed in *Times Literary Supplement* 29 May 1982

1 Each writer is born with a repertory company in his head. Shakespeare has perhaps twenty players, and Tennessee Williams has about five, and Samuel Beckett one—and maybe a clone of that one. I have ten or so, and that's a lot. As you get older, you become more skilful at casting them.

Gore Vidal 1925– : in *Times Herald* (Dallas) 18 June 1978

2 I have to watch my characters crossing the room, lighting a cigarette. I have to see everything they do, even if I don't write it down. So my eyes get tired.

Graham Greene 1904–91: interview with John Mortimer in *Sunday Times* 16 March 1980

3 The main characters in a novel must necessarily have some kinship to the author, they come out of his body as a child comes from the womb, then the umbilical cord is cut.

Graham Greene 1904–91: *Ways of Escape* (1980)

4 She moves out of our minds as easily as she moves out of Harrods.

of Virginia Woolf's 'Mrs Dalloway'

Graham Greene 1904–91: Marie-Françoise Allain *The Other Man, Conversations with Graham Greene* (1983)

5 My characters run away but not far. Their guise is surprises.

Bernard Malamud 1914–86: George Plimpton (ed.) *The Writer's Chapbook* (1989)

6 Show me a character totally without anxieties and I will show you a boring book.

Margaret Atwood 1939– : Geoff Hancock *Canadian Writers at Work* (1986) 'Tightrope-Walking over Niagara Falls'

7 All characters in this story are imaginary and no reference is intended to any living person. Readers who think that they can identify the creations of the author's fancy among their own acquaintance are paying the author an extravagant compliment, which he acknowledges with gratitude.

disclaimer at the beginning of the novel

Robertson Davies 1913–95: *Tempet-tost* (1986)

8 I sometimes lose interest in the characters and get much more interested in the trees and animals.

Toni Morrison 1913– : George Plimpton (ed.) *The Writer's Chapbook* (1989)

9 One never knows enough about characters in real life to put them into novels. One gets started and then, suddenly, one cannot remember what toothpaste they use; what are their views on interior decoration; and one is stuck already. No, major characters emerge; minor ones may be photographed.

Graham Greene 1904–91: attributed

10 I'm not too keen on characters taking over; they do as they are damn well told.

Iain Banks 1954– : Stan Nicholls (ed.) *Wordsmiths of Wonder* (1993)

11 I don't go round looking for material from my life that will make a novel, nor do I turn people whom I know into characters. Once I have invented characters I see things through their eyes.

Graham Swift 1949– : Clare Boylan (ed.) *The Agony and the Ego* (1993); attributed

12 Once a character has gelled it's an unmistakable sensation, like an engine starting up within one's body. From then onwards one is driven by this other person, seeing things through their eyes, shuffling round the shops

Deborah Moggach 1948– : Clare Boylan (ed.) *The Agony and the Ego* (1993)

as a 57-year-old man and practically feeling one has grown a beard.

1 Inventing really evil people is great fun. It is difficult to make a good person attractive and not boring.

Mary Wesley 1912– : attributed, 1995

2 If you haven't got room to make a character, if you give him or her some totally memorable physical characteristic, the character becomes symbolic and stands for itself. Somebody will always come up and say to you, 'that is an absolutely wonderful character you created with that great plait down her back'. In fact, the character consisted only of that plait down her back . . . but it was memorable.

A. S. Byatt 1936– : in *Literary Review* December 1995

Children's Literature

3 What toys, the daily reading of such a book, may work in the will of a young gentleman, or a young maid . . . wise men can judge, and honest men do pity.

of Malory's Le Morte D'Arthur *as unsuitable reading for the young*

Roger Ascham 1515–68: *The Schoolmaster* (1570)

4 As an actor does his part,
So the nurses get by heart
Namby-pamby's little rhymes,
Little jingle, little chimes.

Henry Carey *c.*1687–1743: 'Namby-Pamby' (1725)

5 Too rigid precepts
often fail,
Where short amusing
tales prevail.
The author doubtless
aims aright
Who joins instruction
with delight.

Thomas Boreman fl. 1730–34: in *Oxford Companion to Children's Literature*

6 Babies do not want to hear about babies; they like to be told of giants and castles, and of somewhat which can stretch and stimulate their little minds.

Samuel Johnson 1709–84: Hester Lynch Piozzi *Anecdotes of . . . Johnson* (1786)

7 Remember always that the parents buy the books, and that the children never read them.

Samuel Johnson 1709–84: Hester Lynch Piozzi *Anecdotes of . . . Johnson* (1786)

8 It is children that read children's books (when they are read); but it is parents that choose them.

William Godwin 1756–1836: letter to Charles Lamb, 10 March 1808

9 Never in all my early childhood, did anyone address to me the affecting preamble, 'Once upon a time!' I was told about missionaries, but never about pirates; I was familiar with humming-birds, but I had never heard of fairies.

Edmund Gosse 1849–1928: *Father and Son* (1907)

10 No one can write a book which children will like, unless he write it for himself first.

A. A. Milne 1882–1956: *Once on a Time* (ed. 2, 1925); preface

11 Young people are gluttons for detail and have an acute sense of what is fit and proper in that respect.

John Buchan 1875–1940: *The Novel and the Fairy Tale* (1931)

1 Since the tales had to be read by children, before people realized that they were meant for grown-ups . . . I worked the material in three or four overlaid tints and textures, which might or might not reveal themselves according to the shifting light of sex, youth, and experience. It was like working lacquer and mother o' pearl, a natural combination, into the same scheme as niello and grisaille, and trying not to let the joins show.

Rudyard Kipling 1865–1936: *Something of Myself* (1937)

2 It is worth noting a rather curious fact, and that is that the school story is a thing peculiar to England. So far as I know, there are extremely few school stories in foreign languages.

George Orwell 1903–50: 'Boys' Weeklies' (1939)

3 What do we ever get nowadays from reading to equal the excitement and the revelation in those first fourteen years?

Graham Greene 1904–91: *The Lost Childhood* (1951)

4 Children prefer incident to character; if character is to be drawn, it must be done broadly, in tar or whitewash.

A. A. Milne 1882–1956: *Once on a Time* (1965 ed.); introduction

5 It may be better for them to read some things, especially fairy-stories, that are beyond their measure rather than short of it. Their books like their clothes should allow for growth, and their books at any rate should encourage it.

J. R. R. Tolkien 1892–1973: *Tree and Leaf* (1964) 'On Fairy-Stories'

6 Publishers and authors seem to think that the smaller the child, the larger the book must be—for what reason, since their arms are short and their eyesight usually at its best, it is hard to imagine.

Penelope Mortimer 1918– : 'Thoughts Concerning Children's Books' (1966)

7 Revolts may come, revolts may go, but brats go on forever. And I would like to do a perfectly stunning brat book!

Arthur Ransome 1884–1967: A. N. Wilson *Penfriends from Porlock* (1988)

8 Political history is far too criminal and pathological to be a fit subject of study of the young. Children should acquire their heroes and villains from fiction.

W. H. Auden 1907–73: attributed

9 A children's writer should, ideally, be a dedicated semi-lunatic, a kind of poet with a marvellous idea, who, preferably, when not committing the marvellous idea to paper, does something else of a quite different kind, so as to acquire new and rich experience.

Joan Aiken 1924– : *The Way to Write for Children* (1982)

10 Teenagers are natural pessimists (and who should blame them?) . . . The teenage novel has a duty to portray the successive tidal waves of feeling that wash over adolescents.

Joan Aiken 1924– : *The Way to Write for Children* (1982)

on her preferred childhood reading:

11 Protestant ethic, goal-oriented books I wasn't so keen on. I was much more keen on dragons and magic.

Margaret Atwood 1939– : in an interview, 20 January 1983; Earl G. Ingersoll (ed.) *Margaret Atwood: Conversations* (1990)

12 Children's literature is a strange phenomenon. It is something that virtually all of us come across; it involves millions of pounds changing hands and yet very few adults take it seriously.

Michael Rosen 1946– : introduction to Michael Rosen and Jill Burridge *Treasure Islands 2* (1993)

1 An idea will come to me as a concentrated short burst, comparable to poems as opposed to prose. Then it seems right for a children's book. Sometimes, it's because the matter of which I'm writing is too deep or too metaphysical for adults.

Russell Hoban 1925– : Michael Rosen and Jill Burridge *Treasure Islands 2* (1993)

2 You know how it is in the kids' book world; it's just bunny eat bunny.

Anonymous: unattributed comment; Julia Vitullo-Martin and J. Robert Moskin (eds.) *The Executive's Book of Quotations* (1994)

3 One does not write *for* children. One writes so that children can understand. Which means writing as clearly, vividly and truthfully as possible. Adults might put up with occasional lapses; children are far less tolerant.

Leon Garfield 1921–96: in his obituary, *Daily Telegraph* 4 June 1996

4 When you are writing for children, the story is more important than you are. You can't be self-conscious, you just have to get out of the way.

Philip Pullman 1946– : interview in *Bookseller* 9 August 1996

Choice of Words see also Style

5 A word fitly spoken is like apples of gold in pictures of silver.

Bible: Proverbs

6 You will have written exceptionally well if, by skilful arrangement of your words, you have made an ordinary one seem original.

Horace 65–8 BC: *Ars Poetica*

7 I have revered always not crude verbosity, but holy simplicity.

St Jerome *c.* AD 342–420: letter 'Ad Pammachium'

8 A loose, plain, rude writer . . . I call a spade a spade.

Robert Burton 1577–1640: *The Anatomy of Melancholy* (1621–51)

9 His words . . . like so many nimble and airy servitors trip about him at command.

John Milton 1608–74: *An Apology for Smectymnuus* (1642)

10 A thing well said will be wit in all languages.

John Dryden 1631–1700: *An Essay of Dramatic Poesy* (1668)

11 True ease in writing comes from art, not chance,
As those move easiest who have learned to dance.
'Tis not enough no harshness gives offence,
The sound must seem an echo to the sense.

Alexander Pope 1688–1744: *An Essay on Criticism* (1711)

12 Apt Alliteration's artful aid.

Charles Churchill 1731–64: *The Prophecy of Famine* (1763)

13 Don't, Sir, accustom yourself to use big words for little matters. It would *not* be *terrible*, though I *were* to be detained some time here.

when Boswell said it would be 'terrible' if Johnson should not be able to return speedily from Harwich

Samuel Johnson 1709–84: James Boswell *Life of Samuel Johnson* (1791) 6 August 1763

1 When you read proof, take out adjectives and adverbs wherever you can.

Anton Chekhov 1860–1904: letter, 14 January 1887

2 Her occasional pretty and picturesque use of dialect words—those terrible marks of the beast to the truly genteel.

Thomas Hardy 1840–1928: *The Mayor of Casterbridge* (1886)

3 How often misused words generate misleading thoughts.

Herbert Spencer 1820–1903: *Principles of Ethics* (1879)

4 His life was that of a pearl-diver, breathless in the thick element while he groped for the priceless word, and condemned to plunge again and again. He passed it in reconstructing sentences, exterminating repetitions, calculating and comparing cadences, harmonious *chutes de phrases*, and beating about the bush to deal death to the abominable assonance.
of ***Flaubert***

Henry James 1843–1916: 'Gustave Flaubert' (1893)

5 I knew exactly what I had got to say, put the words firmly in their places like so many stitches, hemmed the edges of chapters round with what seemed to me the graceful flourishes, touched them finally with my cunningest points of colour, and read the work to papa and mamma at breakfast next morning, as a girl shows her sampler.

John Ruskin 1819–1900: in *Dictionary of National Biography* (1917–)

6 An average English word is four letters and a half. By hard, honest labour I've dug all the large words out of my vocabulary and shaved them down till the average is three and a half letters . . . I never write metropolis for seven cents because I can get the same money for city. I never write policeman, because I can get the same money for *Cop*.

Mark Twain 1835–1910: *Mark Twain's Speeches* (1923)

7 The minute a phrase becomes current it becomes an apology for not thinking accurately to the end of the sentence.

Oliver Wendell Holmes Jr. 1841–1935: letter to Harold Laski, 2 July 1917

8 Objectivity and again objectivity, and expression: no hindside-before-ness, no straddled adjectives (as 'addled mosses dank'), no Tennysonianness of speech; nothing—nothing that you couldn't, in some circumstance, in the stress of some emotion, actually say.

Ezra Pound 1885–1972: letter to Harriet Monroe, January 1915

9 The adjective 'cross' as a description of his Jovelike wrath . . . jarred upon Derek profoundly. It was as though Prometheus, with the vultures tearing his liver, had been asked if he were piqued.

P. G. Wodehouse 1881–1975: *Jill the Reckless* (1922)

10 And it is that word 'hummy', my darlings, that marks the first place in 'The House at Pooh Corner' at which Tonstant Weader fwowed up.

Dorothy Parker 1893–1967: review as 'Constant Reader' in *New Yorker* 20 October 1928

11 A phrase is born into the world both good and bad at the same time. The secret lies in a slight, an almost invisible twist. The lever should rest in your hand, getting warm, and you can only turn it once, not twice.

Isaac Babel 1894–1940: *Guy de Maupassant* (1932)

1 All my life I have nearly always known *what* to write, but since I tried to get it all on twelve pages, since I have restricted myself in this way, I have had to pick and choose words that are, first, significant; second, simple; and third, beautiful.

Isaac Babel 1894–1940: interview, Union of Soviet Writers, 28 September 1937

2 Words are chameleons, which reflect the colour of their environment.

Learned Hand 1872–1961: in *Commissioner v. National Carbide Corp.* (1948)

3 We must use words as they are used or stand aside from life.

Ivy Compton-Burnett 1884–1969: *Mother and Son* (1955)

4 The phrase . . . a clutch of words that gives you a clutch at the heart.

when asked about the basic point to all fine writing

Robert Frost 1874–1963: interview in 1960; E. Connery Latham (ed.) *Interviews with Robert Frost* (1967)

5 They're perfect sentences. Very direct sentences, smooth rivers, clear water over granite, no sinkholes.

of ***Hemingway's*** A Farewell to Arms

Joan Didion 1934– : George Plimpton (ed.) *The Writer's Chapbook* (1989)

Closing Lines see also **Opening Lines**

6 *L'amor che muove il sole e l'altre stelle.*

The love that moves the sun and the other stars.

Dante Alighieri 1265–1321: *Divina Commedia* 'Paradiso'

7 And so I betake myself to that course, which is almost as much as to see myself go into my grave—for which, and all the discomforts that will accompany my being blind, the good God prepare me!

Samuel Pepys 1633–1703: *Diary* 31 May 1669; cf. **58:8**

8 Silent, upon a peak in Darien.

John Keats 1795–1821: 'On First Looking into Chapman's Homer' (1817); cf. **304:11**

9 I lingered round them, under that benign sky: watched the moths fluttering among the heath and hare-bells; listened to the soft wind breathing through the grass; and wondered how any one could ever imagine unquiet slumbers for the sleepers in that quiet earth.

Emily Brontë 1818–48: *Wuthering Heights* (1847)

10 And they lived happily ever after.

traditional ending to a fairy story

Anonymous: recorded (with slight variations) from the 1850s

11 'Justice' was done, and the President of the Immortals (in Aeschylean phrase) had ended his sport with Tess.

Thomas Hardy 1840–1928: *Tess of the D'Urbervilles* (1891)

12 After all, tomorrow is another day.

Margaret Mitchell 1900–49: *Gone with the Wind* (1936)

13 The creatures outside looked from pig to man, and from man to pig, and from pig to man again, but already it was impossible to say which was which.

George Orwell 1903–50: *Animal Farm* (1945)

14 So that, in the end, there was no end.

Patrick White 1912–90: *The Tree of Man* (1955)

Comedy see Humour and Comedy

Conversation see Dialogue and Conversation

Creativity see Inspiration and Creativity

Crime and Mystery

1 Detection is, or ought to be, an exact science, and should be treated in the same cold and unemotional manner. You have attempted to tinge it with romanticism, which produces much the same effect as if you worked a love-story or an elopement into the fifth proposition of Euclid.

Arthur Conan Doyle 1859–1930: *The Sign of Four* (1890)

2 Death seems to provide the minds of the Anglo-Saxon race with a greater fund of amusement that any other single subject.

Dorothy L. Sayers 1893–1957: introduction to *The Third Omnibus of Crime* (1935)

of detective story writers of the 'HIBK' ('Had I but known then what I know now') school:

3 And when the killer is finally trapped into a confession by
some elaborate device of the Had I But Known-er some hundred pages later than if they hadn't held their knowledge aloof,
Why, they say, why Inspector I knew all along it was he
but I couldn't tell you, you would have laughed at me unless I had absolute proof.

Ogden Nash 1902–71: 'Don't Guess, Let Me Tell You' (1940)

4 Down these mean streets a man must go who is not himself mean, who is neither tarnished nor afraid.

Raymond Chandler 1888–1959: in *Atlantic Monthly* December 1944 'The Simple Art of Murder'

5 The detective novel is the art-for-art's-sake of our yawning Philistinism, the classic example of a specialized form of art removed from contact with the life it pretends to build on.

V. S. Pritchett 1900–97: in *New Statesman* 16 June 1951

6 Detective stories—the modern fairy tales.

Graham Greene 1904–91: 'Journey into Success' (1952)

7 In the melodrama of the brutal thriller we come as close as it is normally possible for art to come to the pure self-righteousness of the lynching mobs.

Northrop Frye 1912–91: *The Anatomy of Criticism* (1957)

8 Sapper, Buchan, Dornford Yates, practitioners in that school of Snobbery with Violence that runs like a thread of good-class tweed through twentieth-century literature.

Alan Bennett 1934– : *Forty Years On* (1969)

9 Had she told the dicks
How she got in that fix,
I would be much apter
To read the last chapter.

Ogden Nash 1902–71: 'The Spinster Detective'

1 The setting for the crime stories by what we might call the Mayhem Parva school would be a cross between a village and a commuters' dormitory in the South of England, self-contained and largely self-sufficient. It would have a well-attended church, an inn with reasonable accommodation for itinerant detective-inspectors, a village institute, library and shops—including a chemist's where weed killer and hair dye might conveniently be bought.

Colin Watson 1920–83: *Snobbery with Violence* (1971)

2 What the detective story is about is not murder but the restoration of order.

P. D. James 1920– : in *Face* December 1986

3 I've always enjoyed crime fiction. I think that much of the best writing being done today is in crime novels. The plot and discipline essential to a crime novel save it from the terrible traps of being sensitive and stream-of-consciousness and all of that stuff.

John Mortimer 1923– : George Plimpton (ed.) *The Writer's Chapbook* (1989)

4 If you want to show the violence that lives behind the bland faces that most of us present to the world, what better vehicle can you have than the crime novel.

Julian Symons 1912–94: in *Daily Telegraph* 12 May 1990

5 A genre which has traditionally been bedevilled by rules, regulations, and rituals reminiscent of a third-rate Masonic cult.

Michael Dibdin 1947– : preface to *The Picador Book of Crime Fiction* (1993)

6 The fact is that ninety per cent of crime stories, mystery stories, thrillers, are written by people with no feeling for language, place or character.

Julian Symons 1912–94: *Criminal Practices* (1994)

7 It seems to me that the recent American writers, often praised for ruthless realism, produce for the most part sensational or sentimental sex-grills designed to titillate, written in hard-shelled but soft-boiled sub-Hemingway prose.

Julian Symons 1912–94: *Criminal Practices* (1994)

8 It is, it ought to be, it must be a morality.
the views of 'Ellis Peters' on writing a thriller

Edith Pargeter 1913–95: in *Daily Telegraph* 16 October 1995; obituary

9 I had an interest in death from an early age. It fascinated me. When I heard 'Humpty Dumpty sat on a wall,' I thought, 'Did he fall or was he pushed?'

P. D. James 1920– : in *Paris Review* 1995

10 With Agatha Christie ingenuity of plot was paramount—no one looked for subtlety of characterization, motivation, good writing. It was rather like a literary card trick. Today we've moved closer to the mainstream novel, but nevertheless we need plot.

P. D. James 1920– : in *Paris Review* 1995

11 Murder itself is not interesting. It is the impetus to murder, the passions and terrors which bring it to pass and the varieties of feelings surrounding the act that make a sordid or revolting event compulsive fascination. Even the most ardent readers of detective fiction are not much preoccupied with whether a Colt Magnum revolver or a Bowie knife was used to dispatch the victim. The perpetrator's purpose, the 'why', is what impels them to read on. They need to find out what has gone on in his

Ruth Rendell 1930– : introduction to *The Reason Why: An Anthology of the Murderous Mind* (1995)

head, whether revealed through action, dialogue, mental activity or the stream of consciousness. They need to follow what goes on in the minds of others who come within his range, observe him, fear him, or suffer at his hands.

1 By the end he only read novels that began with 'A shot rang out'.
of his father, Kingsley ***Amis***

Martin Amis 1949– : in *Observer* 7 April 1996

Criticism see also **Critics, Reviews, Scholarship**

2 Tear him for his bad verses, tear him for his bad verses.

William Shakespeare 1564–1616: *Julius Caesar* (1599)

3 To judge of poets is only the faculty of poets; and not of all poets, but the best.

Ben Jonson *c.*1573–1637: *Timber, or Discoveries made upon Men and Matter* (1641)

4 One should look long and carefully at oneself before one considers judging others.

Molière 1622–73: *Le Misanthrope* (1666)

5 He hears
On all sides, from innumerable tongues
A dismal universal hiss, the sound
Of public scorn.

John Milton 1608–74: *Paradise Lost* (1667)

6 They who write ill, and they who ne'er durst write,
Turn critics out of mere revenge and spite.

John Dryden 1631–1700: *The Conquest of Granada* (1670)

7 Much malice mingled with a little wit
Perhaps may censure this mysterious writ.

John Dryden 1631–1700: *The Hind and the Panther* (1687)

8 The pleasure of criticism destroys (more literally, removes) in us that of being moved by beautiful things.

Jean de la Bruyère 1645–96: *Les Caractères ou les moeurs de ce siècle* (1688)

9 Yet let not each gay turn thy rapture move,
For fools admire, but men of sense approve.

Alexander Pope 1688–1744: *An Essay on Criticism* (1711)

10 A true critic ought to dwell rather upon excellencies than imperfections, to discover the concealed beauties of a writer, and communicate to the world such things as are worth their observation.

Joseph Addison 1672–1719: *The Spectator* 2 February 1712

11 Criticism is a study by which men grow important and formidable at very small expense.

Samuel Johnson 1709–84: in *The Idler* 9 June 1759

12 You *may* abuse a tragedy, though you cannot write one. You may scold a carpenter who has made you a bad table, though you cannot make a table. It is not your trade to make tables.

Samuel Johnson 1709–84: James Boswell *Life of Samuel Johnson* (1791) 25 June 1763

13 Of all the cants which are canted in this canting world,—though the cant of hypocrites may be the worst,—the cant of criticism is the most tormenting!

Laurence Sterne 1713–68: *Tristram Shandy* (1759–67)

14 If it is abuse,—why one is always sure to hear of it from one damned goodnatured friend or another!

Richard Brinsley Sheridan 1751–1816: *The Critic* (1779)

1 In the character of his Elegy I rejoice to concur with the common reader; for by the common sense of readers uncorrupted with literary prejudices . . . must be finally decided all claim to poetical honours.

Samuel Johnson 1709–84: *Lives of the English Poets* (1779–81) 'Gray'

2 The ultimate end of criticism is much more to establish the principles of writing, than to furnish *rules* how to pass judgement on what has been written by others; if indeed it were possible that the two could be separated.

Samuel Taylor Coleridge 1772–1834: *Biographia Literaria* (1817)

3 Criticism makes its appearance like Ate: it pursues authors, but limpingly.

Johann Wolfgang von Goethe 1749–1832: *Sayings in Prose*

4 I am bound by my own definition of criticism: *a disinterested endeavour to learn and propagate the best that is known and thought in the world.*

Matthew Arnold 1822–88: *Essays in Criticism* First Series (1865) 'The Function of Criticism at the Present Time'

5 We must grant the artist his subject, his idea, his *donnée*: our criticism is applied only to what he makes of it.

Henry James 1843–1916: 'The Art of Fiction' (1888)

6 Criticism is not only medicinally salutary: it has positive popular attractions in its cruelty, its gladiatorship, and the gratification given to envy by its attacks on the great, and to enthusiasm by its praises.

George Bernard Shaw 1856–1950: preface to *Plays Unpleasant* (1898)

7 Works of art are of an infinite solitariness, and nothing is less likely to bring us near to them than criticism. Only love can apprehend and hold them, and can be just towards them.

Rainer Maria Rilke 1875–1926: *Briefe an einen jungen Dichter* (1929) 23 April 1903

8 I always find French criticism of English work very instructive, disconcerting, and tonic.

Arnold Bennett 1867–1931: diary, 25 October 1903

9 The critic's symbol should be the tumble-bug; he deposits his egg in someone else's dung otherwise he could not hatch it.

Mark Twain 1835–1910: *Mark Twain's Notebook* (1935)

10 I will try to account for the degree of my aesthetic emotion. That, I conceive, is the function of the critic.

Clive Bell 1881–1964: *Art* (1914)

11 You don't expect me to know what to say about a play when I don't know who the author is, do you?

George Bernard Shaw 1856–1950: *Fanny's First Play* (1914)

12 The European view of a poet is not of much importance unless the poet writes in Esperanto.

A. E. Housman 1859–1936: in *Cambridge Review* 1915

13 Never trust the artist. Trust the tale. The proper function of a critic is to save the tale from the artist who created it.

D. H. Lawrence 1885–1930: *Studies in Classic American Literature* (1923)

14 Criticism is the art wherewith a critic tries to guess himself into a share of the artist's fame.

George Jean Nathan 1882–1958: *The House of Satan* (1926)

15 Parodies and caricatures are the most penetrating of criticisms.

Aldous Huxley 1894–1963: *Point Counter Point* (1928)

16 How many children had Lady Macbeth?
satirizing the style of criticism represented by A. C. Bradley's 'detective interest' in plot and emphasis on 'character'

L. C. Knights 1906–97: title of essay (1933); cf. **49:4**

1 There's only one kind of critic I do resent . . . The kind that affects to believe that I am writing with my tongue in my cheek.

James Joyce 1882–1941: Frank Budgen *James Joyce and the Making of Ulysses* (1934)

2 The critic's pretence that he can unravel the procedure is grotesque. As well hope to start with a string of sausages and reconstruct the pig.

on a method of biblical exegesis

B. H. Streeter 1874–1937: J. Ashton *Understanding the Fourth Gospel* (1991)

3 An author of talent is his own best critic—the ability to criticize his own work is inseparably bound up with his talent: it *is* his talent.

Graham Greene 1904–91: 'Some Notes on Somerset Maugham' (1935–8)

4 I was never, in the true sense, a critic; never an enlightening judge of excellence. I knew what was good, but I was apt to be puzzled as to the constituents of its goodness, and was a foggy eulogist. Badness is easy game, and to badness I always turned with relief. Badness is auspicious to the shower-off. Its only drawback is that it isn't worth writing about.

Max Beerbohm 1872–1956: letter, *c.*1942

5 Think before you speak is criticism's motto; speak before you think creation's.

E. M. Forster 1879–1970: *Two Cheers for Democracy* (1951)

6 Drama criticism is essentially a fallible verbal reflexion of how a particular entertainment struck a unique mind on one special evening . . . The last thing a critic ought to be concerned with is the people who read him first. He should write for posterity.

Kenneth Tynan 1927–80: unpublished note for speech at Foyles lunch, 21 November 1952; Kathleen Tynan *The Life of Kenneth Tynan* (1987)

7 Poetry is what is lost in translation. It is also what is lost in interpretation.

Robert Frost 1874–1963: Louis Untermeyer *Robert Frost* (1964)

8 Interpretation is not (as some people assume) an absolute value, a gesture of mind situated in some timeless realm of capabilities. Interpretation must be evaluated . . . Like the fumes of the automobile and of heavy industry which befoul the urban atmosphere, the effusion of interpretation of art today poisons our sensibilities. In a culture whose already classic dilemma is the hypertrophy of the intellect at the expense of energy and sensual capability, interpretation is the revenge of the intellect upon art.

Susan Sontag 1933– : in *Evergreen Review* December 1964

9 The work of criticism is rooted in the unconscious of the critic just as the poem is rooted in the unconscious of the poet.

Randall Farrell: *A Sad Heart at the Supermarket* (1965)

10 Drama criticism . . . [is] a self-knowing account of the way in which one's consciousness has been modified during an evening in the theatre.

Kenneth Tynan 1927–80: *Tynan Right and Left* (1967)

11 The important thing is that you make sure that neither the favourable nor the unfavourable critics move into your head and take part in the composition of your next work.

Thornton Wilder 1897–1975: George Plimpton (ed.) *The Writer's Chapbook* (1989)

12 Like thinking about the technique of skiing when you're half-way down a hill.

on writing about her own writing

Margaret Atwood 1939– : in an interview, February 1976; Earl G. Ingersoll (ed.) *Margaret Atwood: Conversations* (1990)

1 Writing criticism is to writing fiction and poetry as hugging the shore is to sailing in the open sea.

John Updike 1932– : foreword to *Hugging the Shore* (1983)

2 No critical display is more offensive than that which praises one author by damning another, as though critical judgement were a seesaw on which one reputation cannot rise unless another is lowered.

Carolyn G. Heilbrun 1926– : *Hamlet's Mother and Other Women* (1990) 'Virginia Woolf and James Joyce'

3 Criticism is a life without risk.

John Lahr 1941– : *Light Fantastic* (1996)

4 Personally I have always thought 'how many children had Lady Macbeth?' a perfectly good question. I am also curious about how old Hamlet is, what subjects he studied at the University of Wittenberg, and what grades he got for his studies there.

John Sutherland 1938– : introduction to *Is Heathcliff a Murderer?* (1996); cf. **47:16**

Critics

5 Critics are like brushers of noblemen's clothes.

Henry Wotton 1568–1639: Francis Bacon *Apophthegms New and Old* (1625)

6 You who scribble, yet hate all who write . . .
And with faint praises one another damn.
of drama critics

William Wycherley c.1640–1716: *The Plain Dealer* (1677)

7 Some have at first for wits, then poets passed,
Turned critics next, and proved plain fools at last.

Alexander Pope 1688–1744: *An Essay on Criticism* (1711)

8 Every good poet includes a critic; the reverse will not hold.

William Shenstone 1714–63: *Works . . .* (1764) 'On Writing and Books'

9 He gets at the substance of a book directly; he tears out the heart of it.
of Samuel ***Johnson***

Mary Knowles 1733–1807: James Boswell *Life of Samuel Johnson* (1791) 15 April 1778

10 A man must serve his time to every trade
Save censure—critics all are ready made.
Take hackneyed jokes from Miller, got by rote,
With just enough of learning to misquote.

Lord Byron 1788–1824: *English Bards and Scotch Reviewers* (1809)

11 He wreathed the rod of criticism with roses.
of Pierre Bayle

Isaac D'Israeli 1766–1848: *Curiosities of Literature* (9th ed., 1834)

12 You know who the critics are? The men who have failed in literature and art.

Benjamin Disraeli 1804–81: *Lothair* (1870)

13 There spoke up a brisk little somebody,
Critic and whippersnapper, in a rage
To set things right.

Robert Browning 1812–89: *Balaustion's Adventure* (1871)

14 What is important, then, is not that the critic should possess a correct abstract definition of beauty for the intellect but a certain kind of temperament, the power of being deeply moved by the presence of beautiful objects.

Walter Pater 1839–94: *Studies in the History of the Renaissance* (1873) 'Preface'

1 The good critic is he who relates the adventures of his soul in the midst of masterpieces.

Anatole France 1844–1924: *La Vie littéraire* (1888)

2 The lot of critics is to be remembered by what they failed to understand.

George Moore 1852–1933: *Impressions and Opinions* (1891) 'Balzac'

3 The principal thrill of reading Saintsbury is the sensation of looking down on literature as with the comparative eye of God.

of the critic G. E. B. Saintsbury

Edmund Wilson 1895–1972: in *New Republic* 8 February 1933; cf. **50:4**

4 For 18 years he *started the day* by reading a French novel (in preparation for his history of them) an act so unnatural to man as to amount almost to genius.

of the critic G. E. B. Saintsbury

Stephen Potter 1900–69: *The Muse in Chains* (1937); cf. **50:3**

5 Remember, a statue has never been set up in honour of a critic!

Jean Sibelius 1865–1957: Bengt de Törne *Sibelius: A Close-Up* (1937)

6 I am the only critic in London who is too small for his boots.

Alan Dent 1905–78: James Agate *Ego 4* (1939)

7 It would be unfair to suggest that one of the most characteristic sounds of the English Sunday is the sound of Harold Hobson barking up the wrong tree.

Penelope Gilliatt 1933– : in *Encore* November-December 1959

8 A critic is a bundle of biases held loosely together by a sense of taste.

Whitney Balliett 1926– : *Dinosaurs in the Morning* (1962)

9 Critics are like eunuchs in a harem; they know how it's done, they've seen it done every day, but they're unable to do it themselves.

Brendan Behan 1923–64: attributed

10 A critic is a man who knows the way but can't drive the car.

Kenneth Tynan 1927–80: in *New York Times Magazine* 9 January 1966

11 No degree of dullness can safeguard a work against the determination of critics to find it fascinating.

Harold Rosenberg 1906–78: *Discovering the Present* (1973)

12 Critics search for ages for the wrong word which, to give them credit, they eventually find.

Peter Ustinov 1921– : Ned Sherrin *Cutting Edge* (1984)

13 There is, perhaps, no more dangerous man in the world than the man with the sensibilities of an artist but without creative talent. With luck such men make wonderful theatrical impresarios and interior decorators, or else they become mass murderers or critics.

Barry Humphries 1934– : *More Please* (1992)

14 Asking a playwright how he felt about critics was like asking a lamppost how it felt about dogs.

Christopher Hampton 1946– : in *The Times* 4 April 1995; cf. **118:9**

15 By the fifties, critic was something you put proudly on your passport. By the sixties, it had transmuted into an agenda, a politics.

Malcolm Bradbury 1932– : in *Daily Telegraph* 28 January 1995 'They Said It'

Death see also **Last Words**

1 *Non omnis moriar.*
I shall not altogether die.

Horace 65–8 BC: *Odes*

2 Rigidly classical, you save
Your praise for poets in the grave.
Forgive me, it's not worth my while
Dying to earn your critical smile.

Martial AD *c*.40–*c*.104: *Epigrammata* tr. James Michie

3 With one foot already in the stirrup.
apprehending his own, imminent death

Cervantes 1547–1616: *Los Trabajos de Persiles y Sigismunda* (1617)

4 When one man dies, one chapter is not torn out of the book, but translated into a better language.

John Donne 1572–1631: *Devotions upon Emergent Occasions* (1624)

5 Any man's death diminishes me, because I am involved in Mankind; And therefore never send to know for whom the bell tolls; it tolls for thee.

John Donne 1572–1631: *Devotions upon Emergent Occasions* (1624)

6 Men fear death as children fear to go in the dark; and as that natural fear in children is increased with tales, so is the other.

Francis Bacon 1561–1626: *Essays* (1625) 'Of Death'

7 Death is still working like a mole,
And digs my grave at each remove.

George Herbert 1593–1633: 'Grace' (1633)

8 See in what peace a Christian can die.
dying words to his stepson Lord Warwick

Joseph Addison 1672–1719: Edward Young *Conjectures on Original Composition* (1759)

9 The body of
Benjamin Franklin, printer,
(Like the cover of an old book,
Its contents worn out,
And stripped of its lettering and gilding)
Lies here, food for worms!
Yet the work itself shall not be lost,
For it will, as he believed, appear once more
In a new
And more beautiful edition,
Corrected and amended
By its Author!

Benjamin Franklin 1706–90: epitaph for himself (1728)

10 Can storied urn or animated bust
Back to its mansion call the fleeting breath?

Thomas Gray 1716–71: *Elegy Written in a Country Churchyard* (1751)

11 It matters not how a man dies, but how he lives. The act of dying is not of importance, it lasts so short a time.

Samuel Johnson 1709–84: James Boswell *Life of Samuel Johnson* (1791) 26 October 1769

12 Tyrawley and I have been dead these two years; but we don't choose to have it known.

Lord Chesterfield 1694–1773: James Boswell *Life of Samuel Johnson* (1791) 3 April 1773

1 I am dying as fast as my enemies, if I have any, could wish, and as easily and cheerfully as my best friends could desire.
in his last illness, to his doctor

David Hume 1711–76: William Smellie *Literary and Characteristical Lives* (1800)

2 When I asked if there was anything she wanted, her answer was that she wanted nothing but death.
of her sister Jane's last illness

Cassandra Austen 1772–1845: letter to Fanny Knight, May 1817

3 When I have fears that I may cease to be
Before my pen has gleaned my teeming brain.

John Keats 1795–1821: 'When I have fears that I may cease to be' (written 1818)

4 Darkling I listen; and, for many a time
I have been half in love with easeful Death,
Called him soft names in many a musèd rhyme,
To take into the air my quiet breath;
Now more than ever seems it rich to die,
To cease upon the midnight with no pain.

John Keats 1795–1821: 'Ode to a Nightingale' (1820)

5 I know the colour of that blood;—it is arterial blood;—I cannot be deceived in that colour; that drop of blood is my death-warrant—I must die.
on coughing up blood and recognizing the fatal symptom of tuberculosis

John Keats 1795–1821: to his friend Charles Armitage Brown; Hyder E. Rollins (ed.) *The Keats Circle* (ed. 2, 1965)

6 I shall soon be laid in the quiet grave—thank God for the quiet grave—O! I can feel the cold earth upon me—the daisies growing over me—O for this quiet—it will be my first.

John Keats 1795–1821: letter from Joseph Severn to John Taylor, 6 March 1821

7 Death cancels everything but truth; and strips a man of everything but genius and virtue. It is a sort of natural canonization.

William Hazlitt 1778–1830: *The Spirit of the Age* (1825) 'Lord Byron'

8 The last breath he drew in he wished might be through a pipe and exhaled in a pun.

Charles Lamb 1775–1834: William Charles Macready diary, 9 January 1834

9 With the dead there is no rivalry. In the dead there is no change. Plato is never sullen. Cervantes is never petulant. Demosthenes never comes unseasonably. Dante never stays too long. No difference of political opinion can alienate Cicero. No heresy can excite the horror of Bossuet.

Lord Macaulay 1800–59: *Essays Contributed to the Edinburgh Review* (1843) 'Lord Bacon'

10 Unless one is a moron, one always dies unsure of one's own value and that of one's works. Virgil himself, as he lay dying, wanted the Aeneid burned.

Gustave Flaubert 1821–80: letter, 19 September 1852

11 Fear death?—to feel the fog in my throat,
The mist in my face.

Robert Browning 1812–89: 'Prospice' (1864)

12 Don't worry, you'll survive. No one dies in the middle of Act Five.

Henrik Ibsen 1828–1906: *Peer Gynt* (1867)

13 It was with many misgivings that I killed my old friend Mrs Proudie. I could not, I think, have done it, but for a resolution taken and declared under circumstances of great momentary pressure.

Anthony Trollope 1815–82: *Autobiography* (1883)

1 For though from out our bourne of time and place
The flood may bear me far,
I hope to see my pilot face to face
When I have crossed the bar.

Alfred, Lord Tennyson 1809–92: 'Crossing the Bar' (1889)

2 I have had a dreadful day; I have killed the Bishop and Felix.

while working simultaneously on her biography of the missionary Bishop Patteson, killed in Melanesia, and her novel Pillars of the House, *in which the death of Felix Underwood is a tragic climax.*

Charlotte Yonge 1823–1901: Margaret Mare and Alicia C. Percival *Victorian Best-Seller* (1947)

3 So here it is at last, the distinguished thing!

on experiencing his first stroke

Henry James 1843–1916: Edith Wharton *A Backward Glance* (1934)

4 Webster was much possessed by death
And saw the skull beneath the skin;
And breastless creatures underground
Leaned backward with a lipless grin.

T. S. Eliot 1888–1965: 'Whispers of Immortality' (1919)

5 The dead don't die. They look on and help.

D. H. Lawrence 1885–1930: letter to J. Middleton Murry, 2 February 1923

6 A man's dying is more the survivors' affair than his own.

Thomas Mann 1875–1955: *The Magic Mountain* (1924)

7 To die will be an awfully big adventure.

J. M. Barrie 1860–1937: *Peter Pan* (1928)

8 Too late for fruit, too soon for flowers.

recovering from an illness during which his life had been in danger

Walter de la Mare 1873–1956: John Bailey diary, 3 April 1928

9 I still go up my 44 stairs two at a time, but that is in hopes of dropping dead at the top.

A. E. Housman 1859–1936: letter to Laurence Housman, 9 June 1935

10 And what the dead had no speech for, when living,
They can tell you, being dead: the communication
Of the dead is tongued with fire beyond the language of
the living.

T. S. Eliot 1888–1965: *Four Quartets* 'Little Gidding' (1942)

11 I want to go on living even after death!

Anne Frank 1929–45: diary, 4 April 1944

12 Do not go gentle into that good night,
Old age should burn and rave at close of day;
Rage, rage against the dying of the light.

Dylan Thomas 1914–53: 'Do Not Go Gentle into that Good Night' (1952)

13 The only thing that really saddens me over my demise is that I shall not be here to read the nonsense that will be written about me . . . There will be lists of apocryphal jokes I never made and gleeful misquotations of words I never said. *What* a pity I shan't be here to enjoy them!

Noël Coward 1899–1973: diary, 19 March 1955

14 I wrote the book because we're all gonna die.

Jack Kerouac 1922–69: *On the Road* (1957)

15 Who wields a poem huger than the grave?

e. e. cummings 1894–1962: 'but if a living dance upon dead minds'; *selected poems 1923–1958*

1 Life is a great surprise. I do not see why death should not be an even greater one.

Vladimir Nabokov 1899–1977: *Pale Fire* (1962)

2 Dying,
Is an art, like everything else.

Sylvia Plath 1932–63: 'Lady Lazarus' (1963)

3 Let me die a youngman's death
Not a clean & in-between-
The-sheets, holy-water death,
Not a famous-last-words
Peaceful out-of-breath death.

Roger McGough 1937– : 'Let Me Die a Youngman's Death' (1967)

4 If there wasn't death, I think you couldn't go on.

Stevie Smith 1902–71: in *Observer* 9 November 1969

5 Death is nothing if one can approach it as such. I was just a tiny night-light, suffocated in its own wax, and on the point of expiring.

E. M. Forster 1879–1970: Philip Gardner (ed.) *E. M. Forster: Commonplace Book* (1985)

6 Death has got something to be said for it:
There's no need to get out of bed for it;
Wherever you may be,
They bring it to you, free.

Kingsley Amis 1922–95: 'Delivery Guaranteed' (1979)

7 And though poets I admire have published poems
Whose imperfections reflect our own decay,
I could never begin a poem; 'When I am dead'
In case it tempted Fate, and Fate gave way.

Roger McGough 1937– : 'When I am Dead' (1982); cf. **205:8**

8 Death is a displaced name for a linguistic predicament.

Paul de Man 1919–83: David Lehman *Signs of the Times* (1991)

9 Death is the great Maecenas, Death is the great angel of writing. You must write because you are not going to live any more.

Carlos Fuentes 1928– : in *Writers at Work* (6th series, 1984)

10 So the last date slides into the bracket,
that will appear in all future anthologies—
And in quiet Cornwall and in London's ghastly racket
We are now Betjemanless.

Gavin Ewart 1916–95: 'In Memoriam, Sir John Betjeman (1906–84)' (1985)

11 Would Hamlet have felt the delicious fascination of suicide if he hadn't had an audience, and lines to speak?

Jean Genet 1910–86: *Prisoner of Love* (1989)

12 Most deaths in novels are there for a reason, so that the death will point up the meaning of the whole story . . . I wanted to say that death isn't like that. It just happens, not necessarily to the person who deserves to be dead.
commenting on the death of a character in her novel Still Life

A. S. Byatt 1936– : in an interview, April 1988; George Greenfield *Scribblers for Bread* (1989)

13 Even death is unreliable: instead of zero it may be some ghastly hallucination, such as the square root of minus one.

Samuel Beckett 1906–89: attributed

14 The poem in the rock and
The poem in the mind
Are not one.
It was in dying
I tried to make them so.

R. S. Thomas 1913– : 'Epitaph'

1 My breath is folded up
Like sheets in lavender.
The end for me
Arrives like nursery tea.

Graham Greene 1904–91: *A World of My Own* (1992)

2 My only regret is to die four pages too soon—if I can finish, then I'm quite happy to go.

Dennis Potter 1935–94: interview with Melvyn Bragg on Channel 4, March 1994, in *Seeing the Blossom* (1994)

3 It's largely passed now, that panic about death. Some people always have it—like Dad and Larkin.

Martin Amis 1949– : interview in *Waterstone's Quarterly Guide* Spring/Summer 1996

Dedications

4 Go, litel bok, go, litel myn tragedye,
Ther God thi makere yet, er that he dye,
So sende myght to make in som comedye!
But litel bok, no makyng thow n'envie,
But subgit be to alle poesye;
And kis the steppes, where as thow seest pace
Virgile, Ovide, Omer, Lucan, and Stace.

Geoffrey Chaucer *c.*1343–1400: *Troilus and Criseyde*

5 If the first heir of my invention prove deformed, I shall be sorry it had so noble a godfather.

William Shakespeare 1564–1616: *Venus and Adonis* (1593) dedication

6 What I have done is yours; what I have to do is yours; being part in all I have, devoted yours.

William Shakespeare 1564–1616: *The Rape of Lucrece* (1594)

7 To the onlie begetter of these insuing sonnets, Mr. W. H.

William Shakespeare 1564–1616: *Sonnets* (1609) dedication (also attributed to Thomas Thorpe, the publisher)

8 Perhaps when you again appear in print you may choose to dedicate your volumes to Prince Leopold: any historical romance, illustrative of the history of the august House of Coburg, would just now be very interesting.

James Stanier Clarke *c.*1765–1834: letter to Jane Austen, 27 March 1816; cf. **101:10**

9 Look with favour
Upon the chapters in your hand . . .
The mind's reflections coldly noted,
The bitter insights of the heart.

Alexander Pushkin 1799–1837: *Eugene Onegin* (1833) 'Dedication' (translated by Babette Deutsch)

10 A dedication, for me, is a serious thing. It is an offering of my thoughts given in affection and esteem.

Joseph Conrad 1857–1924: letter, 29 August 1896

11 To live is to battle with trolls in the vaults of heart and brain. To write: that is to sit in judgement over one's self.
dedicatory lines which Ibsen said he once inscribed in a copy of one of his books

Henrik Ibsen 1828–1906: letter, 16 June 1880

12 To my daughter Leonora without whose never-failing sympathy and encouragement this book would have been finished in half the time.

P. G. Wodehouse 1881–1975: dedication to *The Heart of a Goof* (1926)

1 One can find Evelyn's biography in the dedications to his books, each displaying a further step in his social progress.
a 'cruel contemporary' on Evelyn **Waugh**

Anonymous: in *Time* 12 July 1948

2 I'd be delighted to accept the dedication of *The Contenders*, but Heaven knows when I'll be able to return it—Sunday writers like myself do about a book a decade, and the queue is already in existence.

Philip Larkin 1922–85: letter to John Wain, 15 January 1957

Description

3 The business of a poet, said Imlac, is to examine, not the individual, but the species; to remark general properties and appearances: he does not number the streaks of the tulip, or describe the different shades in the verdure of the forest.

Samuel Johnson 1709–84: *Rasselas* (1759)

4 Damn description, it is always disgusting.

Lord Byron 1788–1824: letter, 6 August 1809

5 Description is always a bore, both to the describer and to the describee.

Benjamin Disraeli 1804–81: letter, 1830; *Home Letters* (1885)

6 Such epithets, like pepper,
Give zest to what you write;
And if you strew them sparely,
They whet the appetite:
But if you lay them on too thick,
You spoil the matter quite!

Lewis Carroll 1832–98: 'Phantasmagoria' (1876)

7 Merely corroborative detail, intended to give artistic verisimilitude to an otherwise bald and unconvincing narrative.

W. S. Gilbert 1836–1911: *The Mikado* (1885)

8 No human being ever spoke of scenery for above two minutes at a time, which makes me suspect we hear too much of it in literature.

Robert Louis Stevenson 1850–94: *Memories and Portraits* (1887)

9 You must describe your women in such a way that the reader feels your tie is off and your waistcoat open. Women and nature both. Let yourself go.

Anton Chekhov 1860–1904: letter, 20 October 1888

10 As to the Adjective: when in doubt, strike it out.

Mark Twain 1835–1910: *Pudd'nhead Wilson* (1894)

11 My attitude towards adjectives is the story of my life. If ever I write my autobiography, I'll call it *The Story of an Adjective*. In my youth I thought that the sumptuous must be conveyed by sumptuous means. But I was wrong. It turned out that one must very often proceed by opposites.

Isaac Babel 1894–1940: interview, Union of Soviet Writers, 28 September 1937

12 There is no need for the writer to eat a whole sheep to be able to tell you what mutton tastes like. It is enough if he eats a cutlet. But he should do that.

W. Somerset Maugham 1874–1965: *A Writer's Notebook* (1949) written in 1941

13 It is easier to describe the threshold of divine revelation than the working of a pair of scissors.

C. S. Lewis 1898–1963: attributed; perhaps summarizing a passage in *Studies in Words* (1960)

1 Our language lacks words to express this offence, the demolition of a man.
of a year spent in Auschwitz

Primo Levi 1919–87: *If This is a Man* (1958)

2 I don't know if you care for descriptions? I don't.
to the novelist Elizabeth Taylor

Ivy Compton-Burnett 1884–1969: Hilary Spurling *Secrets of a Woman's Heart: the Later Life of Ivy Compton-Burnett* (1984)

3 When I describe a scene, I capture it with the moving eye of the cine-camera rather than with the photographer's eye—which leaves it frozen.

Graham Greene 1904–91: Marie-Françoise Allain *The Other Man, Conversations with Graham Greene* (1983)

4 Details fascinate me. I love to pile up details. They create an atmosphere.

Muriel Spark 1918– : *Curriculum Vitae* (1992)

Dialogue and Conversation see also **Speech**

5 Give 'em words;
Pour oil into their ears, and send them hence.

Ben Jonson *c.*1573–1637: *Volpone* (1606)

6 Language most shows a man: Speak, that I may see thee. It springs out of the most retired and inmost parts of us, and is the image of the parent of it, the mind. No glass renders a man's form or likeness so true as his speech.

Ben Jonson *c.*1573–1637: *Timber, or Discoveries made upon Men and Matter* (1641)

7 Then he will talk, Good Gods,
How he will talk.

Nathaniel Lee *c.*1653–92: *The Rival Queens* (1677)

8 A transition from an author's books to his conversation, is too often like an entrance into a large city, after a distant prospect. Remotely, we see nothing but spires of temples, and turrets of palaces, and imagine it the residence of splendour, grandeur, and magnificence; but when we have passed the gates, we find it perplexed with narrow passages, disgraced with despicable cottages, embarrassed with obstructions, and clouded with smoke.

Samuel Johnson 1709–84: in *The Rambler* 5 May 1784

9 'My idea of good company, Mr Elliot, is the company of clever, well-informed people, who have a great deal of conversation; that is what I call good company.' 'You are mistaken,' said he gently, 'that is not good company, that is the best.'

Jane Austen 1775–1817: *Persuasion* (1818)

10 Ye Lilies male! think (as your tea you sip,
While the Town small-talk flows from lip to lip;
Intrigues half-gathered, conversation-scraps,
Kitchen-cabals, and nursery-mishaps,)
If the vast world may not some scene produce,
Some state where your small talents might have use.

George Crabbe 1754–1832: *The Borough* (1810) Letter 3 'The Vicar' l. 69

11 Conversation is a game of circles. In conversation we pluck up the *termini* which bound the common of silence on every side.

Ralph Waldo Emerson 1803–82: *Essays* (1841) 'Circles'

1 They tell me I say ill-natured things. I have a weak voice; if I did not say ill-natured things, no one would hear what I said.

Samuel Rogers 1763–1855: Henry Taylor *Autobiography* (1885) vol. 1

2 One shouldn't talk when one is tired. One Hamletizes, and it seems a lie.

D. H. Lawrence 1885–1930: *Women in Love* (1921)

3 Shaw talked practically the whole time, which is the same thing as saying he talked a damn sight too much . . . I really wanted to have a scrap with Virginia Woolf, but got no chance.
of a dinner party at H. G. ***Wells****'s*

Arnold Bennett 1867–1931: diary, 4 November 1926

4 As soon as the dialogue begins, I become merely a recording instrument, and my hand never hesitates because my mind has not to choose, but only to set down what these stupid or intelligent, lethargic or passionate, people say to each other in a language, and with arguments, that appear to be all their own.

Edith Wharton 1862–1937: *A Backward Glance* (1934)

5 Conversation is imperative if gaps are to be filled, and old age, it is the last gap but one.

Patrick White 1912–90: *The Tree of Man* (1955) ch. 22

6 When the dialogue begins, the tempo slows down to the pace of the story itself. The reader understands very well that he is being drawn close in. He, too, is relieved to hear what the voices are like.

Penelope Fitzgerald 1916– : Clare Boylan (ed.) *The Agony and the Ego* (1993)

7 The Watergate tapes are the most famous and extensive transcripts of real-life speech ever published. When they were released, Americans were shocked, though not all for the same reason. Some people—a very small number—were surprised that Nixon had taken part in a conspiracy to obstruct justice. A few were surprised that the leader of the free world cussed like a stevedore. But one thing that surprised everyone was what ordinary conversation looks like when it is written down verbatim.

Steven Pinker 1954– : *The Language Instinct* (1994)

Diaries

8 And so I betake myself to that course, which is almost as much as to see myself go into my grave.
on being forced by failing eyesight to give up keeping his diary

Samuel Pepys 1633–1703: diary, 31 May 1669; cf. **43:7**

9 What though his head be empty, provided his commonplace book be full.

Jonathan Swift 1667–1745: *A Tale of a Tub* (1704)

10 A page of my Journal is like a cake of portable soup. A little may be diffused into a considerable portion.

James Boswell 1740–95: *Journal of a Tour to the Hebrides* (1785) 13 September 1773

11 I never travel without my diary. One should always have something sensational to read in the train.

Oscar Wilde 1854–1900: *The Importance of Being Earnest* (1895)

1 What sort of diary should I like mine to be? . . . I should like it to resemble some deep old desk, or capacious hold-all, in which one flings a mass of odds and ends without looking them through.

Virginia Woolf 1882–1941: diary, 20 April 1919

2 One need not write in a diary what one is to remember for ever.

Sylvia Townsend Warner 1893–1978: diary, 22 October 1930

3 What is more dull than a discreet diary? One might just as well have a discreet soul.

Henry 'Chips' Channon 1897–1958: diary, 26 July 1935

4 I always say, keep a diary and some day it'll keep you.

Mae West 1892–1980: *Every Day's a Holiday* (1937 film)

5 Now that I am finishing the damned thing I realise that diary-writing isn't wholly good for one, that too much of it leads to living for one's diary instead of living for the fun of living as ordinary people do.

James Agate 1877–1947: letter, 7 December 1946

6 To be a good diarist one must have a little, snouty, sneaky mind.

in reference to ***Pepys***

Harold Nicolson 1886–1968: diary, 9 November 1947

7 After the writer's death, reading his journal is like receiving a long letter.

after reading ***Kafka****'s diary*

Jean Cocteau 1889–1963: diary, 7 June 1953

8 The moment a man sets his thoughts down on paper, however secretly, he is in a sense writing for publication.

Raymond Chandler 1888–1959: working notes on the Julia Wallace murder case; in *Raymond Chandler Speaking* (1962)

9 To write a diary every day is like returning to one's own vomit.

Enoch Powell 1912–98: interview in *Sunday Times* 6 November 1977

10 I am a great believer in diaries, if only in the sense that bar exercises are good for ballet dancers: it's often through personal diaries . . . that the novelist discovers his true bent—that he can narrate real events and distort them to please himself, describe character, observe other beings, hypothesize, invent.

John Fowles 1932– : George Plimpton (ed.) *The Writer's Chapbook* (1989)

11 I have decided to keep a full journal, in the hope that my life will perhaps seem more interesting when it is written down.

Sue Townsend 1946– : *Adrian Mole: The Wilderness Years* (1993)

12 It is a confession. A diary is not trying to establish a reputation but to give people an idea of what you thought at the time.

on his Diaries

Tony Benn 1925– : in *Daily Telegraph* 30 September 1995 'They Said It'

Dictionaries

13 *Lexicographer*. A writer of dictionaries, a harmless drudge.

Samuel Johnson 1709–84: *A Dictionary of the English Language* (1755)

1 *Dull.* To make dictionaries is dull work.
8th definition of 'dull'

Samuel Johnson 1709–84: *A Dictionary of the English Language* (1755)

2 But these were the dreams of a poet doomed at last to wake a lexicographer.

Samuel Johnson 1709–84: *A Dictionary of the English Language* (1755)

3 Every quotation contributes something to the stability or enlargement of the language.
on citations of usage in a dictionary

Samuel Johnson 1709–84: *A Dictionary of the English Language* (1755)

4 All dictionaries are made from dictionaries.

Voltaire 1694–1778: *Philosophical Dictionary* (1764)

5 Dictionaries are like watches, the worst is better than none, and the best cannot be expected to go quite true.

Samuel Johnson 1709–84: letter to Francesco Sastres, 21 August 1784

6 At painful times, when composition is impossible and reading is not *enough*, grammars and dictionaries are excellent for *distraction*.

Elizabeth Barrett Browning 1806–61: letter to Mary Russell Mitford, April 1839

7 When I feel inclined to read poetry I take down my Dictionary. The poetry of words is quite as beautiful as that of sentences. The author may arrange the gems effectively, but their shape and lustre have been given by the attrition of ages.

Oliver Wendell Holmes 1809–94: *The Autocrat of the Breakfast Table* (1858)

8 Neither is a dictionary a bad book to read. There is no cant in it, no excess of explanation, and it is full of suggestion, the raw material of possible poems and histories.

Ralph Waldo Emerson 1803–82: *The Conduct of Life* (1860)

9 They are strange beings, these lexicographers.

John Brown 1810–82: *Horae Subsecivae* (rev. ed. 1884)

10 What a comfort a Dictionary is!

Lewis Carroll 1832–98: *Sylvie and Bruno Concluded* (1893)

11 Here's a book full of words; one can choose as he fancies,
As a painter his tint, as a workman his tool;
Just think! all the poems and plays and romances
Were drawn out of this, like the fish from the pool.

Oliver Wendell Holmes 1809–94: 'A Familiar Letter'

12 Two men wrote a lexicon, Liddell and Scott;
Some parts were clever, but some parts were not.
Hear, all ye learned, and read me this riddle,
How the wrong part wrote Scott, and the right part wrote Liddell.
of Henry Liddell (1811–98) and Robert Scott (1811–87) co-authors of the Greek Lexicon *(1843), Liddell being in the habit of ascribing to his co-author usages which he criticised in his pupils, and which they said that they had culled from the* Lexicon

Edward Waterfield: L. E. Tanner *Westminster School: A History* (1934)

Bywater had managed to find an early instance of poetria *for the* Oxford English Dictionary:

13 It took me some time; but I am sometimes lucky on Sundays.

Ingram Bywater 1840–1914: in *Dictionary of National Biography*

1 I am not a literary man . . . I am a man of science, and I am interested in that branch of Anthropology which deals with the history of human speech.
account of himself by the first Editor of the Oxford English Dictionary

James A. H. Murray 1837–1915: lecture to the Ashmolean History Society, Oxford; K. M. E. Murray *Caught in the Web of Words* (1977)

of the work-room of the New English Dictionary *in the Old Ashmolean, Oxford:*

2 That great dusty workshop, that brownest of brown studies.

J. R. R. Tolkien 1892–1973: *c.*1919; Humphrey Carpenter *J. R. R. Tolkien* (1977)

3 The Dictionary has not attempted to rival some of its predecessors in deliberate humour . . . Such rare occasions for a smile as may be found in it are unintentional.
of the New English Dictionary

W. A. Craigie 1867–1967: in *The Periodical* 15 February 1928

4 Once or twice recently I have looked up a word in the dictionary for fear of being again accused of coining, and have found it there right enough—only to read on and find that the sole authority quoted is myself in a half-forgotten novel.
in conversation with Robert Graves

Thomas Hardy 1840–1928: Robert Graves *Goodbye to All That* (1929)

5 Useful as daylight, firm as stone,
Wet as a fish, dry as a bone,
Heavy as lead, light as a breeze—
Frank Wilstach's book of similes.

Franklin P. Adams 1881–1960: 'Lines on Reading Frank J. Wilstach's *A Dictionary of Similes*'; in *The New York World c.*1922–30

6 O precious codex, volume, tome,
Book, writing, compilation, work
Attend the while I pen a pome,
A jest, a jape, a quip, a quirk.

Franklin P. Adams 1881–1960: 'To a Thesaurus'; in *The New York World c.*1922–30

7 I've been in *Who's Who*, and I know what's what, but it'll be the first time I ever made the dictionary.
on having an inflatable life jacket named after her

Mae West 1892–1980: letter to the RAF, early 1940s; Fergus Cashin *Mae West* (1981)

8 Actually if a writer needs a dictionary he should not write. He should have read the dictionary at least three times from beginning to end.

Ernest Hemingway 1899–1961: letter to Bernard Berenson, 20 March 1953

9 The greatest masterpiece in literature is only a dictionary out of order.

Jean Cocteau 1889–1963: attributed

10 A dictionary is a frozen pantomime. Our problem is only beginning when we consider the pale flowers of that nosegay of faded metaphors that it presses between its pages.

Dwight Bolinger 1907– : 'The Atomization of Meaning' (1965)

11 Dictionaries do not exist to define, but to help people grasp meanings, and for this purpose their main task is to supply a series of hints and associations that will relate the unknown to something known. The orderliness and apparent system in a dictionary are more the result of our instinct to be orderly than of any towering need for system based on subject matter.

Dwight Bolinger 1907– : 'The Atomization of Meaning' (1965)

1 I suppose that so long as there are people in the world, they will publish dictionaries defining what is unknown in terms of something equally unknown.

Flann O'Brien 1911–66: *Myles Away from Dublin* (1990)

2 [The] collective unconscious of the race is the OED.

James Merrill 1926– : in *American Poetry Review* September/October 1979'On James Merrill'

3 Services to Scrabble.
summarizing the work of the OED Supplement

J. I. M. Stewart 1906–94: Anthony Thwaite, obituary of J. I. M. Stewart in *Independent* 15 November 1994

4 Short dictionaries should be improved because they are intended for people who actually need help.

William Empson 1906–84: attributed

5 Big dictionaries are nothing but storerooms with infrequently visited and dusty corners.

Richard W. Bailey 1939– : *Images of English* (1991)

Drama

6 Let a play have five acts, neither more not less.

Horace 65–8 BC: *Ars Poetica*

7 For what's a play without a woman in it?

Thomas Kyd 1558–94: *The Spanish Tragedy* (1592)

8 Can this cockpit hold
The vasty fields of France? or may we cram
Within this wooden O the very casques
That did affright the air at Agincourt?

William Shakespeare 1564–1616: *Henry V* (1599)

9 The play's the thing
Wherein I'll catch the conscience of the king.

William Shakespeare 1564–1616: *Hamlet* (1601)

10 Then to the well-trod stage anon,
If Jonson's learnèd sock be on,
Or sweetest Shakespeare fancy's child,
Warble his native wood-notes wild.

John Milton 1608–74: 'L'Allegro' (1645)

11 I saw Hamlet Prince of Denmark played, but now the old play began to disgust this refined age.

John Evelyn 1620–1706: diary, 26 November 1661

12 *Qu'en un lieu, qu'en un jour, un seul fait accompli*
Tienne jusqu'à la fin le théâtre rempli.

Let a single completed action, all in one place, all in one day, keep the theatre packed to the end of your play.

Nicolas Boileau 1636–1711: *L'Art poétique* (1674)

13 To wake the soul by tender strokes of art,
To raise the genius, and to mend the heart;
To make mankind, in conscious virtue bold,
Live o'er each scene, and be what they behold:
For this the Tragic Muse first trod the stage.

Alexander Pope 1688–1744: Prologue to Addison's *Cato* (1713)

14 There still remains, to mortify a wit,
The many-headed monster of the pit.

Alexander Pope 1688–1744: *Imitations of Horace* (1737)

1 'Do you come to the play without knowing what it is?' 'O yes, Sir, yes, very frequently; I have no time to read play-bills; one merely comes to meet one's friends, and show that one's alive.'

Fanny Burney 1752–1840: *Evelina* (1778)

2 O Lord, Sir—when a heroine goes mad she always goes into white satin.

Richard Brinsley Sheridan 1751–1816: *The Critic* (1779)

3 It is better to have written a damned play, than no play at all—it snatches a man from obscurity.

Frederic Reynolds 1764–1841: *The Dramatist* (1789)

4 I consider it injurious for a dramatic work to be first made available to the public by a stage performance . . . [because it] can never be understood and judged in isolation as a piece of literature. Judgement will always include both the piece and its performance.

Henrik Ibsen 1828–1906: letter, 1872

5 The play was a great success, but the audience was a total failure.

after the first performance of Lady Windermere's Fan

Oscar Wilde 1854–1900: Peter Hay *Theatrical Anecdotes* (1987)

6 NINA: Your play's hard to act, there are no living people in it.
TREPLEV: Living people! We should show life neither as it is nor as it ought to be, but as we see it in our dreams.

Anton Chekhov 1860–1904: *The Seagull* (1896)

7 What the American public always wants is a tragedy with a happy ending.

explaining to Edith **Wharton** *why* The House of Mirth, *her first play, wouldn't run on Broadway*

William Dean Howells 1837–1920: in October 1906; R. W. B. Lewis *Edith Wharton* (1975)

8 The ever-importunate murmur, 'Dramatize it, dramatize it!'

Henry James 1843–1916: *The Altar of the Dead* (1909 ed.) preface

9 My curse on plays
That have to be set up in fifty ways,
On the day's war with every knave and dolt,
Theatre business, management of men.

W. B. Yeats 1865–1939: 'The Fascination of What's Difficult' (1910)

10 If any play has been produced only twice in three hundred years, there must be some good reason for it.

Rupert Hart-Davis 1907– : letter to George Lyttelton, 7 July 1957

11 There is far too much sex and violence gets by in the name of entertainment. I mean, I go to the theatre to be entertained, I want to be taken out of myself, I don't want to see lust and rape and incest and sodomy and so on, I can get all that at home.

Alan Bennett 1934– : Bennett et al. *Beyond the Fringe* (1963) 'Man of Principles'

12 I can do you blood and love without the rhetoric, and I can do you blood and rhetoric without the love, and I can do you all three concurrent or consecutive, but I can't do you love and rhetoric without the blood. Blood is compulsory—they're all blood, you see.

Tom Stoppard 1937– : *Rosencrantz and Guildenstern are Dead* (1967)

13 Depending on shock tactics is easy, whereas writing a good play is difficult.

J. B. Priestley 1894–1984: *Outcries and Asides* (1974)

14 I've never much enjoyed going to plays . . . The unreality of painted people standing on a platform saying things they've said to each other for months is more than I can overlook.

John Updike 1932– : George Plimpton (ed.) *Writers at Work* 4th Series (1977)

1 Drama is life with the dull bits left out.

Alfred Hitchcock 1899–1980: attributed

2 Williams recognized that great theatre begins with great talkers, and that great talkers obey two rules: they never sound like anyone else and they never say anything directly.

of Tennessee ***Williams***

Edmund White 1940– : in *New Republic* 13 May 1985

3 There is . . . a 'wonder' in and of our shrunken mortality and our scrabbling appetites which maybe prayer and maybe drama and maybe just a song or a dance or a breeze in the air can sometimes fleetingly catch hold of.

Dennis Potter 1935–94: James MacTaggart Memorial Lecture in *Seeing the Blossom* (1994)

4 Playwriting is not a job, let alone a career. It's like being an eternal student.

Doug Lucie 1953– : in *Daily Telegraph* 18 March 1995 'They Said It'

5 A play, I think, ought to make sense to commonsense people. Drama is akin to other inventions of man in that it ought to help us to know more, and not merely to spend our feelings.

of The Crucible

Arthur Miller 1915– : attributed, 1996

Drink and Drugs

6 No verse can give pleasure for long, nor last, that is written by drinkers of water.

Horace 65–8 BC: *Epistles*

7 When the wine is in, the wit is out.

Thomas Becon 1512–67: *Catechism* (1560)

8 But that which most doth take my Muse and me
Is a pure cup of rich Canary wine,
Which is the Mermaid's now, but shall be mine.

Ben Jonson *c.*1573–1637: 'Inviting a Friend to Supper' (1616); cf. **65:3**

9 What things have we seen,
Done at the Mermaid! heard words that have been
So nimble, and so full of subtil flame,
As if that every one from whence they came,
Had meant to put his whole wit in a jest,
And had resolved to live a fool, the rest
Of his dull life.

Francis Beaumont 1584–1616: 'Letter to Ben Jonson'; cf. **65:3**

10 I have left off wine and writing; for I really think that a man must be a bold writer who trusts to wit without it.

John Gay 1685–1732: letter to Dean Swift; *Life and Letters* (1921)

11 Let schoolmasters puzzle their brain,
With grammar, and nonsense, and learning,
Good liquor, I stoutly maintain,
Gives genius a better discerning.

Oliver Goldsmith 1728–74: *She Stoops to Conquer* (1773)

12 Claret is the liquor for boys; port, for men; but he who aspires to be a hero (smiling) must drink brandy.

Samuel Johnson 1709–84: James Boswell *Life of Samuel Johnson* (1791) 7 April 1779

1 Freedom and Whisky gang thegither!

Robert Burns 1759–96: 'The Author's Earnest Cry and Prayer' (1786)

2 A man may surely be allowed to take a glass of wine by his own fireside.

on being encountered drinking a glass of wine in the street, while watching his theatre, the Drury Lane, burn down

Richard Brinsley Sheridan 1751–1816: T. Moore *Life of Sheridan* (1825)

3 Souls of poets dead and gone,
What Elysium have ye known,
Happy field or mossy cavern,
Choicer than the Mermaid Tavern?
Have ye tippled drink more fine
Than mine host's Canary wine?

John Keats 1795–1821: 'Lines on the Mermaid Tavern' (1820); cf. **64:8, 64:9**

4 Away! away! for I will fly to thee,
Not charioted by Bacchus and his pards,
But on the viewless wings of Poesy.

John Keats 1795–1821: 'Ode to a Nightingale' (1820)

5 O, for a draught of vintage! that hath been
Cooled a long age in the deep-delvèd earth,
Tasting of Flora and the country green,
Dance, and Provençal song, and sunburnt mirth!

John Keats 1795–1821: 'Ode to a Nightingale' (1820)

6 Gin-and-water is the source of all my inspiration.

Lord Byron 1788–1824: *Conversations* (1824)

7 Thou hast the keys of Paradise, oh just, subtle, and mighty opium!

Thomas De Quincey 1785–1859: *Confessions of an English Opium Eater* (1822, ed. 1856)

8 *L'Opium agrandit ce qui n'a pas de bornes,*
Allonge l'illimité,
Approfondit le temps, creuse la volupté,
Et de plaisirs noirs et mornes
Remplit l'âme au-delà de sa capacité.

Opium magnifies things that have no limits, prolongs the boundless, makes Time more profound, deepens voluptuousness, and fills the soul to overflowing with dark and gloomy pleasures.

Charles Baudelaire 1821–67: 'Le Poison' (1857)

9 To tell the story of Coleridge without the opium is to tell the story of Hamlet without mentioning the ghost.

Leslie Stephen 1832–1904: *Hours in a Library* (1874–9)

10 And malt does more than Milton can
To justify God's ways to man.
Ale, man, ale's the stuff to drink
For fellows whom it hurts to think.

A. E. Housman 1859–1936: *A Shropshire Lad* (1896); cf. **203:7**

11 A pipe for the hour of work; a cigarette for the hour of conception; a cigar for the hour of vacuity.

George Gissing 1857–1903: *Commonplace Book* (1962)

12 This great College, of this ancient University, has seen some strange sights. It has seen Wordsworth drunk and Porson sober. And here am I, a better poet than Porson, and a better scholar than Wordsworth, betwixt and between.

A. E. Housman 1859–1936: speech at Trinity College, Cambridge, 1911

1 After all, most struggling poets drink Camp coffee instead of nectar and find it just as inspiring and much cheaper.

Barbara Pym 1913–80: 'Young Men in Fancy Dress' (written *c.*1930); Hazel Holt *A Lot to Ask* (1990)

2 If you ever get that depressed unable-to-concentrate feeling, try taking Benzedrine Tablets, but not too many.

W. H. Auden 1907–73: letter, April 1940

3 Drink heightens feeling. When I drink, it heightens my emotions and I put it in a story.

F. Scott Fitzgerald 1896–1940: Andrew Turnbull *Scott Fitzgerald* (1962)

4 A man you don't like who drinks as much as you do.
definition of an alcoholic

Dylan Thomas 1914–53: Constantine Fitzgibbon *Life of Dylan Thomas* (1965)

5 A man shouldn't fool with booze until he's fifty; then he's a damn fool if he doesn't.

William Faulkner 1897–1962: James M. Webb and A. Wigfall Green *William Faulkner of Oxford* (1965)

6 Boozing does not necessarily have to go hand in hand with being a writer . . . I therefore solemnly declare to all young men trying to be writers that they do not actually have to become drunkards first.

James Jones 1921–77: in *Writers at Work* (3rd Series, 1967)

7 It's hard to say why writing verse,
Should terminate in drink or worse.

A. P. Herbert 1890–1971: 'Lines for a Worldly Person'

8 LSD? Nothing much happened, but I did get the distinct impression that some birds were trying to communicate with me.

W. H. Auden 1907–73: George Plimpton (ed.) *The Writer's Chapbook* (1989)

9 *The Confidential Agent* . . . was completed in six weeks under the influence of benzedrine.

Graham Greene 1904–91: Marie-Françoise Allain *The Other Man, Conversations with Graham Greene* (1983)

10 Really, I can't imagine the drug scene. My generation are drinkers and smokers; I wouldn't stick a needle into myself for a hatful of golden guineas.

Philip Larkin 1922–85: letter, 15 September 1985

11 No other human being, no woman, no poem or music, book or painting, can replace alcohol in its power to give man the illusion of real creation.

Marguerite Duras 1914– : *Practicalities* (1987, tr. 1990)

12 One simply pulls the cork out of the bottle, waits three minutes, and two thousand or more years of Scottish craftsmanship does the rest.

J. G. Ballard 1930– : George Plimpton (ed.) *The Writer's Chapbook* (1989)

Earning a Living see also **Money**

13 Barefaced poverty drove me to writing verses.

Horace 65–8 BC: *Epistles*

14 Poor starving bard, how small thy gains!

Jonathan Swift 1667–1745: 'On Poetry' (1733)

1 *Patron*. Commonly a wretch who supports with insolence, and is paid with flattery.

Samuel Johnson 1709–84: *A Dictionary of the English Language* (1755)

2 Born in a cellar . . . and living in a garret.

Samuel Foote 1720–77: *The Author* (1757)

3 No man but a blockhead ever wrote, except for money.

Samuel Johnson 1709–84: James Boswell *Life of Samuel Johnson* (1791) 5 April 1776

4 When men write for profit, they are not very delicate.

Horace Walpole 1717–97: letter to Revd William Cole, 1 September 1778

5 What affectionate parent would consent to see his son devote himself to his pen as his profession? . . . Most authors close their lives in apathy or despair, and too many of them live by means which few of them would not blush to describe.

Isaac D'Israeli 1766–1848: *Calamities of Authors* (1812)

6 You will be glad to hear that every copy of *Sense and Sensibility* is sold and that it has brought me £140 besides the copyright, if that should ever be of value.

Jane Austen 1775–1817: letter, 3 July 1813

7 They knew luxury; they knew beggary; but they never knew comfort.

of writers struggling to make a living in Johnson's day

Lord Macaulay 1800–59: *Essays Contributed to the Edinburgh Review* (1843) 'Samuel Johnson'

8 Always waiting and what to do or to say in the meantime I don't know, and who wants poets at all in lean years?

Johann Christian Friedrich Hölderlin 1770–1843: 'Bread and Wine' (1800-01)

9 My object is remuneration.

submitting her first short story for magazine publication

Frances Hodgson Burnett 1849–1924: letter, *c.*1867; Ann Thwaite *Waiting for the Party* (1994)

10 During the last twenty years I have made by literature something near £70,000. As I have said before in these pages, I look upon the result as comfortable, but not splendid.

Anthony Trollope 1815–82: *Autobiography* (1883)

11 Brains that are unbought will never serve the public much. Take away from English authors their copyrights, and you would very soon take away also from England her authors.

Anthony Trollope 1815–82: *Autobiography* (1883)

12 Medicine is my lawful wife and literature is my mistress. When I get tired of one I spend the night with the other.

Anton Chekhov 1860–1904: letter to A. S. Suvorin, 11 September 1888

13 I am the literary man of 1882 . . . I am learning my business. Literature nowadays is a trade. Putting aside men of genius, who may succeed by mere cosmic force, your successful man of letters is your successful tradesman. He thinks first and foremost of the markets;

George Gissing 1857–1903: 'Jasper Milvain' in *New Grub Street* (1891)

when one kind of goods begins to go off slackly, he is ready with something new and appetising.

1 What an insane thing it is to make literature one's only means of support! When the most trivial accident may at any time prove fatal to one's power of work for weeks and months. No, that is the unpardonable sin! To make a trade of art!

George Gissing 1857–1903: 'Edwin Reardon' in *New Grub Street* (1891)

2 The profession of letters is, after all, the only one in which one can make no money without being ridiculous.

Jules Renard 1864–1910: diary, 1906

3 It is a fine world, and I wish I knew how to make £200 a year in it.

Edward Thomas 1878–1917: letter to Gordon Bottomley, 16 June 1915

4 The tip's a good one, as for literature
It gives no man a sinecure.
And no one knows, at sight, a masterpiece.
And give up verse, my boy,
There's nothing in it.

Ezra Pound 1885–1972: *Hugh Selwyn Mauberley* (1920) 'Mr Nixon'

5 Go in for Celtic, lad; there's money in it.
a philologist's advice to the young ***Tolkien***

Joseph Wright 1855–1930: Humphrey Carpenter *J. R. R. Tolkien* (1977)

6 For me I never cared for fame
Solvency was my only aim.

J. C. Squire 1884–1958: at a dinner given in his honour, 15 December 1932; Patrick Howarth *Squire: Most Generous of Men* (1963)

7 There is only one way to make money at writing, and that is to marry a publisher's daughter.

George Orwell 1903–50: *Down and Out in Paris and London* (1933)

8 I had to earn my own living and this is antipathetic to a purely aesthetic view of life.

Louis MacNeice 1907–63: *Modern Poetry* (1938)

9 High-priced commercial writing for the magazines is a very definite trick.

F. Scott Fitzgerald 1896–1940: letter 19 May 1940

10 However toplofty and idealistic a man may be, he can always rationalize his right to earn money.
to his New York literary agent

Raymond Chandler 1888–1959: letter to Carl Brandt, 15 November 1951; *Raymond Chandler Speaking* (1962)

11 I have got to write a damned book but when it's done I'll never again let myself be tempted by large advances to undertake anything my daemon doesn't suggest.
of his biography of Lawrence of Arabia

Richard Aldington 1892–1962: letter to his wife Hilda Doolittle ('H. D.'), 29 May 1951

12 You don't write to support yourself; you work to support your writing.

Alfred Kazin 1915– : Sylvia Plath, letter to her mother, 25 October 1954

13 If you want to write poetry you must earn a living some other way.

T. S. Eliot 1888–1965: attributed, 1958

14 The profession of book writing makes horse racing seem like a solid, stable business.

John Steinbeck 1902–68: in *Newsweek* 24 December 1962

1 It is a sad fact about our culture that a poet can earn much more money writing or talking about his art than he can by practising it.

W. H. Auden 1907–73: *The Dyer's Hand* (1962) foreword

2 The greatest threat to literature is merchant bankers.
a publisher's view

Anonymous: in *Standard* 25 January 1965

3 Who would, for preference
be a bard in an oral culture,
obliged at drunken feasts to improvise a eulogy
of some beefy illiterate burner,
giver of rings, or depend for bread on the moods of a
Baroque Prince, expected
like his dwarf, to amuse?

W. H. Auden 1907–73: 'The Cave of Making' (1965)

4 Nowadays one's agent, and one's solicitor, and one's bank manager only do the irreducible minimum, but unfortunately it is the minimum one cannot do oneself.

Ivy Compton-Burnett 1884–1969: Hilary Spurling *Secrets of a Woman's Heart: the Later Life of Ivy Compton-Burnett* (1984)

5 [Feydeau] had the great traditional stimulant to the industry of an artist, laziness and debt.

John Mortimer 1923– : *Clinging to the Wreckage* (1982)

6 One of my great surprises when I was in America was about twenty-five years ago in Harvard, hearing Randall Jarrell deliver a bitter attack on the way poets were neglected. Yet there were about two thousand people present, and he was being paid five hundred dollars for delivering this attack.

Stephen Spender 1909–95: George Plimpton (ed.) *Writers at Work* (6th series, 1984)

7 Poetry? It's a hobby.
I run model trains.
Mr Shaw there breeds pigeons.
It's not work. You don't sweat.
Nobody pays for it.
You *could* advertise soap.

Basil Bunting 1900–85: 'What the Chairman Told Tom'

8 I have always made it a point of honour to write as though I had a million dollars; that is, I try to write in the most original way I know how, and that feels like a risk each time you do it.

Edmund White 1940– : interview in *Paris Review* 1988

9 I have never written in order to make money. A story comes to me, is given me, as it were, and I write it. But perhaps the need to earn a living and my need to write coincided. I know that I would still write if tomorrow I was given a huge legacy, and I will always be profligate.

Edna O'Brien 1932– : George Plimpton (ed.) *The Writer's Chapbook* (1989)

10 Many books are written . . . for very mundane reasons. It tends to be forgotten, for example, that Johnson wrote *Rasselas* to defray the expenses of his mother's funeral, or that Dumas's terse, interrogative dialogue was the result of his being paid at so many centimes a line.

D. J. Taylor 1960– : *After the War* (1993)

11 Everyone involved with the production of a book—the editors and publishers, the manufacturers of paper, the binders, the van drivers, the accountants, the publicists, the booksellers, the office cleaners—makes a reasonable living except the majority of starry-eyed masochists who

Milton Shulman 1913– : Barry Turner *The Writer's Handbook 1996* (1995)

actually provide the words without which all the others would have to be doing something else.

1 I always earn out my advances and I don't see why I should subsidise his greed simply because he has a divorce to pay for and has just had all his teeth done.
on reports of Martin **Amis***'s demands for a large advance on his new book*

A. S. Byatt 1936– : in *Guardian* 7 January 1995; cf. **276:7**

Editors and Editing see also **Revision**

2 Sir, he was a scoundrel and a coward: a scoundrel, for charging a blunderbuss against religion and morality; a coward, because he had not resolution to fire it off himself, but left half a crown to a beggarly Scotchman, to draw the trigger after his death!
on Bolingbroke's Works *published under the editorship of David Mallett*

Samuel Johnson 1709–84: James Boswell *Life of Samuel Johnson* (1791)

3 The poem will please if it is lively—if it is stupid it will fail—but I will have none of your damned cutting and slashing.

Lord Byron 1788–1824: letter to his publisher John Murray, 6 April 1819

4 That passage is what I call the sublime dashed to pieces by cutting too close with the fiery four-in-hand round the corner of nonsense.
on lines excluded from his own poem Limbo, *written 1817*

Samuel Taylor Coleridge 1772–1834: *Table Talk* (1835) 20 January 1834

5 Did you ever buy your own meat? That cutting down of 30 pages to 20, is what you proposed to the butcher when you asked him to take off the bony bit at the end, and the skinny bit at the other . . . the butcher told you that nature had produced the joint bone and skin as you saw it.
on being asked to make cuts in a short story

Anthony Trollope 1815–82: letter, 9 August 1860

6 Will you tell me my fault, frankly as to yourself, for I had rather wince, than die. Men do not call the surgeon to commend the bone, but to set it, Sir.

Emily Dickinson 1830–86: letter to T. W. Higginson, July 1862

of the compilation of a dictionary of national biography:
7 The editor of such a work must, by the necessity of the case, be autocratic. He will do his best to be a considerate autocrat.

Leslie Stephen 1832–1904: in *Athenaeum* 23 December 1882

8 After my marriage, she edited everything I wrote. And what is more—she not only edited my works—she edited me!
of his wife, Livy

Mark Twain 1835–1910: Van Wyck Brooks *The Ordeal of Mark Twain* (1920)

9 I have done it . . . But it's a bloody trade.
on cutting his Times Literary Supplement *review of Balzac; a similar response to being asked to cut an obituary, 'But yours is a butcher's trade', is also attributed to James*

Henry James 1843–1916: letter to Bruce Richmond, 4 June 1913

10 Whence came the intrusive comma on p. 4? It did not fall from the sky.

A. E. Housman 1859–1936: letter to the Richards Press, 3 July 1930

1 Everything seems now to be right with the book. And you will see, when we send you the page proof, what we have done about the words.
*letter to Ernest **Hemingway** from his editor at Scribners*

Maxwell Perkins 1884–1947: letter to Hemingway, 22 July 1932

2 Again and again in my literary life I have encountered . . . editorial timidity. I think it was Edwin Godkin, then the masterly editor of the New York *Evening Post*, who said that the choice of articles published in American magazines was entirely determined by the fear of scandalizing a non-existent clergyman in the Mississippi Valley.

Edith Wharton 1862–1937: *A Backward Glance* (1934)

3 No passion in the world is equal to the passion to alter someone else's draft.

H. G. Wells 1866–1946: attributed

4 Editing is the same as quarrelling with writers—same thing exactly.

Harold Ross 1892–1951: in *Time* 6 March 1950

5 Some of their editorializing *is* good. The places they pick on to criticize are usually the right places, only they suggest the wrong changes.
of the New Yorker

Elizabeth Bishop 1911–79: letter to Pearl Kazin, 10 February 1953

6 I shook with anger at their august editorial decisions, their fussy little changes and pipsqueak variations on my copy.

S. J. Perelman 1904–79: in 1957; attributed

7 [The editor] should say to himself, 'How can I help this writer to say it better in his own style?' and avoid 'How can I show him how I would write it, if it were my piece?'
memo to New Yorker

James Thurber 1894–1961: in 1959; in *New York Times Book Review* 4 December 1988

on being asked if he agreed with the view that 'most editors are failed writers':

8 Perhaps, but so are most writers.

T. S. Eliot 1888–1965: Robert Giroux in *Sewanee Review* Winter 1966 'A Personal Memoir'

9 If a poet has printed more than one version of his own poem, an editor . . . has the liberty of choice. Sometimes the first is preferable. Wordsworth, in old age, usually spoiled his earlier poems.

Robert Graves 1895–1985: 'Standards of Craftmanship' (Oxford Addresses on Poetry, 1964)

10 Today in publishing editors breed like rabbits gone wild.

Robert Lusty 1909– : speech to the Oxford Book Association, September 1976

11 My definition of a good editor is a man I think charming, who sends me large cheques, praises my work, my physical beauty, and my sexual prowess, and who has a stranglehold on my publisher.

John Cheever 1912–82: George Plimpton (ed.) *The Writer's Chapbook* (1989)

12 What is an editor but a cross between a fall guy and a father figure?

Arthur Koestler 1905–83: George Greenfield *Scribblers for Bread* (1989)

13 Sometimes even sincerity should be edited.

Craig Raine 1944– : in *Literary Review* June 1985

1 I've had great fun doing some stories by phone with certain magazine editors . . . Bargaining goes on, horse-trading. 'You can have the dash if I get the semicolon.'

Margaret Atwood 1939– : in an interview, March 1986; in *Paris Review* Winter 1990

2 There is a difference between a book of two hundred pages from the very beginning, and a book of two hundred pages which is the result of an original eight hundred pages. The six hundred are there. Only you don't see them.

Elie Wiesel 1928– : George Plimpton (ed.) *Writers at Work* (8th series, 1988)

3 I don't write books; I write writers.

asked whether he regretted not having time to write his own books

A. R. Orage 1873–1934: attributed

4 Only budget on what you have earned by direct labour. All unexpected income—from repeats, film options, syndications, etc.—must be designated as 'fairy money' and used to buy treats.

advice to Clare Boylan

Jennifer Johnston 1930– : Clare Boylan introduction to *The Agony and the Ego* (1993)

5 It's a little like going to the tailor or barber. I have never liked haircuts and I don't like being edited, even slightly.

John Updike 1932– : on *Blue Pencil* (BBC Radio 3) 6 August 1995

Effort

6 Give
Me leisure, all the time Maecenas found
For Horace and his Virgil, and I'll try
To build a masterpiece destined to live
And save my name from ashes. When the ground
Is poor, the ox works listlessly; rich soil
Tires, but there's satisfaction then in toil.

Martial AD *c.*40–*c.*104: *Epigrammata* tr. James Michie

7 This manner of writing [prose] wherein knowing myself inferior to myself . . . I have the use, as I may account it, but of my left hand.

John Milton 1608–74: *The Reason of Church Government* (1642) bk. 2, introduction

8 While pensive poets painful vigils keep,
Sleepless themselves, to give their readers sleep.

Alexander Pope 1688–1744: *The Dunciad* (1742)

9 A man may write at any time, if he will set himself doggedly to it.

Samuel Johnson 1709–84: James Boswell *Life of Samuel Johnson* (1791) March 1750

10 I often compare myself to a poor old woman, who having no bellows, lays herself down on her hearth, and with her mouth endeavours to blow up into a faint blaze a little handful of sticks, half green, half dry, in order to warm a mess of pottage, that, after all her pains, hardly keeps life and soul together.

Samuel Richardson 1689–1761: letter 1751

11 You write with ease, to show your breeding,
But easy writing's vile hard reading.

Richard Brinsley Sheridan 1751–1816: 'Clio's Protest' (written 1771, published 1819)

1 What is written without effort is in general read without pleasure.

Samuel Johnson 1709–84: William Seward *Biographia* (1799)

2 There is a pleasure in poetic pains
Which only poets know.

William Cowper 1731–1800: *The Task* (1785) 'The Timepiece'

3 'Tis hard indeed to toil, as we sometimes do, to our own loss and disappointment; to sweat in the field of fame, merely to reap a harvest of chaff, and pile up reams of paper for the worm to dine upon. It is a cruel thing to rack our brains for nothing, run our jaded fancies to a standstill, and then lie down at the conclusion of our race, a carcase for the critics.

Richard Cumberland 1732–1811: *Henry* (1795)

4 I am a galley slave to pen and ink.

Honoré de Balzac 1799–1850: letter 1832

5 Sir, My pa requests me to write to you, the doctors considering it doubtful whether he will ever recuvver the use of his legs which prevents his holding a pen.
Fanny Squeers on behalf of her father

Charles Dickens 1812–70: *Nicholas Nickleby* (1839)

6 When Rogers produces a couplet, he goes to bed, and the knocker is tied—and straw is laid down—and caudle is made—and the answer to inquiries is that Mr Rogers is as well as can be expected.
of the poet Samuel Rogers (1763–1855)

Sydney Smith 1771–1845: Harriet Martineau *Biographical Sketches* (1869)

7 What a heavy oar the pen is, and what a strong current ideas are to row in!

Gustave Flaubert 1821–80: letter, 23 October 1851

8 Look at such of my manuscripts as are in the library at Gad's, and think of the patient hours devoted year after year to single lines.

Charles Dickens 1812–70: letter to his son Harry, 11 February 1868

9 Inscribe all human effort with one word,
Artistry's haunting curse, the Incomplete!

Robert Browning 1812–89: *The Ring and the Book* (1868–9)

10 Forethought is the elbow-grease which a novelist, or poet, or dramatist, requires.

Anthony Trollope 1815–82: *Thackeray* (1879)

11 It bored me hellishly to write the Emigrant; well, it's going to bore others to read it; that's only fair.

Robert Louis Stevenson 1850–94: letter to Sidney Colvin, January 1880

12 What a heavy thing is a pen!

Émile Zola 1840–1902: letter, 25 October 1882

13 Three hours a day will produce as much as a man ought to write.

Anthony Trollope 1815–82: *Autobiography* (1883)

14 After a man has done making love, there is no other thing on earth to make him happy except hard work.

Anthony Trollope 1815–82: *Autobiography* (1883)

15 Tom's most well, now . . . and so there ain't nothing more to write about, and I am rotten glad of it, because if I'd knowed what a trouble it was to make a book I wouldn't a tackled it and ain't agoing to no more.

Mark Twain 1835–1910: *The Adventures of Huckleberry Finn* (1884)

16 I find twenty-five years of practice only make *me* write slower and slower; so that I am rapidly reaching a fine maximum of twenty-five words a day.

Henry James 1843–1916: letter 30 March 1895

1 When I face that fatal manuscript it seems to me that I have forgotten how to think—worse! how to write. It is as if something in my head had given way to let in a cold grey mist. I knock about in it till I am positively, physically sick.

Joseph Conrad 1857–1924: letter, 5 August 1896

2 I can write only by thinking back; I have never written straight from nature. I need to let a subject strain through my memory until only what is important or typical remains as a filter.

Anton Chekhov 1860–1904: letter, 15 December 1897

3 My instinct is to multiply books and articles and plays. I constantly gloat over the number of words I have written in a given period.

Arnold Bennett 1867–1931: diary, 5 April 1908

4 The fascination of what's difficult
Has dried the sap out of my veins, and rent
Spontaneous joy and natural content
Out of my heart.

W. B. Yeats 1865–1939: 'The Fascination of What's Difficult' (1910)

5 I don't think of work, only of gradually regaining my health through reading, rereading, reflecting.

Rainer Maria Rilke 1875–1926: letter, *c.*1911; Donald Prater *A Ringing Glass* (1986)

6 For twenty months . . . I had, like the prophet of old, 'wrestled with the Lord' for my creation . . . These are, perhaps, strong words, but it is difficult to characterize otherwise the intimacy and strain of a creative effort in which mind and will and conscience are engaged to the full, hour after hour, day after day, away from the world, and to the exclusion of all that makes life really lovable and gentle—something for which a material parallel can only be found in the everlasting stress of the westward winter passage round Cape Horn.
on the writing of Nostromo

Joseph Conrad 1857–1924: *A Personal Record* (1912)

7 Determination not to give in, and the sense of an impending shape keep one at it more that anything.
on beginning a new book

Virginia Woolf 1882–1941: diary, 11 May 1920

8 The task I set myself technically in writing a book from eighteen different points of view and in as many styles, all apparently unknown or undiscovered by my fellow tradesmen, that and the nature of the legend chosen would be enough to upset anyone's mental balance.
of writing Ulysses

James Joyce 1882–1941: letter, 24 June 1921

9 A thousand things to be written had I time: had I power. A very little writing uses up my capacity for writing.

Virginia Woolf 1882–1941: *A Writer's Diary* (1953) 18 September 1927

10 Only amateurs say that they write for their own amusement. Writing is not an amusing occupation. It is a combination of ditch-digging, mountain-climbing, treadmill and childbirth. Writing may be interesting, absorbing, exhilarating, racking, relieving. But amusing? Never!

Edna Ferber 1887–1968: *A Peculiar Treasure* (1939)

1 Writing a book is a horrible, exhausting struggle, like a long bout of some painful illness.

George Orwell 1903–50: *Collected Essays* (1968) vol. 1 'Why I Write'

2 The art of writing, like the art of love, runs all the way from a kind of routine hard to distinguish from piling bricks to a kind of frenzy closely related to delirium tremens.

H. L. Mencken 1880–1956: *Minority Report* (1956)

3 Routine, in an intelligent man, is a sign of ambition.

W. H. Auden 1907–73: 'The Life of That-There Poet' (1958)

4 I am constantly meeting ladies who say 'how lovely it must be to write', as though one sat down at the *escritoire* after breakfast, and it poured out like a succession of bread and butter letters, instead of being dragged out, by tongs, a bloody mess, in the small hours.

Patrick White 1912–90: after finishing *The Solid Mandala* (1966); *Letters* (1996)

5 The conditions of writing change absolutely between the first novel and the second: the first is an adventure, the second is a duty.

Graham Greene 1904–91: *A Sort of Life* (1971)

6 I never knew anyone who had a passion for words who had as much difficulty in saying things as I do. I very seldom say them in a manner I like. If I do it's because I don't know I'm trying.

Marianne Moore 1887–1972: George Plimpton (ed.) *The Writer's Chapbook* (1989)

7 READER: Miss Moore, your poetry is very difficult to read.
MARIANNE MOORE: It is very difficult to write.

Marianne Moore 1887–1972: George Plimpton (ed.) *The Writer's Chapbook* (1989)

8 Novelists do not write as birds sing, by the push of nature. It is part of the job that there should be much routine and some daily stuff on the level of carpentry.

William Golding 1911–93: 'Rough Magic', lecture, 16 February 1977; *A Moving Target* (1982)

9 I love being a writer. What I can't stand is the paperwork.

Peter de Vries 1910–93: Laurence J. Peter (ed.) *Quotations for our Time* (1977)

10 For a writer, going back home means back to the pen, pencil, and typewriter—and the blank, implacable sheet of white paper.

Paul Scott 1920–78: Hilary Spurling *Paul Scott* (1990)

11 In my experience, after a few months, an author usually feels that his novel is taking control. There has been the drive at increasing speed of the plane along the runway, then the slow lift and you feel the wheels no longer touch the ground.

Graham Greene 1904–91: *Ways of Escape* (1980)

12 Painful though it is, the best way to think and write is to do nothing else. One is then forced into effort as an escape from boredom and one's own personality.

J. K. Galbraith 1908– : *A Life in our Times* (1981)

13 89% work and worry over work, struggle against lunacy 10%, and friends 1%.
division of his life

Tennessee Williams 1911–83: John Lahr *Light Fantastic* (1996)

1 My real motive is to describe how my brain-damaged life is as normal for me as my friends' able-bodied life is to them. My mind is just like a spin-dryer at full speed; my thoughts fly around my skull while millions of beautiful words cascade down into my lap. Images gunfire across my consciousness and while trying to discipline them I jump in awe at the soulfilled bounty of my mind's expanse. Try then to imagine how frustrating it is to give expression to that avalanche in efforts of one great nod after the other.
of his reasons for writing The Eye of the Clock

Christopher Nolan 1965– : in *Observer* 8 November 1987

2 Many a poetic career begins and ends with poems which do no more than cry out in innocent primary glee, 'Listen, I can do it! Look how well it turned out! And I can do it again! See?'

Seamus Heaney 1939– : *The Government of the Tongue* (1988)

3 I doubt that an overwhelmingly jolly, optimistic person has ever been an artist of any sort. You are made melancholy, more than anything, by the struggle you have with words—the struggle you have with trying to express what sometimes resists expression.

William Trevor 1928– : in *Paris Review* 1989

4 Don't ask a writer what he's working on. It's like asking someone with cancer about the progress of his disease.

Jay McInerney 1955– : *Brightness Falls* (1985)

5 If you're not thinking that a particular situation is an obstacle, then it isn't . . . I had sticking power, which is just as important as literary talent. I just got on with the work. And I think there are such things as writing animals. I simply have to write.

Doris Lessing 1919– : in *Chicago Tribune* 3 January 1993

6 The hours spent writing are like giving a performance on the page, a prolonged one-man show which will grip the audience's attention . . . Writing fiction is exhausting; it's not the mechanical process that tires you out but the stage fright, the tension and the final collapse in the dressing room and the first drink of the evening.

John Mortimer 1923– : Clare Boylan (ed.) *The Agony and the Ego* (1993)

7 Writing's hard work and it's boring, but I like it.

V. S. Pritchett 1900–97: Clare Boylan (ed.) *The Agony and the Ego* (1993)

8 Trying to write with a bit more precision this morning and to come up with the right word, I remember a machine that used to be in every seaside amusement arcade. A big mirrored drum in a glass case slowly revolved and on it some (not very) desirable objects . . . One slid in a penny that activated a grab which one had to manoeuvre over one's chosen prize before at the critical moment releasing the grab to grip the object. Except that it never did. Either the grab moved or failed to grip or the drum revolved what one wanted out of reach. That was what happened this morning.

Alan Bennett 1934– : *Writing Home* (1994)

9 I like stress, you know, even if it kills me.

Fay Weldon 1933– : in *New Yorker* 26 June 1995

Ending see Beginning and Ending

Erotic Writing and Pornography

see also **Sex**

1 Madam, I've warned you many times,
Skip when my book becomes obscene.

Martial AD *c.*40–*c.*104: *Epigrammata*, tr. James Michie

2 My English text is chaste, and all licentious passages are left in the obscurity of a learned language.

parodied as 'decent obscurity' in the Anti-Jacobin, *1797–8*

Edward Gibbon 1737–94: *Memoirs of My Life* (1796)

3 It certainly is my wish, and it has been my study, to exclude from this publication whatever is unfit to be read aloud by a gentleman to a company of ladies.

Thomas Bowdler 1754–1825: preface to *The Family Shakespeare* (1818) ; cf. **34:5**

4 Juan was taught from out the best edition,
Expurgated by learned men, who place
Judiciously, from out the schoolboy's vision
The grosser parts.

Lord Byron 1788–1824: *Don Juan* (1819–24)

5 Smut detected in it by moral men is theirs rather than mine. Scientific truth was my touchstone for every scene, even the most febrile.

of his novel Thérèse Raquin

Émile Zola 1840–1902: preface to second edition, 1868

6 I was thinking the other day, while reading a very sensual love-scene in *Le Lys Rouge* [by Anatole France], that a novelist never describes the dishabille of the male in such scenes; I can't remember an instance where he even hints at it. This shows how incomplete 'realism' is. I see no reason why the appearance of the male should not be described in a manner to assist the charm of the scene. But tradition is decidedly against the practice.

Arnold Bennett 1867–1931: diary, 19 June 1904

7 It is not good enough to spend time and ink in describing the penultimate sensations and physical movements of people getting into a state of rut, we all know them too well.

of D. H. Lawrence's Sons and Lovers

John Galsworthy 1867–1933: letter to Edward Garnett, 13 April 1914

8 We have long passed the Victorian Era when asterisks were followed after a certain interval by a baby.

W. Somerset Maugham 1874–1965: *The Constant Wife* (1926)

9 It is obvious that 'obscenity' is not a term capable of exact legal definition; in the practice of the Courts, it means 'anything that shocks the magistrate'.

Bertrand Russell 1872–1970: *Sceptical Essays* (1928) 'The Recrudescence of Puritanism'

10 At last an unprintable book that is readable.

of Henry Miller's Tropic of Cancer

Ezra Pound 1885–1972: in 1934; attributed

11 Surely the sex business isn't worth all this damned fuss? I've met only a handful of people who cared a biscuit for it.

on reading Lady Chatterley's Lover

T. E. Lawrence 1888–1935: Christopher Hassall *Edward Marsh* (1959)

1 You have left your hero and heroine tied up in a cavern under the Thames for a week, and they are not married.
an editor's complaint to Chesterton's sister-in-law about a serial story

Anonymous: G. K. Chesterton *Autobiography* (1936)

2 Pornography is the attempt to insult sex, to do dirt on it.

D. H. Lawrence 1885–1930: *Phoenix* (1936) 'Pornography and Obscenity'

3 Is it a book you would even wish your wife or your servants to read?
of D. H. Lawrence's Lady Chatterley's Lover

Mervyn Griffith-Jones 1909–79: speech for the prosecution at the Central Criminal Court, Old Bailey, 20 October 1960

4 I think Lawrence tried to portray this [sex] relation as in a real sense an act of holy communion. For him flesh was sacramental of the spirit.
the Bishop of Woolwich as defence witness in the case against Penguin Books for publishing Lady Chatterley's Lover

John Robinson 1919–83: in *The Times* 28 October 1960

5 What pornography is really about, ultimately, isn't sex but death.

Susan Sontag 1933– : in *Partisan Review* Spring 1967

6 A widespread taste for pornography means that nature is alerting us to some threat of extinction.

J. G. Ballard 1930– : *Myths of the Near Future* (1982)

7 Pornography is rather like trying to find out about a Beethoven symphony by having somebody tell you about it and perhaps hum a few bars.

Robertson Davies 1913–95: in 1972; *The Enthusiasms of Robertson Davies* (1990)

8 I emerge from editorial experience knowing more of oral and anal sex, paedophilia, coprophilia, bondage, SM, you name it, I've read about it, than I'll ever need in this life or, hopefully, the next. It is salutary for editors to be occasionally reminded that they are in the erotica business.
*of general publishing in the post-*Lady Chatterley *era*

Robin Denniston 1926– : in 1978; George Greenfield *Scribblers for Bread* (1989)

9 With sex so much harder to write about maybe we'll have more novels about work from now on.
of the post-Aids era

David Lodge 1935– : in *Guardian* 7 March 1987

10 Reading about sex in yesterday's novels is like watching people smoke in old films.

Fay Weldon 1933– : in *Guardian* 1 December 1989

11 Since we no longer write about the union with God, writing about sex has become the ultimate test for the writer: to communicate the incommunicable.

Michèle Roberts 1949– : in *Daily Telegraph* 9 July 1994

12 In adolescence pornography is a substitute for sex, whereas in adulthood sex is a substitute for pornography.

Anonymous: Edmund White *The Burning Library* (1994)

Essays

13 Mere essayists! A few loose sentences, and that's all.

Ben Jonson *c.*1573–1637: *Epicene* (1609)

1 Essays. The word is late but the thing is ancient.

Francis Bacon 1561–1626: *Essays* (1612) 'Dedication to Prince Henry'

2 The wildness of those compositions which go by the name of essays.

Joseph Addison 1672–1719: *The Spectator* no. 476 (5 September 1712)

3 *Essay.* A loose sally of the mind; an irregular indigested piece; not a regular and orderly composition.

Samuel Johnson 1709–84: *A Dictionary of the English Language* (1755)

4 A good essay must have this permanent quality about it; it must draw its curtains round us, but it must be a curtain that shuts us in, not out.

Virginia Woolf 1882–1941: *The Common Reader* (1925) 'The Modern Essay'

5 The essayist . . . can pull on any sort of shirt, be any sort of person, according to his mood or his subject matter—philosopher, scold, jester, raconteur, confidant, pundit, devil's advocate, enthusiast.

E. B. White 1899–1985: *Essays of E. B. White* (1977)

6 Essays come in all shapes and sizes. There are essays on Human Understanding, and essays on What I Did in the Holidays; essays on Truth, and essays on potato crisps . . . Essays that start out as book reviews, and essays that end up as sermons. Even more than most literary forms, the essay defies strict definition. It can shade into the character sketch, the travel sketch, the memoir, the *jeu d'esprit*.

John Gross 1935– : introduction to *The Oxford Book of Essays* (1991)

7 In a way, an essay is just a grown-up version of the tie-breakers in supermarket quizzes: Complete the line 'I think history is bunk because . . . ' in not more than 10,000 words. Essayists are preachers, but also the stand-up comedians of literature: there are no props to fall back on. Neither is there a plot. Novelists require their readers to sign an invisible contract promising to indulge their clever lies. But essayists tell the truth. They just say what they think, as nicely or as brutally as they can.

Robert Winder : in *Independent* 22 June 1996

Fables and Fairy Stories see also Fantasy

8 *Ich weiss nicht, was soll es bedeuten,*
Dass ich so traurig bin;
Ein Märchen aus alten Zeiten,
Das kommt mir nicht aus dem Sinn.

I know not why I am so sad; I cannot get out of my head a fairy-tale of olden times.

Heinrich Heine 1797–1856: 'Die Lorelei' (1826–31)

9 [The reader] must be satisfied with the soup that is set before him, and not desire to see the bones of the ox out of which it has been boiled.

on accepting legends as they are

George Webbe Dasent 1817–96: *Popular Tales from the Norse* (1859)

10 I left fairy stories lying on the floor of the nursery, and I have not found any books so sensible since.

G. K. Chesterton 1874–1936: *Orthodoxy* (1908) 'The Ethics of Elfland'

1 Our folk-tales prefigure our racial temperaments. Every race betrays itself thus in the tales it tells to its own children.

Rudyard Kipling 1865–1936: *A Book of Words* (1928) 'A Thesis'

2 We have always had storytellers and makers of fiction since the days of the cave-man. There is an eternal impulse in human nature to enliven the actual working life by the invention of tales of another kind of life, recognizable by its likeness to ordinary life, but so arranged that things happen more dramatically and pleasingly—which indeed is the world in a glorified and idealized form.

That is the origin of what we call the folk tale or the fairy tale . . . These tales come out of the most distant deeps of human experience and human fancy.

John Buchan 1875–1940: *The Novel and the Fairy Tale* (1931)

3 A myth is, of course, not a fairy story. It is the presentation of facts belonging to one category in the idioms appropriate to another. To explode a myth is accordingly not to deny the facts but to re-allocate them.

Gilbert Ryle 1900–76: *The Concept of Mind* (1949)

4 When I was ten, I read fairy tales in secret, and would have been ashamed of being found doing so. Now that I am fifty, I read them openly. When I became a man, I put away childish things, including the fear of childishness and the desire to be very grown up.

C. S. Lewis 1898–1963: 'On Three Ways of Writing for Children' (1952)

5 The value of fairy-stories is thus not, in my opinion, to be found by considering children in particular. Collections of fairy stories are, in fact, by nature attics and lumber-rooms, only by temporary and local custom playrooms. Their contents are disordered, and often battered, a jumble of different dates, purposes, and tastes; but among them may occasionally be found a thing of permanent value: an old work of art, not too much damaged, that only stupidity would ever have stuffed away.

J. R. R. Tolkien 1892–1973: *Tree and Leaf* (1964) 'On Fairy-Stories'

6 *Grimm's Fairy Tales* was the most influential book I ever read.

Margaret Atwood 1939– : in an interview, March/April 1976; Earl G. Ingersoll (ed.) *Margaret Atwood: Conversations* (1990)

7 Fairy tales, unlike any other sort of literature, direct the child to discover his identity and calling.

Bruno Bettelheim 1903–90: *The Uses of Enchantment* (1976)

8 Myth does not mean something untrue, but a concentration of truth.

Doris Lessing 1919– : *African Laughter: Four Visits to Zimbabwe* (1992)

9 Fairy stories are about one king going to another king to borrow a cup of sugar.

Angela Carter 1940–92: attributed

10 Stories held in common make and remake the world we inhabit.

Marina Warner 1946– : *Little Angels, Little Monsters, Beautiful Beasts and More* (Reith Lectures 1994)

Fairy Stories see Fables and Fairy Stories

Fame see also Reputation and Achievement

1 I have erected a monument more lasting than bronze.
Horace 65–8 BC: *Odes*

2 Thank you, earnest fan
For having granted me the fame
Seldom enjoyed by a dead poet
While I'm alive and here to know it.
Martial AD *c.*40–*c.*104: *Epigrammata*, tr. James Michie

3 Even for learned men, love of fame is the last thing to be given up.
Tacitus AD *c.*56–after 117: *Histories*

4 He that cometh in print because he would be known, is like the fool that cometh into the market because he would be seen.
John Lyly *c.*1554–1606: *Euphues* (1580)

5 Not marble, nor the gilded monuments
Of princes, shall outlive this powerful rhyme;
But you shall shine more bright in these contents
Than unswept stone, besmeared with sluttish time.
William Shakespeare 1564–1616: sonnet 55

6 The universal object and idol of men of letters is reputation.
John Adams 1735–1826: *Discourses on Davila* (1791)

7 My great comfort is, that the temporary celebrity I have wrung from the world has been in the very teeth of all opinions and prejudices. I have flattered no ruling powers; I have never concealed a single thought that tempted me.
Lord Byron 1788–1824: letter to Thomas Moore, 9 April 1814

8 O the flummery of a birth place! Cant! Cant! Cant! It is enough to give a spirit the guts-ache.
*on visiting **Burns**'s birthplace.*
John Keats 1795–1821: letter to John Hamilton Reynolds, 11 July 1818

9 I equally dislike the favour of the public with the love of a woman—they are both a cloying treacle to the wings of independence.
John Keats 1795–1821: letter to John Taylor, 23 August 1819

10 I awoke one morning and found myself famous.
on the instantaneous success of Childe Harold
Lord Byron 1788–1824: Thomas Moore *Letters and Journals of Lord Byron* (1830)

11 Literary fame is the only fame of which a wise man ought to be ambitious, because it is the only lasting and living fame.
Robert Southey 1774–1843: John Forster *Life of Landor* (1876)

12 Ah, did you once see Shelley plain,
And did he stop and speak to you
And did you speak to him again?
How strange it seems, and new!
Robert Browning 1812–89: 'Memorabilia' (1855)

13 I was born in Düsseldorf on Rhine, and note this explicitly in case seven cities after my death—Schilda, Krähwinkel, Polkwitz, Bockum, Dülk, Göttingen and Schöppenstadt—compete for the honour of being my birthplace.
Heinrich Heine 1797–1856: attributed; cf. **304:8, 304:9**

1 Whatever may be the success of my stories, I shall be resolute in preserving my incognito, having observed that a *nom de plume* secures all the advantages without the disagreeables of reputation.

George Eliot 1819–80: letter to William Blackwood, 4 February 1857

2 For several reasons I am very anxious to retain my incognito for some time to come, and to an author not already famous, anonymity is the highest *prestige*. Besides, if George Eliot turns out a dull dog and an ineffective writer—a mere flash in the pan—I, for one, am determined to cut him on the first intimation of that disagreeable fact.

George Eliot 1819–80: letter to John Blackwood, 14 March 1857

3 Enduring fame is promised only to those writers who can offer to successive generations a substance constantly renewed; for every generation arrives upon the scene with its own particular hunger.

André Gide 1869–1951: *Pretexts* (1903)

4 At Tennyson's funeral, Royalty was represented, but Royalty itself was conspicuously absent. The Prince of Wales was at Newmarket, where he personally congratulated a successful jockey.

George Gissing 1857–1903: *Commonplace Book* (1962)

5 The bower we shrined to Tennyson,
Gentlemen,
Is roof-wrecked; damps there drip upon
Sagged seats, the creeper-nails are rust,
The spider is sole denizen;
Even she who voiced those rhymes is dust,
Gentlemen!

Thomas Hardy 1840–1928: 'An Ancient to Ancients' (1922)

advice to a young writer 'who is merely thinking of fame':

6 Concentrate on one subject. Let him, when he is twenty, write about the earthworm. Let him continue for forty years to write of nothing but the earthworm. When he is sixty, pilgrims will make a hollow path with their feet to the door of the world's great authority on the earthworm. They will knock at his door and humbly beg to be allowed to see the Master of the Earthworm.

Hilaire Belloc 1870–1953: Sisley Huddleston *Paris Salons, Cafes, Studios* (1928)

7 A new shade for knickers and nightdresses has been named *Brighton Rock* . . . Is this fame?

his novel Brighton Rock *had been published in the previous year*

Graham Greene 1904–91: letter to his brother Hugh, 7 April 1939

8 It took me fifteen years to discover that I had no talent for writing, but I couldn't give it up because by that time I was too famous.

Robert Benchley 1889–1945: Nathaniel Benchley *Robert Benchley* (1955)

9 I felt a very lonely, foreign midget orating up there, in a huge hall, before all those faces.

on giving poetry readings in the US

Dylan Thomas 1914–53: letter to Caitlin Thomas, 25 February 1950

10 CLARK GABLE: Do you write, Mr Faulkner?
FAULKNER: Yes, Mr Gable. What do you do?

William Faulkner 1897–1962: attributed

11 Fame often makes a writer vain, but seldom makes him proud.

W. H. Auden 1907–73: *The Dyer's Hand* (1962) 'Writing'

1 There's no such thing as bad publicity except your own obituary.

Brendan Behan 1923–64: Dominic Behan *My Brother Brendan* (1965)

2 The libraries of the East fight to own my verses,
The rulers seek me out to fill my mouth with gold,
The angels already know my last couplet by heart
The tools of my art are humiliation and anguish.
from a twelfth century Persian poem

Jorge Luis Borges 1899–1986: *Selected Poems, 1923–1967* (1972) 'The Poet Tells of his Fame', tr. W. S. Merwin

3 A poet's hope: to be,
like some valley cheese,
local, but prized elsewhere.

W. H. Auden 1907–73: 'Shorts II' (1976)

4 Mere wealth, I am above it,
It is the reputation wide,
The playwright's pomp, the poet's pride
That eagerly I covet.

Phyllis McGinley 1905–78: 'A Ballad of Anthologies'

5 Unfortunately many young writers are more concerned with fame than with their own work . . . It's much more important to write than to be written about.

Gabriel García Márquez 1928– : in *Writers at Work* (6th series, 1984)

6 A famous writer who wants to continue writing has to be constantly defending himself against fame.

Gabriel García Márquez 1928– : in *Writers at Work* (6th series, 1984)

7 Celebrity is a mask that eats into the face.

John Updike 1932– : *Self-Consciousness: Memoirs* (1989)

8 The shelf life of the modern hardback writer is somewhere between the milk and the yoghurt.

Calvin Trillin 1935– : in *Sunday Times* 9 June 1991; attributed

9 The best fame is a writer's fame: it's enough to get a table at a good restaurant, but not enough that you get interrupted when you eat.

Fran Lebowitz 1946– : in *Observer* 30 May 1993 'Sayings of the Week'

10 People say that novelists, nowadays, are like rock stars. Where have they been living? It's been that way for years. This is my Fourth World Tour.

Martin Amis 1949– : 'Buy My Book, Please' in *New Yorker* 26 June 1995

Family and Friends

11 Rest in soft peace, and, asked, say here doth lie
Ben Jonson his best piece of poetry.

Ben Jonson *c.*1573–1637: 'On My First Son' (1616)

12 What is the character of a family to an hypothesis? my father would reply.

Laurence Sterne 1713–68: *Tristram Shandy* (1759–67)

13 I should, many a good day, have blown my brains out, but for the recollection that it would have given pleasure to my mother-in-law; and, even *then*, if I could have been certain to haunt her . . .

Lord Byron 1788–1824: letter, 28 January 1817

14 The roaring of the wind is my wife and the stars through the window pane are my children.

John Keats 1795–1821: letter to George and Georgiana Keats, 24 October 1818

15 To one whose sweet voice has often encouraged, and whose taste and judgement have ever guided, its pages; the most severe of critics, but—a perfect wife!

Benjamin Disraeli 1804–81: *Sybil* (1845); dedication

1 Reader, I married him.

Charlotte Brontë 1816–55: *Jane Eyre* (1847)

2 Jack Sprat and his wife in the nursery rhyme, offer an ideal example of adaptation for co-existence.

Robert Louis Stevenson 1850–94: *Memories and Portraits* (1887) 'From his Notebooks'

3 Of all human struggles there is none so treacherous and remorseless as the struggle between the artist man and the mother woman.

George Bernard Shaw 1856–1950: *Man and Superman* (1903)

4 The true artist will let his wife starve, his children go barefoot, his mother drudge for his living at seventy, sooner than work at anything but his art.

George Bernard Shaw 1856–1950: *Man and Superman* (1903)

5 Wives can be an awful handicap. They are constantly telling their husbands to do this, fetch that, and ordering them from the house.
to his mother, c.1926

Terence Rattigan 1911–77: John Lahr *Light Fantastic* (1996)

6 The public does not matter—only one's friends matter.

W. B. Yeats 1865–1939: letter to Edith Shackleton Heald, 18 May 1937

7 It's terrible discovering that your moral plank, i.e. undiluted horror of babies, has crumbled! We're so excited we can hardly speak, and expect a prodigy whose first words will be 'Partisan Review'.
when about to become a father

Robert Lowell 1917–77: letter to J. F. Powers, 16 May 1956

8 She steals, too. She says I never tell her anything, and when I do, she puts it in books. And gives me copies. So that my thoughts aren't mine.
the view of a writer's daughter

A. S. Byatt 1936– : *The Game* (1967)

9 I believe that all those painters and writers who leave their wives have an idea at the back of their minds that their painting or writing will be the better for it, whereas they only go from bad to worse.

Patrick White 1912–90: letter to Barry Humphries, 7 October 1973

10 Until I grew up I thought I hated everybody, but when I grew up I realized it was just children I didn't like.

Philip Larkin 1922–85: in *Observer* 16 December 1979

11 If you are a single father, it's lucky you're a writer, because you can stay at home all the time, you have the time for it.

J. G. Ballard 1930– : Alastair Reid *Whereabouts* (1987) 'Digging Up Scotland'

12 The most terrible thing about children and writing is the total uncertainty of being able to plan ahead. Because the moment you sit down, they fall off a wall, they get measles.

A. S. Byatt 1936– : in an interview, April 1988; George Greenfield *Scribblers for Bread* (1989)

13 Do not be disheartened if no one reads your book. It has already made me a happy woman because it has brought me closer to you.
letter to her daughter Jung Chang, just before the publication of the best-selling Wild Swans

Xia Dehong 1931– : letter, 1991; in *Sunday Telegraph* 26 May 1996

1 With the birth of each child, you lose two novels.

Candia McWilliam 1955– : in *Guardian* 5 May 1993

2 Dad was my ghostly sub-editor. Although he didn't read my books, of course, I read all of his. I dedicated *London Fields* to him and he read about 30 pages. He didn't get it . . . But yeah, I minded it when it was clear he just couldn't finish my novels—it was a generational kind of taste, I think.

Martin Amis 1949– : interview in *Waterstone's Quarterly Guide* Spring/Summer 1996

3 The great obstacle was gone . . . it was as if I had come into my destiny, to be on the front line.

on the death of his father, Kingsley ***Amis***

Martin Amis 1949– : in *Observer* 7 April 1996

4 One day I will write verses about him and see how he likes it.

on his father, A. A. ***Milne***

Christopher Milne 1920–96: attributed; in *The Times* 22 April 1996

5 Writers spend the whole day alone, so you rather depend on friends and a social life.

Piers Paul Read 1941– : in *Daily Telegraph* 10 August 1996

6 I loved my parents (and I had more than the usual number to love).

of Clive and Vanessa Bell, and Duncan Grant

Quentin Bell 1910–96: in *Daily Telegraph* 18 December 1996; obituary

Fantasy see also **Fables and Fairy Stories, Science Fiction**

of the romance as distinct from the novel:

7 A fictitious narrative in prose or verse, the interest of which turns upon marvellous and uncommon incidents.

Sir Walter Scott 1771–1832: *Essay on Romance* (1824); cf. **158:9**

8 I find it difficult to take much interest in a man whose father was a dragon.

apologizing for his inability to appreciate William ***Morris's*** *epic poem* Sigurd the Volsung *(1876)*

Dante Gabriel Rossetti 1828–82: Osbert Sitwell *Noble Essences* (1950)

9 Fantasy deals with things that are not and cannot be. Science fiction deals with things that can be, that some day may be.

Frederic Brown 1906–72: *Angels and Spaceships* (1955)

10 Where a Tolkien prophetically faced the central fact of our time, our capacity to destroy ourselves, the present spate of so-called heroic fantasy, in which Good defeats Evil by killing it with a sword or staff or something phallic, seems to have nothing in mind beyond instant gratification, the avoidance of discomfort, in a fake-medieval past where technology is replaced by magic and wishful thinking works.

Ursula Le Guin 1929– : 'Facing It' (1982)

11 We need metaphors of magic and monsters in order to understand the human condition.

Stephen Donaldson 1947– : Stan Nicholls (ed.) *Wordsmiths of Wonder* (1993)

12 Fantasy is the oldest form of literature and science fiction is just a new twist on it.

Katharine Kerr : Stan Nicholls (ed.) *Wordsmiths of Wonder* (1993)

1 Most modern fantasy just rearranges the furniture in Tolkien's attic.

Terry Pratchett 1948– : Stan Nicholls (ed.) *Wordsmiths of Wonder* (1993)

2 Fantasy literature, in its broadest definition which includes everything from 'Cinderella' to *Beowulf* to Stephen Donaldson, is literature which makes deliberate use of something known to be impossible.

Tom Shippey 1943– : introduction to *Oxford Book of Fantasy Stories* (1994)

3 The trouble is that many people think the boundaries of fantasy lie somewhere north of Camelot and south of Conan the Barbarian, which is like saying that *Star Trek* represents most of science fiction.

Terry Pratchett 1948– : in interview; Terry Pratchett and Stephen Briggs *The Discworld Companion* (1994)

4 I regard fantasy, as distinct from SF, as having a spiritual, or perhaps I mean a religious, or perhaps I mean a metaphysical side. This regard comes from the area whence all memories spring, the personal deeps, compounded of old forgotten stories told and read, alchemic woodcuts, and perhaps a surly reproduction of Dante Gabriel Rossetti's *doppelganger* drawing, *How They Met Themselves*.

Brian Aldiss 1925– : *The Detached Retina* (1995) 'One Hump or Two'

5 I was never inspired by the traditional dragon stories where the dragon ravages the landscape and the hero has to spear it. Nor was I interested in stories where characters are riding about on dragons like horses. I prefer to see fantasy written in a purer way.

Graham Edwards 1965– : interview in *Voyager* (electronic journal) 15 July 1996

Feeling

6 If writing did not exist, what terrible depressions we should suffer from.

Sei Shōnagon *c.*966–*c.*1013: *Pillow Book*

7 I write of melancholy, by being busy to avoid melancholy.

Robert Burton 1577–1640: *The Anatomy of Melancholy* (1621–51) 'Democritus to the Reader'

8 *Much more* lively and affecting . . . must be the style of those who write in the height of a present distress, the mind tortured by pangs of uncertainty (the events then hidden in the womb of fate); than the dry, narrative unanimated style of a person relating difficulties and danger surmounted, can be . . . The relater perfectly at ease; and if himself unmoved by his own story, not likely greatly to affect the reader.

Samuel Richardson 1689–1761: preface to *Clarissa* (1747–8)

9 But, spite of all the criticizing elves,
Those who would make us feel, must feel themselves.

Charles Churchill 1731–64: *The Rosciad* (1761)

10 The black dog I hope always to resist, and in time to drive, though I am deprived of almost all those that used to help me . . . When I rise my breakfast is solitary, the black dog waits to share it, from breakfast to dinner he continues barking, except that Dr Brocklesby for a little keeps him at a distance . . . Night comes at last, and some hours of restlessness and confusion bring me again to a day of

Samuel Johnson 1709–84: letter to Mrs Thrale, 28 June 1783

solitude. What shall exclude the black dog from a habitation like this?

on his attacks of melancholia; more recently associated with Winston Churchill, who used the phrase 'black dog' when alluding to his own periodic bouts of depression

1 Poetry is the spontaneous overflow of powerful feelings: it takes its origin from emotion recollected in tranquillity.

William Wordsworth 1770–1850: *Lyrical Ballads* (2nd ed., 1802)

2 To be *thoroughly* conversant with a man's heart, is to take our final lesson in the iron-clasped volume of despair.

Edgar Allan Poe 1809–49: 'Marginalia'; in *Southern Literary Messenger* (Richmond, Virginia) June 1849

on being found in tears by a friend, having received the last number of The Old Curiosity Shop*:*

3 Little Nelly, Boz's little Nelly, is dead.

Francis, Lord Jeffrey 1773–1850: Julian Charles Young *A Memoir of Charles Mayne Young* (1871) vol. 2; cf. **87:4, 87:10**

on reading of the death of Little Nell:

4 I have never read printed words that gave me so much pain.

William Macready 1793–1873: diary, 1850; Edgar Johnson *Charles Dickens: His Tragedy and Triumph* (1952); cf. **87:3**

5 Only habit of persistent work can make one continually content; it produces an opium that numbs the soul.

Gustave Flaubert 1821–80: letter, 26 July 1851

6 The poisoning of Bovary made me throw up into my chamber pot; the assault on Carthage is giving me aches and pains in my arms.

Gustave Flaubert 1821–80: letter, 25 September 1861

7 A man of letters should be as objective as a chemist; he has to renounce ordinary subjectivity and realize that manure plays a very respectable role in a landscape and that evil passions are as inherent in life as good ones.

Anton Chekhov 1860–1904: letter, 14 January 1887

8 I wrote such melancholy things when I was young that I am obliged to be unusually cheerful and robust in my old age.

Christina Rossetti 1830–94: Jan Marsh *Christina Rossetti* (1994)

9 Analysis is an abominable business. I am quite sure that people who work out subjects thoroughly are disagreeable wretches. One only feels as one should when one doesn't know much about the matter.

of the effect of the research done for his book The Stones of Venice *(1851–3) on his sense of 'the charm of the place'*

John Ruskin 1819–1900: in *Dictionary of National Biography* (1917–)

10 One must have a heart of stone to read the death of Little Nell without laughing.

Oscar Wilde 1854–1900: Ada Leverson *Letters to the Sphinx* (1930); cf. **87:3**

11 I tell you there is such a thing as creative hate!

Willa Cather 1873–1947: *The Song of the Lark* (1915)

12 I like to feel that a writer is perfectly cool and detached, regarding other people's feelings or his own, like a God who has got beyond them.

T. S. Eliot 1888–1965: letter 19 September 1917

1 Poetry is not a turning loose of emotion, but an escape from emotion; it is not the expression of personality but an escape from personality. But, of course, only those who have personality and emotions know what it means to want to escape from these things.

T. S. Eliot 1888–1965: *The Sacred Wood* (1920) 'Tradition and Individual Talent'

2 Whatever is felt upon the page without being specifically named there—that, one might say, is created. It is the inexplicable presence of the thing not named, of the overtone divined by the ear but not heard by it, the verbal mood, the emotional aura of the fact or the thing or the deed, that gives high quality to the novel or the drama, as well as to poetry itself.

Willa Cather 1873–1947: *The Novel Démeublé* (1922)

3 I may as well tell you, here and now, that if you are going about the place thinking things pretty, you will never make a modern poet. Be poignant, man, be poignant!

P. G. Wodehouse 1881–1975: *The Small Bachelor* (1927)

4 Only an aching heart
Conceives a changeless work of art.

W. B. Yeats 1865–1939: 'The Tower' (1928)

5 How one likes to suffer. Anyway writers do; it is their income.

W. H. Auden 1907–73: Berlin diary, April 1929

6 Enthusiasm is taken through the prism of the intellect and spread on the screen in colour, all the way from hyperbole or overstatement at one end to understatement at the other end. It is a long strip of dark lines and many colours. I would be willing to throw away everything but that: enthusiasm tamed by metaphors.

Robert Frost 1874–1963: 'Education by Poetry' in *Amherst Graduates' Quarterly* February 1931

7 Experience has taught me, when I am shaving of a morning, to keep watch over my thoughts, because, if a line of poetry strays into my memory, my skin bristles so that the razor ceases to act . . . The seat of this sensation is the pit of the stomach.

A. E. Housman 1859–1936: lecture at Cambridge, 9 May 1933

8 No tears in the writer, no tears in the reader. No surprise for the writer, no surprise for the reader.

Robert Frost 1874–1963: *Collected Poems* (1939) 'The Figure a Poem Makes'

9 Now that my ladder's gone
I must lie down where all ladders start
In the foul rag and bone shop of the heart.

W. B. Yeats 1865–1939: 'The Circus Animals' Desertion' (1939)

10 Each venture
Is a new beginning, a raid on the inarticulate
With shabby equipment always deteriorating
In the general mess of imprecision of feeling.

T. S. Eliot 1888–1965: *Four Quartets* 'East Coker' (1940) pt. 5

11 I had to feel anything and everything that for me was existing so intensely that I could put it down in writing as a thing in itself without at all necessarily using its name.

Gertrude Stein 1874–1946: *Look at me Now and Here I am: Writings and Lectures, 1909–45* (1971)

12 It is closing time in the gardens of the West and from now on an artist will be judged only by the resonance of his solitude or the quality of his despair.

Cyril Connolly 1903–74: in *Horizon* December 1949—January 1950

1 The more acute the experience, the less articulate its expression.

Harold Pinter 1930– : in his 1960 programme notes to *The Room* and *The Dumb Waiter*; Malcolm Bradbury and James McFarlane (eds.) *Modernism* (1991)

2 Sentimentality is the emotional promiscuity of those who have no sentiment.

Norman Mailer 1923– : *Cannibals and Christians* (1966)

3 Writing is not observation—it is feeling.

Paul Scott 1920–78: Hilary Spurling *Paul Scott* (1990)

4 What in the world is this emotion? What is the bearing of supremely great works of art on my life which makes me feel so glad?

after reading King Lear

Rebecca West 1892–1983: *Rebecca West—A Celebration* (1978) 'The Strange Necessity'

5 I think writing about unhappiness is probably the source of my popularity, if I have any—after all most people *are* unhappy, don't you think?

Philip Larkin 1922–85: *Required Writing* (1983)

6 People always ask what do you teach in creative writing? People insist: there's nothing to teach. Well, of course, there is something you can teach; you teach people to find ways of tapping their own emotions.

Edmund White 1940– : in interview in *Paris Review* 1988

7 Sometimes poetry is emotion recollected in a highly
emotional state.

Wendy Cope 1945– : 'An Argument with Wordsworth' (1992); cf. **87:1**

Fiction

8 Refuse profane and old wives' fables, and exercise thyself rather unto godliness.

Bible: I Timothy

9 Storys to rede ar delitabill,
Suppos that thai be nocht bot fabill.

John Barbour *c.*1320–95: *The Bruce* (1375)

10 If this were played upon a stage now, I could condemn it as an improbable fiction.

William Shakespeare 1564–1616: *Twelfth Night* (1601)

11 Poets . . . though liars by profession, always endeavour to give an air of truth to their fictions.

David Hume 1711–76: *A Treatise upon Human Nature* (1739)

12 I hate things all *fiction* . . . there should always be some foundation of fact for the most airy fabric and pure invention is but the talent of a liar.

Lord Byron 1788–1824: letter to John Murray, 2 April 1817

13 'Tis strange—but true; for truth is always strange;
Stranger than fiction.

Lord Byron 1788–1824: *Don Juan* (1819–24)

14 No author, without a trial, can conceive of the difficulty of writing a romance about a country where there is no shadow, no antiquity, no mystery, no picturesque and gloomy wrong, nor anything but a commonplace prosperity, in broad and simple daylight, as is happily the case with my dear native land.

Nathaniel Hawthorne 1804–64: preface to *The Marble Faun* (1860)

1 Fiction is to the grown man what play is to the child; it is there that he changes the atmosphere and tenor of his life.

Robert Louis Stevenson 1850–94: *Memories and Portraits* (1887) 'Gossip on Romance'

2 The good ended happily, and the bad unhappily. That is what fiction means.

Oscar Wilde 1854–1900: *The Importance of Being Earnest* (1895)

3 Literature is a luxury; fiction is a necessity.

G. K. Chesterton 1874–1936: *The Defendant* (1901) 'A Defence of Penny Dreadfuls'

4 Fiction, at the point of development at which it has arrived, demands from the writer a spirit of scrupulous abnegation. The only legitimate basis of creative work lies in the courageous recognition of all the irreconcilable antagonisms that make our life so enigmatic, so burdensome, so fascinating, so dangerous—so full of hope. They exist! And this is the only fundamental truth of fiction.

Joseph Conrad 1857–1924: letter 2 August 1901

5 The house of fiction has in short not one window, but a million . . . but they are, singly or together, as nothing without the posted presence of the watcher.

Henry James 1843–1916: *The Portrait of a Lady* (1908 ed.); cf. **90:12**

6 Reality, as usual, beats fiction out of sight.
commenting on 'this wartime atmosphere'

Joseph Conrad 1857–1924: letter 11 August 1915

7 Fiction is Truth's elder sister. Obviously. No one in the world knew what truth was till somebody had told a story.

Rudyard Kipling 1865–1936: *A Book of Words* (1928) 'Fiction'

8 Fiction, imaginative work that is, is not dropped like a pebble upon the ground, as science maybe; fiction is like a spider's web, attached ever so lightly perhaps, but still attached to life at all four corners. Often the attachment is scarcely perceptible.

Virginia Woolf 1882–1941: *A Room of One's Own* (1929)

9 For me a work of fiction exists only in so far as it affords me what I shall bluntly call aesthetic bliss, that is a sense of being somehow, somewhere, connected with other states of being where art (curiosity, tenderness, kindness, ecstasy) is the norm.

Vladimir Nabokov 1899–1977: *Lolita* (1955) 'On a book entitled *Lolita*'

10 Fiction to me is a kind of parable. You have got to make up your mind it's not true. Some kind of truth emerges from it, but it's not fact.

Muriel Spark 1918– : 'My Conversion' (1961)

11 I write fiction because it's a way of making statements I can disown, and I write plays because dialogue is the most respectable way of contradicting myself.

Tom Stoppard 1937– : in a television interview; in *Guardian* 21 March 1973

12 Of course, as Henry James says, the house of fiction has many windows. Your trouble is you seem to have stood in front of most of them.

Malcolm Bradbury 1932– : *The History Man* (1975); cf. **90:5**

13 Writing fiction is of course the act of an impostor.

Paul Scott 1920–78: letter 1975; Hilary Spurling *Paul Scott* (1990)

14 There is no longer any such thing as fiction or non-fiction; there's only narrative.

E. L. Doctorow 1931– : in *New York Times Book Review* 27 January 1988

1 Good fiction often takes the banal around us and defamiliarizes it.

Edmund White 1940– : in interview in *Paris Review* 1988

2 Writers of fiction are collectors of useless information. They are the opposite of good, solid, wise citizens who collect good information and put it to good use. Fiction writers remember tiny little details, some of them almost malicious, but very telling.

William Trevor 1928– : in *Paris Review* 1989

3 The acceptance that all that is solid has melted into air, that reality and morality are not givens but imperfect human constructs, is the point from which fiction begins.

Salman Rushdie 1947– : 'Is Nothing Sacred?' (Herbert Read Memorial Lecture) 6 February 1990

4 Fiction is nothing less than the subtlest instrument for self-examination and self-display that mankind has invented yet.

John Updike 1932– : *Odd Jobs* (1991)

5 Fiction is not the story of my life or the lives of people I have known. It is a struggle to write novels which will in some way reflect my own experience through the adventures of my characters, novels which permit me to re-examine beliefs I no longer hold and search for some meaning in my life.

Brian Moore 1921– : Clare Boylan (ed.) *The Agony and the Ego* (1993)

6 In the long run, fiction bruises character.

Cynthia Ozick 1928– : *Portrait of the Artist as a Bad Character* (1996)

Figures of Speech

7 By far the most important thing to master is the use of metaphor. This is one thing that cannot be learnt from anyone else, and it is the mark of great natural ability, for the ability to use metaphor implies a perception of resemblances.

Aristotle 384–322 BC: *Poetics*

8 The speaking in a perpetual hyperbole is comely in nothing but in love.

Francis Bacon 1561–1626: *Essays* (1625) 'Of Love'

9 For rhetoric he could not ope
His mouth, but out there flew a trope.

Samuel Butler 1612–80: *Hudibras* pt. 1 (1663)

10 What an image that is—*sea-shouldering whales*!
to his friend Charles Cowden-Clarke, while reading The Faerie Queene

John Keats 1795–1821: Charles Cowden-Clarke *Recollections of Writers* (1878)

11 All slang is metaphor, and all metaphor is poetry.

G. K. Chesterton 1874–1936: *Defendant* (1901) 'Defence of Slang'

12 There comes a time in one man's life, if he is unlucky and has a full life, when he has a secret so dirty that he knows he will never get rid of it. Shakespeare knew this and tried to say it, but he said it just as badly as anyone has ever said it. 'All the perfumes of Arabia' makes you think of all the perfumes of Arabia and nothing more. It is the trouble with all metaphors where human behaviour is concerned. People are not ships, chess men, flowers, racehorses, oil

John O'Hara 1905–70: *Butterfield 8* (1935)

paintings, excrement or musical instruments, or anything else but people. Metaphors are all right to give you an idea.

1 I am a painstaking, conscientious, involved and devious craftsman in words . . . I use everything to make my poems work and move in the directions I want them to: old tricks, new tricks, puns, portmanteau-words, paradox, allusion, paranomasia, paragram, catachresis, slang, assonantal rhymes, vowel rhymes, sprung rhythm . . . Poets have got to enjoy themselves sometimes.

Dylan Thomas 1914–53: 'Poetic Manifesto' (1951)

2 It takes a sound realist to make a convincing symbolist.

D. J. Enright 1920– : *The Apothecary's Shop* (1957)

3 For twenty years I've stared my level best
To see if evening—any evening —would suggest
A patient etherized upon a table;
In vain. I simply wasn't able.

on contemporary poetry, as exemplified by T. S. ***Eliot's*** *'Prufrock'*

C. S. Lewis 1898–1963: 'A Confession' (1964)

4 It's a rare metaphor that doesn't become a bore after about three lines.

Philip Larkin 1922–85: letter, 1 November 1970

5 I was much tempted, perhaps because of my admiration for Metaphysical poets, by exaggerated similes.

Graham Greene 1904–91: *A Sort of Life* (1971)

6 You who with fierce joy celebrated swords hammered out
of iron,
The Norseman's shame,
The banquet of raven and eagle,
Gathering in your military ode
The ritual metaphors of your kin.

Jorge Luis Borges 1899–1986: 'To a Saxon Poet' (1972), tr. Norman Thomas di Giovanni

7 The cure for mixed metaphors, I have always found, is for the patient to be obliged to draw a picture of the result.

Bernard Levin 1928– : *In These Times* (1986)

8 I'm still suffering from the big dénouement in [Jeffrey Archer's book] Not A Penny More when 'the three stood motionless like sheep in the stare of a python.' The whole thing keeps me awake at night. Here are these sheep, gambolling about in the Welsh jungle, when up pops a python. A python, what's more, who thinks he's a cobra.

Nancy Banks-Smith : in *Guardian* 26 March 1990

Food

9 Though each dish
Is lavish and superb, the pleasure's nil
Since you recite your poems! To hell with brill,
Mushrooms and two-pound turbots! I don't need
Oysters: give me a host who doesn't read.

Martial AD *c.*40–*c.*104: *Epigrammata*, tr. James Michie

10 *Equi et poetae alendi, non saginandi.*
Horses and poets should be fed, not overfed.

Charles IX 1550–94: saying

1 When . . . [people] imagine that their food is only a cover for poison, and when they neither love nor trust the hand that serves it, it is not the name of the roast beef of old England that will persuade them to sit down to the table that is spread for them.

Edmund Burke 1729–97: *Thoughts on the Cause of the Present Discontents* (1770)

2 There is more reason for saying grace before a new book than before dinner.

Charles Lamb 1775–1834: *Elia* 'Grace before Meat'

3 HERBERT BEERBOHM TREE: Let us give Shaw a beefsteak and put some red blood into him.
MRS PATRICK CAMPBELL: For heaven's sake, don't. He is bad enough as it is; but if you give him meat no woman in London will be safe.
of the vegetarian G. B. ***Shaw***

Mrs Patrick Campbell 1865–1940: Frank Harris *Contemporary Portraits* (1919)

4 Food comes first, then morals.

Bertolt Brecht 1898–1956: *Die Dreigroschenoper* (1928)

5 And now with some pleasure I find that it's seven; and must cook dinner. Haddock and sausage meat. I think it is true that one gains a certain hold on sausage and haddock by writing them down.

Virginia Woolf 1882–1941: diary, 8 March 1941

6 Take away that pudding — it has no theme.

Winston Churchill 1874–1965: Lord Home *The Way the Wind Blows* (1976)

Friends see Family and Friends

Genius and Talent

7 When a true genius appears in the world, you may know him by this sign, that the dunces are all in confederacy against him.

Jonathan Swift 1667–1745: *Thoughts on Various Subjects* (1711)

8 There is more beauty in the works of a great genius who is ignorant of all the rules of art, than in the works of a little genius, who not only knows but scrupulously observes them.

Joseph Addison 1672–1719: in *The Spectator* 10 September 1714

9 Good God! what a genius I had when I wrote that book.
of A Tale of a Tub

Jonathan Swift 1667–1745: Sir Walter Scott (ed.) *Works of Swift* (1814)

10 True Genius, like Armida's wand,
Can raise the spring from barren land.
While all the art of Imitation,
Is pilf'ring from the first creation.

Robert Lloyd: 'Shakespeare' (1762)

11 The true genius is a mind of large general powers, accidentally determined to some particular direction.

Samuel Johnson 1709–84: *Lives of the English Poets* (1779–81) 'Cowley'

1 It were hyper-criticism, it were pseudo-philosophy to expect from the soul of high-toned genius, the grovellings of a common mind.—The coruscations of talent, elicited by impassioned feeling in the breast of man, are perhaps incompatible with some of the prosaic decencies of life.

Jane Austen 1775–1817: 'Sir Edward Denham' in *Sanditon* (1925 ed.)

2 I really cannot know whether I am or am not the genius you are pleased to call me, but I am very willing to put up with the mistake, it if be one. It is a title dearly enough bought by most men, to render it endurable, even when not quite clearly made out, which it never *can* be till the posterity, whose decisions are merely dreams to ourselves, has sanctioned or denied it, while it can touch us no further.

Lord Byron 1788–1824: letter to Isaac D'Israeli, 10 June 1822; Leslie Marchand (ed.) *Byron's Letters and Journals* (1979) vol. 9

3 The works of genius are watered with its tears.

Honoré de Balzac 1799–1850: *Lost Illusions* (1837–43)

4 What is genius—but the power of expressing a new individuality?

Elizabeth Barrett Browning 1806–61: letter to Mary Russell Mitford, 14 January 1843

5 Genius, all over the world, stands hand in hand, and one shock of recognition runs the whole circle round.

Herman Melville 1819–91: *Hawthorne and His Mosses* (1850)

6 Since when was genius found respectable?

Elizabeth Barrett Browning 1806–61: *Aurora Leigh* (1857)

7 Genius does what it must, and Talent does what it can.

Owen Meredith 1831–91: 'Last Words of a Sensitive Second-Rate Poet' (1868)

8 Does genius burn, Jo?
her family's habitual enquiry to Jo March when engaged in writing

Louisa M. Alcott 1832–88: *Good Wives* (1869)

9 Unless one is a genius, it is best to aim at being intelligible.

Anthony Hope 1863–1933: *The Dolly Dialogues* (1894)

10 I have nothing to declare except my genius.
at the New York Custom House

Oscar Wilde 1854–1900: Frank Harris *Oscar Wilde* (1918)

11 Mediocrity knows nothing higher than itself, but talent instantly recognizes genius.

Arthur Conan Doyle 1859–1930: *The Valley of Fear* (1915)

12 I have known no man of genius who had not to pay, in some affliction or defect either physical or spiritual, for what the gods had given him.

Max Beerbohm 1872–1956: *And Even Now* (1920)

13 A man of genius makes no mistakes. His errors are volitional and are the portals of discovery.

James Joyce 1882–1941: *Ulysses* (1922)

14 The Scots are incapable of considering their literary geniuses purely as writers or artists. They must be either an excuse for a glass or a text for the next sermon.

George Malcolm Thomson 1899– : *Caledonia* (1927)

15 It takes a lot of time to be a genius, you have to sit around so much doing nothing, really doing nothing.

Gertrude Stein 1874–1946: *Everybody's Autobiography* (1937)

16 Talent without genius comes to little. Genius without talent is *nothing*.

Paul Valéry 1871–1945: *At Moments* 'The Beautiful is Negative'

1 Nature is monstrously unjust. There is no substitute for talent. Industry and all the virtues are of no avail.

Aldous Huxley 1894–1963: George Greenfield *Scribblers for Bread* (1989)

2 Geniuses are the luckiest of mortals because what they must do is the same as what they most want to do.

W. H. Auden 1907–73: Dag Hammarskjöld *Markings* (1964)

3 What Romantic terminology called genius or talent or inspiration is nothing other than finding the right road empirically, following one's nose, taking shortcuts.

Italo Calvino 1923–85: 'Cybernetics and Ghosts', lecture in Turin, November 1969; *The Literature Machine* (1987)

4 I doubt that there is a writer over 40 who does not realize in his heart of hearts that literary genius, in prose, consists of proportions more on the order of 65 per cent material and 35 per cent the talent in the sacred crucible.

Tom Wolfe 1931– : 'Stalking the Billion-Footed Beast' (1989)

5 What to do with all this talent, how to stay alive until I've gotten it down. I still feel that.

Saul Bellow 1915– : to his biographer on 30 August 1992; in *New Yorker* 26 June 1995

6 If a man is going to behave like a bastard, he'd better be a genius.

discussing H. G. ***Wells*** *with her husband, Michael Foot*

Jill Craigie : on *Bookmark* (BBC2) 24 August 1996

Ghost Stories

7 A sad tale's best for winter.
I have one of sprites and goblins.

William Shakespeare 1564–1616: *The Winter's Tale* (1610–11)

8 The only supernatural agents which can in any manner be allowed to us moderns, are ghosts; but of these I would advise an author to be extremely sparing. These are indeed like arsenic, and other dangerous drugs in physic, to be used with the utmost caution; nor would I advise the introduction of them at all in those works, or by those authors, to which or to whom a horse-laugh in the reader would be any great prejudice or mortification.

Henry Fielding 1707–54: *Tom Jones* (1749)

9 We can no longer get a good ghost story, either for love nor money. The materialists have it all their own way . . . That cold-blooded demon called Science has taken the place of all the other demons.

William Gilmore Simms 1806–70: *Murder Will Out* (1842)

10 The past, the more or less remote past, of which the prose is clean obliterated by distance—that is the place to get our ghosts from.

Vernon Lee 1856–1935: *Hauntings* (1890) preface

11 Whenever five or six English-speaking people meet round a fire on Christmas Eve, they start telling each other ghost stories.

Jerome K. Jerome 1859–1927: *Told After Supper* (1891) introduction

12 How are we to account for the strange human craving for the pleasure of feeling afraid which is so much involved in our love of ghost stories?

Virginia Woolf 1882–1941: in *Times Literary Supplement* 31 January 1918 'Across the Border'

1 We must admit that Henry James has conquered. That courtly worldly, sentimental old gentleman can still make us afraid of the dark.

Virginia Woolf 1882–1941: in *Times Literary Supplement* 22 December 1921 'The Ghost Stories of Henry James'

2 Let us, then, be introduced to the actors in a placid way; let us see them going about their ordinary business, undisturbed by forebodings, pleased with their surroundings; and into this calm environment let the ominous thing put out its head, unobtrusively at first, and then more insistently, until it holds the stage.

M. R. James 1862–1936: *Ghosts and Marvels* (1924) introduction

3 The success of a ghost story may be judged by its thermometrical quality; if it sends a cold shiver down one's spine, it has done its job and done it well.

Edith Wharton 1862–1937: M. Cox and R. Gilbert (eds.) *Oxford Book of Ghost Stories* (1986) introduction

4 To be successful, a ghost story has to be terrifying, and it is much easier to be ingenious than to be terrifying. The writer of detective stories must present his readers with a crime and an ingenious solution for it. But the writer of ghost stories must freeze his reader's marrow, and that is anything but easy.

Robertson Davies 1913–95: in 1942; *The Enthusiasms of Robertson Davies* (1990)

5 The greatest of ghost-story writers have examined the terror and defined it—this is partly why we like to read them: round their circles of light, our fears gather.

Anne Ridler 1912– : *Best Ghost Stories* (1945) prefatory note

6 [The ghost story] is certainly the most exacting form of literary art, and perhaps the only one in which there is almost no intermediate step between success and failure. Either it comes off or it is a flop.

L. P. Hartley 1895–1972: Cynthia Asquith (ed.) *The Third Ghost Book* (1955) introduction

7 It gathers its strength through obliquity and operates most powerfully through a series of openings whose horror lies in their being just, just out of true.

Elizabeth Bowen 1899–1973: attributed

8 Ghost stories . . . tell us about things that lie hidden within all of us, and which lurk outside all around us.

Susan Hill 1942– : *Ghost Stories* (1983) introduction

Good and Bad Writing see also **Style**

9 *Namque tu solebas*
Meas esse aliquid putare nugas.

For you used to think my trifles were worth something.

Catullus *c.*84–*c.*54 BC: *Carmina* no. 1

10 Not gods, nor men, nor even booksellers have put up with poets being second-rate.

Horace 65–8 BC: *Ars Poetica*

11 There is scarcely any book so bad that nothing can be learnt from it.

his father's customary remark

Pliny the Younger AD *c.*61–*c.*112: *Epistulae*

12 Pure and neat language I love, yet plain and customary. A barbarous phrase hath often made me out of love with a good sense, and doubtful writing hath wracked me beyond my patience.

Ben Jonson *c.*1573–1637: *Timber, or Discoveries made upon Men and Matter* (1641)

1 Sure the poet . . . spewed up a good lump of clotted nonsense at once.

John Dryden 1631–1700: *Notes and Observations on the Empress of Morocco* [by Elkanah Settle] (1674) 'The First Act'

2 What woeful stuff this madrigal would be,
In some starved hackney sonneteer, or me?
But let a Lord once own the happy lines,
How the wit brightens! how the style refines!

Alexander Pope 1688–1744: *An Essay on Criticism* (1711)

3 I am convinced more and more day by day that fine writing is next to fine doing the top thing in the world.

John Keats 1795–1821: letter to J. H. Reynolds, 24 August 1819

4 It is a wretched taste to be gratified with mediocrity when the excellent lies before us.

Isaac D'Israeli 1766–1848: *Curiosities of Literature. Second Series* (1823)

5 Too many flowers . . . too little fruit.
describing the work of Felicia Hemans

Sir Walter Scott 1771–1832: letter to Joanna Baillie, 18 July 1823

6 Clear writers, like clear fountains, do not seem so deep as they are; the turbid look the most profound.

Walter Savage Landor 1775–1864: *Imaginary Conversations* (1824) 'Southey and Porson'

7 People don't deserve to have good writing, they are so pleased with bad.

Ralph Waldo Emerson 1803–82: *Journals* 1841

8 The amount of a certain sort of emasculate twaddle produced in the United States is not encouraging.

Henry James 1843–1916: letter, 14 September 1879

9 The best is the best, though a hundred judges have declared it so.

Arthur Quiller-Couch 1863–1944: *Oxford Book of English Verse* (1900) preface

10 The literary gift is a mere accident—is as often bestowed on idiots who have nothing to say worth hearing as it is denied to strenuous sages.

Max Beerbohm 1872–1956: letter to George Bernard Shaw, 21 September 1903

11 A good novel tells us the truth about its hero; but a bad novel tells us the truth about its author.

G. K. Chesterton 1874–1936: *Heretics* (1905)

12 This of course is not what he was trying to say, but the pen is mightier than the wrist.

A. E. Housman 1859–1936: in *Classical Review* 1920; cf. **186:12**

13 It is far easier to write ten passably effective sonnets, good enough to take in the not too inquiring critic, than one effective advertisement that will take in a few thousand of the uncritical buying public.

Aldous Huxley 1894–1963: *On the Margin* (1923) 'Advertisement'

14 We are nauseated by the sight of trivial personalities decomposing in the eternity of print.

Virginia Woolf 1882–1941: *The Common Reader* (1925) 'The Modern Essay'

15 It is with noble sentiments that bad literature gets written.

André Gide 1869–1951: letter to François Mauriac, 1928

16 A bad book is as much of a labour to write as a good one; it comes as sincerely from the author's soul.

Aldous Huxley 1894–1963: *Point Counter Point* (1928)

17 What I like in a good author is not what he says, but what he whispers.

Logan Pearsall Smith 1865–1946: *All Trivia* (1933) 'Afterthoughts'

1 A great writer creates a world of his own and his readers are proud to live in it. A lesser writer may entice them in for a moment, but soon he will watch them filing out.

Cyril Connolly 1903–74: *Enemies of Promise* (1938)

2 All good writing is *swimming under water* and holding your breath.

F. Scott Fitzgerald 1896–1940: letter (undated) to Frances Scott Fitzgerald

3 The more books we read, the sooner we perceive that the only function of a writer is to produce a masterpiece. No other task is of any consequence.

Cyril Connolly 1903–74: *The Unquiet Grave* (1944)

4 You should only read what is truly good or what is frankly bad.

Gertrude Stein 1874–1946: Ernest Hemingway *A Moveable Feast* (1964)

5 There are only four kinds of books. There are good books that do sell and good books that don't sell; bad books that do sell and bad books that don't sell.

J. C. Squire 1884–1958: in 1948; George Greenfield *Scribblers for Bread* (1989)

6 Good poets have a weakness for bad puns.

W. H. Auden 1907–73: 'The Shield of Achilles' (1955)

7 The world is over-stocked with people who are ready and eager to teach other people to write. It seems astonishing that so much bad writing should find its way into print when so much good advice is to be had.

Robertson Davies 1913–95: in 1959; *The Enthusiasms of Robertson Davies* (1990)

8 You know you're writing well when you're throwing good stuff into the wastebasket.

Ernest Hemingway 1899–1961: attributed

9 There's only one real sin, and that is to persuade oneself that the second-best is anything but the second-best.

Doris Lessing 1919– : *Golden Notebook* (1962)

10 Mediocrity is more dangerous in a critic than in a writer.

Eugène Ionesco 1912–94: attributed, 1966

11 This is not a novel to be tossed aside lightly. It should be thrown with great force.

Dorothy Parker 1893–1967: R. E. Drennan *Wit's End* (1973)

12 I suspect that the reason that the ability to write good prose and good dialogue go hand-in-hand is simply that a good writer knows how to listen.

John Braine 1922–86: *Writing a Novel* (1974)

13 For a writer, the bad elements stand out like a boil. It's all very well to recognize that a boil is only a part of the body, it's still disproportionately obtrusive.

Graham Greene 1904–91: Marie-Françoise Allain *The Other Man, Conversations with Graham Greene* (1983)

14 Nothing we write, if we hope to be any good, will ever turn out as we first thought.

Lillian Hellman 1905–84: attributed

15 When I finish a book I really like, no matter what the subject matter, or see a play or film, like Kurosawa's *Ran*, which is swimming in blood and totally pessimistic, but so well done, I feel very good. It's the well-doneness that has that effect on me.

Margaret Atwood 1939– : in an interview, December 1986; Earl G. Ingersoll (ed.) *Margaret Atwood: Conversations* (1990)

explaining why in his view Vikram Seth's acclaimed A Suitable Boy *had not been shortlisted for the 1993 Booker Prize:*

16 All the wrong bits are in and the right bits are out.

Lord Gowrie 1939– : in *Guardian* 9 March 1994

The Gothic see **Horror and the Gothic**

Grammar and Usage see also **Spelling**

1 *Multa renascentur quae iam cecidere, cadentque*
Quae nunc sunt in honore vocabula, si volet usus,
Quem penes arbitrium est et ius et norma loquendi.

Many terms which have now dropped out of favour will be revived, and those that are at present respectable will drop out, if usage so choose, with whom lies the decision, the judgement, and the rule of speech.

Horace 65–8 BC: *Ars Poetica*

2 Grammer, the ground of al.

William Langland *c.*1330–*c.*1400: *The Vision of Piers Plowman*

3 Syllables govern the world.

John Selden 1584–1654: *Table Talk* (1689)

4 I have laboured to refine our language to grammatical purity, and to clear it from colloquial barbarisms, licentious idioms, and irregular combinations.

Samuel Johnson 1709–84: in *The Rambler* 14 March 1752

5 An aspersion upon my parts of speech!

Richard Brinsley Sheridan 1751–1816: *The Rivals* (1775)

6 In language, the ignorant have prescribed laws to the learned.

Richard Duppa 1770–1831: *Maxims* (1830)

7 Correct English is the slang of prigs who write history and essays. And the strongest slang of all is the slang of poets.

George Eliot 1819–80: *Middlemarch* (1871–2)

8 For first you write a sentence,
And then you chop it small;
Then mix the bits, and sort them out
Just as they chance to fall:
The order of the phrases makes
No difference at all.

Lewis Carroll 1832–98: 'Phantasmagoria' (1876)

9 I will not go down to posterity talking bad grammar.
while correcting proofs of his last Parliamentary speech, 31 March 1881

Benjamin Disraeli 1804–81: Robert Blake *Disraeli* (1966)

10 Good intentions are invariably ungrammatical.

Oscar Wilde 1854–1900: attributed

11 Prefer geniality to grammar.

H. W. Fowler 1858–1933 and **F. G. Fowler** 1870–1918: *The King's English* (1906)

12 Damn the subjunctive. It brings all our writers to shame.

Mark Twain 1835–1910: *Notebook* (1935)

13 Only presidents, editors, and people with tapeworms have the right to use the editorial 'we'.

Mark Twain 1835–1910: attributed

14 Progress through its clumsy and invertebrate sentences is like plodding over a ploughed field of clay.
of the chapter on Edmund Burke in the Cambridge History of English Literature

A. E. Housman 1859–1936: in *Cambridge Review* 1915

1 I don't want to talk grammar, I want to talk like a lady.

George Bernard Shaw 1856–1950: *Pygmalion* (1916)

2 Adjectives are the sugar of literature and adverbs the salt.

Henry James 1843–1916: Theodora Bosanquet *Henry James at Work* (1924)

3 The English-speaking world may be divided into (1) those who neither know nor care what a split infinitive is; (2) those who do not know, but care very much; (3) those who know and condemn; (4) those who know and distinguish. Those who neither know nor care are the vast majority, and are a happy folk, to be envied by most of the minority classes.

H. W. Fowler 1858–1933: *Modern English Usage* (1926)

4 The subjunctive mood is in its death throes, and the best thing to do is to put it out of its misery as soon as possible.

W. Somerset Maugham 1874–1965: *A Writer's Notebook* (1949) written in 1941

5 One can cure oneself of the *not un-* formation by memorizing this sentence: A not unblack dog was chasing a not unsmall rabbit across a not ungreen field.

George Orwell 1903–50: in *Horizon* April 1946

6 Would you convey my compliments to the purist who reads your proofs and tell him or her that I write in a sort of broken-down patois which is something like the way a Swiss waiter talks, and that when I split an infinitive, God damn it, I split it so it will stay split.

Raymond Chandler 1888–1959: letter to Edward Weeks, 18 January 1947

7 This is the sort of English up with which I will not put.

Winston Churchill 1874–1965: Ernest Gowers *Plain Words* (1948)

8 My mother . . . pointed out that one could not say 'a green great dragon', but had to say 'a great green dragon'. I wondered why, and still do.
of the first story he wrote, aged seven

J. R. R. Tolkien 1892–1973: letter to W. H. Auden, 7 June 1955

9 The notion 'grammatical' cannot be identified with 'meaningful' or 'significant' in any semantic sense. Sentences (1) and (2) are equally nonsensical, but . . . only the former is grammatical.
(1) Colourless green ideas sleep furiously.
(2) Furiously sleep ideas green colourless.

Noam Chomsky 1928– : *Syntactic Structures* (1957)

10 You shall know a word by the company it keeps.

J. R. Firth 1890–1960: 'A Synopsis of Linguistic Theory' (1957)

11 You can be a little ungrammatical if you come from the right part of the country.

Robert Frost 1874–1963: in *Atlantic Monthly* January 1962

12 The sentence, that dignified entity with subject and predicate, is shortly to be made illegal. It probably already is in Torremolinos.

Alan Bennett 1934– : *Getting On* (1972)

13 Sentence structure is innate but whining is acquired.

Woody Allen 1935– : 'Remembering Needleman' (1976)

14 There are little constellations of language here and there, and the meaning of a word changes according to its context in the constellation.

Margaret Atwood 1939– : in an interview, July 1978; Earl G. Ingersoll (ed.) *Margaret Atwood: Conversations* (1990)

1 One has a few private rules: never split an adjective and its noun, for instance.

Philip Larkin 1922–85: in 1979; *Required Writing* (1983)

2 The beastly adverb—far more damaging to a writer than an adjective.

Graham Greene 1904–91: *Ways of Escape* (1980)

3 As far as I'm concerned, 'whom' is a word that was invented to make everyone sound like a butler.

Calvin Trillin 1935– : in *The Nation* 8 June 1985

4 I am quite capable of speaking, unprepared, a sentence containing anything up to forty subordinate clauses all embedded in their neighbours like those wooden Russian dolls, and many a native of these islands, speaking English as to the manner born, has followed me trustingly into the labyrinth only to perish miserably trying to find the way out.

Bernard Levin 1928– : *In These Times* (1986)

5 Women, fire, and dangerous things.
a grammatical classification in Dyirbal, an Australian Aboriginal language, taken as an illustration of the tendency of human beings to perceive categories generally

George Lakoff : title of book (1987)

6 Save the gerund and screw the whale.

Tom Stoppard 1937– : *The Real Thing* (1988 rev. ed.)

7 Every sentence he manages to utter scatters its component parts like pond water from a verb chasing its own tail.
of George Bush

Clive James 1939– : *The Dreaming Swimmer* (1992)

8 Language is more fashion than science, and matters of usage, spelling and pronunciation tend to wander around like hemlines.

Bill Bryson 1951– : in *Independent* 17 December 1994 (Quote Unquote)

9 The word *glamour* comes from the word *grammar*, and since the Chomskyan revolution the etymology has been fitting. Who could not be dazzled by the creative power of the mental grammar, by its ability to convey an infinite number of thoughts with a finite set of rules.

Steven Pinker 1954– : *The Language Instinct* (1994)

Historical Fiction

10 I am fully sensible that an historical romance, founded on the House of Saxe Coburg, might be much more to the purpose of profit or popularity than such pictures of domestic life in country villages as I deal in. But I could no more write a romance than an epic poem. I could not sit seriously down to write a serious romance under any other motive than to save my life; and if it were indispensable for me to keep it up and never relax into laughing at myself or other people, I am sure I should be hung before I had finished the first chapter.

Jane Austen 1775–1817: letter to James Stanier Clarke, 1 April 1816; cf. **55:8**

11 It is said that Shakespeare depicted the Romans superbly. I don't see this. They are sheer, inveterate Englishmen, but they are truly human, fundamentally human, and so the Roman toga suits them well enough.

Johann Wolfgang von Goethe 1749–1832: 'Shakespeare without End' (1815)

1 All the time I was at work on the Two Cities, I read no books but such as had the air of time in them.
of writing A Tale of Two Cities

Charles Dickens 1812–70: letter to John Forster, 2 May 1860

2 He took all history for his province, from that of ancient Egypt in 'The Cat of Bubastes' . . . to that of current affairs in 'With Roberts to Pretoria'.
of the writer for boys, G. A. Henty (1832–1902)

Anonymous: in *Dictionary of National Biography* (1917–)

3 Those who put the historical novel in a category apart are forgetting that what every novelist does is only to interpret, by means of the technique which his period affords, a certain number of past events; his memories, whether consciously or unconsciously recalled, whether personal or impersonal, are all woven of the same stuff as history itself.

Marguerite Yourcenar 1903–87: *Memoirs of Hadrian* (1955)

4 There is no book which is not of its own time; the painstaking historical novel *Salammbô*, whose characters are mercenaries during the Punic Wars, is a typical nineteenth-century French novel. The one thing we know for sure about Carthaginian literature, which may have been very rich, is that it could not have had a book like Flaubert's.

Jorge Luis Borges 1899–1986: in 1969; James Woodall *The Man in the Mirror of the Book* (1996)

5 All forms of sexual loving become acceptable if the lovers wear togas or wolfskins.

Naomi Mitchison 1897– : Mary Chamberlain (ed.) *Writing Lives* (1988)

6 *Black Robe* is an historical novel, in a way, but it doesn't give you the heavy padding that historical novels do. They do a lot of research and then they must put the research in. I don't believe in that. Do a minimum of research, and then keep it out. Don't let it impede the story.

Brian Moore 1921– : Rosemary Hartill *Writers Revealed* (1989)

7 It had never occurred to me that to shift the scene of a novel to another age . . . and to cast it in an English some degrees pleasanter than the current, put me in a disreputable genre. I met some very astonishing statements—such as that I was a writer of *adventure stories.*

Patrick O'Brian 1914– : interview in *Independent on Sunday* 15 March 1992

Historical Writing

8 The absence of romance in my history will, I fear, detract somewhat from its interest; but I shall be content if it is judged useful by those inquirers who desire an exact knowledge of the past as an aid to the interpretation of the future.

Thucydides *c.*460–400 BC: *The History of the Peloponnesian War*

9 History is philosophy from examples.

Dionysius of Halicarnassus fl. 30–7 BC: *Ars Rhetorica*

10 If history record good things of good men, the thoughtful hearer is encouraged to imitate what is good; or if it records evil of wicked men, the devout religious listener or reader is encouraged to avoid all that is sinful and perverse

The Venerable Bede AD 673–735: *Ecclesiastical History of the English People* preface

and to follow what he knows to be good and pleasing to God.

1 Should the reader discover any inaccuracies in what I have written, I humbly beg that he will not impute them to me, because, as the laws of history require, I have laboured honestly to transmit whatever I could ascertain from common report for the instruction of posterity.

The Venerable Bede AD 673–735: *Ecclesiastical History of the English People* preface

2 In winter's tedious nights sit by the fire
With good old folks, and let them tell thee tales
Of woeful ages, long ago betid.

William Shakespeare 1564–1616: *Richard II* (1595)

3 Whosoever, in writing a modern history, shall follow truth too near the heels, it may happily strike out his teeth.

Walter Ralegh *c.*1552–1618: *The History of the World* (1614)

4 Historians desiring to write the actions of men, ought to set down the simple truth, and not say anything for love or hatred; also to choose such an opportunity for writing as it may be lawful to think what they will, and write what they think, which is a rare happiness of the time.

Walter Ralegh *c.*1552–1618: 'A Collection of Political Observations'; *The Works of Sir Walter Raleigh* (1751) vol. 1

5 Memoirs are true and useful stars, whilst studied histories are those stars joined in constellations, according to the fancy of the poet.

Samuel Pepys 1633–1703: J. R. Tanner (ed.) *Samuel Pepys's Naval Minutes* (1926)

6 They maintained the dignity of history.
of Thucydides and Xenophon

Henry St John, Lord Bolingbroke 1678–1751: *Letters on the Study and Use of History* (1752)

7 Great abilities are not requisite for an historian . . . imagination is not required in any high degree.

Samuel Johnson 1709–84: James Boswell *Life of Samuel Johnson* (1791) 6 July 1763

8 One of the few books which selection of sentiment and elegance of diction have been able to preserve, though written upon a subject flux and transitory.
of Thomas Sprat's History of the Royal Society *(1667)*

Samuel Johnson 1709–84: in *Dictionary of National Biography* (1917–)

9 History . . . is, indeed, little more than the register of the crimes, follies, and misfortunes of mankind.

Edward Gibbon 1737–94: *The Decline and Fall of the Roman Empire* (1776–88)

10 The life of the historian must be short and precarious.

Edward Gibbon 1737–94: *Memoirs of My Life* (1796)

11 'I am fond of history.'
'I wish I were too. I read it a little as a duty, but it tells me nothing that does not vex or weary me. The quarrels of popes and kings, with wars and pestilences, in every page; the men all so good for nothing, and hardly any women at all.'

Jane Austen 1775–1817: *Northanger Abbey* (1818)

12 This province of literature is a debatable line. It lies on the confines of two distinct territories. It is under the jurisdiction of two hostile powers; and like other districts similarly situated it is ill-defined, ill-cultivated, and ill-regulated. Instead of being equally shared between its two rulers, the Reason and the Imagination, it falls alternately

Lord Macaulay 1800–59: 'History' (1828)

under the sole and absolute dominion of each. It is sometimes fiction. It is sometimes theory.

1 Read no history: nothing but biography, for that is life without theory.

Benjamin Disraeli 1804–81: *Contarini Fleming* (1832); cf. **104:3**

2 History is the essence of innumerable biographies.

Thomas Carlyle 1795–1881: *Critical and Miscellaneous Essays* (1838) 'On History'

3 There is properly no history; only biography.

Ralph Waldo Emerson 1803–82: *Essays* (1841) 'History'; cf. **104:1**

4 History is a gallery of pictures in which there are few originals and many copies.

Alexis de Tocqueville 1805–59: *L'Ancien régime* (1856)

5 Anybody can make history. Only a great man can write it.

Oscar Wilde 1854–1900: *Intentions* (1891) 'The Critic as Artist'

6 It has been said that though God cannot alter the past, historians can; it is perhaps because they can be useful to Him in this respect that He tolerates their existence.

Samuel Butler 1835–1902: *Erewhon Revisited* (1901)

7 If I write nothing but fiction for some time I begin to get stupid, and to feel rather as if it had been a long meal of sweets; then history is a rest, for research or narration brings a different part of the mind into play.

Charlotte Yonge 1823–1901: Georgina Battiscombe *Charlotte Mary Yonge* (1943)

8 The historian, essentially, wants more documents than he can really use; the dramatist only wants more liberties than he can really take.

Henry James 1843–1916: *The Aspern Papers* (1909 ed.) preface

9 History repeats itself. Historians repeat each other.

Philip Guedalla 1889–1944: *Supers and Supermen* (1920)

10 And even I can remember
A day when the historians left blanks in their writings,
I mean for things they didn't know.

Ezra Pound 1885–1972: *Draft of XXX Cantos* (1930)

11 Exiled Thucydides knew
All that a speech can say
About Democracy,
And what dictators do,
The elderly rubbish they talk
To an apathetic grave;
Analysed all in his book,
The enlightenment driven away,
The habit-forming pain,
Management and grief.

W. H. Auden 1907–73: 'September 1, 1939' (1940)

12 The highest history combines scholarship and art.

A. J. P. Taylor 1906–90: in *New Statesman and Nation* 13 November 1947

13 Historian—An unsuccessful novelist.

H. L. Mencken 1880–1956: *A Mencken Chrestomathy* (1949)

14 Since the work of the artist is openly subjective, and 'feigned' history, what matters is not what happened to him, but what he has made his experience into.

W. H. Auden 1907–73: 'History of a Historian' (1955)

1 Man is a history-making creature who can neither repeat his past nor leave it behind.

W. H. Auden 1907–73: *The Dyer's Hand* (1962) 'D. H. Lawrence'

2 History gets thicker as it approaches recent times.

A. J. P. Taylor 1906–90: *English History 1914–45* (1965) bibliography

3 It would be a valuable practice for the historian to rise each morning saying to himself three times slowly and with emphasis, 'I do not know.'

J. L. Martyn 1925– : J. Ashton *Understanding the Fourth Gospel* (1991)

4 You can't get at the truth by writing history; only the novelist can do that.
on being asked to write the Spanish volume in the Oxford History of Europe

Gerald Brenan 1894–1987: in *Times Literary Supplement* 28 November 1986

Horror and the Gothic

5 But that I am forbid
To tell the secrets of my prison-house,
I could a tale unfold whose lightest word
Would harrow up thy soul, freeze thy young blood,
Make thy two eyes, like stars, start from their spheres,
Thy knotted and combinèd locks to part,
And each particular hair to stand on end,
Like quills upon the fretful porpentine:
But this eternal blazon must not be
To ears of flesh and blood. List, list, O, list!

William Shakespeare 1564–1616: *Hamlet* (1601)

6 Every drop of ink in my pen ran cold.

Horace Walpole 1717–97: letter to George Montagu, 30 July 1752

7 I have heard that something very shocking indeed, will soon come out in London.

Jane Austen 1775–1817: *Northanger Abbey* (1818)

8 Charming as were all Mrs Radcliffe's works, and charming even as were the works of her imitators, it was not in them that human nature, at least in the midland counties of England, was to be looked for. Of the Alps and Pyrenees, with their pine forests and their vices, they might give a faithful delineation; and Italy, Switzerland, and the South of France, might be as fruitful in horrors as they were there represented. Catherine dared not doubt beyond her own country, and even of that, if hard pressed, would have yielded the northern and western extremities. But in the central part of England there was surely some security . . . in the laws of the land, and the manners of the age.

Jane Austen 1775–1817: *Northanger Abbey* (1818)

9 I wants to make your flesh creep.
the Fat Boy's aspiration

Charles Dickens 1812–70: *Pickwick Papers* (1837)

10 I'm interested in the Gothic novel because it's very much a woman's form. Why is there such a wide readership for books that essentially say, 'Your husband is trying to kill you'?

Margaret Atwood 1939– : in an interview, July 1978; Earl G. Ingersoll (ed.) *Margaret Atwood: Conversations* (1990)

1 Terror . . . often arises from a pervasive sense of disestablishment; that things are in the unmaking.

Stephen King 1947– : *Danse Macabre* (1981)

2 The site where the late-18th century buried its nuclear waste of repression and neurosis.
of Gothic literature

John Carey 1934– : in *Sunday Times* 1992

3 The great horror stories of the 19th century—starting with Radcliffe, then entering the popular bloodstream with Mary Shelley's *Frankenstein*, Robert Louis Stevenson's *The Strange Case of Dr Jekyll and Mr Hyde* (1886), Bram Stoker's *Dracula* (1897) and Sir Arthur Conan Doyle's *The Hound of the Baskervilles* (1901)—represent the most significant contribution by British writers of the past century to the mass culture of this one.

Christopher Frayling 1946– : in *Sunday Times* 8 December 1996

The Human Race

4 *Quidquid agunt homines, votum timor ira voluptas*
Gaudia discursus nostri farrago libelli est.

Everything mankind does, their hope, fear, rage, pleasure, joys, business, are the hotch-potch of my little book.

Juvenal AD *c.*60–*c.*130: *Satires*

5 Man is man's A.B.C. There is none that can
Read God aright, unless he first spell Man.

Francis Quarles 1592–1644: *Hieroglyphics of the Life of Man* (1638)

6 The world may be divided into people that read, people that write, people that think, and fox-hunters.

William Shenstone 1714–63: *Works* (1764) 'On Writing and Books'

7 Mankind are the creatures of books.

Leigh Hunt 1784–1859: *A Book for a Corner* (1852)

8 Man is a creature who lives not upon bread alone, but principally by catchwords.

Robert Louis Stevenson 1850–94: *Virginibus Puerisque* (1881)

9 I am content to sympathize with common mortals . . . their hearts—like ours—must endure the load of the gifts from heaven: the curse of facts and the blessing of illusions, the bitterness of our wisdom and the deceptive consolation of our folly.

Joseph Conrad 1857–1924: *Almayer's Folly* (1895) author's note

10 The human race, to which so many of my readers belong.

G. K. Chesterton 1874–1936: *The Napoleon of Notting Hill* (1904)

11 We must wash literature off ourselves. We want to be men above all, to be human.

Antonin Artaud 1896–1948: *Les Oeuvres et les Hommes* (unpublished MS, 17 May 1922)

12 If a writer writes truthfully out of individual experience then what is written inevitably speaks for other people. For thousands of years storytellers have taken for granted that their experiences must be general. It never occurred to them that it is possible to divorce oneself from life.

Doris Lessing 1919– : in *Partisan Review* fall, 1992 (special issue) 'Unexamined Mental Attitudes Left Behind by Communism'

Humour and Comedy see also **Irony, Wit and Satire**

1 Comedy represents the worse types of men; worse, however, not in the sense that it embraces any and every kind of badness, but in the sense that the ridiculous is a species of ugliness or badness. For the ridiculous consists in some form of error or ugliness that is not painful or injurious; the comic mask, for example, is distorted and ugly, but causes no pain.

Aristotle 384–322 BC: *Poetics*

2 Comedy is an imitation of the common errors of our life.

Philip Sidney 1554–86: *The Defence of Poetry* (1595)

3 A jest's prosperity lies in the ear
Of him that hears it, never in the tongue
Of him that makes it.

William Shakespeare 1564–1616: *Love's Labour's Lost* (1595)

4 As vinegar is not accounted good until the wine be corrupted, so jests that are true and natural seldom raise laughter with the beast, the multitude.

Ben Jonson *c.*1573–1637: *Timber, or Discoveries made upon Men and Matter* (1641)

5 It's an odd job, making decent people laugh.

Molière 1622–73: *La Critique de l'école des femmes* (1663)

6 It is the business of a comic poet to paint the vices and follies of human kind.

William Congreve 1670–1729: *The Double Dealer* (1694)

7 Among all kinds of writing, there is none in which authors are more apt to miscarry than in works of humour, as there is none in which they are more ambitious to excel.

Joseph Addison 1672–1719: *The Spectator* 10 April 1711

8 Comedy naturally wears itself out—destroys the very food on which it lives; and by constantly and successfully exposing the follies and weaknesses of mankind to ridicule, in the end leaves itself nothing worth laughing at.

William Hazlitt 1778–1830: 'On Modern Comedy'; *The Round Table* (1817)

9 My way of joking is to tell the truth. It's the funniest joke in the world.

George Bernard Shaw 1856–1950: *John Bull's Other Island* (1907)

10 Humorists of the 'mere' sort cannot survive. Humour must not professedly teach and it must not professedly preach, but it must do both if it would live forever. By forever, I mean thirty years.

Mark Twain 1835–1910: *The Autobiography of Mark Twain* (1924)

11 There are several kinds of stories, but only one difficult kind—the humorous.

Mark Twain 1835–1910: attributed

12 I did not intend to write a funny book, at first. I did not know I was a humorist. I have never been sure about it. In the middle ages, I should probably have gone about preaching and got myself burnt or hanged.

Jerome K. Jerome 1859–1927: *My Life and Times* (1926)

13 Afraid of losing themselves in the larger flight of the two-volume novel, they stick to short accounts of their misadventures. They lead, as a matter of fact, an existence of jumpiness and apprehension. They sit on the edge of the chair of Literature. In the house of Life they have the feeling that they have never taken off their overcoats.
of writers of humorous sketches

James Thurber 1894–1961: *My Life and Hard Times* (1937) preface

1 The strongest should come first in comedy because once a character is really established as funny everything he does becomes funny. At least it's that way in life.

F. Scott Fitzgerald 1896–1940: letter, 9 March 1940

2 The funniest thing about comedy is that you never know why people laugh. I know *what* makes them laugh but trying to get your hands on the *why* of it is like trying to pick an eel out of a tub of water.

W. C. Fields 1880–1946: R. J. Anobile *A Flask of Fields* (1972)

3 Good taste and humour . . . are a contradiction in terms, like a chaste whore.

Malcolm Muggeridge 1903–90: in *Time* 14 September 1953

4 Comedy is the noblest form of Stoicism.

W. H. Auden 1907–73: 'Crying Spoils the Appearance' (1957)

5 Humour is the difference between man's aspiration and his achievement.

during his editorship of Punch

Malcolm Muggeridge 1903–90: attributed

6 There are those who, in their pride and their innocence, dedicate their careers to writing humorous pieces. Poor dears, the world is stacked against them from the start, for everybody in it has the right to look at their work and say, 'I don't think that's funny.'

Dorothy Parker 1893–1967: introduction to *The Most of S. J. Perelman* (1959)

7 Humour is emotional chaos remembered in tranquillity.

James Thurber 1894–1961: in *New York Post* 29 February 1960; see **87:1**

8 Comedy is felt to be artificial and escapist; tragedy, toughly real. The opposite view seems more accurate. Tragedy is tender to man's dignity and self-importance, and preserves the illusion that he is a noble creature.

John Carey 1934– : *The Violent Effigy* (1973)

9 [Comedy is] the kindly contemplation of the incongruous.

P. G. Wodehouse 1881–1975: attributed

10 Humour consists of the collision of two different frames of reference.

Arthur Koestler 1905–83: in 1982; attributed

11 Comedy is tragedy that happens to *other* people.

Angela Carter 1940–92: *Wise Children* (1991)

12 I have sat, at the moment of purest heartbreak, in mental agony, and put my thoughts on paper, and then I have taken those thoughts and allocated them to one of my characters, largely for comic effect.

Hilary Mantel 1952– : Clare Boylan (ed.) *The Agony and the Ego* (1993)

13 The world dwindles daily for the humorist . . . Jokes are fast running out, for a joke must transform real life in some perverse way, and real life has begun to perform the same operation perfectly professionally upon itself.

Craig Brown 1957– : *Craig Brown's Greatest Hits* (1993)

14 Anyone like myself who thinks making jokes is a serious matter must regret the eclipse of the Book of Common Prayer because it has diminished the common stock of shared reference on which jokes—and of course it's not only jokes—depend.

Alan Bennett 1934– : *Writing Home* (1994)

Imagination

1 The lunatic, the lover, and the poet,
Are of imagination all compact:
One sees more devils than vast hell can hold,
That is, the madman; the lover, all as frantic,
Sees Helen's beauty in a brow of Egypt:
The poet's eye, in a fine frenzy rolling,
Doth glance from heaven to earth, from earth to heaven.

William Shakespeare 1564–1616: *A Midsummer Night's Dream* (1595–6)

2 And, as imagination bodies forth
The forms of things unknown, the poet's pen
Turns them to shapes, and gives to airy nothing
A local habitation and a name.

William Shakespeare 1564–1616: *A Midsummer Night's Dream* (1595–6)

3 Tell me where is fancy bred.
Or in the heart or in the head?

William Shakespeare 1564–1616: *The Merchant of Venice* (1596–8)

4 That fairy kind of writing which depends only upon the force of imagination.

John Dryden 1631–1700: *King Arthur* (1691)

5 Imagination . . . is the mother of sentiment, the great distinction of our nature, the only purifier of the passions.—Animals have a portion of reason, and equal, if not more exquisite, senses; but no trace of imagination, or of her offspring taste, appears in any of their actions.

Mary Wollstonecraft 1759–97: letter *c.*1795

6 But oh! each visitation
Suspends what nature gave me at my birth,
My shaping spirit of imagination.

Samuel Taylor Coleridge 1772–1834: 'Dejection: an Ode' (1802)

7 Whither is fled the visionary gleam?
Where is it now, the glory and the dream?

William Wordsworth 1770–1850: 'Ode. Intimations of Immortality' (1807)

8 The mind can make
Substance, and people planets of its own
With beings brighter than have been, and give
A breath to forms which can outlive all flesh.

Lord Byron 1788–1824: 'The Dream' (1816)

9 Heard melodies are sweet, but those unheard
Are sweeter.

John Keats 1795–1821: 'Ode on a Grecian Urn' (1820)

10 Such writing is a sort of mental masturbation—he is always f—gg—g his *imagination.*—I don't mean that he is indecent but viciously soliciting his own ideas into a state which is neither poetry nor any thing else but a Bedlam vision produced by raw pork and opium.

of ***Keats***

Lord Byron 1788–1824: letter to John Murray, 9 November 1820

11 The great instrument of moral good is the imagination; and poetry administers to the effect by acting on the cause.

Percy Bysshe Shelley 1792–1822: *A Defence of Poetry* (written 1821)

12 The longing to invent stories grew with violence; everything I heard or read became food for my distemper. The simplicity of truth was not enough for me; I must needs embroider imagination upon it . . . Even now, tho' watched, prayed and striven against, this is still the sin that most easily besets me.

Emily Gosse 1806–57: diary, *c.*1835; Edmund Gosse *Father and Son* (1907)

1 Imagination, which in truth,
Is but another name for absolute power
And clearest insight, amplitude of mind,
And Reason, in her most exalted mood.

William Wordsworth 1770–1850: *The Prelude* (1850)

2 His imagination resembled the wings of an ostrich. It enabled him to run, though not to soar.

Lord Macaulay 1800–59: 'John Dryden' (1828)

3 He said he should prefer not to know the sources of the Nile, and that there should be some unknown regions preserved as hunting-grounds for the poetic imagination.

George Eliot 1819–80: *Middlemarch* (1871–2)

4 Where there is no imagination there is no horror.

Arthur Conan Doyle 1859–1930: *A Study in Scarlet* (1888)

5 For art to exist, for any sort of aesthetic activity or perception to exist, a certain physiological precondition is indispensable: intoxication.

Friedrich Nietzsche 1844–1900: *Twilight of the Idols* (1889)

6 Poets do not go mad; but chess-players do. Mathematicians go mad, and cashiers; but creative artists very seldom. I am not, as will be seen, in any sense attacking logic: I only say that this danger does lie in logic, not in imagination.

G. K. Chesterton 1874–1936: *Orthodoxy* (1908)

7 The balloon of experience is in fact of course tied to the earth, and under that necessity we swing, thanks to a rope of remarkable length, in the more or less commodious car of the imagination; but it is by the rope we know where we are, and from the moment that cable is cut we are at large and unrelated.

Henry James 1843–1916: *The American* (1909 ed.) preface

8 Only in men's imagination does every truth find an effective and undeniable existence. Imagination, not invention, is the supreme master of art, as of life.

Joseph Conrad 1857–1924: *Some Reminiscences* (1912)

9 We had fed the heart on fantasies,
The heart's grown brutal from the fare.

W. B. Yeats 1865–1939: 'Meditations in Time of Civil War' no. 6 'The Stare's Nest by my Window' (1928)

10 In writing novels I have never been able to place much importance upon the distinction between real and imagined. A novelist . . . makes as much or as little use of the real world as he needs to project his vision of life.

Angus Wilson 1913–91: *The Wild Garden* (1963)

11 Imagination is not enough. Knowledge is necessary.

Paul Scott 1920–78: Hilary Spurling *Paul Scott* (1990)

12 The imagination is a kind of electronic machine that takes account of all possible combinations and chooses the ones that are appropriate to a particular purpose, or are simply the most interesting, pleasing, or amusing.

Italo Calvino 1923–85: *Six Memos for the Next Millennium* (1992)

13 To find the psychic energy to pursue a long career, it seems to me, a writer must juggle between a vigorous, recording curiosity about the world and how it works and the ongoing process of self-creation. It is the imagination, of course, that negotiates between reality and the ego.

Edmund White 1940– : *The Burning Library* (1994)

1 Creative writing classes . . . cannot teach the spirit of light that wakes the imagination—kick-starts it like an electric charge.

Jane Gardam 1928– : Clare Boylan (ed.) *The Agony and the Ego* (1993)

2 A true writer's imagination is always bigger than he is, it outreaches his personality. Sometimes this can be felt palpably and thrillingly in the very act of writing, and perhaps it is for this infrequent but soaring sensation that writers, truly, write.

Graham Swift 1949– : Clare Boylan (ed.) *The Agony and the Ego* (1993)

3 The imagination conjures gifts; what the ungrateful, unsentimental part of the mind has to do is to unwrap them, find fault with them, see them for what they are and then alter them.

Rose Tremain 1943– : Clare Boylan (ed.) *The Agony and the Ego* (1993)

4 Invention despoils observation, insinuation invalidates memory. A stewpot of bad habits, all of it—so that imaginative writers wind up, by and large, a shifty crew, sunk in distortion, misrepresentation, illusion, imposture, fakery.

Cynthia Ozick 1928– : *Portrait of the Artist as a Bad Character* (1996)

Inspiration and Creativity see also

Motivation,Writer's Block

5 What is beauty saith my sufferings, then?
If all the pens that ever poets held
Had fed the feeling of their masters' thoughts,
And every sweetness that inspired their hearts,
Their minds, and muses on admired themes:
If all the heavenly quintessence they still
From their immortal flowers of Poesy,
Wherein as in a mirror we perceive
The highest reaches of a human wit;
If these had made one poem's period,
And all combined in beauty's worthiness,
Yet should there hover in their restless heads
One thought, one grace, one wonder at the least,
Which into words no virtue can digest.

Christopher Marlowe 1564–93: *Tamburlaine the Great* (1590)

6 Assist me some extemporal god of rime, for I am sure I shall turn sonneter. Devise, wit; write, pen; for I am for whole volumes in folio.

William Shakespeare 1564–1616: *Love's Labour's Lost* (1595)

7 O! for a Muse of fire, that would ascend
The brightest heaven of invention.

William Shakespeare 1564–1616: *Henry V* (1599)

8 Our poesy is as a gum, which oozes
From whence 'tis nourished: the fire i' the flint
Shows not till it be struck; our gentle flame
Provokes itself.

William Shakespeare 1564–1616: *Timon of Athens* (c.1607)

1 It came from mine own heart, so to my head,
And thence into my fingers tricklèd;
Then to my pen, from whence immediately
On paper I did dribble it daintily.

John Bunyan 1628–88: *The Holy War* (1682) 'Advice to the Reader'

2 What judgement I had increases rather than diminishes; and thoughts, such as they are, come crowding in so fast upon me, that my only difficulty is to choose or reject; to run them into verse or to give them the other harmony of prose.

John Dryden 1631–1700: *Fables Ancient and Modern* (1700)

3 Me . . . no Muse of heav'nly birth inspires,
No judgement tempers when rash genius fires,
Who boast no merit but mere knack of rhyme,
Short gleams of sense, and satire out of time.

Charles Churchill 1731–64: *The Prophecy of Famine* (1763)

4 Just now I've taen the fit o' rhyme,
My barmie noddle's working prime.

Robert Burns 1759–96: 'To J. S[mith]' (1786)

5 It was at Rome, on the fifteenth of October, 1764, as I sat musing amidst the ruins of the Capitol, while the barefoot friars were singing vespers in the Temple of Jupiter, that the idea of writing the decline and fall of the city first started to my mind.

Edward Gibbon 1737–94: *Memoirs of My Life* (1796)

6 On awaking he . . . instantly and eagerly wrote down the lines that are here preserved. At this moment he was unfortunately called out by a person on business from Porlock.

Samuel Taylor Coleridge 1772–1834: 'Kubla Khan' (1816) preliminary note; cf. **114:11, 270:1**

7 I have come to this resolution—never to write for the sake of writing, or making a poem, but from running over with any little knowledge or experience which many years of reflection may perhaps give me—otherwise I shall be dumb.

John Keats 1795–1821: letter to B. R. Haydon, 8 March 1819

8 'We will each write a ghost story,' said Lord Byron; and his proposition was acceded to. There were four of us . . . *Have you thought of a story?* I was asked each morning, and each morning I was forced to reply with a mortifying negative . . . On the morrow I announced that I had *thought of a story* . . . At first I thought but of a few pages—of a short tale; but Shelley urged me to develop the idea at greater length.
on beginning Frankenstein

Mary Shelley 1797–1851: introduction to *Frankenstein* (ed. 3, 1831)

9 Write while the heat is in you . . . The writer who postpones the recording of his thoughts uses an iron which has cooled to burn a hole with. He cannot inflame the minds of his audience.

Henry David Thoreau 1817–62: letter, 10 February 1852

10 From eight o'clock in the morning till half-past four in the evening, Pierre sits there in his room . . . Sometimes the intent ear of Isabel in the next room, overhears the alternate silence, and then the long lonely scratch of his pen. It is as if she heard the busy claw of some midnight mole in the ground . . . In the heart of such silence, surely something is at work? Is it creation, or destruction? Builds

Herman Melville 1819–91: *Pierre* (1852)

Pierre the noble world of a new book? or does the Pale Haggardness unbuild the lungs and the life in him?

1 Urge and urge and urge,
Always the procreant urge of the world.

Walt Whitman 1819–92: 'Song of Myself' (written 1855)

2 Stung by the splendour of a sudden thought.

Robert Browning 1812–89: 'A Death in the Desert' (1864)

3 I kept a scorpion in an empty beer bottle on my table. Now and then the animal was sick; then I used to throw it a piece of soft fruit, which it hurled itself on with fury and into which it poured out its poison; then it became healthy again.

Is there not something similar in us poets? The laws of Nature hold for the intellectual field as well.

Henrik Ibsen 1828–1906: letter, 1870

4 I have many irons on the fire, and am bursting with writableness.

Henry James 1843–1916: letter 29 May 1878

5 To me it would not be more absurd if the shoemaker were to wait for inspiration, or the tallow-chandler for the divine moment of melting.

Anthony Trollope 1815–82: *Autobiography* (1883)

6 Giving birth to a book is always an abominable torture for me, because it cannot answer my imperious need for universality and totality.

Émile Zola 1840–1902: letter, 26 January 1892

7 All fine imaginative work is self-conscious and deliberate.

Oscar Wilde 1854–1900: attributed

8 In Ireland, for a few years more, we have a popular imagination that is fiery and magnificent and tender, so that those of us who wish to write start with a chance that is not given to writers in places where the springtime of the local life has been forgotten and the harvest is a memory only, and the straw has been turned into bricks.

John Millington Synge 1871–1909: introduction to *The Playboy of the Western World* (1907)

9 And least of all can you condemn an artist pursuing, however humbly and imperfectly, a creative aim. In that interior world where his thought and his emotions go seeking for the experience of imagined adventures, there are no policemen, no law, no pressure of circumstance or dread of opinion to keep him within bounds.

Joseph Conrad 1857–1924: *A Personal Record* (1912)

10 A lady beside me made in the course of talk one of those allusions that I have always found myself recognizing on the spot as 'germs' . . . the stray suggestion, the wandering word, the vague echo, at touch of which the novelist's imagination winces as at the prick of some sharp point.

of the effect of a chance remark by a dinner companion

Henry James 1843–1916: preface to *The Spoils of Poynton* (New York edition, 1907–17)

11 Real books should be the offspring not of daylight and casual talk but of darkness and silence.

Marcel Proust 1871–1922: *Time Regained* (1926)

12 The old literature of Ireland . . . has been the chief illumination of my imagination all my life.

W. B. Yeats 1865–1939: speech in the Irish Senate on Irish manuscripts, 1923

13 As an experience, madness is terrific . . . and in its lava I still find most of the things I write about.

Virginia Woolf 1882–1941: letter to Ethel Smyth, 22 June 1930

1 Tempt me no more; for I
Have known the lightning's hour,
The poet's inward pride,
The certainty of power.

C. Day-Lewis 1904–72: *The Magnetic Mountain* (1933)

2 Let us now consider the Personal Daemon of Aristotle and others, of whom it has been truthfully written . . . :
This is the doom of the Makers—their Daemon lives in their pen.
If he be absent or sleeping, they are even as other men . . . Mine came to me early when I sat bewildered among other notions, and said, 'Take this and no other.' I obeyed and was rewarded.

Rudyard Kipling 1865–1936: *Something of Myself* (1937)

3 My Daemon was with me in the *Jungle Books*, *Kim*, and both Puck books, and good care I took to walk delicately lest he should withdraw. I know that he did not, because when these books were finished they said so themselves with, almost, the water-hammer click of a tap turned off.

Rudyard Kipling 1865–1936: *Something of Myself* (1937)

4 Like a piece of ice on a hot stove the poem must ride on its own melting. A poem may be worked over once it is in being, but may not be worried into being.

Robert Frost 1874–1963: 'The Figure a Poem Makes' (1939)

5 I have that continuous uncomfortable feeling of 'things' in the head, like icebergs or rocks or awkwardly placed pieces of furniture. It's as if all the nouns were there but the verbs were lacking . . . And I can't help having the theory that if they are joggled around hard enough and long enough some kind of electricity will occur just by friction.

Elizabeth Bishop 1911–79: letter to Marianne Moore, 11 September 1940

6 I never consciously invented with a pen in my hand; I waited until the story had told itself and then wrote it down, and, since it was already a finished thing, I wrote it fast.

John Buchan 1875–1940: *Memory-Hold-the-Door* (1940)

7 From this the poem springs: that we live in a place
That is not our own and, much more, not ourselves
And hard it is in spite of blazoned days.

Wallace Stevens 1879–1955: 'Notes Towards a Supreme Fiction' (1942)

8 I believe I've got a *book* coming. I feel so excited . . . I walked up Piccadilly and back and went into a Gent's in Brick Street, and suddenly in the Gent's, I saw the three chunks, the beginning, the middle and the end.
on the genesis of The Third Man

Graham Greene 1904–91: letter to Catherine Walston, 30 September 1947

9 Every creative writer worth our consideration, every writer who can be called in the wide eighteenth century use of the term a poet, is a victim: a man given over to an obsession.

Graham Greene 1904–91: 'Walter De La Mare's Short Stories' (1948)

10 I don't know anything about inspiration because I don't know what inspiration is—I've heard about it, but I never saw it.

William Faulkner 1897–1962: interview in *Paris Review* Spring 1956

11 I long for the Person from Porlock
To bring my thoughts to an end,
I am growing impatient to see him
I think of him as a friend.

Stevie Smith 1902–71: 'Thoughts about the "Person from Porlock" ' (1962); cf. **112:6**

1 The impulse to write a novel comes from a momentary unified vision of life.

Angus Wilson 1913–91: *The Wild Garden* (1963)

2 Why does my Muse only speak when she is unhappy?
She does not, I only listen when I am unhappy
When I am happy I live and despise writing
For my Muse this cannot but be dispiriting.

Stevie Smith 1902–71: 'My Muse' (1964)

3 I think I feel on the whole that something's there trying to get out . . . It's sort of trying to get out and wants help.

Ivy Compton-Burnett 1884–1969: Kay Dick *Ivy and Stevie* (1971)

describing the creation of The Lord of the Rings:

4 One writes such a story not out of the leaves of trees still to be observed, nor by means of botany and soil-science; but it grows like a seed in the dark out of the leaf-mould of the mind: out of all that has been seen or thought or read, that has long ago been forgotten, descending into the deeps. No doubt there is much selection, as with a gardener: what one throws on one's personal compost-heap; and my mould is evidently made largely of linguistic matter.

J. R. R. Tolkien 1892–1973: Humphrey Carpenter *J. R. R. Tolkien* (1977)

5 Poets or artists are sometimes married happily to their muse; and sometimes they have a very difficult life with her.

in conversation with Isaiah Berlin

W. H. Auden 1907–73: interview with Isaiah Berlin, *Daily Telegraph* 3 August 1996

6 The artist brings something into the world that didn't exist before, and . . . he does it without destroying something else.

John Updike 1932– : George Plimpton (ed.) *Writers at Work* (4th series, 1977)

7 I imagined the poet in him as an unborn twin, one that could be cruel to him as well as kind.

Paul Scott 1920–78: 'Barbie Batchelor' on her father; *The Towers of Silence* (1971)

8 Deprivation is for me what daffodils were for Wordsworth.

Philip Larkin 1922–85: *Required Writing* (1983)

9 One knows poetry can't be written to order. One waits for something to come through from The Management upstairs and The Management can be very capricious.

responding to the lukewarm reception given to his celebratory poem on the wedding of Princess Anne

John Betjeman 1906–84: attributed

10 'The Wreck of the Deutschland' would have been markedly inferior if Hopkins had been a survivor from the passenger list.

Philip Larkin 1922–85: attributed

asked why he wrote The Name of the Rose:

11 I felt like poisoning a monk.

Umberto Eco 1932– : George Plimpton (ed.) *The Writer's Chapbook* (1989)

12 It's inevitably the case that whatever idea impels you to write a novel turns out to appear in the book as an afterthought.

Douglas Adams 1952– : Stan Nicholls (ed.) *Wordsmiths of Wonder* (1993)

13 If I feel the need for inspiration I read the OED.

Anthony Burgess 1917–93: Clare Boylan (ed.) *The Agony and the Ego* (1993)

1 I came across a letter of Thackeray's in which he talked of a novel 'a-boilin' up in my interior' . . . But now, fifteen years later, I know they don't always boil up: sometimes the purpose can come before the inspiration.

Margaret Forster 1938– : Clare Boylan (ed.) *The Agony and the Ego* (1993)

2 The movement is from delight to wisdom and not vice versa. The felicity of a cadence, the chain reaction of a rhyme, the pleasuring of an etymology, such things can proceed happily and as it were autistically, in an area of mental operations cordoned off by and from the critical sense.

Seamus Heaney 1939– : *The Redress of Poetry* (1995)

3 Very little experience, the merest whiff of a situation or story, may be sufficient stimulus for a writer's imagination. Stendhal found the germ of *Scarlet and Black* in a newspaper report a couple of paragraphs long. Tolstoy also found his inspiration for *Anna Karenina* in a similarly brief report.

Allan Massie 1938– : Barry Turner *The Writer's Companion* (1996)

4 I say a prayer and God gives me a plot immediately. I write almost as if it was dictated by him.

Barbara Cartland 1901– : in *Sunday Times* 10 March 1996

5 I wrote *Cider with Rosie* in an attic in London; I couldn't have written it here [in Gloucestershire] . . . You can't write about love while you're still in bed. You can't write a love story in a bedroom. I had to be in London, I had to get the atmospheres blowing through the distance of time.

Laurie Lee 1914– : in *Guardian* 22 June 1996

Intelligence see **Knowledge and Intelligence**

Irony see also **Humour, Wit and Satire**

6 There may be men so diabolic,
To think my praise is hyperbolic;
Or venture, with an envious leer
I write these lines in *yronia*.

Nicolas de Bibera fl. 13th century AD: *Carmen Satyricum* (*c.*1281–2), tr. Dilwyn Knox

7 By his needle he understands ironia,
That with one eye looks two ways at once.

Thomas Middleton *c.*1580–1627: *The World Tossed at Tennis* (with William Rowley, 1620)

8 An irony is a nipping jest, or a speech that hath the honey of pleasantness in its mouth, and a sting of rebuke in its tail.

Edward Reyner 1600–68: *Rules for the Government of the Tongue* (1656)

9 A mode of speech of which the meaning is contrary to the words.
definition of irony

Samuel Johnson 1709–84: *A Dictionary of the English Language* (1755)

10 Irony is that little grain of salt which alone renders the dish palatable.

Johann Wolfgang von Goethe 1749–1832: attributed

11 A drayman, in a passion, calls out, 'You are a pretty fellow,' without suspecting that he is uttering irony.

Lord Macaulay 1800–59: 'Lord Bacon' (1843)

12 Remember . . . that women, children, and revolutionists hate irony, which is the negation of all faith, of all devotion, of all action.

Joseph Conrad 1857–1924: Sophia Antonovna in *Under Western Eyes* (1911)

1 Finding the inappropriate word—the device upon which irony depends.

John Carey 1934– : *The Violent Effigy* (1973)

2 Irony . . . may be defined as what people miss.

Julian Barnes 1946–: *A History of the World in 10½ Chapters* (1989)

Journalism see also **Newpapers**

3 All accounts of gallantry, pleasure and entertainment, shall be under the article of White's Chocolate-house; poetry, under Will's Coffee-house; learning, under the title of Graecian; foreign and domestic news, you will have from St James's Coffee-house; and what else I shall on any subject offer, shall be dated from my own apartment.
what ***Steele*** *intended* The Tatler *to provide*

Richard Steele 1672–1729: *The Tatler* 12 April 1709

4 In a time of war . . . the task of news-writers is easy; they have nothing to do but to tell that the battle is expected, and afterwards that a battle has been fought, in which we and our friends, whether conquering or conquered, did all, and our enemies did nothing.

Samuel Johnson 1709–84: in *The Idler* 11 November 1758

5 The journalists have constructed for themselves a little wooden chapel, which they also call the Temple of Fame, in which they put up and take down portraits all day long and make such a hammering you can't hear yourself speak.

Georg Christoph Lichtenberg 1742–99: A. Leitzmann *Georg Christoph Lichtenberg Aphorismen* (1904)

6 The man must have a rare recipe for melancholy, who can be dull in Fleet Street.

Charles Lamb 1775–1834: letter to Thomas Manning, 15 February 1802

7 Newspaper writing is a thing *sui generis*; it is to literature what brandy is to beverage.

Thomas Barnes 1785–1841: P. Howard *We Thundered Out* (1985)

8 All newspaper and journalistic activity is an intellectual brothel from which there is no retreat.

Leo Tolstoy 1828–1910: letter to Prince V. P. Meshchersky, 22 August 1871

9 To any young writer who solicited my advice I would say: 'As you learn to swim by flinging yourself into water, so learn to write by flinging yourself into journalism.' It is the only virile school we have; it is there that one measures oneself against other men, and there . . . that one forges one's style on the terrible anvil of daily deadlines.

Émile Zola 1840–1902: *Le Figaro* 1881

10 I hate journalists. There is nothing in them but tittering, jeering emptiness. They have all made what Dante calls the Great Refusal. That is, they have ceased to be self-centred, have given up their individuality.

W. B. Yeats 1865–1939: letter to Katharine Tynan, 1888

11 Journalism largely consists in saying 'Lord Jones Dead' to people who never knew that Lord Jones was alive.

G. K. Chesterton 1874–1936: *The Wisdom of Father Brown* (1914)

12 Journalists say a thing that they know isn't true, in the hope that if they keep on saying it long enough it *will* be true.

Arnold Bennett 1867–1931: *The Title* (1918)

1 Comment is free, but facts are sacred.

C. P. Scott 1846–1932: in *Manchester Guardian* 5 May 1921; cf. **00:00**

2 The art of newspaper paragraphing is to stroke a platitude until it purrs like an epigram.

Don Marquis 1878–1937: E. Anthony *O Rare Don Marquis* (1962)

3 You cannot hope
to bribe or twist,
thank God! the
British journalist.
But, seeing what
the man will do
unbribed, there's
no occasion to.

Humbert Wolfe 1886–1940: 'Over the Fire' (1930)

4 Journalism's a shrew and scold; I like her.
She makes you sick, she makes you old; I like her.
She's daily trouble, storm and strife;
She's love and hate and death and life;
She ain't no lady—she's my wife; I like her.

Franklin P. Adams 1881–1960: in *The New York World* 27 February 1931 (final issue)

5 It is questionable whether anyone who has had long experience as a freelance journalist ought to become an editor. It is too like taking a convict out of his cell and making him governor of a prison.

George Orwell 1903–50: in *Tribune* 31 January 1947

6 The first aim of the journalist is to interest; of the historian it is to instruct—of course the good journalist and the good historian try to do both.

A. J. P. Taylor 1906–90: BBC broadcast 13 January 1948

7 Usually he confined himself to written comments. His later famed 'What mean?' 'Who he?' and the like began to appear on manuscripts and proofs.
of Harold Ross (1892–1951) as editor of the New Yorker

Dale Kramer 1936– : *Ross and The New Yorker* (1952)

8 If your sons are not inclined to the Church, send them into journalism.

Lord Beaverbrook 1879–1964: attributed, 1955

9 Journalist is to politician as dog is to lamppost.

H. L. Mencken 1880–1956: attributed; cf. **50:14**

10 It is really more like manufacturing synthetic whipped cream out of the by-products of a plastic factory than anything remotely connected with writing—even journalistic writing.
of writing under contract to Life *magazine*

Elizabeth Bishop 1911–79: letter to Pearl Kazin, 13 August 1961

11 In journalism one has to be so brash and glib with generalities and labels.

Philip Larkin 1922–85: letter, 8 April 1963

12 Journalism is still an underdeveloped profession and, accordingly, newspapermen are quite often regarded as were surgeons and musicians a century ago, as having the rank, roughly speaking, of barbers and riding masters.

Walter Lippmann 1889–1974: attributed, 1965

13 Success in journalism can be a form of failure. Freedom comes from lack of possessions. The truth-divulging paper must imitate the tramp and sleep under a hedge.

Graham Greene 1904–91: in *New Statesman* 31 May 1968

1 Comment is free but facts are on expenses.

Tom Stoppard 1937– : *Night and Day* (1978); cf. **00:00**

2 The media. It sounds like a convention of spiritualists.

Tom Stoppard 1937– : *Night and Day* (1978)

3 Rock journalism is people who can't write interviewing people who can't talk for people who can't read.

Frank Zappa 1940–93: Linda Botts *Loose Talk* (1980)

4 Every journalist should be a dissident.

John Pilger 1939– : in *Guardian* 16 October 1989

5 Journalists belong in the gutter because that is where the ruling classes throw their guilty secrets.

Gerald Priestland 1927–91: in *Observer* 22 May 1988 'Sayings of the Week'

6 I used to tell young reporters that if they wanted to learn to write magnificent NEWSPAPER English they should learn to write like Daniel Defoe. None of them did.

Robertson Davies 1913–95: in *Paris Review* 1989

7 Journalism could be described as turning one's enemies into money.

Craig Brown 1957– : in *Daily Telegraph* 28 September 1990

8 What the man in the street wants to read is not what he has said already but what he would like to have said if he had thought of it first.

Keith Waterhouse 1929– : in *Intercity* 26 October 1990

9 Fleet Street can scent the possibilities of sex like a tile-tripping tomcat.

Julian Barnes 1946– : *Letters from London* (1995)

10 Many people . . . would no more think of entering journalism than the sewage business, which at least does us all some good.

Stephen Fry 1957– : in *Independent* 25 February 1995 'Quote Unquote'

11 Journalism encourages haste . . . and haste is the enemy of art.

Jeanette Winterson 1959– : *Art Objects* (1995)

Knowledge and Intelligence

12 Whence is thy learning? Hath thy toil
O'er books consumed the midnight oil?

John Gay 1685–1732: *Fables* (1727)

13 There is a North-west passage to the intellectual World.

Laurence Sterne 1713–68: *Tristram Shandy* (1759–67)

14 If the doors of perception were cleansed everything would appear to man as it is, infinite.

William Blake 1757–1827: *The Marriage of Heaven and Hell* (1790–3)

15 The petrifactions of a plodding brain.

Lord Byron 1788–1824: *English Bards and Scotch Reviewers* (1809)

16 Negative Capability, that is when man is capable of being in uncertainties, mysteries, doubts, without any irritable reaching after fact and reason.

John Keats 1795–1821: letter to George and Thomas Keats, 21 December 1817

17 You, for example, clever to a fault,
The rough and ready man who write apace,
Read somewhat seldomer, think perhaps even less.

Robert Browning 1812–89: 'Bishop Blougram's Apology' (1855)

1 So complete was my father's reliance on the influence of reason over the mind of mankind, whenever it is allowed to reach them, that he felt as if all would be gained if the whole population were taught to read, if all sorts of opinions were allowed to be addressed to them by word and in writing, and if, by means of the suffrage, they could nominate a legislation to give effect to the opinions they adopted.

John Stuart Mill 1806–73: *Autobiography* (1873)

2 The intellect is not a serious thing, and never has been. It is an instrument on which one plays, that is all.

Oscar Wilde 1854–1900: *A Woman of No Importance* (1893)

3 The nihilists, the intellectual, hopeless people—Ibsen, Flaubert, Hardy—represent the dream we are waking from.

D. H. Lawrence 1885–1930: in *Rhythm* March 1913 'Georgian Poetry'

4 *La trahison des clercs.*

The treachery of the intellectuals.

Julien Benda 1867–1956: title of book (1927)

5 What is a highbrow? He is a man who has found something more interesting than women.

Edgar Wallace 1875–1932: in *New York Times* 24 January 1932

6 The test of a first-rate intelligence is the ability to hold two opposed ideas in the mind at the same time, and still retain the ability to function.

F. Scott Fitzgerald 1896–1940: in *Esquire* February 1936, 'The Crack-Up'

7 To the man-in-the-street, who, I'm sorry to say,
Is a keen observer of life,
The word 'Intellectual' suggests straight away
A man who's untrue to his wife.

W. H. Auden 1907–73: *New Year Letter* (1941)

8 There can be no two opinions as to what a highbrow is. He is the man or woman of thoroughbred intelligence who rides his mind at a gallop across country in pursuit of an idea.

Virginia Woolf 1882–1941: *The Death of the Moth* (1942) 'Middlebrow'

9 An intellectual is someone whose mind watches itself.

Albert Camus 1913–60: *Carnets, 1935–42* (1962)

10 Knowledge is a polite word for dead but not buried imagination.

e. e. cummings 1894–1962: *Jottings* in *Wake* (1951)

11 A spirit of national masochism prevails, encouraged by an effete corps of impudent snobs who characterize themselves as intellectuals.

Spiro T. Agnew 1918–96: speech in New Orleans, 19 October 1969

12 Intellectuals are people who believe that ideas are of more importance than values. That is to say, their own ideas and other people's values.

Gerald Brenan 1894–1987: *Thoughts in a Dry Season* (1978) 'Life'

13 But I'm such a bad scholar, I feel like a man with a white cane knocking into knowledge.

Peter Carey 1943– : in *Sunday Times* 20 March 1988

14 When an old man dies, a library burns down.

Anonymous: African proverb

Language see also **Grammar, Languages**

15 The chief merit of language is clearness, and we know that nothing detracts so much from this as do unfamiliar terms.

Galen AD 129–99: *On the Natural Faculties*

1 It has been well said, that heart speaks to heart, whereas language only speaks to the ears.

St Francis of Sales 1567–1622: letter to the Archbishop of Bourges, 5 October 1604, which John Henry Newman paraphrased for his motto as *'cor ad cor loquitur* [heart speaks to heart]'

2 He tickles this age that can
Call Tullia's ape a marmasyte
And Leda's goose a swan.

Anonymous: 'Fara diddle dyno'; Thomas Weelkes *Airs or Fantastic Spirits* (1608)

3 Lovely enchanting language, sugar-cane,
Honey of roses!

George Herbert 1593–1633: 'The Forerunners' (1633)

4 Good heavens! For more than forty years I have been speaking prose without knowing it.

Molière 1622–73: *Le Bourgeois Gentilhomme* (1671)

5 Words may be false and full of art,
Sighs are the natural language of the heart.

Thomas Shadwell *c.*1642–92: *Psyche* (1675)

6 The true use of speech is not so much to express our wants as to conceal them.

Oliver Goldsmith 1728–74: in *The Bee* 20 October 1759 'On the Use of Language'

7 Language is the dress of thought.

Samuel Johnson 1709–84: *Lives of the English Poets* (1779–81); cf. **121:10**

8 He gave man speech, and speech created thought,
Which is the measure of the universe.

Percy Bysshe Shelley 1792–1822: *Prometheus Unbound* (1820)

9 Every age has a language of its own; and the difference in the words is often far greater than in the thoughts. The main employment of authors, in their collective capacity, is to translate the thoughts of other ages into the language of their own.

Augustus Hare 1834–1903: *Guesses at Truth* (1827)

10 Language is called the garment of thought: however, it should rather be, language is the flesh-garment, the body, of thought.

Thomas Carlyle 1795–1881: *Sartor Resartus* (1834); cf. **121:7**

11 Under all speech that is good for anything there lies a silence that is better. Silence is deep as Eternity; speech is shallow as Time.

Thomas Carlyle 1795–1881: *Critical and Miscellaneous Essays* (1838) 'Sir Walter Scott'

12 Language is fossil poetry.

Ralph Waldo Emerson 1803–82: *Essays. Second Series* (1844) 'The Poet'

13 Human speech is like a cracked kettle on which we tap crude rhythms for bears to dance to, while we long to make music that will melt the stars.

Gustave Flaubert 1821–80: *Madame Bovary* (1857)

14 Speech is the small change of silence.

George Meredith 1828–1909: *The Ordeal of Richard Feverel* (1859)

15 Take care of the sense, and the sounds will take care of themselves.

Lewis Carroll 1832–98: *Alice's Adventures in Wonderland* (1865)

16 The bond between the signifier and the signified is arbitrary.

Ferdinand de Saussure 1857–1913: *Course in General Linguistics* (1916)

1 Language is a system of interdependent terms in which the value of each term results solely from the simultaneous presence of the others.

Ferdinand de Saussure 1857–1913: *Course in General Linguistics* (1916)

2 In language there are only differences.

Ferdinand de Saussure 1857–1913: *Course in General Linguistics* (1916)

3 Language can . . . be compared with a sheet of paper: thought is the front and sound the back; one cannot cut the front without cutting the back at the same time.

Ferdinand de Saussure 1857–1913: *Course in General Linguistics* (1916)

4 The limits of my language mean the limits of my world.

Ludwig Wittgenstein 1889–1951: *Tractatus Logico-Philosophicus* (1922)

5 What can be said at all can be said clearly; and whereof one cannot speak thereof one must be silent.

Ludwig Wittgenstein 1889–1951: *Tractatus Logico-Philosophicus* (1922)

6 There's a cool web of language winds us in,
Retreat from too much joy or too much fear.

Robert Graves 1895–1985: 'The Cool Web' (1927)

7 Since our concern was speech, and speech impelled us
To purify the dialect of the tribe
And urge the mind to aftersight and foresight.

T. S. Eliot 1888–1965: *Four Quartets* 'Little Gidding' (1942)

8 Don't you see that the whole aim of Newspeak is to narrow the range of thought? In the end we shall make thoughtcrime literally impossible, because there will be no words in which to express it.

George Orwell 1903–50: *Nineteen Eighty-Four* (1949)

9 The great enemy of clear language is insincerity. When there is a gap between one's real and one's declared aims, one turns as it were instinctively to long words and exhausted idioms, like a cuttlefish squirting out ink.

George Orwell 1903–50: *Shooting an Elephant* (1950) 'Politics and the English Language'

10 The linguistic philosophy, which cares only about language, and not about the world, is like the boy who preferred the clock without the pendulum because, although it no longer told the time, it went more easily than before and at a more exhilarating pace.

Bertrand Russell 1872–1970: foreword to Ernest Gellner *Words and Things* (1959)

11 Slang is a language that rolls up its sleeves, spits on its hands and goes to work.

Carl Sandburg 1878–1967: in *New York Times* 13 February 1959

12 Different persons growing up in the same language are like different bushes trimmed and trained to take the shape of identical elephants. The anatomical details of twigs and branches will fulfill the elephantine shape differently from bush to bush, but the overall outward results are alike.

W. V. Quine 1908– : *Word and Object* (1960)

13 Language is a form of human reason, and has its reasons which are unknown to man.

Claude Lévi-Strauss 1908– : *La Pensée sauvage* (1962)

14 It is language which speaks, not the author.

Roland Barthes 1915–80: *The Death of the Author* (1968)

15 A language is a dialect with an army and a navy.

Max Weinreich 1894–1969: Steven Pinker *The Language Instinct* (1994)

1 The unconscious is structured like a language.

Jacques Lacan 1901–81: *Écrits* (1966)

2 Linguistic analysis. A lot of chaps pointing out that we don't always mean what we say, even when we manage to say what we meant.

Tom Stoppard 1937– : *Professional Foul* (1978)

3 As long as our language is inadequate, our vision remains formless.

Adrienne Rich 1929– : *On Lies, Secrets, and Silence* (1980)

4 The polymorphic visions of the eyes and the spirit are contained in uniform lines of small or capital letters, periods, commas, parentheses—pages of signs, packed as closely together as grains of sand, representing the many-coloured spectacle of the world on a surface that is always the same and always different, like dunes shifted by the desert wind.

Italo Calvino 1923–85: *Six Memos for the Next Millennium* (1992)

5 Literature . . . is the Promised Land in which language becomes what it really ought to be.

Italo Calvino 1923–85: *Six Memos for the Next Millennium* (1992)

6 Language tethers us to the world; without it we spin like atoms.

Penelope Lively 1933– : *Moon Tiger* (1987)

7 Language is obviously as different from other animals' communication systems as the elephant's trunk is different from other animals' nostrils.

Steven Pinker 1954– : *The Language Instinct* (1994)

8 A word, in a word, is complicated.

Steven Pinker 1954– : *The Language Instinct* (1994)

9 A book is a riverbank for the river of language. Language without the riverbank is only television talk—a free fall, a loose splash, a spill.

Cynthia Ozick 1928– : *Portrait of the Artist as a Bad Character* (1996)

Languages see also Language

10 Ye knowe ek that in forme of speche is chaunge
Withinne a thousand yeer, and wordes tho
That hadden pris, now wonder nyce and straunge
Us thinketh hem, and yet thei spake hem so.

Geoffrey Chaucer *c.*1343–1400: *Troilus and Criseyde*

11 So now they have made our English tongue a gallimaufry or hodgepodge of all other speeches.

Edmund Spenser *c.*1552–99: *The Shepherd's Calendar* (1579)

12 Away with him! away with him! he speaks Latin.

William Shakespeare 1564–1616: *Henry VI, Part 2* (1592)

13 Poets that lasting marble seek
Must carve in Latin or in Greek.

Edmund Waller 1606–87: 'Of English Verse' (1645)

14 To speak English, one must place the tongue between the teeth, and I have lost my teeth
*to James **Boswell**, 24 December 1764*

Voltaire 1694–1778: Frederick A Pottle (ed.) *Boswell on the Grand Tour* (1953)

15 I am not like a lady at the court of Versailles, who said: 'What a dreadful pity that the bother at the tower of Babel should have got language all mixed up; but for that, everyone would always have spoken French.'

Voltaire 1694–1778: letter to Catherine the Great, 26 May 1767

1 I am always sorry when any language is lost, because languages are the pedigree of nations.

Samuel Johnson 1709–84: James Boswell *Journal of a Tour to the Hebrides* (1785) 18 September 1773

2 Philologists, who chase
A panting syllable through time and space,
Start it at home, and hunt it in the dark,
To Gaul, to Greece, and into Noah's ark.

William Cowper 1731–1800: 'Retirement' (1782)

3 What is not clear is not French.

Antoine de Rivarol 1753–1801: *Discours sur l'Universalité de la Langue Française* (1784)

4 I like that ancient Saxon phrase, which calls
The burial-ground God's-Acre!

Henry Wadsworth Longfellow 1807–82: 'God's-Acre' (1841)

5 I must learn Spanish, one of these days,
Only for that slow sweet name's sake.

Robert Browning 1812–89: 'The Flower's Name' (1845)

6 None of your live languages for Miss Blimber. They must be dead—stone dead—and then Miss Blimber dug them up like a Ghoul.

Charles Dickens 1812–70: *Dombey and Son* (1848)

7 The great breeding people had gone out and multiplied; colonies in every clime attest our success; French is the *patois* of Europe; English is the language of the world.

Walter Bagehot 1826–77: in *National Review* January 1856 'Edward Gibbon'

8 Life is short and art is long, indeed nearly impossible when one is writing in a language that is worn to the point of being threadbare, so worm-eaten that it frays at every touch.

Gustave Flaubert 1821–80: letter, 18 February 1859; cf. **6:9**

9 Speak in French when you can't think of the English for a thing.

Lewis Carroll 1832–98: *Through the Looking-Glass* (1872)

10 I once heard a Californian student in Heidelberg say, in one of his calmest moods, that he would rather decline two drinks than one German adjective.

Mark Twain 1835–1910: *A Tramp Abroad* (1880)

11 The knowledge of the ancient languages is mainly a luxury.

John Bright 1811–89: letter in *Pall Mall Gazette* 30 November 1886

12 Nobody can say a word against Greek: it stamps a man at once as an educated gentleman.

George Bernard Shaw 1856–1950: *Major Barbara* (1907)

13 There is no language like the Irish for soothing and quieting.

John Millington Synge 1871–1909: *The Aran Islands* (1907)

14 Remember that you are a human being with a soul and the divine gift of articulate speech: that your native language is the language of Shakespeare and Milton and The Bible; and don't sit there crooning like a bilious pigeon.

George Bernard Shaw 1856–1950: *Pygmalion* (1916)

15 Written English is now inert and inorganic: not stem and leaf and flower, not even trim and well-joined masonry, but a daub of untempered mortar.

A. E. Housman 1859–1936: in *Cambridge Review* 1917

1 By being so long in the lowest form [at Harrow] I gained an immense advantage over the cleverer boys. They all went on to learn Latin and Greek . . . . But I was taught English. . . . Thus I got into my bones the essential structure of the ordinary British sentence — which is a noble thing. . . . Naturally I am biased in favour of boys learning English. I would make them all learn English: and then I would let the clever ones learn Latin as an honour, and Greek as a treat.

Winston Churchill 1874–1965: *My Early Life* (1930)

2 Learning French is some trouble, but after that you have a clear and beautiful language; in English the undergrowth is part of the language and listed in NED.

NED = the New *(later the* Oxford*)* English Dictionary

William Empson 1906–84: in *Spectator* 14 June 1935

3 Heinrich Heine so loosened the corsets of the German language that even little salesmen can fondle her breasts.

Karl Kraus 1874–1936: *Half-truths and One-and-a-half Truths* 'Riddles'

4 It is a difficulty in writing English that the sound of the living voice dominates the look of the printed word.

W. Somerset Maugham 1874–1965: *The Summing Up* (1938)

5 The great tragedy of the classical languages is to have been born twins.

Geoffrey Madan 1895–1947: *Geoffrey Madan's Notebooks* (1981)

6 For sheer dirtiness of fighting, the feud between the inventors of the international languages would take a lot of beating.

George Orwell 1903–50: Robert Pearce (ed.) *The Sayings of George Orwell* (1994)

7 England and America are two countries divided by a common language.

George Bernard Shaw 1856–1950: attributed in this and other forms, but not found in Shaw's published writings

8 Greek the language they gave me;
poor the house on Homer's shores.
My only care my language on Homer's shores.

Odysseus Elytēs 1911–96: 'The Axion Esti' (1959)

9 I don't know why you waste your time with Anglo-Saxon, instead of studying something useful like Latin or Greek!

to her son, Jorge Luis ***Borges****, c.*1964

Leonor Acevedo Borges 1876–1975: Alberto Manguel *A History of Reading* (1996); cf. **125:12, 141:11**

10 Waiting for the German verb is surely the ultimate thrill.

Flann O'Brien 1911–66: *The Hair of the Dogma* (1977)

11 At various times I have asked myself what reasons
Moved me to study while my night came down,
Without particular hope of satisfaction,
The language of the blunt-tongued Anglo-Saxons.

Jorge Luis Borges 1899–1986: 'Poem Written in a Copy of Beowulf' (1972), tr. Alastair Reid

12 All praise to the inexhaustible
Labyrinth of cause and effect
Which, before unveiling to me the mirror
Where I shall see no one or shall see some other self,
Has granted me this perfect contemplation
Of a language at its dawn.

Jorge Luis Borges 1899–1986: 'Embarking on the Study of Anglo-Saxon Grammar' (1972), tr. Alastair Reid; cf. **125:9**

1 The fluidity of Greek, punctuated by hardness, and with its surface glitter captivated me. But part of the attraction was antiquity and alien remoteness (from me): it did not touch home.

J. R. R. Tolkien 1892–1973: Humphrey Carpenter *J. R. R. Tolkien* (1977)

of his discovery of Finnish:

2 It was like discovering a wine-cellar filled with bottles of amazing wine of a kind and flavour never tasted before. It quite intoxicated me.

J. R. R. Tolkien 1892–1973: Humphrey Carpenter *J. R. R. Tolkien* (1977)

3 Stylists used to revere 'pure' English, but in reality English is about as pure as factory effluent, and has displayed its mongrel toughness over the centuries by cannibalizing a picturesque array of foreign tongues from Greek to Polynesian.

John Carey 1934– : in *Sunday Times* 27 January 1985

4 Italian is the only language in which the word *vago* (vague) also means 'lovely, attractive'.

Italo Calvino 1923–85: *Six Memos for the Next Millennium* (1992)

5 We are walking lexicons. In a single sentence of idle chatter we preserve Latin, Anglo-Saxon, Norse; we carry a museum inside our heads, each day we commemorate peoples of whom we have never heard.

Penelope Lively 1933– : *Moon Tiger* (1987)

6 Others may speak and read English—more or less—but it is our language, not theirs. It was made in England by the English and it remains our distinctive property, however widely it is learnt or used.

Enoch Powell 1912–98: speech to the Royal Society of St George, April 1988; in *Sunday Times* 14 January 1990

7 To deny a boy or girl the opportunity to read and write Latin is cruelty to children.

Enoch Powell 1912–98: in *Independent* 2 June 1990

8 Because the Welsh language has survived the oppression of the English language there are older words than Anglo-Saxon ones which are still heard on Welsh rugby touchlines.

view of the author of 'the first erotic novel to be written in Welsh'

Andrew Bennett : in *Daily Telegraph* 8 October 1994 'They Said It'

9 There is no such thing as an ugly language. Today I hear every language as if it were the only one, and when I hear of one that is dying, it overwhelms me as though it were the death of the earth.

Elias Canetti 1905–94: *The Secret Heart of the Clock* (1994)

10 English is the great vacuum cleaner of languages: it sucks in anything it can get.

David Crystal 1941– : in *Daily Telegraph* 30 December 1995 'They Said It In 1995'

Last Words see also **Death**

11 What Cato did, and Addison approved,
Cannot be wrong.

lines found on his desk after he, too, had taken his own life

Eustace Budgell 1686–1737: Colley Cibber *Lives of the Poets* (1753) vol. 5 'Life of Eustace Budgell'

12 This is no time for making new enemies.

on being asked to renounce the Devil on his deathbed

Voltaire 1694–1778: attributed

1 Here lies one whose name was writ in water.
epitaph for himself

John Keats 1795–1821: Richard Monckton Milnes *Life, Letters and Literary Remains of John Keats* (1848)

2 Well, I've had a happy life.

William Hazlitt 1778–1830: W. C. Hazlitt *Memoirs of William Hazlitt* (1867)

3 More light!

Johann Wolfgang von Goethe 1749–1832: attributed; actually 'Open the second shutter, so that more light can come in'

4 God will pardon me, it is His trade.

Heinrich Heine 1797–1856: Alfred Meissner *Heinrich Heine. Erinnerungen* (1856)

5 It's been so long since I've had champagne.
after which, he slowly drank the glass and died

Anton Chekhov 1860–1904: Henri Troyat *Chekhov* (1984)

6 On the contrary.
after a nurse had said that he 'seemed to be a little better'

Henrik Ibsen 1828–1906: Michael Meyer *Ibsen* (1967)

7 In this life there's nothing new in dying,
But nor, of course, is living any newer.
Yesenin's final poem, written in his own blood the day before he hanged himself in his Leningrad hotel room, 28 December 1925

Sergei Yesenin 1895–1925: 'Goodbye, my Friend, Goodbye', translated by Gordon McVay

8 If this is dying, then I don't think much of it.

Lytton Strachey 1880–1932: Michael Holroyd *Lytton Strachey* vol. 2 (1968)

9 On limestone quarried near the spot
By his command these words are cut:
Cast a cold eye
On life, on death.
Horseman pass by!
the last three lines are used as Yeats's own epitaph

W. B. Yeats 1865–1939: 'Under Ben Bulben' (1939)

10 And were an epitaph to be my story
I'd have a short one ready for my own.
I would have written of me on my stone:
I had a lover's quarrel with the world.

Robert Frost 1874–1963: 'The Lesson for Today' (1942)

11 Just before she [Stein] died she asked, 'What *is* the answer?' No answer came. She laughed and said, 'In that case what is the question?' Then she died.

Gertrude Stein 1874–1946: Donald Sutherland *Gertrude Stein, A Biography of her Work* (1951)

12 The woman is perfected
Her dead
Body wears the smile of accomplishment.
opening lines of her last poem, written a week before her suicide

Sylvia Plath 1932–63: 'Edge'

13 Below my window . . . the blossom is out in full now . . . I *see* it is the whitest, frothiest, blossomiest blossom that there ever could be, and I can see it. Things are both more trivial than they ever were, and more important than they

Dennis Potter 1935–94: interview with Melvyn Bragg on Channel 4, March 1994, in *Seeing the Blossom* (1994)

ever were, and the difference between the trivial and the important doesn't seem to matter. But the nowness of everything is absolutely wondrous.

on his heightened awareness of things, in the face of his imminent death

1 Lord take my soul, but the struggle continues.

last words before he was hanged

Ken Saro-Wiwa 1941–95: in *Daily Telegraph* 13 November 1995

Letters

2 Ye see how large a letter I have written unto you with mine own hand.

Bible: Galatians

3 There is nothing to write about, you say. Well then, write and let me know just this—that there is nothing to write about; or tell me in the good old style if you are well.

Pliny the Younger AD *c.*61–*c.*112: *Letters*

4 . . . *Verbosa et grandis epistula venit*
A Capreis.

A huge wordy letter came from Capri.

on the Emperor Tiberius's letter to the Senate, which caused the downfall of Sejanus in AD *31*

Juvenal AD *c.*60–*c.*130: *Satires*

5 Sir, more than kisses, letters mingle souls.

John Donne 1572–1631: 'To Sir Henry Wotton' (1597–8)

6 I knew one that when he wrote a letter he would put that which was most material in the postscript, as if it had been a bymatter.

Francis Bacon 1561–1626: *Essays* (1625) 'Of Cunning'

7 All letters, methinks, should be free and easy as one's discourse, not studied as an oration, nor made up of hard words like a charm.

Dorothy Osborne 1627–95: letter to William Temple, September 1653

8 A woman seldom writes her mind but in her postscript.

Richard Steele 1672–1729: in *The Spectator* 31 May 1711

9 An odd thought strikes me:—we shall receive no letters in the grave.

Samuel Johnson 1709–84: James Boswell *Life of Samuel Johnson* (1791) December 1784

10 I have now attained the true art of letter-writing, which we are always told is to express on paper exactly what one would say to the same person by word of mouth.

Jane Austen 1775–1817: letter to her sister Cassandra, 3 January 1801

11 My dear Isa, I now sit down on my botom to answer all your kind and beloved letters which you was so good as to write to me.

Marjory Fleming 1803–11: letter to Isabella; *Journals, Letters and Verses* (ed. A. Esdaile, 1934)

12 She'll vish there wos more, and that's the great art o' letter writin'.

Charles Dickens 1812–70: *Pickwick Papers* (1837)

13 Correspondences are like small-clothes before the invention of suspenders; it is impossible to keep them up.

Sydney Smith 1771–1845: letter to Catherine Crowe, 31 January 1841

1 Life is too precious to be spent in this weaving and unweaving of false impressions, and it is better to live quietly under some degree of misrepresentation than to attempt to remove it by the uncertain process of letter-writing.

George Eliot 1819–80: letter to Mrs Peter Taylor, 8 June 1856

2 I would any day as soon kill a pig as write a letter.
on his dislike of personal correspondence

Alfred, Lord Tennyson 1809–92: remark made in the 1850s; Ann Thwaite *Emily Tennyson* (1996)

3 The slowest and most intermittent talker must *seem* fluent in letter-writing. He may have taken half-an-hour to compose his second sentence; but there it is, close after the first!

Lewis Carroll 1832–98: *Sylvie and Bruno Concluded* (1893)

4 Letter writing is a terrible venture of a man's soul . . . You may have changed your mind, or seen reason to feel quite coldly towards your correspondent, long before your production finds its way into his hands.

Robert Louis Stevenson 1850–94: Roger C. Swearingen (ed.) *An Old Song and Edifying Letters of the Rutherford Family* (1982)

5 You don't know a woman until you have had a letter from her.

Ada Leverson 1865–1936: *Tenterhooks* (1912)

6 It is wonderful how much news there is when people write every other day; if they wait for a month, there is nothing that seems worth telling.

O. Douglas 1877–1948: *Penny Plain* (1920)

7 Ah, but when the post knocks and the letter comes always the miracle seems repeated—speech attempted.

Virginia Woolf 1882–1941: *Jacob's Room* (1922)

8 Letters of thanks, letters from banks,
Letters of joy from girl and boy,
Receipted bills and invitations
To inspect new stock or to visit relations,
And applications for situations,
And timid lovers' declarations,
And gossip, gossip from all the nations.

W. H. Auden 1907–73: 'Night Mail' (1936)

9 It does me good to write a letter which is not a response to a demand, a gratuitous letter, so to speak, which has accumulated in me like the waters of a reservoir.

Henry Miller 1891–1980: *The Books in My Life* (1951)

10 I am sorry for people who can't write letters. But I suspect also that you and I . . . love to write them because it's kind of like working without really doing it.

Elizabeth Bishop 1911–79: letter to Kit and Ilse Barker, 5 September 1953

11 A man seldom puts his authentic self into a letter. He writes it to amuse a friend or to get rid of a social or business obligation, which is to say, a nuisance.

H. L. Mencken 1880–1956: *Minority Report* (1956)

12 Beware of writing to me. I always answer . . . My father spent the last 20 years of his life writing letters. If someone thanked him for a present, he thanked them for thanking him and there was no end to the exchange but death.

Evelyn Waugh 1903–66: letter to Lady Mosley, 30 March 1966

13 Don't think that this is a letter. It is only a small eruption of a disease called friendship.

Jean Renoir 1894–1979: letter to Janine Bazin, 12 June 1974

1 A man who publishes his letters becomes a nudist—nothing shields him from the world's gaze except his bare skin.

E. B. White 1899–1985: letter to Corona Machemer, 11 June 1975

2 Letters . . . exclude not only the reader as co-writer, or predictor, or guesser, but they exclude the reader as reader, they are written, if they are true letters, for *a* reader.

A. S. Byatt 1936– : *Possession* (1990)

Libraries and Librarians see also **Borrowing Books**

3 Let your bookcases and your shelves be your gardens and your pleasure-grounds. Pluck the fruit that grows therein, gather the roses, the spices and the myrrh.

Judah Ibn Tibbon 1120–90: Israel Abrahams *Jewish Life in the Middle Ages* (1932)

4 Come, and take choice of all my library,
And so beguile thy sorrow.

William Shakespeare 1564–1616: *Titus Andronicus* (1590)

5 My library
Was dukedom large enough.

William Shakespeare 1564–1616: *The Tempest* (1611)

6 Affect not as some do that bookish ambition to be stored with books and have well-furnished libraries, yet keep their heads empty of knowledge; to desire to have many books, and never to use them, is like a child that will have a candle burning by him all the while he is sleeping.

Henry Peacham *c.*1576–*c.*1643: *The Compleat Gentleman* (1622)

7 No place affords a more striking conviction of the vanity of human hopes, than a public library.

Samuel Johnson 1709–84: in *The Rambler* 23 March 1751

8 Madam, a circulating library in a town is as an evergreen tree of diabolical knowledge; it blossoms throughout the year. And depend on it . . . that they who are so fond of handling the leaves, will long for the fruit at last.

Richard Brinsley Sheridan 1751–1816: *The Rivals* (1775)

9 It is almost everywhere the case that soon after it is begotten the greater part of human wisdom is laid to rest in *repositories*.

Georg Christoph Lichtenberg 1742–99: A. Leitzmann (ed.) *Georg Christoph Lichtenberg Aphorismen* (1904)

10 Lo! all in silence, all in order stand,
And mighty folios first, a lordly band;
Then quartos their well-ordered ranks maintain,
And light octavos fill a spacious plain;
See yonder, ranged in more frequented rows,
A humbler band of duodecimos.

George Crabbe 1754–1832: 'The Library' (1808)

11 We only know that you are our Librarian by seeing your name attached to the receipts for your salary.

letter from an unidentified director of the London Institution to the Librarian, Richard Porson (1759–1808)

Anonymous: as reported by William Maltby, Porson's successor as Librarian; Samuel Rogers *Table Talk* (1903)

12 In his library he had been always sure of leisure and tranquillity; and though prepared . . . to meet with folly and conceit in every other room in the house, he was used to be free of them there.

Jane Austen 1775–1817: *Pride and Prejudice* (1813)

1 What a sad want I am in of libraries, of books to gather facts from! Why is there not a Majesty's library in every county town? There is a Majesty's jail and gallows in every one.

Thomas Carlyle 1795–1881: letter, 18 May 1832

2 We do not subscribe to a circulating library at Haworth, and consequently 'new novels' rarely indeed come in our way.

Charlotte Brontë 1816–55: letter to Ellen Nussey, 26 June 1848

3 We call ourselves a rich nation, and we are filthy and foolish enough to thumb each other's books out of circulating libraries!

John Ruskin 1819–1900: *Sesame and Lilies* (1865)

4 A man should keep his little brain attic stocked with all the furniture that he is likely to use, and the rest he can put away in the lumber room of his library, where he can get it if he wants it.

Arthur Conan Doyle 1859–1930: *The Adventures of Sherlock Holmes* (1892)

5 Here Greek and Roman find themselves
Alive along these crowded shelves;
And Shakespeare treads again his stage,
And Chaucer paints anew his age.

John Greenleaf Whittier 1807–92: 'The Library'

6 Every library should try to be complete on something, if it were only the history of pinheads.

Oliver Wendell Holmes 1809–94: *The Poet at the Breakfast-Table* (1872)

7 Mr Quarmby laughed in a peculiar way, which was the result of long years of mirth-subdual in the Reading-room.

George Gissing 1857–1903: *New Grub Street* (1891)

8 The fog grew thicker; she looked up at the windows beneath the dome and saw that they were a dusky yellow. Then her eye discerned an official walking along the upper gallery, and in pursuance of her grotesque humour, her mocking misery, she likened him to a black, lost soul, doomed to wander in an eternity of vain research along endless shelves. Or again, the readers who sat here at these radiating lines of desks, what were they but hapless flies caught in a huge web, its nucleus the great circle of the Catalogue?

'Marian Yule' in the Reading Room of the British Museum

George Gissing 1857–1903: *New Grub Street* (1891)

9 We should burn all libraries and allow to remain only that which everyone knows by heart. A beautiful age of the legend would then begin.

Hugo Ball 1886–1927: *Flight out of Time: A Dada Diary* 9 January 1917

10 The London Library, for a private library, is surprisingly good; its terms are generous and its manners gracious.

T. S. Eliot 1888–1965: letter October 1919

11 I've been drunk for about a week now, and I thought it might sober me up to sit in a library.

F. Scott Fitzgerald 1896–1940: *The Great Gatsby* (1925)

12 Tuppenny dram-shops.

the small suburban circulating libraries of the twenties and thirties

Q. D. Leavis 1906–81: *Fiction and the Reading Public* (1932)

13 A family library is a breeding-place of character.

Graham Greene 1904–91: 'Background for Heroes' (1937)

14 Even in houses commonly held to be 'booky' one finds, nine times out of ten, not a library but a book-dump.

Edith Wharton 1862–1937: attributed

1 The library annoyed him with its look
Of calm belief in being really there;
He threw away a rival's silly book,
And clattered panting up the spiral stair.

W. H. Auden 1907–73: 'The Quest' (1941)

2 I ransack public libraries, and find them full of sunk treasure.

Virginia Woolf 1882–1941: Hermione Lee *Virginia Woolf* (1996)

3 A broad and firm foundation of books of reference constantly replenished and kept up to date; all the still *living* classics, in Greek, Latin and the principal modern languages, and an annual influx of the best in current letters.

the principles he employed in building up his library

Bernard Berenson 1865–1959: attributed

4 Some on commission, some for the love of learning,
Some because they have nothing better to do
Or because they hope these walls of books will deaden
The drumming of the demon in their ears.

Louis MacNeice 1907–63: 'The British Museum Reading Room'

5 There can be few more unrewarding tasks for the educated man of curiosity than the routine duties of librarianship; while for the higher rungs of bibliography I soon realized that an avid taste for the contents of books was a hindrance.

Angus Wilson 1913–91: *The Wild Garden* (1963)

6 Cultures of East and West, the entire atlas,
Encyclopedias, centuries, dynasties,
Symbols, the cosmos, and cosmogonies
Are offered from the walls.

Jorge Luis Borges 1899–1986: 'Poem of the Gifts' (1972), tr. Alastair Reid

7 What is more important in a library than anything else—than everything else—is the fact that it exists.

Archibald MacLeish 1892–1982: 'The Premise of Meaning' in *American Scholar* 5 June 1972

8 It's a librarian's duty to distinguish between poetry and a sort of belle-litter.

Tom Stoppard 1937– : *Travesties* (1975)

9 Being a librarian doesn't help. I've always found them close relatives of the walking dead.

Alan Bennett 1934– : Anthony Thwaite *Larkin at Sixty* (1982)

10 On the whole, as I am fond of saying, libraries are feminine: they respond, they do not initiate.

Philip Larkin 1922–85: *Required Writing* (1983)

11 He looked into the water and saw that it was made up of a thousand thousand thousand and one different currents, each one a different colour, weaving in and out of each other like a liquid tapestry of breathtaking complexity; and Iff explained that these were the Streams of Story, that each colour strand represented and contained a single tale. Different parts of the Ocean contained different sorts of stories, and as all the stories that had ever been told and many that were still in the process of being invented could be found here, the Ocean of the Streams of Story was in fact the biggest library in the world. And because the stories were held here in liquid form, they retained the ability to change, to become new versions of themselves, to join up with other stories and so become yet other

Salman Rushdie 1947– : *Haroun and the Sea of Stories* (1990)

stories; so that unlike a library of books, the Ocean of the Stream of Stories was much more than a storeroom of yarns. It was not dead but alive.

1 The Librarian was, of course, very much in favour of reading in general, but readers in particular got on his nerves . . . He liked people who loved and respected books, and the best way to do that, in the Librarian's opinion, was to leave them on the shelves where Nature intended them to be.

Terry Pratchett 1948– : *Men at Arms* (1993)

2 Whatever classifications have been chosen, every library tyrannizes the act of reading, and forces the reader—the curious reader, the alert reader—to *rescue* the book from the category to which it has been condemned.

Alberto Manguel 1948– : *A History of Reading* (1996)

Life

3 My soul, sit thou a patient looker-on;
Judge not the play before the play is done:
Her plot hath many changes; every day
Speaks a new scene; the last act crowns the play.

Francis Quarles 1592–1644: *Emblems* (1635) 'Respice Finem'

4 No arts; no letters; no society; and which is worst of all, continual fear and danger of violent death; and the life of man, solitary, poor, nasty, brutish, and short.

Thomas Hobbes 1588–1679: *Leviathan* (1651)

5 When I consider how my light is spent,
E're half my days, in this dark world and wide,
And that one talent which is death to hide
Lodged with me useless . . .
Doth God exact day-labour, light denied,
I fondly ask; but patience to prevent
That murmur, soon replies, God doth not need
Either man's work or his own gifts, who best
Bear his mild yoke, they serve him best, his state
Is kingly. Thousands at his bidding speed
And post o'er land and ocean without rest:
They also serve who only stand and wait.

John Milton 1608–74: *Sonnet* 16 'When I consider how my light is spent' (1673)

6 This world is a comedy to those that think, a tragedy to those that feel.

Horace Walpole 1717–97: letter to Anne, Countess of Upper Ossory, 16 August 1776

7 I should have no objection to go over the same life from its beginning to the end: requesting only the advantage authors have, of correcting in a second edition the faults of the first.

Benjamin Franklin 1706–90: *Autobiography* (1868)

8 A man's life of any worth is a continual allegory.

John Keats 1795–1821: letter to George and Georgiana Keats, 19 February 1819

9 I strove with none; for none was worth my strife;
Nature I loved, and, next to Nature, Art.

Walter Savage Landor 1775–1864: 'Dying Speech of an Old Philosopher' (1853)

1 Our life is frittered away by detail . . . Simplify, simplify.

Henry David Thoreau 1817–62: *Walden* (1854)

2 Human life is a sad show, undoubtedly: ugly, heavy and complex. Art has no other end, for people of feeling, than to conjure away the burden and bitterness.

Gustave Flaubert 1821–80: letter to Amelie Bosquet, July 1864

3 If we had a keen vision and feeling of all ordinary human life, it would be like hearing the grass grow and the squirrel's heart beat, and we should die of that roar which lies on the other side of silence.

George Eliot 1819–80: *Middlemarch* (1871–2)

4 Books are good enough in their own way, but they are a mighty bloodless substitute for life.

Robert Louis Stevenson 1850–94: *Virginibus Puerisque* (1881) 'An Apology for Idlers'

5 And anyway no literature can outdo real life when it comes to cynicism. You're not going to get a person drunk with a jigger when he's just polished off a barrel.

Anton Chekhov 1860–1904: letter to M. V. Kiseleva, 14 January 1887

6 One can read when one is middle-aged or old; but one can mingle in the world with fresh perceptions only when one is young. The great thing is to be *saturated*, with something—that is, in one way or another, with life.

Henry James 1843–1916: letter 29 October 1888

7 My life has been in my poems . . . I have seen others enjoying, while I stand alone with myself—commenting, commenting—a mere dead mirror on which things reflect themselves.

W. B. Yeats 1865–1939: letter to Katharine Tynan, 1888

8 All that I desire to point out is the general principle that Life imitates Art far more than Art imitates Life.

Oscar Wilde 1854–1900: *Intentions* (1891)

9 The life of every man is a diary in which he means to write one story, and writes another; and his humblest hour is when he compares the volume as it is with what he vowed to make it.

J. M. Barrie 1860–1937: *The Little Minister* (1891)

10 Do you want to know the great drama of my life? It's that I have put my genius into my life; all I've put into my works is my talent.

Oscar Wilde 1854–1900: André Gide *Oscar Wilde* (1910)

11 Life being all inclusion and confusion, and art being all discrimination and selection.

Henry James 1843–1916: preface to *The Spoils of Poynton* (1909 ed.)

12 The perfect delight of writing tales where so many lives come and go at the cost of one which slips imperceptibly away.

Joseph Conrad 1857–1924: *A Personal Record* (1912)

13 Life deceives us so much that we come to believing that literature has no relation with it and we are astonished to observe that the wonderful ideas books have presented to us are gratuitously exhibited in everyday life, without risk of being spoilt by the writer.

Marcel Proust 1871–1922: *Time Regained* (1926)

14 Most of life is so dull that there is nothing to be said about it, and the books and talk that would describe it as interesting are obliged to exaggerate, in the hope of justifying their own existence.

E. M. Forster 1879–1970: *A Passage to India* (1924)

1 Life is not a series of gig lamps symmetrically arranged; life is a luminous halo, a semi-transparent envelope surrounding us from the beginning of consciousness to the end.

Virginia Woolf 1882–1941: *The Common Reader* (1925) 'Modern Fiction'

2 I enjoy almost everything. Yet I have some restless searcher in me. Why is there not a discovery in life? Something one can lay one's hands on and say 'This is it'?

Virginia Woolf 1882–1941: diary, 27 February 1926

3 The intellect of man is forced to choose
Perfection of the life, or of the work.

W. B. Yeats 1865–1939: 'Coole Park and Ballylee, 1932' (1933)

4 For the majority of creative people, life is a pretty mean trick.

F. Scott Fitzgerald 1896–1940: Jeffrey Meyers *Scott Fitzgerald* (1994)

5 Constantly I desire to point with delight to the blessed motley of this world, but equally constantly to bring to mind the fact that at the basis of this motley there lies a unity; constantly I desire to show that beautiful and ugly, light and dark, sin and sanctity are opposites only momentarily, and that they continually pass over into each other.

Hermann Hesse 1877–1962: Richard B. Matzig *Hermann Hesse* (1947)

6 No art can completely reject reality. Real literary creation uses . . . reality and only reality with all its warmth and blood, its passion and its outcries. It simply adds something which transfigures reality.

Albert Camus 1913–60: *The Rebel* (1951)

7 An old teapot, used daily, can tell me more of my past than anything I recorded of it.
Continuity . . . continuity . . . it is that which we cannot write down, it is that we cannot compass, record or control.

Sylvia Townsend Warner 1893–1978: letter to Alyse Gregory, 26 May 1953

8 Timeless fictional worlds
Of self-evident meaning
Would not delight
Were not our own
A temporal one, where nothing
Is what it seems.

W. H. Auden 1907–73: 'The Cave of Making' (1965)

9 Let no one demean to tears or reproach
This declaration of the skill of God
Who with such magnificent irony
Gave me at the same time darkness and the books.

Jorge Luis Borges 1899–1986: 'Poem of the Gifts' (1972) tr. Alastair Reid

10 Books say: she did this because. Life says: she did this. Books are where things are explained to you; life is where things aren't . . . Books make sense of life. The only problem is that the lives they make sense of are other people's lives, never your own.

Julian Barnes 1946– : *Flaubert's Parrot* (1984)

11 Life is a means of extracting fiction.

Robert Stone 1937– : George Plimpton (ed.) *Writers at Work* (8th series, 1988)

1 Though I liked reading (and showed off at it), it was soon borne in upon me that the world of books was only distantly related to the world in which I lived.

Alan Bennett 1934– : *Writing Home* (1994)

2 There is no point to life, though there is a point to art.
said the month before he died

Kingsley Amis 1922–95: attributed, 1995

3 Well there you are. This is life. What I've found as a writer is that you have to keep taming it down, making it less improbable in order to fit it into some sort of fictional context.

John Mortimer 1923– : in *Paris Review* 1995

Literary Theory

4 *Il n'y a pas de hors-texte.*
There is nothing outside of the text.

Jacques Derrida 1930– : *Of Grammatology* (1967)

5 It attempts to make the not-seen accessible to sight.
on deconstructive reading

Jacques Derrida 1930– : *Of Grammatology* (1967)

6 A text is not a line of words releasing a single 'theological' meaning (the 'message' of the Author-God) but a multi-dimensional space in which a variety of writings, none of them original, blend and clash.

Roland Barthes 1915–80: *The Death of the Author* (1968)

7 Once the Author is removed, the claim to decipher a text becomes quite futile.

Roland Barthes 1915–80: *The Death of the Author* (1968)

8 Interpretation is nothing but the possibility of error.

Paul de Man 1919–83: *Blindness and Insight* (1971)

9 The literary work has two poles, which we might call the artistic and the aesthetic: the artistic refers to the text created by the author, and the aesthetic to the realization accomplished by the reader. From this polarity it follows that the literary work cannot be completely identical with the text, or with the realization of the text, but in fact must lie half-way between the two.

Wolfgang Iser: 'The Reading Process' (1972)

10 Two people gazing at the night sky may both be looking at the same collection of stars, but one will see the image of a plough, and the other will make out a dipper. The 'stars' in a literary text are fixed; the lines that join them are variable.

Wolfgang Iser: 'The Reading Process' (1972)

11 All reading is misreading.

J. Hillis Miller 1928– : 'Walter Pater: a Partial Portrait' (1976)

12 The deconstructive critic seeks to find . . . the element in the system studied which is alogical, the thread in the text in question which will unravel it all, or the loose stone which will pull down the whole building. The deconstruction, rather, annihilates the ground on which the building stands by showing that the text has already

J. Hillis Miller 1928– : 'Stevens' Rock and Criticism as Cure: II' (1976)

annihilated that ground, knowingly or unknowingly. Deconstruction is not a dismantling of the structure of a text but a demonstration that it has dismantled itself.

1 Incredulity towards metanarratives.
a definition of postmodernism

Jean-François Lyotard: *The Postmodern Condition* (1979)

2 Structuralism is not a subject that grips the ordinary reader much. Its articles of faith are likely to strike him as a mixture of the self-evident and the impossible. Thus the proposition, solemnly repeated by structuralists, that language is a system of signs (or 'signifiers') seems to him too obvious to remark. Who ever imagined otherwise? On the other hand, the ideas floated by the wilder type of structuralist—that literary texts ought to mean anything we require them to, or that authors do not create their works but are created by them—pretty clearly call for a spell of sedation and devoted nursing.

John Carey 1934– : in *Sunday Times* 1981

3 Deconstruction is in one sense an extraordinarily modest proposal: a sort of patient, probing reformism of the text, which is not, so to speak, to be confronted over the barricades but cunningly waylaid in the corridors and suavely chivvied into revealing its ideological hand. Stoically convinced of the unbreakable grip of the metaphysical closure, the deconstructionist, like any responsible trade union bureaucrat confronting management, must settle for that and negotiate what he or she can within the left-overs and stray contingencies casually unabsorbed by the textual power system. But to say no more than this is to do deconstruction a severe injustice. For it ignores that other face of deconstruction which is its hair-raising *radicalism*—the nerve and daring with which it knocks the stuffing out of every smug concept and leaves the well-groomed text shamefully dishevelled. It ignores, in short, the *madness* and violence of deconstruction, its scandalous urge to think the unthinkable, the flamboyance with which it poses itself on the very brink of meaning and dances there, pounding away at the crumbling cliff-edge beneath its feet and prepared to fall with it into the sea of unlimited semiosis or schizophrenia.

Terry Eagleton 1943– : *Walter Benjamin or Towards a Revolutionary Criticism* (1981)

4 I tried for the longest time to find out what *deconstructionism* was. Nobody was able to explain it to me clearly. The best answer I got was from a writer, who said, 'Honey, it's bad news for you and me.'

Margaret Atwood 1939– : in an interview, December 1986; Earl G. Ingersoll (ed.) *Margaret Atwood: Conversations* (1990)

5 Theory on a dramatic scale happens when it is both possible and necessary for it to do so—when the traditional rationales which have silently underpinned our daily practices stand in danger of being discredited, and need either to be revised or discarded . . . Theory is just a practice forced into a new form of self-reflectiveness on account of certain grievous problems it has encountered.

Terry Eagleton 1943– : *The Significance of Theory* (1990)

Like small lumps on the neck, it is a symptom that all is not well.

1 Though it often apes scientific language, critical theory would not be recognized as theory by any scientist, since it does not open itself to experimental verification. Composed purely of assertions, not testable hypotheses, it can have no bearing on reality, and no explanatory value.

John Carey 1934– : in *Sunday Times* 7 August 1994

Literature see also **Literatures**

2 Your true lover of literature is never fastidious.

Robert Southey 1774–1843: *The Doctor* (1812)

3 A losing trade, I assure you, sir: literature is a drug.

George Borrow 1803–81: *Lavengro* (1851)

4 But literature, though the grandest occupation in the world for a man's leisure, is, I take it, a slavish profession.

Anthony Trollope 1815–82: *The Bertrams* (1859)

5 It takes a great deal of history to produce a little literature.

Henry James 1843–1916: *Hawthorne* (1879)

6 *Et tout le reste est littérature.*

All the rest is mere fine writing.

Paul Verlaine 1844–96: 'Art poétique' (1882)

7 *La pensée est à la littérature ce que la lumière est à la peinture.*

Ideas are to literature what light is to painting.

Paul Bourget 1852–1935: *La Physiologie de l'Amour Moderne* (1890)

8 Literature is a splendid mistress, but a bad wife.

advice to Edgar Wallace, c.1897

Rudyard Kipling 1865–1936: Margaret Lane *Edgar Wallace* (1964)

9 Oh literature, oh the glorious Art, how it preys upon the marrow of our bones. It scoops the stuffing out of us and chucks us aside. Alas!

D. H. Lawrence 1885–1930: letter to Walter de la Mare, 10 June 1912

10 Literature is a method of sudden arrangement of commonplaces. *The suddenness* makes us forget the commonplace.

T. E. Hulme 1883–1917: in *Criterion* 1925 vol. 3 'Notes on Language and Style'

11 The rest, called *literature*, is a dossier of human imbecility for the guidance of future professors.

Tristan Tzara 1896–1963: in *Dada* 4/5 Zurich May 1919

12 Literature flourishes best when it is half a trade and half an art.

William Ralph Inge 1860–1954: *Victorian Age* (1922)

13 All literature is, finally, autobiographical.

Jorge Luis Borges 1899–1986: in 1926; James Woodall *The Man in the Mirror of the Book* (1996)

14 Our American professors like their literature clear and cold and pure and very dead.

Sinclair Lewis 1885–1951: *The American Fear of Literature* (Nobel Prize Address, 12 December 1930)

1 Great literature is simply language charged with meaning to the utmost possible degree.

Ezra Pound 1885–1972: *How To Read* (1931)

2 Remarks are not literature.

Gertrude Stein 1874–1946: *Autobiography of Alice B. Toklas* (1933)

3 Literature is news that STAYS news.

Ezra Pound 1885–1972: *The ABC of Reading* (1934)

4 Literature is the art of writing something that will be read twice; journalism what will be read once.

Cyril Connolly 1903–74: *Enemies of Promise* (1938)

5 My theories and views of literature vary with the lateness of the hour, the quality of my companions, and the quantity of liquor.

James Thurber 1894–1961: Fred B. Millett *Contemporary American Authors* (1940)

6 *Longtemps, longtemps*, la voix humaine *fut base et condition de la* littérature . . .
Un jour vint où l'on sut lire des yeux sans épeler, sans entendre, et la littérature en fut tout altérée.

For a long, long time, *the human voice* was the foundation and condition of all *literature* . . .
A day came when the reader could read with his eyes alone without having to spell things out, or hear them, and literature was completely transformed by this.

Paul Valéry 1871–1945: *Tel Quel 1* (1941)

7 To turn events into ideas is the function of literature.

George Santayana 1863–1952: attributed

8 Literature is the orchestration of platitudes.

Thornton Wilder 1897–1975: in *Time* 12 January 1953

9 The illusion of art is to make one believe that great literature is very close to life, but exactly the opposite is true. Life is amorphous, literature is formal.

Françoise Sagan 1935– : Malcolm Cowley (ed.) *Writers at Work* (1958) 1st series

10 He knew everything about literature except how to enjoy it.

Joseph Heller 1923– : *Catch-22* (1961)

11 Literature is mostly about having sex and not much about having children. Life is the other way round.

David Lodge 1935– : *The British Museum is Falling Down* (1965)

12 The world must be all fucked up when men travel first class and literature goes as freight.

Gabriel García Márquez 1928– : *One Hundred Years of Solitude* (1967)

13 The image of literature to be found in ordinary culture is tyrannically centred on the author, his person, his life, his tastes, his passions.

Roland Barthes 1915–80: *The Death of the Author* (1968)

14 The virtue of much literature is that it is dangerous and may do you extreme harm.

John Mortimer 1923– : C. H. Rolph *Books in the Dock* (1969)

15 The central function of imaginative literature is to make you realise that other people act on moral convictions different from your own.

William Empson 1906–84: *Milton's God* (1981)

1 Any writer worth his salt knows that only a small proportion of literature does more than partly compensate people for the damage they have suffered in learning to read.

Rebecca West 1892–1983: Peter Vansittart *Path from a White Horse* (1985); epigraph

2 In the . . . congested times that await us, literature must aim at the maximum concentration of poetry and thought.

Italo Calvino 1923–85: *Six Memos for the Next Millennium* (1992)

3 Among the values I would like passed on to the next millennium, there is this above all: a literature that has absorbed the taste for mental orderliness and exactitude, the intelligence of poetry, but at the same time that of science and of philosophy.

Italo Calvino 1923–85: *Six Memos for the Next Millennium* (1992)

4 Literature is the one place in any society where, within the secrecy of our own heads, we can hear *voices talking about everything in every possible way.*

Salman Rushdie 1947– : lecture 'Is Nothing Sacred' 6 February 1990

5 To me literature is forever blowing a horn, singing about youth when youth is irretrievably gone, singing about your homeland when in the schizophrenia of the times you find yourself in a land that lies over the ocean, a land—no matter how hospitable and friendly—where your heart is not, because you landed on those shores too late.

Josef Škvorecký 1924– : foreword to *The Bass Saxophone* (1994)

Literatures see also Literature

6 *Satura quidem tota nostra est.*

Verse satire indeed is entirely our own.
meaning Roman as opposed to Greek

Quintilian AD *c.*35–*c.*96: *Institutio Oratoria*

7 The language of the age is never the language of poetry, except among the French, whose verse, where the thought or image does not support it, differs in nothing from prose.

Thomas Gray 1716–71: letter to Richard West, 8 April 1742

8 The character of American literature is, generally speaking, pretty justly appreciated in Europe. The immense exhalation of periodical trash, which penetrates into every cot and corner of the country, and which is greedily sucked in by all ranks, is unquestionably one cause of its inferiority.

Frances Trollope 1780–1863: *Domestic Manners of the Americans* (1832)

9 Has Canada no poet to describe the glories of his parent land—no painter that can delineate her matchless scenery of land and wave? Are her children dumb and blind, that they leave to strangers the task of singing her praise? The standard literature of Canada must be looked for in the newspapers.

Susannah Moodie 1803–85: *Mark Hudlestone* (1853); introduction

10 Of these two literatures [French and German], as of the intellect of Europe in general, the main effort, for now many years, has been a *critical* effort; the endeavours, in all branches of knowledge—theology, philosophy, history, art, science—to see the object as in itself it really is.

Matthew Arnold 1822–88: *On Translating Homer* (1861)

1 The more I reflect on the destiny of Canadian literature, the less chance I find for its leaving a mark in history. Canada lacks its own language. If we spoke Iroquois or Huron, our literature would live.

Octave Crémazie 1827–79: letter to Abbé Henri-Raymond Casgrain, 29 January 1867

2 It would seem that in our great unendowed, unfurnished, unentertained and unentertaining continent [of North America], where we all sit sniffing, as it were, the very earth of our foundations, we ought to have leisure to turn out something handsome from the very heart of simple nature.

Henry James 1843–1916: letter, 14 January 1874

3 The floods of tepid soap and water which under the name of novels are being vomited forth in England, seem to me, by contrast [with French fiction], to do little honour to our race.

Henry James 1843–1916: letter, 21 February 1884

4 In France literature divides itself into schools, movements, and circles . . . In England . . . each man works by himself and for himself, for England is a land of literary Ishmaels.

W. B. Yeats 1865–1939: 'The Celt in London' (1892)

5 Alone, perhaps, among the nations of Europe we are in our ballad or epic age . . . Our poetry is still a poetry of the people in the main, for it still deals with the tales and thoughts of the people.

W. B. Yeats 1865–1939: 'Nationality and Literature', lecture 19 May 1893

6 Roman literature is Greek literature written in Latin.

Heinrich von Treitschke 1834–96: attributed

7 Sir Walter Scott gave Highland legends and Highland excitability so great a mastery over all romance that they seem romance itself.

W. B. Yeats 1865–1939: 'The Celtic Element in Literature' (1897)

8 What most offends an Englishman in the heroes of French fiction is the peculiar dastardliness to women they are capable of.

George Gissing 1857–1903: *Commonplace Book* (1962)

9 It is the dull man who is always sure, and the sure man who is always dull. The more a man dreams, the less he believes. A great literature is thus chiefly the product of doubting and inquiring minds in revolt against the immovable certainties of the nation.

H. L. Mencken 1880–1956: *Prejudices* (2nd series, 1920) 'The National Letters'

10 Many people now search for the epic in Western movies and in their hard riders. More than in the Greeks and Romans and in the Lay of the Nibelungs, I have found the epic in the prose and poetry of the North.

Jorge Luis Borges 1899–1986: *Seis poemas escandinavos* (1966) preface

11 I had always thought of English literature as the richest in the world; the discovery now of a secret chamber at the very threshold of that literature came to me as an additional gift.

Jorge Luis Borges 1899–1986: *The Aleph and Other Stories* (1971) 'Autobiographical Essay'; cf. **125:9**

12 In [my] preference for short literary forms I am only following the true vocation of Italian literature, which is poor in novelists but rich in poets.

Italo Calvino 1923–85: *Six Memos for the Next Millennium* (1992)

13 The Channel is a slipper bath of irony through which we pass these serious Continentals in order not to be infected by their gloom.

Alan Bennett 1934– : *Writing Home* (1994)

1 The novels created below the thirty-fifth parallel, though a bit foreign to European taste, are the extension of the history of the European novel, of its form and of its spirit, and are even astonishingly close to its earliest beginnings. Nowhere else today does the old Rabelaisian sap run so joyfully as in the work of these non-European writers.

Milan Kundera 1929– : *Testaments Betrayed* (1995)

2 Obsessive denigration of English fiction is the dying chirrup of some sort of imperial misery.
speech at the Booker awards, 29 October 1996

Carmen Callil 1938– : in *Daily Telegraph* 30 October 1996

Love

3 Dumb swans, not chattering pies, do lovers prove;
They love indeed who quake to say they love.

Philip Sidney 1554–86: *Astrophel and Stella* (1591)

4 From women's eyes this doctrine I derive:
They are the ground, the books, the academes,
From whence doth spring the true Promethean fire.

William Shakespeare 1564–1616: *Love's Labour's Lost* (1595)

5 For these fellows of infinite tongue, that can rhyme themselves into ladies' favours, they do always reason themselves out again.

William Shakespeare 1564–1616: *Henry V* (1599)

6 If all the earth were paper white
And all the sea were ink
'Twere not enough for me to write
As my poor heart doth think.

John Lyly *c.*1554–1606: 'If all the earth were paper white'

7 Love made me poet,
And this I writ;
My heart did do it,
And not my wit.

Elizabeth, Lady Tanfield *c.*1565–1628: epitaph for her husband, in Burford Parish Church, Oxfordshire

8 I am two fools, I know,
For loving, and for saying so
In whining poetry.

John Donne 1572–1631: 'The Triple Fool'

9 She that with poetry is won,
Is but a desk to write upon.

Samuel Butler 1612–80: *Hudibras* pt. 2 (1664)

10 No one would ever have fallen in love unless he had first read about it.

Duc de la Rochefoucauld 1613–80: Edmund White *The Burning Library* (1994); attributed

11 I court others in verse: but I love thee in prose:
And they have my whimsies, but thou hast my heart.

Matthew Prior 1664–1721: 'A Better Answer' (1718)

12 Unlearn'd, he knew no schoolman's subtle art,
No language, but the language of the heart.
of his own father

Alexander Pope 1688–1744: 'An Epistle to Dr Arbuthnot' (1735)

13 Thro' all the drama—whether damned or not—
Love gilds the scene, and women guide the plot.

Richard Brinsley Sheridan 1751–1816: *The Rivals* (1775)

14 I have met with women whom I really think would like to be married to a poem and to be given away by a novel.

John Keats 1795–1821: letter to Fanny Brawne, 8 July 1819

15 Think you, if Laura had been Petrarch's wife,
He would have written sonnets all his life?

Lord Byron 1788–1824: *Don Juan* (1819–24)

1 When amatory poets sing their loves
In liquid lines mellifluously bland,
And pair their rhymes as Venus yokes her doves,
They little think what mischief is in hand.

Lord Byron 1788–1824: *Don Juan* (1819–24)

2 The ideal story is that of two people who go into love step for step, with a fluttered consciousness, like a pair of children venturing together into a dark room.

Robert Louis Stevenson 1850–94: *Virginibus Puerisque* (1881) 'El Dorado'

3 Only connect! . . . Only connect the prose and the passion, and both will be exalted, and human love will be seen at its height.

E. M. Forster 1879–1970: *Howards End* (1910)

4 Friendship is useless in the development of the artist. Only love (that is, jealousy) can train the writer's mind, since constant suspicious questioning of every motive, every movement, and the conversion of each innocent story into a guilty alibi — only this restless and piercing scrutiny can teach the writer to observe.

Marcel Proust 1871–1922: Edmund White *The Burning Library* (1994)

5 Should poets bicycle-pump the human heart
Or squash it flat?
Man's love is of man's life a thing apart;
Girls aren't like that.

Kingsley Amis 1922–95: 'A Bookshop Idyll' (1956)

6 We men have got love well weighed up; our stuff
Can get by without it.
Women don't seem to think that's good enough;
They write about it.

Kingsley Amis 1922–95: 'A Bookshop Idyll' (1956)

7 Beware, madam, of the witty devil,
The arch intriguer who walks disguised
In a poet's cloak, his gay tongue oozing evil.

Robert Graves 1895–1985: 'Beware, Madam!'

8 In our culture, love needs a mixer before it qualifies as a subject for literature. Pour it out neat, and you get Mills & Boon.

John Carey 1934– : in *Sunday Times* 11 February 1996

Magazines see **Newspapers and Magazines**

Meaning

9 And this is the writing that was written, MENE, MENE, TEKEL, UPHARSIN.
This is the interpretation of the thing: MENE; God hath numbered thy kingdom, and finished it.
TEKEL; Thou art weighed in the balances and art found wanting.
PERES; Thy kingdom is divided, and given to the Medes and Persians.

Bible: Daniel

10 I pray thee, understand a plain man in his plain meaning.

William Shakespeare 1564–1616: *The Merchant of Venice* (1596–8)

1 In all speech, words and sense are as the body and the soul. The sense is as the life and soul of language, without which all words are dead.

Ben Jonson *c.*1573–1637: *Timber, or Discoveries made upon Men and Matter* (1641)

2 Where more is meant than meets the ear.

John Milton 1608–74: 'Il Penseroso' (1645)

3 Still follow sense, of ev'ry art the soul,
Parts answering parts shall slide into a whole.

Alexander Pope 1688–1744: *Epistles to Several Persons* 'To Lord Burlington' (1731)

4 Egad I think the interpreter is the hardest to be understood of the two!

Richard Brinsley Sheridan 1751–1816: *The Critic* (1779)

5 God and I both knew what it meant once; now God alone knows.

also attributed to ***Browning****, apropos* Sordello, *in the form 'When it was written, God and Robert Browning knew what it meant; now only God knows'*

Friedrich Klopstock 1724–1803: C. Lombroso *The Man of Genius* (1891)

6 Better the rudest work that tells a story or records a fact, than the richest without meaning.

John Ruskin 1819–1900: *Seven Lamps of Architecture* (1849)

7 'Then you should say what you mean,' the March Hare went on. 'I do,' Alice hastily replied; 'at least—at least I mean what I say—that's the same thing, you know.' 'Not the same thing a bit!' said the Hatter. 'Why, you might just as well say that "I see what I eat" is the same thing as "I eat what I see!" '

Lewis Carroll 1832–98: *Alice's Adventures in Wonderland* (1865)

8 Be sure that you go to the author to get at his meaning, not to find yours.

John Ruskin 1819–1900: *Sesame and Lilies* (1865)

9 And this song is considered a perfect gem,
And as to the meaning, it's what you please.

C. S. Calverley 1831–84: 'Ballad' (1872)

10 'There's glory for you!' 'I don't know what you mean by "glory",' Alice said. 'I meant, "there's a nice knock-down argument for you!" ' 'But "glory" doesn't mean "a nice knock-down argument",' Alice objected. 'When *I* use a word,' Humpty Dumpty said in a rather scornful tone, 'it means just what I choose it to mean—neither more nor less.'

Lewis Carroll 1832–98: *Through the Looking-Glass* (1872)

11 You see it's like a portmanteau—there are two meanings packed up into one word.

Lewis Carroll 1832–98: *Through the Looking-Glass* (1872)

12 The meaning doesn't matter if it's only idle chatter of a
transcendental kind.

W. S. Gilbert 1836–1911: *Patience* (1881)

13 No one means all he says, and yet very few say all they mean, for words are slippery and thought is viscous.

Henry Brooks Adams 1838–1918: *The Education of Henry Adams* (1907)

14 I do not know which to prefer,
The beauty of inflections
Or the beauty of innuendoes,
The blackbird whistling
Or just after.

Wallace Stevens 1879–1955: 'Thirteen Ways of Looking at a Blackbird' (1923)

1 The little girl had the making of a poet in her who, being told to be sure of her meaning before she spoke, said, 'How can I know what I think till I see what I say?'

Graham Wallas 1858–1932: *The Art of Thought* (1926)

2 Great literature is simply language charged with meaning to the utmost possible degree.

Ezra Pound 1885–1972: *How to Read* (1931)

3 Even when poetry has a meaning, as it usually has, it may be inadvisable to draw it out . . . Perfect understanding will sometimes almost extinguish pleasure.

A. E. Housman 1859–1936: *The Name and Nature of Poetry* (1933)

4 Any general statement is like a cheque drawn on a bank. Its value depends on what is there to meet it.

Ezra Pound 1885–1972: *The ABC of Reading* (1934)

5 That was a way of putting it—not very satisfactory:
A periphrastic study in a worn-out poetical fashion,
Leaving one still with the intolerable wrestle
With words and meanings.

T. S. Eliot 1888–1965: *Four Quartets* 'East Coker' (1940)

6 I distrust the incommunicable: it is the source of all violence.

Jean-Paul Sartre 1905–80: 'Qu'est-ce que la littérature?' in *Les Temps Modernes* July 1947

7 She understood, as women often do more easily than men, that the declared meaning of a spoken sentence is only its overcoat, and the real meaning lies underneath its scarves and buttons.

Peter Carey 1943– : *Oscar and Lucinda* (1989)

8 Often what a poet does not say is as important as what he does.

at a reading in Prague of Seamus Heaney's poetry, April 1996

Miroslav Holub 1923– : in *Sunday Times* 28 April 1996

Mishaps

9 *To The Reader* Christian Reader, I must advertise thee, that, either through the negligence of the printer, or for want of a diligent corrector, many faults have escaped in the printing of this book. Diverse of them are very gross, and do quite mar the sense of the place, which I would pray thee to amend with thy pen, before thou begin to read. As for the rest which be but literal, I would intreat thee in love to pardon them, or to correct them as thou readest. Amongst other things, I think it not amiss, here in this place, to admonish thee of one in particular, namely that the figures set to number the pages are very faultily set.

Robert Parker 1564?–1614: *A Scholastical Discourse Against Symbolizing with Antichrist in Ceremonies* (1607)

10 O Diamond! Diamond! thou little knowest the mischief done!

to a dog, who knocked over a candle which set fire to some papers and thereby 'destroyed the almost finished labours of some years'

Isaac Newton 1642–1727: Thomas Maude *Wensley-Dale . . . a Poem* (1773); probably apocryphal

11 The play-bill, which is said to have announced the tragedy of Hamlet, the character of the Prince of Denmark being left out.

commonly alluded to as 'Hamlet without the Prince'

Sir Walter Scott 1771–1832: *The Talisman* (1825)

1 I began *again* at the beginning. Early the day after tomorrow (after a hard and quite novel kind of battle) I count on having the First Chapter on paper a second time, no worse than it was, though considerably different.
after John Stuart Mill's housemaid had accidentally burnt the manuscript of ***Carlyle's*** The French Revolution

Thomas Carlyle 1795–1881: letter to his brother John Carlyle, 23 March 1835

2 What do you think of this for a misprint: 'idle vistas and melancholy nooks'—'*idle sisters and melancholy monks*'!!

Henry James 1843–1916: letter, 13 June 1874

3 Last night the lamp exploded here and before I could run back into the room the whole round table was in a blaze, books, cigarettes, MS—alas. The whole second part of *End of the Tether* . . . This morning looking at the pile of charred paper—MS and typed copy—my head swam; it seemed to me the earth was turning backwards.

Joseph Conrad 1857–1924: letter to Ford Madox Ford, 24 June 1902; cf. **240:7**

4 It is nice, but in one of the chapters the author made a mistake. He describes the sun as rising twice on the same day.
comment on the ***Dostoevsky's*** *novel* Crime and Punishment

Paul Dirac 1902–84: G. Gamow *Thirty Years that Shook Physics* (1966)

5 I can only suppose that I was so intent on *misprints* I never saw staggering great absurdities; this is a kind of mistake I never thought to guard against. Nor do I well see how I could. *But how many more are there?* I can see myself joining Bowdler and Grainger: '*to larkinise*, v.t., to omit that part of poem printed on verso and subsequent pages, from a notorious anthology published in later half of 20th century'.
on his accidentally omitting sections of two poems from the Oxford Book of Twentieth-Century Verse

Philip Larkin 1922–85: letter, 11 April 1973

Money see also **Earning a Living**

6 What! all this for a song?
to Queen Elizabeth, on being ordered to make a gratuity of £100 to ***Spenser*** *in return for some poems*

William Cecil 1520–98: Edmund Spenser *The Faerie Queene* (1751 ed.) 'The Life of Mr Edmund Spenser' by Thomas Birch

7 It is much more easy to write on money than to obtain it, and those who gain it jest much at those who only write about it.

Voltaire 1694–1778: *Philosophical Dictionary* (1764)

8 I have imbibed such a love for money that I keep some sequins in a drawer to count, and cry over them once a week.

Lord Byron 1788–1824: letter, 27 January 1819

9 Money, which represents the prose of life, and which is hardly spoken of in parlours without an apology, is, in its effects and laws, as beautiful as roses.

Ralph Waldo Emerson 1803–82: *Essays. Second Series* (1844) 'Nominalist and Realist'

10 I'm tired of Love: I'm still more tired of Rhyme.
But Money gives me pleasure all the time.

Hilaire Belloc 1870–1953: 'Fatigued' (1923)

1 'And what dun they gi'e thee for that, lad?'
'Fifty pounds, father.'
'Fifty pounds!' He was dumbfounded, and looked at me with shrewd eyes, as if I were a swindler. 'Fifty pounds! An' tha's niver done a day's hard work in thy life.'
on hearing what his son, D. H. ***Lawrence****, had received for* The White Peacock

John Arthur Lawrence d. 1924: *c.*1911; D. H. Lawrence *The Phoenix* (1936)

2 If you want to get rich from writing, write the sort of thing that's read by persons who move their lips when reading.

Don Marquis 1878–1937: attributed

3 I should like to see the custom introduced of readers who are pleased with a book sending the author some small cash token: anything between half-a-crown and a hundred pounds . . . Not more than a hundred pounds—that would be bad for my character—not less than half-a-crown—that would do no good to yours.

Cyril Connolly 1903–74: *Enemies of Promise* (1938)

4 If there's no money in poetry, neither is there poetry in money.

Robert Graves 1895–1985: speech at London School of Economics, 6 December 1963

5 Of all novelists in any country, Trollope best understands the role of money. Compared with him, even Balzac is too romantic.

W. H. Auden 1907–73: *Forewords and Afterwords* (1973)

6 It is well known that, when two authors meet, they at once start talking about money—like everyone else.

V. S. Pritchett 1900–97: in *The Author* Spring 1978

7 We all need money, but there are degrees of desperation.

Anthony Burgess 1917–93: in *Face* December 1984

8 Money doesn't mind if we say it's evil, it goes from strength to strength. It's a fiction, and addiction, and a tacit conspiracy.

Martin Amis 1949– : John Haffenden (ed.) *Novelists in Interview* (1985)

9 People are always surprised when writers receive money, as if they don't have mortgages to pay.

Helen Dunmore 1952– : in *Guardian* 16 May 1996

Morality

10 He who would not be frustrate of his hope to write well hereafter in laudable things, ought himself to be a true poem.

John Milton 1608–74: *An Apology for Smectymnuus* (1642)

11 Upon the accuracy with which similitude in dissimilitude, and dissimilitude in similitude are perceived, depend our taste and moral feelings.

William Wordsworth 1770–1850: preface to *Lyrical Ballads* (1800)

12 The reading or non-reading a book—will never keep down a single petticoat.

Lord Byron 1788–1824: letter to Richard Hoppner, 29 October 1819

13 We know no spectacle so ridiculous as the British public in one of its periodical fits of morality.

Lord Macaulay 1800–59: *Essays Contributed to the Edinburgh Review* (1843) 'Moore's *Life of Lord Byron*'

1 Conventionality is not morality. Self-righteousness is not religion. To attack the first is not to assail the last. To pluck the mask from the face of the Pharisee, is not to lift an impious hand to the Crown of Thorns.

Charlotte Brontë 1816–55: *Jane Eyre* (2nd ed., 1848) preface

2 It is a noble grand book, whoever wrote it—but Miss Evans' life taken at the best construction, does so jar against the beautiful book that one cannot help hoping against hope.

on first hearing of the true identity of 'George ***Eliot****', author of* Adam Bede

Elizabeth Gaskell 1810–65: letter to George Smith, 4 August 1859

3 But a man or woman who publishes writings inevitably assumes the office of teacher or influences the public mind . . . He can no more escape influencing the moral taste, and with it the action of the intelligence, than a setter of fashion in furniture and dress can fill the shops with his designs and leave the garniture of persons and houses unaffected by his industry.

George Eliot 1819–80: attributed

4 There is no such thing as a moral or an immoral book. Books are well written, or badly written.

Oscar Wilde 1854–1900: *The Picture of Dorian Gray* (1891)

5 I believe that literature is the principal voice of the conscience, and it is its duty age after age to affirm its morality against the specific moralities of clergymen and churches; and of kings and parliaments and peoples.

W. B. Yeats 1865–1939: letter to the Editor of the *Freeman's Journal*, 14 November 1901

6 As my poor father used to say
In 1863,
Once people start on all this Art
Goodbye, moralitee!

A. P. Herbert 1890–1971: 'Lines for a Worthy Person' (1930)

7 Morality in the novel is the trembling instability of the balance. When the novelist puts his thumb in the scale, to pull down the balance to his own predilection, that is immorality.

D. H. Lawrence 1885–1930: *Phoenix* (1936) 'Morality and the Novel'

8 Art may be served by morality: it can never be its servant. For the principles of art are eternal, while the principles of morality fluctuate with the spiritual ebb and flow of the ages.

Arthur Symons 1865–1945: Edmund White *The Burning Library* (1994); attributed

9 As I grow older and older,
And totter towards the tomb,
I find that I care less and less
Who goes to bed with whom.

Dorothy L. Sayers 1893–1957: 'That's Why I Never Read Modern Novels'; Janet Hitchman *Such a Strange Lady* (1975)

10 Morality's *not* practical. Morality's a gesture. A complicated gesture learned from books.

Robert Bolt 1924–95: *A Man for All Seasons* (1960)

11 Leavis demands moral earnestness; I prefer morality . . . I mean I'd sooner live among people who don't cheat at cards than among people who are earnest about not cheating at cards.

C. S. Lewis 1898–1963: 'Unreal Estates'; Kingsley Amis and Robert Conquest (eds.) *Spectrum IV* (1965)

12 That a piece of writing is good doesn't override other considerations—moral considerations—when it comes to damaging others.

A. S. Byatt 1936– : *The Game* (1967)

1 The humanity of an artist's work is no guarantee that he is a decent human being.

Peter Hall 1930– : diary, 21 May 1978

2 Even fabulist fictions are moral. They are among the most moral of things. What's more moral than a fairy tale? Science fiction is dripping with message.

Margaret Atwood 1939– : in an interview, December 1986; Earl G. Ingersoll (ed.) *Margaret Atwood: Conversations* (1990)

Motivation

3 Even if nature says no, indignation makes me write verse.

Juvenal AD *c.*60–*c.*130: *Satires*

4 The multitude of books is a great evil. There is no measure or limit to this fever of writing; everyone must be an author; some out of vanity to acquire celebrity; others for the sake of lucre or gain.

Martin Luther 1483–1546: *Table-Talk* (1569)

5 Some rhyme a neebor's name to lash;
Some rhyme (vain thought!) for needfu' cash;
Some rhyme to court the countra clash,
An' raise a din;
For me, an aim I never fash;
I rhyme for fun.

Robert Burns 1759–96: 'To J. S[mith]' (1786)

6 An old literary truth: What we write pleases us, otherwise we surely wouldn't have written it.

Johann Wolfgang von Goethe 1749–1832: *On Morphology* (1817) 'The Fate of the Manuscript'

7 The port from which I set out was, I think, that of the *essential loneliness of my life.*

Henry James 1843–1916: letter, 2 October 1900

8 God, what a hell of a profession to be a writer. One is one simply because one can't help it.

F. Scott Fitzgerald 1896–1940: letter, August 1935

9 The ruling fantasy which drove him to write: a sense of evil religious in its intensity.
*of Henry **James***

Graham Greene 1904–91: 'Henry James: the Private Universe' (1936)

10 I was driven into writing because I found it was the only way a lazy and ill-educated man could make a decent living. I am not complaining about the wages. They always seem to me disproportionately high. What I mind so much is the work.

Evelyn Waugh 1903–66: in *Nash's Pall Mall Magazine* March 1937

11 You don't write because you want to say something; you write because you've got something to say.

F. Scott Fitzgerald 1896–1940: Edmund Wilson (ed.) *The Crack-Up* (1945) 'Note-Books'

*the young Stephen **Spender** had told **Eliot** of his wish to become a poet:*

12 I can understand your wanting to write poems, but I don't quite know what you mean by 'being a poet' . . .

T. S. Eliot 1888–1965: Stephen Spender *World within World* (1951)

13 In the same way that a woman becomes a prostitute. First I did it to please myself, then I did it to please my friends, and finally I did it for money.
when asked how he became a writer

Ferenc Molnar 1878–1972: attributed

1 There are three reasons for becoming a writer. The first is that you need the money; the second, that you have something to say that you think the world should know; and the third is that you can't think what to do with the long winter evenings.

Quentin Crisp 1908– : *The Naked Civil Servant* (1968)

2 One needs a mentor, otherwise it's very lonely. You need someone to tell you to go on.

Paul Scott 1920–78: Hilary Spurling *Paul Scott* (1990)

3 What's writing? A way of escape, like travelling to a war, or to see the Mau Mau. Escaping what? Boredom. Death.

Graham Greene 1904–91: interview with John Mortimer, in *Sunday Times* 16 March 1980

4 It's probably a form of childish curiosity that keeps me going as a fiction writer. I . . . want to open everybody's bureau drawers and see what they keep in there. I'm nosy.

Margaret Atwood 1939– : in an interview, December 1986; Earl G. Ingersoll (ed.) *Margaret Atwood: Conversations* (1990)

5 Every writing career starts as a personal quest for sainthood, for self-betterment. Sooner or later, and as a rule quite soon, a man discovers that his pen accomplishes a lot more than his soul.

Joseph Brodsky 1940–96: *Less than One* (1986)

6 I sometimes get interested in stories because I notice a sort of blank—why hasn't anyone written about this? *Can* it be written about?

Margaret Atwood 1939– : in an interview, November 1989; Earl G. Ingersoll (ed.) *Margaret Atwood: Conversations* (1990)

7 Write to amuse? What an appalling suggestion!
I write to make people anxious and miserable and to
  worsen their indigestion.

Wendy Cope 1945– : 'Serious Concerns' (1992)

8 I think writing does come out of a deep well of loneliness and a desire to fill some gap. No one in his right mind would sit down to write a book if he were a well-adjusted, happy man.

Jay McInerney 1955– : in *Independent on Sunday* 19 April 1992

Movements and Trends

9 Come leave the loathsome stage,
And the more loathsome age
Where pride and impudence in faction knit,
Usurp the chair of wit . . .
Say that thou pour'st them wheat,
And they would acorns eat;
Twere simple fury, still thyself to waste
On such as have no taste.

Ben Jonson *c.*1573–1637: 'Ode to Himself'

10 The next Augustan age will dawn on the other side of the Atlantic. There will, perhaps, be a Thucydides at Boston, a Xenophon at New York, and, in time, a Virgil at Mexico, and a Newton at Peru. At last, some curious traveller from Lima will visit England and give a description of the ruins of St Paul's, like the editions of Balbec and Palmyra.

Horace Walpole 1717–97: letter to Horace Mann, 24 November 1774

1 About the beginning of the seventeenth century appeared a race of writers that may be termed the metaphysical poets . . . The metaphysical poets were men of learning, and to show their learning was their whole endeavour.

Samuel Johnson 1709–84: *Lives of the English Poets* (1779–81) 'Cowley'

2 It is proper that I should mention one other circumstance which disfigures these poems from the popular poetry of the day . . . The subject is indeed important! For the human mind is capable of excitement without the application of gross and violent stimulants.
on the new popular literature

William Wordsworth 1770–1850: preface to *Lyrical Ballads* (1800)

3 The metaphysical school, which marred a good poet in Cowley and found its proper direction in Butler, expired in Norris of Bemerton.

Robert Southey 1774–1843: in *Quarterly Review* vol. 12 1814

4 The classical is health, the romantic sickness.

Johann Wolfgang von Goethe 1749–1832: *Sayings in Prose*

5 Wordsworth, Tennyson and Browning; or, pure, ornate, and grotesque art in English poetry.

Walter Bagehot 1826–77: in *National Review* November 1864, essay title

6 In literature the period may be defined as that in which men had ceased to write for students, and had not begun to write for women.
of the eighteenth century

Walter Bagehot 1826–77: in *National Review* January 1856 'Edward Gibbon'

7 To say the word Romanticism is to say modern art–that is, intimacy, spirituality, colour, aspiration towards the infinite, expressed by every means available to the arts.

Charles Baudelaire 1821–67: *Curiosités Esthétiques* (1868)

8 Though the Philistines may jostle, you will rank as an
apostle in the high aesthetic band,
If you walk down Piccadilly with a poppy or a lily in your
medieval hand.

W. S. Gilbert 1836–1911: *Patience* (1881)

9 Consciousness, then, does not appear to itself chopped up in bits . . . It is nothing jointed; it flows. A 'river' or a 'stream' are the metaphors by which it is most naturally described. In talking of it hereafter, let us call it the stream of thought, of consciousness, or of *subjective life*.

William James 1842–1910: *Principles of Psychology* (1890) vol. 1

10 The nineteenth century dislike of Realism is the rage of Caliban seeing his own face in the glass.

Oscar Wilde 1854–1900: *The Picture of Dorian Gray* (1891)

11 It was only with the modern poets, with Goethe and Wordsworth and Browning, that poetry gave up the right to consider all things in the world as a dictionary of types and symbols and began to call itself a critic of life and an interpreter of things as they are.

W. B. Yeats 1865–1939: 'The Autumn of the Body' (1898)

12 Spliced cinematography in paintings and diarrhoea in writing.
describing Futurism

Ezra Pound 1885–1972: letter to James Joyce, 6 September 1915

1 In the seventeenth century a dissociation of sensibility set in, from which we have never recovered; and this dissociation, as is natural, was due to the influence of the two most powerful poets of the century, Milton and Dryden.

T. S. Eliot 1888–1965: 'The Metaphysical Poets' (1921)

2 A Movement in the Arts—*any* movement—leavens a whole Nation with astonishing rapidity: its ideas pour through the daily, the weekly and the monthly press with the rapidity of water pouring through interstices, until at last they reach the Quarterlies and disturb even the Academicians asleep over their paper baskets.

Ford Madox Ford 1873–1939: *Thus to Revisit* (1921)

3 The European moderns are all *trying* to be extreme. The great Americans just were it.

D. H. Lawrence 1885–1930: *Studies in Classic American Literature* (1923)

4 I am touched at your sending me a copy, for I feel that to your generation, which has taken such a flying leap into the future, I must represent the literary equivalent of tufted furniture and gas chandeliers.

to F. Scott ***Fitzgerald****, who had sent her a copy of* The Great Gatsby

Edith Wharton 1862–1937: letter to F. Scott Fitzgerald, 8 June 1925

5 All our youth they hung about the houses of our minds like Uncles, the Big Four: H. G. Wells, George Bernard Shaw, John Galsworthy and Arnold Bennett.

Rebecca West 1892–1983: *The Strange Necessity* (1928)

6 Sodomhipped young men, with the inevitable sidewhiskers and cigarettes, the faulty livers and the stained teeth, reading Lawrence as an aphrodisiac and Marie Corelli in their infrequent baths, spew onto paper and canvas their ignorance and perversions, wetting the bed of their brains with discharges of fungoid verse. This is the art of today.

Dylan Thomas 1914–53: letter to Pamela Hansford Johnson, November 1933

7 As the world grows smaller, so the minds of men grow smaller, more compact, and more empty. These are the machine-minders of literature.

Raymond Chandler 1888–1959: letter to Charles W. Morton, 5 January 1947

8 The poets of the Romantic Movement gave an outlet to new ideas . . . beneath the crust of their age, just as the Metaphysicals had done for the new ideas of their time.

C. Day-Lewis 1904–72: *The Colloquial Element in English Poetry* (1947)

9 It is affectation that makes so many of today's writings, even the best among them, unbearable to me. The author takes on a tone that is not natural to him.

André Gide 1869–1951: *Ainsi Soit-il* (1952)

10 The French fathered the Modern Movement, which slowly moved beyond the Channel and then across the Irish Sea until the Americans finally took it over, bringing to it their own demonic energy, extremism and taste for the colossal.

Cyril Connolly 1903–74: *The Modern Movement* (1965)

11 I think the emotional content of twentieth century English verse so far has been on the whole thinner than that of previous centuries.

Larkin had edited the Oxford Book of Twentieth-Century Verse *(1954)*

Philip Larkin 1922–85: letter 20 January 1966

1 This solemn pledge to abstain from truth was called socialist realism.

Alexander Solzhenitsyn 1918– : *The Oak and the Calf* (1980)

2 Post-modernism may be seen as the tendency to make ironic use of the stock images of the mass media, or to inject the taste for the marvellous inherited from the literary tradition into narrative mechanisms that accentuate its alienation.

Italo Calvino 1923–85: *Six Memos for the Next Millennium* (1992)

3 No writer is really part of a group sensibility. You can record one and sympathize with it but, when you're writing, you're on your own.

A. S. Byatt 1936– : in an interview, April 1988; George Greenfield *Scribblers for Bread* (1989)

4 The morbid marriage of love and death which is the hallmark of the Romantic approach to life.

A. N. Wilson 1950– : *Penfriends from Porlock* (1988)

5 The introduction of realism into literature in the 18th century by Richardson, Fielding and Smollett was like the introduction of electricity into engineering.

Tom Wolfe 1931– : 'Stalking the Billion-Footed Beast' (1989)

6 For a serious young writer to stick with realism after 1960 required contrariness and courage.

Tom Wolfe 1931– : 'Stalking the Billion-Footed Beast' (1989)

7 The way of telling the tale may and must change, but is the tale really a new one? If the writer thinks of himself not as a successor to the Georgians, but as one of the line of Aesop and Scheherazade and the tirelessly inventive author of *The Golden Legend*, he need not worry too much about the latest literary fashions from the Parisian literary couturiers.

Robertson Davies 1913–95: Clare Boylan (ed.) *The Agony and the Ego* (1993)

8 [Roger Fry] gave us the term 'Post-Impressionist', without realising that the late twentieth century would soon be entirely fenced in with posts.

Jeanette Winterson 1959– : *Art Objects* (1995)

of the 'romanticism' of Rider Haggard, Robert Louis ***Stevenson****, and Rudyard* ***Kipling****:*

9 I think . . . they were the first British writers who woke up and said, My God, we've got an Empire and it stretches right round the world. We shouldn't still be writing parish pump novels.

Hammond Innes 1913– : interview in *Daily Telegraph* 3 August 1996

Mystery see **Crime and Mystery**

Names

10 If you should have a boy do not christen him John . . . 'Tis a bad name and goes against a man. If my name had been Edmund I should have been more fortunate.

John Keats 1795–1821: letter to his sister-in-law, 13 January 1820

11 Call me Ishmael.

Herman Melville 1819–91: *Moby Dick* (1851)

1 Fiction-mongers collect proper names, surnames, etc.—make notes and lists of any odd or unusual, as handsome or ugly ones they see or hear—in newspapers (columns of births, deaths, marriages, etc.) or in directories and signs of shops or elsewhere; fishing out of these memoranda in time of need the one that strikes them as good for a particular case.
to a Mr Capadose, who had written to James about his use of the name in 'The Liar'

Henry James 1843–1916: letter 13 October 1896

2 I have fallen in love with American names,
The sharp, gaunt names that never get fat,
The snakeskin-titles of mining-claims,
The plumed war-bonnet of Medicine Hat,
Tucson and Deadwood and Lost Mule Flat.

Stephen Vincent Benét 1898–1943: 'American Names' (1927)

3 My characters always appear with their names. Sometimes these names seem to me affected, sometimes almost ridiculous; but I am obliged to own that they are never fundamentally unsuitable. And the proof that they are not, that they really belong to the people, is the difficulty I have in trying to substitute other names. For many years the attempt always ended fatally; any character I unchristened instantly died on my hands, as if it were some kind of sensitive crustacean, and the name it brought with it were its shell.

Edith Wharton 1862–1937: *A Backward Glance* (1934)

4 Bingo Bolger-Baggins a bad name. Let Bingo = Frodo.
on the first draft of The Lord of the Rings

J. R. R. Tolkien 1892–1973: note, *c.*1938; Humphrey Carpenter *J. R. R. Tolkien* (1977)

on being asked by William Carlos Williams how he had chosen the name 'West':

5 Horace Greeley said, 'Go West, young man. So I did.'

Nathanael West 1903–40: Jay Martin *Nathanael West* (1970)

6 He [James Joyce] liked to think how some day, way off in Tibet or Somaliland, some boy or girl reading that little book would be pleased to come upon the name of his or her home river.
***Joyce** had worked 350 river names into the Anna Livia Plurabelle section of* Finnegan's Wake

Richard Ellman 1918–87: *James Joyce* (1959)

7 If one uses an initial for one's principal character, people begin to talk about Kafka.

Graham Greene 1904–91: *In Search of a Character* (1961)

8 Proper names are poetry in the raw. Like all poetry they are untranslatable.

W. H. Auden 1907–73: *A Certain World* (1970)

9 There is a magical quality in names—to change the name is to change the character.

Graham Greene 1904–91: *Ways of Escape* (1980)

10 Names have to be appropriate. Therefore I spend a lot of time reading up on the meanings of names, in books like *Name Your Baby*.

Margaret Atwood 1939– : in an interview, December 1986; Earl G. Ingersoll (ed.) *Margaret Atwood: Conversations* (1990)

1 Names, once they are in common use, quickly become mere sounds, their etymology being buried, like so many of the earth's marvels, beneath the dust of habit.

Salman Rushdie 1947– : *The Satanic Verses* (1988)

2 Why should people I have never met, who read me in bed and in the bathtub, think of me as 'Sam'.

insisting that his first name be represented by the initial 'S.' on the title-pages of his books

Samuel ('Sam') Schoenbaum 1927–96: in *The Times* 25 April 1996; obituary

Narrative see **Plot and Narrative**

Nature

3 Nature never set forth the earth in so rich tapestry as diverse poets have done . . . her world is brazen, the poets only deliver a golden.

Philip Sidney 1554–86: *The Defence of Poetry* (1595)

4 And this our life, exempt from public haunt,
Finds tongues in trees, books in the running brooks,
Sermons in stones, and good in everything.

William Shakespeare 1564–1616: *As You Like It* (1599); cf. **342:10**

5 I have learned
To look on nature, not as in the hour
Of thoughtless youth; but hearing oftentimes
The still, sad music of humanity.

William Wordsworth 1770–1850: 'Lines composed . . . above Tintern Abbey' (1798)

6 I believe a leaf of grass is no less than the journey-work of the stars,
And the pismire is equally perfect, and a grain of sand, and the egg of the wren,
And the tree toad is a chef-d'oeuvre for the highest,
And the running blackberry would adorn the parlours of heaven.

Walt Whitman 1819–92: 'Song of Myself' (written 1855)

7 What a book a devil's chaplain might write on the clumsy, wasteful, blundering, low, and horridly cruel works of nature!

Charles Darwin 1809–82: letter to J. D. Hooker, 13 July 1856

8 No matter how often you knock at nature's door, she won't answer in words you can understand—for Nature is dumb. She'll vibrate and moan like a violin, but you mustn't expect a song.

Ivan Turgenev 1818–83: *On the Eve* (1860)

9 Nature is not a temple, but a workshop, and man's the workman in it.

Ivan Turgenev 1818–83: *Fathers and Sons* (1862)

10 Poems are made by fools like me,
But only God can make a tree.

Joyce Kilmer 1886–1918: 'Trees' (1914)

11 What happens when you idealize the soil, the mother-earth, and really go back to it? Then with overwhelming conviction it is borne in upon you, as it was upon Thomas Hardy, that the whole scheme of things is against you.

D. H. Lawrence 1885–1930: *Studies in Classic American Literature* (1923)

12 Nature and letters seem to have a natural antipathy . . . they tear each other to pieces.

Virginia Woolf 1882–1941: *Orlando* (1928)

1 After reading Thoreau I felt how much I have lost by leaving nature out of my life.

F. Scott Fitzgerald 1896–1940: letter 11 March 1939

2 Landscape is a passive creature which lends itself to an author's mood.

T. S. Eliot 1888–1965: *After Strange Gods* (1934) 'Thomas Hardy'

3 I'm replacing some of the timber used up by my books. Books are just trees with squiggles on them.
on growing trees

Hammond Innes 1913– : interview in *Radio Times* 18 August 1984

Newspapers and Magazines see also **Journalism**

4 It is to be noted that when any part of this paper appears dull there is a design in it.

Richard Steele 1672–1729: in *The Tatler* 7 July 1709

5 The liberty of the press is the *Palladium* of all the civil, political, and religious rights of an Englishman.

'Junius': *The Letters of Junius* (1772 ed.)

6 The newspapers! Sir, they are the most villainous—licentious—abominable—infernal—Not that I ever read them—No—I make it a rule never to look into a newspaper.

Richard Brinsley Sheridan 1751–1816: *The Critic* (1779)

7 The influence of the press, if you believe writers and printers, is the one sufficient condition of social well-being. Your newspaper people are the only traders that thrive upon convulsion. In quiet times who cares for the paper? In times of tumult, who does not? . . . Take in *The Times*, and you will see it assumed that every year ought to be an era. 'The government does nothing' is the indignant cry, and simple people in the country don't know that this is merely a civilized façon de parler for 'I have nothing to say'.

Walter Bagehot 1826–77: in *Inquirer* 1852 'The French Newspaper Press'

8 The purchaser [of a newspaper] desires an article which he can appreciate at sight; which he can lay down and say, 'An excellent article, very excellent; exactly *my own* sentiments.'

Walter Bagehot 1826–77: in *National Review* July 1856 'The Character of Sir Robert Peel'

the founder of the New York Herald *justifying as legitimate hoaxes the paragraphs of fictitious news which appeared in his paper:*

9 I am always serious in my aims, but full of frolic in my means.

James Gordon Bennett 1800–72: in *Dictionary of National Biography* (1917–)

10 Newspaper editors sport daily with the names of men of whom they do not hesitate to publish almost the severest words that can be uttered; but let an editor be himself attacked, even without his name, and he thinks that the thunderbolt of heaven should fall upon the offender.

Anthony Trollope 1815–82: *Phineas Redux* (1874)

11 The screeching newspapers . . . for me, the danger that overtops all others.

Henry James 1843–1916: letter 20 April 1898

1 One of the many reasons why I should like to be a highly instructed Frenchman is, that I might have the luxury of appreciating as an exotic the peculiar blackguardism of an English sporting paper.

George Gissing 1857–1903: *Commonplace Book* (1962)

2 The Pope may launch his Interdict,
The Union its decree,
But the bubble is blown and the bubble is pricked
By Us and such as We.
Remember the battle and stand aside
While Thrones and Powers confess
That King over all the children of pride
Is the Press—the Press—the Press!

Rudyard Kipling 1865–1936: 'The Press' (1917)

3 We have in modern society a huge journalistic organism the 'critical' or review press which *must* be fed—there simply is not enough, nowhere near enough, good creative work to feed the 'critical' machine, and so reputations are manufactured to feed it, and works born perfectly dead enjoy an illusory life.

T. S. Eliot 1888–1965: letter 12 January 1920

4 It is the duty of newspapers to advocate a policy of optimism in the broadest sense and to declare almost daily their belief in the future of England.

Lord Beaverbrook 1879–1964: in 1922; Matthew Engel *Tickle the Public* (1996)

5 Of all the literary scenes
Saddest this sight to me:
The graves of little magazines
Who died to make verse free.

Keith Preston 1884–1927: 'The Liberators'

6 I do not know where the British and American papers get their scare headlines about me. I have never given an interview in my life and do not receive journalists. Nor do I understand why they should consider an unread writer as good copy.

James Joyce 1882–1941: letter, 10 November 1932

7 Small and obscure papers and reviews keep critical thought alive, and encourage authors of original talent.

T. S. Eliot 1888–1965: in *Criterion* January 1939

8 The *New Yorker* will be the magazine which is not edited for the old lady in Dubuque.

Harold Ross 1892–1951: James Thurber *The Years with Ross* (1959)

9 A good newspaper, I suppose, is a nation talking to itself.

Arthur Miller 1915– : in *Observer* 26 November 1961

10 News is whatever a good editor chooses to print.

Arthur MacEwen : Daniel J. Boorstin *The Image* (1961)

11 On the whole I would not say that our press is obscene. I would say that it trembles on the brink of obscenity.

Lord Longford 1905– : attributed, 1963

12 If you want to make mischief come and work on my papers.

Lord Beaverbrook 1879–1964: to Anthony Howard, in *Radio Times* 27 June (1981); attributed

13 A licence to steal money forever.
of American newspapers

Rupert Murdoch 1931– : in *Washington Post* 24 July 1977

1 If they have a popular thought they have to go into a darkened room and lie down until it passes.
of the editors of 'quality' newspapers

Kelvin Mackenzie 1946– : in *Independent* 19 September 1989

2 I think our newspapers have high moral values, absolutely, and if they don't, they should have.

Rupert Murdoch 1931– : attributed, 1989

3 But how can you bear the responsibility of telling people what to *think*?
to a newspaper editor

Keith Joseph 1918–94: in *Observer* 14 October 1990

4 Interdepartmental memoranda for the elite.
of quality newspaper journalism

A. J. P. Taylor 1906–90: attributed

of his editorship of the science fiction magazine New Worlds*:*

5 It . . . had to have essentially a loony dictator, which is what I was. Every publication has to have a personality in that way, somebody who can't really tell the difference between themselves and the magazine.

Michael Moorcock 1939– : Stan Nicholls (ed.) *Wordsmiths of Wonder* (1993)

6 House organ of the Eurotrash.
of Vanity Fair

Calvin Trillin 1935– : in *Sunday Times* 9 April 1995

The Novel see also **Fiction**

7 Sure no one will contend, that the epistolary style is in general the most proper to a novelist, or that it hath been used by the best writers of this kind.

Henry Fielding 1707–54: preface to Sarah Fielding *Familiar Letters* (1747)

8 'Oh! it is only a novel! . . . only Cecilia, or Camilla, or Belinda:' or, in short, only some work in which the most thorough knowledge of human nature, the happiest delineation of its varieties, the liveliest effusions of wit and humour are conveyed to the world in the best chosen language.

Jane Austen 1775–1817: *Northanger Abbey* (1818)

9 A fictitious narrative, differing from the romance, because the events are accommodated to the ordinary train of human events, and the modern state of society.

Sir Walter Scott 1771–1832: *Essay on Romance* (1824); cf. **85:7**

10 A novel is a mirror which passes over a highway. Sometimes it reflects to your eyes the blue of the skies, at others the churned-up mud of the road.

Stendhal 1783–1842: *Le Rouge et le noir* (1830)

11 The novel is a subjective epic in which the author requests permission to treat the world in his own way. So the only question is whether he has a way; the rest of it will follow of itself.

Johann Wolfgang von Goethe 1749–1832: *Art and Antiquity* (1816–32)

12 It is the test of a novel writer's art that he conceals his snake-in-the-grass; but the reader may be sure that it is always there. No man or woman with a conscience,—no man or woman with intellect sufficient to produce amusement, can go on from year to year without the desire of teaching.

Anthony Trollope 1815–82: *Ralph the Heir* (1871)

13 The regular resource of people who don't go enough into the world to live a novel is to write one.

Thomas Hardy 1840–1928: *A Pair of Blue Eyes* (1873)

1 The advantages of the letter-system of telling a story (passing over the disadvantages) are that, hearing what one side has to say, you are led constantly to the imagination of what the other side must be feeling, and at last are anxious to know if the other side does really feel what you imagine.

Thomas Hardy 1840–1928: notebook, April 1878

2 When I want to read a novel, I write one.

Benjamin Disraeli 1804–81: W. Monypenny and G. Buckle *Life of Benjamin Disraeli* (1920) vol. 6

3 I am of the opinion that the epistolary form is an antiquated affair. It is all right when the gist of the matter is in the letters themselves (e.g., in the case of a district policeman who loves letter-writing), but as a literary form it is no good in many respects: it puts the author into a frame—that is its main weakness.

Anton Chekhov 1860–1904: letter 4 March 1886

4 One should not be too severe on English novels; they are the only relaxation of the intellectually unemployed.

Oscar Wilde 1854–1900: in *Pall Mall Gazette* 4 August 1886

5 A novel which does moral injury to a dozen imbeciles, and has bracing results upon a thousand intellects of normal vigour, can justify its existence; and probably a novel was never written by the purest minded author for which there could not be found some moral invalid or other whom it was capable of harming.

Thomas Hardy 1840–1928: in *The Forum* March 1888 'The Profitable Reading of Fiction'

6 The only obligation to which in advance we may hold a novel, without incurring the accusation of being arbitrary, is that it be interesting.

Henry James 1843–1916: 'The Art of Fiction' (1888)

7 A novel is a living thing, all one and continuous, like any other organism, and in proportion as it lives will it be found, I think, that in each of the parts there is something of each of the other parts.

Henry James 1843–1916: 'The Art of Fiction' (1888)

8 A triple-headed monster, sucking the blood of English novelists.

'Jasper Milvain' on the three-volume novel system

George Gissing 1857–1903: *New Grub Street* (1891)

9 A novel is an impression, not an argument.

Thomas Hardy 1840–1928: *Tess of the D'Urbervilles* (5th ed., 1892) preface

10 Essential characteristic of the really great novelist: a Christ-like all-embracing compassion.

Arnold Bennett 1867–1931: diary, 15 October 1896

11 Fair held the breeze behind us—twas warm with lovers'
prayers.
We'd stolen wills for ballast and a crew of missing heirs.
They shipped as Able Bastards till the wicked nurse
confessed,
And they worked the old three-decker to the Islands of the
Blest.

responding to the statement that 'the three-volume novel is extinct'

Rudyard Kipling 1865–1936: 'The Three-Decker' (1896)

12 A good novel tells us the truth about its hero; but a bad novel tells us the truth about its author.

G. K. Chesterton 1874–1936: *Heretics* (1905)

1 What is a novel if not a conviction of our fellow-men's existence strong enough to take upon itself a form of imagined life clearer than reality and whose accumulated verisimilitude of selected episodes puts to shame the pride of documentary history?

Joseph Conrad 1857–1924: *A Personal Record* (1912)

2 I believe that all novels . . . deal with character, and that it is to express character—not to preach doctrines, sing songs, or celebrate the glories of the British Empire, that the form of the novel, so clumsy, verbose, and undramatic, so rich, elastic, and alive, has been evolved.

Virginia Woolf 1882–1941: 'Mr. Bennett and Mrs. Brown' (1924)

3 One consequence of the modern novel's shift away from realism and humanized representation is that art tends to become a game or a delightful fraud.

José Ortega y Gasset 1883–1955: *The Dehumanization of Art* (1925)

4 Yes—oh dear yes—the novel tells a story.

E. M. Forster 1879–1970: *Aspects of the Novel* (1927)

5 And here lies the vast importance of the novel, properly handled. It can inform and lead into new places the flow of our sympathetic consciousness and it can lead our sympathy away in recoil from things gone dead.

D. H. Lawrence 1885–1930: *Lady Chatterley's Lover* (1928)

6 A novelist must preserve a childlike belief in the importance of things which common sense considers of no great consequence.

W. Somerset Maugham 1874–1965: *A Writer's Notebook* (1949) written in 1933

7 Anyone could write a novel given six weeks, pen, paper, and no telephone or wife.

Evelyn Waugh 1903–66: Henry 'Chips' Channon diary, 16 December 1934

8 If you try to nail anything down in the novel, either it kills the novel, or the novel gets up and walks away with the nail.

D. H. Lawrence 1885–1930: *Phoenix* (1936) 'Morality and the Novel'

9 The novel is the one bright book of life.

D. H. Lawrence 1885–1930: *Phoenix* (1936) 'Why the novel matters'

10 And in his own weak person, if he can,
Dully put up with all the wrongs of Man.

W. H. Auden 1907–73: 'The Novelist' (1938)

11 A good novel should leap like a fish at the end of a line.

perhaps summarizing Woolf's vision of a woman writer as a figure 'in a attitude of contemplation, like a fisherwoman, sitting on the bank of a lake . . . letting her imagination down into the depths of her consciousness'

Virginia Woolf 1882–1941: attributed; perhaps a summary of an extended metaphor in the essay 'Professions for Woman' (1931)

12 Lady Peabury was in the morning room reading a novel; early training gave a guilty spice to this recreation, for she had been brought up to believe that to read a novel before luncheon was one of the gravest sins it was possible for a gentlewoman to commit.

Evelyn Waugh 1903–66: *Work Suspended* (1942) 'An Englishman's Home'

13 It can be said that all prose fiction is a variation on the theme of *Don Quixote* . . . the poverty of the Don suggests that the novel is born with the appearance of money as a social element—money, the great solvent of the solid fabric of the old society, the great generator of illusion. Or,

Lionel Trilling 1905–75: *The Liberal Imagination* (1950) 'Manners, Morals and the Novel'

which is to say much the same thing, the novel is born in response to snobbery.

1 What, in fact, is a novel but a universe in which action is endowed with form, where final words are pronounced, where people possess one another completely and where life assumes the aspect of destiny?

Albert Camus 1913–60: *The Rebel* (1951) 'Rebellion and the Novel'

2 In our time the novel devours all other forms; one is almost forced to use it as the medium of expression.

Marguerite Yourcenar 1903–87: *Memoirs of Hadrian* (1955)

3 You can declare at the very start that it's impossible to write a novel nowadays, but then, behind your back, so to speak, give birth to a whopper, a novel to end all novels.

Günter Grass 1927– : *The Tin Drum* (1959)

4 I found that the novel enabled me to express the comic side of my mind and at the same time work out some serious theme.

Muriel Spark 1918– : 'How I Became a Novelist' (1960)

5 The economy of a novelist is a little like that of a careful housewife, who is unwilling to throw away anything that might perhaps serve its turn. Or perhaps the comparison is closer to the Chinese cook who leaves hardly any part of a duck unserved.

Graham Greene 1904–91: *In Search of a Character* (1961)

6 A great many novels nowadays are just travel books disguised, just travel books really.

Ivy Compton-Burnett 1884–1969: Hilary Spurling *Secrets of a Woman's Heart: the Later Life of Ivy Compton-Burnett* (1984)

7 A novel is balanced between a few true impressions and the multitude of false ones that make up most of what we call life. It tells us that for every human being there is a diversity of existences, that the single existence is itself an illusion in part . . . it promises us meaning, harmony, and even justice.

Saul Bellow 1915– : speech on receiving the Nobel Prize, 1976

8 The word 'novel', at root, means 'news', and no novelist, even though he explore no further than the closets and back stairs of his own home, can be without some news he wishes to bring.

John Updike 1932– : 'Melville's Withdrawal' (1981)

9 It is a waste of a novelist's energy to have ideas. All one remembers from good novels is the extent to which they have believably captured human character, or been able to describe emotions, places and things.

A. N. Wilson 1950– : in *Spectator* 31 July 1982

10 I still think novels are much more interesting than poems—a novel is so spreading, it can be so fascinating and so difficult.

Philip Larkin 1922–85: *Required Writing* (1983)

11 A novel that does not uncover a hitherto unknown segment of existence is immoral. Knowledge is the novel's only morality.

Milan Kundera 1929– : in *New York Review of Books* 19 July 1984

12 Writing novels preserves you in a state of innocence—a lot passes you by—simply because your attention is otherwise diverted.

Anita Brookner 1938– : John Haffenden (ed.) *Novelists in Interview* (1985)

1 Writing a novel is not merely going on a shopping expedition across the border to an unreal land: it is hours and years spent in the factories, the streets, the cathedrals of the imagination.

Janet Frame 1924– : *The Envoy from Mirror City* (1985)

2 I . . . see the novel as a vehicle for looking at society—an interface between language and what we choose to call reality.

Margaret Atwood 1939– : in an interview, March 1986; in *Paris Review* Winter 1990

3 I would say a novelist's proper job is to be sensitive to the way things look; I agree with Conrad that fiction is primarily a visual medium, and that there is something very concrete and valuable and eternal in any accurate description of the way things look.

Edmund White 1940– : interview in *Paris Review* 1988

4 Writing a novel is actually searching for victims. As I write I keep looking for casualties. The stories uncover the casualties.

John Irving 1942– : George Plimpton (ed.) *Writers at Work* 8th Series 1988

5 People assume that because a novel's invented it isn't true. In fact the reverse is the case. Biography and memoirs can never be wholly true, since they cannot include every conceivable circumstance of what happened. The novel can do that.

Anthony Powell 1905– : in *Independent* 25 November 1989

6 When you're a novelist, you're writing a play but you're acting all the parts, you're controlling the lights and the scenery and the whole business, and it's your show.

Robertson Davies 1913–95: in *Paris Review* 1989

7 All great novels, all true novels, are bisexual.

Milan Kundera 1929– : in *The Times* 16 May 1991

8 The novel is an unknown man and I have to find him.

Graham Greene 1904–91: attributed

9 Put simply, the novel stands between us and the hardening concept of statistical man. There is no other medium in which we can live for so long and intimately with a character. That is the service a novel renders. It performs no less an act than the rescue and preservation of the individuality and dignity of the single being, be it man, woman or child.

William Golding 1911–93: attributed

10 Every novel is a story, but life isn't one, more of a sprawl of incidents.

Doris Lessing 1919– : *Under My Skin* (1994)

11 For me being a novelist was more than just working in one 'literary genre' rather than another; it was an outlook, a wisdom, a position; a position that would rule out identification with any politics, any religion, any ideology, any moral doctrine, any group.

Milan Kundera 1929– : *Testaments Betrayed* (1995)

12 A novelist must systematically desystematize his thought, kick at the barricade that he himself has erected around his ideas.

Milan Kundera 1929– : *Testaments Betrayed* (1995)

13 The word 'novel' itself now makes me feel ill.

V. S. Naipaul 1932– : in 1995; Salman Rushdie in *Observer* 18 August 1996

1 What novel can compete with the best of reportage?
to the centenary conference of the British Publishers' Association, 1996

George Steiner 1929– : Salman Rushdie in *Observer* 18 August 1996

2 In the compact between novelist and reader, the novelist promises to lie, and the reader promises to allow it.

Cynthia Ozick 1928– : *Portrait of the Artist as a Bad Character* (1996)

Opening Lines see also **Closing Lines**

3 *Arma virumque cano.*
I sing of arms and the man.

Virgil 70–19 BC: *Aeneid*

4 *Nel mezzo del cammin di nostra vita.*
Midway along the path of our life.

Dante Alighieri 1265–1321: *Divina Commedia* 'Inferno'

5 Whan that Aprill with his shoures soote
The droghte of March hath perced to the roote.

Geoffrey Chaucer c.1343–1400: *The Canterbury Tales* 'The General Prologue'

6 Once upon a time . . .
traditional opening to a story, especially a fairy story

Anonymous: recorded from 1595

7 O! for a Muse of fire, that would ascend
The brightest heaven of invention.

William Shakespeare 1564–1616: *Henry V* (1599)

8 If music be the food of love, play on.

William Shakespeare 1564–1616: *Twelfth Night* (1601)

9 Yet once more, O ye laurels, and once more
Ye myrtles brown, with ivy never sere.

John Milton 1608–74: 'Lycidas' (1638)

10 Of man's first disobedience, and the fruit
Of that forbidden tree, whose mortal taste
Brought death into the world, and all our woe,
With loss of Eden.

John Milton 1608–74: *Paradise Lost* (1667)

11 As I walked through the wilderness of this world.

John Bunyan 1628–88: *The Pilgrim's Progress* (1678) pt. 1

12 It is a truth universally acknowledged, that a single man in possession of a good fortune, must be in want of a wife.

Jane Austen 1775–1817: *Pride and Prejudice* (1813)

13 Much have I travelled in the realms of gold,
And many goodly states and kingdoms seen.

John Keats 1795–1821: 'On First Looking into Chapman's Homer' (1817); cf. **199:9**

14 Oh, what can ail thee knight at arms
Alone and palely loitering?

John Keats 1795–1821: 'La belle dame sans merci' (1820)

15 Season of mists and mellow fruitfulness,
Close bosom-friend of the maturing sun.

John Keats 1795–1821: 'To Autumn' (1820)

16 I shall not say why and how I became, at the age of fifteen, the mistress of the Earl of Craven.

Harriette Wilson 1789–1846: *Memoirs* (1825); cf. **165:7**

17 It was a dark and stormy night.

Edward George Bulwer-Lytton 1803–73: *Paul Clifford* (1830)

1 There was no possibility of taking a walk that day.
Charlotte Brontë 1816–55: *Jane Eyre* (1847)

2 The boy stood on the burning deck
Whence all but he had fled.
Felicia Hemans 1793–1835: 'Casabianca' (1849)

3 Call me Ishmael.
Herman Melville 1819–91: *Moby Dick* (1851)

4 It was the best of times, it was the worst of times.
Charles Dickens 1812–70: *A Tale of Two Cities* (1859)

5 'Christmas won't be Christmas without any presents,' grumbled Jo, lying on the rug.
Louisa May Alcott 1832–88: *Little Women* (1868–9)

6 All happy families resemble one another, but each unhappy family is unhappy in its own way.
Leo Tolstoy 1828–1910: *Anna Karenina* (1875–7)

7 It is Christmas Day in the Workhouse.
George R. Sims 1847–1922: 'In the Workhouse—Christmas Day' (1879)

8 The opening was barred by a black bank of clouds, and the tranquil waterway leading to the uttermost ends of the earth flowed sombre under an overcast sky—seemed to lead into the heart of an immense darkness.
Joseph Conrad 1857–1924: *Heart of Darkness* (1902)

9 When Mary Lennox was sent to Misselthwaite Manor to live with her uncle, everybody said she was the most disagreeable-looking child ever seen.
Frances Hodgson Burnett 1849–1924: *The Secret Garden* (1911)

10 'Is there anybody there?' said the Traveller,
Knocking on the moonlit door.
Walter de la Mare 1873–1956: 'The Listeners' (1912)

11 If I should die, think only this of me:
That there's some corner of a foreign field
That is for ever England.
Rupert Brooke 1887–1915: 'The Soldier' (1914)

12 When Gregor Samsa awoke one morning from uneasy dreams he found himself transformed in his bed into a gigantic insect.
Franz Kafka 1883–1924: *The Metamorphosis* (1915)

13 Once upon a time and a very good time it was there was a moocow coming down along the road and this moocow that was down along the road met a nicens little boy named baby tuckoo.
James Joyce 1882–1941: *A Portrait of the Artist as a Young Man* (1916)

14 In a hole in the ground there lived a hobbit.
J. R. R. Tolkien 1892–1973: *The Hobbit* (1937)

15 Last night I dreamt I went to Manderley again.
Daphne Du Maurier 1907–89: *Rebecca* (1938)

16 In my beginning is my end.
T. S. Eliot 1888–1965: *Four Quartets* 'East Coker' (1940)

17 *Aujourd'hui, maman est morte. Ou peut-être hier, je ne sais pas.*

Mother died today. Or perhaps it was yesterday, I don't know.
Albert Camus 1913–60: *L'Étranger* (1944)

18 It was a bright cold day in April, and the clocks were striking thirteen.
George Orwell 1903–50: *Nineteen Eighty-Four* (1949)

1 The past is a foreign country: they do things differently there.

L. P. Hartley 1895–1972: *The Go-Between* (1953)

2 To begin at the beginning: It is spring, moonless night in the small town, starless and bible-black.

Dylan Thomas 1914–53: *Under Milk Wood* (1954)

3 Lolita, light of my life, fire of my loins. My sin, my soul. Lo-lee-ta: the tip of the tongue taking a trip of three steps down the palate to tap, at three, on the teeth. Lo. Lee. Ta.

Vladimir Nabokov 1899–1977: *Lolita* (1955)

4 'Take my camel, dear,' said my aunt Dot, as she climbed down from this animal on her return from High Mass.

Rose Macaulay 1881–1958: *The Towers of Trebizond* (1956)

5 If I am out of my mind, it's all right with me, thought Moses Herzog.

Saul Bellow 1915– : *Herzog* (1961)

6 It was the afternoon of my eighty-first birthday, and I was in bed with my catamite when Ali announced that the archbishop had come to see me.

Anthony Burgess 1917–93: *Earthly Powers* (1980)

7 At the age of fifteen my grandmother became the concubine of a warlord general.

Jung Chang 1952– : *Wild Swans* (1991); cf. **163:16**

Originality

8 The saying of the noble and glorious Aeschylus, who declared that his tragedies were large cuts taken from Homer's mighty dinners.

Aeschylus *c.*525–456 BC: Athenaeus *Deipnosophistae*

9 Nothing has yet been said that's not been said before.

Terence *c.*190–159 BC: *Eunuchus*

10 It is hard to utter common notions in an individual way.

Horace 65–8 BC: *Ars Poetica*

11 Not wrung from speculations and subtleties, but from common sense, and observation; not picked from the leaves of any author, but bred among the weeds and tares of mine own brain.

Thomas Browne 1605–82: *Religio Medici* (1643)

12 The original writer is not he who refrains from imitating others, but he who can be imitated by none.

François-René Chateaubriand 1768–1848: *Le Génie du Christianisme* (1802)

13 Never forget what I believe was observed to you by Coleridge, that every great and original writer, in proportion as he is great and original, must himself create the taste by which he is to be relished.

William Wordsworth 1770–1850: letter to Lady Beaumont, 21 May 1807

14 An original something, fair maid, you would win me
To write—but how shall I begin?
For I fear I have nothing original in me—
Excepting Original Sin.

Thomas Campbell 1777–1844: 'To a Young Lady, Who Asked Me to Write Something Original for Her Album' (1843)

15 When Shakespeare is charged with debts to his originals, Landor replies, 'Yet he was more original than his originals. He breathed upon dead bodies and brought them life.'

Ralph Waldo Emerson 1803–82: *Letters and Social Aims* (1876)

1 Perhaps the hardest thing in all literature—at least *I* have found it so: by no voluntary effort can I accomplish it: I have to take it as it comes—is to write anything *original*. And perhaps the easiest is, when once an original line has been struck out, to follow it up, and to write any amount more of the same.

Lewis Carroll 1832–98: preface to *Sylvie and Bruno* (1889)

2 Blank cheques of intellectual bankruptcy.
definition of catch-phrases

Oliver Wendell Holmes 1809–94: attributed

3 The history of art is the history of revivals.

Samuel Butler 1835–1902: *Notebooks* (1912)

4 It is not permitted to a man who takes up pen or chisel to seek originality, for passion is his only business, and he cannot but mould or sing after a new fashion because no disaster is like another.

W. B. Yeats 1865–1939: *Per Amica Silentia Lunae* (1918)

5 Another unsettling element in modern art is that common symptom of immaturity, the dread of doing what has been done before.

Edith Wharton 1862–1937: *The Writing of Fiction* (1925)

6 *Étonne-moi.*

Astonish me.
to Jean Cocteau

Sergei Diaghilev 1872–1929: Wallace Fowlie (ed.) *Journals of Jean Cocteau* (1956)

7 You merely loop the loop on a commonplace and come down between the lines.
when asked how to make an epigram by a young man in the flying corps

W. Somerset Maugham 1874–1965: *A Writer's Notebook* (1949) written in 1933

8 Where in this small-talking world can I find
A longitude with no platitude?

Christopher Fry 1907– : *The Lady's not for Burning* (1949)

9 Tching prayed on the mountain and
wrote MAKE IT NEW
on his bath tub.
Day by day make it new
cut underbrush,
pile the logs
keep it growing.

Ezra Pound 1885–1972: *Cantos* (1954)

10 The literary world is not conducted according to Marquis of Queensberry rules; if you find someone's private papers, you immediately rootle through them, looking for raw material. This is something non-literary people never understand. They are apt to confuse it with a vulgar, prying nature. Moral: when you have authors in the house you needn't lock up your spoons or your daughters, but get your diaries into the Safe Deposit.

Robertson Davies 1913–95: in 1959; *The Enthusiasms of Robertson Davies* (1990)

11 It is sometimes necessary to repeat what we all know. All mapmakers should place the Mississippi in the same location, and avoid originality.

Saul Bellow 1915– : *Mr Sammler's Planet* (1970)

12 Strong poets make . . . history by misreading one another, so as to clear imaginative space for themselves.

Harold Bloom 1930– : *The Anxiety of Influence* (1973)

13 Let's have some new clichés.

Sam Goldwyn 1882–1974: attributed, perhaps apocryphal

1 What obsesses a writer starting out on a lifetime's work is the panic-stricken search for a voice of his own.

John Mortimer 1923– : *Clinging to the Wreckage* (1982)

2 The task of the artist at any time is uncompromisingly simple—to discover what has not yet been done, and to do it.

Craig Raine 1944– : in *Observer* 21 August 1988 'Sayings of the Week'

Plagiarism

3 *Sic vos non vobis mellificatis apes.*
Sic vos non vobis nidificatis aves.
Sic vos non vobis vellera fertis oves.

Thus you bees make honey not for yourselves. Thus you birds build nests not for yourselves. Thus you sheep bear fleeces not for yourselves.

on Bathyllus claiming authorship of certain lines by **Virgil**

Virgil 70–19 BC: attributed

4 *O imitatores, servum pecus.*

O imitators, you slavish herd.

Horace 65–8 BC: *Epistles*

5 Whatever is well said by another, is mine.

Seneca ('the Younger') *c.*4 BC–AD 65: *Epistulae ad Lucilium*

6 In comparing various authors with one another, I have discovered that some of the gravest and latest writers have transcribed, word for word, from former works, without making acknowledgement.

Pliny the Elder AD 23–79: dedication to *Natural History*

7 He buys up poems for recital
And then as 'author' reads.
Why not? the purchase proves the title.
Our words become his deeds.

Martial AD *c.*40–*c.*104: *Epigrammata*, tr. James Michie

8 It could be said of me that in this book I have only made up a bunch of other men's flowers, providing of my own only the string that ties them together.

Montaigne 1533–92: *Essais* (1580)

9 So all my best is dressing old words new,
Spending again what is already spent.

William Shakespeare 1564–1616: sonnet 76

10 They lard their lean books with the fat of others' works.

Robert Burton 1577–1640: *The Anatomy of Melancholy* (1621–51)

11 So, naturalists observe, a flea
Hath smaller fleas that on him prey;
And these have smaller fleas to bite 'em,
And so proceed *ad infinitum*.
Thus every poet, in his kind,
Is bit by him that comes behind.

Jonathan Swift 1667–1745: 'On Poetry' (1733)

12 Damn them! They will not let my play run, but they steal my thunder!

on hearing his new thunder effects used at a performance of Macbeth, *following the withdrawal of one of his own plays after only a short run*

John Dennis 1657–1734: William S. Walsh *A Handy-Book of Literary Curiosities* (1893)

1 I hate like death the situation of the plagiarist; the glass I drink from is not large, but at least it is my own.

Alfred de Musset 1810–57: *La Coupe et les lèvres* (1832)

2 The truth is that the propensity of man to imitate what is before him is one of the strongest parts of his nature.

Walter Bagehot 1826–77: *Physics and Politics* (1872) 'Nation-Making'

3 When 'Omer smote 'is bloomin' lyre,
He'd 'eard men sing by land an' sea;
An' what he thought 'e might require,
'E went an' took—the same as me!

Rudyard Kipling 1865–1936: 'When 'Omer smote 'is bloomin' lyre' (1896)

4 Great writers create; writers of smaller gifts copy.

W. Somerset Maugham 1874–1965: *A Writer's Notebook* (1949) written in 1917

5 Immature poets imitate; mature poets steal.

T. S. Eliot 1888–1965: *The Sacred Wood* (1920) 'Philip Massinger'

6 We writers all act and react on one another; and when I see a good thing in another man's book I react on it at once.

Stephen Leacock 1869–1944: *My Discovery of England* (1922) 'Impressions of London'

7 If you steal from one author, it's plagiarism; if you steal from many, it's research.

Wilson Mizner 1876–1933: Alva Johnston *The Legendary Mizners* (1953)

8 No plagiarist can excuse the wrong by showing how much of his work he did not pirate.

Learned Hand 1872–1961: *Sheldon v. Metro-Goldwyn Pictures Corp.* 1936

9 Plagiarize! Let no one else's work evade your eyes,
Remember why the good Lord made your eyes.

Tom Lehrer 1928– : 'Lobachevski' (1953 song)

10 The history of literature is a history of appropriation . . . Literature, like property, is theft.

in 1993, defending the writer David Leavitt against the charge of plagiarizing Stephen ***Spender****'s* World Within World

James Atlas : in *Daily Telegraph* 20 July 1996

11 All writers are thieves; theft is a necessary tool of the trade.

Nina Bawden 1925– : *Mothers: Reflections by Daughters* (1995)

12 It felt as if I had walked into my house and found a complete stranger in the kitchen helping himself to a beer from my fridge.

on encountering what he believed to be a case of plagiarism

Ken Follett 1949– : in *Sunday Telegraph* 15 September 1996

Plot and Narrative

13 Of plots and actions, the episodic are the worst. I call a plot 'episodic' in which the episodes or acts succeed one another without probable or necessary sequence.

Aristotle 384–322 BC: *Poetics*

14 With a tale forsooth he [the poet] cometh unto you, with a tale which holdeth children from play, and old men from the chimney corner.

Philip Sidney 1554–86: *The Defence of Poetry* (1595)

15 What a devil is the plot good for, but to bring in fine things?

George Villiers, 2nd Duke of Buckingham 1628–87: *The Rehearsal* (1672)

1 Ay, now the plot thickens very much upon us.

George Villiers, 2nd Duke of Buckingham 1628–87: *The Rehearsal* (1672)

2 The French writers do not burden themselves too much with plot, which has been reproached to them as a fault.

John Dryden 1631–1700: attributed

3 Digressions, incontestably, are the sunshine;—they are the life, the soul of reading;—take them out of this book for instance,—you might as well take the book along with them.

Laurence Sterne 1713–68: *Tristram Shandy* (1759–67)

4 I abhor a mystery. I would fain, were it possible, have my tale run through from its little prologue to the customary marriage in its last chapter, with all the smoothness incidental to ordinary life. I have no ambition to surprise my reader.

Anthony Trollope 1815–82: *The Bertrams* (1859)

5 In telling a tale it is, I think, always well to sink the personal pronoun. The old way, 'Once upon a time', with slight modifications is the best way of telling a story.

Anthony Trollope 1815–82: letter, 24 May 1868

6 We want incident, interest, action: to the devil with your philosophy.

Robert Louis Stevenson 1850–94: letter to John Meiklejohn, February 1880

7 Make-'em-laugh, make-'em-cry, make-'em-wait.
formula for a successful novel

Charles Reade 1814–84: attributed

8 Literature, above all in its most typical mood, the mood of narrative, similarly flees the direct challenge and pursues instead an independent and creative aim. So far as it imitates at all, it imitates not life but speech: not the facts of human destiny, but the emphasis and the suppressions with which the human actor tells of them.

Robert Louis Stevenson 1850–94: 'A Humble Remonstrance' (1884)

9 The whole secret of fiction and the drama—in the constructional part—lies in the adjustment of things unusual to things eternal and universal.

Thomas Hardy 1840–1928: notebook 23 February 1893

10 Remember you shot a seagull? A man happened to come along, saw it and killed it, just to pass the time. A plot for a short story.

Anton Chekhov 1860–1904: *The Seagull* (1896)

11 The Story is just the spoiled child of art.

Henry James 1843–1916: *The Ambassadors* (1909 ed.) preface

on being asked if novelists found plot-making their hardest task:
12 All ladies find it so except Miss Austen.

Charlotte Yonge 1823–1901: Christabel Coleridge *Charlotte Mary Yonge* (1903)

13 'The king died and then the queen died', is a story. 'The king died and then the queen died of grief' is a plot.

E. M. Forster 1879–1970: *Aspects of the Novel* (1927)

14 Intimacy is gained but at the expense of illusion and nobility. It is like standing a man a drink so that he may not criticize your opinions.
on direct address to the reader

E. M. Forster 1879–1970: *Aspects of the Novel* (1927)

1 Stories tend to get out of hand, and this one has taken an unpremeditated turn.
of the unplanned introduction of the 'Black Rider' into the story that was to become The Lord of the Rings

J. R. R. Tolkien 1892–1973: letter to his publisher, spring 1938; Humphrey Carpenter *J. R. R. Tolkien* (1977)

2 A plot is like the bones of a person, not interesting like expression or signs of experience, but the support of the whole.

Ivy Compton-Burnett 1884–1969: 'A Conversation Between I. Compton-Burnett and M. Jourdain' (1945)

3 The structure of a play is always the story of how the birds came home to roost.

Arthur Miller 1915– : in *Harper's Magazine* August 1958

4 When in doubt have a man come through the door with a gun in his hand.

Raymond Chandler 1888–1959: attributed

5 No opera plot can be sensible, for in sensible situations people do not sing. An opera plot must be, in both senses of the word, a melodrama.

W. H. Auden 1907–73: in *Times Literary Supplement* 2 November 1967

6 The plot is not very important to me, though a novel must have one, of course. It's just a line to hang the washing on.

Ivy Compton-Burnett 1884–1969: Hilary Spurling *Secrets of a Woman's Heart: the Later Life of Ivy Compton-Burnett* (1984)

7 What I am trying to achieve is a voice sitting by a fireplace telling you a story on a winter's evening.

Truman Capote 1924–84: attributed

8 With me it's story, story, story.

Bernard Malamud 1914–86: attributed

9 The narrative impulse is always with us; we couldn't imagine ourselves through a day without it.

Robert Coover 1932– : in *Time Out* 7 May 1986

10 If you're a writer, a real writer, you're a descendant of those medieval storytellers who used to go into the square of a town and spread a little mat on the ground and sit on it and beat on a bowl and say, 'If you give me a copper coin I will tell you a golden tale.'

Robertson Davies 1913–95: in *Paris Review* 1989

11 I don't have ugly ducklings turning into swans in my stories. I have ugly ducklings turning into confident ducks.

Maeve Binchy 1940– : in *Current Biography* November 1995

12 A book has a pattern; it starts slowly, then rises to a small crisis and a slightly larger one, then comes up to the real crisis, which is where you hold the attention. A true storyteller is always dramatic.

Rumer Godden 1907– : Michael Rosen and Jill Burridge *Treasure Islands 2* (1993)

13 You do not think up a plot. You do not invent, you relate. The story is led by character. The character describes himself without knowing it.

V. S. Pritchett 1900–97: Clare Boylan (ed.) *The Agony and the Ego* (1993)

14 Story-telling is an instinct to come to terms with mystery, chaos, mess.

Graham Swift 1949– : Clare Boylan (ed.) *The Agony and the Ego* (1993); attributed

15 If I were asked what is the essence of storytelling I would say it is a simple thing: the relating of something strange.

Graham Swift 1949– : Clare Boylan (ed.) *The Agony and the Ego* (1993)

1 When I am thickening my plots, I like to think 'What if . . . What *if* . . . '

Patricia Highsmith 1921–95: Clare Boylan (ed.) *The Agony and the Ego* (1993)

2 Outlining is dangerous. I always describe a plot of a book as like footprints left in the snow after someone's run by. You must not put those footprints ahead of the person.

Michael Moorcock 1939– : Stan Nicholls (ed.) *Wordsmiths of Wonder* (1993)

3 In adult literary fiction, stories are there on sufferance. Other things are felt to be more important: technique, style, literary knowingness. The present day would-be George Eliots take up their stories as if with a pair of tongs. They're embarrassed by them. If they could write novels without stories in them, they would.
view of a children's author

Philip Pullman 1946– : in *Independent* 18 July 1996

4 It is a ruse . . . which could not be achieved on film or television: long live the written word!
on a plot device employed by Ruth Rendell in The Keys to the Street *(1996)*

Antonia Fraser 1932– : in *Daily Telegraph* 7 September 1996

Poetry see also **Rhyme and Rhythm**

5 Painting is silent poetry, poetry is eloquent painting.

Simonides *c.*556–468 BC: Plutarch *Moralia*

6 So poetry is something more philosophical and more worthy of serious attention than history, for while poetry is concerned with universal truths, history treats of particular facts.

Aristotle 384–322 BC: *Poetics*

7 *At non effugies meos iambos.*
But you shall not escape my iambics.

Catullus *c.*84–*c.*54 BC: R. A. B. Mynors (ed.) *Catulli Carmina* (1958) Fragment 3

8 Skilled or unskilled, we all scribble poems.

Horace 65–8 BC: *Epistles*

9 Poetry is devil's wine.

St Augustine AD 354–430: *Contra Academicos*; cf. **172:1**

10 The poet ranks far below the painter in the representation of visible things, and far below the musician in that of invisible things.

Leonardo da Vinci 1452–1519: Irma A. Richter (ed.) *Selections from the Notebooks of Leonardo da Vinci* (1952)

11 Poetry therefore, is an art of *imitation* . . . that is to say, a representing, counterfeiting, or figuring forth to speak metaphorically. A speaking picture, with this end: to teach and delight.

Philip Sidney 1554–86: *The Defence of Poetry* (1595)

12 Poesy was ever thought to have some participation of divineness, because it doth raise and erect the mind, by submitting the shows of things to the desires of the mind; whereas reason doth buckle and bow the mind unto the nature of things.

Francis Bacon 1561–1626: *The Advancement of Learning* (1605)

1 Did not one of the fathers in great indignation call poesy *vinum daemonum*?

Francis Bacon 1561–1626: *The Advancement of Learning* (1605); *vinum daemonum* the wine of devils; cf. **171:9**

2 We have watered our houses in Helicon.
occasionally misread 'We have watered our horses in Helicon'

George Chapman *c.*1559–1634: *May-Day* (1611)

3 All poets are mad.

Robert Burton 1577–1640: *The Anatomy of Melancholy* (1621–51) 'Democritus to the Reader'

4 Blest pair of Sirens, pledges of heaven's joy,
Sphere-born harmonious sisters, Voice, and Verse.

John Milton 1608–74: 'At a Solemn Music' (1645)

5 Things unattempted yet in prose or rhyme.

John Milton 1608–74: *Paradise Lost* (1667)

6 So poetry, which is in Oxford made
An art, in London only is a trade.

John Dryden 1631–1700: 'Prologue to the University of Oxon . . . at the Acting of *The Silent Woman*' (1673)

7 Poetry's a mere drug, Sir.

George Farquhar 1678–1707: *Love and a Bottle* (1698)

8 He [the poet] must write as the interpreter of nature, and the legislator of mankind, and consider himself as presiding over the thoughts and manners of future generations; as a being superior to time and place.

Samuel Johnson 1709–84: *Rasselas* (1759)

9 BOSWELL: Sir, what is poetry?
JOHNSON: Why Sir, it is much easier to say what it is not. We all *know* what light is; but it is not easy to *tell* what it is.

Samuel Johnson 1709–84: James Boswell *Life of Samuel Johnson* (1791) 12 April 1776

10 You will never be alone with a poet in your pocket.

John Adams 1735–1826: letter to John Quincy Adams, 14 May 1781

11 In common things that round us lie
Some random truths he can impart,—
The harvest of a quiet eye
That broods and sleeps on his own heart.

William Wordsworth 1770–1850: 'A Poet's Epitaph' (1800)

requirement for a great poet:
12 The touch of a blind man feeling the face of a darling child.

Samuel Taylor Coleridge 1772–1834: letter, 13 July 1802

13 We poets in our youth begin in gladness;
But thereof comes in the end despondency and madness.

William Wordsworth 1770–1850: 'Resolution and Independence' (1807)

14 I by no means rank poetry high in the scale of intelligence—this may look like affectation—but it is my real opinion—it is the lava of the imagination whose eruption prevents an earthquake.

Lord Byron 1788–1824: letter to Annabella Milbanke, 29 November 1813

15 A long poem is a test of invention which I take to be the polar star of poetry, as fancy is the sails, and imagination the rudder.

John Keats 1795–1821: letter to Benjamin Bailey, 8 October 1817

1 She ventured to hope he did not always read only poetry; and to say, that she thought it was the misfortune of poetry, to be seldom safely enjoyed by those who enjoyed it completely; and that the strong feelings which alone could estimate it truly, were the very feelings which ought to taste it but sparingly.

Jane Austen 1775–1817: *Persuasion* (1818)

2 That willing suspension of disbelief for the moment, which constitutes poetic faith.

Samuel Taylor Coleridge 1772–1834: *Biographia Literaria* (1817)

3 The two cardinal points of poetry, the power of exciting the sympathy of the reader by a faithful adherence to the truth of nature, and the power of giving the interest of novelty by the modifying colours of imagination.

Samuel Taylor Coleridge 1772–1834: *Biographia Literaria* (1817)

4 Poetry should surprise by a fine excess, and not by singularity—it should strike the reader as a wording of his own highest thoughts, and appear almost a remembrance.

John Keats 1795–1821: letter to John Taylor, 27 February 1818

5 Most wretched men
Are cradled into poetry by wrong:
They learn in suffering what they teach in song.

Percy Bysshe Shelley 1792–1822: 'Julian and Maddalo' (1818)

6 We hate poetry that has a palpable design upon us—and if we do not agree, seems to put its hand in its breeches pocket. Poetry should be great and unobtrusive, a thing which enters into one's soul, and does not startle it or amaze it with itself, but with its subject.

John Keats 1795–1821: letter to J. H. Reynolds, 3 February 1818

7 If poetry comes not as naturally as the leaves to a tree it had better not come at all.

John Keats 1795–1821: letter to John Taylor, 27 February 1818

8 As to the poetical character itself, (I mean that sort of which, if I am any thing, I am a member; that sort distinguished from the Wordsworthian or egotistical sublime; which is a thing *per se* and stands alone) it is not itself—it has no self . . . It has as much delight in conceiving an Iago as an Imogen.

John Keats 1795–1821: letter to Richard Woodhouse, 27 October 1818

9 A poet is the most unpoetical of any thing in existence, because he has no identity; he is continually in for—and filling some other body.

John Keats 1795–1821: letter to Richard Woodhouse, 27 October 1818

10 The poet and the dreamer are distinct,
Diverse, sheer opposite, antipodes.
The one pours out a balm upon the world,
The other vexes it.

John Keats 1795–1821: 'The Fall of Hyperion' (written 1819)

11 Chameleons feed on light and air:
Poets' food is love and fame.

Percy Bysshe Shelley 1792–1822: 'An Exhortation' (1820)

12 Poetry is the record of the best and happiest moments of the happiest and best minds.

Percy Bysshe Shelley 1792–1822: *A Defence of Poetry* (written 1821)

13 Poets are the unacknowledged legislators of the world.

Percy Bysshe Shelley 1792–1822: *A Defence of Poetry* (written 1821)

14 Perhaps no person can be a poet, or even enjoy poetry, without a certain unsoundness of mind.

Lord Macaulay 1800–59: 'Milton' (1825)

1 Scorn not the Sonnet; Critic, you have frowned,
Mindless of its just honours; with this key
Shakespeare unlocked his heart.

William Wordsworth 1770–1850: 'Scorn not the Sonnet' (1827); cf. **326:10**

2 Poetry is certainly something more than good sense, but it must be good sense at all events; just as a palace is more than a house, but it must be a house, at least.

Samuel Taylor Coleridge 1772–1834: *Table Talk* (1835) 9 May 1830

3 Vex not thou the poet's mind
With thy shallow wit:
Vex not thou the poet's mind;
For thou canst not fathom it.

Alfred, Lord Tennyson 1809–92: 'The Poet's Mind' (1830)

4 Poetry, in the most comprehensive application of the term, I take to be the flower of any kind of experience, rooted in truth, and issuing forth into beauty.

Leigh Hunt 1784–1859: *The Story of Rimini* (1832 ed.)

5 Poetry's unnat'ral; no man ever talked in poetry 'cept a beadle on boxin' day.
spoken by 'Mr Weller'

Charles Dickens 1812–70: *Pickwick Papers* (1837)

6 What is a modern poet's fate?
To write his thoughts upon a slate;
The critic spits on what is done,
Gives it a wipe—and all is gone.

Thomas Hood 1799–1845: 'A Joke'; Hallam Tennyson *Alfred Lord Tennyson* (1897)

7 Not deep the Poet sees, but wide.

Matthew Arnold 1822–88: 'Resignation' (1849)

8 Everything you invent is true: you can be sure of that. Poetry is a subject as precise as geometry.

Gustave Flaubert 1821–80: letter to Louise Colet, 14 August 1853

9 We do not enjoy poetry unless we know it to be poetry.

Henry David Thoreau 1817–62: diary, 1 October 1856

10 What is poetry? . . . The suggestion, by the imagination, of noble grounds for the noble emotions.

John Ruskin 1819–1900: *Modern Painters* (1856)

11 Nay, if there's room for poets in this world
A little overgrown (I think there is)
Their sole work is to represent the age,
Their age, not Charlemagne's.

Elizabeth Barrett Browning 1806–61: *Aurora Leigh* (1857)

12 The poet is like the prince of the clouds, who rides out the tempest and laughs at the archer. But when he is exiled on the ground, amidst the clamour, his giant's wings prevent him from walking.

Charles Baudelaire 1821–67: *Les fleurs du mal* (1857) 'L'Albatross'—'Spleen et idéal'

13 The business of a poet is fundamentally to *see*, not to analyse.

Henrik Ibsen 1828–1906: letter, 1871

14 A sonnet is a moment's monument,—
Memorial from the Soul's eternity
To one dead deathless hour.

Dante Gabriel Rossetti 1828–82: *The House of Life* (1881)

15 Poetry is at bottom a criticism of life.

Matthew Arnold 1822–88: *Essays in Criticism* Second Series (1888) 'Wordsworth'

1 More and more mankind will discover that we have to turn to poetry to interpret life for us, to console us, to sustain us. Without poetry, our science will appear incomplete; and most of what now passes with us for religion and philosophy will be replaced by poetry.

Matthew Arnold 1822–88: *Essays in Criticism* Second Series (1888) 'The Study of Poetry'

2 The difference between genuine poetry and the poetry of Dryden, Pope, and all their school, is briefly this: their poetry is conceived and composed in their wits, genuine poetry is conceived and composed in the soul.

Matthew Arnold 1822–88: *Essays in Criticism* Second Series (1888) 'Thomas Gray'

3 You explain nothing, O poet, but thanks to you all things become explicable.

Paul Claudel 1868–1955: *La Ville* (1897)

4 We who with songs beguile your pilgrimage
And swear that beauty lives though lilies die,
We poets of the proud old lineage
Who sing to find your hearts, we know not why,—
What shall we tell you? Tales, marvellous tales
Of ships and stars and isles where good men rest.

James Elroy Flecker 1884–1915: *The Golden Journey to Samarkand* (1913) 'Prologue'

5 Poets in our civilization, as it exists at present, must be *difficult*.

T. S. Eliot 1888–1965: 'The Metaphysical Poets' (1921)

6 A poet's mind . . . is constantly amalgamating disparate experience; the ordinary man's experience is chaotic, irregular, fragmentary. The latter falls in love, or reads Spinoza, and these two experiences have nothing to do with each other, or with the noise of the typewriter or the smell of cooking; in the mind of the poet these experiences are always forming new wholes.

T. S. Eliot 1888–1965: 'The Metaphysical Poets' (1921)

7 Words in search of a meaning.

Roman Jakobson 1896–1982: 'The Newest Russian Poetry' (1919; revised 1921)

8 Poetry is a comforting piece of fiction set to more or less lascivious music.

H. L. Mencken 1880–1956: *Prejudices* (1922)

9 Poetry is the achievement of the synthesis of hyacinths and biscuits.

Carl Sandburg 1878–1967: in *Atlantic Monthly* March 1923

10 Poetry is the opening and closing of a door, leaving those who look through to guess about what is seen during a moment.

Carl Sandburg 1878–1967: in *Atlantic Monthly* March 1923

11 We make out of the quarrel with others, rhetoric, but of the quarrel with ourselves, poetry.

W. B. Yeats 1865–1939: *Essays* (1924) 'Anima Hominis'

12 Poetry has no role to play except beyond philosophy.

André Breton 1896–1966: *Les Pas Perdus* (1924)

13 A Poem should be palpable and mute
As a globed fruit
Dumb
As old medallions to the thumb
Silent as the sleeve-worn stone
Of casement ledges where the moss has grown—
A poem should be wordless
As the flight of birds.

Archibald MacLeish 1892–1982: 'Ars Poetica' (1926)

1 A poem should not mean
But be.

Archibald MacLeish 1892–1982: 'Ars Poetica' (1926)

2 It [poetry] is capable of saving us; it is a perfectly possible means of overcoming chaos.

I. A. Richards 1893–1979: *Science and Poetry* (1926)

3 The poet produces something beautiful by fixing his attention on something real.

Simone Weil 1909–43: *Gravity and Grace* (1927)

4 Genuine poetry can communicate before it is understood.

T. S. Eliot 1888–1965: *Dante* (1929)

5 Poetry is simply literature reduced to the essence of its active principle. It is purged of idols of every kind, of realistic illusions, or any conceivable equivocation between the language of 'truth' and the language of 'creation'.

Paul Valéry 1871–1945: *Literature* (1930)

6 The poet is a bird of strange moods. He descends from his lofty domain to tarry among us, singing; if we do not honour him he will unfold his wings and fly back to his dwelling place.

Khalil Gibran 1883–1931: *Thoughts and Meditations* (1960) 'The Poet from Baalbek'

7 The poet's business is not to describe things to us, or to tell us about things, but to create in our minds the very things themselves.

Lascelles Abercrombie 1881–1938: *Poetry: Its Music and Meaning* (1932)

8 I, too, dislike it: there are things that are important
beyond all this fiddle.
Reading it, however, with a perfect contempt for it, one
discovers in it, after all, a place for the genuine.

Marianne Moore 1887–1972: 'Poetry' (1935)

9 Nor till the poets among us can be
'literalists of
the imagination'—above
insolence and triviality and can present
for inspection, imaginary gardens with real toads in them,
shall we have
it.

Marianne Moore 1887–1972: 'Poetry' (1935)

10 And poems are all that matter. The utmost of ambition is to lodge a few poems where they will be hard to get rid of.

Robert Frost 1874–1963: letter to Louis Untermeyer 21 August 1935

11 Writing a book of poetry is like dropping a rose petal down the Grand Canyon and waiting for the echo.

Don Marquis 1878–1937: E. Anthony *O Rare Don Marquis* (1962)

12 I would have a poet able-bodied, fond of talking, a reader of the newspapers, capable of pity and laughter, informed in economics, appreciative of women, involved in personal relationships, actively interested in politics, susceptible to physical impressions.

Louis MacNeice 1907–63: *Modern Poetry* (1938)

13 Burdened with the complexity of the lives we lead, fretting over appearances, netted in with anxieties and apprehensions, half smothered in drifts of tepid thoughts and tepid feelings, we may refuse what poetry has to give; but under its influence serenity returns to the troubled mind, the world crumbles, loveliness shines like flowers

Walter de la Mare 1873–1956: *Behold This Dreamer* (1939) 'Dream and Imagination'

after rain, and the further reality is once more charged with mystery.

1 A poem begins with a lump in the throat; a home sickness or a love sickness. It is a reaching-out toward expression; an effort to find fulfilment. A complete poem is one where an emotion has found its thought and the thought has found the words . . . My definition of poetry (if I were forced to give one) would be this: words that have become deeds.

Robert Frost 1874–1963: Lawrence Thompson *Fire and Ice* (1942)

2 My method is simple: not to bother about poetry. It must come of its own accord. Merely whispering its name drives it away.

Jean Cocteau 1889–1963: on 26 August 1945; *Professional Secrets* (1972)

3 An age which is incapable of poetry is incapable of any kind of literature except the cleverness of a decadence.

Raymond Chandler 1888–1959: letter to Charles W. Morton, 5 January 1947

4 The function of poetry is religious invocation of the Muse; its use is the experience of mixed exultation and horror that her presence excites.

Robert Graves 1895–1985: *The White Goddess* (1948)

5 For God-sake don't call me a poet,
For I've never been guilty of that.

Robert Service 1874–1958: 'A Verseman's Apology' (1949)

6 He [the poet] may be used as the barometer, but let us not forget he is also part of the weather.

Lionel Trilling 1905–75: *The Sense of the Past* (1950)

7 [Poetry] is a violence from within that protects us from a violence without.

Wallace Stevens 1879–1955: 'The Noble Rider And The Sounds Of Words' (1951)

8 A verbal art like poetry is reflective. It stops to think. Music is immediate: it goes on to become.

W. H. Auden 1907–73: Aaron Copland *Music and Imagination* (1952)

9 Poetry is a religion with no hope.

Jean Cocteau 1889–1963: *Journal d'un inconnu* (1953) 'De l'invisibilité'

10 Peotry is sissy stuff that rhymes. Weedy people sa la and fie and swoon when they see a bunch of daffodils.

Geoffrey Willans 1911–58 and **Ronald Searle** 1920– : *Down with Skool!* (1953)

11 A true sonnet goes eight lines and then takes a turn for better or worse and goes six or eight lines more.

Robert Frost 1874–1963: remark made on TV, 29 March 1954

12 The poet is the priest of the invisible.

Wallace Stevens 1879–1955: 'Adagia' (1957)

13 I know that poetry is indispensable, but for what I could not say.

Jean Cocteau 1889–1963: attributed, 1955

14 You need not fear to be a poet.

Walter de la Mare 1873–1956: attributed

15 I like a man with poetry in him, but not a poet.

Marilyn Monroe 1926–62: attributed, 1956

1 Poetry is so emotional and very tiring.

Edith Sitwell 1887–1964: attributed, 1957

2 Doctors in verse
Being scarce now, most poets
Are their own patients, compelled to treat
Themselves first, their complaint being
Peculiar always.

R. S. Thomas 1913– : 'The Cure' (1958)

3 Poetry is a way of taking life by the throat.

Robert Frost 1874–1963: Elizabeth S. Sergeant *Robert Frost* (1960)

4 Poetry is the revelation of a feeling that the poet believes to be interior and personal but which the reader recognises as his own.

Salvatore Quasimodo 1901–68: in *New York Times* 14 May 1960

5 Poetry is the only art people haven't yet learnt to consume like soup.

W. H. Auden 1907–73: in *New York Times* 1960

6 Even when the poet seems most himself . . . he is never the bundle of accident and incoherence that sits down to breakfast; he has been reborn as an idea, something intended, complete.

W. B. Yeats 1865–1939: *Essays and Introductions* (1961) 'A General Introduction for my Work'

7 Most people ignore most poetry
because
most poetry ignores most people.

Adrian Mitchell 1932– : *Poems* (1964)

8 And scribbled lines like fallen hopes
On backs of tattered envelopes.

Francis Hope 1938–74: 'Instead of a Poet' (1965)

9 When in public poetry should take off its clothes and wave to the nearest person in sight; it should be seen in the company of thieves and lovers rather than that of journalists and publishers.

Brian Patten 1946– : *Little Johnny's Confession* (1967)

10 Poetry before breakfast would be rather grisly.

Roy Fuller 1912–91: attributed, 1968

11 Ink runs from the corners of my mouth.
There is no happiness like mine.
I have been eating poetry.

Mark Strand 1934– : 'Eating Poetry' (1968)

12 I don't think poetry expresses emotion. It evokes emotion from the reader, and that is a very different thing. As someone once said, 'If you want to express emotion, scream.'

Margaret Atwood 1939– : in an interview, 4 April 1972; Earl G. Ingersoll (ed.) *Margaret Atwood: Conversations* (1990)

13 Too many people in the modern world view poetry as a luxury, not a necessity like petrol. But to me it's the oil of life.

John Betjeman 1906–84: attributed, 1974

14 My favourite poem is the one that starts 'Thirty days hath September' because it actually tells you something.

Groucho Marx 1895–1977: Ned Sherrin *Cutting Edge* (1984); attributed

1 This passion for poetry readings has led to a kind of poetry that you *can* understand first go: easy rhythms, easy emotions, easy syntax. I don't think it stands up on the page.

Philip Larkin 1922–85: *Required Writing* (1983)

2 I used to think all poets were Byronic —
Mad, bad and dangerous to know.
And then I met a few. Yes it's ironic —
I used to think all poets were Byronic.
They're mostly wicked as a ginless tonic
And wild as pension plans.

Wendy Cope 1945– : 'Triolet' (1986); cf. **287:3**

3 I think poetry should be alive. You should be able to dance it.

Benjamin Zephaniah 1958– : in *Sunday Times* 23 August 1987

4 The fact that poetry is not of the slightest economic or political importance, that it has no attachment to any of the powers that control the modern world, may set it free to do the only thing that in this age it can do—to keep some neglected parts of the human experience alive until the weather changes; as in some unforeseeable way it may do.

Graham Hough 1908– : Malcolm Bradbury and James McFarlane (eds.) *Modernism* (1991)

5 In no other job have I ever had to deal with such utterly abnormal people. Yes, it is true, poetry does something to them.
on working for the Poetry Society

Muriel Spark 1918– : *Curriculum Vitae* (1992)

6 I think people are born with a specific temperament . . . To become a poet you must, above all, be yourself.

Seamus Heaney 1939– : interviewed in *Athens News* 8 October 1995

7 Poetry cannot afford to lose its fundamentally self-delighting inventiveness, its joy in being a process of language as well as a representation of things in the world.

Seamus Heaney 1939– : *The Redress of Poetry* (1995)

Poetry versus Prose

8 All that is not prose is verse; and all that is not verse is prose.

Molière 1622–73: *Le Bourgeois Gentilhomme* (1671)

9 And this unpolished rugged verse I chose
As fittest for discourse and nearest prose.

John Dryden 1631–1700: *Religio Laici* (1682)

10 WITWOUD: Madam, do you pin up your hair with all your letters?
MILLAMANT: Only with those in verse, Mr Witwoud. I never pin up my hair with prose.

William Congreve 1670–1729: *The Way of the World* (1700)

11 And he, whose fustian's so sublimely bad,
It is not poetry, but prose run mad.

Alexander Pope 1688–1744: 'An Epistle to Dr Arbuthnot' (1735)

12 Is there then, it will be asked, no essential difference between the language of prose and metrical composition? I answer that there neither is nor can be any essential difference.

William Wordsworth 1770–1850: preface to *Lyrical Ballads* (1800)

1 The habits of a poet's mind are not those of industry or research: his images come to him, he does not go to them; and in prose-subjects, and dry matters of fact and close reasoning, the natural stimulus that at other times warms and rouses, deserts him altogether. He sees no unhallowed visions, he is inspired by no daydreams. All is tame, literal, and barren, without the Nine. Nor does he collect his strength to strike fire from the flint by the sharpness of collision, by the eagerness of his blows.

William Hazlitt 1778–1830: *The Plain Speaker* (1826) vol. 1 'On the Prose Style of Poets'

2 Prose = words in their best order;—poetry = the *best* words in the best order.

Samuel Taylor Coleridge 1772–1834: *Table Talk* (1835) 12 July 1827

3 Prose is when all the lines except the last go on to the end. Poetry is when some of them fall short of it.

Jeremy Bentham 1748–1832: M. St. J. Packe *The Life of John Stuart Mill* (1954)

4 To write prose, one must have something to say; but he who has nothing to say can still make verses and rhymes, where one word suggests the other, and finally something comes out which in fact is nothing but looks as if it were something.

Johann Wolfgang von Goethe 1749–1832: Johann Peter Eckermann *Conversations with Goethe* (1836–48)

5 Prose was born yesterday—this is what we must tell ourselves. Poetry is pre-eminently the medium of past literatures. All the metrical combinations have been tried but nothing like this can be said of prose.

Gustave Flaubert 1821–80: letter to Louise Colet, 24 April 1852

6 Prose on certain occasions can bear a great deal of poetry: on the other hand, poetry sinks and swoons under a moderate weight of prose.

Walter Savage Landor 1775–1864: *Imaginary Conversations* 'Archdeacon Hare and Walter Landor' in *The Last Fruit off an Old Tree* (1853)

7 I shall be found by the fire, suppose,
O'er a great wise book as beseemeth age,
While the shutters flap as the cross-wind blows
And I turn the page, and I turn the page,
Not verse now, only prose!

Robert Browning 1812–89: 'By the Fireside' (1855)

8 They shut me up in prose—
As when a little girl
They put me in the closet—
Because they liked me 'still'.

Emily Dickinson 1830–86: 'They shut me up in prose' (*c.*1862)

9 Outside prose, no salvation.

Émile Zola 1840–1902: letter, 18 August 1864

10 Prose is for ideas, verse for visions.

Henrik Ibsen 1828–1906: 'Rhymed Letter for Fru Heiberg' (1871)

11 In the past 7–8 years, I have scarcely written a single verse, but exclusively cultivated the incomparably more difficult art of writing purely realistic everyday language.

Henrik Ibsen 1828–1906: letter, 1883

12 Mr Stone's hexameters are verses of no sort, but prose in ribands.

A. E. Housman 1859–1936: in *Classical Review* 1899

1 Prose wanders around with a lantern and laboriously schedules and verifies the details and particulars of a valley and its frame of crags and peaks, then Poetry comes, and lays bare the whole landscape with a single splendid flash.

Mark Twain 1835–1910: H. N. Smith and W. H. Gibson (eds.) *Mark Twain–Howells Letters* (1960) vol. 2

2 Poetry must be *as well written as prose*.

Ezra Pound 1885–1972: letter to Harriet Monroe, January 1915

3 ACQUAINTANCE: How are you?
YEATS: Not very well. I can only write prose today.

W. B. Yeats 1865–1939: attributed

4 I don't think anyone can write succinct prose unless they have at least tried and failed to write a good iambic pentameter sonnet, and read Browning's short dramatic poems.

F. Scott Fitzgerald 1896–1940: letter (undated) to Frances Scott Fitzgerald

5 Poetry is to prose as dancing is to walking.

John Wain 1925–94: BBC radio broadcast, 13 January 1976

6 If you tell a novelist, 'Life's not like that', he has to do something about it. The poet simply replies, 'No, but *I* am.'

Philip Larkin 1922–85: speech as Chairman of the Booker Prize judges, 1977; *Required Writing* (1983)

7 In poetry words are like notes from a flute, the tracery of a tune, whereas in fiction words are like notes of a symphony orchestra—compositional, the integers of a giant calculus.

Edmund White 1940– : in (1981); Edmund White *The Burning Library* (1994)

8 I am convinced that writing prose should not be any different from writing poetry. In both cases it is a question of looking for the unique expression, one that is concise, concentrated, and memorable.

Italo Calvino 1923–85: *Six Memos for the Next Millennium* (1992)

Point of View

9 The only means of strengthening one's intellect is to make up one's mind about nothing—to let the mind be a thoroughfare for all thoughts. Not a select party.

John Keats 1795–1821: letter to George and Georgiana Keats, 24 September 1819

10 Subjectivity is a terrible thing. It is bad in this alone, that it reveals the author's hands and feet.

Anton Chekhov 1860–1904: letter to Alexander Chekhov, April 1883

11 A writer must be as objective as a chemist: he must abandon the subjective line; he must know that dung-heaps play a very reasonable part in a landscape, and that evil passions are as inherent in life as good ones.

Anton Chekhov 1860–1904: letter to M. V. Kiselev, 14 January 1887

12 If I introduce subjectivity, the image becomes blurred and the story will not be as compact as all short stories ought to be. When I write, I reckon entirely upon the reader to add for himself the subjective elements that are lacking in the story.

Anton Chekhov 1860–1904: letter to A. S. Suvorin, 1 April 1890

13 We Cromwellian Directors laid down this principle twenty-five years ago, and have not departed from it: never accept or reject a play because of its opinions.

W. B. Yeats 1865–1939: in *Dublin Magazine* 1926

1 I am a camera with its shutter open, quite passive, recording, not thinking.

Christopher Isherwood 1904–86: *Goodbye to Berlin* (1939) 'Berlin Diary' Autumn 1930

2 A novelist must preserve a child-like belief in the importance of things which common-sense considers of no great consequence. He must never entirely grow up . . . The novelist is dead in the man who has become aware of the triviality of human affairs.

W. Somerset Maugham 1874–1965: *A Writer's Notebook* (1949) written in 1933

3 Time that with this strange excuse
Pardoned Kipling and his views,
And will pardon Paul Claudel,
Pardons him for writing well.

W. H. Auden 1907–73: *Another Time* (1940) 'In Memory of W. B. Yeats'

4 At bottom it is always a writer's tendency, his 'purpose', his 'message', that makes him liked or disliked. The proof of this is the extreme difficulty of seeing any literary merit in a book that seriously damages your deepest beliefs.

George Orwell 1903–50: *Inside the Whale* (1940)

5 If you can't annoy somebody with what you write, I think there's little point in writing.

Kingsley Amis 1922–95: in *Radio Times* 1 May 1971

6 A writer has to conform to two conflicting requirements: he must be involved in his novel and detached from himself.

Graham Greene 1904–91: Marie-Françoise Allain *The Other Man, Conversations with Graham Greene* (1983)

7 Beware the writer who puts forward his concern for you to embrace, who leaves you in no doubt of his worthiness, his usefulness, his altruism, who declares that his heart is in the right place and ensures that it can be seen in full view, a pulsating mass where his characters ought to be.

Harold Pinter 1930– : in *Observer* 16 October 1988

8 Journalism is about working yourself up into a lather over things you previously felt nothing about. It is diametrically opposed to what you do as a novelist, which is very slowly to discover what it is you really think about things.

Kazuo Ishiguro 1954– : in *Guardian* 15 May 1996

Politics

9 Politics in the middle of things that concern the imagination are like a pistol-shot in the middle of a concert.

Stendhal 1783–1842: *Scarlet and Black* (1830)

10 The English poet Thomson wrote a very good poem on the Seasons, but a very bad one on Liberty, and that not from want of poetry in the poet but from want of poetry in the subject. As soon as a poet exerts himself politically, he must give himself up to a party; and once he does that, he is lost as a poet; he must say farewell to his freedom of spirit, his impartial outlook, and pull over his ears the cap of bigotry and blind hatred.

Johann Wolfgang von Goethe 1749–1832: Johann Peter Eckermann *Conversations with Goethe* (1836–48)

1 God help the Minister that meddles with art!

Lord Melbourne 1779–1848: Lord David Cecil *Lord M* (1954)

2 True literature can exist only where it is created not by diligent and trustworthy officials, but by madmen, heretics, dreamers, rebels and sceptics. But when a writer must be sensible . . . there can be no bronze literature, there can only be a newspaper literature, which is read today, and used for wrapping soap tomorrow.

Yevgeny Zamyatin 1884–1937: 'I am Afraid' (1921)

3 The proletarian state must bring up thousands of excellent 'mechanics of culture', 'engineers of the soul'.

Maxim Gorky 1868–1936: speech at the Writers' Congress 1934; cf. **183:10**

4 I never dared be radical when young
For fear it would make me conservative when old.

Robert Frost 1874–1963: 'Precaution' (1936)

5 Those who publish books on their experience in public life have often a rather delicate task to perform. That is to offer their thanks in a suitably subtle way to the individual who actually wrote the book, while somehow minimizing this considerable delegation.

J. K. Galbraith 1908– : *World Economy Since the Wars* (1944)

6 Political writing in our time consists almost entirely of prefabricated phrases bolted together like the pieces of a child's Meccano set.

George Orwell 1903–50: 'The Prevention of Literature' (1946)

7 Political language . . . is designed to make lies sound truthful and murder respectable, and to give an appearance of solidity to pure wind.

George Orwell 1903–50: *Shooting an Elephant* (1950) 'Politics and the English Language'

8 Letting a hundred flowers blossom and a hundred schools of thought contend is the policy for promoting progress in the arts and the sciences and a flourishing socialist culture in our land.

Mao Zedong 1893–1976: speech in Peking, 27 February 1957

9 Dictators are as scared of books as they are of cannon.

Harry Golden 1902–81: *Only in America* (1958)

10 In free society art is not a weapon . . . Artists are not engineers of the soul.

John F. Kennedy 1917–63: speech at Amherst College, Mass., 26 October 1963; cf. **183:3**

11 When power leads man toward arrogance, poetry reminds him of his limitations. When power narrows the areas of man's concern, poetry reminds him of the richness and diversity of his existence. When power corrupts, poetry cleanses. For art establishes the basic human truths which must serve as the touchstone of our judgement.

John F. Kennedy 1917–63: speech at Amherst College, Mass., 26 October 1963

12 If ten or twelve Hungarian writers had been shot at the right moment, there would have been no revolution.

Nikita Khrushchev 1894–1971: attributed

13 The only thing politics and poetry have in common is the letter 'p' and the letter 'o'.

Joseph Brodsky 1940–96: in *Newsweek* 15 May 1986

1 It's very different from living in academia in Oxford. We called someone vicious in the *Times Literary Supplement*. We didn't know what vicious was.
on returning to Burma (Myanmar)

Aung San Suu Kyi 1945– : in *Observer* 25 September 1988 'Sayings of the Week'

2 One of the things I'm writing about is that I'm convinced the further left you go, the more right wing you become.

Alan Bleasdale 1946– : in *Independent* 2 May 1990

3 Not every fiction writer entering a relation with politics trades imagination for the hair shirt of the party hack.

Nadine Gordimer 1923– : Clare Boylan (ed.) *The Agony and the Ego* (1993)

4 If you want to find out what is happening in an age or in a nation, find out what is happening to the writers, the town criers.
on the death sentence passed on Ken Saro-Wiwa in Nigeria

Ben Okri 1959– : in *Observer* 5 November 1995

Popular Fiction see also **Best-sellers**

5 I wonder how anybody can find any pleasure in reading the books which are Lady Mary's chief favourites!
on Lady Mary Wortley Montagu's fondness for novels and romances; cf. **184:6**

Lady Walpole 1709–81: to Joseph Spence in 1740; Robert Halsband (ed.) *Complete Letters of Lady Mary Wortley Montagu* (1966) vol. 2

6 I thank God my taste still continues for the gay part of reading; wiser people may think it trifling, but it serves to sweeten life to me, and is, at worst, better than the generality of conversation.
on her liking for romances and novels; cf. **184:5**

Lady Mary Wortley Montagu 1689–1762: letter to her daughter, Lady Bute, 24 December 1750

7 Quick, my dear Lucy, hide these books. Quick, quick! Fling 'Peregrine Pickle' under the toilette—throw 'Roderick Random' into the closet—put 'The Innocent Adultery' into 'The Whole Duty of Man'; thrust 'Lord Aimworth' under the sofa! cram 'Ovid' behind the bolster; there—put 'The Man of Feeling' into your pocket. Now for them.

Richard Brinsley Sheridan 1751–1816: *The Rivals* (1775)

8 A masquerade, a murdered peer,
His throat just cut from ear to ear—
A rake turned hermit—a fond maid
Run mad, by some false loon betrayed—
These stores supply the female pen,
Which writes them o'er and o'er again,
And readers likewise may be found
To circulate them round and round.

Mary Alcock *c.*1742–98: 'A Receipt for Writing a Novel'

9 I am no indiscriminate novel-reader. The mere trash of the common circulating library, I hold in the highest contempt. You will never hear of me advocating those puerile emanations which detail nothing but discordant principles incapable of amalgamation, or those vapid tissues of ordinary occurrences from which no useful deductions can be drawn.

Jane Austen 1775–1817: 'Sir Edward Denham' in *Sanditon* (1925 ed.)

1 It is a shame to women so to write; and it is a shame to the women who read and accept as a true representation of themselves and their ways the equivocal talk and fleshly inclinations herein attributed to them. Their patronage of such books is in reality an adoption and acceptance of them.
of the 'sensation novels' of the period

Margaret Oliphant 1828–97: in *Blackwood's Magazine* 1867 'Novels'

2 No *man* would have dared to write and publish such books . . . no *man could* have written such delineations of female passion . . . No! They are women, who by their writings have been doing the work of the enemy of souls . . . Women . . . who might have been bright and shining lights in their generation.

Francis E. Paget 1806–82: *Lucretia* (1868)

3 For I've read in many a novel that, unless they've souls
that grovel,
Folks *prefer* in fact a hovel to your dreary marble halls.

C. S. Calverley 1831–84: 'In the Gloaming' (1872)

4 The amount of crime, treachery, murder, slow poisoning, and general infamy required by the halfpenny reader is something terrible.

Mary Elizabeth Braddon 1837–1915: to Bulwer Lytton; R. L. Woolf *Sensational Victorian* (1979)

5 Bad literature of the sort called amusing is spiritual gin.

George Eliot 1819–80: *Leaves from a Note-book: Authorship* (1879) 'The Impressions of Theophrastus Such'

6 My books are water; those of the great geniuses are wine. Everybody drinks water.

Mark Twain 1835–1910: notebook, 11 December 1885; *Mark Twain's Notebook* (1935)

7 It is only the fiction that lives that can hope for a triumph in this latter-day appeal at sixpence to the masses. Their knowledge extends to the books which cry from the heights, as it were, but it does not yet penetrate into the highways and byways of literature. In other words, the masses want what is of proved interest, the established story—that and that only.
on the commercial success of his sixpenny paperbacks and the new cheap fiction

Andrew Chatto : in *Author* 1 October 1900 'The Sixpenny Book'

8 Here is one of the fundamental defects of American fiction—perhaps the one character that sets it off sharply from all other known kinds of contemporary fiction. It habitually exhibits, not a man of delicate organization in revolt against the the inexplicable tragedy of existence, but a man of low sensibilities and elemental desires yielding himself gladly to his environment, and so achieving what, under a third-rate civilization, passes for success.

H. L. Mencken 1880–1956: *Prejudices* (2nd series, 1920) 'The National Letters'

9 Don't read too much now: the dude
Who lets the girl down before
The hero arrives, the chap
Who's yellow and keeps the store,
Seem far too familiar. Get stewed:
Books are a load of crap.

Philip Larkin 1922–85: 'Study of Reading Habits' (1964)

1 Good relaxing reading is a matter of personal choice . . . I'd rather have cloth-of-gold wedding dresses, quotations from *Urne Buriall* and tigerish passion in crime writers acquitted of murder, than brown frocks, knitted socks in clerical grey, and cauliflower cheese.
comparing Dorothy L. ***Sayers*** *and Barbara* ***Pym*** *as providers of escape literature*

A. S. Byatt 1936– : in 1986; *Passions of the Mind* (1991)

2 He can't write fiction and he can't write non-fiction, so he's invented a bogus category in between.
of Jeffrey Archer's new 'novelography'

Ian Hislop 1960– : in *Observer* 14 April 1996 'Sayings of the Week'

Pornography see Erotic Writing and Pornography

The Power of the Pen

3 Write the vision, and make it plain upon tables, that he may run that readeth it.

Bible: Habakkuk

4 And now I have finished the work, which neither the wrath of Jove, nor fire, nor the sword, nor devouring age shall be able to destroy.

Ovid 43 BC–AD c.17: *Metamorphoses*

5 Let none presume to tell me that the pen is preferable to the sword.

Cervantes 1547–1616: *Don Quixote* (1605)

6 Your tale, sir, would cure deafness.

William Shakespeare 1564–1616: *The Tempest* (1611)

7 So long as men can breathe, or eyes can see,
So long lives this, and this gives life to thee.

William Shakespeare 1564–1616: sonnet 18

8 A good book is the precious life-blood of a master spirit, embalmed and treasured up on purpose to a life beyond life.

John Milton 1608–74: *Areopagitica* (1644)

9 To endeavour to work upon the vulgar with fine sense, is like attempting to hew blocks with a razor.

Alexander Pope 1688–1744: *Miscellanies* (1727) 'Thoughts on Various Subjects'

10 It is, however, with books as it is with men: a very small number play a great part; the rest are confounded with the multitude.

Voltaire 1694–1778: *A Philosophical Dictionary* (1764–70) 'Books'

11 The true antithesis to knowledge, in this case, is not *pleasure*, but *power*. All that is literature seeks to communicate power; all that is not literature, to communicate knowledge.
De Quincey adds that he is indebted for this distinction to 'many years' conversation with Mr ***Wordsworth****'*

Thomas De Quincey 1785–1859: *Letters to a Young Man whose Education has been Neglected*, in the *London Magazine* January–July 1823

12 Beneath the rule of men entirely great
The pen is mightier than the sword.

Edward George Bulwer-Lytton 1803–73: *Richelieu* (1839); cf. **97:12**

1 We need books of this tart cathartic virtue, more than books of political science or of private economy.
on Plutarch's Lives

Ralph Waldo Emerson 1803–82: *Essays* (1841) 'Heroism'

2 It is splendid to be a great writer, to put men into the frying pan of your words and make them pop like chestnuts.

Gustave Flaubert 1821–80: letter, 3 November 1851

3 There is first the literature of *knowledge*, and secondly, the literature of *power*.

Thomas De Quincey 1785–1859: review of the *Works of Pope* (1847 ed.) in *North British Review* August 1848

4 So you're the little woman who wrote the book that made this great war!
on meeting Harriet Beecher Stowe, author of Uncle Tom's Cabin *(1852)*

Abraham Lincoln 1809–65: Carl Sandburg *Abraham Lincoln: The War Years* (1936)

5 Dreamer of dreams, born out of my due time,
Why should I strive to set the crooked straight?
Let it suffice me that my murmuring rhyme
Beats with light wing against the ivory gate,
Telling a tale not too importunate
To those who in the sleepy region stay,
Lulled by the singer of an empty day.

William Morris 1834–96: *The Earthly Paradise* (1868–70) 'An Apology'

6 In our times, the task of every piece of literature is to move the frontier post.

Henrik Ibsen 1828–1906: attributed

7 All books are either dreams or swords,
You can cut, or you can drug, with words.

Amy Lowell 1874–1925: 'Sword Blades and Poppy Seed' (1914)

8 This is not the age of pamphleteers. It is the age of the engineers. The spark-gap is mightier than the pen.

Lancelot Hogben 1895–1975: *Science for the Citizen* (1938)

9 All that I have said and done,
Now that I am old and ill,
Turns into a question till
I lie awake night after night
And never get the answers right.
Did that play of mine send out
Certain men the English shot?

W. B. Yeats 1865–1939: 'The Man and the Echo' (1939)

10 Books can not be killed by fire. People die, but books never die. No man and no force can abolish memory . . . In this war, we know, books are weapons. And it is a part of your dedication always to make them weapons for man's freedom.

Franklin D. Roosevelt 1882–1945: 'Message to the Booksellers of America' 6 May 1942

11 What makes the poet the potent figure that he is, or was, or ought to be, is that he creates the world to which we turn incessantly and without knowing it and that he gives to life the supreme fictions without which we are unable to conceive of it.

Wallace Stevens 1879–1955: *The Noble Rider and the Sound of Words* (1942)

1 I suggest that the only books that influence us are those for which we are ready, and which have gone a little farther down our particular path than we have yet got ourselves.

E. M. Forster 1879–1970: *Two Cheers for Democracy* (1951) 'Books That Influenced Me'

2 The book is alive and potent and fructifying and able to promote thought and discussion *only* when its plan and shape and intention are not understood, because that moment of seeing the shape and plan and intention is also the moment when there isn't anything more to be got out of it.

Doris Lessing 1919– : *The Golden Notebook* (1962) preface

3 I believe that Brecht did nothing for Communism, that the revolution was not provoked by Beaumarchais's *The Marriage of Figaro*. The closer a work of art is to perfection, the more it turns in on itself. Still worse, it awakens a taste for the past.

Jean Genet 1910–86: in the periodical *Le Nouvel Observateur* 1971

4 To be arrested for the power of your writing is one of the highest compliments an author can be paid, if an unwelcome one.

on being jailed without trial, in 1977

Ngugi wa Thiong'o 1938– : attributed; in *Assistant Librarian* September 1986

5 A writer is not so powerless as he usually feels, and a pen, as well as a silver bullet, can draw blood.

*in relation to President Duvalier's anger at the portrayal of Haiti in **Greene**'s* The Comedians

Graham Greene 1904–91: *Ways of Escape* (1980)

6 Dead dictators are my speciality. I discovered to my horror that all the political figures most featured in my writing—Mrs G, Sanjay Gandhi, Bhutto, Zia—have now come to sticky ends. It's the grand slam really. This is a service I can perform, perhaps. A sort of literary contract.

Indira Gandhi, Prime Minister of India, was assassinated, Zulfikar Ali Bhutto was ousted as Prime Minister of Pakistan and subsequently hanged, and his successor Zia ul-Haq and Sanjay Gandhi both died in air crashes

Salman Rushdie 1947– : interview in *Independent* 10 September 1988

7 It would be absurd to think that a book can cause riots.

Salman Rushdie 1947– : to Indian interviewer in September 1988; in *Sunday Times* 23 July 1989; cf. **35:14**

8 I've never read a political poem that's accomplished anything. Poetry makes things happen, but rarely what the poet wants.

Howard Nemerov 1920–91: in *International Herald Tribune* 14 October 1988

9 I really do inhabit a system in which words are capable of shaking the entire structure of government, where words can prove mightier than ten military divisions.

speech in Germany accepting a peace prize, October 1989

Václav Havel 1936– : in *Independent* 9 December 1989

10 The men who ordained and supervised this show of shame, this tragic charade, are frightened by the word, the power of ideas, the power of the pen . . . They are so scared of the word that they do not read. And that will be their funeral.

shortly before his execution in 1995

Ken Saro-Wiwa 1941–95: in *London Review of Books* 4 April 1996

1 I've used my talents as a writer to enable the Ogoni people to confront their tormentors. I was not able to do it as a politician or a businessman. My writing did it . . . I think I have the moral victory.
letter, shortly before his execution in 1995, to William Boyd

Ken Saro-Wiwa 1941–95: in *London Review of Books* 4 April 1996

Praise see **Admiration and Praise**

Prizes

2 It has been usual to catch a mouse or two (for form's sake) in public once a year.
on refusing the Laureateship

Thomas Gray 1716–71: letter to William Mason, 19 December 1757

3 Were I my own man . . . I would refuse this offer (with all gratitude); but as I am situated, L.300 or L.400 a-year is not to be sneezed at.
on being offered the Laureateship

Sir Walter Scott 1771–1832: letter to James Ballantyne, 24 August 1813

4 Just for a handful of silver he left us,
Just for a riband to stick in his coat.
*of **Wordsworth**'s implied abandonment of radical principles by his acceptance of the Laureateship*

Robert Browning 1812–89: 'The Lost Leader' (1845)

5 Had they sent me ¼ lb of good tobacco, the addition to my happiness had probably been suitabler and greater!
on being awarded the Prussian Order of Merit

Thomas Carlyle 1795–1881: letter to his brother John Carlyle, 14 February 1874

6 In the end I accepted the honour, because during dinner Venables told me, that, if I became Poet Laureate, I should always when I dined out be offered the liver-wing of a fowl.
on being made Poet Laureate in 1850

Alfred, Lord Tennyson 1809–92: in *Alfred Lord Tennyson: A Memoir by his Son* (1897) vol. 1

objecting to having been appointed a Companion of Honour without his consent:

7 How would you like it if you woke up and found yourself Archbishop of Canterbury?

Rudyard Kipling 1865–1936: letter to Bonar Law, 1917; Charles Carrington *Rudyard Kipling* (1978)

8 The award of a pure gold medal for poetry would flatter the recipient unduly: no poem ever attains such carat purity.

Robert Graves 1895–1985: *Address to the Oxford University Philological Society* January 1960

9 A writer must refuse, therefore, to allow himself to be transformed into an institution.

Jean-Paul Sartre 1905–80: refusing the Nobel Prize at Stockholm, 22 October 1964

10 I want to be read by people who feel like reading my books. Not by celebrity collectors.
on refusing the 1964 Nobel prize in literature

Jean-Paul Sartre 1905–80: interview in *Paris-Press-L'Intransigeant* 24 October 1964

11 The Nobel is a ticket to one's funeral. No one has ever done anything after he got it.

T. S. Eliot 1888–1965: attributed

on being awarded the Order of Merit in 1977:

1 I've only two things to say about it. First I deserve it. Second, they've been too long about giving me it. There'll be another vacancy very soon.

J. B. Priestley 1894–1984: in a radio interview, October 1977; John Braine *J. B. Priestley* (1978)

2 After our work was over, the Secretary told me that I had been the weakest chairman they had ever had. He didn't put it quite like that, of course; what he said was that never before had members of the panel been encouraged to make so full a contribution.

of chairing the judges for the Booker Prize

Philip Larkin 1922–85: in 1977; *Required Writing* (1983)

3 It is extraordinary, an act of illiterates, to give prizes for literature.

Geoffrey Grigson 1905–85: *The Private Art* (1982)

4 I was on the Booker Prize Committee twice. It almost drove me mad.

Rebecca West 1892–1983: interview in George Plimpton (ed) *Writers at Work* (1984) 6th series

5 The Booker Prize, like British politics, is half a crusade and half a sporting event.

Norman St John Stevas 1929– : attributed, 1985

6 To be a [Booker Prize] judge you don't have to know about books, you have to be skilled at picking shrapnel out of your head.

Joanna Lumley 1946– : in *Observer* 17 November 1985

7 It is the prize, not the novelist, that grabs the attention of the fiction business now.

Anonymous: in *Economist* 25 October 1986

8 It really means nothing in this country whatsoever—but then being a writer here means nothing either.

William Golding 1911–93: in *Observer* 31 May 1987

9 I don't think literature is ever finished in any country which has more writers than it has prizes.

Gore Vidal 1925– : in *Observer* 27 September 1987 'Sayings of the Week'

10 I got to the point where I couldn't read a laundry list without considering it for the Booker Prize.

on being a judge for the 1986 Booker Prize

Bernice Rubens 1928– : Rosemary Hartill *Writers Revealed* (1989)

11 That one book is better than another is nothing more than a matter of taste. I find it difficult to accept that it's something that can be decided by a panel of judges.

Graham Swift 1949– : in *Observer* 24 June 1990 'Sayings of the Week'

12 I didn't think about the critics when I was writing. If I had, I would have been paralyzed.

on winning the Booker Prize 1995

Pat Barker 1943– : in *Athens News* 9 November 1995

13 Prizes are like sashes, you can wear them and be Miss World for a bit . . . I've been royally dissed by prizes.

Martin Amis 1949– : interview in *Waterstone's Quarterly Guide* Spring/Summer 1996

14 The whole idea of an award just for women fills me with horror.

on the Orange prize for women's fiction

Anita Brookner 1938– : in *Sunday Times* 21 April 1996; cf. **261:1**

15 It's about money and power, and that's what gets the column inches.

on establishing the Orange prize for women's fiction

Sarah Dunant 1950– : in *Sunday Times* 21 April 1996

1 There were honourable exceptions, but so many books were about domestic obsessions, marriages, and obsessions with boring lives.
an Orange Prize judge on the short list

Susan Hill 1942– : in *Observer* 21 April 1996 'Sayings of the Week'

2 My father [Kingsley] always had doubts about the Booker prize although they evaporated on the announcement that he had won it.

Martin Amis 1949– : in *Independent on Sunday* 28 April 1996

3 With all those prizes the most interesting thing is getting on to the shortlist, because that tells you who people see as your peers.

David Malouf 1934– : in *Daily Telegraph* 7 September 1996

4 The Booker is murder. Absolutely nothing would be lost if it withered away and died.
view of the 1971 winner of the Booker Prize at the time of the 1996 awards

V. S. Naipaul 1932– : in *Guardian* 30 October 1996

Publishers and Publishing

5 Frail book, although there's room for you to stay
Snug on my shelves, you'd rather fly away
To the bookshops and be published.

Martial AD *c.*40–*c.*104: *Epigrammata*, tr. James Michie

6 I, according to my copy, have done set it in imprint, to the intent that noble men may see and learn the noble acts of chivalry, the gentle and virtuous deeds that some knights used in those days.

William Caxton *c.*1421–91: Thomas Malory *Le Morte D'Arthur* (1485) prologue

7 I love a ballad in print, a-life, for then we are sure they are true.

William Shakespeare 1564–1616: *The Winter's Tale* (1610–11)

8 Some said, John, print it; other said, Not so:
Some said, It might do good; others said, No.

John Bunyan 1628–88: *The Pilgrim's Progress* (1678) pt. 1, 'Author's Apology'

9 I find all your trade are sharpers.
to the publisher Jacob Tonson, c.1697

John Dryden 1631–1700: Ian Hamilton *Keepers of the Flame* (1992)

10 Never literary attempt was more unfortunate than my Treatise of Human Nature. It fell *dead-born from the press.*

David Hume 1711–76: *My Own Life* (1777)

11 You shall see them on a beautiful quarto page where a neat rivulet of text shall meander through a meadow of margin.

Richard Brinsley Sheridan 1751–1816: *The School for Scandal* (1777)

12 Thou god of our idolatry, the press . . .
Thou fountain, at which drink the good and wise;
Thou ever-bubbling spring of endless lies;
Like Eden's dread probationary tree,
Knowledge of good and evil is from thee.

William Cowper 1731–1800: 'The Progress of Error' (1782)

13 EDMUND BURKE: You must remember that booksellers deal in commodities they are not supposed to understand.
ARTHUR MURPHY: True, some of 'em do deal in morality.

Arthur Murphy 1727–1805: in *Thraliana* (1942, ed. K. C. Balderston)

1 I'll publish, right or wrong:
Fools are my theme, let satire be my song.

Lord Byron 1788–1824: *English Bards and Scotch Reviewers* (1809)

2 Gentlemen, you must not mistake me. I admit that the French Emperor is a tyrant. I admit he is a monster. I admit that he is the sworn foe of our nation, and, if you will, of the whole human race. But, gentlemen, we must be just to our great enemy. We must not forget that he once shot a bookseller.

proposing a toast to Napoleon at a literary dinner during the Napoleonic Wars

Thomas Campbell 1777–1844: G. O. Trevelyan *The Life of Lord Macaulay* (1876)

3 Publish and be damned.

replying to Harriette Wilson's blackmail threat, c. 1825

Duke of Wellington 1769–1852: attributed

4 Now Barabbas was a publisher.

paraphrasing the biblical verse 'Now Barabbas was a robber'; cf. **194:1**

Thomas Campbell 1777–1844: attributed, in Samuel Smiles *A Publisher and his Friends* (1891); also attributed, wrongly, to Byron

5 I suppose publishers are untrustworthy. They certainly always look it.

Oscar Wilde 1854–1900: letter, February 1898

6 I have seen enough of my publishers to know that they have no ideas of their own about literature save what they can clutch at as believing it to be a straight tip from a business point of view.

Samuel Butler 1835–1902: *Notebooks* (1912)

7 Only one thing, is impossible for God: to find any sense in any copyright law on the planet.

Mark Twain 1835–1910: notebook 23 May 1903

8 University printing presses exist, and are subsidised by the Government for the purpose of producing books which no one can read; and they are true to their high calling.

Francis M. Cornford 1874–1943: *Microcosmographia Academica* (1908)

9 All a publisher has to do is write cheques at intervals, while a lot of deserving and industrious chappies rally round and do the real work.

P. G. Wodehouse 1881–1975: *My Man Jeeves* (1919)

10 For several days after my first book was published I carried it about in my pocket, and took surreptitious peeps at it to make sure that the ink had not faded.

J. M. Barrie 1860–1937: speech at the Critics' Circle in London, 26 May 1922

11 The illustrations, which are far more numerous and less apposite than comports with the dignity of history, may be imputed to the publishers, for publishers seek to attract readers whom authors would wish to repel.

A. E. Housman 1859–1936: in *Cambridge Review* 1923

12 Publishers and printers alike seemed to agree among themselves, no matter how divergent their points of view were in other matters, not to publish anything of mine as I wrote it.

James Joyce 1882–1941: letter, 2 April 1932

13 It is so unpleasant and ugly, both in narration and incident, that I wonder the printers did not go on strike while printing it.

on a cheap edition of Boy *by James Hanley*

Hugh Walpole 1884–1941: in 1934; Anthony Burgess introduction to James Hanley *Boy* (1990 ed.)

1 In my capacity as reader, I applaud the Penguin Books; in my capacity as writer I pronounce them anathema . . . The result may be a flood of cheap reprints which will cripple the lending libraries (the novelist's foster-mother) and check the output of new novels. This would be a fine thing for literature but a very bad thing for trade.

George Orwell 1903–50: in 1935; Hans Schmoller *The Paperback Revolution* (1974)

2 As repressed sadists are supposed to become policemen or butchers, so those with an irrational fear of life become publishers.

Cyril Connolly 1903–74: *Enemies of Promise* (1938)

3 You cannot or at least you should not try to argue with authors. Too many are like children whose tears can suddenly be changed to smiles if they are handled in the right way.
a publisher's view

Michael Joseph 1897–1958: *The Adventure of Publishing* (1949)

on the requirement as a publisher to compose blurbs for book jackets:

4 I don't know how to grow asparagus, or how to improve your lawn tennis, or the best diet for a 6-month old baby, but I have to write blurbs about them.

T. S. Eliot 1888–1965: reported by Milton Shulman in *Evening Standard* 8 August 1950

5 Publishing is merely a matter of saying Yes and No at the right time.

Michael Joseph 1897–1958: speaking at the Foyle's Jubilee Dinner, 1954

6 Being published by the Oxford University Press is rather like being married to a duchess: the honour is almost greater than the pleasure.

G. M. Young 1882–1959: Rupert Hart-Davis, letter to George Lyttelton, 29 April 1956

7 Very harsh things have been said about publishers, but there can be nothing but good in the heart of a man who regales an author with figgy pudding.
after lunching with his publisher

Robertson Davies 1913–95: in 1959; *The Enthusiasms of Robertson Davies* (1990)

8 English publishers being what they are (i.e., chary about wasting stamps), I never get to find out what the press says about any book of mine until years later, and then only in red ink on the publisher's statement.

S. J. Perelman 1904–79: letter, 7 January 1960

9 I am told that printer's readers no longer exist because clergymen are no longer unfrocked for sodomy.

Evelyn Waugh 1903–66: letter to Tom Driberg, 11 June 1960

10 The lions looked like so many publishers satiated on a diet of mutual agreement over terms.
after a visit to Longleat

Paul Scott 1920–78: letter, 15 June 1968

11 Publishers are in business to make money, and if your books do well they don't care whether you are male, female, or an elephant.

Margaret Atwood 1939– : Graeme Gibson *Eleven Canadian Novelists* (1973) 'Dissecting the Way a Writer Works'

12 If your publisher promises you a full-page ad in the *New York Times*, get it in writing.

Bill Adler : *Inside Publishing* (1982)

13 A publisher who writes is like a cow in a milk bar.

Arthur Koestler 1905–83: attributed, 1982

1 I always thought Barabbas was a much misunderstood man . . .
a publisher's view
Peter Grose: letter, 25 May 1983; cf. **192:4**

2 Publishers should not have the Garter.
to Kenneth Rose after declining the honour
Harold Macmillan 1894–1986: Alistair Horne *Harold Macmillan* (1991) vol. 2

3 If I had been someone not very clever, I would have done an easier job like publishing. That's the easiest job I can think of.
A. J. Ayer 1910–89: attributed

4 I'd like the company to continue. I think it will, provided someone doesn't do anything silly. Someone might suddenly decide they want to *educate* the public. Bloody disaster. The public don't want to be educated by us. They want to be amused.
view of the chairman of Mills and Boon, publishers of romantic fiction
John Boon 1916–96: in 1989; in obituary, *Daily Telegraph* 16 July 1996

5 It is not wise to solicit the opinions of publishers—they become proud if you do.
Gore Vidal 1925– : George Greenfield *Scribblers for Bread* (1989)

6 Four happy publishers
Out on a spree.
Someone had to pay the bill
And then there were three.
Wendy Cope 1945– : 'Two Hand-Rhymes for Grown-ups' (1992)

7 All her life to labour and labour for Faber and Faber.
of a Faber's editor
Seamus Heaney 1939– : attributed; in *Sunday Telegraph* 24 September 1995

8 It's an editor's world. However cross an editor makes you, you cannot afford to quarrel. Swear after you've put the phone down and not before.
Susan Elkin : Barry Turner *The Writer's Companion* (1996)

9 The novels of Virginia Woolf or Elizabeth Bowen or Henry Green would get nowhere in today's world: people would say, 'We loved *The Waves*, but why not try to write a book about the sex life of George Eliot?'
A. N. Wilson 1950– : in *Bookseller* 5 July 1996

10 I'm not saying all publishers have to be literary, but *some* interest in books would help.
A. N. Wilson 1950– : in *Bookseller* 5 July 1996

11 The whole world of publishing has changed. The accountants have moved in. It's now the bottom line, not is it a good book?
Hammond Innes 1913– : interview in *Daily Telegraph* 3 August 1996

Punctuation

12 Another sport which wastes unlimited time is comma-hunting. Once start a comma and the whole pack will be off, full cry, especially if they have had a literary training.
on academic committees
Francis M. Cornford 1874–1943: *Microcosmographia Academica* (1908)

13 Cast iron rules will not answer . . . what is one man's colon is another man's comma.
Mark Twain 1835–1910: Charles Neider (ed.) *Life as I Find It* (1961)

1 Punctuation ought to be exact. Under ordinary circumstances, it is as hard for me to alter punctuation as to alter words, though I will admit that at times I am heady and irresponsible.

Marianne Moore 1887–1972: letter to Ezra ***Pound***, 19 January 1919

2 No iron can stab the heart with such force as a full stop put just at the right place.

Isaac Babel 1894–1940: *Guy de Maupassant* (1932)

3 I have a certain system of punctuation which has no authority except in so far as it is founded on the Authorized Version of the Bible, which is not consistent . . . In the Bible there is not from beginning to end a single dash or inverted comma. If you met with either in it you would be shocked . . . I argue that if the Bible could do without dashes and inverted commas, both being disfigurements of the printer's work, any book can.

George Bernard Shaw 1856–1950: letter to May Morris, 13 April 1936

4 Cut out all these exclamation points. An exclamation point is like laughing at your own joke.
correcting a radio script by Sheilah Graham

F. Scott Fitzgerald 1896–1940: Sheilah Graham and Gerald Frank *Beloved Infidel* (1959)

5 The punctuation is pitiable but it never becomes unintelligible so I just shouldn't try. It is clearly not your subject—like theology.
of Love in a Cold Climate

Evelyn Waugh 1903–66: letter to Nancy Mitford, 24 October 1948

6 Do not be afraid of the semicolon; it can be most useful.

Ernest Gowers 1880–1966: *The Complete Plain Words* (1954)

7 The failure of English masters, at all the schools I attended, to give me any comprehension of the purpose of punctuation is splendidly evident in that story.
of his first short story, 'Raspberry Jam' (1946)

Angus Wilson 1913–91: *The Wild Garden* (1963)

8 I dictate everything to a secretary who is good at punctuation. Then a schoolmaster friend reads it all again, for grammar *and* punctuation.

Barbara Cartland 1901– : in *Bookseller* 21 January 1978

9 If you take hyphens seriously you will surely go mad.

Anonymous: said to be from a style book in use with Oxford University Press, New York; perhaps apocryphal

10 Commas in *The New Yorker* fall with the precision of knives in a circus act, outlining the victim.

E. B. White 1899–1985: George Plimpton (ed.) *Writers at Work* 8th Series (1988)

11 Unconventional punctuation is, in fact, one of the most obvious and universal signs of Modernism in prose fiction.

David Lodge 1935– : Malcolm Bradbury and James McFarlane (eds.) *Modernism* (1991)

Quotation and Allusion

12 Confound those who have said our remarks before us.

Aelius Donatus fl. 4th century AD: St Jerome *Commentary on Ecclesiastes*

1 He ranged his tropes, and preached up patience;
Backed his opinion with quotations.

Matthew Prior 1664–1721: 'Paulo Purganti and his Wife' (1709)

2 Some for renown on scraps of learning dote,
And think they grow immortal as they quote.

Edward Young 1683–1765: *The Love of Fame* (1725–8)

3 Classical quotation is the *parole* of literary men all over the world.

Samuel Johnson 1709–84: James Boswell *Life of Samuel Johnson* (1791) 8 May 1781

4 He liked those literary cooks
Who skim the cream of others' books;
And ruin half an author's graces
By plucking bon-mots from their places.

Hannah More 1745–1833: *Florio* (1786)

5 No Greek; as much Latin as you like: never French in any circumstance: no English poet unless he has completed his century.

advice for House of Commons quotations

Charles James Fox 1749–1806: J. A. Gere and John Sparrow (eds.) *Geoffrey Madan's Notebooks* (1981)

6 His works contain nothing worth quoting; and a book that furnishes no quotations is, *me judice*, no book—it's a plaything.

Thomas Love Peacock 1785–1866: *Crotchet Castle* (1831)

7 A proverb is one man's wit and all men's wisdom.

Lord John Russell 1792–1878: R. J. Mackintosh *Sir James Mackintosh* (1835)

8 I hate quotation. Tell me what you know.

Ralph Waldo Emerson 1803–82: diary, May 1849

9 To be occasionally quoted is the only fame I care for.

Alexander Smith 1830–67: *Dreamthorp* (1863) 'Men of Letters'

10 Next to the originator of a good sentence is the first quoter of it.

Ralph Waldo Emerson 1803–82: *Letters and Social Aims* (1876)

11 He wrapped himself in quotations—as a beggar would enfold himself in the purple of emperors.

Rudyard Kipling 1865–1936: *Many Inventions* (1893)

12 Shake was a dramatist of note;
He lived by writing things to quote.

H. C. Bunner 1855–96: *Shake, Mulleary and Go-ethe*

13 OSCAR WILDE: How I wish I had said that.
WHISTLER: You will, Oscar, you will.

James McNeill Whistler 1834–1903: R. Ellman *Oscar Wilde* (1987)

14 Pretentious quotations being the surest road to tedium.

H. W. Fowler 1858–1933 and **F. G. Fowler** 1870–1918: *The King's English* (1906)

15 You must not treat my immortal works as quarries to be used at will by the various hacks whom you may employ to compile anthologies.

A. E. Housman 1859–1936: letter to his publisher Grant Richards, 29 June 1907

16 What a good thing Adam had. When he said a good thing he knew nobody had said it before.

Mark Twain 1835–1910: *Notebooks* (1935)

17 Ah, yes! I wrote the 'Purple Cow'—
I'm sorry, now, I wrote it!
But I can tell you anyhow,
I'll kill you if you quote it!

Gelett Burgess 1866–1951: 'Confessional' (1914)

1 An anthology is like all the plums and orange peel picked out of a cake.
Walter Raleigh 1861–1922: letter to Mrs Robert Bridges, 15 January 1915

2 I know heaps of quotations, so I can always make quite a fair show of knowledge.
O. Douglas 1877–1948: *The Setons* (1917)

3 But I have long thought that if you knew a column of advertisements by heart, you could achieve unexpected felicities with them. You can get a happy quotation anywhere if you have the eye.
Oliver Wendell Holmes Jr. 1841–1935: letter to Harold Laski, 31 May 1923

4 Quotations in my work are like wayside robbers who leap out armed and relieve the stroller of his conviction.
Walter Benjamin 1892–1940: *One-Way Street* (1928) 'Hardware'

5 It is a good thing for an uneducated man to read books of quotations.
Winston Churchill 1874–1965: *My Early Life* (1930)

6 I always have a quotation for everything—it saves original thinking.
Dorothy L. Sayers 1893–1957: *Have His Carcase* (1932)

7 Misquotation is, in fact, the pride and privilege of the learned. A widely-read man never quotes accurately, for the rather obvious reason that he has read too widely.
Hesketh Pearson 1887–1964: *Common Misquotations* (1934)

8 The surest way to make a monkey of a man is to quote him.
Robert Benchley 1889–1945: *My Ten Years in a Quandary* (1936)

9 To-day I am a lamppost against which no anthologist lifts his leg.
James Agate 1877–1947: diary, 21 August 1941

10 In the dying world I come from quotation is a national vice. No one would think of making an after-dinner speech without the help of poetry. It used to be the classics, now it's lyric verse.
Evelyn Waugh 1903–66: *The Loved One* (1948)

11 A great many complimentary things have been said about the faculty of memory, and if you look in a good quotation book you will find them neatly arranged.
Robertson Davies 1913–95: in 1956; *The Enthusiasms of Robertson Davies* (1990)

12 It seems pointless to be quoted if one isn't going to be quotable . . . It's better to be quotable than honest.
Tom Stoppard 1937– : in *Guardian* 21 March 1973

13 The nice thing about quotes is that they give us a nodding acquaintance with the originator which is often socially impressive.
Kenneth Williams 1926–88: *Acid Drops* (1980)

14 I am not against anthologies, as long as they are not attempts to enforce a poor idea of poetry, as long as they discover, and as long as they are born of excitement and generosity.
Geoffrey Grigson 1905–85: *The Private Art* (1982)

15 A quotation is what a speaker wants to say—unlike a soundbite which is all that an interviewer allows you to say.
Tony Benn 1925– : letter to Antony Jay, August 1996

16 In mobilizing support for a project or policy it is especially agreeable to be able to call upon the distinguished dead; their distinction adds intellectual weight and moral force to the argument, and their death makes it impossible for them to appear on television later and say that they meant something completely different.
Antony Jay 1930– : introduction to *Oxford Dictionary of Political Quotations* (1996)

Reading

1 Take up and read, take up and read.

St Augustine AD 354–430: *Confessions* (AD 397–8)

2 And as for me, though that I konne but lyte,
On bokes for to rede I me delyte,
And to hem yive I feyth and ful credence,
And in myn herte have hem in reverence
So hertely, that ther is game noon
That fro my bokes maketh me to goon.

Geoffrey Chaucer c.1343–1400: *The Legend of Good Women* 'The Prologue'

3 I have sought for happiness everywhere, but I have found it nowhere except in a little corner with a little book.

Thomas à Kempis c.1380–1471: attributed; Gerald Donaldson *Books* (1981)

4 He hath not fed of the dainties that are bred in a book; he hath not eat paper, as it were; he hath not drunk ink.

William Shakespeare 1564–1616: *Love's Labour's Lost* (1595)

5 POLONIUS: What do you read, my lord?
HAMLET: Words, words, words.

William Shakespeare 1564–1616: *Hamlet* (1601)

6 Read not to contradict and confute, nor to believe and take for granted, nor to find talk and discourse, but to weigh and consider.

Francis Bacon 1561–1626: *Essays* (1625) 'Of Studies'

7 Reading maketh a full man.

Francis Bacon 1561–1626: *Essays* (1625) 'Of Studies'

8 Some books are to be tasted, others to be swallowed, and some few to be chewed and digested; that is, some books are to be read only in parts; others to be read but not curiously; and some few to be read wholly, and with diligence and attention. Some books also may be read by deputy, and extracts made of them by others.

Francis Bacon 1561–1626: *Essays* (1625) 'Of Studies'

9 I wish thee as much pleasure in the reading, as I had in the writing.

Francis Quarles 1592–1644: *Emblems* (1635) 'To the Reader'

10 Who reads
Incessantly, and to his reading brings not
A spirit and judgement equal or superior
(And what he brings, what needs he elsewhere seek?)
Uncertain and unsettled still remains,
Deep-versed in books and shallow in himself.

John Milton 1608–74: *Paradise Regained* (1671)

11 Choose an author as you choose a friend.

Wentworth Dillon, Lord Roscommon c.1633–1685: *Essay on Translated Verse* (1684)

12 He had read much, if one considers his long life; but his contemplation was much more than his reading. He was wont to say that if he had read as much as other men, he should have known no more than other men.

John Aubrey 1626–97: *Brief Lives* 'Thomas Hobbes'

13 Reading is to the mind what exercise is to the body.

Richard Steele 1672–1729: in *The Tatler* 18 March 1710

14 The bookful blockhead, ignorantly read,
With loads of learned lumber in his head.

Alexander Pope 1688–1744: *An Essay on Criticism* (1711)

1 A reader seldom peruses a book with pleasure until he knows whether the writer of it be a black man or a fair man, of a mild or choleric disposition, married or a bachelor.

Joseph Addison 1672–1719: in *The Spectator* 1 March 1711

2 I have too much indulged my sedentary humour and have been a rake in reading.

Lady Mary Wortley Montagu 1689–1762: letter to her daughter, Lady Bute, 11 April 1759

3 A man ought to read just as inclination leads him; for what he reads as a task will do him little good.

Samuel Johnson 1709–84: James Boswell *Life of Samuel Johnson* (1791) 14 July 1763

4 ELPHINSTON: What, have you not read it through?
JOHNSON: No, Sir, do *you* read books *through*?

Samuel Johnson 1709–84: James Boswell *Life of Samuel Johnson* (1791) 19 April 1773

5 People in general do not willingly read, if they can have anything else to amuse them.

Samuel Johnson 1709–84: James Boswell *Life of Samuel Johnson* (1791)

6 There is an art of reading, as well as an art of thinking, and an art of writing.

Isaac D'Israeli 1766–1848: *The Literary Character* (1795)

7 But who shall be the master? The writer or the reader?

Denis Diderot 1713–84: *Jacques le Fataliste et son maître* (1796)

8 The time to read is any time: no apparatus, no appointment of time and place, is necessary.

John Aikin 1747–1822: *Letters from a Father to his Son* (1796)

9 Much have I travelled in the realms of gold,
And many goodly states and kingdoms seen.

John Keats 1795–1821: 'On First Looking into Chapman's Homer' (1817); cf. **163:13**

10 There are three kinds of readers: one, who enjoys without judging; a third, who judges without enjoying; another in the middle, who judges while enjoying and enjoys while judging. The last class truly reproduces a work of art anew; its members are not numerous.

Johann Wolfgang von Goethe 1749–1832: letter to Johann Friedrich Rochlitz, 13 June 1819

11 For those who have tasted the profound activity of writing, reading is no more than a secondary pleasure.

Stendhal 1783–1842: *De l'Amour* (1822)

12 One must be an inventor to read well.

Ralph Waldo Emerson 1803–82: *The American Scholar* (1837)

13 Books must be read as deliberately and reservedly as they are written.

Henry David Thoreau 1817–62: *Walden* (1854) 'Reading'

14 Read in order to live.

Gustave Flaubert 1821–80: letter to Mademoiselle de Chantepie, June 1857

on the books she was planning to read:

15 I have not had time yet. But I look at them as a child looks at a cake,—with glittering eyes and watering mouth, imagining the pleasure that awaits him!

Elizabeth Gaskell 1810–65: letter to George Smith, 4 August 1859

16 I do not know any reading more easy, more fascinating, more delightful than a catalogue.

Anatole France 1844–1924: *The Crime of Sylvestre Bonnard* (1881)

1 *La chair est triste, hélas! et j'ai lu tous les livres.*
The flesh, alas, is wearied; and I have read all the books there are.

Stéphane Mallarmé 1842–98: 'Brise Marin' (1887)

2 It is absurd to have a hard and fast rule about what one should read and what one shouldn't. More than half of modern culture depends on what one shouldn't read.

Oscar Wilde 1854–1900: *The Importance of Being Earnest* (1895)

3 The misery of having no time to read a thousand glorious books.

George Gissing 1857–1903: *Commonplace Book* (1962)

4 I would never read a book if it were possible to talk for half an hour with the man who wrote it.

Woodrow Wilson 1856–1924: speech to students at Princeton University in 1910

5 Only sheer ennui sometimes drives [the middle class] to seek distraction in the artist's work.

Arnold Bennett 1867–1931: *Books and Persons* (1917) 'Middle-Class'

6 Reading, that unpunished vice.

Logan Pearsall Smith 1865–1946: *Trivia* (1918)

7 Reading other people's books is better than having to read one's own: and it's much better doing something than nothing.

D. H. Lawrence 1885–1930: letter to Lady Cynthia Asquith, 1922

8 Every reader is, when he reads, reading only about himself.

Marcel Proust 1871–1922: Malcolm Bradbury and James McFarlane (eds.) *Modernism* (1991)

9 'She reads at such a pace,' she complained, 'and when I asked her *where* she had learnt to read so quickly, she replied "On the screens at cinemas."'

Ronald Firbank 1886–1926: *The Flower Beneath the Foot* (1923)

10 The desire to read, like all the other desires that distract our unhappy souls, is capable of analysis.

Virginia Woolf 1882–1941: 'Sir Thomas Browne' (1923)

11 The pain of living and the drug of dreams
Curl up the small soul in the window seat
Behind the *Encyclopedia Britannica*.

T. S. Eliot 1888–1965: 'Animula' (1929)

12 People say that life is the thing, but I prefer reading.

Logan Pearsall Smith 1865–1946: *Afterthoughts* (1931) 'Myself'

13 The reading habit is now often a form of the drug habit.

Q. D. Leavis 1906–81: *Fiction and the Reading Public* (1932)

14 I have sometimes dreamt that when the Day of Judgement dawns and the great conquerors and lawyers and statesmen come to receive their rewards—their crowns, their laurels, their names carved indelibly upon imperishable marble—the Almighty will turn to Peter and will say, not without a certain envy when He sees us coming with our books under our arms, 'Look, these need no reward. We have nothing to give them. They have loved reading.'

Virginia Woolf 1882–1941: *The Common Reader* (2nd ser., 1932)

15 The mere brute pleasure of reading—the sort of pleasure a cow must have in grazing.

G. K. Chesterton 1874–1936: Dudley Barker *G. K. Chesterton* (1973)

1 I would sooner read a time-table or a catalogue than nothing at all . . . They are much more entertaining than half the novels that are written.

W. Somerset Maugham 1874–1965: *Summing Up* (1938)

2 I wish you read books (you know those things that look like blocks but come apart on one side).

F. Scott Fitzgerald 1896–1940: letter to his wife Zelda, 4 May 1940

3 I have only ever read one book in my life, and that is *White Fang*. It's so frightfully good I've never bothered to read another.

'Uncle Matthew' as reader

Nancy Mitford 1904–73: *The Pursuit of Love* (1945)

4 Have you read any good books lately?

Richard Murdoch 1907–90 and **Kenneth Horne** 1900–69: catch-phrase used by Richard Murdoch in radio comedy series *Much-Binding-in-the-Marsh* (first broadcast 2 January 1947)

5 Imaginative readers rewrite books to suit their own taste, omitting and mentally altering what they read.

Robert Graves 1895–1985: *The Reader over your Shoulder* (1947)

6 What really knocks me out is a book that, when you're all done reading it, you wish the author that wrote it was a terrific friend of yours and you could call him up on the phone whenever you felt like it.

J. D. Salinger 1919– : *Catcher in the Rye* (1951)

7 Persons with manners do not read at table.

Anonymous: saying used by Dylan Thomas in *Under Milk Wood* (1954)

8 In a country like England of strictly rationed petrol I was marooned almost each night for almost four years. Even a long acquired capacity to use books as an opiate could not entirely banish many hours of self-communing.

Angus Wilson 1913–91: *The Wild Garden* (1963)

9 I can turn from a classic to a thriller without any mental disruption.

Clement Attlee 1883–1967: attributed, 1964

10 Reading isn't an occupation we encourage among police officers. We try to keep the paper work down to a minimum.

Joe Orton 1933–67: *Loot* (1967)

11 The birth of the reader must be at the cost of the death of the Author.

Roland Barthes 1915–80: *The Death of the Author* (1968)

12 Curiously enough, one cannot *read* a book: one can only reread it. A good reader, a major reader, an active and creative reader is a rereader.

Vladimir Nabokov 1899–1977: *Lectures on Literature* (1980) 'Good Readers and Good Writers'

13 Reading means approaching something that is just coming into being.

Italo Calvino 1923–85: *If on a Winter's Night a Traveller* (1979)

14 The allegory of reading narrates the impossibility of reading.

Paul de Man 1919–83: *The Allegory of Reading* (1979)

15 Reading a book is like rewriting it for yourself . . . You bring to . . . anything you read, all your experience of the world. You bring your history and you read it in your own terms.

Angela Carter 1940–92: in *Marxism Today* January 1985

1 I read for pleasure, and that is the moment at which I learn most. Subliminal learning.

Margaret Atwood 1939– : in an interview, December 1986; Earl G. Ingersoll (ed.) *Margaret Atwood: Conversations* (1990)

2 Many people go on reading now as the equivalent of turning on a television channel for white noise in the background.

Gardner Dozois 1947– : Stan Nicholls (ed.) *Wordsmiths of Wonder* (1993)

3 In a Jeffrey Archer story you get everything in the first page. You don't have to read the rest of the book. You know the whole story on page one. My secret is to try to hold you there for the next four hundred pages.

Jeffrey Archer 1940– : in an interview, November 1987; George Greenfield *Scribblers for Bread* (1989)

4 We may be the last generation, or the last few generations, that regard reading as anything more than a very specific, highly specialized entertainment interest. Like dressing up in cowboy clothes and going to Nashville.

Michael Moorcock 1939– : Stan Nicholls (ed.) *Wordsmiths of Wonder* (1993)

5 Home video is taking over because it is much easier to watch something than to read. No-one is going to sit down and read *Bleak House* to the family any more, but they can all huddle up happily in front of Charles Bronson.

Martin Amis 1949– : Barry Turner *The Writer's Handbook 1994* (1993)

6 And, gentle reader, you as well,
The fountainhead of all remittance.
Buy me before good sense insists
You'll strain your purse and sprain your wrists.

Vikram Seth 1952– : 'A Word of Thanks', at the beginning of *A Suitable Boy* (1993)

7 I too read in bed. In the long succession of beds in which I spent the nights of my childhood . . . the combination of bed and book granted me a sort of home which I knew I could go back to, night after night, under whichever skies.

Alberto Manguel 1948– : *A History of Reading* (1996)

8 After three days without reading, talk becomes flavourless.

Anonymous: Chinese proverb

9 If you believe everything you read, better not read.

Anonymous: Japanese proverb

Rejection

10 After being turned down by numerous publishers, he had decided to write for posterity.

George Ade 1866–1944: *Fables in Slang* (1900)

11 No less than twenty-two publishers and printers read the manuscript of *Dubliners* and when at last it was printed some very kind person bought out the entire edition and had it burnt in Dublin.

James Joyce 1882–1941: letter, 2 April 1932

12 My story 'The Sea and Its Shore' came back from *The Criterion* with *two* rejection slips enclosed, which seems unnecessarily cruel.

Elizabeth Bishop 1911–79: letter to Marianne Moore, 25 February 1937

13 It isn't easy for an author to remain a pleasant human being: both success and failure are usually of a crippling kind.

Graham Greene 1904–91: 'The Poker-Face' (1943)

1 To receive a bitter blow on an early Spring evening (such as that Cape don't want to publish *An Unsuitable Attachment*—but it might be that someone doesn't love you any more)—is it worse than on an Autumn or Winter evening?

Barbara Pym 1913–80: diary, 24 March 1963

a publisher's reader commenting on the manuscript of J. G. Ballard's novel Crash *(published 1973):*

2 This author is beyond psychiatric help . . . do not publish.

Anonymous: in *Independent on Sunday* 16 June 1996; perhaps apocryphal

3 The letter I wrote to *The Author* about not getting published was never published, which seems to be the final accolade of failure.

Barbara Pym 1913–80: letter to Philip Larkin, 19 July 1974

4 These little setbacks, amounting sometimes to thousands of dollars' worth of time wasted, writers must learn to take like Spartans.

Patricia Highsmith 1921–95: *Plotting and Writing Suspense Stories* (1983)

Religion

5 If these writings of the Greeks agree with the book of God, they are useless and need not be preserved; if they disagree, they are pernicious and ought to be destroyed.
on burning the library of Alexandria, AD *c.641*

Caliph Omar AD *c.*581–644: Edward Gibbon *The Decline and Fall of the Roman Empire* (1776-88)

6 A verse may find him, who a sermon flies,
And turn delight into a sacrifice.

George Herbert 1593–1633: 'The Church Porch' (1633)

7 What in me is dark
Illumine, what is low raise and support;
That to the height of this great argument
I may assert eternal providence,
And justify the ways of God to men.

John Milton 1608–74: *Paradise Lost* (1667); cf. **65:10**

8 God is the perfect poet,
Who in his person acts his own creations.

Robert Browning 1812–89: *Paracelsus* (1835)

of the novels of Jane **Austen***:*

9 What vile creatures her parsons are.

John Henry Newman 1801–90: letter to Mrs John Morley, 10 January 1837

10 The word is the Verb, and the Verb is God.

Victor Hugo 1802–85: *Contemplations* (1856)

11 There are many who would laugh at the idea of a novelist teaching either virtue or nobility . . . I have regarded my art from so different a point of view that I have ever thought of myself as a preacher of sermons, and my pulpit as one which I could make both salutary and agreeable to my audience.

Anthony Trollope 1815–82: *Autobiography* (1883)

12 Our religion has materialized itself in the fact, in the supposed fact; it has attached its emotions to the fact, and now the fact is failing it. But for poetry the idea is everything; the rest is a world of illusion, of divine illusion.

Matthew Arnold 1822–88: *Essays in Criticism* Second Series (1888) 'The Study of Poetry'

Poetry attaches its emotion to the idea; the idea *is* the fact. The strongest part of our religion today is its unconscious poetry.

1 I see land! Mr Kendal is just going to be confirmed.
engrossed in Charlotte Yonge's novel The Young Stepmother, *in which the happiness of the family is dependent on their being full members of the Anglican church*

Alfred, Lord Tennyson 1809–92: Alethea Hayter *Charlotte Yonge* (1996)

2 There's no reason to bring religion into it. I think we ought to have as great a regard for religion as we can, so as to keep it out of as many things as possible.

Sean O'Casey 1880–1964: *The Plough and the Stars* (1926)

3 We know too much and are convinced of too little. Our literature is a substitute for religion, and so is our religion.

T. S. Eliot 1888–1965: *Selected Essays* (1932) 'A Dialogue on Dramatic Poetry' (1928)

4 If God exists, why write literature?
And if he doesn't, why write literature?

Eugène Ionesco 1912–94: *Non* (1934)

5 If God were a poet or took poetry seriously (or science for that matter), he would never have given man free will.

W. H. Auden 1907–73: *Poets at Work* (1948) 'Squares and Oblongs'

6 The poet is the priest of the invisible.

Wallace Stevens 1879–1955: 'Adagia' (1957)

7 Religion, oh, just another of those numerous failures resulting from an attempt to popularize art.

Ezra Pound 1885–1972: undated letter to Mary Moore; Humphrey Carpenter *A Serious Character* (1988)

8 In the eyes of God, Who cuts through appearances and goes beyond them, there is no novel, no art, for art thrives on appearances.

Jean-Paul Sartre 1905–80: Edmund White *The Burning Library* (1994)

9 Religion to me has always been the wound, not the bandage.

Dennis Potter 1935–94: interview with Melvyn Bragg on Channel 4, March 1994, in *Seeing the Blossom* (1994)

10 I'm sure there is a paper to be written on the evidence of the Prayer Book in the world of Bertie Wooster, and another on the influence of the Prayer Book on English detective fiction.

Alan Bennett 1934– : *Writing Home* (1994)

Reputation and Achievement see also **Admiration, Fame**

11 It is harder to make one's name by a perfect work than it is for a mediocre one to win esteem through the name one already has.

Jean de la Bruyère 1645–96: *Les Caractères ou les moeurs de ce siècle* (1688)

12 One of our late great poets is sunk in his reputation, because he could never forgive any conceit which came in his way; but swept like a drag-net, great and small. There was plenty enough, but the dishes were ill-sorted; whole

John Dryden 1631–1700: *Fables Ancient and Modern* (1700) preface; cf. **293:4**

pyramids of sweetmeats, for boys and women; but little of solid meat for men.
*on Abraham **Cowley***

1 I hold it as certain, that no man was ever written out of reputation but by himself.
Richard Bentley 1662–1742: William Warburton (ed.) *The Works of Alexander Pope* (1751)

2 I had done all that I could; and no man is well pleased to have his all neglected, be it ever so little.
Samuel Johnson 1709–84: letter to Lord Chesterfield, 7 February 1755

3 Oh, fond attempt to give a deathless lot
To names ignoble, born to be forgot!
William Cowper 1731–1800: 'On Observing Some Names of Little Note Recorded in the Biographia Britannica' (1782)

4 Then my verse I dishonour, my pictures despise,
My person degrade and my temper chastise;
And the pen is my terror, the pencil my shame;
And my talents I bury, and dead is my fame.
William Blake 1757–1827: letter to Thomas Butts, 16 August 1803

5 'If I should die,' said I to myself, 'I have left no immortal work behind me—nothing to make my friends proud of my memory—but I have loved the principle of beauty in all things, and if I had had time I would have made myself remembered.'
John Keats 1795–1821: letter to Fanny Brawne, *c.*February 1820

6 The effect of studying masterpieces is to make me admire and do otherwise.
Gerard Manley Hopkins 1844–89: letter to Robert Bridges, 25 September 1888

7 A louse in the locks of literature.
of the critic John Churton Collins (1848–1908)
Alfred, Lord Tennyson 1809–92: Evan Charteris *Life and Letters of Sir Edmund Gosse* (1931)

8 When I am dead, I hope it may be said:
'His sins were scarlet, but his books were read.'
Hilaire Belloc 1870–1953: 'On His Books' (1923); cf. **54:7**

9 There can be nothing so gratifying to an author as to arouse the respect and esteem of the reader. Make him laugh and he will think you a trivial fellow, but bore him in the right way and your reputation is assured.
W. Somerset Maugham 1874–1965: *Gentleman in the Parlour* (1930)

10 Parnassus after all is not a mountain,
Reserved for A.1. climbers such as you;
It's got a park, it's got a public fountain.
The most I ask is leave to share a pew
With Bradford or with Cottam, that will do.
W. H. Auden 1907–73: *Letter to Lord Byron* (1936)

11 Whom the gods wish to destroy they first call promising.
Cyril Connolly 1903–74: *Enemies of Promise* (1938)

12 A writer's ambition should be . . . to trade a hundred contemporary readers for ten readers in ten years' time and for one reader in a hundred years.
Arthur Koestler 1905–83: in *New York Times Book Review* 1 April 1951

13 The difference in England is that they want us to be distinguished, to be good.
*in conversation with Gore **Vidal***
Stephen Spender 1909–95: in *The Nation* 2 January 1960

14 Some books are undeservedly forgotten; none are undeservedly remembered.
W. H. Auden 1907–73: *The Dyer's Hand* (1962) 'Reading'

1 American writers want to be not good but great; and so are neither.

Gore Vidal 1925– : *Two Sisters* (1970)

2 If there is anything worse for a writer than missing the bus, it is being thought twenty years later, to have got on the wrong one.

Paul Scott 1920–78: 'Literature and the Social Conscience' (1972)

3 I don't want to go around pretending to be me.
of being a 'great man of letters'

Philip Larkin 1922–85: interview in *Observer* 16 December 1979

4 Were those real poems you read or did you write them yourself?
child's question at a poetry reading, giving title to article 'Are Those Real Poems?'

Anonymous: in *New York Times Book Review* 12 February 1995 'Are Those Real Poems?'

5 I doubt whether I will be remembered after my brother has been forgotten, but at least I've made a small contribution to the history of my time, as all authors, even minor ones, do.
comment by John Major's brother on his own memoirs

Terry Major-Ball 1932– : *Major-Major* (ed. 2, 1996)

6 Minor poets are lucky. Minor novelists are totally forgotten, but if you get a poem into an anthology they remember you.

Geoffrey Dearmer 1893–1996: in *The Times* 20 August 1996; obituary

Reviews see also Criticism

7 Reviewers are usually people who would have been poets, historians, biographers, &c., if they could; they have tried their talents at one or at the other, and have failed; therefore they turn critics.

Samuel Taylor Coleridge 1772–1834: *Seven Lectures on Shakespeare and Milton* (delivered 1811–12)

8 Send me no more reviews of any kind.—I will read no more of evil or good in that line.—Walter Scott has not read a review of *himself* for *thirteen years.*

Lord Byron 1788–1824: letter to his publisher John Murray, 3 November 1821

9 'Tis strange the mind, that very fiery particle,
Should let itself be snuffed out by an article.
*on **Keats** 'who was killed off by one critique'*

Lord Byron 1788–1824: *Don Juan* (1819–24)

10 He took the praise as a greedy boy takes apple pie, and the criticism as a good dutiful boy takes senna-tea.
of Bulwer Lytton, whose novels he had criticized

Lord Macaulay 1800–59: letter, 5 August 1831

11 We cannot sum up the merits of the stupendous mass of paper which lies before us, better than by saying, that it consists of about two thousand closely printed pages, that it occupies fifteen hundred inches cubic measure, and that it weighs sixty pounds avoirdupois.
reviewing Edward Nares's three-volume Memoirs of William Cecil, Lord Burghley

Lord Macaulay 1800–59: in *Edinburgh Review* April 1832

12 I never read a book before reviewing it; it prejudices a man so.

Sydney Smith 1771–1845: H. Pearson *The Smith of Smiths* (1934)

1 People who like this sort of thing will find this the sort of thing they like.
judgement of a book

Abraham Lincoln 1809–65: G. W. E. Russell *Collections and Recollections* (1898)

2 It is with utter indifference that I regard the critical disturbance and all the insanity written about *Ghosts*. I was prepared for this . . . There were screams about *Peer Gynt*, and not less against *Pillars of Society* and *A Doll's House*. The screams will die away on this occasion as they did previously.

Henrik Ibsen 1828–1906: letter to Hegel, 1882

3 If this sort of thing continues no more novel-writing for me. A man must be a fool to deliberately stand up and be shot at.
of a hostile review of Tess of the D'Urbervilles, *1891*

Thomas Hardy 1840–1928: Florence Hardy *The Early Life of Thomas Hardy* (1928)

4 I am strongly of opinion that an author had far better not read any reviews of his books: the unfavourable ones are almost certain to make him cross, and the favourable ones conceited; and neither of these results is desirable.

Lewis Carroll 1832–98: *Sylvie and Bruno Concluded* (1893)

5 Browning made the verses
Your servant the critique
Browning couldn't sing at all
I fancy I could speak.
Although his book was clever
(To give the deil his due)
I wasn't pleased with Browning's verse
Nor he with my review.

Robert Louis Stevenson 1850–94: 'Light Verse'

6 A sound-headed costermonger who did not know the word *critic* would give better judgement.
on hack reviewers

George Gissing 1857–1903: *Commonplace Book* (1962)

7 I am sitting in the smallest room of my house. I have your review before me. In a moment it will be behind me.
responding to a savage review by Rudolph Louis in Münchener Neueste Nachrichten, *7 February 1906*

Max Reger 1873–1916: Nicolas Slonimsky *Lexicon of Musical Invective* (1953)

8 When I read reviews I crush the columns together to get at one or two sentences; is it a good book or a bad? And then I discount those two sentences according to what I know of the book and of the reviewer. But when I write a review I write every sentence as if it were going to be tried before three Chief Justices: I can't believe that I am crushed together and discounted.

Virginia Woolf 1882–1941: diary, 18 February 1922

9 From the moment I picked up your book until I laid it down, I was convulsed with laughter. Some day I intend reading it.
blurb written for S. J. Perelman's 1928 book Dawn Ginsberg's Revenge

Groucho Marx 1895–1977: Hector Arce *Groucho* (1979)

10 This fictional account of the day-by-day life of an English gamekeeper is still of considerable interest to outdoor-minded readers, as it contains many passages on pheasant raising, the apprehending of poachers, ways to control vermin, and other chores and duties of the professional gamekeeper. Unfortunately one is obliged to wade through

Anonymous: review of D. H. Lawrence *Lady Chatterley's Lover*, attributed to *Field and Stream*, *c.* 1928

many pages of extraneous material in order to discover and savour these sidelights on the management of a Midlands shooting estate, and in this reviewer's opinion this book cannot take the place of J. R. Miller's *Practical Gamekeeping.*

1 The professional reviewers: the light men who bubble at the mouth with enthusiasm because they see other bubbles floating around; the dumb men who regularly mistake your worst stuff for your best and your best for your worst, and, most of all, the cowards who straddle and the leeches who review your books in terms that they have cribbed out of the book itself, like scholars under some extraordinary dispensation which allows them to heckle the teacher.

F. Scott Fitzgerald 1896–1940: letter, 10 May 1934

2 [Castorley] went out of his way to review one of Manallace's books with an intimacy of unclean deduction (this was before the days of Freud) which long stood as a record.

Rudyard Kipling 1865–1936: *Limits and Renewals* (1932) 'Dayspring Mishandled'

3 *House Beautiful* is play lousy.

Dorothy Parker 1893–1967: review of play in *New Yorker*, 1933; Phyllis Hartnoll *Plays and Players* (1984)

4 I stay very close to the text—no soaring eagle but a low-swung basset who hunts by scent and keeps his nose to the ground.

Cyril Connolly 1903–74: introduction to *The Condemned Playground* (1945)

5 Whoso maintains that I am humbled now
(Who wait the Awful Day) is still a liar;
I hope to meet my Maker brow to brow
And find my own the higher.

Frances Cornford 1886–1960: 'Epitaph for a Reviewer' (1954)

6 One cannot review a bad book without showing off.

W. H. Auden 1907–73: *Dyer's Hand* (1962) 'Reading'

7 Writing reviews can be fun, but I don't think the practice is very good for the character.

W. H. Auden 1907–73: George Plimpton (ed.) *Writers at Work* 1977 4th series

8 A writer writes and the reviewer then tells the writer what he or she meant. And what she has managed to do.

Bernice Rubens 1928– : Rosemary Hartill *Writers Revealed* (1989)

9 The ones who get under my skin are the academic critics whose whole training is to detect faults. They call them 'flaws'. I call them 'flawyers'.
on reviewers

Robertson Davies 1913–95: in *Paris Review* 1989

10 Kingsley Amis said 'You should let a bad review ruin your breakfast but not your lunch'. I tend to move that forward a bit: let it ruin your lunch but not your dinner 'cause I probably get up later than him.

Arthur Smith : in *Independent on Sunday* 5 February 1995 'Overheard'

11 I have spent years as a professional writer and what I know now is that the only review that is no use to me is a review that lies.

Kazuo Ishiguro 1954– : in *Guardian* 15 May 1996

Revision see also **Choice of Words, Style**

1 Now, O king, establish the decree, and sign the writing, that it be not changed, according to the law of the Medes and Persians, which altereth not.
Bible: Daniel

2 In the mind, as in the body, there is the necessity of getting rid of waste, and a man of active literary habits will write for the fire as well as for the press.
Jerome Cardan 1501–76: William Osler *Aequanimites* (1904); epigraph

3 I had not time to lick it into form, as she [a bear] doth her young ones.
Robert Burton 1577–1640: *The Anatomy of Melancholy* (1621–51)

4 I have made this [letter] longer than usual, only because I have not had the time to make it shorter.
Blaise Pascal 1623–62: *Lettres Provinciales* (1657)

5 Of every four words I write, I strike out three.
Nicolas Boileau 1636–1711: *Satire (2). A M. Molière* (1665)

6 I write I neither know how nor why, and always make worse what I try to amend.
Horace Walpole 1717–97: letter to Rev. William Mason, 11 May 1769

7 Read over your compositions, and where ever you meet with a passage which you think is particularly fine, strike it out.
Samuel Johnson 1709–84: quoting a college tutor, James Boswell *Life of Samuel Johnson* (1791) 30 April 1773

8 Remove at least fifty superlatives in each chapter. Never say 'Oliver's burning passion for Helen'. The poor novelist has to make us believe in the burning passion without ever naming it: that would be immodest.
Stendhal 1783–1842: letter to Mme Gaulthier, 4 May 1834

9 Not that the story need be long, but it will take a long while to make it short.
Henry David Thoreau 1817–62: letter to Harrison Blake, 16 November 1857

10 If I don't rewrite them it's because I don't see how to write them better, not because I don't think they should be.
Robert Louis Stevenson 1850–94: letter to W. E. Henley, April 1879

11 Sometimes the three hours' labour of a morning resulted in half a dozen lines, corrected into illegibility.
George Gissing 1857–1903: of 'Edwin Reardon' in *New Grub Street* (1891)

12 I generally go back and do over my yesterday's work, much like the snail in the arithmetical problem, who climbed four feet each day and slipped back three each night, besides sometimes going back to write whole masses again . . . I am happier rewriting than blocking out.
Charlotte Yonge 1823–1901: Georgina Battiscombe *Charlotte Mary Yonge* (1943)

13 I said 'a line will take us hours maybe,
Yet if it does not seem a moment's thought
Our stitching and unstitching has been naught.'
W. B. Yeats 1865–1939: 'Adam's Curse' (1904)

14 The friends that have it I do wrong
Whenever I remake a song,
Should know what issue is at stake:
It is myself that I remake.
W. B. Yeats 1865–1939: 'The friends that have it I do wrong' (1908)

15 The business of selection and revision is simply hell for me—my efforts to cut out 50,000 words may sometimes result in my adding 75,000.
Thomas Wolfe 1900–38: letter to Maxwell Perkins, his editor at Scribner's, 17 November 1928

1 I published it in the waste-paper basket.

Rudyard Kipling 1865–1936: Thomas Pinney in *Times Literary Supplement* 7 April 1995

2 A tale from which pieces have been raked out is like a fire that has been poked. One does not know that the operation has been performed, but everyone feels the effect.

Rudyard Kipling 1865–1936: *Something of Myself* (1937)

3 I often covered more than a hundred sheets of paper with drafts, revisions, rewritings, ravings, doodlings, and intensely concentrated work to construct a single verse.

Dylan Thomas 1914–53: letter, 25 May 1948

4 The manuscript was a delight to read . . . but isn't a book at all yet. No more 40 hour week. Blood, sweat and tears. That is to say if you want to produce a work of art. There is a work of art there, lurking in a hole, occasionally visible to the tip of its whiskers.

having read the manuscript of Nancy Mitford's Love in a Cold Climate

Evelyn Waugh 1903–66: letter to Nancy Mitford, 24 October 1948

5 Now none of this. No complaints about headaches. Revision is just as important as any other part of writing and must be done con amore.

Evelyn Waugh 1903–66: letter to Nancy Mitford, 31 March 1951

6 Tell them the author giveth and the author taketh away.

to a playwright afraid to tell the cast of cuts he had made

George S. Kaufman 1889–1961: Howard Teichmann *George S. Kaufman* (1973)

7 I constantly rewrite—an incinerator is a writer's best friend.

Thornton Wilder 1897–1975: in *New York Times* 6 November 1961

8 A writer is unfair to himself when he is unable to be hard on himself.

Marianne Moore 1887–1972: George Plimpton (ed.) *Writers at Work* (2nd series, 1963)

9 I do a lot of revising. Certain chapters six or seven times . . . I usually write to a point where the work is getting worse rather than better. That's the point to stop and the time to publish.

John Dos Passos 1896–1970: George Plimpton (ed.) *The Writer's Chapbook* (1989)

10 First drafts are for learning what your novel or story is about. Revision is working with that knowledge to enlarge and enhance an idea, to re-form it . . . Revision is one of the true pleasures of writing.

Bernard Malamud 1914–86: George Plimpton (ed.) *Writers at Work* (6th series, 1984)

11 If it sounds like writing, I rewrite it.

Elmore Leonard 1925– : interview in *Newsweek* 22 April 1985

12 The waste-paper basket is the writer's best friend.

Isaac Bashevis Singer 1904–91: George Plimpton (ed.) *The Writer's Chapbook* (1989)

13 I do a lot of rewriting. I find that the more versions you see of, say, the beginning of a chapter—blue paper, white paper, typed, longhand—the more you get it right in the end.

William Trevor 1928– : in *Paris Review* 1989

1 I correct or change words, but I can't rewrite a scene or make a major change because there's a sense then of someone looking over my shoulder.

Eudora Welty 1909– : George Plimpton (ed.) *The Writer's Chapbook* (1989)

2 Let alone rewrite, he doesn't even reread.

Clive James 1939– : *The Dreaming Swimmer* (1992)

Rhyme and Rhythm see also **Poetry**

3 Of its own accord my song would come in the right rhythms, and what I was trying to say was poetry.

Ovid 43 BC–AD *c.*17: *Tristia*

4 'By God,' quod he, 'for pleynly, at a word,
Thy drasty rymyng is nat worth a toord!'

Geoffrey Chaucer *c.*1343–1400: *The Canterbury Tales* 'Sir Thopas'

5 For rhyme the rudder is of verses,
With which like ships they steer their courses.

Samuel Butler 1612–80: *Hudibras* pt. 1 (1663)

6 Rhyme being no necessary adjunct or true ornament of poem or good verse, in longer works especially, but the invention of a barbarous age, to set off wretched matter and lame metre.

John Milton 1608–74: *Paradise Lost* (1667) 'The Verse' (preface, added 1668)

7 The troublesome and modern bondage of rhyming.

John Milton 1608–74: *Paradise Lost* (1667) 'The Verse' (preface, added 1668)

8 Rhyme is the rock on which thou art to wreck.

John Dryden 1631–1700: *Absalom and Achitophel* (1681)

9 But when loud surges lash the sounding shore,
The hoarse, rough verse should like the torrent roar.
When Ajax strives, some rock's vast weight to throw,
The line too labours, and the words move slow.

Alexander Pope 1688–1744: *An Essay on Criticism* (1711)

10 A needless Alexandrine ends the song,
That, like a wounded snake, drags its slow length along.

Alexander Pope 1688–1744: *An Essay on Criticism* (1711)

11 Let your little verses flow
Gently, sweetly, row by row;
Let the verse the subject fit,
Little subject, little wit.

Henry Carey *c.*1687–1743: 'Namby-Pamby: or, A Panegyric on the New Versification' (1725)

12 Iambics march from short to long;—
With a leap and a bound the swift Anapaests throng.

Samuel Taylor Coleridge 1772–1834: 'Metrical Feet' (1806)

13 Trochee trips from long to short.

Samuel Taylor Coleridge 1772–1834: 'Metrical Feet' (1806)

14 O lovely O most charming pug
Thy graceful air and heavenly mug . . .
His noses cast is of the roman
He is a very pretty weoman
I could not get a rhyme for roman
And was oblidged to call it weoman.

Marjory Fleming 1803–11: 'Sonnet'

1 Prose poets like blank-verse. I'm fond of rhyme,
Good workmen never quarrel with their tools.

Lord Byron 1788–1824: *Don Juan* (1819–24)

2 There is something magical about rhythm; it even makes us believe we have taken possession of the sublime.

Johann Wolfgang von Goethe 1749–1832: *Art and Antiquity* (1816–32)

3 Mysterious and strong effects lie in different poetical forms. If the content of my *Roman Elegies* were transposed into the tone and metre of Byron's *Don Juan*, then what is said would sound quite infamous.

Johann Wolfgang von Goethe 1749–1832: Johann Peter Eckermann *Conversations with Goethe* (1836–48)

4 Keeping time, time, time,
In a sort of Runic rhyme,
To the tintinnabulation that so musically wells
From the bells, bells, bells, bells.

Edgar Allan Poe 1809–49: 'The Bells' (1849)

5 Here lies that peerless paper peer Lord Peter,
Who broke the laws of God and man and metre.

John Gibson Lockhart 1794–1854: epitaph for Patrick ('Peter'), Lord Robertson, in *The Journal of Sir Walter Scott* (1890) vol. 1

6 No reasonable little Child expects
A Grown-up Man to make a rhyme on X.

Hilaire Belloc 1870–1953: *A Moral Alphabet* (1899)

7 In our language rhyme is a barrel. A barrel of dynamite. The line is a fuse. The line smoulders to the end and explodes; and the town is blown sky-high in a stanza.

Vladimir Mayakovsky 1893–1930: 'Conversation with an Inspector of Taxes about Poetry' (1926)

8 The author's conviction on this day of New Year is that music begins to atrophy when it departs too far from the dance; that poetry begins to atrophy when it gets too far from music.

Ezra Pound 1885–1972: *The ABC of Reading* (1934)

9 The useful trick of rhyming stressed with unstressed syllables, which I introduced into English poetry.

Robert Graves 1895–1985: letter, 1 September 1943

10 I'd as soon write free verse as play tennis with the net down.

Robert Frost 1874–1963: Edward Lathem *Interviews with Robert Frost* (1966)

11 One salient consequence of my blindness was my gradual abandonment of free verse in favour of classical metrics. In fact, blindness made me take up the writing of poetry again. Since rough drafts were denied me, I had to fall back on memory. It is obviously easier to remember verse than prose, and to remember regular verse forms rather than free ones. Regular verse is, so to speak, portable.

Jorge Luis Borges 1899–1986: *The Aleph and Other Stories* (1971) 'Autobiographical Essay'

12 Don't let this aid to rhyming bitch your talent or your timing.

in a rhyming dictionary given to Lionel Bart

Noël Coward 1899–1973: attributed

13 The notion of expressing sentiments in short lines having similar sounds at their ends seems as remote as mangoes on the moon.

Philip Larkin 1922–85: letter to Barbara Pym, 22 January 1975

14 Metrical poetry is ultimately allied to song, and I like the connection. Free verse is ultimately allied to conversation, and I like that connection too.

Thom Gunn 1929– : in *Paris Review* 1995

Rivalry see also **Admiration and Praise**

1 My desire is . . . that mine adversary had written a book.

Bible: Job

2 *Multa fero, ut placem genus irritabile vatum.*
I have to put up with a lot, to please the touchy breed of poets.

Horace 65–8 BC: *Epistles*

3 Readers and listeners like my books,
Yet a certain poet calls them crude.
What do I care? I serve up food
To please my guests, not fellow cooks.

Martial AD c.40–c.104: *Epigrammata*, tr. James Michie

4 Sei Shōnagon . . . was dreadfully conceited. She thought herself so clever and littered her writings with Chinese characters; but if you examined them closely, they left a good deal to be desired . . . People who go out of their way to try and be sensitive in the most unpromising situations, trying to capture every moment of interest, however slight, are bound to look ridiculous and superficial.
one literary Japanese court lady's view of another

Murasaki Shikibu c.978–c.1031: diary, c.1010; cf. **237:7**

5 The readers and the hearers like my books,
But yet some writers cannot them digest;
But what care I? for when I make a feast
I would my guests should praise it, not the cooks.

John Harington 1561–1612: *Epigrams* (1618) 'Of Writers who Carp and Other Men's Books'

6 Envy's a sharper spur than pay,
No author ever spared a brother,
Wits are gamecocks to one another.

John Gay 1685–1732: *Fables* (1727) 'The Elephant and the Bookseller'

7 Hot, envious, noisy, proud, the scribbling fry
Burn, hiss and bounce, waste paper, stink, and die.

Edward Young 1683–1765: *The Love of Fame* (1725–8)

8 What poet would not grieve to see
His brother write as well as he?
But rather than they should excel,
Would wish his rivals all in Hell?

Jonathan Swift 1667–1745: 'Verses on the Death of Dr Swift' (1731)

9 The infamous trade of vilifying one's colleagues to earn a little money should be left to cheap journalists . . . It is those wretches who have made of literature an arena for gladiators.

Voltaire 1694–1778: letter to a friend, 20 February 1767

10 I think none but pikes and poets prey upon their kind.

William Warburton 1698–1779: to David Garrick, 22 April 1762

11 How odious all authors are, and how doubly so to each other!

Henry Fox, Lord Holland d. 1859: letter, 3 January 1821

12 In general I do not draw well with literary men—not that I dislike them but—I never know what to say to them after I have praised their last publication.

Lord Byron 1788–1824: 'Detached Thoughts' 15 October 1821

13 Authors are like cattle going to a fair: those of the same field can never move on without butting one another.

Walter Savage Landor 1775–1864: *Imaginary Conversations* (1824–9) 'Archdeacon Hare and Walter Landor'

1 Success in literature? What on earth does George Lewes know about success in literature?
on learning that Lewes had contributed articles on the theme of 'Success in Literature'

Charles Dickens 1812–70: Peter Ackroyd *Dickens* (1990)

2 The hateful spirit of literary rancour . . . enough to make all literature appear a morbid excrescence upon human life.

George Gissing 1857–1903: *New Grub Street* (1891)

3 Hateful as is the struggle for life in every form, this rough-and-tumble of the literary arena seems to me sordid and degrading beyond all others. Oh, your prices per thousand words! Oh, your paragraphs and your interviewings! and oh, the black despair that awaits those down-trodden in the fray.

George Gissing 1857–1903: *The Private Papers of Henry Ryecroft* (1903)

4 But where's the wild dog that has praised his fleas?

W. B. Yeats 1865–1939: 'To a Poet, Who would have Me Praise certain bad Poets, Imitators of His and of Mine' (1910)

5 I was jealous of her writing—the only writing I have ever been jealous of.
shortly after the death of Katherine ***Mansfield***

Virginia Woolf 1882–1941: letter, 16 January 1923

6 Do we want laurels for ourselves most,
Or most that no one else shall have any?

Amy Lowell 1874–1925: *What's O'Clock* (1925) 'La Ronde du Diable'

7 Poets arguing about modern poetry: jackals snarling over a dried-up well.

Cyril Connolly 1903–74: *The Unquiet Grave* (1944)

8 My personal animosity against a writer never affects my opinion of what he writes. Nobody could be more anxious than myself, for instance, that Alan Alexander Milne should trip over a loose bootlace and break his bloody neck, yet I reread his early stuff at regular intervals with all the old enjoyment.
A. A. ***Milne*** *had written a hostile letter to the* Daily Telegraph *on the report of* ***Wodehouse****'s broadcasting from Germany*

P. G. Wodehouse 1881–1975: letter, 27 November 1945

9 I started out very quiet and I beat Mr Turgenev. Then I trained hard and I beat Mr de Maupassant. I've fought two draws with Mr Stendhal, and I think I had an edge in the last one. But nobody's going to get me in any ring with Mr Tolstoy unless I'm crazy or I keep getting better.

Ernest Hemingway 1899–1961: in *New Yorker* 13 May 1950

10 I had the freak of luck to start high on the mountain, and go down sharp while others were passing me.
of the period after the publication of his novel The Barbary Shore

Norman Mailer 1923– : Gore Vidal in *The Nation* 2 January 1960

of her time as editor of Poetry Review:

11 Their petty ambitions and their cut-throat behaviour was amazing, I had never seen anything like it. I could see how literature works up people's passions and ambitions for success—any little success, publication, anything.

Muriel Spark 1918– : on *Bookstand*, 1961 television programme; repeated on BBC2 *Bookmark* 9 March 1996

1 I thought I'd begin with a sonnet by Shakespeare but then I thought why should I? He never reads any of mine.

Spike Milligan 1918– : remark at Poetry and Jazz concert, Hampstead Town Hall 1961

2 No poet or novelist wishes he were the only one who ever lived, but most of them wish they were the only one alive, and quite a number fondly believe their wish has been granted.

W. H. Auden 1907–73: *The Dyer's Hand* (1962) 'Writing'

3 Whenever a friend succeeds, a little something in me dies.

Gore Vidal 1925– : in *Sunday Times Magazine* 16 September 1973

4 Let Shakespeare do it his way, I'll do it mine. We'll see who comes out better.

Mae West 1892–1980: G. Eells and S. Musgrove *Mae West* (1989)

5 The book of my enemy has been remaindered
And I rejoice . . .
What avail him now his awards and prizes,
The praise expended upon his meticulous technique,
His individual new voice?

Clive James 1939– : 'The Book of My Enemy has been Remaindered' (1986)

6 Writers seldom wish other writers well.

Saul Bellow 1915– : attributed, 1989

of appreciations of other writers in Kingsley ***Amis's*** Memoirs*:*

7 It is as if Amis is swimming slowly but surely under water, carefully slogging through the praise stroke by stroke, when all of a sudden he feels he can't go any further without rising to the surface and taking a quick slug of the air of misanthropy.

Craig Brown 1957– : *Craig Brown's Greatest Hits* (1993)

8 Being a minor poet is like being minor royalty. And no one, as a former lady-in-waiting to Princess Margaret once explained to me, is happy as that.

Stephen Spender 1909–95: in *Daily Telegraph* 18 July 1995; obituary

9 For a writer who has been quietly getting on with her work for over 30 years with malice towards none, it is shocking to discover how much ill-will and envy of the successful bubbles beneath the surface.

P. D. James 1920– : in *Daily Telegraph* 30 September 1995 'They Said It'

10 Good writing has always been attacked, notably by other good writers.

Salman Rushdie 1947– : interview in *Observer* 18 August 1996

11 There is a kind of political correctness about most of our literary assessment. Abroad yes, here no. Guarded praise is the most one is permitted. The sulphur of envy, particularly from newspapers, wraps itself around writers' lives.

Carmen Callil 1938– : speech at the Booker awards, 29 October 1996, in *Daily Telegraph* 30 October 1996

Romantic Fiction see also **Popular Fiction**

12 The novels which I approve are such as display human nature with grandeur—such as show her in the sublimities of intense feeling—such as exhibit the progress of strong passion from the first germ of incipient susceptibility to the utmost energies of reason half-dethroned,—where we see the strong spark of woman's

Jane Austen 1775–1817: 'Sir Edward Denham' in *Sanditon* (1925 ed.)

captivations elicit such fire in the soul of man as lead him—(though at the risk of some aberration from the strict line of primitive obligations)—to hazard all, dare all, achieve all, to obtain her.

1 And what's romance? Usually, a nice little tale where you have everything As You Like It, where rain never wets your jacket and gnats never bite your nose and it's always daisy-time.

D. H. Lawrence 1885–1930: *Studies in Classic American Literature* (1924)

2 When a customer demanded a book of this category or that, . . . 'Sex' or 'Crime' or 'Wild West' or 'Romance' (always with the accent on the *o*) Gordon was ready with expert advice.

George Orwell 1903–50: *Keep the Aspidistra Flying* (1936)

3 It's our *own* story *exactly*! He bold as a hawk, she soft as the dawn.

James Thurber 1894–1961: cartoon caption in *New Yorker* 25 February 1939

4 As artists they're rot, but as providers they're oil wells; they gush.
on lady novelists

Dorothy Parker 1893–1967: Malcolm Cowley *Writers at Work* 1st Series (1958)

5 That scene in bodice-ripper romances where the vulnerable heroine meets the rakehell hero.

Erica Jong 1942– : *Parachute and Kisses* (1984)

6 We ought to be prescribed by the NHS. We're better than valium.
view of the chairman of Mills and Boon, publishers of romantic fiction

John Boon 1916–96: in 1989; in obituary, *Daily Telegraph* 16 July 1996

7 You can't lose if you give them handsome highwaymen, duels, 3-foot fountains and whacking great horses and dogs all over the place.

Barbara Cartland 1901– : in *Attitude*; in *Guardian* 26 April 1996

Satire see **Wit and Satire**

Scholarship and Academe

8 Of making many books there is no end; and much study is a weariness of the flesh.

Bible: Ecclesiastes

9 *Atque inter silvas Academi quaerere verum.*
And seek for truth in the groves of Academe.

Horace 65–8 BC: *Epistles*

10 In the usual course of study I had come to a book of a certain Cicero.

St Augustine AD 354–430: *Confessions* (AD 397–8)

11 And gladly wolde he lerne and gladly teche.

Geoffrey Chaucer *c.*1343–1400: *The Canterbury Tales* 'The General Prologue'

12 O, tis a precious apothegmatical pedant, who will find matter enough to dilate a whole day of the first invention of *Fy, fa, fum*, I smell the blood of an Englishman.

Thomas Nashe 1567–1601: *Have with you to Saffron-walden* (1596)

1 I would I had bestowed that time in the tongues that I have in fencing, dancing, and bear-baiting. O! had I but followed the arts!

William Shakespeare 1564–1616: *Twelfth Night* (1601)

2 Whilst others have been at the balloo, I have been at my book, and am now past the craggy paths of study, and come to the flowery plains of honour and reputation.

Ben Jonson *c.*1573–1637: *Volpone* (1606)

3 And let a scholar all Earth's volumes carry,
He will be but a walking dictionary.

George Chapman *c.*1559–1634: *The Tears of Peace* (1609)

4 Studies serve for delight, for ornament, and for ability.

Francis Bacon 1561–1626: *Essays* (1625) 'Of Studies'

5 I have not wished to enrich the edition with any references, as some have desired me to do, because the learned do not need such things, and the others do not bother about them.

St Francis of Sales 1567–1622: J. H. Adels *Wisdom of the Saints* (1987) frontispiece

6 Learning hath gained most by those books by which the printers have lost.

Thomas Fuller 1608–61: *The Holy State and the Profane State*

7 What song the Syrens sang, or what name Achilles assumed when he hid himself among women, though puzzling questions, are not beyond all conjecture.

Thomas Browne 1605–82: *Hydriotaphia* (Urn Burial, 1658)

8 But for the most part, women are not educated as they should be, I mean those of quality; oft their education is only to dance, sing, and fiddle, to write complimental letters, to read romances, to speak some languages that is not their native . . . their parents take more care of their feet than their head, more of their words than their reason.

Margaret Cavendish *c.*1624–74: *Sociable Letters* (1664)

9 I am not ambitious to appear a man of letters: I could be content the world should think I had scarce looked upon any other book than that of nature.

Robert Boyle 1627–91: *Philosophical Works* (1738) vol. 1

10 How science dwindles, and how volumes swell,
How commentators each dark passage shun,
And hold their farthing candle to the sun.

Edward Young 1683–1765: *The Love of Fame* (1725–8)

11 There mark what ills the scholar's life assail,
Toil, envy, want, the patron, and the jail.

Samuel Johnson 1709–84: *The Vanity of Human Wishes* (1749)

12 It is a great fault of commentators that they are apt to be silent or at most very concise where there is any difficulty, and to be very prolix and tedious where there is none.

Thomas Newton 1704–82: introduction to *Paradise Lost* (1749)

13 I have always suspected that the reading is right, which requires many words to prove it wrong; and the emendation wrong, that cannot without so much labour appear to be right.

Samuel Johnson 1709–84: *Plays of William Shakespeare* (1765)

14 Notes are often necessary, but they are necessary evils.

Samuel Johnson 1709–84: *Plays of William Shakespeare* (1765) preface

15 Take care not to understand editions and title-pages too well. It always smells of pedantry, and not always of learning . . . Beware of the *bibliomanie.*

Lord Chesterfield 1694–1773: *Letters to his Son* (1774)

1 Gie me ae spark o' Nature's fire,
That's a' the learning I desire.

Robert Burns 1759–96: 'Epistle to J. L[aprai]k' (1786)

2 Our meddling intellect
Mis-shapes the beauteous forms of things:—
We murder to dissect.
Enough of science and of art;
Close up these barren leaves;
Come forth, and bring with you a heart
That watches and receives.

William Wordsworth 1770–1850: 'The Tables Turned' (1798)

3 A votary of the desk—a notched and cropt scrivener—one that sucks his substance, as certain sick people are said to do, through a quill.

Charles Lamb 1775–1834: *Essays of Elia* (1823) 'Oxford in the Vacation'

4 The true University of these days is a collection of books.

Thomas Carlyle 1795–1881: *On Heroes, Hero-Worship, and the Heroic* (1841)

5 A classic lecture, rich in sentiment,
With scraps of thundrous epic lilted out
By violet-hooded Doctors, elegies
And quoted odes, and jewels five-words-long,
That on the stretched forefinger of all Time
Sparkle for ever.

Alfred, Lord Tennyson 1809–92: *The Princess* (1847)

6 A whaleship was my Yale College and my Harvard.

Herman Melville 1819–91: *Moby Dick* (1851)

7 You will find it a very good practice always to verify your references, sir!

Martin Joseph Routh 1755–1854: John William Burgon *Lives of Twelve Good Men* (1888 ed.)

8 And I have written three books on the soul,
Proving absurd all written hitherto,
And putting us to ignorance again.

Robert Browning 1812–89: 'Cleon' (1855)

9 Nor can I do better, in conclusion, than impress upon you the study of Greek literature, which not only elevates above the vulgar herd, but leads not infrequently to positions of considerable emolument.

Thomas Gaisford 1779–1855: Christmas Day Sermon in the Cathedral, Oxford; W. Tuckwell *Reminiscences of Oxford* (2nd ed., 1907)

10 I think aesthetic teaching is the highest of all teaching, because it deals with life in its highest complexity. But if it ceases to be purely aesthetic—if it lapses anywhere from the picture to the diagram—it becomes the most offensive of all teaching.

George Eliot 1819–80: letter, 15 August 1866

11 Fred's studies are not very deep . . . he is only reading a novel.

George Eliot 1819–80: 'Rosamond Vincy' in *Middlemarch* (1871–2)

12 The clever men at Oxford
Know all that there is to be knowed.
But they none of them know one half as much
As intelligent Mr Toad!

Kenneth Grahame 1859–1932: *The Wind in the Willows* (1908)

1 It is terrible news that Miss Watts has 'thousands of letters'! I wish they would be burned in one great heap. The world is infinitely too full of such documents.
while working on his biography of ***Swinburne***

Edmund Gosse 1849–1928: letter to T. J. Wise, 1915; Ann Thwaite 'Writing Lives' (1988)

2 All shuffle there; all cough in ink;
All wear the carpet with their shoes;
All think what other people think;
All know the man their neighbour knows.
Lord, what would they say
Did their Catullus walk that way?

W. B. Yeats 1865–1939: 'The Scholars' (1919)

3 They hunt a reference in dusty tomes; or wrestle wearily with cumbrous files of years-old newspapers, to earn the sorry pittance paid to those who gather long-forgotten facts from print.

Charles Inge 1868–1957: *Flashes of London* (1920) 'Sisters of Fear'

4 The proper study of mankind is books.

Aldous Huxley 1894–1963: *Crome Yellow* (1921)

5 The material for this book was collected directly from nature at great personal risk by the author.
in capitals, on the flyleaf of her book

Helen Rowland 1875–1950: *A Guide to Men* (1922)

6 I dreamt last night that Shakespeare's ghost
Sat for a Civil Service post;
The English paper for the year
Had several questions on *King Lear*
Which Shakespeare answered very badly
Because he hadn't read his Bradley.

Guy Boas b. 1896: in 1926; in *Spectator* 27 January 1990

7 This ain't your silly English Literature, you ass. It's our marks.

Rudyard Kipling 1865–1936: *The Complete Stalky and Co* (1929) 'The Propagation of Knowledge'

8 Weep not for little Léonie
Abducted by a French Marquis!
Though loss of honour was a wrench
Just think how it's improved her French.

Harry Graham 1874–1936: *More Ruthless Rhymes for Heartless Homes* (1930) 'Compensation'

9 Pedantry is the dotage of knowledge.

Holbrook Jackson 1874–1948: *Anatomy of Bibliomania* (1930) vol. 1

10 One learns more from a good scholar in a rage than from a score of lucid and laborious drudges.

Rudyard Kipling 1865–1936: *Something of Myself* (1937)

11 I've put in so many enigmas and puzzles that it will keep the professors busy for centuries arguing over what I meant, and that's the only way of insuring one's immortality.
of Ulysses

James Joyce 1882–1941: Richard Ellmann *James Joyce* (1982)

12 The primary object of a student of literature is to be delighted. His duty is to enjoy himself: his efforts should be directed to developing his faculty of appreciation.

Lord David Cecil 1902–86: *Reading as one of the Fine Arts* (1949)

1 Being a professor of poetry is rather like being a Kentucky colonel. It's not really a subject one can profess—unless one hires oneself out to write pieces of poetry for funerals or the marriages of dons.

W. H. Auden 1907–73: attributed, 1960

2 'What . . . is a text course?' 'One that uses books, of course . . . You remember books? They're what we used to read before we started discussing what we ought to read.'

Amanda Cross 1926– : *Poetic Justice* (1970)

3 A writer who lives long enough becomes an academic subject and almost qualified to teach it himself.

Harold Rosenberg 1906–78: *Discovering the Present* (1973)

4 I had measles at the age of four. I remember because I had to give up reading the *Encyclopedia Britannica* at the time.

Enoch Powell 1912–98: in *Observer* 7 October 1990 'Sayings of the Week'

5 Milton and Dante are the most pugnacious of the greatest Western writers. Scholars somehow manage to evade the ferocity of both poets and even dub them pious.

Harold Bloom 1930– : *The Western Canon* (1995)

6 At least one of my children did one of my plays at A-level. I think he got a 'B' with my help.
on being a set text

Tom Stoppard 1937– : attributed, 1995

Science and Literature

7 If the labours of the men of science should ever create any material revolution, direct or indirect, in our condition, and in the impressions which we habitually receive, the poet will sleep no more than at present, but he will be ready to follow the steps of the man of science, not only in those general indirect effects, but he will be at his side, carrying sensation into the midst of the objects of the science itself. The remotest discoveries of the chemist, the botanist, or mineralogist, will be as proper objects of the poet's art as any upon which it can be employed, if the time should ever come when these things shall be familiar to us, and the relations under which they are contemplated by the followers of these respective sciences shall be manifestly and palpably material to us as enjoying and suffering beings.

William Wordsworth 1770–1850: preface to *Lyrical Ballads* (1800)

8 In science, read, by preference, the newest works; in literature, the oldest.

Edward George Bulwer-Lytton 1803–73: *Caxtoniana* (1863) 'Hints on Mental Culture'

9 A contemporary poet has characterized this sense of the personality of art and of the impersonality of science in these words—'Art is myself; science is ourselves'.

Claude Bernard 1813–78: *Introduction à l'Étude de la Médecin Experiméntale* (1865)

10 Science is meaningless because it gives no answer to our question, the only question important for us: 'What shall we do and how shall we be?'

Leo Tolstoy 1828–1910: Lewis Wolpert *The Unnatural Nature of Science* (1993)

11 Why is it that the scholar is the only man of science of whom it is ever demanded that he should display taste and feeling?

A. E. Housman 1859–1936: 'Cambridge Inaugural Lecture' (1911)

1 Even if I could be Shakespeare, I think I should still choose to be Faraday.

Aldous Huxley 1894–1963: in 1925; R. Weber *More Random Walks in Science* (1982)

2 When science arrives it expels literature.

Goldsworthy Lowes Dickinson 1862–1932: *Plato and his Dialogues* (1931)

3 Every good poem, in fact, is a bridge built from the known, familiar side of life over into the unknown. Science too, is always making expeditions into the unknown. But this does not mean that science can supersede poetry. For poetry enlightens us in a different way from science; it speaks directly to our feelings or imagination. The findings of poetry are no more and no less true than science.

C. Day-Lewis 1904–72: *Poetry for You* (1944)

4 Art is meant to disturb, science reassures.

Georges Braque 1882–1963: *Le Jour et la nuit: Cahiers 1917–52*

5 The intellectual life of the whole of western society is increasingly being split into two polar groups . . . Literary intellectuals at one pole—at the other scientists, and as the most representative, the physical scientists. Between the two a gulf of mutual incomprehension.

C. P. Snow 1905–80: *The Two Cultures and the Scientific Revolution* (1959 Rede Lecture)

6 The true men of action in our time, those who transform the world, are not the politicians and statesmen, but the scientists. Unfortunately poetry cannot celebrate them, because their deeds are concerned with things, not persons, and are, therefore, speechless. When I find myself in the company of scientists, I feel like a shabby curate who has strayed by mistake into a drawing room full of dukes.

W. H. Auden 1907–73: *The Dyer's Hand* (1962) 'The Poet and the City'

7 The precondition of any fruitful relationship between literature and science is knowledge.

Aldous Huxley 1894–1963: *Literature and Science* (1963)

8 People who write obscurely are either unskilled in writing or up to mischief.

Peter Medawar 1915–87: *Pluto's Republic* (1984) 'Science and Literature'

9 Shakespeare would have grasped wave functions, Donne would have understood complementarity and relative time. They would have been excited. What richness! They would have plundered this new science for their imagery. And they would have educated their audiences too. But you 'arts' people, you're not only ignorant of these magnificent things, you're rather proud of knowing nothing.

Ian McEwan 1948– : *The Child in Time* (1987)

10 If Watson and Crick had not discovered the nature of DNA, one can be virtually certain that other scientists would eventually have determined it. With art—whether painting, music or literature — it is quite different. If Shakespeare had not written *Hamlet*, no other playwright would have done so.

Lewis Wolpert 1929– : *The Unnatural Nature of Science* (1993)

1 Why have the sciences yielded great explainers like Richard Dawkins and Stephen Jay Gould, while the arts routinely produce some of the worst writing known to history?

Brian Eno 1948– : in *Daily Telegraph* 9 December 1995 'They Said It'

2 One of the disabling weaknesses of current Western literature is its unwillingness or inability to engage with the dance of the spirit in the sciences. Music and the arts are equipped to do better.

George Steiner 1929– : *A Festival Overture* (Edinburgh University Festival Lecture, August 1996)

Science Fiction

3 Science fiction is a kind of archaeology of the future.

Clifton Fadiman 1904– : *Selected Writings* (1955)

4 Science Fiction is no more written for scientists than ghost stories are written for ghosts.

Brian Aldiss 1925– : introduction to *Penguin Science Fiction* (1962)

5 If some fatal process of applied science enables us in fact to reach the moon, the real journey will not at all satisfy the impulse which we now seek to gratify by writing such stories.

C. S. Lewis 1898–1963: *Of Other Worlds* (1966)

6 Everything is becoming science fiction. From the margins of an almost invisible literature has sprung the intact reality of the 20th century.

J. G. Ballard 1930– : 'Fictions of Every Kind' in *Books and Bookmen* February 1971

7 I have been a soreheaded occupant of a file drawer labelled 'Science Fiction' . . . and I would like out, particularly since so many serious critics regularly mistake the drawer for a urinal.

Kurt Vonnegut Jr. 1922– : *Wampeters, Foma and Granfallons* (1974)

8 Hubris clobbered by Nemesis.

Brian Aldiss 1925– : introduction to *Science Fiction Art* (1975)

9 Science fiction writers foresee the inevitable, and although problems and catastrophes may be inevitable, solutions are not.

Isaac Asimov 1920–92: 'How Easy to See the Future' in *Natural History* April 1975

10 Don't read science fiction books. It'll look bad if you die in bed with one on the nightstand. Always read stuff that will make you look good if you die in the middle of the night.

P. J. O'Rourke 1947– : attributed, 1979

11 If science fiction is the myth of modern technology, then its myth is tragic.

Ursula Le Guin 1929– : 'The Carrier Bag Theory of Fiction' (written 1986); *Dancing at the Edge of the World* (1989)

12 Science fiction, like Brazil, is where the nuts come from.

Thomas M. Disch 1940– : in *Observer* 23 August 1987

13 Space or science fiction has become a dialect for our time.

Doris Lessing 1919– : in *Guardian* 7 November 1987

14 Science fiction is the literature of *might be*.

C. J. Cherryh 1942– : Stan Nicholls (ed.) *Wordsmiths of Wonder* (1993)

1 Science fiction and rock and roll were the two areas, as a kid, where there was no adult interest.

Michael Moorcock 1939– : Stan Nicholls (ed.) *Wordsmiths of Wonder* (1993)

2 Until the 60s, sf was a hole-in-the-wall fringe literature, the kind of thing you wrapped in a brown paper bag if you read it on the bus.

Stan Nicholls : introduction to *Wordsmiths of Wonder* (1993)

3 What you get in science fiction is what someone once called 'the view from a distant star'. It helps us to see our world from outside.

Frederik Pohl 1919– : Stan Nicholls (ed.) *Wordsmiths of Wonder* (1993)

4 The only genuine consciousness-expanding drug.

Arthur C. Clarke 1917– : letter claiming coinage in *New Scientist* 2 April 1994

5 We live in a world where emissions from our refrigerators have caused the ozone layer to evaporate and we'll get skin cancer if we sunbathe. If that's not a science fiction scenario, I don't know what is.

William Gibson 1948– : 'Perspectives' in *Newsweek* 5 June 1995

Screenwriting see **Adaptation and Screenwriting**

Self-doubt and Self-esteem see also **Fame, Reputation, Rivalry**

6 I have never yet known a poet who did not think himself super-excellent.

Cicero 106–43 BC: *Tusculanae Disputationes*

7 *Quodsi me lyricis vatibus inseres,*
Sublimi feriam sidera vertice.

And if you include me among the lyric poets, I'll hold my head so high it'll strike the stars.

Horace 65–8 BC: *Odes*

8 *Odi profanum vulgus et arceo;*
Favete linguis; carmina non prius
Audita Musarum sacerdos
Virginibus puerisque canto.

I hate the common herd and keep them off. Hush your tongues; as a priest of the Muses, I sing songs never heard before to virgin girls and boys.

Horace 65–8 BC: *Odes*

9 May I present myself—the man
You read, admire, and long to meet,
Known the world over for his neat
And witty epigrams? The name
is Martial.

Martial AD *c.*40–*c.*104: *Epigrammata*, tr. James Michie

10 Oft-times nothing profits more
Than self esteem, grounded on just and right
Well managed.

John Milton 1608–74: *Paradise Lost* (1667)

1 Faith, that's as well said, as if I had said it myself.

Jonathan Swift 1667–1745: *Polite Conversation* (1738)

2 For ne'er
Was flattery lost on poet's ear:
A simple race! they waste their toil
For the vain tribute of a smile.

Sir Walter Scott 1771–1832: *The Lay of the Last Minstrel* (1805)

3 As for conceit, what man will do any good who is not conceited? Nobody holds a good opinion of a man who has a low opinion of himself.

Anthony Trollope 1815–82: *Orley Farm* (1862)

4 I always have to pretend to forget when people talk to me about my own books. It looks modest . . . But the writer never forgets.

Anthony Trollope 1815–82: letter, 5 December 1881

5 It is the peculiar fate of literary hens to lay solid gold eggs at night, only to discover, in the cruel pallor of dawn, that the eggs have gilt shells and are as hollow as drums.

Ernest L. Meyer 1892–1952: 'The Columnist's Lot' in *Capital Times* 4 May 1928

6 Literature is strewn with the wreckage of men who have minded beyond reason the opinions of others.

Virginia Woolf 1882–1941: *A Room of One's Own* (1929)

7 Better to write for yourself and have no public, than to write for the public and have no self.

Cyril Connolly 1903–74: in *New Statesman* 25 February 1933

8 What I have done is *excellent*. I don't think it could be better. Very gruesome. Rather like Webster in modern idiom.
of his novel A Handful of Dust

Evelyn Waugh 1903–66: letter to Lady Diana Cooper, January 1934

9 How rare, how precious is frivolity! How few writers can prostitute all their powers! They are always implying, 'I am capable of higher things.'

E. M. Forster 1879–1970: *Abinger Harvest* (1936)

10 Every genius needs praise.

Gertrude Stein 1874–1946: Edmund White *The Burning Library* (1994)

11 A confessional passage has probably never been written that didn't stink a little bit of the writer's pride in having given up his pride.

J. D. Salinger 1919– : *Catcher in the Rye* (1951)

12 What matters finally is not the world's judgement of oneself but one's judgement of the world. Any writer who lacks this final arrogance will not survive very long in America.

Gore Vidal 1925– : in *The Nation* 2 January 1960

13 Most people enjoy the sight of their own handwriting as they enjoy the smell of their own farts.

W. H. Auden 1907–73: *The Dyer's Hand* (1962)

14 However strong or egotistical your writing personality is, the *alter ego*—the reflection of you that looks at what you are writing and have written—must be a critic that is almost impossible to please, or get a good mark from.

Paul Scott 1920–78: Hilary Spurling *Paul Scott* (1990); advice to students of his writing class in Tulsa, Oklahoma

15 I don't lack confidence in what I can do, only in what is going to happen to it.

Paul Scott 1920–78: Hilary Spurling *Paul Scott* (1990)

1 I used to know several eminent writers who were given to boasting of the speed with which they created. It's not a lovable attribute, to put it mildly, and I'm afraid our acquaintanceship has languished.

S. J. Perelman 1904–79: George Plimpton (ed.) *The Writer's Chapbook* (1989)

2 Literature can do with any amount of egoism; but the merest pinch of narcissism spoils the broth.

John Updike 1932– : *Hugging the Shore* (1983)

3 When starting to think about any novel, part of the motive is: I'm going to show them, this time. Without that, a lot of what passes under the name of creative energy would be lost.

Kingsley Amis 1922–95: George Greenfield *Scribblers for Bread* (1989)

4 I tend to write in a fragile, edgy, doubtful sort of way, trying things out all the time, never confident that I've got something right.

William Trevor 1928– : in *Paris Review* 1989

5 Most people are vain, so I try to ensure that any author who comes to stay will find at least one of their books in their room.

Duke of Devonshire 1920– : in *Spectator* 22 January 1994

6 No one working in the English language now comes close to my exuberance, my passion, my fidelity to words.
on being asked to name the best living author writing in English

Jeanette Winterson 1959– : in *Sunday Times* 13 March 1994

Selling Books

7 No doubt you often go
Down Booksellers' Row.
Well, then, opposite Caesar's Forum there's a shop
With door-posts plastered with advertisements from
bottom to top,
So that at a glance you can read
The list of available poets.

Martial AD *c.*40–*c.*104: *Epigrammata*, tr. James Michie

8 If I were to paint Sloth . . . I swear, I would draw it like a stationer that I know, with his thumb under his girdle, who if a man comes to his stall and asks him for a book, never stirs his head, or looks upon him, but stands stone still, and speaks not a word: only with his little finger points backwards to his boy, who must be his interpreter, and so all the day, gaping like a dumb image, he sits without motion.

Thomas Nashe 1567–1601: *Pierce Pennilesse* (1592)

9 Well! it is now public, and you will stand for your privileges we know: to read, and censure. Do so, but buy it first. That doth best commend a book, the stationer says.

John Heming 1556–1630 and **Henry Condell** d. 1627: First Folio Shakespeare (1623)

10 Write what will sell! To this Golden rule every minor canon must be subordinate.

Edward Coplestone : *Advice to a Young Reviewer* (1807)

11 Our book is found to be a drug, no man needs it or heeds it. In the space of a year our publisher has disposed but of two copies.

Charlotte Brontë 1816–55: letter to De Quincey, 16 June 1847

1 Where is human nature so weak as in the bookstore?

Henry Ward Beecher 1813–87: *Star Papers* (1855) 'Subtleties of Book Buyers'

2 How long would most people look at the best book before they would give the price of a large turbot for it?

John Ruskin 1819–1900: *Sesame and Lilies* (1865)

3 Yon second-hand bookseller is second to none in the worth of the treasures which he dispenses.

Leigh Hunt 1784–1859: *On the Beneficence of Bookstalls* (1899)

4 What we want above all things is not more books, not more publishers, not more education, not more literary genius, but simply and prosaically more shops.

George Bernard Shaw 1856–1950: in *The Author* 1903

5 When I get hold of a first issue of *Last Poems* I insert the missing stops on p. 52. I believe that this destroys the value of the book for bibliophiles, so you can bring an action against me if you like.

A. E. Housman 1859–1936: letter, 13 June 1929

6 Between the GARDENING and the COOKERY
Comes the brief POETRY shelf.

Kingsley Amis 1922–95: *A Case of Samples* (1956) 'A Bookshop Idyll'

7 They praised the book in Leeds and Pimlico,
In Leicester Square and Paternoster Row,
Filling the town with tidings of its wit
Till even booksellers got wind of it,
And this unwelcome thought their slumbers shook,
That now at last they'd have to sell a book.

Gerald Bullett 1894–1958: attributed; George Greenfield *Scribblers for Bread* (1989)

Sex see also **Erotic Writing and Pornography**

8 Everyone should study at least enough philosophy and *belles lettres* to make his sexual experience more delectable.

Georg Christoph Lichtenberg 1742–99: *The Lichtenberg Reader* (1959)

9 If people will stop at the first tense of the verb 'aimer' they must not be surprised if one finishes the conjugation with somebody else.

Lord Byron 1788–1824: letter, 13 January 1814

10 Is it not *life*, is it not *the thing*?—Could any man have written it—who has not lived in the world?—and tooled in a post-chaise? in a hackney coach? in a gondola? Against a wall? in a court carriage? in a *vis-à-vis*?—on a table?—and under it?
of Don Juan

Lord Byron 1788–1824: letter to Douglas Kinnaird, 26 October 1819

11 Not even the advocates of freedom [from censorship] seek to justify the free treatment of sexual matters in any other than a high moral-pointing vein. The notion that sexual themes might allowably be treated in the mere aim of amusement does not seem to have occurred to anybody at all.

Arnold Bennett 1867–1931: diary, 31 October 1907

12 While we think of it, and talk of it
Let us leave it alone, physically, keep apart.
For while we have sex in the mind, we truly have none in the body.

D. H. Lawrence 1885–1930: 'Leave Sex Alone' (1929)

1 It's not true the more sex that you have, the more it interferes with your work. I find that the more sex you have, the better work you do.
to Michael Foot, c.1938

H. G. Wells 1866–1946: Jill Craigie on *Bookmark* (BBC2) 24 August 1996

2 Sex can be indicated with asterisks. I've always felt that was as good a way as any.

John Dos Passos 1896–1970: George Plimpton (ed.) *The Writer's Chapbook* (1989)

3 Lord Longford is against us reading or seeing things that keep our minds below the navel.

William Hardcastle 1918–75: in *Punch* 1 December 1972

4 Sexual intercourse began
In nineteen sixty-three
(Which was rather late for me) —
Between the end of the *Chatterley* ban
And the Beatles' first LP.

Philip Larkin 1922–85: 'Annus Mirabilis' (1974)

5 Sex is more exciting on the screen and between the pages than between the sheets.

Andy Warhol 1927–87: *From A to B and Back Again* (1975)

6 Sex as an institution, sex as a general notion, sex as a problem, sex as a platitude—all this is something I find too tedious for words. Let's skip sex.

Vladimir Nabokov 1899–1977: attributed

7 I've led a good rich sexual life, and I don't see why it should be left out.

Henry Miller 1891–1980: George Plimpton (ed.) *The Writer's Chapbook* (1989)

8 It's a trade off; more brain or more penis. You can't have everything.

J. Philippe Rushton : in *Rolling Stone* 20 October 1994

9 If you don't know about sex at my age, you never will. I am always asked questions about why I write about sex because I am so ancient.

Mary Wesley 1912– : attributed, 1995

10 H. G. Wells thought that the creative urge was the sexual urge . . . I was a bit scared that if it started to ease up, and one didn't think about sex, then maybe one couldn't write any more.

Beryl Bainbridge 1933– : interview in *Daily Telegraph* 10 September 1996; cf. **00:00**

Short Stories

11 The dénouement of a long story is nothing; it is just a 'full close', which you may approach and accompany as you please—it is a coda, not an essential member in the rhythm; but the body and end of a short story is bone of the bone and blood of the blood of the beginning.

Robert Louis Stevenson 1850–94: letter to Sidney Colvin, September 1891

12 Poetic tautness and clarity are so essential to it that it may be said to stand on the edge of prose.

Elizabeth Bowen 1899–1973: introduction to *Faber Book of Modern Stories* (1937)

13 The first necessity for the short story, at the set out, is *necessariness*. The story, that is to say, must spring from an impression or perception pressing enough, acute enough, to have made the writer write.

Elizabeth Bowen 1899–1973: introduction to *Faber Book of Modern Stories* (1937)

1 Atmosphere and precision, however subtly concealed, are in fact two of the cardinal points in the art of the short-story writer.

H. E. Bates 1905–74: *The Modern Short Story* (1941)

2 The things I like to find in a story are punch and poetry.

Sean O'Faolain 1900–91: *The Short Story* (1948) foreword

3 From time to time there is an urge not to speed up and condense events and character development, which is what one does in a play, but to hold them frozen and to see things isolated in stillness, which I think is the great strength of a good short story.

Arthur Miller 1915– : *I Don't Need You Any More* (1967); foreword

4 I think it is the art of the glimpse. If the novel is like an intricate Renaissance painting, the short story is an Impressionist painting. It *should* be an explosion of truth.

William Trevor 1928– : in *Paris Review* 1989

5 The key to a short story is tension. At the end of a short story the reader's imagination should be able to take the story on in his mind, but at the end of a novel he is entitled to expect a rounding-off.

William Trevor 1928– : interview in *Sunday Telegraph* 21 January 1990

6 A short story is like a stripped-down racer; there's no room for anything extra in there.

Robert Asprin : Stan Nicholls (ed.) *Wordsmiths of Wonder* (1993)

7 The greatest masters of the form of the short story . . . have all tended to seek their material in the realm of the unremarkable—which turns out, under their patient illumination, to be remarkable after all.

John Wain 1925–94: attributed

8 The novel tends to tell us everything, whereas the short story tells us only one thing, and that intensely.

V. S. Pritchett 1900–97: attributed

Society and Social Responsibility see also **The Power of the Pen**

9 The only time a human being is free is when he or she makes a work of art.

Friedrich von Schiller 1759–1805: Edmund White *The Burning Library* (1994)

10 The more indignant I make the bourgeois, the happier I am.

Gustave Flaubert 1821–80: letter, 25 July 1842; cf. **229:1**

11 I have no wish to withhold justice from writers who give that proof of their sincerity which is implied by the publication of an octavo volume.

Robert Peel 1788–1850: in the House of Commons 1844

12 I regard him as the first social regenerator of the day—as the very master of that working corps who would restore to rectitude the warped system of things.
of William Makepeace ***Thackeray***

Charlotte Brontë 1816–55: *Jane Eyre* (2nd ed., 1848) preface

13 Cast aside your allegories
And empty hypotheses!
Give us straight answers
To the accursed questions.

Heinrich Heine 1797–1856: 'Zum Lazarus'

1 *Il faut épater le bourgeois.*
One must astonish the bourgeois.

Charles Baudelaire 1821–67: attributed; also attributed to Privat d'Anglemont (*c.*1820–59) in the form '*Je les ai épatés, les bourgeois* [I flabbergasted them, the bourgeois]'; cf. **228:10**

2 [Russian literature is] one uninterrupted indictment of Russian reality.

Alexander Herzen 1812–70: Isaiah Berlin *Personal Impressions* (1982); attributed

3 I am not in the habit of getting excited over novels that I read, but there is one thing in fiction which always moves me to an excess of rage—It is, Mrs Pendennis's treatment of Fanny Bolton.

in Thackeray's novel Pendennis, *the hero's mother fears that her son will marry the working-class Fanny*

George Gissing 1857–1903: *Commonplace Book* (1962)

4 When the soul of a man is born in this country, there are nets flung at it to hold it back from flight. You talk to me of nationality, language, religion. I shall try to fly by those nets.

James Joyce 1882–1941: *A Portrait of the Artist as a Young Man* (1916)

5 Our duty is to blare like brazen-throated horns in the fog of philistinism and in seething storms. The poet is always indebted to the universe, paying interest and fines on sorrow.

Vladimir Mayakovsky 1893–1930: 'Conversation with an Inspector of Taxes about Poetry' (1926)

6 And only my own kind will kill me.

Osip Mandelstam 1892–1938: Doris Lessing *The Wind Blows Away Our Words* (1987)

7 Now Ireland has her madness and her weather still,
For poetry makes nothing happen: it survives
In the valley of its saying where executives
Would never want to tamper, flows on south
From ranches of isolation and the busy griefs,
Raw towns that we believe and die in; it survives,
A way of happening, a mouth.

W. H. Auden 1907–73: 'In Memory of W. B. Yeats' (1940)

8 The best of the communications an author has to make is to his own generation, and he is wise to let the generation that succeeds his choose its own exponent.

on the falling off of a writer's powers in old age

W. Somerset Maugham 1874–1965: *A Writer's Notebook* (1949) written in 1944

9 There's nothing in the world for which a poet will give up writing, not even when he is a Jew and the language of his poems is German.

Paul Celan 1920–70: letter to relatives, 2 August 1948

10 It is barbarous to write a poem after Auschwitz.

Theodor Adorno 1903–69: I. Buruma *Wages of Guilt* (1994)

11 Nothing I wrote in the thirties saved one Jew from Auschwitz.

W. H. Auden 1907–73: attributed

12 I've often thought we'd have a utopia in this country if every community adopted all the advice we offered from time to time.

in 1972, at a reception at the White House for the 50th birthday of Reader's Digest

DeWitt Wallace: attributed

1 It cannot have escaped teachers of English literature that much of their time is spent unfitting their pupils for the lives they will eventually have to lead. Most twentieth-century authors, and in particular the greats like Yeats, Eliot and Lawrence, who regularly feature in A-level and undergraduate syllabuses, inculcate an attitude of contempt for ordinary, bread-earning citizens, which must inevitably unsettle youngsters who are on the point of choosing a career, unless they are mercifully too dense to get the modernists' message at all.

John Carey 1934– : in *Listener* 1974

2 For me the novel is a social vehicle. It reflects society.

Margaret Atwood 1939– : in an interview, 1979; Earl G. Ingersoll (ed.) *Margaret Atwood: Conversations* (1990)

3 Russian literature saved my soul. When I was a young girl in school and I asked what is good and what is evil, no one in that corrupt system could show me.

Irina Ratushinskaya 1954– : in *Observer* 15 October 1989 'Sayings of the Week'

4 We shouldn't trust writers, but we should read them.

Ian McEwan 1948– : in *The Late Show* (BBC2) 7 February 1990

5 One glibly despises the photographer who zooms in on the starving child or the dying soldier without offering help. Writing is not different.

Alan Bennett 1934– : *Writing Home* (1994)

6 If we read the Western Canon in order to form our social, political, or personal moral values, I firmly believe we will become monsters of selfishness and exploitation.

Harold Bloom 1930– : *The Western Canon* (1995)

7 What literature can and should do is change the people who teach the people who don't read the books.

A. S. Byatt 1936– : interview in *Newsweek* 5 June 1995

Speech

8 Then said they unto him, Say now Shibboleth: and he said Sibboleth: for he could not frame to pronounce it right. Then they took him, and slew him.

Bible: Judges

9 Somwhat he lipsed, for his wantownesse,
To make his Englissh sweete upon his tonge.

Geoffrey Chaucer *c.*1343–1400: *The Canterbury Tales* 'The General Prologue'

10 He pronounced the letter R (*littera canina*) very hard—a certain sign of a satirical wit.

John Aubrey 1626–97: *Brief Lives* 'John Milton'

11 And, when you stick on conversation's burrs,
Don't strew your pathway with those dreadful *urs.*

Oliver Wendell Holmes 1809–94: 'A Rhymed Lesson' (1848)

12 To Trinity Church, Dorchester. The rector in his sermon delivers himself of mean images in a very sublime voice, and the effect is that of a glowing landscape in which clothes are hung up to dry.

Thomas Hardy 1840–1928: *Notebooks* 1 February 1874

13 Can the most accomplished pronouncer of English get through the foll. without a mistake of h's: 'It's he who owes you, not you who owe him.'

George Gissing 1857–1903: *Commonplace Book* (1962)

1 If, sir, I possessed, as you suggest, the power of conveying unlimited sexual attraction through the potency of my voice, I would not be reduced to accepting a miserable pittance from the BBC for interviewing a faded female in a damp basement.
reply to Mae West's manager who asked 'Can't you sound a bit more sexy when you interview her?'

Gilbert Harding 1907–60: S. Grenfell *Gilbert Harding by his Friends* (1961)

Speeches and Speech-making

2 . . . *I, demens, et saevas curre per Alpes*
Ut pueris placeas et declamatio fias.

Off you go, madman, and hurry across the horrible Alps, duly to delight schoolboys and become a subject for practising speech-making.
on Hannibal

Juvenal AD *c.*60–*c.*130: *Satires*

3 Speak the speech, I pray you, as I pronounced it to you, trippingly on the tongue; but if you mouth it, as many of your players do, I had as lief the town-crier spoke my lines.

William Shakespeare 1564–1616: *Hamlet* (1601)

4 Talking and eloquence are not the same: to speak, and to speak well, are two things.

Ben Jonson *c.*1573–1637: *Timber, or Discoveries made upon Men and Matter* (1641)

5 Continual eloquence is tedious.

Blaise Pascal 1623–62: *Pensées* (1670)

6 His tongue
Dropped manna, and could make the worse appear
The better reason.

John Milton 1608–74: *Paradise Lost* (1667)

7 His words came feebly, from a feeble chest,
Yet each in solemn order followed each,
With something of a lofty utterance drest;
Choice words, and measured phrase; above the reach
Of ordinary men; a stately speech!
Such as grave Livers do in Scotland use.

William Wordsworth 1770–1850: 'Resolution and Independence' (1807) st. 15

8 He is one of those orators of whom it was well said, 'Before they get up, they do not know what they are going to say; when they are speaking, they do not know what they are saying; and when they have sat down, they do not know what they have said.'
of Lord Charles Beresford

Winston Churchill 1874–1965: speech, House of Commons, 20 December 1912

9 If I am to speak for ten minutes, I need a week for preparation; if fifteen minutes, three days; if half an hour, two days; if an hour, I am ready now.

Woodrow Wilson 1856–1924: Josephus Daniels *The Wilson Era* (1946)

10 He mobilized the English language and sent it into battle to steady his fellow countrymen and hearten those Europeans upon whom the long dark night of tyranny had descended.
of Winston Churchill

Ed Murrow 1908–65: broadcast, 30 November 1954

1 Do you remember that in classical times when Cicero had finished speaking, the people said, 'How well he spoke', but when Demosthenes had finished speaking, they said, 'Let us march.'
introducing John F. Kennedy in 1960

Adlai Stevenson 1900–65: Bert Cochran *Adlai Stevenson*

2 Poetry has everything to do with speeches, a knowledge that words are magic, that words, like children, have the power to make dance the dullest beanbag of a heart.
a speechwriter's view

Peggy Noonan 1950– : in *Observer* 22 January 1989 'Sayings of the Week'

Spelling see also **Grammar**

3 Thou whoreson zed! thou unnecessary letter!

William Shakespeare 1564–1616: *King Lear* (1605–6)

4 'Do you spell it with a "V" or a "W"?' inquired the judge. 'That depends upon the taste and fancy of the speller, my Lord,' replied Sam [Weller].

Charles Dickens 1812–70: *Pickwick Papers* (1837)

5 They spell it Vinci and pronounce it Vinchy; foreigners always spell better than they pronounce.

Mark Twain 1835–1910: *The Innocents Abroad* (1869)

6 My spelling is Wobbly. It's good spelling but it Wobbles, and the letters get in the wrong places.

A. A. Milne 1882–1956: *Winnie-the-Pooh* (1926)

7 The impertinent compositors have taken it upon themselves to correct, as they suppose, my spelling and grammar: altering throughout *dwarves* to *dwarfs*; *elvish* to *elfish*; *further* to *farther*; and worst of all, *elven-* to *elfin*.
of the galley proofs of The Lord of the Rings

J. R. R. Tolkien 1892–1973: letter to Christopher Tolkien, 4 August 1953

8 So you're the boy who doesn't know how to spell.
to Norman Mailer on his liberal use of the word 'fug' in The Naked and the Dead

Tallulah Bankhead 1903–68: attributed

Structure

9 A whole is that which has a beginning, a middle, and an end. A beginning is that which does not itself follow anything by causal necessity, but after which something naturally is or comes to be. An end, on the contrary, is that which itself naturally follows some other thing, either by necessity, or as a rule, but has nothing following it. A middle is that which follows something as some other thing follows it. A well-constructed plot, therefore, must neither begin not end at haphazard, but conform to these principles.

Aristotle 384–322 BC: *Poetics*; cf. **233:7**

10 The famous rules, which the French call *Des Trois Unitez*, or, the Three Unities, which ought to be observed in every regular play; namely, of Time, Place, and Action.

John Dryden 1631–1700: *A Essay of Dramatic Poesy* (1668)

11 Homer to preserve the unity of his action hastens into the midst of things.

Joseph Addison 1672–1719: *The Spectator* no. 267 (1712)

1 It is fortunate for tale-tellers that they are not tied down like theatrical writers to the unities of time and place.

Sir Walter Scott 1771–1832: *Tales of My Landlord* (1st series, 1816) 'Old Mortality'

2 Two years . . . is a terrible gap in a story, but in these days the unities are not much considered.

Anthony Trollope 1815–82: *The Bertrams* (1859)

3 Don't let anyone persuade you . . . that Form *is* [not] substance to that degree that there is absolutely no substance without it. Form alone *takes*, and holds and preserves, substance.

Henry James 1843–1916: letter to Hugh Walpole, 19 May 1912

4 You would do better, or at least no worse, to obliterate texts then to blacken margins, to fill in the holes of words till all is blank and flat and the whole ghastly business looks like what it is, senseless, speechless, issueless misery.

Samuel Beckett 1906–89: *Molloy* (1951)

5 To find a form that accommodates the mess, that is the task of the artist now.

Samuel Beckett 1906–89: *Proust* (1961)

6 Style and structure are the essence of a book; great ideas are hogwash.

Vladimir Nabokov 1899–1977: George Plimpton (ed.) *Writers at Work* (4th series, 1977)

7 A beginning, a muddle, and an end.
on the 'classic formula' for a novel

Philip Larkin 1922–85: in *New Fiction* January 1978; cf. **232:9**

8 Sicilian storytellers use the formula '*lu cuntu nun metto tempo*' (time takes no time in a story) when they want to leave out links or indicate gaps of months or even years.

Italo Calvino 1923–85: *Six Memos for the Next Millennium* (1992)

9 We are driven
By endings as by hunger. We *must know*
How it comes out, the shape o' the whole, the thread
Whose links are weak or solid, intricate
Or boldly welded in great clumsy loops
Of primitive workmanship. We feel our way
Along the links and we cannot let go
Of this bright chain of curiosity
Which is become our fetter.

A. S. Byatt 1936– : poem by 'Randolph Ash' in *Possession* (1990)

Style see also **Choice of Words, Revision**

10 Works of serious purpose and grand promises often have a purple patch or two stitched on, to shine far and wide.

Horace 65–8 BC: *Ars Poetica*; cf. **235:9**

11 An honest tale speeds best being plainly told.

William Shakespeare 1564–1616: *Richard III* (1591)

12 More matter with less art.

William Shakespeare 1564–1616: *Hamlet* (1601)

13 I do not much dislike the matter, but
The manner of his speech.

William Shakespeare 1564–1616: *Antony and Cleopatra* (1606–7)

14 When we see a natural style, we are quite surprised and delighted, for we expected to see an author and we find a man.

Blaise Pascal 1623–62: *Pensées* (1670)

1 A good writer, and one who writes with care, often finds that the expression he's spent a long time hunting for without finding it, and which he finds at last, turns out to be the simplest and most natural one, which looks as if it ought to have occurred to him at the beginning, without any effort.

Jean de la Bruyère 1645–96: *Les Caractères ou les moeurs de ce siècle* (1688)

2 Style is the dress of thought; a modest dress,
Neat, but not gaudy, will true critics please.

Samuel Wesley 1662–1735: 'An Epistle to a Friend concerning Poetry' (1700)

3 Proper words in proper places, make the true definition of a style.

Jonathan Swift 1667–1745: *Letter to a Young Gentleman lately entered into Holy Orders* 9 January 1720

4 All styles are good except the tiresome kind.

Voltaire 1694–1778: *L'Enfant prodigue* (1736)

5 These things [subject matter] are external to the man; style is the man.

Comte de Buffon 1707–88: *Discours sur le style*; address given to the Académie Française, 25 August 1753

6 One should only write when one has something important or profoundly beautiful to say, but then one must say it as simply as possible, as if one were trying one's best to prevent it being noticed.

Stendhal 1783–1842: letter to his sister Pauline, 20 August 1805

7 He read all the Essays, Letters, Tours and Criticisms of the day—and with the same ill-luck which made him derive only false principles from lessons of morality, and incentives to vice from the history of its overthrow, he gathered only hard words and involved sentences from the style of our most approved writers.

Jane Austen 1775–1817: 'Sir Edward Denham' in *Sanditon* (1926 ed.)

8 I know of only one rule: style cannot be too *clear*, too *simple*.

Stendhal 1783–1842: letter to Balzac, 30 October 1840

9 I would rather omit a touch of truth than fall into the abominable fault, now so common, of dropping into declamation.

Stendhal 1783–1842: *La Vie de Henri Brulard* (1890)

10 Style is life! It is the very life-blood of thought! Boileau was a little river, narrow, not very deep, but beautifully clear and well embanked. That's why his waters never run dry.

Gustave Flaubert 1821–80: letter to Louise Colet, 7 September 1853

11 Nothing has raised more questioning among my critics than these words—noble, the grand style . . . I think it will be found that the grand style arises in poetry, when a noble nature, poetically gifted, treats with simplicity or with severity a serious subject.

Matthew Arnold 1822–88: *On Translating Homer. Last Words* (1862)

12 When you read proof, take out adjectives and adverbs wherever you can.

Anton Chekhov 1860–1904: letter, 14 January 1887

13 Life has taught me not to believe in well-turned phrases.

Henrik Ibsen 1828–1906: *A Doll's House* (1879)

1 I have been asked whether anything in the way of 'literary style' is to be admitted. If style means superfluous ornament, I say emphatically, No. But style, and even high literary ability, is required for lucid and condensed narrative, and of such style I shall be anxious to get as much as I can.
as editor of the Dictionary of National Biography

Leslie Stephen 1832–1904: in *Athenaeum* 23 December 1882; cf. **32:8**

2 The web, then, or the pattern; a web at once sensuous and logical, an elegant and pregnant texture: that is style, that is the foundation of the art of literature.

Robert Louis Stevenson 1850–94: *The Art of Writing* (1905) 'On some technical Elements of Style in Literature' (written 1885)

3 People think that I can teach them style. What stuff it all is! Have something to say, and say it as clearly as you can. That is the only secret of style.

Matthew Arnold 1822–88: G. W. E. Russell *Collections and Recollections* (1898)

4 I don't wish to sign my name, though I am afraid everybody will know who the writer is: one's style is one's signature always.
sending a letter for publication

Oscar Wilde 1854–1900: letter to the *Daily Telegraph*, 2 February 1891

5 You have so many modifiers that the reader has a hard time determining what deserves his attention, and it tires him out. If I write 'A man sat down on the grass,' it is understandable because it is clear and doesn't require a second reading. But it would be hard to follow and brain-taxing were I to write, 'A tall, narrow-chested, red-bearded man of medium height sat down noiselessly, looking around timidly and in fright, on a patch of green grass that had once been trampled by pedestrians.' The brain can't grasp all that at once, and the art of fiction ought to be immediately, instantly graspable.

Anton Chekhov 1860–1904: letter to Maxim Gorky, 2 September 1899

6 *Circumlocution*, n. A literary trick whereby the writer who has nothing to say breaks it gently to the reader.

Ambrose Bierce 1842–*c.*1914: *The Devil's Dictionary* (1911)

7 I hate the sort of licence that English people give themselves . . . to spread over and flop and roll about. I feel as fastidious as though I wrote with acid.

Katherine Mansfield 1888–1923: letter to John Middleton Murry, 19 May 1913

8 I haven't quite reached the ruthless artistry which would let me cut out an exquisite bit that had no place in the context.

F. Scott Fitzgerald 1896–1940: letter, 9 August 1925

9 I know what you mean about purple patches. My new book is black with them but then I live by my pen as they say and you don't.

Evelyn Waugh 1903–66: letter to Henry Yorke, July 1929; cf. **233:10**

10 You praise the firm restraint with which they write—
I'm with you there, of course:
They use the snaffle and the curb all right,
But where's the bloody horse?

Roy Campbell 1901–57: 'On Some South African Novelists' (1930)

11 Backward ran sentences until reeled the mind.
satirizing the style of Time *magazine*

Wolcott Gibbs 1902–58: in *New Yorker* 28 November 1936 'Time . . . Fortune . . . Life . . . Luce'

1 An author arrives at a good style when his language performs what is required of it without shyness.

Cyril Connolly 1903–74: *Enemies of Promise* (1938)

2 The Mandarin style . . . is beloved by literary pundits, by those who would make the written word as unlike as possible to the spoken one. It is the style of those writers whose tendency is to make their language convey more than they mean or more than they feel, it is the style of most artists and all humbugs.

Cyril Connolly 1903–74: *Enemies of Promise* (1938)

3 'Feather-footed through the plashy fen passes the questing vole' . . . 'Yes,' said the Managing Editor. 'That must be good style.'

Evelyn Waugh 1903–66: *Scoop* (1938)

4 A good style doesn't form unless you absorb half a dozen top-flight authors every year. Or rather it *forms* but, instead of being a subconscious amalgam of all that you have admired, it is simply a reflection of the last writer you have read, a watered-down journalese.

F. Scott Fitzgerald 1896–1940: letter, 18 July 1940

5 The test of good prose is that the reader does not notice it any more than a man looking through a window at a landscape notices the glass.

W. H. Auden 1907–73: 'Who Shall Plan the Planners?' (1940); cf. **236:8**

6 For God's sake don't talk politics. I'm not interested in politics. The only thing that interests me is style.

James Joyce 1882–1941: Richard Ellmann *James Joyce* (1982)

7 The final elegance, not to console
Nor sanctify, but plainly to propound.

Wallace Stevens 1879–1955: 'Notes Towards a Supreme Fiction' (1942)

8 Good prose is like a window-pane.

George Orwell 1903–50: *Collected Essays* (1968) vol. 1 'Why I Write'; cf. **236:5**

9 Be subtle, various, ornamental, clever,
And do not listen to those critics ever
Whose crude provincial gullets crave in books
Plain cooking made still plainer by plain cooks.

W. H. Auden 1907–73: 'The Shield of Achilles' (1955)

10 I am well aware that an addiction to silk underwear does not necessarily imply that one's feet are dirty. Nonetheless, style, like sheer silk, too often hides eczema.

Albert Camus 1913–60: *The Fall* (1956)

11 In literature, vulgarity is preferable to nullity, just as grocer's port is preferable to distilled water.

W. H. Auden 1907–73: 'Reading' (1964)

12 The day of the jewelled epigram is passed and, whether one likes it or not, one is moving into the stern puritanical era of the four-letter word.

Noel Annan 1916– : in the House of Lords, 1966; George Greenfield *Scribblers for Bread* (1989)

13 My style flows from the fingers. The eye and ear approve or amend.

Bernard Malamud 1914–86: George Plimpton (ed.) *The Writer's Chapbook* (1989)

14 I loved those novels so much that I was paralyzed by them for a long time. All those possibilities. All that perfectly reconciled style. It made me afraid to put words down.
*of the novels of Henry **James***

Joan Didion 1934– : George Plimpton (ed.) *The Writer's Chapbook* (1989)

1 Lyrically passionate writing should always be resisted, especially by the writer. A real idea slows you down, by demanding that you make yourself as plain as possible.

Clive James 1939– : *The Dreaming Swimmer* (1992)

2 Every author of some value *transgresses* against 'good style', and in that transgression lies the originality (and hence the raison d'être) of his art.

Milan Kundera 1929– : *Testaments Betrayed* (1995)

Subject and Theme

3 Grasp the subject, the words will follow.

Cato the Elder 234–149 BC: Caius Julius Victor *Ars Rhetorica*

4 *Sicelides Musae, paulo maiora canamus!*
Non omnis arbusta iuvant humilesque myricae;
Si canimus silvas, silvae sint consule dignae.
Ultima Cumaei venit iam carminis aetas;
Magnus ab integro saeclorum nascitur ordo.
Iam redit et virgo, redeunt Saturnia regna,
Iam nova progenies caelo demittitur alto.

Sicilian Muses, let us sing of rather greater things. Bushes and low tamarisks do not please everyone; if we sing of the woods, let them be woods of consular dignity. Now has come the last age according to the oracle at Cumae; the great series of lifetimes starts anew. Now too the virgin goddess returns, the golden days of Saturn's reign return, now a new race is sent down from high heaven.

Virgil 70–19 BC: *Eclogues*

5 *Navita de ventis, de tauris narrat arator,*
Enumerat miles vulnera, pastor oves.

The seaman tells stories of winds, the ploughman of bulls; the soldier details his wounds, the shepherd his sheep.

Propertius *c.*50–after 16 BC: *Elegies*

6 *Quidquid agunt homines, votum timor ira voluptas*
Gaudia discursus nostri farrago libelli est.

Everything mankind does, their hope, fear, rage, pleasure, joys, business, are the hotch-potch of my little book.

Juvenal AD *c.*60–*c.*130: *Satires*

a list of poetic subjects:

7 The capital city. Arrowroot. Water-bur. Colts. Hail. Bamboo grass. The round-leaved violet. Club moss. Water oats. Flat river-boats. The mandarin duck. The scattered *chigaya* reed. Lawns. The green vine. The pear tree. The jujube tree. The althea.

Sei Shōnagon *c.*966–*c.*1013: *Pillow Book*; cf. **213:4**

8 Anything whatsoever may become the subject of a novel, provided only that it happens in this mundane life and not in some fairyland beyond our human ken.

Murasaki Shikibu *c.*978–*c.*1031: *The Tale of Genji*

9 A mere tale of a tub, my words are idle.

John Webster *c.*1580–*c.*1625: *The White Devil* (1612)

1 I describe not men, but manners; not an individual, but a species.

Henry Fielding 1707–54: *Joseph Andrews* (1742)

2 Johnson had said that he could repeat a complete chapter of 'The Natural History of Iceland' . . . the whole of which was exactly thus:—'Chap. lxxii. *Concerning Snakes*. There are no snakes to be met with throughout the whole island.'

the origin of the allusive 'snakes in Iceland', the type of something posited only to be dismissed as non-existent

James Boswell 1740–95: *Life of Samuel Johnson* (1791)

3 The moving accident is not my trade;
To freeze the blood I have no ready arts:
'Tis my delight, alone in summer shade,
To pipe a simple song for thinking hearts.

William Wordsworth 1770–1850: 'Hart-Leap Well' (1800)

4 Let other pens dwell on guilt and misery. I quit such odious subjects as soon as I can.

Jane Austen 1775–1817: *Mansfield Park* (1814)

5 3 or 4 families in a country village is the very thing to work on.

Jane Austen 1775–1817: letter to Anna Austen, 9 September 1814

6 I cannot write books handling the topics of the day; it is of no use trying. Nor can I write a book for its moral.

Charlotte Brontë 1816–55: letter to George Smith, 30 October 1852

7 The author has provided himself with a moral—the truth, namely, that the wrongdoing of one generation lives into the successive ones.

Nathaniel Hawthorne 1804–64: preface to *The House of the Seven Gables* (1851)

8 Shut not your doors to me proud libraries,
For that which was lacking on all your well-fill'd shelves,
yet needed most, I bring
Forth from the war emerging, a book I have made,
The words of my book nothing, the drift of it everything,
A book separate, not link'd with the rest nor felt by the intellect,
But you ye untold latencies will thrill to every page.

Walt Whitman 1819–92: *Leaves of Grass* (1867) 'Shut Not Your Doors'

9 Everything that I have written is closely related to something that I have lived through.

Henrik Ibsen 1828–1906: letter, 1880

10 The business of the poet and novelist is to show the sorriness underlying the grandest things, and the grandeur underlying the sorriest things.

Thomas Hardy 1840–1928: notebook entry for 19 April 1885

11 NOTICE: Persons attempting to find a motive in this narrative will be prosecuted; persons attempting to find a moral in it will be banished; persons attempting to find a plot in it will be shot. BY ORDER OF THE AUTHOR.

Mark Twain 1835–1910: *The Adventures of Huckleberry Finn* (1884)

12 The life of man is not the subject of novels, but the inexhaustible magazine from which subjects are to be selected.

Robert Louis Stevenson 1850–94: *Memories and Portraits* (1887) 'A Humble Remonstrance'

13 Every good story is of course both a picture and an idea, and the more they are interfused the better the problem is solved.

Henry James 1843–1916: 'Guy de Maupassant' (1888)

1 Romance! Those first-class passengers they like it very well,
Printed, an' bound in little books; but why don't poets tell?
I'm sick of all their quirks an' turns—the loves an' doves they dream—
Lord, send a man like Robbie Burns to sing the Song o' Steam!

Rudyard Kipling 1865–1936: 'McAndrew's Hymn' (1896)

2 Am writing an essay on the life-history of insects and have abandoned the idea of writing on 'How Cats Spend their Time'.

W. N. P. Barbellion 1889–1919: *Journal of a Disappointed Man* (1919) 3 January 1903

3 This is an important book, the critic assumes, because it deals with war. This is an insignificant book because it deals with the feelings of women in a drawing-room.

Virginia Woolf 1882–1941: *A Room of One's Own* (1929)

4 Even to want to write about so-called artists who spend on sodomy what they have gained by sponging betrays a kind of spiritual inadequacy.
reviewing Cyril Connolly's The Rock Pool

George Orwell 1903–50: in *New English Weekly* 23 July 1936

5 Irish poets, learn your trade,
Sing whatever is well made.

W. B. Yeats 1865–1939: 'Under Ben Bulben' (1939)

6 A writer should never write about the extraordinary. That is for the journalist.

James Joyce 1882–1941: letter to Djuna Barnes; Richard Ellman *James Joyce* (1959)

7 The hardest part is having something to write about that succeeds in drawing words from your inner mind—that is very important, as one can always think of *subjects*, but they have to *matter* in that peculiar way that produces words and some kind of development of thought or theme, or else there's no poem in thought or words.

Philip Larkin 1922–85: letter, 10 April 1961

8 Solitary sensitive boys have been the stuff of novels from Dickens' blacking factory onwards. It may be said that they have paid diminishing artistic returns since that day.

Angus Wilson 1913–91: *The Wild Garden* (1963)

9 When I become interested in a subject, say old age, then the world is peopled for me—just peopled with them. And it's a narrow little small world, but it's full of old people, full of whatever I'm studying.

Muriel Spark 1918– : 'The House of Fiction' (1963)

10 The main concern of the fiction writer is with mystery as it is incarnated in real life.

Flannery O'Connor 1925–64: 'Catholic Novelists and their Readers' (1964)

11 To be shockingly original with your first novel you don't have to discover a new technique: simply write about people as they are and not as the predominantly liberal and humanist literary Establishment believes that they ought to be.

John Braine 1922–86: *Writing a Novel* (1974)

12 The first twenty-five years, or even sixteen, provide a rich enough quarry to exploit for the rest of life.

Graham Greene 1904–91: Marie-Françoise Allain *The Other Man, Conversations with Graham Greene* (1983)

1 Novels are about other people and poems are about yourself.

Philip Larkin 1922–85: *Required Writing* (1983)

2 For a novelist, a given historic situation is an *anthropologic laboratory* in which he explores his basic question: *What is human existence?*

Milan Kundera 1929– : *Life is Elsewhere* (postscript, 1986 ed.)

on hearing that Watership Down *was a novel about rabbits written by a civil servant:*

3 I would rather read a novel about civil servants written by a rabbit.

Craig Brown 1957– : attributed; probably apocryphal

replying to the question 'what is Rosencrantz and Guildenstern are Dead *about?' (after its first night in New York):*

4 It's about to make me rich.

Tom Stoppard 1937– : in *Independent* 2 December 1995

5 My subject matter may be grim, but I'm in search of delight, always of delight.

Martin Amis 1949– : *Waterstone's Quarterly Guide* Spring/Summer 1996

Talent see Genius and Talent

Theme see Subject and Theme

Titles see also Borrowed Titles

6 *The Ancient Mariner* would not have taken so well if it had been called *The Old Sailor*.

Samuel Butler 1835–1902: attributed

7 A thing I am trying to write now called *The End of the Tether*—an inept title to heartbreaking bosh.

Joseph Conrad 1857–1924: letter, 10 June 1902; cf. **146:3**

8 The little importance of names of sterling books is shown by Charlotte Brontë's novels. Never had novel a worse title than 'Villette'.

George Gissing 1857–1903: *Commonplace Book* (1962)

9 *Author Hunting* is an excellent title. But I think there should be a hyphen between the two words. Otherwise people might think the book was an account of Anthony Trollope in his off-moments.

Max Beerbohm 1872–1956: letter, 16 July 1934

10 I always start with a title . . . and then work round different meanings. A novel is, for me, always an elaboration of a title.

Muriel Spark 1918– : in *Scotsman* 1962

11 Rereading Hardy, I was struck by his titles—just looking them over in the index—and thought what wonderful titles a lot of them would have made for Wallace Stevens, too—some even for Eliot—but with such differences in the poems.

Elizabeth Bishop 1911–79: letter, 21 December 1965

1 I think the title 'Four Point Turn' a little smart for so moving a book: it needs something sadder, more compassionate.
on a possible title for Barbara ***Pym's*** *novel* Quartet in Autumn

Philip Larkin 1922–85: letter to Barbara Pym, 26 September 1976

2 Title: *Last Quartet* is better than *Four Point Turn*, but I still wish for something less literary, more striking, more . . . oh, I don't know. Titles are so very personal, one hesitates to plunge: *For the Dark*, *The Way into Winter*, *Doors into Dark*, something about *age*, something *poetic*.
on a possible title for Quartet in Autumn

Philip Larkin 1922–85: letter to Barbara Pym, 26 September 1976

3 I thought of a splendid title for a novel *Blind Mouths at the Nipple*.
watching a cat feeding her kittens

Barbara Pym 1913–80: letter to Philip Larkin, 1 May 1979

4 The most important part of the title is the comma. Because it seems to me that I am that comma.
explaining the name of his forthcoming book East, West

Salman Rushdie 1947– : in *Daily Telegraph* 6 August 1994

5 I think they were rather shamefaced about altering the title, but they seemed to be quite serious when they explained that the *Henry V* film brought a number of enquiries about what had become of one to four.
on changing The Madness of George III *to* The Madness of King George *for the American market*

Alan Bennett 1934– : in *The Times* 3 December 1994

6 The title is possibly a mistake: *Endure* would have been better, though hardly a crowd-puller.
of his ill-fated play Enjoy

Alan Bennett 1934– : *Writing Home* (1994)

7 In my case the title comes either very early on, with no problem, or takes a long time and is found with difficulty.

P. D. James 1920– : in *Paris Review* 1995

Tools of the Trade

8 Is not this a lamentable thing, that of the skin of an innocent lamb should be made parchment? that parchment, being scribbled o'er, should undo a man?

William Shakespeare 1564–1616: *Henry VI, Part 2* (1592)

9 It is well to observe the force and virtue and consequence of discoveries, and these are to be seen nowhere more conspicuously than in those three which were unknown to the ancients, and of which the origins, though recent, are obscure and inglorious; namely, printing, gunpowder, and the mariner's needle [compass]. For these three have changed the whole face and state of things throughout the world.

Francis Bacon 1561–1626: *Novum Organum* (1620); cf. **242:3**

10 I like writing with a peacock's quill; because its feathers are all eyes.

Thomas Fuller 1654—1734: *Gnomologia* (1732)

11 I was in a printing house in Hell, and saw the method in which knowledge is transmitted from generation to generation.

William Blake 1757–1827: *The Marriage of Heaven and Hell* (1790–3) 'A Memorable Fancy' plates 15–17

1 Oh! nature's noblest gift—my grey goose quill:
Slave of my thoughts, obedient to my will.
Torn from thy parent bird to form a pen.
That mighty instrument of little men!

Lord Byron 1788–1824: *English Bards and Scotch Reviewers* (1809)

2 For you know, dear—I may, without vanity, hint—
Though an angel should write, still 'tis *devils* must print.

Thomas Moore 1779–1852: *The Fudges in England* (1835)

3 The three great elements of modern civilization, Gunpowder, Printing, and the Protestant Religion.

Thomas Carlyle 1795–1881: *Critical and Miscellaneous Essays* (1838) 'The State of German Literature'; cf. **241:9**

4 RIDDLE: *Je suis le capitaine de vingt-quatre soldats, et sans moi Paris serait pris?*
ANSWER: *A.*
RIDDLE: I am the captain of twenty-four soldiers, and without me Paris would be taken?
ANSWER: A [i.e. 'Paris' minus 'a' = *pris* taken].

the saying 'With twenty-six lead soldiers [the characters of the alphabet set up for printing] *I can conquer the world' may derive from this riddle, but probably arose independently*

Anonymous: in Hugh Rowley *Puniana: or, Thoughts wise and otherwise* (1867)

5 It came as a boon and a blessing to men,
The peaceful, the pure, the victorious PEN!

almost certainly the inspiration for the advertisement by MacNiven and H. Cameron Ltd., 'It came as a boon and a blessing to men, /The Pickwick, the Owl, and the Waverley pen'

J. C. Prince: E. W. Cole (ed.) *The Thousand Best Poems in the World* (1891)

6 When the doorbell announced the first visitor, he would throw a thin swatch of red silk over his worktable, hiding the paper mess and the tools of his trade, which were as sacred to him as liturgical objects to a priest.

*on **Flaubert**'s reception of visitors to Sunday lunch*

Guy de Maupassant 1850–93: *Complete Works* (1910)

7 The sight of an inkwell and of a pen fills me with anger and horror.

Joseph Conrad 1857–1924: letter, 20 December 1896

8 The printing press is either the greatest blessing or the greatest curse of modern times, one sometimes forgets which.

J. M. Barrie 1860–1937: *Sentimental Tommy* (1896)

9 I am trying to make use of an accursed 'fountain' pen—but it's a vain struggle, it beats me.

Henry James 1843–1916: letter, 2 January 1908

*on the difficulties of reading the novels of Sir Walter **Scott**:*

10 He shouldn't have written in such small print.

O. Douglas 1877–1948: *The Setons* (1917)

11 Henry James must altogether have spent several thousands of the hours of his declining years in apologising for use of the typewriting machine.

Max Beerbohm 1872–1956: letter, 21 May 1921

12 Eeyore was saying to himself, 'This writing business. Pencils and what-not. Over-rated, if you ask me. Silly stuff. Nothing in it.'

A. A. Milne 1882–1956: *Winnie-the-Pooh* (1926)

1 Having found and bought, at a local paper-shop, a number of copy-books similar to those I had used at school, I set to work. The heavy grey-ruled pages, the vertical red line of margins, the black cover and its inset medallion and the ornamental title, *Le Calligraphe*, reawakened the urge, a sort of itch in my fingers.
on starting to write the 'Claudine' novels

Colette 1873–1954: *My Appenticeships* (1936)

2 The only thing that goes missing in Nature is a pencil.

Robert Benchley 1889–1945: attributed, perhaps apocryphal

3 The [*or* A] quick brown fox jumps over the lazy dog.
used by keyboarders to ensure that all letters of the alphabet are functioning

Anonymous: R. Hunter Middleton's introduction to *The Quick Brown Fox* (1945) by Richard H. Templeton Jr.

4 The biggest obstacle to professional writing is the necessity for changing a typewriter ribbon.

Robert Benchley 1889–1945: *Chips off the old Benchley* (1949) 'Learn to Write'

5 I have known the inexorable sadness of pencils,
Neat in their boxes, dolour of pad and paper-weight,
All the misery of manilla folders and mucilage,
Desolation in immaculate public places.

Theodore Roethke 1908–63: 'Dolour' (1948)

6 I wrote all my formal communications to the press in longhand. I have never had the secret knack of typewriters. Typewriters can't spell, you know.

Max Beerbohm 1872–1956: S. N. Behrman *Converations with Max* (1960)

7 My own experience has been that the tools I need for my work are paper, tobacco, food and a little whiskey.

William Faulkner 1897–1962: Malcolm Cowley (ed.) *Writers at Work* (1st series, 1958)

8 Much as I loathe the typewriter, I must admit that it is a help in self-criticism. Typescript is so impersonal and hideous to look at, if I type out a poem, I immediately see defects which I missed when I looked through it in manuscript.

W. H. Auden 1907–73: *The Dyer's Hand* (1962)

9 I never write except with a writing board. I've never had a table in my life. And I use all sorts of things. Write on the sole of my shoe.

Robert Frost 1874–1963: George Plimpton (ed.) *The Writer's Chapbook* (1989)

10 The medium is the message.

Marshall McLuhan 1911–80: *Understanding Media* (1964)

11 From the Olivetti portable,
the dictionaries, (the very
best money can buy), the heaps of paper, it is evident
what must go on. Devoid of
flowers and family photographs, all is subordinate
here to a function.

W. H. Auden 1907–73: 'The Cave of Making' (1965)

12 Between my finger and my thumb
The squat pen rests.
I'll dig with it.

Seamus Heaney 1939– : 'Digging' (1966)

1 From the time I was nine or ten, it was a toss-up whether I was going to be a writer or a painter, and I discovered by the time I was sixteen or seventeen that paints cost too much money, so I became a writer because you could be a writer with a pencil and a penny notebook.

Frank O'Connor 1903–66: George Plimpton (ed.) *The Writer's Chapbook* (1989)

2 The typewriter holding up its dismembered black bits of words like some elaborate machine of torture.

Alison Lurie 1926– : *Real People* (1969)

3 My single-lined foolscap—a word which already had an ominous ring to it.

Graham Greene 1904–91: *A Sort of Life* (1971)

4 The typewriter separated me from a deeper intimacy with poetry, and my hand brought me closer to that intimacy again.

Pablo Neruda 1904–73: in *Writers at Work* (5th series, 1981)

5 I put a sheet of paper in the typewriter and curse a bit.
on his method of writing

P. G. Wodehouse 1881–1975: attributed

6 I sat down before the blank sheets of foolscap . . . I had abandoned the single-lined variety where the lines seemed to me now like the bars on a prison window.

Graham Greene 1904–91: *Ways of Escape* (1980)

7 My memory is certainly in my hands. I can remember things only if I have a pencil and I can write with it and play with it. I think your hand concentrates for you.

Rebecca West 1892–1983: George Plimpton (ed.) *The Writer's Chapbook* (1989)

8 How very bold of you to buy an electric typewriter; the only time I tried one I was scared to death, as it seemed to be running away with me. I felt as if I had been put at the controls of Concorde after five minutes' tuition.

Philip Larkin 1922–85: letter to Anthony Powell, 7 August 1985

9 I don't use a typewriter. It's too heavy, too much trouble. I use a notebook, and I write in bed. Ninety-five percent of everything I've written has been done in bed.

Paul Bowles 1910– : George Plimpton (ed.) *The Writer's Chapbook* (1989)

10 To scrutinise the trivial can be to discover the monumental.
the principle behind his writing a history of the pencil

Henry Petroski 1942– : in *New Statesman* 9 November 1990

11 The PC is the LSD of the 90s.

Timothy Leary 1920–96: remark made in the early 1990s; in *Guardian* 1 June 1996

12 I use white paper in A4 size and I always use a black drawing pen with a very fine nib. The vital accessories to my work are my reference books, such as the complete Shakespeare and a prayer book, and a large black refuse bin.

Beryl Bainbridge 1933– : Clare Boylan (ed.) *The Agony and the Ego* (1993)

13 Electric typewriters keep going 'mmmmmmm—what are you waiting for?

Anthony Burgess 1917–93: Clare Boylan (ed.) *The Agony and the Ego* (1993)

14 I've got an assortment of rotting pens that have run out of ink. I type after an appalling three-fingered fashion, but all my manuscripts are done by hand.

V. S. Pritchett 1900–97: Clare Boylan (ed.) *The Agony and the Ego* (1993)

15 The dead-pan cloudiness of a word processor.

Seamus Heaney 1939– : *The Redress of Poetry* (1995)

1 The internet is an elite organisation; most of the population of the world has never even made a phone call.

Noam Chomsky 1928– : in *Observer* 18 February 1996

2 Means of artistic expression that require large quantities of finance and sophisticated technology—films, plays, records—become, by virtue of that dependence, easy to censor and to control. But what one writer can make in the solitude of one room is something no power can easily destroy.

Salman Rushdie 1947– : interview in *Observer* 18 August 1996

Tradition see also The Western Canon

3 Turn the pages of your Greek models night and day.

Horace 65–8 BC: *Ars Poetica*

4 [A] requisite in our poet or maker is imitation, *imitatio*, to be able to convert the substance or riches of another poet to his own use. To make choice of one excellent man above the rest, and so to follow him . . . Not as a creature that swallows what it takes in, crude, raw and undigested; but that feeds with an appetite, and hath a stomach to concoct, divide, and turn all into nourishment.

Ben Jonson *c.*1573–1637: *Timber, or Discoveries made upon Men and Matter* (1641)

5 Nothing is more ridiculous than to make an author a dictator, as the schools have done with Aristotle.

Ben Jonson *c.*1573–1637: *Timber, or Discoveries made upon Men and Matter* (1641)

6 Everything has been said, and one arrives too late after more than seven thousand years of human history and thought.

Jean de la Bruyère 1645–96: *Les Caractères ou les moeurs de ce siècle* (1688)

7 We feed on the ancients and the talented among the moderns, we squeeze them and extract all we can from them, we use them to blow up our works; and when finally we are authors and believe we can walk by ourselves, we turn against them, we mistreat them, like those children who have grown tough and strong from the milk they were given, and who attack their nurse.

Jean de la Bruyère 1645–96: *Les Caractères ou les moeurs de ce siècle* (1688)

8 Books, like proverbs, receive their chief value from the stamp and esteem of ages through which they have passed.

William Temple 1628–99: *Miscellanea. The Second Part* (1690) 'Ancient and Modern Learning'

9 Books are the legacies that a great genius leaves to mankind, which are delivered down from generation to generation, as presents to the posterity of those who are yet unborn.

Joseph Addison 1672–1719: *The Spectator* 10 September 1711

10 Speak of the moderns without contempt, and of the ancients without idolatry.

Lord Chesterfield 1694–1773: *Letters to his Son* (1774)

11 Meek young men grow up in libraries, believing it their duty to accept the views which Cicero, which Locke, which Bacon have given, forgetful that Cicero, Locke and Bacon were only young men in libraries when they wrote these books.

Ralph Waldo Emerson 1803–82: *The American Scholar* (1837)

1 Men grind and grind in the mill of a truism, and nothing comes out but what was put in. But the moment they desert the tradition for a spontaneous thought, then poetry, wit, hope, virtue, learning, anecdote, all flock to their aid.

Ralph Waldo Emerson 1803–82: *Literary Ethics* (1838)

2 It takes an old civilization to set a novelist in motion—a proposition that seems to me so true as to be a truism. It is on manners, customs, usages, habits, forms, upon all these things matured and established, that a novelist lives—they are the very stuff his work is made of.

Henry James 1843–1916: letter, 31 January 1880

3 I cannot read the old books!
They always bore me so.
I *never* read the old books,
They are so dull and slow.
Dickens and Scott are awful rot
Lytton's pure fiddlededee.
I cannot read the old books
They give the hump to me.

Punch 1841–1992: 'The Song of the New Novel Reader' 15 February 1896

4 '*Classic.*' A book which people praise and don't read.

Mark Twain 1835–1910: *Following the Equator* (1897)

5 Someone said: 'The dead writers are remote from us because we *know* so much more than they did.' Precisely, and they are that which we know.

T. S. Eliot 1888–1965: *The Sacred Wood* (1920) 'Tradition and Individual Talent'

6 A classic . . . is a successful book that has survived the reaction of the next period or generation. Then it's safe, like a style in architecture or furniture. It's acquired a picturesque dignity to take the place of its fashion.

F. Scott Fitzgerald 1896–1940: *The Beautiful and the Damned* (1922)

7 I have, then, given my hostages. What I think and judge I have stated as responsibly and clearly as I can. Jane Austen, George Eliot, Henry James, Conrad, and D. H. Lawrence: the great tradition of the British novel is there.

F. R. Leavis 1895–1978: introduction to *The Great Tradition* (1948)

8 You're familiar with the tragedies of antiquity, are you? The great homicidal classics?

Tom Stoppard 1937– : *Rosencrantz and Guildenstern are Dead* (1967)

9 A glorious place, a glorious age, I tell you! A very Neon Renaissance—And the myths that actually touched you at that time—not Hercules, Orpheus, Ulysses and Aeneas—but Superman, Captain Marvel, Batman.

Tom Wolfe 1931– : *The Electric Kool-Aid Acid Test* (1968)

10 Thus when I started to verse,
I presently sat at the feet of
Hardy and *Thomas* and *Frost*.
Falling in love altered that,
now Someone, at least, was important:
Yeats was a help, so was *Graves* . . .
. . . Fondly I ponder You all:
Without you I couldn't have managed
even my weakest of lines.

W. H. Auden 1907–73: 'A Thanksgiving' (1974)

11 A classic is a book that has never finished saying what it has to say.

Italo Calvino 1923–85: *The Literature Machine* (1987)

1 Great literature cannot grow from a neglected soil. Only if we actually tend or care will it transpire that every hundred years or so we might get a *Middlemarch*.

P. D. James 1920– : in *Daily Telegraph* 14 April 1988

2 No story comes from nowhere; new stories are born from old—it is the new combinations that make them new.

Salman Rushdie 1947– : *Haroun and the Sea of Stories* (1990)

3 Tradition is not only a handing-down or process of benign transmission; it is also a conflict between past genius and present aspiration, in which the prize is literary survival or canonical inclusion.

Harold Bloom 1930– : *The Western Canon* (1995)

4 Poems, stories, novels, plays come into being as a response to prior poems, stories, novels, and plays, and that response depends upon acts of reading and interpretation by the later writers, acts that are identical with the new works.

Harold Bloom 1930– : *The Western Canon* (1995)

5 Writers have to start out as readers, and before they put pen to paper, even the most disaffected of them will have internalized the norms and forms of the tradition from which they wish to secede.

Seamus Heaney 1939– : *The Redress of Poetry* (1995)

6 It adds a new terror to the death of the novelist.
of the vogue for sequels

Peter Ackroyd 1949– : in *Independent on Sunday* 22 September 1996

7 Nowadays the real danger to dead authors isn't the malicious biography but the avaricious sequel.

David Grylls 1947– : in *Sunday Times* 13 October 1996

Tragedy

8 Tragedy is thus a representation of an action that is worth serious attention, complete in itself and of some amplitude . . . by means of pity and fear bringing about the purgation of such emotions.

Aristotle 384–322 BC: *Poetics*

9 The composition of a tragedy requires *testicles*.
on being asked why no woman had ever written 'a tolerable tragedy'

Voltaire 1694–1778: letter from Byron to John Murray, 2 April 1817

10 One of Edward's Mistresses was Jane Shore, who has had a play written about her, but it is a tragedy and therefore not worth reading.

Jane Austen 1775–1817: *The History of England* (written 1791)

11 We do not expect people to be deeply moved by what is not unusual. That element of tragedy which lies in the very fact of frequency, has not yet wrought itself into the coarse emotion of mankind.

George Eliot 1819–80: *Middlemarch* (1871–2)

12 Tragedy is like strong acid—it dissolves away all but the very gold of truth.

D. H. Lawrence 1885–1930: letter, 1 April 1911

13 None but a poet can write a tragedy. For tragedy is nothing less than pain transmuted into exaltation by the alchemy of poetry.

Edith Hamilton 1867–1963: *The Greek Way* (1930)

1 Show me a hero and I will write you a tragedy.

F. Scott Fitzgerald 1896–1940: Edmund Wilson (ed.) *The Crack-Up* (1945) 'Note-Books E'

2 The spring is wound up tight. It will uncoil of itself. That is what is so convenient in tragedy. The least little turn of the wrist will do the job. Anything will set it going.

Jean Anouilh 1910–87: *Antigone* (1944)

3 A tragic situation exists when virtue does not *triumph* but when it is still felt that man is nobler than the forces that destroy him.

George Orwell 1903–50: 'Lear, Tolstoy and the Fool' (1947)

4 The bad end unhappily, the good unluckily. That is what tragedy means.

Tom Stoppard 1937– : *Rosencrantz and Guildenstern are Dead* (1967)

Translation and Translators

5 When I recalled how knowledge of Latin had previously decayed throughout England, and yet many could still read things written in English, I then began, amidst the various and multifarious afflictions of this kingdom, to translate into English the book which in Latin is called *Pastoralis*, in English 'Shepherd-book', sometimes word for word, sometimes sense for sense.

Alfred the Great AD 849–99: preface to the Anglo-Saxon version of St Gregory's *Pastoral Care* (translated by S. Keynes and M. Lapidge, 1983)

6 Translation it is that openeth the window, to let in the light; that breaketh the shell, that we may eat the kernel; that putteth aside the curtain, that we may look into the most holy place; that removeth the cover of the well, that we may come by the water.

Bible: Authorized Version (1611) 'The Translators to the Reader'

7 Such is our pride, our folly, or our fate,
That few, but such as cannot write, translate.

John Denham 1615–69: 'To Richard Fanshaw' (1648)

8 He is translation's thief that addeth more,
As much as he that taketh from the store
Of the first author.

Andrew Marvell 1621–78: 'To His Worthy Friend Dr Witty' (1651)

9 Some hold translations not unlike to be
The wrong side of a Turkey tapestry.

James Howell 1594?–1666: *Familiar Letters* (1645–55)

10 It is a pretty poem, Mr Pope, but you must not call it Homer.

*when pressed by **Pope** to comment on 'My Homer', i.e. his translation of **Homer**'s* Iliad

Richard Bentley 1662–1742: John Hawkins (ed.) *The Works of Samuel Johnson* (1787)

11 The vanity of translation; it were as wise to cast a violet into a crucible that you might discover the formal principle of its colour and odour, as seek to transfuse from one language to another the creations of a poet. The plant must spring again from its seed, or it will bear no flower.

Percy Bysshe Shelley 1792–1822: *A Defence of Poetry* (written 1821)

12 Translators are like busy pimps extolling the surpassing charms of some half-veiled beauty. They excite an irresistible desire for the original.

Johann Wolfgang von Goethe 1749–1832: *Art and Antiquity* (1816–32)

1 Wordsworth says somewhere that wherever Virgil seems to have composed 'with his eye on the object', Dryden fails to render him. Homer invariably composes 'with his eye on the object', whether the object be a moral or a material one: Pope composes with his eye on his style, into which he translates his object, whatever it is.

Matthew Arnold 1822–88: *On Translating Homer* (1861)

2 I do not hesitate to read . . . all good books in translations. What is really best in any book is translatable—any real insight or broad human sentiment.

Ralph Waldo Emerson 1803–82: *Society and Solitude* (1870) 'Books'

3 I believe that a poem ought to be translated in the way the poet himself would have composed it, had he belonged to the nation for which he is being translated.

Henrik Ibsen 1828–1906: letter, 1872

4 These pearls of thought in Persian gulfs were bred,
Each softly lucent as a rounded moon;
The diver Omar plucked them from their bed,
Fitzgerald strung them on an English thread.

James Russell Lowell 1819–91: 'In a Copy of Omar Khayyám'

5 The only tribute a French translator can pay Shakespeare is not to translate him—even to please Sarah [Bernhardt].

Max Beerbohm 1872–1956: in *Saturday Review* 17 June 1899

6 A translation is no translation unless it will give you the music of a poem along with the words of it.

John Millington Synge 1871–1909: *The Aran Islands* (1907)

7 I have a prejudice against people who print things in a foreign language and add no translation. When I am the reader, and the author considers me able to do the translating myself, he pays me quite a nice compliment—but if he would do the translating for me I would try to get along without the compliment.

Mark Twain 1835–1910: A. B. Paine (ed.) *Moments with Mark Twain* (1920)

8 An idea does not pass from one language to another without change.

Miguel de Unamuno 1864–1936: *Tragic Sense of Life* (1913)

9 The original Greek is of great use in elucidating Browning's translation of the *Agamemnon*.

Robert Yelverton Tyrrell 1844–1914: Ulick O'Connor *Oliver St John Gogarty* (1964)

10 Translation is the purest procedure by which the poetic skill can be recognized.

Rainer Maria Rilke 1875–1926: in conversation in 1924; Albert Manguel *A History of Reading* (1996)

11 Humour is the first of the gifts to perish in a foreign tongue.

Virginia Woolf 1882–1941: *The Common Reader* (1st series, 1925) 'On Not Knowing Greek'

12 I understand that you are to translate *Ulysses*, and I have come from Paris to tell you not to alter a single word.
to a prospective translator

James Joyce 1882–1941: Richard Ellmann *James Joyce* (1982)

13 I do love translating it is the pure pleasure of writing without the misery of inventing.
while translating La Princesse de Clèves

Nancy Mitford 1904–73: letter to Evelyn Waugh, 11 January 1949

1 Translations (like wives) are seldom strictly faithful if they are in the least attractive.

Roy Campbell 1901–57: in *Poetry Review* June-July 1949

2 Pastiche and face-powder.

on T. E. Lawrence's translation of the Odyssey, *of which* ***Beerbohm*** *said that he 'would rather not have been that translator than have driven the Turks out of Arabia'*

Max Beerbohm 1872–1956: in June 1955; S. N. Behrman *Conversations with Max* (1960)

3 [Wallace] Stevens says in his letters . . . that translating is a waste of time—but I don't agree with him completely. It gets one to going through dictionaries, and that is a helpful activity.

Elizabeth Bishop 1911–79: letter to May Swenson, 16 November 1968

4 It has never occurred to Anderson that one foreign language can be translated into another. He assumes that every strange tongue exists only by virtue of its not being English.

Tom Stoppard 1937– : *Where Are They Now?* (1973)

5 The original is unfaithful to the translation.

on Henley's translation of Beckford's Vathek

Jorge Luis Borges 1899–1986: *Sobre el 'Vathek' de William Beckford*; in *Obras Completas* (1974)

6 Poets belong to the language, not to the world.

Seamus Heaney 1939– : interviewed in *Athens News* 8 October 1995

Travel Writing

7 The travel-book, if to be done at all, would cost me very little trouble, and surely would go very far to pay charges, whenever published.

Charles Dickens 1812–70: letter, 2 November 1843

8 Our instructed vagrancy, which has hardly time to linger by the hedgerows, but runs away early to the tropics, and is at home with palms and banyans—which is nourished on books of travel, and stretches the theatre of its imagination to the Zambesi.

George Eliot 1819–80: *The Mill on the Floss* (1860)

9 Travel writing as a genre is *per se* almost impossible. To eliminate all repetitions you would have had to refrain from telling what you saw.

Gustave Flaubert 1821–80: letter, November 1866

10 It would have been a capital volume, if there had been no letterpress.

of Thomas Dibdin's lavishly illustrated account of his travels, Bibliographical, Antiquarian, and Picturesque Tour *(1821)*

Anonymous: in *Dictionary of National Biography* (1917–)

11 Moryson had spent three years in making an abstract of the history of the twelve countries which he had visited, but his manuscript proved so bulky that with a consideration rare in authors he destroyed it, and turned his attention to a briefer record of his experiences of travel.

of Fynes Moryson's compilation of his Itinerary *(1617)*

Anonymous: in *Dictionary of National Biography* (1917–)

1 Of all possible subjects, travel is the most difficult for an artist, as it is the easiest for a journalist.

W. H. Auden 1907–73: *The Dyer's Hand* (1962)

2 The travel writer seeks the world we have lost—the lost valleys of the imagination.

Alexander Cockburn 1941– : in *Harper's* August 1985

3 Writing about travels is nearly always tedious, travelling being, like war and fornication, exciting but not interesting.

Malcolm Muggeridge 1903–90: in *Observer* 5 September 1976

4 Life, as the most ancient of all metaphors insists, is a journey; and the travel book, in its deceptive simulation of the journey's fits and starts, rehearses life's own fragmentation. More even than the novel, it embraces the contingency of things.

Jonathan Raban 1942– : *For Love and Money* (1987)

5 It is not travel that narrows the mind but travel writing.

James Buchan 1916– : in *Spectator* 11 August 1990

Trends see **Movement and Trends**

Truth

6 A poem, whose subject is not truth, but things like truth.

George Chapman *c.*1559–1634: *The Revenge of Bussy D'Ambois* (1613) dedication

7 Who says that fictions only and false hair
Become a verse? Is there in truth no beauty?
Is all good structure in a winding stair?

George Herbert 1593–1633: 'Jordan (1)' (1633)

8 Beholding the bright countenance of truth in the quiet and still air of delightful studies.

John Milton 1608–74: *The Reason of Church Government* (1642)

9 Though all the winds of doctrine were let loose to play upon the earth, so Truth be in the field, we do injuriously by licensing and prohibiting to misdoubt her strength. Let her and Falsehood grapple; who ever knew Truth put to the worse, in a free and open encounter?

John Milton 1608–74: *Areopagitica* (1644)

10 In lapidary inscriptions a man is not upon oath.

Samuel Johnson 1709–84: James Boswell *Life of Samuel Johnson* (1791) 1775

11 I am certain of nothing but the holiness of the heart's affections and the truth of imagination—what the imagination seizes as beauty must be truth—whether it existed before or not.

John Keats 1795–1821: letter to Benjamin Bailey, 22 November 1817

12 'Tis strange—but true; for truth is always strange;
Stranger than fiction.

Lord Byron 1788–1824: *Don Juan* (1819–24)

13 The hero of my tale—whom I love with all the power of my soul, whom I have tried to portray in all his beauty, who has been, is, and will be beautiful—is Truth.

Leo Tolstoy 1828–1910: *Sevastopol in May* (1855)

1 You will say to me, perhaps, 'Are you sure that your tale is a true one?' What do I care about the reality of the world around me, if only it helps me to live, to feel I exist and to know what I am.

Charles Baudelaire 1821–67: *The Windows*

2 There was things which he stretched, but mainly he told the truth.

Mark Twain 1835–1910: *The Adventures of Huckleberry Finn* (1884)

3 There are two duties incumbent upon any man who enters on the business of writing: truth to the fact and a good spirit in the treatment.

Robert Louis Stevenson 1850–94: *Essays Literary and Critical* (1923) 'Morality of the Profession of Letters'

4 The folly of mistaking a paradox for a discovery, a metaphor for a proof, a torrent of verbiage for a spring of capital truths, and oneself for an orator, is inborn in us.

Paul Valéry 1871–1945: *Introduction to the Method of Leonardo da Vinci* (1895)

5 The truth is rarely pure, and never simple.

Oscar Wilde 1854–1900: *The Importance of Being Earnest* (1895)

6 There are no such things as facts, only interpretation.
found in Nietzsche's posthumous papers

Friedrich Nietzsche 1844–1900: Malcolm Bradbury and James McFarlane (eds.) *Modernism* (1991)

7 The art of fiction has this great ethical importance that it enables one to tell the truth about human beings in a way which is impossible in actual life . . . Thackeray's moral usefulness is especially great in that respect.

George Gissing 1857–1903: *Commonplace Book* (1962)

8 Though leaves are many, the root is one;
Through all the lying days of my youth
I swayed my leaves and flowers in the sun;
Now I may wither into the truth.

W. B. Yeats 1865–1939: 'The Coming of Wisdom with Time' (1910)

9 Scepticism the tonic of minds, the tonic of life, the agent of truth—the way of art and salvation.

Joseph Conrad 1857–1924: letter, 11 November 1911

10 Nothing is poorer than a truth expressed as it was thought. Committed to writing in such cases, it is not even a bad photograph . . . Truth wants to be startled abruptly, at one stroke, from her self-immersion, whether by uproar, music or cries for help.

Walter Benjamin 1892–1940: *One-Way Street* (1928) 'Technical Aid'

11 Thought does not crush to stone.
The great sledge drops in vain.
Truth never is undone;
Its shafts remain.

Theodore Roethke 1908–63: 'The Adamant' (1941)

12 It doesn't have to be the truth, just your vision of it, written down.

Virginia Woolf 1882–1941: attributed

13 At some time in the future, if the human mind becomes something totally different from what it now is, we may learn to separate literary creation from intellectual honesty. At present we know only that the imagination, like certain wild animals, will not breed in captivity.

George Orwell 1903–50: 'The Prevention of Literature' in *Polemic* January 1946

1 A poem is a witness to man's knowledge of evil as well as good. It is not the duty of a witness to pass moral judgement on the evidence he has to give, but to give it clearly and accurately; the only crime of which a witness can be guilty is perjury.

W. H. Auden 1907–73: *The Dyer's Hand* (1962)

2 All your life you live so close to truth, it becomes a permanent blur in the corner of your eye, and when something nudges it into outline it is like being ambushed by a grotesque.

Tom Stoppard 1937– : *Rosencrantz and Guildenstern are Dead* (1967)

3 Errors are of greater value than truths: truth is machine-like, error is alive; truth reassures, error unsettles. And even if the answers are quite impossible, so much the better: to ask answered questions is the privilege of minds constructed on the same principle as the cow's stomach, which is ideally suited, as well we know, to chewing the cud.

on Babel and Zamyatin and their refusal to conform to the demands of Socialist Realism

Mihajlo Mihajlov 1934– : *Russian Themes* (1968)

4 Truth is always duller than fiction.

Piers Paul Read 1941– : in *Observer* 1981

5 We don't go in for nondenominationalism and tolerance, we go in for strict truth and let the other guy be tolerant of us.

Garrison Keillor 1942– : *Leaving Home* (1988)

6 I'm merely a reporter whose truth lies
In diction clear as water.

Georges Szirtes 1948– : *Bridge Passages* (1991) 'Street Entertainment'

7 The disturbing thing about false and erroneous statements is that well-meaning scholars tend to repeat one another. Lies are like fleas hopping from here to there, sucking the blood of the intellect.

Muriel Spark 1918– : *Curriculum Vitae* (1992)

8 The best we can do is write words from which a kind of truth emerges.

Muriel Spark 1918– : Clare Boylan (ed.) *The Agony and the Ego* (1993); attributed

Usage see Grammar and Usage

War

9 Our swords shall play the orators for us.

Christopher Marlowe 1564–93: *Tamburlaine the Great* (1590)

10 Among the calamities of war may be jointly numbered the diminution of the love of truth, by the falsehoods which interest dictates and credulity encourages.

Samuel Johnson 1709–84: in *The Idler* 11 November 1758; possibly the source of 'When war is declared, Truth is the first casualty', epigraph to Arthur Ponsonby's *Falsehood in Wartime* (1928); attributed also to Hiram

Johnson, speaking in the US Senate, 1918, but not recorded in his speech

1 The Minstrel Boy to the war is gone,
In the ranks of death you'll find him;
His father's sword he has girded on,
And his wild harp slung behind him.

Thomas Moore 1779–1852: *Irish Melodies* (1807) 'The Minstrel Boy'

2 The cudgel of the people's war was lifted with all its menacing and majestic might, and caring nothing for good taste and procedure, with dull-witted simplicity but sound judgement it rose and fell, making no distinctions.

Leo Tolstoy 1828–1910: *War and Peace* (1868–9)

3 The real war will never get in the books. And so goodbye to the war.

written after the American Civil war

Walt Whitman 1819–92: *Specimen Days* (1882) 'The Real War Will Never Get in the Books'

4 How is the world ruled and led to war? Diplomats lie to journalists and believe these lies when they see them in print.

Karl Kraus 1874–1936: *Nachts* (1918)

5 All a poet can do today is warn.

Wilfred Owen 1893–1918: preface (written 1918) in *Poems* (1963)

6 My subject is War, and the pity of War.
The Poetry is in the pity.

Wilfred Owen 1893–1918: preface (written 1918) in *Poems* (1963)

7 If you could hear, at every jolt, the blood
Come gargling from the froth-corrupted lungs,
Obscene as cancer, bitter as the cud
Of vile, incurable sores on innocent tongues,—
My friend, you would not tell with such high zest
To children ardent for some desperate glory,
The old Lie: Dulce et decorum est
Pro patria mori.

Wilfred Owen 1893–1918: 'Dulce et Decorum Est'

8 I think it better that at times like these
We poets keep our mouths shut, for in truth
We have no gift to set a statesman right.

W. B. Yeats 1865–1939: 'On being asked for a War Poem' (1919)

9 Who live under the shadow of a war,
What can I do that matters?

Stephen Spender 1909–95: 'Who live under the shadow of a war' (1933)

10 As soon as war is declared it will be impossible to hold the poets back. Rhyme is still the most effective drum.

Jean Giraudoux 1882–1944: *La Guerre de Troie n'aura pas lieu* (1935)

11 Passive suffering is not the theme for poetry. If war is necessary in our time, best to forget its suffering as we forget the discomfort of fever.

W. B. Yeats 1865–1939: introduction to *Oxford Book of Modern Poetry* (1936)

12 I have a distaste for certain poems written in the Great War. The writers were officers. They felt bound to plead the suffering of their men. In poems written in the first person, they made that suffering their own.

W. B. Yeats 1865–1939: introduction to *Oxford Book of Modern Poetry* (1936)

*on being asked by Stephen **Spender** in the 1930s how best a poet could serve the Communist cause:*

1 Go to Spain and get killed. The movement needs a Byron.

Harry Pollitt 1890–1960: Frank Johnson *Out of Order* (1982); attributed, perhaps apocryphal

2 Remember that the Patriots are in the right and are going to win . . . But they must win quickly. The British public has no interest in a war that drags on indecisively. A few sharp victories, some conspicuous acts of personal bravery on the Patriot side and a colourful entry into the capital. That is *The Beast* Policy for the war.

Evelyn Waugh 1903–66: *Scoop* (1938)

3 We only watch, and indicate and make our scribbled
pencil notes.
We do not wish to moralize, only to ease our dusty
throats.

Donald Bain 1922– : 'War Poet'; Brian Gardner *The Terrible Rain: The War Poets 1939–45* (1966)

4 I understand the hero keeps getting in bed with women, and the war wasn't fought that way.

*of **Hemingway's*** A Farewell to Arms

Harold Ross 1892–1951: James Thurber *The Years with Ross* (1959)

5 War is, after all, the universal perversion . . . war stories, the pornography of war.

John Rae 1931– : *The Custard Boys* (1960)

6 We French, we English, never lost our civil war,
endure it still, a bloodless civil bore;
no wounded lying about, no Whitman wanted.
It's only by our lack of ghosts we're haunted.

Earle Birney 1904– : 'Can. Lit.' (1962)

7 War is capitalism with the gloves off and many who go to war know it but they go to war because they don't want to be a hero.

Tom Stoppard 1937– : *Travesties* (1975)

8 A 'war' poet is not one who chooses to commemorate or celebrate a war but one who reacts against having a war thrust upon him.

Philip Larkin 1922–85: *Required Writing* (1983)

The Western Canon

9 If you like poetry let it be first-rate; Milton, Shakespeare, Thomson, Goldsmith, Pope (if you will, though I don't admire him), Scott, Byron, Campbell, Wordsworth, and Southey.

Charlotte Brontë 1816–55: letter to Ellen Nussey, 4 July 1834

10 The great tradition.

F. R. Leavis 1895–1978: title of book (1948)

11 Western culture . . . was a grand ancestral property that educated men had inherited from their intellectual forefathers, while their female relatives, like characters in a Jane Austen novel, were relegated to modest dower houses on the edge of the estate.

Sandra M. Gilbert 1936– : 'What Do Feminist Critics Want?' (1980)

12 I believe in the established canon of English and American literature and in the validity of the concept of privileged texts. I think it is more important to read Spenser, Shakespeare, or Milton than to read Borges in translation, or even, to say the truth, to read Virginia Woolf.

J. Hillis Miller 1928– : Sandra M. Gilbert 'What Do Feminist Critics Want?' (1980)

1 There was . . . a necessary period around about the mid-seventies of a kind of demystificatory criticism, which one felt to be essential when . . . the canon was riding high and certain interpretations were going uncriticized.

Terry Eagleton 1943– : in an interview with Michael Payne; *The Significance of Theory* (1990)

2 The only surviving Old English epic, thank God . . . the most shitty and boring part of one's heritage.
on Beowulf

Kingsley Amis 1922–95: remark, 15 April 1993; in *Sunday Times* 17 March 1996

3 The western canon.

Harold Bloom 1930– : title of book, 1995

4 [English departments where] Batman comics, Mormon theme parks, television, movies and rock will replace Chaucer, Shakespeare, Milton, Wordsworth and Wallace Stevens.

Harold Bloom 1930– : *The Western Canon* (1995)

on an early twentieth century immigrant child's being given ***Scott's*** The Lady of the Lake *to read as a school assigment:*

5 What *The Lady of the Lake* stood for, in the robes and tapestries of its particular English, was the received tradition.

Cynthia Ozick 1928– : *Portrait of the Artist as a Bad Character* (1996)

Wit and Satire see also **Humour and Comedy**

6 How easy it is to call rogue and villain, and that wittily! But how hard to make a man appear a fool, a blockhead, or a knave, without using any of those opprobrious terms! To spare the grossness of the names, and to do the thing yet more severely, is to draw a full face, and to make the nose and cheeks stand out, and yet not to employ any depth of shadowing.

John Dryden 1631–1700: *Of Satire* (1693)

7 True wit is Nature to advantage dressed,
What oft was thought, but ne'er so well expressed.

Alexander Pope 1688–1744: *An Essay on Criticism* (1711)

8 Satire is a sort of glass, wherein beholders do generally discover everybody's face but their own; which is the chief reason for that kind of reception it meets in the world, and that so very few are offended with it.

Jonathan Swift 1667–1745: *The Battle of the Books* (1704), preface

9 Unlike my subject will I frame my song,
It shall be witty and it sha'n't be long.
epigram on 'Long' Sir Thomas Robinson

Lord Chesterfield 1694–1773: in *Dictionary of National Biography* (1917–)

10 A man who could make so vile a pun would not scruple to pick a pocket.

John Dennis 1657–1734: *The Gentleman's Magazine* (1781); editorial note

11 What is an Epigram? a dwarfish whole,
Its body brevity, and wit its soul.

Samuel Taylor Coleridge 1772–1834: 'Epigram' (1809)

12 [A pun] is a pistol let off at the ear; not a feather to tickle the intellect.

Charles Lamb 1775–1834: *Last Essays of Elia* (1833) 'Popular Fallacies'

13 Flippancy, the most hopeless form of intellectual vice.

George Gissing 1857–1903: *New Grub Street* (1891)

1 Don't try to be witty in the writing, unless it's natural—just true and real.

F. Scott Fitzgerald 1896–1940: letter, 7 July 1938

2 Reality goes bounding past the satirist like a cheetah laughing as it lopes ahead of the greyhound.

Claud Cockburn 1904–81: *Crossing the Line* (1958)

3 Ridicule is the only honourable weapon we have left.

Muriel Spark 1918– : 'The Desegregation of Art' (1971)

4 The English are very fond of humour, but they are afraid of wit. For wit is like a sword, but humour is like a jester's bladder.

J. B. Morton ('Beachcomber') 1893–1975: attributed

5 There is parody, when you make fun of people who are smarter than you; satire, when you make fun of people who are richer than you; and burlesque, when you make fun of both while taking off your clothes.

P. J. O'Rourke 1947– : in 1980; *Age and Guile* (1995)

6 I shouldn't call myself a satirist. To be a satirist, you have to know better than everyone else, and I've never done that.

Philip Larkin 1922–85: A. N. Wilson *Penfriends from Porlock* (1988)

7 Satire is dependent on strong beliefs, and on strong beliefs wounded.

Anita Brookner 1938– : in *Spectator* 23 March 1989

8 To hear some people talk, you would think humour was an aspect of satire, instead of the other way round. Satire is simply humour in uniform.

Paul Jennings 1918–89: in obituary in *Guardian* 1 January 1990

9 I'm not a social punster. I tether them to the page.

Roger McGough 1937– : interview in *Sunday Telegraph* 12 May 1996

Women and Literature

10 I am obnoxious to each carping tongue,
Who says my hand a needle better fits,
A poet's pen, all scorn, I should thus wrong;
For such despite they cast on female wits:
If what I do prove well, it won't advance,
They'll say it's stolne, or else, it was by chance.

Anne Bradstreet *c.*1612–72: 'The Prologue' (1650)

11 I'm hither come, but what d'ye think to say?
A woman's pen presents you with a play:
Who smiling told me I'd be sure to see
That once confirmed, the house would empty be.

Frances Boothby fl. 1670: *Marcelia* (1670) prologue

12 All I ask, is the privilege for my masculine part the poet in me . . . If I must not, because of my sex, have this freedom . . . I lay down my quill, and you shall hear no more of me.

Aphra Behn 1640–89: preface to *The Lucky Chance* (1686)

13 But of all plagues, the greatest is untold,
The book-learned wife in Greek and Latin bold,
The critic-dame, who at her table sits,
Homer and Virgil quotes, and wrights their wits.

John Dryden 1631–1700: translation of Juvenal *Satires*

14 The carping malice of the vulgar world; who think it a proof of sense to dislike every thing that is writ by Women.

Susannah Centlivre *c.*1669–1723: *The Platonic Lady* (1707)

1 Alas! a woman that attempts the pen
Such an intruder on the rights of men,
Such presumptuous creature is esteemed
The fault can by no virtue be redeemed.

Anne Finch, Lady Winchilsea 1661–1720: 'The Introduction' (1713)

2 Regularity and Decorum. 'Tis what we women-authors, in particular, have been thought greatly deficient in; and I should be concerned to find it an objection not to be removed.

Elizabeth Cooper fl. 1730: preface to *The Rival Widows* (1735)

3 Men have had every advantage of us in telling their own story. Education has been theirs in so much higher a degree; the pen has been in their hands.

Jane Austen 1775–1817: *Persuasion* (1818)

4 Except some professional scholars, I have often observed that women in general read much more than men; but, for want of a plan, a method, a fixed object, their reading is of little benefit to themselves, or others.

Edward Gibbon 1737–94: *Autobiography* (1827)

5 Literature cannot be the business of a woman's life, and it ought not to be.

Robert Southey 1774–1843: letter to Charlotte Brontë, 1836

6 Oh! . . . that ladies would make puddings and mend stockings! That they would not meddle with religion, except to pray to God, to live quietly among their families.

reviewing Fanny Trollope's novel The Vicar of Wrexhill

William Makepeace Thackeray 1811–63: in *Fraser's Magazine* (1837)

7 To such critics I would say, To you I am neither man nor woman—I come before you as an author only.

Charlotte Brontë 1816–55: letter to W. S. Williams, 16 August 1849

8 I wish critics would judge me as an *author*, not as a woman.

Charlotte Brontë 1816–55: letter to George Henry Lewes, 19 January 1850

9 *All* women, as authors, are feeble and tiresome. I wish they were forbidden to write, on pain of having their faces deeply scarified with an oyster shell.

Nathaniel Hawthorne 1804–64: letter to his publisher, 1852

10 America is now given over to a d—d mob of scribbling women, and I should have no chance of success while the public taste is occupied with their trash—and should be ashamed of myself if I did succeed.

Nathaniel Hawthorne 1804–64: letter, 1854

11 If those two volumes, or part of them, were not written by a woman, then should I begin to believe that I am a woman myself.

of George ***Eliot****'s* Scenes of Clerical Life

Charles Dickens 1812–70: letter to J. Langford, 18 January 1858

12 Women are capable only of a certain delicacy and sensitivity. Everything that is truly sublime, truly great, escapes them.

Gustave Flaubert 1821–80: letter, 11 January 1859

13 There is no good end attained by trying to persuade ourselves that women are all incorporeal, angelic, colourless, passionless, helpless creatures . . . Women have especial need, as the world goes, to be shrewd, self-reliant, and strong; and we do all we can in our literature to render them helpless, imbecile, and idiotic.

Justin McCarthy 1830–1912: in *Westminster Review* 1864

14 It is hard for a woman to define her feelings in language which is chiefly made by men to express theirs.

Thomas Hardy 1840–1928: *Far from the Madding Crowd* (1874)

1 To say in print what she thinks is the last thing the woman novelist or journalist is so rash as to attempt . . . Her publishers are not women.

Elizabeth Robins 1862–1952: in 1908, as first president of the Women Writers' Suffrage League

2 I have nothing to say to 'charming' women. I feel like a cat among tigers.
on her dislike of social occasions

Katherine Mansfield 1888–1923: John Middleton Murry *Between Two Worlds* (1935)

3 I struggle to keep the writing as much as possible in male hands, as I distrust the feminine in literature.
on editing The Egoist

T. S. Eliot 1888–1965: letter, 31 October 1917

4 A woman must have money and a room of her own if she is to write fiction.

Virginia Woolf 1882–1941: *A Room of One's Own* (1929)

5 Far from the vulgar haunts of men
Each sits in her 'successful room',
Housekeeping with her fountain pen
And writing novels with her broom.

Roy Campbell 1901–57: 'On Some South African Novelists'

6 The sniffs I get from the ink of the women are always fey, old-bat, Quaintsy, Gaysy, tiny, too dykily psychotic, crippled, creepish fashionable, frigid, outer-Baroque, maquille in mannequin's whimsey, or else bright and stillborn.

Norman Mailer 1923– : *Advertisements for Myself* (1959)

7 To be a woman and a writer
is double mischief, for
the world will slight her
who slights 'the servile house', and who would rather
make odes than beds.

Dilys Laing 1906–60: 'Sonnet to a Sister in Error'

8 Dr Leavis believed he could identify a woman writer by her style, even though necessarily all that she wrote must have been a parody of some man's superior achievement. After all, there was not much wrong with Virginia Woolf except that she was a woman.

Germaine Greer 1939– : *The Female Eunuch* (1970)

9 WHY 'Women in Literature'? No—It's *The Women Poets in English*, I see. But still, WHY? Why not *Men Poets in English*? . . . Literature is literature, no matter who produces it.
having been asked to contribute to an anthology of women poets

Elizabeth Bishop 1911–79: letter to May Swenson, 7 November 1971

10 'She writes because she *must*,
My gifted daughter Ann.'
How nice! We won't pretend
She writes because she can.

William Plomer 1903–73: 'Gifted Daughter'

11 Women must write through their bodies, they must invent the impregnable language that will wreck partitions, classes, and rhetorics, regulations and codes, they must submerge, cut through, get beyond the ultimate reserve-discourse, including the one that laughs at the very idea of pronouncing the word 'silence'.

Hélène Cixous 1937–'The Laugh of the Medusa' (1975)

1 Who says vaginas can't have teeth? Some do. Dentate vaginas . . . vaginae dentatae . . . All those literary ladies from the rubyfruit jungle.
lashing out at the 'feminist buzz saws'

Edward Abbey 1927–89: in *New York Times* 1979; attributed

2 Before we can even begin to ask how the literature of women would be different and special, we need to reconstruct its past, to rediscover the scores of women novelists, poets and dramatists whose work has been obscured by time, and to establish the continuity of the female tradition from decade to decade, rather than from Great Woman to Great Woman.

Elaine Showalter 1941– : 'Towards a Feminist Poetics' (1979)

3 Re-vision—the act of looking back, of seeing with fresh eyes, of entering an old text from a new critical direction—is for women more than a chapter in cultural history: it is an act of survival.

Adrienne Rich 1929– : *On Lies, Secrets, and Silence* (1980)

4 Men's novels are about men. Women's novels are about men too but from a different point of view. You can have a men's novel with no women in it except possibly the landlady or the horse, but you can't have a women's novel with no men in it. Sometimes men put women in men's novels but they leave out some of the parts: the heads, for instance, or the hands. Women's novels leave out parts of the men as well. Sometimes it's the stretch between the belly button and the knees, sometimes it's the sense of humour. It's hard to have a sense of humour in a cloak, in a high wind, on a moor.

Margaret Atwood 1939– : *Murder in the Dark* (1984) 'Women's Novels'

5 If you want your writing to be taken seriously, don't marry and have kids, and above all, don't die. But if you have to die, commit suicide. They approve of that.

Ursula Le Guin 1929– : 'Prospects for Women in Writing' (1986); *Dancing at the Edge of the World* (1989)

6 Men like women who write. Even though they don't say so. A writer is a foreign country.

Marguerite Duras 1914– : *Practicalities* (1987)

7 Men in suits took notes and my goose was cooked.
of a speech given to women at Harper & Row, her publishers

Andrea Dworkin 1946– : *Letters from a War Zone* (1988)

8 I think it's a question which particularly arises over women writers: whether it's better to have a happy life or a good supply of tragic plots.

Wendy Cope 1945– : in *Independent* 9 March 1992

9 I keep things up pretty well. But there's apt to be chaos underneath—in the backs of closets or cupboards—and it's the knowledge of this chaos which I use to keep myself from writing. I can get into housework very, very quickly, because I get a whole lot of virtuous feelings not from writing but from cleaning.

Alice Munro 1931– : in *New Yorker* 26 June 1995

10 One reason why women are good at writing detective stories may be our feminine eye for detail; clue-making demands attention to the detail of everyday life.

P. D. James 1920– : in *Paris Review* 1995

11 The solitary genius in the garret is a male myth, as he would undoubtedly have been supported by several unacknowledged women who cooked and ironed.

Michèle Roberts 1949– : in *Independent on Sunday* 4 February 1996

1 I am against sexism. I am against positive discrimination. I think literature is without gender.
refusing to enter for the Orange fiction award, reserved for women

Anita Brookner 1938– : in *Sunday Times* 18 February 1996; cf. **190:14**

Words

2 Winged words.

Homer: *The Iliad*

3 The words of his mouth were softer than butter, having war in his heart: his words were smoother than oil, and yet they be very swords.

Bible: Psalm 55

4 *Proicit ampullas et sesquipedalia verba.*

He throws aside his paint-pots and his words a foot and a half long.

Horace 65–8 BC: *Ars Poetica*

5 *Et semel emissum volat irrevocabile verbum.*

And once sent out a word takes wing beyond recall.

Horace 65–8 BC: *Epistles*

6 A gloton of wordes.

William Langland *c.*1330–*c.*1400: *The Vision of Piers Plowman*

7 Throughout the world, if it were sought,
Fair words enough a man shall find.
They be good cheap; they cost right naught;
Their substance is but only wind.
But well to say and so to mean—
That sweet accord is seldom seen.

Thomas Wyatt *c.*1503–42: 'Throughout the world, if it were sought' (1557)

8 The words of Mercury are harsh after the songs of Apollo.

William Shakespeare 1564–1616: *Love's Labour's Lost* (1595)

9 But words are words; I never yet did hear
That the bruised heart was piercèd through the ear.

William Shakespeare 1564–1616: *Othello* (1602–4)

10 Words are the tokens current and accepted for conceits, as moneys are for values.

Francis Bacon 1561–1626: *The Advancement of Learning* (1605)

11 Words are women, deeds are men.

George Herbert 1593–1633: *Outlandish Proverbs* (1640)

12 Words are wise men's counters, they do but reckon by them: but they are the money of fools, that value them by the authority of an Aristotle, a Cicero, or a Thomas, or any other doctor whatsoever, if but a man.

Thomas Hobbes 1588–1679: *Leviathan* (1651)

13 Oaths are but words, and words but wind.

Samuel Butler 1612–80: *Hudibras* pt. 2 (1664)

14 Thy genius calls thee not to purchase fame
In keen iambics, but mild anagram:
Leave writing plays, and choose for thy command
Some peaceful province in Acrostic Land.
There thou mayest wings display and altars raise,
And torture one poor word ten thousand ways.

John Dryden 1631–1700: *MacFlecknoe* (1682)

1 Th' artillery of words.

Jonathan Swift 1667–1745: 'Ode to Dr William Sancroft' (written 1692)

2 A barren superfluity of words.

Samuel Garth 1661–1719: *The Dispensary* (1699)

3 Grant me some wild expressions, Heavens, or I shall burst— . . . Words, words or I shall burst.

George Farquhar 1678–1707: *The Constant Couple* (1699)

4 For the idiom of words very little she heeded,
Provided the matter she drove at succeeded,
She took and gave languages just as she needed.

Matthew Prior 1664–1721: 'Jinny the Just' (after 1700)

5 Words are men's daughters, but God's sons are things.

Samuel Madden 1686–1765: *Boulter's Monument* (1745)

6 I am not yet so lost in lexicography as to forget that words are the daughters of earth, and that things are the sons of heaven. Language is only the instrument of science, and words are but the signs of ideas: I wish, however, that the instrument might be less apt to decay, and that signs might be permanent, like the things which they denote.

Samuel Johnson 1709–84: *A Dictionary of the English Language* (1755)

7 It's exactly where a thought is lacking
That, just in time, a word shows up instead.

Johann Wolfgang von Goethe 1749–1832: *Faust* (1808)

8 A single word even may be a spark of inextinguishable thought.

Percy Bysshe Shelley 1792–1822: *A Defence of Poetry* (written 1821)

9 For words, like Nature, half reveal
And half conceal the Soul within.

Alfred, Lord Tennyson 1809–92: *In Memoriam A. H. H.* (1850)

10 We talk about the tyranny of words, but we like to tyrannise over them too; we are fond of having a large superfluous establishment of words to wait upon us on great occasions; we think it looks important, and sounds well.

Charles Dickens 1812–70: *David Copperfield* (1850)

11 Oh, indelicate! How I do hate that word. If any word in the language reminds me of a whited sepulchre it is that:—all clean and polished outside with filth and rottenness within. Are your thoughts delicate? That's the thing.

Anthony Trollope 1815–82: 'Kate Vavasour' in *Can You Forgive Her?* (1864)

12 They've a temper, some of them—particularly verbs: they're the proudest—adjectives you can do anything with, but not verbs—however, I can manage the whole lot of them!

Lewis Carroll 1832–98: *Through the Looking-Glass* (1872)

13 All the charm of all the Muses
often flowering in a lonely word.

Alfred, Lord Tennyson 1809–92: 'To Virgil' (1882)

14 The vulgarity of the son of a Tory Duke having talked about 'pooh-poohing' something or other in the House of Commons: a vile new verb, unworthy of that high assembly.

Henry James 1843–1916: letter, 14 April 1884

15 Words alone are certain good.

W. B. Yeats 1865–1939: 'The Song of the Happy Shepherd' (1885)

1 Some word that teems with hidden meaning—like Basingstoke.

W. S. Gilbert 1836–1911: *Ruddigore* (1887)

2 Words are always getting conventionalized to some secondary meaning. It is one of the works of poetry to take the truants into custody and bring them back to their right senses. Poets are the policemen of language, they are always arresting those old reprobates the words.

W. B. Yeats 1865–1939: letter to Ellen O'Leary, 1889

3 All the words that I gather,
And all the words that I write,
Must spread out their wings untiring,
And never rest in their flight,
Till they come where your sad, sad heart is,
And sing to you in the night,
Beyond where the waters are moving
Storm-darkened or starry bright.

W. B. Yeats 1865–1939: 'Where My Books Go' (1892)

4 A definition is the enclosing a wilderness of idea within a wall of words.

Samuel Butler 1835–1902: *Notebooks* (1912)

5 I keep six honest serving-men
(They taught me all I knew);
Their names are What and Why and When
And How and Where and Who.

Rudyard Kipling 1865–1936: *Just So Stories* (1902) 'The Elephant's Child'

6 To illustrate calling a simple thing by a hard name, say that 'Baby, baby bunting' is written in Ithyphallics.

George Gissing 1857–1903: *Commonplace Book* (1962)

7 'Sesquippledan,' he would say. 'Sesquippledan verboojuice.'

H. G. Wells 1866–1946: *The History of Mr Polly* (1909)

8 Words, as is well known, are the great foes of reality.

Joseph Conrad 1857–1924: *Under Western Eyes* (1911)

9 A swear-word in a rustic slum
A simple swear-word is to some,
To Masefield something more.

Max Beerbohm 1872–1956: *Fifty Caricatures* (1912)

10 The war has used up words; they have weakened, they have deteriorated like motor-car tyres; they have like millions of other things, been more overstrained and knocked about and voided of the happy semblance during the last six months than in all the long ages before, and we are now confronted with a depreciation of all our terms, or otherwise speaking, with a loss of expression through increase of limpness, that may well make us wonder what ghosts will be left to walk.

Henry James 1843–1916: in *New York Times* 21 March 1915

11 One of our defects as a nation is a tendency to use what have been called 'weasel words'. When a weasel sucks eggs the meat is sucked out of the egg. If you use a 'weasel word' after another, there is nothing left of the other.

Theodore Roosevelt 1858–1919: speech in St Louis, 31 May 1916

12 Summer afternoon—summer afternoon . . . the two most beautiful words in the English language.

Henry James 1843–1916: Edith Wharton *A Backward Glance* (1934)

13 I fear those big words, Stephen said, which make us so unhappy.

James Joyce 1882–1941: *Ulysses* (1922)

1 Words are, of course, the most powerful drug used by mankind.

Rudyard Kipling 1865–1936: speech, 14 February 1923

2 Slang is, at least, vigorous and apt. Probably most of our vital words were once slang.

presidential address to the English Association in 1924

John Galsworthy 1867–1933: *Castles in Spain and Other Screeds* (1927)

3 The Americans are doing what the Elizabethans did—they are coining new words . . . In England, save for the impetus given by war, the word-coining power has lapsed.

Virginia Woolf 1882–1941: 'American Fiction' (1925)

4 'Well,' said Owl, 'the customary procedure in such cases is as follows.' 'What does Crustimoney Proseedcake mean?' said Pooh. 'For I am a Bear of Very Little Brain, and long words Bother me.'

A. A. Milne 1882–1956: *Winnie-the-Pooh* (1926)

5 One picture is worth ten thousand words.

Frederick R. Barnard: in *Printers' Ink* 10 March 1927

6 The Greeks had a word for it.

Zoë Akins 1886–1958: title of play (1930)

7 When I cannot see words curling like rings of smoke round me I am in darkness—I am nothing.

Virginia Woolf 1882–1941: *The Waves* (1931)

8 I gotta use words when I talk to you.

T. S. Eliot 1888–1965: *Sweeney Agonistes* (1932)

9 Words strain,
Crack and sometimes break, under the burden,
Under the tension, slip, slide, perish,
Decay with imprecision, will not stay in place,
Will not stay still.

T. S. Eliot 1888–1965: *Four Quartets* 'Burnt Norton' (1936)

10 I think that the deliberate invention of words is at least worth thinking over.

George Orwell 1903–50: 'New Words' (1940)

11 Do not become embittered by waiting and tears. Speak with calmness and serenity, and do as our holy sages have done—pour forth words and cast them into letters. Then the holy souls of your brothers and sisters will remain alive. These evil ones scheme to blot out their names from the face of the earth; but a man cannot destroy letters. For words have wings; they mount up to the heavenly heights and they endure for eternity.

a rabbi to his students in 1940, as the Germans were entering Kovno

Nachum Yanchiker : attributed

12 There is no use indicting words, they are no shoddier than what they peddle.

Samuel Beckett 1906–89: *Malone Dies* (1958)

13 Man does not live by words alone, despite the fact that he sometimes has to eat them.

Adlai Stevenson 1900–65: *The Wit and Wisdom of Adlai Stevenson* (1965)

14 MIKE: There's no word in the Irish language for what you were doing.
WILSON: In Lapland they have no word for snow.

Joe Orton 1933–67: *The Ruffian on the Stair* (rev. ed. 1967)

15 Don't swear, boy. It shows a lack of vocabulary.

Alan Bennett 1934– : *Forty Years On* (1969)

1 If there's one word that sums up everything that's gone wrong since the War, it's Workshop.

Kingsley Amis 1922–95: *Jake's Thing* (1979)

2 I think that words are an around-the-world, ox-cart way of doing things, awkward instruments, and they will be laid aside eventually, probably sooner than we think.

William S. Burroughs 1914–97: George Plimpton (ed.) *The Writer's Chapbook* (1989)

3 The mad . . . more than anyone proceed by punning. The word in action. The deranged pursue their sanity down the only alley known to them: giving language more meaning, more significance, than it was ever meant to have.

Fay Weldon 1933– : *The Cloning of Joanna May* (1989)

4 Words are undervalued as a means of expression. Pictures tend to trivialise experience.

Arthur Miller 1915– : attributed, 1990

Writers see also **Writing**

5 He has gained every point who has mixed profit with pleasure, by delighting the reader at the same time as instructing him.

Horace 65–8 BC: *Ars Poetica*

6 *Tenet insanabile multos*
Scribendi cacoethes et aegro in corde senescit.

Many suffer from the incurable disease of writing, and it becomes chronic in their sick minds.

Juvenal AD *c.*60–*c.*130: *Satires*

7 Authors are judged by strange capricious rules
The great ones are thought mad, the small ones fools.

Alexander Pope 1688–1744: prologue to *Three Hours after Marriage* (1717)

8 But those who cannot write, and those who can,
All rhyme, and scrawl, and scribble, to a man.

Alexander Pope 1688–1744: *Imitations of Horace* (1737)

9 I love to write to the moment.

Samuel Richardson 1689–1761: *Clarissa* (1747–8)

10 I do think . . . the mighty stir made about scribbling and scribes, by themselves and others—a sign of effeminacy, degeneracy, and weakness. Who would write, who had any thing better to do?

Lord Byron 1788–1824: diary, 24 November 1813

11 Until you understand a writer's ignorance, presume yourself ignorant of his understanding.

Samuel Taylor Coleridge 1772–1834: *Biographia Literaria* (1817)

12 All clean and comfortable I sit down to write.

John Keats 1795–1821: letter to George and Georgiana Keats, 17 September 1819

13 I know no person so perfectly disagreeable and even dangerous as an author.

William IV 1765–1837: Philip Ziegler *King William IV* (1971)

14 When once the itch of literature comes over a man, nothing can cure it but the scratching of a pen.

Samuel Lover 1797–1868: *Handy Andy* (1842)

15 An author in his book must be like God in his universe, present everywhere and visible nowhere.

Gustave Flaubert 1821–80: letter, 9 December 1852

1 Pray know that when a man begins writing a book he never gives over. The evil with which he is beset is as inveterate as drinking—as exciting as gambling.

Anthony Trollope 1815–82: letter to an unknown correspondent, *c.*1855; *Letters* (1983) vol. 1

2 Writers, like teeth, are divided into incisors and grinders.

Walter Bagehot 1826–77: *Estimates of some Englishmen and Scotchmen* (1858) 'The First Edinburgh Reviewers'

3 We authors, Ma'am.
to Queen Victoria after the publication of Leaves from the Journal of our Life in the Highlands *in 1868*

Benjamin Disraeli 1804–81: Elizabeth Longford *Victoria R.I.* (1964)

4 One man is as good as another until he has written a book.

Benjamin Jowett 1817–93: Evelyn Abbott and Lewis Campbell (eds.) *Life and Letters of Benjamin Jowett* (1897)

5 We work in the dark—we do what we can—we give what we have. Our doubt is our passion and our passion is our task. The rest is the madness of art.

Henry James 1843–1916: 'The Middle Years' (short story, 1893)

6 The Llama is a woolly sort of fleecy hairy goat,
With an indolent expression and an undulating throat
Like an unsuccessful literary man.

Hilaire Belloc 1870–1953: *More Beasts for Worse Children* (1897) 'The Llama'

7 An artist is a dreamer consenting to dream of the actual world.

George Santayana 1863–1952: *The Life of Reason* (1905)

8 Can anything be more bitter than to be doomed to a life of literature and hot-water bottles when one's a pirate at heart?.

Lytton Strachey 1880–1932: to George Mallory, 1913; Michael Holroyd *Lytton Strachey* (1994 rev. ed.)

9 I have often thought that the best mode of life for me would be to sit in the innermost room of a spacious locked cellar with my writing things and my lamp. Food would be brought and always put down far away from my room . . . For who am I?

Franz Kafka 1883–1924: attributed

10 In this
most Christian of worlds all poets
are Jews.

Marina Tsvetaeva 1892–1941: 'Poem of the End' (1924)

11 Every author really wants to have letters printed in the papers. Unable to make the grade, he drops down a rung of the ladder and writes novels.

P. G. Wodehouse 1881–1975: *Louder and Funnier* (1932)

12 A serious writer is not to be confounded with a solemn writer. A serious writer may be a hawk or a buzzard or even a popinjay, but a solemn writer is always a bloody owl.

Ernest Hemingway 1899–1961: *Death in the Afternoon* (1932)

13 A writer wastes nothing.

F. Scott Fitzgerald 1896–1940: Sheilah Graham and Gerald Frank *Beloved Infidel* (1959)

1 Master of nuance and scruple
Pray for me and for all writers living or dead;
Because there are many whose works
Are in better taste than their lives; because there is no end
To the vanity of our calling: make intercession
For the treason of all clerks.

W. H. Auden 1907–73: 'At the Grave of Henry James' (1945)

2 An artist is his own fault.

John O'Hara 1905–70: *The Portable F. Scott Fitzgerald* (1945)

3 The great mass of human beings are not acutely selfish. After the age of about thirty they abandon individual ambition—in many cases, indeed, they almost abandon the sense of being individuals at all—and live chiefly for others, or are simply smothered under drudgery. But there is also the minority of gifted, wilful people who are determined to live their own lives to the end, and writers belong in this class.

George Orwell 1903–50: 'Why I Write' (1946)

4 Coleridge was a drug addict. Poe was an alcoholic. Marlowe was stabbed by a man whom he was treacherously trying to stab. Pope took money to keep a woman's name out of a satire then wrote a piece so that she could still be recognized anyhow. Chatterton killed himself. Byron was accused of incest. Do you still want to be a writer—and if so, why?

Bennett Cerf 1898–1971: *Shake Well Before Using* (1948)

5 He [the writer] must teach himself that the basest of all things is to be afraid and, teaching himself that, forget it forever, leaving no room in his workshop for anything but the old verities and truths of the heart, the old universal truths lacking which any story is ephemeral and doomed—love and honor and pity and pride and compassion and sacrifice.

William Faulkner 1897–1962: Nobel Prize speech, 1950

6 The greatest advantage of being a writer is that you can *spy* on people. You're there listening to every word, but part of you is observing. Everything is useful to a writer, you see—every scrap, even the longest and most boring of luncheon parties.

to Michael Korda on Alexander Korda's yacht, Antibes, 1950

Graham Greene 1904–91: in *New Yorker* 25 March 1996

7 There is only one position for an artist anywhere: and that is, upright.

Dylan Thomas 1914–53: *Quite Early One Morning* (1954) 'Wales and the Artist'

8 Artists are the antennae of the race, but the bullet-headed many will never learn to trust their great artists.

Ezra Pound 1885–1972: *Literary Essays* (1954)

9 Writing is not a profession but a vocation of unhappiness.

Georges Simenon 1903–89: interview in *Paris Review* Summer 1955

10 The writer's only responsibility is to his art. He will be completely ruthless if he is a good one. He has a dream. It anguishes him so much he must get rid of it. He has no peace until then. Everything goes by the board . . . If a writer has to rob his mother, he will not hesitate; the *Ode on a Grecian Urn* is worth any number of old ladies.

William Faulkner 1897–1962: in *Paris Review* Spring 1956

1 The most essential gift for a good writer is a built-in, shock-proof shit detector. This is the writer's radar and all great writers have had it.

Ernest Hemingway 1899–1961: in *Paris Review* Spring 1958

2 Every educated man should write verse, even if he cannot paint a picture.

Lord Hailsham 1907– : attributed, 1962

3 The author is a modern figure, a product of our society insofar as, emerging from the Middle Ages with English empiricism, French rationalism and the personal faith of the Reformation, it discovered the prestige of the individual, or, as it is more nobly put, the 'human person'.

Roland Barthes 1915–80: *The Death of the Author* (1968)

4 Some writers take to drink, others take to audiences.

Gore Vidal 1925– : in *Paris Review* 1981

5 The writer must be universal in sympathy and an outcast by nature: only then can he see clearly.

Julian Barnes 1946– : *Flaubert's Parrot* (1984)

6 When I was a little boy, they called me a liar, but now that I am grown up, they call me a writer.

Isaac Bashevis Singer 1904–91: in *Bibliophile* July 1986

7 You should find that your writing overcomes the besetting feeling of vagueness and ennui which is characteristic of everyday life.

Edmund White 1940– : in interview in *Paris Review* 1988

8 All experience is good for writers—except for physical pain.

William Trevor 1928– : in *Paris Review* 1989

9 Writing is neither profession nor vocation, but an incurable illness. Those who give up are not writers and never were; those who persevere do so not from pluck or determination, but because they cannot help it: they are sick and advice is an impertinence.

Hugh Leonard 1926– : *Out After Dark* (1989)

10 One of the things a writer is for is to say the unsayable, speak the unspeakable and ask difficult questions.

Salman Rushdie 1947– : in *Independent on Sunday* 10 September 1995 'Quotes of the Week'

Writer's Block

11 It's almost a month now, and I've scarcely finished
A single page.

Martial AD c.40–c.104: *Epigrammata*, tr. James Michie

12 But words came halting forth, wanting Invention's stay;
Invention, Nature's child, fled step-dame Study's
blows . . .
Biting my truant pen, beating myself for spite,
'Fool,' said my Muse to me; 'look in thy heart and write.'

Philip Sidney 1554–86: *Astrophil and Stella* (1591) sonnet 1

13 Invention flags, his brain goes muddy,
And black despair succeeds brown study.

William Congreve 1670–1729: *An Impossible Thing* (1720)

14 You beat your pate, and fancy wit will come:
Knock as you please, there's nobody at home.

Alexander Pope 1688–1744: 'Epigram: You beat your pate' (1732)

1 Tom Birch is as brisk as a bee in conversation; but no sooner does he take a pen in his hand, than it becomes a torpedo to him, and benumbs all his faculties.

Samuel Johnson 1709–84: James Boswell *Life of Samuel Johnson* (1791) 1743

2 Poetry is a distinct faculty—it won't come when called—you may as well whistle for a wind.

Lord Byron 1788–1824: E. J. Trelawny *Records of Shelley, Byron and the Author* (1878)

3 But I must say to the Muse of fiction, as the Earl of Pembroke said to the ejected nun of Wilton, 'Go spin, you jade, go spin!'

Sir Walter Scott 1771–1832: diary, 8 February 1826

4 Two or three years ago . . . he wouldn't sit at his desk after a night of conjugal effusion, knowing beforehand he couldn't construct a sentence, write a line. Now it's the opposite. After eight or ten days of mediocre work, coitus induces a slight fever that unblocks him.

of Zola

Edmond de Goncourt 1822–96: diary, 4 April 1875

5 If one waits for the right time to come before writing, the right time never comes.

James Russell Lowell 1819–91: letter to Charles Eliot Norton, 22 April 1883

6 Birds build—but not I build; no, but strain,
Time's eunuch, and not breed one work that wakes.
Mine, O thou lord of life, send my roots rain.

Gerard Manley Hopkins 1844–89: 'Thou art indeed just, Lord' (written 1889)

7 Reardon . . . walked in the darkness round the outer circle of Regent's Park, racking his fagged brain in a hopeless search for characters, situations, motives.

George Gissing 1857–1903: *New Grub Street* (1891)

8 I sit down for eight hours every day—and sitting down is all. In the course of that working day of eight hours I write three sentences which I erase before leaving the table in despair.

Joseph Conrad 1857–1924: letter to Edward Garnett, 29 March 1898

9 No pen, no ink, no table, no room, no time, no quiet, no inclination.

James Joyce 1882–1941: letter to his brother, 7 December 1906

10 All things can tempt me from this craft of verse.

W. B. Yeats 1865–1939: 'All Things Can Tempt Me' (1909)

11 In barrenness, at any rate, I hold a high place among English poets, excelling even Gray.

A. E. Housman 1859–1936: letter, 28 February 1910

12 Full 3 weeks—no two consecutive ideas, no six consecutive words to be found anywhere in the world. I would prefer a red hot gridiron to that cold blankness.

Joseph Conrad 1857–1924: letter to Galsworthy, May 1911

13 For the last two weeks I have written scarcely anything. I have been idle. I have *failed.*

Katherine Mansfield 1888–1923: diary, 13 November 1921

14 I am overcome by my own amazing sloth . . . Can you please forgive me and believe that it is really because I want to do something well that I don't do it at all?

Elizabeth Bishop 1911–79: letter to Marianne Moore, 25 February 1937

15 If you are in difficulties with a book, try the element of surprise: attack it at an hour when it isn't expecting it.

H. G. Wells 1866–1946: attributed

1 Coleridge received the Person from Porlock
And ever after called him a curse,
Then why did he hurry to let him in?
He could have hid in the house.
It was not right of Coleridge in fact it was wrong
(But often we all do wrong)
As the truth is I think he was already stuck
With Kubla Khan . . .

Stevie Smith 1902–71: 'Thoughts about the "Person from Porlock" ' (1962); cf. **112:6**

2 An hour at a poem without adding a single (sodding) *word* . . . One never gets any better at this lark.

Philip Larkin 1922–85: letter, 2 May 1974

3 Any memory of pain is deeply buried, and there is nothing more painful for a writer than an inability to work.

John Cheever 1912–82: in *Writers at Work* (5th series, 1981)

4 At the beginning of the 'block' one says to oneself, 'This time it's the *coup de grâce*; it's the end' . . . Only dreams enable me to fight these painful blocks.

Graham Greene 1904–91: Marie-Françoise Allain *The Other Man, Conversations with Graham Greene* (1983)

5 I am afraid the compulsion to write poems left me about seven years ago, since when I have written virtually nothing. Naturally this is a disappointment, but I would sooner write no poems than bad poems.

Philip Larkin 1922–85: letter, 11 August 1984

6 You can always write something. You write limericks. You write a love letter. You do something to get you into the habit of writing again, to bring back the desire.

Erskine Caldwell 1903–87: George Plimpton (ed.) *The Writer's Chapbook* (1989)

7 I often read, with amazement, of people who suffer from writer's block; I might enjoy a wee block, just to have time to catch my breath.

Robertson Davies 1913–95: in *Paris Review* 1989

Writing see also **Writers**

8 Be a scribe! Engrave this in your heart!
So that your name might live on like theirs!
The scroll is better than the carved stone.
A man has died: his corpse is dust,
And his people have passed from the land.
It is a book which makes him be remembered
In the mouth of the speaker who reads him.
composed by an Ancient Egyptian scribe, c.1300 BC

Anonymous: M. Lichtheim *Ancient Egyptian Literature* (1973) vol. 1

9 I and Pangur Bán, my cat,
'Tis a like task we are at;
Hunting mice is his delight,
Hunting words I sit all night.
Better far than praise of men
'Tis to sit with book and pen;
Pangur bears me no ill will,
He too plies his simple skill . . .
. . . So in peace our tasks we ply,
Pangur Bán, my cat, and I;
In our arts we find our bliss,
I have mine and he has his.

Anonymous: 'Pangur Bán', Latin poem found in the margins of an 8th-century *Epistles of St Paul* belonging to an Austrian monastery founded by Irish monks; translated 1931 by Robin Flower

Practice every day has made
Pangur perfect in his trade;
I get wisdom day and night
Turning darkness into light.

1 He that will write well in any tongue, must follow this counsel of Aristotle, to speak as the common people do, to think as wise men do; and so should every man understand him, and the judgement of wise men allow him.

Roger Ascham 1515–68: *Toxophilus* (1545)

2 Making a book is a craft, as is making a clock; it takes more than wit to become an author.

Jean de la Bruyère 1645–96: *Les Caractères ou les moeurs de ce siècle* (1688) 'Des Ouvrages de l'esprit'

3 Learn to write well, or not to write at all.

John Sheffield, Duke of Buckingham and Normanby 1648–1721: 'An Essay upon Satire' (1689)

4 Eye Nature's walks, shoot Folly as it flies,
And catch the Manners living as they rise.
Laugh where we must, be candid where we can;
But vindicate the ways of God to man.

Alexander Pope 1688–1744: *An Essay on Man* Epistle 1 (1733)

5 Instruction, Madam, is the pill; amusement is the gilding.

Samuel Richardson 1689–1761: letter 22 September 1755

6 The only end of writing is to enable the readers better to enjoy life, or better to endure it.

Samuel Johnson 1709–84: *A Free Enquiry* (1757)

7 [I] will go through almost anything with a degree of satisfaction if I am to put an account of it in writing.

James Boswell 1740–95: diary, 1762–3; Frank Brady *James Boswell* (1984)

8 Writing, when properly managed (as you may be sure I think mine is) is but a different name for conversation.

Laurence Sterne 1713–68: *Tristram Shandy* (1759–67)

9 Any fool may write a most valuable book by chance, if he will only tell us what he heard and saw with veracity.

Thomas Gray 1716–71: letter to Horace Walpole, 25 February 1768

10 The greatest part of a writer's time is spent in reading, in order to write: a man will turn over half a library to make one book.

Samuel Johnson 1709–84: James Boswell *Life of Samuel Johnson* (1791) 6 April 1775

11 It is very difficult to depict from memory that which is *natural* in us; one too easily depicts that which is *factitious*, that which is *acted*, because the effort needed to *act* it imprints it on the memory. Training myself to recall my natural sentiments is a study which could give me the talent of Shakespeare.

Stendhal 1783–1842: diary, 1805

12 The artist must be in his work as God is in creation, invisible and all-powerful; one must sense him everywhere but never see him.

Gustave Flaubert 1821–80: letter to Mademoiselle Leroyer de Chantepie, 18 March 1857

13 My writing is simply a set of experiments in life—an endeavour to see what our thought and emotion may be capable of.

George Eliot 1819–80: letter, 25 January 1876

1 I finished on Thursday the novel I was writing, and on Friday I began another. Nothing really frightens me but the idea of enforced idleness. As long as I can write books even though they be not published, I think that I can be happy.

Anthony Trollope 1815–82: letter, 21 December 1880

2 The writer's problem is, how to strike the balance between the uncommon and the ordinary so as on the one hand to give interest, on the other to give reality.

Thomas Hardy 1840–1928: notebook July 1881

3 You are right in demanding that an artist should take a conscious attitude to his work, but you confuse two conceptions: *the solution of a question and the correct setting of a question*. The latter alone is obligatory for the artist. In *Anna Karenina* and *Onegin* not a single problem is solved, but they satisfy completely because all the problems are set correctly. The court is obliged to submit the case fairly, but let the jury do the deciding, each according to its own judgement.

Anton Chekhov 1860–1904: letter to Alexei Suvorin, 27 October 1888

4 My task which I am trying to achieve is by the power of the written word, to make you hear, to make you feel—it is, before all, to make you *see*. That—and no more, and it is everything.

Joseph Conrad 1857–1924: *The Nigger of the Narcissus* (1897) preface

5 When I was writing 'The Shadow of the Glen', some years ago, I got more aid than any learning could have given me from a chink in the floor of the old Wicklow house where I was staying, that let me hear what was being said by the servant girls in the kitchen.

John Millington Synge 1871–1909: *Playboy of the Western World* preface

6 Neither Christ nor Buddha nor Socrates wrote a book, for to do that is to exchange life for a logical process.

W. B. Yeats 1865–1939: *Estrangement* (1909)

7 Writing is not a recreation I care for.

W. G. Grace 1848–1915: in introduction to *Cricketing Reminiscences and Personal Recollections* (1980)

8 The artist, like the God of the creation, remains within or behind or beyond or above his handiwork, invisible, refined out of existence, indifferent, paring his fingernails.

James Joyce 1882–1941: *A Portrait of the Artist as a Young Man* (1916)

9 My theory of writing I can sum up in one sentence. An author ought to write for the youth of his own generation, the critics of the next, and the schoolmasters of ever after.

F. Scott Fitzgerald 1896–1940: letter to the Booksellers' Convention, April 1920

10 Probably . . . the larger part of the labour of an author in composing his work is critical labour; the labour of sifting, combining, constructing, expunging, correcting, testing: this frightful toil is as much critical as creative.

T. S. Eliot 1888–1965: 'The Function of Criticism' (1923)

11 First I write one sentence: then I write another. That's how I write. But I have a feeling writing ought to be like running through a field.

Lytton Strachey 1880–1932: in conversation with Max Beerbohm; Virginia Woolf *A Writer's Diary* (1953) 1 November 1938

1 All good books are alike in that they are truer than if they had really happened and after you are finished reading one you will feel that all that happened to you and afterwards it all belongs to you: the good and the bad, the ecstasy, the remorse and sorrow, the people and the places and how the weather was. If you can get so that you can give that to people, then you are a writer.

Ernest Hemingway 1899–1961: in *Esquire* December 1934 'Old Newsman Writes'

2 Often I think writing is a sheer paring away of oneself leaving always something thinner, barer, more meagre.

F. Scott Fitzgerald 1896–1940: letter to his daughter Scottie (Frances Scott Fitzgerald), 27 April 1940

3 By an epiphany he meant a sudden spiritual manifestation, whether in vulgarity of speech or of gesture or in a memorable phase of the mind itself. He believed that it was for the man of letters to recover these epiphanies with extreme care, seeing that they themselves are the most delicate and evanescent of moments.

James Joyce 1882–1941: *Stephen Hero* (1944); part of a first draft of *A Portrait of the Artist as a Young Man*

4 An author is like a horse pulling a coal-cart down an icy hill; he ought to stop, but when he reflects that it would probably kill him to try, he goes right on, neighing and rolling his eyes.

Robertson Davies 1913–95: in 1959; *The Enthusiasms of Robertson Davies* (1990)

5 Writing is the destruction of every voice, of every point of origin. Writing is that neutral, composite, oblique space where our subject slips away, the negative where all identity is lost, starting with the very identity of the body writing.

Roland Barthes 1915–80: *The Death of the Author* (1968)

6 The responsibility of a writer is to excavate the experience of the people who produced him.

James Baldwin 1924–87: *A Dialogue* (1973)

7 Writing is like getting married. One should never commit oneself until one is amazed at one's luck.

Iris Murdoch 1919– : *The Black Prince* 'Bradley Pearson's Foreword' (1973)

8 I love writing. I never feel really comfortable unless I am either actually writing or have a story going. I could not stop writing.

P. G. Wodehouse 1881–1975: George Plimpton (ed.) *The Writer's Chapbook* (1989)

9 The slow discovery by a novelist of his individual method can be exciting, but a moment comes in middle age when he feels he no longer controls his method; he has become its prisoner.

Graham Greene 1904–91: *Ways of Escape* (1980)

10 If you don't spend every morning of your life writing, it's awfully difficult to know what to do otherwise.

Anthony Powell 1905– : interview in *Observer* 3 April 1984

11 Writing is very improvisational. It's like trying to fix a broken sewing machine with safety pins and rubber bands. A lot of tinkering.

Margaret Atwood 1939– : in an interview, December 1986; Earl G. Ingersoll (ed.) *Margaret Atwood: Conversations* (1990)

12 Oh, I used to read the Sears and Roebuck catalogue, every year when it came out. But I learned early in life that you can be a reader or a writer. I decided to be a writer.

Erskine Caldwell 1903–87: George Plimpton (ed.) *The Writer's Chapbook* (1989)

1 Writing is *play* in the same way that playing the piano is 'play', or putting on a theatrical 'play' is play. Just because something's fun doesn't mean it isn't serious.

Margaret Atwood 1939– : in an interview, November 1989; Earl G. Ingersoll (ed.) *Margaret Atwood: Conversations* (1990)

2 All novelists know their art proceeds by indirection. When tempted by didacticism, the writer should imagine a spruce sea-captain eyeing the storm ahead, bustling from instrument to instrument in a catherine wheel of gold braid, expelling crisp orders down the speaking tube. But there is nobody below decks; the engine-room was never installed, and the rudder broke off centuries ago.

Julian Barnes 1946– : *A History of the World in 10½ Chapters* (1989) 'Parenthesis'

3 I can't imagine not needing to write. I should be very unhappy if I couldn't write.

Iris Murdoch 1919– : Rosemary Hartill *Writers Revealed* (1989)

4 One *must* avoid ambition *in order to* write. Otherwise something else is the goal: some kind of power beyond the power of language. And the power of language, it seems to me, is the only kind of power a writer is entitled to.

Cynthia Ozick 1928– : George Plimpton (ed.) *The Writer's Chapbook* (1989)

5 Writing a novel was like driving to Edinburgh (from London). You knew the first 10 miles very well. You knew where you were heading. And you knew a few of the places along the way. The rest you filled in as you went along, or perhaps discovered.

Kingsley Amis 1922–95: remark, 11 December 1992, in *Sunday Times* 17 March 1996

6 You don't give up writing until writing gives you up.

Rumer Godden 1907– : Michael Rosen and Jill Burridge *Treasure Islands 2* (1993)

7 My Catholic girlhood taught me two disciplines that are invaluable, I think, for writing: the daily examination of conscience and the meditation on holy pictures.

Marina Warner 1946– : Clare Boylan (ed.) *The Agony and the Ego* (1993)

on his discovery of writing:

8 It was sorta like being an athlete and using only the left side of your body, and then finding a game where you could use your whole body.

David Foster Wallace 1962– : interview in *Daily Telegraph* 29 June 1996

9 I've always thought people write because they are not living properly.

Beryl Bainbridge 1933– : interview in *Daily Telegraph* 10 September 1996

10 If imagination cannot be taught, the craft of writing can.

Andrew Motion 1952– : Barry Turner *The Writer's Companion* (1996)

Writers and their Works

Joseph Addison 1672–1719

1 Whoever wishes to attain an English style, familiar but not coarse, and elegant but not ostentatious, must give his days and nights to the volumes of Addison.

Samuel Johnson 1709–84: *Lives of the English Poets* (1779–81) 'Addison'

Kingsley Amis 1922–95 see also **46:1, 85:3**

2 *Lucky Jim* is a remarkable novel. It has been greatly praised and widely read, but I have not noticed that any of the reviewers have remarked on its ominous significance. I am told that today rather more than 60 per cent of the men who go to the universities go on a Government grant. This is a new class that has entered upon the scene . . . They are scum.

W. Somerset Maugham 1874–1965: in *Sunday Times* 25 December 1955

3 When it comes down to it, Lucky Jim is Just William, bigger and bespectacled, literate and funny, but scarcely grown-up. What Christine is to the one, a bag of bulls' eyes is to the other.

Simon Gray 1936– : in *The Times* 3 February 1966

4 That's Kingsley Amis, and there's no known cure.
on spotting him looking disgruntled at a party

Robert Graves 1895–1985: attributed

5 Kingsley Amis never writes a novel without bellyaching about something. It's an awful bore.

Robertson Davies 1913–95: in *Independent on Sunday* 9 April 1995

Martin Amis 1949–

6 A kind of male turkeycocking which is extremely bad for the industry.
on Martin Amis's demands for a large advance on a new book; cf. **70:1**

A. S. Byatt 1936– : in *Sunday Times* 8 January 1995

7 If I was reviewing Martin under a pseudonym, I would say he works too hard and it shows.

Kingsley Amis 1922–95: in *Guardian* 26 August 1995

8 Each of his sentences bears its manufacturer's logo.

Adam Mars-Jones 1954– : in *Waterstone's Quarterly Guide* Spring/Summer 1996; attributed

9 The greatest pyrotechnician of his generation . . . he's got serious, he's got ideas. The GUT—Great Universal Themes—are all there now, aren't they.

Craig Raine 1944– : in *Waterstone's Quarterly Guide* Spring/Summer 1996; attributed

Maya Angelou 1928–

10 What I would really like said about me is that I dared to love.

Maya Angelou 1928– : interview in *USA Today* 5 March 1985

1 In all my work what I try to say is that as human beings we are more alike than we are unalike.

Maya Angelou 1928– : interview in *New York Times* 20 January 1993

Matthew Arnold 1822–88

2 I met Matthew Arnold and had a few words with him. He is not as handsome as his photographs—or as his poetry.

Henry James 1843–1916: letter to Charles Eliot Norton, 31 March 1873

3 Arnold is a dandy Isaiah, a poet without passion, whose verse, written in a surplice, is for freshmen and for gentle maidens who will be wooed to the arms of these future rectors.

George Meredith 1828–1909: in *Fortnightly Review* July 1909

W. H. Auden 1907–73

4 I sometimes think of his poetry as a great war, admire intensely the mature, religious, and logical fighter, and deprecate the boy bushranger.

Dylan Thomas 1914–53: in *New Verse* November 1937

5 The high-water mark, so to speak, of Socialist literature is W. H. Auden, a sort of gutless Kipling.

George Orwell 1903–50: *The Road to Wigan Pier* (1937)

6 The most violent action he ever saw was when he was playing table tennis at Tossa del Mar on behalf of the Spanish Republicans—apart from the violent exercise he got with his knife and fork.

commenting on Auden's war record

Roy Campbell 1901–57: *Nine* (1950)

7 He is the dirtiest man I have ever liked.

Igor Stravinsky 1882–1971: Richard Davenport-Hines *W. H. Auden* (1995)

8 He makes me suffer and commit follies, without which I should soon become like the later Tennyson.

of his partner, Chester Kallman

W. H. Auden 1907–73: Richard Davenport-Hines *W. H. Auden* (1995)

9 My face looks like a wedding-cake left out in the rain.

W. H. Auden 1907–73: Humphrey Carpenter *W. H. Auden* (1981)

10 People sometimes divide others into those you laugh at and those you laugh with. The young Auden was someone you could laugh-at-with.

Stephen Spender 1909–95: *W. H. Auden* (1973)

11 As if life itself had delineated a kind of face-scape to make manifest the 'heart's invisible furies'.

of W. H. Auden's famous wrinkles

Hannah Arendt 1906–75: Richard Davenport-Hines *W. H. Auden* (1995)

12 He didn't love God, just fancied him.

Anonymous: unattributed comment; John Mortimer *In Character* (1983)

13 Auden of the last years, when he had begun to resemble in his own person an ample, flopping, ambulatory volume of the *OED* in carpet slippers.

Seamus Heaney 1939– : in *London Review of Books* 4 June 1987

Jane Austen 1775–1817 see also 3:8, 55:8, 203:9

1 I think I may boast myself to be, with all possible vanity, the most unlearned and uninformed female who ever dared to be an authoress.

Jane Austen 1775–1817: letter, 11 December 1815

2 Till 'Pride and Prejudice' showed what a precious gem was hidden in that unbending case, she was no more regarded in society than a poker or a fire-screen, or any other thin upright piece of wood or iron that fills its corner in peace and quietness. The case is very different now: she is still a poker—but a poker of whom everyone is afraid.

Mary Russell Mitford 1787–1855: letter, 1815

3 What should I do with your strong, manly, spirited sketches, full of variety and glow?—How could I possibly join them on to the little bit (two inches wide) of ivory on which I work with so fine a brush, as produces little effect after much labour?

Jane Austen 1775–1817: letter to J. Edward Austen, 16 December 1816

4 The Big Bow-Wow strain I can do myself like any now going; but the exquisite touch, which renders ordinary commonplace things and characters interesting, from the truth of the description and the sentiment, is denied to me.

Sir Walter Scott 1771–1832: W. E. K. Anderson (ed.) *Journals of Sir Walter Scott* (1972) 14 March 1826

5 Miss Austen being, as you say, without 'sentiment', without *poetry*, maybe *is* sensible, real (more *real* than *true*), but she cannot be great.

Charlotte Brontë 1816–55: letter to George Henry Lewes, 18 January 1848

6 When I take up one of Jane Austen's books . . . I feel like a barkeeper entering the kingdom of heaven. I know what his sensation would be and his private comments. He would not find the place to his taste, and he would probably say so.

Mark Twain 1835–1910: Q. D. Leavis *Fiction and the Reading Public* (1932)

7 You could not shock her more than she shocks me;
Beside her Joyce seems innocent as grass,
It makes me most uncomfortable to see
An English spinster of the middle class
Describe the amorous effects of 'brass',
Reveal so frankly and with such sobriety
The economic basis of society.

W. H. Auden 1907–73: *Letter to Lord Byron* (1936)

8 Regulated hatred.

D. W. Harding 1906– : title of an article on the novels of Jane Austen, in *Scrutiny* March 1940

9 Her novels are the Maxims of La Rochefoucauld set in motion.

Giuseppe di Lampedusa 1896–1957: *The Sirens and Selected Writings* (translated by David Gilmour, 1995)

10 Austen's peculiar tone of grave seriousness towards morals and satirical benevolence towards manners.

Edmund White 1940– : *Review of Contemporary Literature* (1986)

11 I hope she knows how big she is in Uruguay.
accepting an Oscar for the screenplay of Sense and Sensibility *(1995 film)*

Emma Thompson 1959– : in Los Angeles, 26 March 1996; in *Daily Telegraph* 27 March 1996

1 Jane Austen finds sex as demonic as Sade does. She finds it demonic and therefore locks it out.

J. M. Coetzee 1940– : *Giving Offence* (1996)

Francis Bacon 1561–1626

2 The fear of every man that heard him was, lest he should make an end.

Ben Jonson c.1573–1637: *Timber, or Discoveries made upon Men and Matter* (1641) 'Dominus Verulamius'

3 He was no striped frieze; he was shot silk.

Lytton Strachey 1880–1932: *Elizabeth and Essex* (1928)

Honoré de Balzac 1799–1850 see also 3:14

4 If I'm not a genius, I'm done for.

Honoré de Balzac 1799–1850: letter to his sister Laure, 1819

5 Between you and me, I am not deep, but I am very wide, and it takes time to walk around me.

Honoré de Balzac 1799–1850: letter to Countess Maffei, 1837

6 The Russians make us debate some point of view peculiar to the author, Flaubert etherealizes all with his conviction that life is no better than a smell of cooking through a grating. But Balzac leaves us when the book is closed amid the crowd that fills the boxes and the galleries of grand opera.

W. B. Yeats 1865–1939: 'Louis Lambert' (July, 1934)

7 I am inclined to think that Balzac's reputation rests on a lot of neat generalizations about life.

James Joyce 1882–1941: Frank Budgen *James Joyce and the Making of Ulysses* (1934)

8 Balzac observed all the things that Marx did not.

Régis Debray 1940– : *Teachers, Writers, Celebrities* (1981)'Balzac, or Zoology Today'

9 Someone once said Balzac's only fault is that he makes all of his characters into geniuses, like himself. What a wonderful fault!

Edmund White 1940– : interview in *Paris Review* 1988

J. M. Barrie 1860–1937

10 A little child whom the Gods have whispered to.

Mrs Patrick Campbell 1865–1940: letter to G. B. Shaw, January 1913

11 The cheerful clatter of Sir James Barrie's cans as he went round with the milk of human kindness.

Philip Guedalla 1889–1944: *Supers and Supermen* (1920) 'Some Critics'

Charles Baudelaire 1821–67 see also 3:13

12 The only downright repulsive face of a poet that I am yet acquainted with is that of Baudelaire.

George Gissing 1857–1903: *Commonplace Book* (1962)

Simone de Beauvoir 1908–86

1 Miss de Beauvoir has written an enormous book about women and it is soon clear that she does not like being a woman.
reviewing The Second Sex

Stevie Smith 1902–71: in *World Review* 1950s; Jack Barbera and William McBrien *Stevie* (1985)

Samuel Beckett 1906–89

2 A special virtue attaches to plays which remind the drama of how much it can do without and still exist. By all the known criteria, Samuel Beckett's 'Waiting for Godot' is a dramatic vacuum. Pity the critic who sees a chink in its armour, for it is all chink.

Kenneth Tynan 1927–80: *Curtains* (1961) 'Waiting for Godot'

3 I couldn't have done it otherwise, gone on I mean. I could not have gone on through the awful wretched mess of life without having left a stain upon the silence.

Samuel Beckett 1906–89: Deirdre Bair *Samuel Beckett* (1978)

Max Beerbohm 1872–1956

4 The younger generation is knocking at the door, and as I open it there steps spritely in the incomparable Max.
on handing over the theatre review column to Max Beerbohm

George Bernard Shaw 1856–1950: in *Saturday Review* 21 May 1898 'Valedictory'

5 Tell me, when you are alone with Max, does he take off his face and reveal his mask?

Oscar Wilde 1854–1900: W. H. Auden *Forewords and Afterwords* (1973)

6 He has the most remarkable and seductive genius—and I should say about the smallest in the world.

Lytton Strachey 1880–1932: letter to Clive Bell, 4 December 1917

Hilaire Belloc 1870–1953

7 Wells and I, contemplating the Chesterbelloc, recognize at once a very amusing pantomime elephant, the front legs being that very exceptional and un-English individual Hilaire Belloc, and the hind legs that extravagant freak of French nature, G. K. Chesterton.

George Bernard Shaw 1856–1950: in *New Age* 15 February 1908

Saul Bellow 1915–

8 My eyes are on eternity.
to his biographer James Atlas, who is thinking 'He really doesn't keep up'

Saul Bellow 1915– : to his biographer on 30 August 1992; in *New Yorker* 26 June–3 July 1995

Alan Bennett 1934–

1 Winsome, lose some.
cancelling an interview with the Independent *after the paper described him as winsome*

Alan Bennett 1934– : in *Daily Telegraph* 18 March 1995 'They Said It'

2 There was a time when I thought my only connection with the literary world would be that I had once delivered meat to T. S. Eliot's mother-in-law.

Alan Bennett 1934– : *Writing Home* (1994)

3 I'm less genial than people think, but I'm too timid to seem nasty.

Alan Bennett 1934– : in *Observer* 22 October 1995

Arnold Bennett 1867–1931

4 I'd like to write an essay on [Arnold] Bennett—sort of pig in clover.

D. H. Lawrence 1885–1930: letter to Aldous Huxley, 27 March 1928

5 It was perhaps a part of his competent autonomy that Bennett was so remarkably free from the normal infantilism of the human male. He was not so dependent upon women for his comfort and self-respect as most of us are; he was not very deeply interested in them from that point of view. And he had not that capacity for illusion about them which is proper to our sex. The women in his books are for the most part good hard Staffordshire ware, capable, sisterly persons with a tang to their tongues.

H. G. Wells 1866–1946: *Experiment in Autobiography* (1934)

6 Arnold Bennett knew his eggs. Whatever his interest in good writing, he never showed the public anything but AVARICE. Consequently they adored him.

Ezra Pound 1885–1972: letter to Laurence Pollinger, May 1937

John Betjeman 1906–84 see also 54:10

7 The quickest way to start a punch-up between two British literary critics is to ask them what they think of the poems of Sir John Betjeman.

Philip Larkin 1922–85: *Required Writing* (1983)

8 His output was utterly staggering considering he was always having lunch and quite a lot to drink.
a daughter's view

Candida Lycett Green 1942– : in *Independent on Sunday* 22 October 1995 'Quotes of the Week'

William Blake 1757–1827

9 Blake saw a treefull of angels at Peckham Rye,
And his hands could lay hold on the tiger's terrible heart.
Blake knew how deep is Hell, and Heaven how high,
And could build the universe from one tiny part.

William Rose Benét 1886–1950: 'Mad Blake' (1918)

10 Or that William Blake
Who beat upon the wall
Till truth obeyed his call.

W. B. Yeats 1865–1939: 'An Acre of Grass' (*c.*1938)

Jorge Luis Borges 1899–1986

1 Although at my age almost everyone I know is dead, I prefer to live my life looking forward. The past is a subject for poems, for elegies, but I try not to think about the past. I would rather spend my time thinking of the future, although quite possibly I have little future left. But I hope to conserve my mind; I hope to continue dreaming and writing. I come from a sad country.

Jorge Luis Borges 1899–1986: in 1984; James Woodall *The Man in the Mirror of the Book* (1996)

James Boswell 1740–95

2 Were you to die, it would be a limb lopped off.

Samuel Johnson 1709–84: A. N. Wilson *Penfriends from Porlock* (1988); attributed

3 It is the story of a mountebank and his zany.
of Boswell's Tour of the Hebrides

Horace Walpole 1717–97: letter to Hon. Henry Conway, 6 October 1785

4 Before I read his book [Boswell's *Life of Johnson*] I thought he was a gentleman who had the misfortune to be mad: I now think he is a madman who has the misfortune not to be a gentleman.

Lord Monboddo 1714–99: E. L. Cloyd *James Burnett, Lord Monboddo* (1972)

5 The Life of Johnson is assuredly a great, a very great work. Homer is not more decidedly the first of heroic poets, Shakespeare is not more decidedly the first of dramatists, Demosthenes is not more decidedly the first of orators, than Boswell is the first of biographers.

Lord Macaulay 1800–59: *Essays Contributed to the Edinburgh Review* (1843) vol. 1 'Samuel Johnson'

6 Sensible, respectable acquaintances such as . . . Fanny Burney began to . . . portray him in their diaries, as the caricature of an acolyte, as a drunken gambling fawning played-out fool whose only purpose was to punctuate whoring and drinking with prowling after Samuel Johnson, pen and tablet clutched in shaking hands.

Roger Hutchinson 1949– : *All the Sweets of Being* (1995)

Elizabeth Bowen 1899–1973

7 She wasn't just a brilliant writer. She was a proper countrywoman. She rode beautifully and gave great, ordinary hunting lunches.

Molly Keane 1904–96: in *Independent* 1 June 1996

Marjorie Bowen 1886–1952

8 Enormous romping vitality and a love for the beauty of language in which one would believe more thoroughly if she did not so frequently split her infinitives neatly down the middle.

Rebecca West 1892–1983: in 1915; *The Young Rebecca* (1982)

1 It was as if I had been supplied once and for all with a subject . . . Goodness has only once found a perfect incarnation in a human body and never will again, but evil can always find a home there. Human nature is not black and white but black and grey. I read all that in *The Viper of Milan* and I looked round and I saw that it was so.
of reading Marjorie Bowen's novel The Viper of Milan *at the age of fourteen*

Graham Greene 1904–91: 'The Lost Childhood' (1951)

Bertolt Brecht 1898–1956

2 I don't regard Brecht as a man of iron-grey purpose and intellect, I think he is a theatrical whore of the first quality.

Peter Hall 1930– : attributed, 1962

Charlotte Brontë 1816–55

3 Here at Haworth . . . one day resembles another—and all have heavy lifeless physiognomies . . . I shall soon be 30—and I have done nothing yet . . . I feel as if we were all buried here —.

Charlotte Brontë 1816–55: letter to Ellen Nussey, 24 March 1845

4 Charlotte has been writing a book, and it is much better than likely.
to his daughters Anne and Emily, on first reading Jane Eyre; *in a letter of August 1850, Mrs Gaskell gives the wording as 'Charlotte has been writing a book–and I think it is a better one than I expected'*

Patrick Brontë 1777–1861: Elizabeth Gaskell *The Life of Charlotte Brontë* (1857)

5 [I have] lost (or won if you like) a whole day in reading it . . . It is a fine book though—the man and woman capital . . . The plot of the story is one with which I am familiar. Some of the love passages made me cry—to the astonishment of John who came in with the coals . . . It is a woman's writing, but whose? . . . Give my respects and thanks to the author.
on reading Jane Eyre *for the first time*

William Makepeace Thackeray 1811–63: letter to W. S. Williams, 23 October 1847

6 She showed that abysses may exist inside a governess and eternities inside a manufacturer.

G. K. Chesterton 1874–1936: *Twelve Types* (1902)

Emily Brontë 1818–48

7 It is rustic all through. It is moorish, and wild, and knotty as a root of heath.
on the setting of Emily Brontë's Wuthering Heights

Charlotte Brontë 1816–55: preface to the 1850 edition

Rupert Brooke 1887–1915

1 A young Apollo, golden-haired,
Stands dreaming on the verge of strife,
Magnificently unprepared
For the long littleness of life.

Frances Cornford 1886–1960: 'Youth' (1910)

2 *The Morning Post*, which has always hitherto disapproved of him, is now loud in his praises because he has conformed to their stupid axiom of literary criticism that the only stuff of poetry is violent physical experience, by dying on active service.

having seen the notice of Brooke's death in The Morning Post

Charles Sorley 1895–1915: letter, April 1915

3 He energized the Garden-Suburb ethos with a certain original talent and the vigour of a prolonged adolescence. His verse exhibits . . . something that is rather like Keats's vulgarity with a Public School accent.

F. R. Leavis 1895–1978: *New Bearings in English Poetry* (1932)

Elizabeth Barrett Browning 1806–61

4 Mrs Browning's death is rather a relief to me, I must say: no more Aurora Leighs, thank God! A woman of real genius, I know; but what is the upshot of it all? She and her sex had better mind the kitchen and their children; and perhaps the poor: except in such things as little novels, they only devote themselves to what men do much better, leaving that which men do worse or not at all.

Edward Fitzgerald 1809–83: letter to W. H. Thompson, 15 July 1861; cf. **284:6**

5 The simple truth is that she was the poet, and I the clever person by comparison.

Robert Browning 1812–89: letter to Isa Blagden, 19 August 1871

6 Ay, dead! and were yourself alive, good Fitz,
How to return your thanks would pass my wits.
Kicking you seems the common lot of curs—
While more appropriate greeting lends you grace:
Surely to spit there glorifies your face—
Spitting from lips once sanctified by Hers.

rejoinder to Edward Fitzgerald, who had 'thanked God my wife was dead'

Robert Browning 1812–89: in *Athenaeum* 13 July 1889; cf. **284:4**

Robert Browning 1812–89 see also 249:9

7 A great gossip and a very 'sympathetic' easy creature.

Henry James 1843–1916: letter, 31 January 1877

8 One of my latest sensations was going one day to Lady Airlie's to hear Browning read his own poems—with the comfort of finding that, at least, if you don't understand them, he himself apparently understands them even less. He read them as if he hated them and would like to bite them to pieces.

Henry James 1843–1916: letter, 26 July 1880

1 When it was written, God and Robert Browning knew what it meant; now only God knows.
of Sordello

Robert Browning 1812–89: attributed

2 Meredith's a prose Browning, and so is Browning.

Oscar Wilde 1854–1900: *Intentions* (1891) 'The Critic as Artist'

3 Chaos, illumined by flashes of lightning.
on Robert Browning's 'style'

Oscar Wilde 1854–1900: Ada Leverson *Letters to the Sphinx* (1930); cf. **316:2**

Arthur Bryant 1899–1985

4 He is no Thucydides.
on being asked whether he thought Arthur Bryant was a great historian, on the occasion of Bryant's 80th birthday

Hugh Trevor-Roper 1914– : Andrew Roberts *Eminent Churchillians* (1994)

5 This Uriah Heep of historical writing.

Andrew Roberts 1963– : *Eminent Churchillians* (1994)

John Buchan 1875–1940

6 I had some of my Gothic corners smoothed away, but . . . there remained a large spice of the Shorter Catechist in my make-up.

John Buchan 1875–1940: *Memory-Hold-the-Door* (1940); cf. **331:6**

John Bunyan 1628–88

7 'Pilgrim's Progress', about a man that left his family it didn't say why . . . The statements was interesting, but tough.

Mark Twain 1835–1910: *The Adventures of Huckleberry Finn* (1884)

8 A tinker out of Bedford,
A vagrant oft in quod,
A private under Fairfax,
A minister of God—
Two hundred years and thirty
Ere Armageddon came
His single hand portrayed it,
And Bunyan was his name! . . .

A pedlar from a hovel,
The lowest of the low—
The Father of the Novel,
Salvation's first Defoe—
Eight blinded generations
Ere Armageddon came,
He showed us how to meet it,
And Bunyan was his name!

Rudyard Kipling 1865–1936: 'The Holy War' (1917)

1 Just as Oliver Cromwell aimed to bring about the kingdom of God on earth and founded the British Empire, so Bunyan wanted the millennium and got the novel.

Christopher Hill 1912– : *A Turbulent, Seditious, and Factious People: John Bunyan and his Church, 1628-1688* (1988)

Edmund Burke 1729–97

2 If a man were to go by chance at the same time with Burke under a shed, to shun a shower, he would say—'this is an extraordinary man.'

Samuel Johnson 1709–84: James Boswell *Life of Samuel Johnson* (1791) 15 May 1784

3 [Edmund Burke] is not affected by the reality of distress touching his heart, but by the showy resemblance of it striking his imagination. He pities the plumage, but forgets the dying bird.

on Burke's Reflections on the Revolution in France

Thomas Paine 1737–1809: *The Rights of Man* (1791)

4 As he rose like a rocket, he fell like the stick.

on Burke's losing the debate on the French Revolution to Charles James Fox, in the House of Commons

Thomas Paine 1737–1809: *Letter to the Addressers on the late Proclamation* (1792)

5 I had reason for my prejudice in favour of this author. To understand an adversary is some praise: to admire him is more. I thought I did both: I knew I did one. From the first time I cast my eyes on anything of Burke's . . . I said to myself, 'This is true eloquence: this is a man pouring out his mind on paper.' All other styles seemed to me pedantic and impertinent . . . I conceived too that he might be wrong in his main argument, and yet deliver fifty truths in arriving at a false conclusion.

William Hazlitt 1778–1830: 'On Reading Old Books' (1826)

Frances Hodgson Burnett 1849–1924

6 She is a fatally deluded little woman, and I'm afraid cunning hands are plucking her of her downy plumage. I wish she would gather up her few remaining feathers while there is yet time and flutter them westward, where she has, after all, a husband and a child.

Henry James 1843–1916: letter to Mrs Hugh Bell, 7 January 1892

Robert Burns 1759–96

7 The Poetic Genius of my Country found me as the prophetic bard Elijah did Elisha — at the plough; and threw her inspiring mantle over me.

Robert Burns 1759–96: *Poems* 1787 (2nd ed.); dedication

8 What an antithetical mind!—tenderness, roughness—delicacy, coarseness—sentiment, sensuality—soaring and grovelling, dirt and deity—all mixed up in that one compound of inspired clay!

Lord Byron 1788–1824: diary, 13 December 1813

1 He is a myth evolved by the popular imagination, a communal poetic creation, a Protean figure: we can all shape him to our likeness, for the myth is endlessly adaptable.

Edwin Muir 1887–1959: 'The Burns Myth' (1947)

2 The perfection of the old achieving the shock and immediacy of the new.
on Robert Burns' ear for lyric

Thomas Crawford 1920– : *Burns* (1960)

Lord Byron 1788–1824 see also 5:7

3 Mad, bad, and dangerous to know.
after their first meeting at a ball in March 1812

Lady Caroline Lamb 1785–1828: diary, 1812; Elizabeth Jenkins *Lady Caroline Lamb* (1932); cf. **179:2**

4 It still saddens me that Lord Byron, who showed such impatience with the fickle public, wasn't aware of how well the Germans can understand him and how highly they esteem him. With us the moral and political tittle-tattle of the day falls away, leaving the man and the talent standing alone in all their brilliance.

Johann Wolfgang von Goethe 1749–1832: letter to John Murray, 29 March 1831

5 Lord Byron is great only as a poet; as soon as he reflects, he is a child.

Johann Wolfgang von Goethe 1749–1832: Johann Peter Eckermann *Conversations with Goethe* (1836–48)

6 From the poetry of Lord Byron they drew a system of ethics, compounded of misanthropy and voluptuousness, a system in which the two great commandments were, to hate your neighbour, and to love your neighbour's wife.

Lord Macaulay 1800–59: *Essays Contributed to the Edinburgh Review* (1843) 'Moore's *Life of Lord Byron*'

7 What helps it now, that Byron bore,
With haughty scorn which mocked the smart,
Through Europe to the Aetolian shore
The pageant of his bleeding heart?
That thousands counted every groan,
And Europe made his woe her own?

Matthew Arnold 1822–88: 'Stanzas from the Grande Chartreuse' (1855)

8 Always looking at himself in mirrors to make sure he was sufficiently outrageous.

Enoch Powell 1912–98: in *Sunday Times* 8 May 1988

Jane Welsh Carlyle 1801–66 see also 288:4

9 Jenny kissed me when we met,
Jumping from the chair she sat in;
Time, you thief, who love to get
Sweets into your list, put that in:
Say I'm weary, say I'm sad,
Say that health and wealth have missed me,
Say I'm growing old, but add,
Jenny kissed me.
having been warmly welcomed by Jane Carlyle, who had been anxious for his health in an influenza epidemic

Leigh Hunt 1784–1859: 'Rondeau' (1838)

1 As soon as that man's tongue stops, that woman's begins!
*of Jane and Thomas **Carlyle** at one of Samuel Rogers's breakfast parties*

Samuel Rogers 1763–1855: Francis Espinasse *Literary Recollections and Sketches* (1893)

Thomas Carlyle 1795–1881

2 Carlyle is a poet to whom nature has denied the faculty of verse.

Alfred, Lord Tennyson 1809–92: letter to W. E. Gladstone, *c.*1870

3 Rugged, mountainous, volcanic, he was himself more a French revolution than any of his volumes.

Walt Whitman 1819–92: *Specimen Days* 10 February 1881

4 It was very good of God to let Carlyle and Mrs Carlyle marry one another and so make only two people miserable instead of four.

Samuel Butler 1835–1902: letter, 21 November 1884

5 Carlyle was so poisonous it's a wonder his mind didn't infect his bloodstream.

John Carey 1934– : in *Sunday Times* 1983

Catullus *c.*84–*c.*54 BC

6 *Gratias tibi maximas Catullus*
Agit pessimus omnium poeta,
Tanto pessimus omnium poeta,
Quanto tu optimus omnium's patronum.

Catullus gives you warmest thanks,
And he the worst of poets ranks;
As much the worst of bards confessed,
As you of advocates the best.
letter of thanks to Cicero

Catullus *c.*84–*c.*54 **bc**: *Carmina* no. 49, tr. William Marris

7 There beneath the Roman ruin where the purple flowers grow,
Came that 'Ave atque Vale' of the Poet's hopeless woe,
Tenderest of Roman poets nineteen-hundred years ago,
'Frater Ave atque Vale'—as we wander'd to and fro
Gazing at the Lydian laughter of the Garda Lake below
Sweet Catullus's all-but-island, olive-silvery Sirmio!

Alfred, Lord Tennyson 1809–92: *Tiresias* (1885) 'Frater Ave atque Vale'

Raymond Chandler 1888–1959

8 If my books had been any worse, I should not have been invited to Hollywood, and if they had been any better, I should not have come.

Raymond Chandler 1888–1959: letter to Charles W. Morton, 12 December 1945

9 Having just read the admirable profile of Hemingway in the *New Yorker* I realize that I am much too clean to be a genius, much too sober to be a champ, and far, far too clumsy with a shotgun to live the good life.

Raymond Chandler 1888–1959: Philip Durham *Down These Mean Streets a Man Must Go* (1963)

Thomas Chatterton 1752–70

1 He was an instance that a complete genius and a complete rogue can be formed before a man is of age.

Horace Walpole 1717–97: letter to William Mason, 24 July 1778

2 I thought of Chatterton, the marvellous boy,
The sleepless soul that perished in its pride.

William Wordsworth 1770–1850: 'Resolution and Independence' (1807)

Geoffrey Chaucer *c.*1343–1400

3 The worshipful father and first founder and embellisher of ornate eloquence in our English, I mean Master Geoffrey Chaucer.

William Caxton *c.*1421–91: Caxton's edition (*c.*1478) of Chaucer's translation of Boethius *De Consolacione Philosophie*

4 Dan Chaucer, well of English undefiled,
On Fame's eternal beadroll worthy to be filed.

Edmund Spenser *c.*1552–99: *The Faerie Queen* (1596)

5 'Tis sufficient to say, according to the proverb, that here is God's plenty.

John Dryden 1631–1700: *Fables Ancient and Modern* (1700)

6 Of all English writers Chaucer is the clearest. He is as precise and slick as a Frenchman.

James Joyce 1882–1941: Frank Budgen *James Joyce and the Making of Ulysses* (1934)

Anton Chekhov 1860–1904

7 My country house is full of people, they never leave me alone; if only they would go away I could be a good writer.

written towards the end of his life

Anton Chekhov 1860–1904: attributed

8 You know I can't stand Shakespeare's plays, but yours are even worse.

remark to Chekhov, after seeing Uncle Vanya

Leo Tolstoy 1828–1910: P. P. Gnedich *Kniga Zhizni Vospominaniya* (1929)

9 All Russians are brutal, except Chekhov. People dislike his plays as they are all about nothing. *I* like them very much.

in conversation with fellow-novelist Elizabeth Taylor

Ivy Compton-Burnett 1884–1969: A. N. Wilson *Penfriends from Porlock* (1988)

10 What Chekhov saw in our failure to communicate was something positive and precious: the private silence in which we live, and which enables us to endure our own solitude. We live, as his characters do, beyond any tale we happen to enact.

V. S. Pritchett 1900–97: *Myth Makers* (1979) 'Chekhov, a doctor'

11 Chekhov must have been the sanest person in 19th-century Europe. He was sanity raised to the power of genius.

John Carey 1934– : in *Sunday Times* 1987

12 Chekhov had the art of showing us art as inverted poetry.

V. S. Pritchett 1900–97: *Chekhov: A Spirit Set Free* (1988)

G. K. Chesterton 1874–1936 see also **280:7**

1 Remote and ineffectual Don
That dared attack my Chesterton.

Hilaire Belloc 1870–1953: 'Lines to a Don' (1910)

2 Chesterton is like a vile scum on a pond . . . all his slop—it is really modern Catholicism to a great extent, the *never* taking a hedge straight, the mumbo-jumbo of superstition dodging behind clumsy fun and paradox . . . I believe he creates a milieu in which art is impossible.

Ezra Pound 1885–1972: letter to John Quinn, 21 August 1917

3 Chesterton's resolute conviviality is about as genial as an *auto da fé* of teetotallers.

George Bernard Shaw 1856–1950: *Pen Portraits and Reviews* (1932)

4 My real judgement of my own work is that I have spoilt a number of jolly good ideas in my time.

G. K. Chesterton 1874–1936: *Autobiography* (1936)

5 Poor G.K.C., his day is past—
Now God will know the truth at last.
mock epitaph

E. V. Lucas 1868–1938: Dudley Barker *G. K. Chesterton* (1973)

6 Chesterton had a body like a slag heap, but a mind like the dawn sky. He saw the world new, as if he'd just landed from another planet.

John Carey 1934– : in *Sunday Times* 1978

Agatha Christie 1890–1976

7 Agatha's best work is, like P. G. Wodehouse and Noel Coward's best work, the most characteristic pleasure-writing of this epoch and will appear one day in all decent literary histories. As *writing* it is not distinguished, but as *story* it is superb.

Robert Graves 1895–1985: letter, 16 July 1944

8 I'm a sausage machine, a perfect sausage machine.

Agatha Christie 1890–1976: G. C. Ramsey *Agatha Christie* (1972)

9 She shows us the ace of spades face up. Then she turns it over, but we still know where it is, so how has it been transformed into the five of diamonds?

Julian Symons 1912–94: *Bloody Murder* (1972)

10 She . . . wanted a detective of a type that had not been used before. She eventually decided that he should be a Belgian refugee . . . Torquay was full of Belgian refugees, bewildered and suspicious, who wanted to be left alone.

Janet Morgan 1945– : *Agatha Christie* (1984)

Samuel Taylor Coleridge 1772–1834

11 Cultivate simplicity, Coleridge.

Charles Lamb 1775–1834: letter to Coleridge, 8 November 1796

12 Coleridge dined with us. He brought his ballad [*The Ancient Mariner*] finished. A beautiful evening, very starry, the horned moon.

Dorothy Wordsworth 1771–1855: 'Alfoxden Journal' 23 March 1798

13 An Archangel a little damaged.

Charles Lamb 1775–1834: letter to Wordsworth, 26 April 1816

1 The Prince of preparatory authors!

William Hazlitt 1778–1830: in *Examiner* 8 September 1816

2 The rogue gives you Love Powders, and then a strong horse drench to bring 'em off your stomach that they mayn't hurt you.

Charles Lamb 1775–1834: letter to Wordsworth, 23 September 1816

3 Coleridge, for instance, would let go by a fine isolated verisimilitude caught from the penetralium of mystery, from being incapable of remaining content with half knowledge.

John Keats 1795–1821: letter to George and Thomas Keats, 21 December 1817

4 He talked on for ever; and you wished him to talk on for ever.

William Hazlitt 1778–1830: *Lectures on the English Poets* (1818)

5 You will see Coleridge—he who sits obscure
In the exceeding lustre and the pure
Intense irradiation of a mind,
Which, with its own internal lightning blind,
Flags wearily through darkness and despair—
A cloud-encircled meteor of the air,
A hooded eagle among blinking owls.

Percy Bysshe Shelley 1792–1822: 'Letter to Maria Gisborne' (1820)

6 And Coleridge, too, has lately taken wing,
But, like a hawk encumbered with his hood,
Explaining metaphysics to the nation—
I wish he would explain his explanation.

Lord Byron 1788–1824: *Don Juan* (1819–24)

7 The owner of a mind which keeps open house, and entertains all comers.

William Hazlitt 1778–1830: *Spirit of the Age* (1825)

8 His forehead was prodigious—a great piece of placid marble; and his fine eyes, in which all the activity of his mind seemed to concentrate, moved under it with a sprightly ease, as if it was pastime to them to carry all that thought.

Leigh Hunt 1784–1859: *Autobiography* (1850)

9 Amputated kind of completeness.
of Coleridge's fragmentary 'The Ballad of the Dark Ladie'

Ted Hughes 1930–98: *A Choice of Coleridge's Verse* (ed. Hughes, 1996)

Joan Collins 1933–

10 I've written bits of novels since I was six or seven. I was always very good at English at school.

Joan Collins 1933– : in *Observer* 16 October 1988 'Sayings of the Week'

Ivy Compton-Burnett 1884–1969

11 It is Miss Compton-Burnett's special gift as a novelist to show us what melodramatic lives quite ordinary people lead without suspecting it.

Robertson Davies 1913–95: in 1950; *The Enthusiasms of Robertson Davies* (1990)

12 There's not much to say. I haven't been at all deedy.
on being asked about herself

Ivy Compton-Burnett 1884–1969: in *The Times* 30 August 1969

1 She saw life in the relentless terms of a Greek tragedy, its cruelties, ironies—above all its passions—played out against a background of triviality and ennui.

Anthony Powell 1905– : in *Spectator* 6 September 1969

William Congreve 1670–1729

2 William Congreve is the only sophisticated playwright England has produced; and like Shaw, Sheridan and Wilde, his nearest rivals, he was brought up in Ireland.

Kenneth Tynan 1927–80: *Curtains* (1961) 'The Way of the World'

Cyril Connolly 1903–74

3 Apes are considerably preferable to Cyril.

Virginia Woolf 1882–1941: attributed

4 He gave pleasure a bad name.

E. M. Forster 1879–1970: Noel Annan *Our Age* (1990)

Joseph Conrad 1857–1924

5 A Polish nobleman, cased in British tar!
self-description

Joseph Conrad 1857–1924: letter, 22 May 1890

6 For me, writing—*the only possible writing*—is just simply the conversion of nervous force into phrases.

Joseph Conrad 1857–1924: letter, October 1903

7 You knock about in the wide waters of expression like the raciest and boldest of privateers.

Henry James 1843–1916: letter to Conrad, 1 November 1906

8 The secret casket of his genius contains a vapour rather than a jewel.
reviewing Conrad's Notes on Life and Letters *(1921)*

E. M. Forster 1879–1970: Cedric Watts *Joseph Conrad* (1994)

9 Conrad spent a day finding the *mot juste*; then killed it.

Ford Madox Ford 1873–1939: Robert Lowell *Notebook 1967–68* (1969)

10 Joseph Conrad's *Heart of Darkness* prophetically inaugurated the twentieth century.

Thomas Mann 1875–1955: attributed

11 He thought of civilized and morally tolerable human life as a dangerous walk on a thin crust of barely cooled lava that might break and let the unwary sink into fiery depths.

Bertrand Russell 1872–1970: Norman Sherry *Conrad and his World* (1972)

12 He seems to write books about the sea, the Malay archipelago and the Congo, but he is really writing about the desperate, convoluted, hopeless heart of man.

Anthony Burgess 1917–93: in *Observer* 6 May 1979

13 The Salieri of letters.

Jeanette Winterson 1959– : *Art Objects* (1995)

James Fenimore Cooper 1789–1851

1 *Deerslayer* is just simply a literary *delirium tremens*.

Mark Twain 1835–1910: 'Fenimore Cooper's Literary Offences' (1895)

Noël Coward 1899–1973

2 Baring his teeth as if unveiling a grotesque memorial, and cooing like a baritone dove, he displays his two weapons—wit and sentimentality.

Kenneth Tynan 1927–80: 'A Tribute to Mr Coward' (1953)

3 There are only two great playwrights in Britain today, Terence Rattigan and myself.

Noël Coward 1899–1973: attributed, 1964

Abraham Cowley 1618–67 see also 204:12

4 He more had pleased us, had he pleased us less.

Joseph Addison 1672–1719: *An Account of the Greatest English Poets* (1694)

5 Who now reads Cowley? if he pleases yet,
His moral pleases, not his pointed wit.

Alexander Pope 1688–1744: *Imitations of Horace* (1737)

Dante Alighieri 1265–1321

6 He stood bewildered, not appalled, on that dark shore which separates the ancient and the modern world . . . He is power, passion, self-will personified.

William Hazlitt 1778–1830: *Lectures on the English Poets* (1818) 'On Poetry in General'

7 Dante, who loved well because he hated,
Hated wickedness that hinders loving.

Robert Browning 1812–89: 'One Word More' (1855)

8 A complete understanding of Dante is neither possible nor desirable. His work resonates more than you know.
on a film of The Inferno

Tom Phillips : in *Observer* 29 July 1990 'Sayings of the Week'

Charles Dickens 1812–70 see also 87:3, 87:4, 333:10

9 There is no contemporary English writer whose works are read so generally through the whole house, who can give pleasure to the servants as well as to the mistress, to the children as well as to the master.

Walter Bagehot 1826–77: in *National Review* 7 October 1858 'Charles Dickens'

10 He describes London like a special correspondent for posterity.

Walter Bagehot 1826–77: in *National Review* 7 October 1858 'Charles Dickens'

11 The greatest of superficial novelists . . . It were, in our opinion, an offence against humanity to place Mr Dickens among the greatest novelists.

Henry James 1843–1916: 'Our Mutual Friend' (1865)

1 He had a large loving mind and the strongest sympathy with the poorer classes. He felt sure a better feeling, and much greater union of classes, would take place in time. And I pray earnestly it may.

Queen Victoria 1819–1901: diary, 11 June 1870

2 Of all the Victorian novelists, he was probably the most antagonistic to the Victorian age itself.

Edmund Wilson 1895–1972: *The Wound and the Bow* (1941) 'The Two Scrooges'

3 Dickens was not the first or the last novelist to find virtue more difficult to portray than the wish for it.

V. S. Pritchett 1900–97: *Books in General* (1953) 'Oliver Twist'

4 My own experience in reading Dickens . . . is to be bounced between violent admiration and violent distaste almost every couple of paragraphs, and this is too uncomfortable a condition to be much alleviated by an inward recital of one's duty not to be fastidious, to gulp the stuff down in gobbets like a man.

Kingsley Amis 1922–95: *What Became of Jane Austen?* (1970)

5 We were put to Dickens as children but it never quite took. That unremitting humanity soon had me cheesed off.

Alan Bennett 1934– : *The Old Country* (1978)

6 It does not matter that Dickens' world is not lifelike; it is alive.

Lord David Cecil 1902–86: *Early Victorian Novelists* (1978)

7 Heartlessness masked by a style overflowing with feeling.
of Dickens's novels

Milan Kundera 1929– : *Testaments Betrayed* (1995)

Emily Dickinson 1830–86

8 You who desired so much—in vain to ask—
Yet fed your hunger like an endless task,
Dared dignify the labour, bless the quest—
Achieved that stillness ultimately best,
Being, of all, least sought for: Emily, hear!

Hart Crane 1899–1932: 'To Emily Dickinson' (1927)

John Donne 1572–1631

9 Donne, for not keeping of accent, deserved hanging.

Ben Jonson *c.*1573–1637: in *Conversations with William Drummond of Hawthornden* (written 1619) no. 3

10 Dr Donne's verses are like the peace of God; they pass all understanding.

James I 1566–1625: remark recorded by Archdeacon Plume (1630–1704)

11 The Muses' garden with pedantic weeds
O'erspread, was purged by thee; the lazy seeds
Of servile imitation thrown away,
And fresh invention planted.

Thomas Carew *c.*1595–1640: 'An Elegy upon the Death of Dr John Donne' (1640)

12 But God, who is able to prevail, wrestled with him, as the Angel did with Jacob, and marked him; marked him for his own.

Izaak Walton 1593–1683: *Life of Donne* (1670 ed.)

1 With Donne, whose muse on dromedary trots,
Wreathe iron pokers into true-love knots.

Samuel Taylor Coleridge 1772–1834: 'On Donne's Poetry' (1818)

2 Tennyson and Browning are poets, and they think; but they do not feel their thought as immediately as the odour of a rose. A thought to Donne was an experience; it modified his sensibility.

T. S. Eliot 1888–1965: 'The Metaphysical Poets' (1921)

3 But Shakespeare's cut and thrust,
I allow you, was a must
on my bookshelves: and after,
Donne's thin, cerebral laughter.

R. S. Thomas 1913– : *Laboratories of the Spirit* (1975)

Fedor Dostoevsky 1821–81

4 The humour of Dostoevsky is the humour of a bar-loafer who ties a kettle to a dog's tail.

W. Somerset Maugham 1874–1965: *A Writer's Notebook* (1949) written in 1917

5 He has the look of a man who has been in hell and seen there, not a hopeless suffering, but meanness and frippery.

W. Somerset Maugham 1874–1965: *A Writer's Notebook* (1949) written in 1917

6 No matter how much of a shabby animal you may be, you can learn from Dostoevsky and Chekhov etc., how to have the most tender, unique, and coruscating soul on earth.

D. H. Lawrence 1885–1930: 'Preface to Mastro-don Gesualdo' (1923)

7 The grimacing, haunted creature . . . fierce mouthings from prehistoric ages.

Joseph Conrad 1857–1924: Cedric Watts *Joseph Conrad: Writers and ther Work* (1994)

8 The novels of Dostoevsky are seething whirlpools, gyrating sandstorms, waterspouts which hiss and boil and suck us in. They are composed purely and wholly of the stuff of the soul. Against our wills we are drawn in, whirled round, blinded and suffocated, and at the same time filled with a giddy rapture.

Virginia Woolf 1882–1941: *The Common Reader* (1925) 'The Russian Point of View'

John Dryden 1631–1700 see also **110:2**

9 Ev'n copious Dryden, wanted, or forgot,
The last and greatest art, the art to blot.

Alexander Pope 1688–1744: *Imitations of Horace* (1737)

10 Remember Dryden, and be blind to all his faults.

Thomas Gray 1716–71: letter to James Beattie, 2 October 1765

11 His mind was of a slovenly character,—fond of splendour, but indifferent to neatness. Hence most of his writings exhibit the sluttish magnificence of a Russian noble, all vermin diamonds, dirty linen and inestimable sables.

Lord Macaulay 1800–59: in *Edinburgh Review* January 1828 'John Dryden'

12 Dryden's genius was of that sort which catches fire by its own motion: his chariot-wheels got hot by driving fast.

Samuel Taylor Coleridge 1772–1834: *Table Talk* (1836)

1 He is the most masculine of our poets; his style and rhythms lay the strongest stress of all our literature on the naked thew and sinew of the English language.

Gerard Manley Hopkins 1844–89: letter to Robert Bridges, 6 November 1887

2 If Dryden's plays had been as good as their prefaces he would have been a dramatist indeed.

Harley Granville-Barker 1877–1946: *On Dramatic Method* (1931)

3 There *Dryden* sits with modest smile,
The master of the middle style.

W. H. Auden 1907–73: *New Year Letter* (1941)

Gerald Durrell 1925–95

4 Don't you think the little devil writes well? His style's like fresh, crisp lettuce.
an elder brother's view

Lawrence Durrell 1912–90: in *Guardian* 31 January 1995; obituary

Lawrence Durrell 1912–90

5 Larrie writes for posterity. I write for money.
a younger brother's view

Gerald Durrell 1925–95: in *Daily Telegraph* 31 January 1995; obituary of Gerald Durrell

George Eliot 1819–80 see also **3:8, 148:2**

6 She is magnificently ugly—deliciously hideous. She has a low forehead, a dull grey eye, a vast pendulous nose . . . Now in this vast ugliness resides a most powerful beauty which, in a very few minutes steals forth and charms the mind, so that you end as I ended, in falling in love with her. Yes behold me literally in love with this great horse-faced blue-stocking.

Henry James 1843–1916: letter, 10 May 1869

7 A marvellous mind *throbs* in every page of *Middlemarch*. It raises the standard of what is to be expected of women . . . We know all about the female heart; but apparently there is a female brain, too.

Henry James 1843–1916: letter, 5 March 1873

8 [She] is sometimes heavy—sometimes abstruse, sometimes almost dull, but always like an egg, full of meat.

Anthony Trollope 1815–82: letter, 18 September 1874

9 She was one whose private life should be left in privacy, as may be said of all who have achieved fame by literary merits.

Anthony Trollope 1815–82: letter, 17 January 1881

10 She told me that, in all she considered her best writing there was a 'not herself' which took possession of her, and that she felt her own personality to be merely the instrument through which the spirit as it were was acting.
of his wife George Eliot

J . W. Cross 1840–1924: *Life of George Eliot* (1884)

11 She was a made woman . . . made by self-manipulation, as one makes a statue or a vase. I have never known anyone who seemed to me so purely artificial as George Eliot.

Mrs Lynn Lynton 1822–98: *My Literary Life* (1899)

T. S. Eliot 1888–1965

1 Many of my colleagues . . . think a banker has no business whatever to be a poet. They don't think the two things can combine. But I believe that anything a man does, whatever his *hobby* may be, it's all the better if he is really keen on it and does well. I think it helps him with his work . . . I don't see why—in time, of course, in time—he mightn't even become a Branch Manager.
view of a senior official of Lloyds Bank where Eliot was employed

Anonymous: in conversation *c.*1920; I. A. Richards 'On T.S.E.' in *T. S. Eliot: the Man and His Work* (1967)

2 He is without pose and full of poise. he makes one feel that all cleverness is an excuse for thinking hard.

Harold Nicolson 1886–1968: *Diaries and Letters, 1930–1939* 2 March 1932

3 How unpleasant to meet Mr Eliot!
With his features of clerical cut,
And his brow so grim
And his mouth so prim
And his conversation, so nicely
Restricted to What Precisely
And If and Perhaps and But.

T. S. Eliot 1888–1965: 'Five-Finger Exercises' (1936); cf. **313:7**

4 [*The Waste Land*] was only the relief of a personal and wholly insignificant grouse against life; it is just a piece of rhythmical grumbling.

T. S. Eliot 1888–1965: *The Waste Land* (ed. Valerie Eliot, 1971) epigraph

5 I myself owe Mr Symons a great debt: but for having read his book, I should not, in the year 1908, have heard of Laforgue or Rimbaud; I should probably not have begun to read Verlaine: and but for reading Verlaine, I should not have heard of Corbière. So the Symons book is one of those which have affected the course of my life.

T. S. Eliot 1888–1965: Edmund White *The Burning Library* (1994)

6 'Mr Eliot' was a fictional character and Tom himself helped to create him. Among the roles the poet deftly played were The Anglican Clergyman, The Formidable Professor, Dr Johnson and the Genteel Bostonian.

Edmund Wilson 1895–1972: attributed

7 Self-contempt, well-grounded.
on the foundation of T. S. Eliot's work

F. R. Leavis 1895–1978: in *Times Literary Supplement* 21 October 1988

8 Even the greatest poets need something to cling to. Keats had Beauty; Milton had God. T. S. Eliot's standby was Worry.

John Carey 1934– : in *Sunday Times* 25 September 1988

Ralph Waldo Emerson 1803–82

9 I called him a wrinkled and toothless baboon, who, first hoisted in notoriety on the shoulders of Carlyle, now spits and splutters on a filthier platform of his own finding and fouling.
account of a letter, sent to Emerson, which did not receive a reply

Algernon Charles Swinburne 1837–1909: in conversation with Edmund Gosse; Evan Charteris *Life and Letters of Sir Edmund Gosse* (1931)

Gavin Ewart 1916–95

1 They'll say (if I'm lucky):
He wrote some silly poems, and some of them were funny.

Gavin Ewart 1916–95: 'Afterwards'

Henry Fielding 1707–54

2 How charming, how wholesome, Fielding always is! To take him up after Richardson is like emerging from a sick room heated by stoves into an open lawn, on a breezy day in May.

Samuel Taylor Coleridge 1772–1834: *Table Talk* (1836)

3 The most singular genius which their island ever produced, whose works it has long been the fashion to abuse in public and to read in secret.

George Borrow 1803–81: *The Bible in Spain* (1843)

4 [Thackeray] resembles Fielding as an eagle does a vulture: Fielding could stoop on carrion, but Thackeray never does.

Charlotte Brontë 1816–55: *Jane Eyre* (2nd ed., 1848) preface; cf. **333:8**

F. Scott Fitzgerald 1896–1940

5 I have lived so long within the circle of this book [*Tender is the Night*] that often it seems to me that the real world does not exist but that only these characters exist.

F. Scott Fitzgerald 1896–1940: letter, 4 March 1934

6 I think he was more interested in capturing time and freezing it. I think very early on he decided that he'd been to a dance and danced with a girl, and even if he couldn't remember which dance or which girl, that it represented some glorious high point of his life, and everything he did was an attempt to recapture that moment. I don't think he was much interested in more general issues.

Jay McInerney 1955– : in *Guardian* 1 June 1996

Gustave Flaubert 1821–80 see also **42:4, 242:6, 279:6**

7 My deplorable mania for analysis exhausts me. I doubt everything, even my doubt.

Gustave Flaubert 1821–80: letter, 8–9 August 1846

8 Writing this book I am like a man playing the piano with lead balls attached to his knuckles.
of Madame Bovary

Gustave Flaubert 1821–80: letter, 26 July 1856; cf. **16:6**

9 A great, stout, simple, kindly, elderly fellow, rather embarrassed at having a stranger presented to him, and bothering himself over what he can say or do . . . He looks like some weather-beaten old military man.

Henry James 1843–1916: letter 20 December 1875

10 *Madame Bovary, c'est moi.*
Madame Bovary is myself.

Gustave Flaubert 1821–80: attributed

1 A kind of opera in prose.
of Salammbô

Guy de Maupassant 1850–93: preface to *Lettres de Gustave Flaubert à George Sand* (1884)

2 It was in his nature to be more conscious of one broken spring in the couch of fate, more wounded by a pin-prick, more worried by an assonance, than he could ever be warmed or pacified from within. Literature and life were a single business to him, and the 'torment of style' that might occasionally intermit in one place was sufficiently sure to break out in another.

Henry James 1843–1916: 'Gustave Flaubert' (1893); cf. **16:6**

3 And there was that sucker Flaubert rolling around on his floor for three days looking for the right word.

Dorothy Parker 1893–1967: Malcolm Cowley (ed.) *Writers at Work* (1958) 1st Series

4 Flaubert was a perpetual adolescent. His distinction lay in never outgrowing the hatred and contempt that the normal teenager feels when confronted with adult human beings.

John Carey 1934– : in *Sunday Times* 2 April 1989

Ford Madox Ford 1873–1939

5 Is it any better in Heaven, my friend Ford,
Than you found it in Provence?

William Carlos Williams 1883–1963: 'To Ford Madox Ford in Heaven' (1944)

E. M. Forster 1879–1970

6 E. M. Forster never gets any further than warming the teapot. He's a rare fine hand at that. Feel this teapot. Is it not beautifully warm? Yes, but there ain't going to be no tea.

Katherine Mansfield 1888–1923: diary, May 1917

7 His style has not, like Henry James's or Meredith's or Hemingway's, spawned; it is not mannered enough for that, and the mind behind it is too rare to be successfully aped. His influence rather permeates, like a dye, than an outside model that can be copied.

Rose Macaulay 1881–1958: 'The Writings of E. M. Forster' (1938)

8 The elusive colt of a dark horse.

John Maynard Keynes 1883–1946: Michael Holroyd *Lytton Strachey* (1994 rev. ed.)

9 The trouble began with Forster. After him it was considered ungentlemanly to write more than five or six novels.

Anthony Burgess 1917–93: in *Guardian* 24 February 1989

10 He was always in court, seated on the high bench, passing judgements, a black cloth on his head.

Gore Vidal 1925– : *Palimpsest* (1995)

John Galsworthy 1867–1933

1 I first read The Forsyte Saga at the age of 15 with great respect and pleasure. I reread it in my late 20s with less respect but still great pleasure. I reread it last week with no respect and precious little pleasure.

Angus Wilson 1913–91: *Diversity and Depth in Fiction* (1983)

Elizabeth Gaskell 1810–65

2 A natural unassuming woman whom they have been doing their best to spoil by making a lioness of her.

Jane Welsh Carlyle 1801–66: letter, 17 May 1849

3 I wish to Heaven, her people would keep a little firmer on their legs!

on the constitutional lack of physical stamina shown by Mrs Gaskell's characters, in such stories as 'The Heart of John Middleton'

Charles Dickens 1812–70: letter to W. H. Wills, 12 December 1850

4 I have spent all my spare moments during the last week reading with avidity *Cranford*.

while serving on the Western Front; he was killed by a sniper two months later

Charles Sorley 1895–1915: letter, August 1915

John Gay 1685–1732

5 This play . . . was first offered to Cibber and his brethren at Drury-Lane, and rejected; it being then carried to Rich had the effect, as was ludicrously said, of making Gay *rich*, and Rich *gay*.

of Gay's The Beggar's Opera

Samuel Johnson 1709–84: *Lives of the English Poets* (1779–81) 'John Gay'

6 A pastoral of an hundred lines may be endured, but who will hear of sheep and goats, and myrtle bowers and purling rivulets through five acts?

of Gay's productions, other than the Beggars' Opera

Samuel Johnson 1709–84: *Lives of the English Poets* (1779–81) 'John Gay'

Edward Gibbon 1737–94 see also **32:4**

when his apparently flattering reference to Gibbon as the 'luminous' author of The Decline and Fall *was queried:*

7 Luminous! oh, I meant—voluminous.

Richard Brinsley Sheridan 1751–1816: during the trial of Warren Hastings in 1785; Samuel Rogers *Table Talk* (1903)

8 Johnson's style was grand and Gibbon's elegant; the stateliness of the former was sometimes pedantic, and the polish of the latter was occasionally finical. Johnson marched to kettle-drums and trumpets; Gibbon moved to flute and hautboys: Johnson hewed passages through the Alps, while Gibbon levelled walks through parks and gardens.

George Colman, the Younger 1762–1836: *Random Records* (1830)

1 When I read a chapter in Gibbon, I seem to be looking through a luminous haze or fog; figures come and go, I know not how or why, all larger than life, or distorted and discoloured; nothing is real, vivid, true; all is scenical, and, as it were, exhibited by candlelight.

Samuel Taylor Coleridge 1772–1834: *Table Talk* (1836)

André Gide 1869–1951

2 An elderly fallen angel travelling incognito.

Peter Quennell 1905–93: *The Sign of the Fish* (1960)

Elinor Glyn 1864–1943

3 Would you like to sin
With Elinor Glyn
On a tigerskin?
Or would you prefer
To err
With her
On some other fur?

Anonymous: 1907 rhyme, in A. Glyn *Elinor Glyn* (1955)

Johann Wolfgang von Goethe 1749–1832

4 If Goethe really died saying 'more light', it was very silly of him: what *he* wanted was more warmth.

Charles Sorley 1895–1915: letter, July 1914; cf. **127:3**

Oliver Goldsmith 1730–74

5 Here lies Nolly Goldsmith, for shortness called Noll,
Who wrote like an angel, but talked like poor Poll.

David Garrick 1717–79: 'Impromptu Epitaph' (written 1773/4)

Maxim Gorky 1868–1936

6 The question of what man *is* really meant, for Gorky, what man can become.

Eugene Lampert 1913– : Malcolm Bradbury and James McFarlane (eds.) *Modernism* (1991)

Robert Graves 1895–1985

7 Writing a poem for me is putting myself in a very odd state indeed in which I am excessively sensitive to interruption—I can hear, or think I can hear, people doing disturbing things behind shut doors three houses off—and really suffer very painfully, as though I were performing a major operation on my own skull.

Robert Graves 1895–1985: letter, 31 July 1942

1 Robert Graves was unique. He followed no fads and set no fashions. He had a mind like an alchemist's laboratory: everything that got into it came out new, weird and gleaming.

John Carey 1934– : in *Sunday Times* 8 December 1985

2 He was fond of declaring that 'he bred show dogs in order to be able to afford a cat', the dogs being prose, the cat poetry.

Alastair Reid 1926– : *Whereabouts* (1987)

Thomas Gray 1716–71

3 The General . . . repeated nearly the whole of Gray's Elegy . . . adding, as he concluded, that he would prefer being the author of that poem to the glory of beating the French to-morrow.

James Wolfe 1727–59: J. Playfair *Biographical Account of J. Robinson* (1815)

4 I shall be but a shrimp of an author.

Thomas Gray 1716–71: letter to Horace Walpole, 25 February 1768

5 The *Church-yard* abounds with images which find a mirror in every mind, and with sentiments to which every bosom returns an echo.

on Gray's 'Elegy in a Country Churchyard'

Samuel Johnson 1709–84: *Lives of the English Poets* (1779–81) 'Gray'

6 Gray, a born poet, fell upon an age of reason.

Matthew Arnold 1822–88: *Essays in Criticism* (1865–88) 'Gray'

Graham Greene 1904–91

7 I wouldn't give up writing about God at this stage, if I was you. It would be like P. G. Wodehouse dropping Jeeves half way through the Wooster series.

Evelyn Waugh 1903–66: to Graham Greene; Christopher Sykes *Evelyn Waugh* (1975)

8 *Brighton Rock* I began in 1937 as a detective story and continued, I am sometimes tempted to think, as an error of judgement.

Graham Greene 1904–91: *Ways of Escape* (1980)

Thomas Hardy 1840–1928

9 Hardy went down to botanize in the swamp, while Meredith climbed towards the sun. Meredith became, at his best, a sort of daintily dressed Walt Whitman: Hardy became a sort of village atheist brooding and blaspheming over the village idiot.

G. K. Chesterton 1874–1936: *The Victorian Age in Literature* (1912)

10 What a commonplace genius he has, or a genius for the commonplace, I don't know which. He doesn't rank so terribly high, really. But better than Bernard Shaw, even then.

D. H. Lawrence 1885–1930: letter to Martin Secker, 24 July 1928

11 No one has written worse English than Mr Hardy in some of his novels—cumbrous, stilted, ugly and inexpressive—yes, but at the same time so strangely expressive of something attractive to us in Mr Hardy himself that we

Virginia Woolf 1882–1941: *The Moment and Other Essays* (1947) 'Personalities'

would not change it for the perfection of Sterne at his best. It becomes coloured by its surroundings; it becomes literature.

Nathaniel Hawthorne 1804–64

1 My sensation throughout is of pity for the poor fellow, who had to feed his soul on such raw material.
on reading Hawthorne's Notebooks

George Gissing 1857–1903: *Commonplace Book* (1962)

William Hazlitt 1778–1830

receiving an apology from John Lamb, who had knocked him down:

2 I am a metaphysician, and do not mind a blow; nothing but an *idea* hurts me.

William Hazlitt 1778–1830: Thomas Moore diary, 9 September 1820

Joseph Heller 1923–

3 When I read something saying I've not done anything as good as *Catch-22* I'm tempted to reply, Who has?'

Joseph Heller 1923– : in *The Times* 9 June 1993

Lilian Hellman 1905–84

4 Every word she writes is a lie, including 'and' and 'the'.

Mary McCarthy 1912–89: in *New York Times* 16 February 1980

Ernest Hemingway 1899–1961 see also 43:5, 255:4

5 Ernest's quality of a stick hardened in the fire.

F. Scott Fitzgerald 1896–1940: letter, 1 September 1930

6 [*The Sun Also Rises* is about] bullfighting, bullslinging, and bull—.

Zelda Fitzgerald 1900–47: Marion Meade *What Fresh Hell Is This?* (1988)

7 What other culture could have produced someone like Hemingway and *not* seen the joke?

Gore Vidal 1925– : *Pink Triangle and Yellow Star* (1982)

George Herbert 1593–1633

8 For three centuries and more, George Herbert exemplified the body heat of a healthy Anglican life.

Seamus Heaney 1939– : *The Redress of Poetry* (1995)

Robert Herrick 1591–1674

1 The Ariel of poets, sucking 'Where the bee sucks' from the rose-heart of nature, and reproducing the fragrance idealized.

Elizabeth Barrett Browning 1806–61: *The Greek Christian Poets and the English Poets* (1842)

2 I think the most indigestible poets are the purely lyrical, poetical ones. Very few people can swallow Herrick. He is so small they bolt him in pellets.

Sylvia Townsend Warner 1893–1978: diary, 26 August 1929

3 How enviable Herrick's
Fourteen hundred lyrics!
Though, as the Scot complained when they dealt him all
The trumps, a lot of them were small.

Roy Fuller 1912–91: 'Quatrains of an Elderly Man: Poetry and Whist'

James Hogg 1770–1835

4 The said Hogg is a strange being, but of great, though uncouth, powers. I think very highly of him, as a poet; but he, and half of these Scotch and Lake troubadours, are spoilt by living in little circles and petty societies.

Lord Byron 1788–1824: letter to Thomas Moore, 3 August 1814

5 The honest grunter.

Sir Walter Scott 1771–1832: diary, 12 December 1825

Homer

6 *Indignor quandoque bonus dormitat Homerus.*

I'm aggrieved when sometimes even excellent Homer nods.

Horace 65–8 BC: *Ars Poetica*

7 In the Odyssey one may liken Homer to the setting sun, of which the grandeur remains without the intensity.

Longinus fl. 1st century AD: *On the Sublime* (supposedly by Longinus)

8 Seven cities warred for Homer, being dead,
Who, living, had no roof to shroud his head.

Thomas Heywood c.1574–1641: 'The Hierarchy of the Blessed Angels' (1635); cf. **81:13, 304:9**

9 Seven wealthy towns contend for HOMER dead
Through which the living HOMER begged his bread.

Anonymous: epilogue to *Aesop at Tunbridge; or, a Few Selected Fables in Verse* By No Person of Quality (1698); cf. **304:8**

10 As learned commentators view
In Homer more than Homer knew.

Jonathan Swift 1667–1745: 'On Poetry' (1733)

11 Oft of one wide expanse had I been told
That deep-browed Homer ruled as his demesne;
Yet never did I breathe its pure serene
Till I heard Chapman speak out loud and bold:
Then felt I like some watcher of the skies
When a new planet swims into his ken;
Or like stout Cortez when with eagle eyes
He stared at the Pacific—and all his men

John Keats 1795–1821: 'On First Looking into Chapman's Homer' (1817); cf. **43:8**

Looked at each other with a wild surmise—
Silent, upon a peak in Darien.

1 Mr Gladstone read Homer for fun, which I thought served him right.

Winston Churchill 1874–1965: *My Early Life* (1930)

Horace 65–8 BC

2 *Horatii curiosa felicitas.*
Horace's careful felicity.

Petronius d. AD 65: *Satyricon*

3 C— taught me to loathe Horace for two years; to forget him for twenty, and then to love him for the rest of my days and through many sleepless nights.
of his school classics master, the model for 'King' in Stalky & Co

Rudyard Kipling 1865–1936: *Something of Myself*

A. E. Housman 1859–1936

4 Housman was Masefield with a dash of Theocritus.

George Orwell 1903–50: *Inside the Whale* (1940)

5 Housman was not taciturn because he had nothing to say but because his first and last characteristic was inscrutability—a buried life that he was determined to keep buried.

Percy Withers : *A Buried Life* (1940)

6 To my generation, no other English poet seemed so perfectly to express the sensibility of a male adolescent.

W. H. Auden 1907–73: Humphrey Carpenter *W. H. Auden* (1981)

7 Housman was a kind of human cactus. Hard and prickly outside, and mushy in the middle, he flowered briefly and surprisingly about twice a year. The poems he produced on these rare occasions are among the most beautiful and miserable in the language.

John Carey 1934– : in *Sunday Times* 1979

8 Housman is the poet of unhappiness; no one else has reiterated his single message so plangently.

Philip Larkin 1922–85: in 1979; *Required Writing* (1983)

Ted Hughes 1930–

9 We had the old crow over at Hull recently, looking like a Christmas present from Easter Island.

Philip Larkin 1922–85: letter, 1975

10 Hughes's voice, I think, is in rebellion against a certain kind of demeaned, mannerly voice . . . I mean, the voice of a generation—the Larkin voice, the Movement voice, even the Eliot voice, the Auden voice—the manners of that speech, the original voices behind that poetic voice, are those of literate English middle-class culture, and I think Hughes's great cry and call and bawl is that English language and English poetry is longer and deeper than that.

Seamus Heaney 1939– : John Haffenden (ed.) *Viewpoints* (1981)

1 As our leading nature poet, he might find some sort of inspiration from the wild life of Balmoral.
greeting the appointment of Ted Hughes as Poet Laureate

David Holloway 1924– : in *Daily Telegraph* 1984

Victor Hugo 1802–85

2 *Victor Hugo était un fou qui se croyait Victor Hugo.*
Victor Hugo was a madman who thought he was Victor Hugo.

Jean Cocteau 1889–1963: *Opium* (1930)

3 *Hugo—hélas!*
Hugo—alas!
when asked who was the greatest 19th-century poet

André Gide 1869–1951: Claude Martin *La Maturité d'André Gide* (1977)

Aldous Huxley 1894–1963

4 People will call Mr Aldous Huxley a pessimist; in the sense of one who makes the worst of it. To me he is that far more gloomy character; the man who makes the best of it.

G. K. Chesterton 1874–1936: *The Common Man* (1950)

5 He is at once the truly clever person and the stupid person's idea of the clever person; he is expected to be relentless, to administer intellectual shocks.

Elizabeth Bowen 1899–1973: in *Spectator* 11 December 1936

6 You could always tell by his conversation which volume of the *Encyclopedia Britannica* he'd been reading. One day it would be Alps, Andes and Apennines, and the next it would be the Himalayas and the Hippocratic Oath.

Bertrand Russell 1872–1970: letter to R. W. Clark, July 1965

Henrik Ibsen 1828–1906

7 Ibsen strikes me as an extraordinary curiosity, and every time he sounds his note the miracle, to my perception, is renewed. I call it a miracle because it is the result of so dry a view of life . . . There is a positive odour of spiritual paraffin.

Henry James 1843–1916: in *Harper's Weekly* 15 January 1897

8 In *Rosmersholm* . . . there is symbolism and a stale odour of spilt poetry.

W. B. Yeats 1865–1939: *The Trembling of the Veil* (1922)

9 I resented being invited to admire dialogue so close to modern educated speech that music and style were impossible . . . As time passed Ibsen became in my eyes the chosen author of very clever young journalists who, condemned to their treadmill of abstraction, hated music and style.

W. B. Yeats 1865–1939: *Autobiographies* (1955)

Christopher Isherwood 1904–86

1 Like all truly honest people, he is as ready to praise as to blame himself.
of Isherwood's 'My Guru and His Disciple'

Edmund White 1940– : in *New York Times* 1 June 1980

Henry James 1843–1916 see also **96:1, 149:9, 236:14**

2 He chaws more than he bites off.

Mrs Henry Adams 1843–85: letter to her father, 4 December 1881

3 Mr Henry James writes fiction as if it were a painful duty.

Oscar Wilde 1854–1900: *Intentions* (1891) 'The Decay of Lying'

4 It is leviathan retrieving pebbles. It is a magnificent but painful hippopotamus resolved at any cost, even at the cost of its dignity, upon picking up a pea which has got into a corner of its den.

H. G. Wells 1866–1946: *Boon* (1915)

5 The thing his [Henry James's] novel is *about* is always there. It is like a church lit but without a congregation to distract you, with every light and line focussed on the high altar. And on the altar, very reverently placed, intensely there, is a dead kitten, an egg-shell, a bit of string.

H. G. Wells 1866–1946: *Boon* (1915)

6 The work of Henry James has always seemed divisible by a simple dynastic arrangement into three reigns: James I, James II, and the Old Pretender.

Philip Guedalla 1889–1944: *Supers and Supermen* (1920)

7 Poor Henry, he's spending eternity wandering round and round a stately park and the fence is just too high for him to peep over and they're having tea just too far away for him to hear what the countess is saying.

W. Somerset Maugham 1874–1965: *Cakes and Ale* (1930)

8 James was a strange unnatural human being, a sensitive man lost in an immensely abundant brain, which had had neither a scientific nor a philosophical training, but which was by education and natural aptitude alike, formal, formally aesthetic, conscientiously fastidious and delicate. Wrapped about in elaborations of gesture and speech, James regarded his fellow creatures with a face of distress and a remote effort at intercourse, like some victim of enchantment placed in the centre of an immense bladder.

H. G. Wells 1866–1946: *Experiment in Autobiography* (1934)

9 It was worth losing a train (and sometimes you had to do that) while he rummaged for the right word.

J. M. Barrie 1860–1937: *The Greenwood Hat* (1937)

10 A curious talent. One has to respect him. But how one would like to give him a push.

Ivy Compton-Burnett 1884–1969: Hilary Spurling *Secrets of a Woman's Heart: the Later Life of Ivy Compton-Burnett* (1984)

Samuel Johnson 1709–84

1 That great Cham of literature, Samuel Johnson.

Tobias Smollett 1721–71: letter to John Wilkes, 16 March 1759

2 I have seen some extracts from Johnson's Preface to his 'Shakespeare' . . . No feeling nor pathos in him! Altogether upon the high horse, and blustering about Imperial Tragedy!

John Brown 1715–66: letter to David Garrick, 27 October 1765

3 Dr Johnson's sayings would not appear so extraordinary, were it not for his bow-wow way.

Henry Herbert, 10th Earl of Pembroke 1734–94: James Boswell *Life of Samuel Johnson* (1791) 27 March 1775

4 Oh! I could thresh his old jacket till I made his pension jingle in his pockets.
on Johnson's inadequate treatment of Paradise Lost

William Cowper 1731–1800: letter to the Revd William Unwin, 31 October 1779

5 Here lies Sam Johnson:—Reader, have a care,
Tread lightly, lest you wake a sleeping bear:
Religious, moral, generous, and humane
He was: but self-sufficient, proud, and vain,
Fond of, and overbearing in, dispute,
A Christian and a scholar—but a brute.

Soame Jenyns 1704–87: suggested epitaph for Dr Johnson, 1784

6 Ay, now that the old lion is dead, every ass thinks he may kick at him.

Samuel Parr 1747–1825: James Boswell *Life of Samuel Johnson* (1791) 20 December 1784

7 Johnson hewed passages through the Alps, while Gibbon levelled walks through parks and gardens.

George Colman, the Younger 1762–1836: *Random Records* (1830)

8 The gigantic body, the huge massy face, seamed with the scars of disease, the brown coat, the black worsted stockings, the grey wig with the scorched foretop, the dirty hands, the nails bitten and pared to the quick.

Lord Macaulay 1800–59: *Essays Contributed to the Edinburgh Review* (1843) vol. 1 'Samuel Johnson'

Ben Jonson *c.*1573–1637

9 He invades authors like a monarch; and what would be theft in other poets, is only victory in him.

John Dryden 1631–1700: *Essay of Dramatic Poesy* (1668)

10 I can't read Ben Jonson, especially his comedies. To me he appears to move in a wide sea of glue.

Alfred, Lord Tennyson 1809–92: Hallam Tennyson *Alfred Lord Tennyson* (1897)

11 The comedies of Ben Jonson are clearly no laughing matter if we compare them with Shakespeare.

Nevill Coghill 1899–1980: *Collected Papers of Nevill Coghill* (1988) 'The Basis of Shakespearian Comedy'

12 Pioneer of the bizarre, racy, and often grotesque urban poetry of modern life.

Craig Raine 1944– : *Haydn and the Valve Trumpet* (1990)

James Joyce 1882–1941

1 It is not my fault that the odour of ashpits and old weeds and offal hangs round my stories. I seriously believe that you will retard the course of civilization in Ireland by preventing the Irish people from having one good look at themselves in my nicely polished looking-glass.

James Joyce 1882–1941: letter, 23 June 1906

2 I am inclined to think that Mr Joyce is riding his method to death.

Ford Madox Ford 1873–1939: *Thus to Revisit* (1921)

3 The scratching of pimples on the body of the bootboy at Claridges.
of Ulysses

Virginia Woolf 1882–1941: letter to Lytton Strachey, 24 April 1922

4 A cruel playful mind like a great soft tiger cat—I hear, as I read, the report of the rebel sergeant in '98: 'O he was a fine fellow, a fine fellow. It was a pleasure to shoot him.'

W. B. Yeats 1865–1939: letter to Olivia Shakespear, 8 March 1922

5 A dogged attempt to cover the universe with mud, an inverted Victorianism, an attempt to make crossness and dirt succeed where sweetness and light failed.
of Ulysses

E. M. Forster 1879–1970: *Aspects of the Novel* (1927)

6 I do not know whether Joyce's *Ulysses* is a great work of literature. I have puzzled a great deal over that question . . . All I will say is that it is the work of an heroic mind.

W. B. Yeats 1865–1939: speech in the Irish Senate on copyright protection, 1927

7 He abused the English and they applauded him for it.

Italo Svevo 1861–1928: attributed

8 My God, what a clumsy *olla putrida* James Joyce is! Nothing but old fags and cabbage-stumps of quotations from the Bible and the rest, stewed in the juice of deliberate, journalistic dirty-mindedness.

D. H. Lawrence 1885–1930: letter to Aldous and Maria Huxley, 15 August 1928

9 When a young man came up to him in Zurich and said, 'May I kiss the hand that wrote *Ulysses?*' Joyce replied, somewhat like King Lear, 'No, it did lots of other things too.'

James Joyce 1882–1941: Richard Ellmann *James Joyce* (1959)

Franz Kafka 1883–1924 see also 9:7

10 Kafka was a tough, neurasthenic unetiolated visionary who lived from the inside out, spinning his writing out of his guts.

D. J. Enright 1920– : in *Observer* 5 August 1984

11 Kafka could never have written as he did had he lived in a house. His writing is that of someone whose whole life was spent in apartments, with lifts, stairwells, muffled voices behind closed doors, and sounds through walls. Put him in a nice detached villa and he'd never have written a word.

Alan Bennett 1934– : *Writing Home* (1994)

12 For our century, it is he who gave legitimacy to the implausible in the art of the novel.

Milan Kundera 1929– : *Testaments Betrayed* (1995)

Molly Keane 1904–96

ascribing her 'limited talent to amuse' to her Irish Ascendancy background:

1 All the Protestants were poor and had big houses. We entertained a lot but we had poor food, bad wine and no heat. It was an absolute duty to be amusing.

Molly Keane 1904–96: in *Independent* 1 June 1996

John Keats 1795–1821 see also **206:9**

2 It is a better and a wiser thing to be a starved apothecary than a starved poet; so back to the shop Mr John, back to 'plasters, pills, and ointment boxes.'
reviewing Endymion

John Gibson Lockhart 1794–1854: in *Blackwood's Edinburgh Magazine* August 1818

*on Keats's enthusiasm for **Spenser**'s* The Faerie Queene:

3 He went through it as a young horse would through a spring meadow—ramping!

Charles Cowden-Clarke 1787–1877: *Recollections of Writers* (1878)

4 In Endymion, I leaped headlong into the sea, and thereby have become better acquainted with the soundings, the quicksands, and the rocks, than if I had stayed upon the green shore, and piped a silly pipe, and took tea and comfortable advice.

John Keats 1795–1821: letter to James Hessey, 8 October 1818

5 It is true that in the height of enthusiasm I have been cheated into some fine passages but that is nothing.

John Keats 1795–1821: letter to B. R. Haydon, 8 March 1819

6 Johnny Keats's piss-a-bed poetry.

Lord Byron 1788–1824: letter to John Murray, 12 October 1820

7 Keats is a miserable creature, hungering after sweets which he can't get; going about saying, 'I am so hungry; I should so like something pleasant!'

Thomas Carlyle 1795–1881: Wemyss Reid *Life of Richard Monckton Milnes* (1891)

8 I see a schoolboy when I think of him
With face and nose pressed to a sweet-shop window,
For certainly he sank into his grave
His senses and his heart unsatisfied,
And made—being poor, ailing and ignorant,
Shut out from all the luxury of the world,
The ill-bred son of a livery stable-keeper—
Luxuriant song.

W. B. Yeats 1865–1939: 'Ego Dominus Tuus' (1917)

9 For awhile after you quit Keats all other poetry seems to be only whistling or humming.

F. Scott Fitzgerald 1896–1940: letter to his daughter Scottie (Frances Scott Fitzgerald), 3 August 1940

10 Except for his unpleasant emphasis on the *palate*, he strikes me as almost everything a poet should have been in his day.

Elizabeth Bishop 1911–79: letter to Robert Lowell, 30 March 1959

11 He reversed the traditional metaphor by making Poetry, as a dominant female, pursue the shrinking, womanish poet with masculine lustfulness.

Robert Graves 1895–1985: attributed

James Kelman 1946–

1 Rambling monologue of Glaswegian low life, narrated by the sort of lumpen proletarian Scottish drunk one might cross Sauchiehall Street to avoid. It is politically angry, remote from genteel London experience and rough. Anyone who can reach the coarser four-letter words has already read a fair part of the book.

of How Late It Was, How Late *by James Kelman, winner of the 1994 Booker Prize*

Anonymous: in *Athens News* 13 October 1994

Rudyard Kipling 1865–1936

2 Will there never come a season
Which shall rid us from the curse
Of a prose which knows no reason
And an unmelodious verse . . .
When there stands a muzzled stripling,
Mute, beside a muzzled bore:
When the Rudyards cease from kipling
And the Haggards ride no more.

J. K. Stephen 1859–92: 'To R.K.' (1891)

3 In his earliest times I thought he perhaps contained the seeds of an English Balzac, but . . . he has come down steadily from the simple in subject to the more simple—from the Anglo-Indian to the natives, from the natives to the Tommies, from the Tommies to the quadrupeds, from the quadrupeds to the fish, and from the fish to the engines and screws.

Henry James 1843–1916: letter to Grace Norton, 25 December 1897

4 He is a most remarkable man—and I am the other one. Between us we cover all knowledge; he knows all that can be known and I know the rest.

Mark Twain 1835–1910: *Autobiography* (1924)

5 I have always thought it was a sound impulse by which he [Kipling] was driven to put his 'Recessional' into the waste-paper basket, and a great pity that Mrs Kipling fished it out and made him send it to *The Times*.

Max Beerbohm 1872–1956: letter, 30 October 1913

6 Rudyard the dud yard,
Rudyard the false measure,
Told 'em that glory
Ain't always a pleasure,
But said it wuz glorious nevertheless
To lick the boots of the bloke
That makes the worst mess.

Ezra Pound 1885–1972: 'Poems of Alfred Venison: Alf's Fourth Bit' (1949)

7 His virtuosity with language is not unlike that of one of his drill sergeants with an awkward squad . . . The vulgarest words learn to wash behind their ears and to execute complicated movements at the word of command, but they can hardly be said to learn to think for themselves.

W. H. Auden 1907–73: in *New Republic* 24 October 1943

1 Kipling is intensely loved and hated. Hardly any reader likes him a little.

C. S. Lewis 1898–1963: in 1950; Roger Lancelyn Green *Kipling: the Critical Heritage* (1971)

2 I came to the conclusion that Kipling was a homosexual after carrying out a great deal of serious research. He did, after all, go to a public school.

Martin Seymour-Smith 1928– : in *Daily Telegraph* 30 December 1989 'Things They Said In 1989'

Thomas Kyd 1558–1594

3 Sporting Kyd.

Ben Jonson *c.*1573–1637: 'To the Memory of . . . Shakespeare' (1623); see **3:9**

4 Murderous topics were always congenial to the dramatist.

Anonymous: in *Dictionary of National Biography* (1971–)

Charles Lamb 1775–1834

5 His sayings are generally like women's letters; all the pith is in the postscript.

William Hazlitt 1778–1830: *Conversations of James Northcote* (1826–7)

Philip Larkin 1922–85

6 I very much feel the need to be on the periphery of things.

Philip Larkin 1922–85: in *Observer* 16 December 1979

7 His attitude to most accredited sources of pleasure would make Scrooge seem unduly frolicsome.

John Carey 1934– : in *Sunday Times* 1983

8 If poems can teach one anything, Larkin's teach that there is no desolation so bleak that it cannot be made habitable by style. If we live inside a bad joke, it is up to us to learn, at best and worst, to tell it well.

Jonathan Raban 1942– : *Coasting* (1986)

9 Larkin was so English that he didn't even care much about Britain, and he rarely mentioned it.

Clive James 1939– : *The Dreaming Swimmer* (1992)

10 Made a habit of being 60; he made a profession of it. Like Lady Dumbleton, he has been 60 for the last 25 years.

Alan Bennett 1934– : *Writing Home* (1995)

D. H. Lawrence 1885–1930 see also 78:3, 78:4, 207:10

11 I like to write when I feel spiteful; it's like having a good sneeze.

D. H. Lawrence 1885–1930: letter to Lady Cynthia Asquith, *c.*25 November 1913

1 I do not claim to be a literary critic, but I know dirt when I smell it and here it is in heaps—festering putrid heaps which smell to high heaven.
review of Women in Love

W. Charles Pilley : in *John Bull* 17 September 1921

2 He was a bum poet, of course, being a bum person.

Robert Graves 1895–1985: letter to Liddell Hart, 21 December 1935

3 He had a glowing gift for nature, a real feeling for nature, and in this he was at his best. But through his landscapes cantered hallucinations.

Max Beerbohm 1872–1956: in June 1955; S. N. Behrman *Conversations with Max* (1960)

4 His descriptive powers were remarkable, but his ideas cannot too soon be forgotten.

Bertrand Russell 1872–1970: *Autobiography* (1967)

5 Gradually I discovered that he had no wish to make the world better but only to indulge in eloquent soliloquy about how bad it was.

Bertrand Russell 1872–1970: Noel Annan *Our Age* (1990)

6 Lawrence's passion for travel was only equalled by his dislike of the places he arrived at. He would have been a tour operator's nightmare.

John Carey 1934– : in *Sunday Times* 1987

Edward Lear 1812–88

7 'How pleasant to know Mr Lear!'
Who has written such volumes of stuff!
Some think him ill-tempered and queer,
But a few think him pleasant enough.

Edward Lear 1812–88: *Nonsense Songs* (1871) preface; cf. **297:3**

8 Children swarmed to him like settlers. He became a land.

W. H. Auden 1907–73: 'Edward Lear' (1939)

F. R. Leavis 1895–1978

9 A Roundhead? I'd have been Cromwell.
replying to a student who had asked him whether he would have been a Roundhead in the Civil War

F. R. Leavis 1895–1978: attributed

10 He cultivated to perfection the sneer which he used like an oyster-knife, inserting it into the shell of his victim, exposing him with a quick turn of the wrist, and finally flipping him over and inviting his audience to discard him as tainted and inedible.

Noel Annan 1916– : *Our Age* (1990)

Mikhail Lermontov 1814–41

11 No, I'm not Byron, it's my role
To be an undiscovered wonder,
Like him, a persecuted wand'rer,
But furnished with a Russian soul.

Mikhail Lermontov 1814–41: 'No, I'm not Byron' (1832)

Henry Wadsworth Longfellow 1807–82

1 The New World meets the Old World and the sentiments expressed
Are melodiously mingled in my warm New England breast.

John Betjeman 1906–84: 'Longfellow's Visit to Venice' (1958)

Lord Macaulay 1800–59 see also 16:9

2 Macaulay is well for a while, but one wouldn't *live* under Niagara.

Thomas Carlyle 1795–1881: R. M. Milnes *Notebook* (1838)

3 I wish I was as cocksure of anything as Tom Macaulay is of everything.

Lord Melbourne 1779–1848: Lord Cowper's preface to *Lord Melbourne's Papers* (1889)

4 He [Macaulay] has occasional flashes of silence, that make his conversation perfectly delightful.

Sydney Smith 1771–1845: Lady Holland *Memoir* (1855) vol. 1

5 His object is to strike, and he attains it; but it is by scene-painting—he aims at stronger effects than truth warrants, and so caricatures many of his personages as to leave it unaccountable how they have done what they did.

John Stuart Mill 1806–73: letter to Arthur Hardy, September 1856

6 A sentence of Macaulay's . . . may have no more sense in it than a blot pinched between doubled paper.

John Ruskin 1819–1900: *Praeterita* (1887)

Roger McGough 1937–

7 I feel like a poet when I'm writing a poem. Otherwise I feel that I'm on the outside of things.

Roger McGough 1937– : interview in *Sunday Telegraph* 12 May 1996

Louis MacNeice 1907–63

8 When we were young . . . his poetry was the poetry of our everyday life, of shop-windows, traffic policemen, ice-cream soda, lawn mowers, and an uneasy awareness of what the newsboys were shouting. In addition he displayed a sophisticated sentimentality about falling leaves and lipsticked cigarette stubs: he could have written the words of 'These Foolish Things'. We were grateful to him for having found a place in poetry for these properties.

Philip Larkin 1922–85: in *New Statesman* 1963

François Malherbe 1555–1628

9 *Ce que Malherbe escrit dure eternellement.*
What Malherbe writes will endure forever.

François Malherbe 1555–1628: 'Sonnet au Roy'

1 *Enfin Malherbe vint, et, le premier en France,*
Fit sentir dans les vers une juste cadence.

At last came Malherbe, and he was the first in France to give poetry a proper flow.

Nicolas Boileau 1636–1711: *L'Art poétique* (1674)

André Malraux 1901–76

2 His life, not his writings, is his chef d'oeuvre.

Anonymous: quoted in *Literary Review* July 1995

3 The life and works of André Malraux suggest a man restricted to the heights of experience.

Anonymous: in *Literary Review* July 1995

Katherine Mansfield 1888–1973 see also 214:5

4 Her mind is a very thin soil, laid an inch or two upon very barren rock.

Virginia Woolf 1882–1941: *A Writer's Diary* (1953) 7 August 1918

Christopher Marlowe 1564–93

5 Marlowe's mighty line.

Ben Jonson *c.*1573–1637: 'To the Memory of . . . Shakespeare' (1623)

6 A kind of cross between Oscar Wilde and Jack the Ripper.

Seamus Heaney 1939– : *The Redress of Poetry* (1995)

W. Somerset Maugham 1874–1965

7 It is this preoccupation with physical appetite, which he doesn't feel, that makes Maugham's work so intensely vulgar—rather like Balzac's to the rich, or Evelyn Waugh's to the highly born, or like Graham Greene's to the good.

Malcolm Muggeridge 1903–90: Noel Annan *Our Age* (1990)

Guy de Maupassant 1850–93

8 No one but a Frenchman can write such pages as that—but no one but a Frenchman *would*, either.

of de Maupassant's description of 'the love-making of poor Madame Walter' in Bel Ami

Henry James 1843–1916: letter, 29 May 1885

Herman Melville 1819–91

1 Herman Melville who split the atom of the traditional novel in the effort to make whaling a universal metaphor.

David Lodge 1935– : *Changing Places* (1975)

George Meredith 1828–1909

2 Meredith! Who can define him? His style is chaos illuminated by flashes of lightning.

Oscar Wilde 1854–1900: 'The Decay of Lying' (1891); cf. **285:3**

3 Meredith became, at his best, a sort of daintily dressed Walt Whitman.

G. K. Chesterton 1874–1936: *The Victorian Age in Literature* (1912)

A. A. Milne 1882–1956 see also **42:10**

4 Milne is so far out of the literary fashion that he failed to detest his parents. His parents had previously failed to ill-treat and misunderstand him. He failed to detest his school and his schoolfellows. He failed to have furtive adolescent sexual misadventures which left him with a burning hatred of all females and an illicit love for some fellow male. He married early, and his marriage failed to be a failure. He had one son, who failed to disappoint or to hate him. And his life failed to be disagreeable in every particular, perhaps because he has failed to be as unpleasant as possible to every person he met.

Frank Swinnerton 1884–1982: *The Georgian Literary Scene* (1939)

John Milton 1608–74

5 Oval face. His eye a dark grey. He had auburn hair. His complexion exceeding fair—he was so fair that they called him *the lady of* Christ's College.

John Aubrey 1626–97: *Brief Lives* 'John Milton'

6 The living throne, the sapphire-blaze,
Where angels tremble, while they gaze,
He saw; but blasted with excess of light,
Closed his eyes in endless night.

Thomas Gray 1716–71: *The Progress of Poesy* (1757)

7 Its perusal is a duty rather than a pleasure.

Samuel Johnson 1709–84: *Lives of the English Poets* (1779–81) 'Milton'

8 Milton, Madam, was a genius that could cut a Colossus from a rock; but could not carve heads upon cherry-stones.

to Hannah More, who had expressed a wonder that the poet who had written Paradise Lost *should write such poor sonnets*

Samuel Johnson 1709–84: James Boswell *Life of Samuel Johnson* (1791) 13 June 1784

9 The reason Milton wrote in fetters when he wrote of Angels and God, and at liberty when of Devils and Hell, is because he was a true Poet, and of the Devil's party without knowing it.

William Blake 1757–1827: *The Marriage of Heaven and Hell* (1790–3)

1 Milton! thou shouldst be living at this hour:
England hath need of thee: she is a fen
Of stagnant waters: altar, sword, and pen,
Fireside, the heroic wealth of hall and bower,
Have forfeited their ancient English dower
Of inward happiness.

William Wordsworth 1770–1850: 'Milton! thou shouldst be living at this hour' (1807)

2 I have but lately been on my guard against Milton. Life to him would be death to me. Miltonic verse cannot be written but in the vein of art—I wish to devote myself to another sensation.

John Keats 1795–1821: letter to George and Georgiana Keats, 17 September 1819

3 O mighty-mouth'd inventor of harmonies,
O skilled to sing of Time or Eternity,
God-gifted organ-voice of England,
Milton, a name to resound for ages.

Alfred, Lord Tennyson 1809–92: 'Milton' (1847)

4 No man can get the full flavour of Milton's poetry who is not able, by knowledge of Latin, to derive the words as he goes on.

George Gissing 1857–1903: *Commonplace Book* (1962)

5 He was the first of the masculinists. He deals in horror and immensity and squalor and sublimity but never in the passions of the human heart. Has any great poem ever let in so little light upon one's own joys and sorrows? I get no help in judging life; I scarcely feel that Milton lived or knew men and women.

Virginia Woolf 1882–1941: diary, 1918; *Diary of Virginia Woolf* (1977) vol. 1

6 After the erection of the Chinese Wall of Milton, blank verse has suffered not only arrest but retrogression.

T. S. Eliot 1888–1965: *Selected Essays* (1932) 'Christopher Marlowe'

7 Nearly every sentence in Milton has that power which physicists sometimes think we shall have to attribute to matter—the power of action at a distance.

C. S. Lewis 1898–1963: *A Preface to Paradise Lost* (1942)

Molière 1622–73

8 *Il plaît à tout le monde, et ne sauroit se plaire.*
He pleases all the world, but cannot please himself.

Nicolas Boileau 1636–1711: 'À M. de Molière'

Marianne Moore 1887–1972

9 If she speaks of a chair you can practically sit on it.

Elizabeth Bishop 1911–79: notebook, *c.*1934/5; D. Kalstone *Becoming a Poet* (1989)

William Morris 1834–96

10 I can't understand how a man who, on the whole, enjoys dinner—and breakfast—and supper—to that extent of fat—can write such lovely poems about Misery.

John Ruskin 1819–1900: letter to Joan Agnew, 21 January 1870

1 Of course he was a wonderful all-round man, but the act of walking round him has always tired me.

Max Beerbohm 1872–1956: letter to S. N. Behrman *c.*1953, in *Conversations with Max* (1960)

Iris Murdoch 1919–

2 She is like a character out of Hieronymus Bosch—the very nicest character.

Rachel Billington 1942– : profile in *The Times* 25 April 1983

Vladimir Nabokov 1899–1977

3 I think like a genius, I write like a distinguished author, and I speak like a child.

Vladimir Nabokov 1899–1977: *Strong Opinions* (1973)

V. S. Naipaul 1932–

4 I am the kind of writer that people think other people are reading.

V. S. Naipaul 1932– : in *Radio Times* 14 March 1979

George Orwell 1903–50

5 He could not blow his nose without moralising on the state of the handkerchief industry.

Cyril Connolly 1903–74: in *Sunday Times* 29 September 1968

John Osborne 1929–94

6 I never deliberately set out to shock, but when people don't walk out of my plays I think there is something wrong.

John Osborne 1929–94: attributed, 1975

7 Thank you, I've already made it.
*when invited by Kenneth **Tynan** to 'make history' at the National Theatre*

John Osborne 1929–94: in *The Times* 27 December 1994; attributed

8 He had to be plied with extremely expensive champagne. He became more and more like the old Edwardian father he kept attacking in *Look Back in Anger*. That was what he always wanted to be. His fury in the 1950s was that he wasn't a rich squire.
recording a 60th birthday TV interview, which was never used

Jonathan Miller 1934– : in *The Times* 27 December 1994

9 Lessons in feeling.
his own description of his plays

John Osborne 1929–94: in *Guardian* 27 December 1994

Ovid 43 BC–AD c.17

1 Here are only numbers ratified; but, for the elegancy, facility, and golden cadence of poesy, *caret*. Ovidius Naso was the man: and why, indeed, Naso, but for smelling out the odoriferous flowers of fancy, the jerks of invention?

William Shakespeare 1564–1616: *Love's Labour's Lost* (1595)

2 Ovid, the soft philosopher of love.

John Dryden 1631–1700: *Love Triumphant* (1694)

3 As Ovid has sweetly in parable told,
We harden like trees, and like rivers grow cold.

Lady Mary Wortley Montagu 1689–1762: *Six Town Eclogues* (1747) 'The Lover'

4 Ovid remained classical even in exile: he looked for his suffering not in himself, but in his separation from the capital of the world.

Johann Wolfgang von Goethe 1749–1832: *Sayings in Prose*

Wilfred Owen 1893–1918

on his exclusion of Owen from The Oxford Book of Modern Verse*:*

5 I did not know I was excluding a revered sandwich-board man of the revolution and that somebody has put his worst and most famous poem in a glass-case at the British Museum—however if I had known it I would have excluded him just the same. He is all blood, dirt and sucked sugar stick.

W. B. Yeats 1865–1939: letter to Dorothy Wellesley, 21 December 1936

Dorothy Parker 1893–1967

6 She is so odd a blend of Little Nell and Lady Macbeth. It is not so much the familiar phenomenon of a hand of steel in a velvet glove as a lacy sleeve with a bottle of vitriol concealed in its folds.

Alexander Woollcott 1887–1943: *While Rome Burns* (1934)

7 Four be the things I'd been better without:
Love, curiosity, freckles, and doubt.

Dorothy Parker 1893–1967: 'Inventory' (1937)

8 Everything I've ever said will be credited to Dorothy Parker.

George S. Kaufman 1889–1961: attributed

Walter Pater 1839–94

9 His prose has none of the freshness of life about it, resembling, in its elaborately cautious movements, a person in poor health making his way upstairs backwards on crutches.

John Carey 1934– : in *Sunday Times* 25 June 1978

Harold Pinter 1930–

10 The weasel under the cocktail cabinet.
on being asked what his plays were about

Harold Pinter 1930– : J. Russell Taylor *Anger and After* (1962) *on being telephoned by the* Evening News *to ask if he had any comment to offer on the occasion of Harold Pinter's fiftieth birthday:*

1 I don't; it's only later I realize I could have suggested two minutes' silence.

Alan Bennett 1934– : *Writing Home* (1994) diary, 1 October 1980

2 Oh, this dread word Pinteresque. It makes people reach for their guns. Or behave as if they were going to church. But when the audience is actually there, I am always gratified when I hear laughter. There is a great deal of humour in my plays.

Harold Pinter 1930– : in *Sunday Times* 9 July 1995

Sylvia Plath 1932–63

3 I see her as a kind of Hammer Films poet.

Philip Larkin 1922–85: letter, 15 November 1981

4 Her last poems . . . present themselves with all the pounce and irrefutability of a tiger lashing its tail.

Seamus Heaney 1939– : *The Government of the Tongue* (1988)

Edgar Allan Poe 1809–49

5 Poe is a kind of Hawthorne and *delirium tremens*.

Leslie Stephen 1832–1904: *Hours in a Library* (1874)

6 There comes Poe, with his raven, like Barnaby Rudge,
Three-fifths of him genius, and two-fifths sheer fudge . . .
Who has written some things quite the best of their kind.
But somehow the heart seems squeezed out by the mind.

James Russell Lowell 1819–91: *Poe and Longfellow* 'A Fable for Critics'

7 Poe is the only impeccable writer. He was never mistaken.

Paul Valéry 1871–1945: Julian Symons *The Tell-Tale Heart* (1978)

8 Poor Poe! At first so forgotten that his grave went without a tombstone twenty-six years . . . today in danger of becoming the life study of a few professors.

W. H. Auden 1907–73: introduction to *Edgar Allan Poe* (1950)

9 Poe . . . was perhaps the first great nonstop literary drinker of the American nineteenth century. He made the indulgences of Coleridge and De Quincey seem like a bit of mischief in the kitchen with the cooking sherry.

James Thurber 1894–1961: *Alarms and Diversions* (1957)

Alexander Pope 1688–1744

10 He hardly drank tea without a stratagem.

Samuel Johnson 1709–84: *Lives of the English Poets* (1779–81) 'Pope'

11 But he (his musical finesse was such,
So nice his ear, so delicate his touch)
Made poetry a mere mechanic art,
And ev'ry warbler has his tune by heart.

William Cowper 1731–1800: 'Table Talk' (1782)

1 To escape from the grotesque tragedy which was his body, Pope perfected a series of immaculate masks and voices.

John Carey 1934– : in *Sunday Times* 1985

Dennis Potter 1935–94

2 The women were weird. The witch, a bitch and a fool.
of Vote, Vote, Vote for Nigel Barton

Nancy Banks-Smith : in *The Sun* 9 December 1965

Ezra Pound 1885–1972

3 Ezra was right half the time, and when he was wrong, he was so wrong you were never in any doubt about it.

Ernest Hemingway 1899–1961: in *New Republic* 11 November 1936

4 A village explainer, excellent if you were a village, but if you were not, not.

Gertrude Stein 1874–1946: Janet Hobhouse *Everyone who was Anybody* (1975)

5 He behaved like Baden-Powell getting everyone under canvas.
on Pound's marshalling poets under the banner of 'Imagisme' c.1912

Wyndham Lewis 1882–1957: Malcolm Bradbury and James McFarlane (eds.) *Modernism* (1991)

Marcel Proust 1871–1922

6 The little lickspittle wasn't satirizing, he really thought his pimps, buggers and opulent idiots were *important*, instead of the last mould on the dying cheese.

Ezra Pound 1885–1972: letter, 23 November 1933

7 His greatness lay in his art, his incredible littleness in the quality of his social admirations.

Edith Wharton 1862–1937: *A Backward Glance* (1934)

8 [Proust] is an exquisite writer but for pomposity and intricacy of style he makes Henry James and Osbert Sitwell look like Berta Ruck.

Noël Coward 1899–1973: diary, 25 July 1950

9 After Proust, there are certain things that simply cannot be done again. He marks off for you the boundaries of your talent.

Françoise Sagan 1935– : Malcolm Cowley (ed.) *Writers at Work* (1958) 1st series

Alexander Pushkin 1799–1837

10 A pair of boots is in every sense better than Pushkin, because . . . Pushkin is mere luxury and nonsense.
frequently quoted in the form 'A pair of boots is worth more than Shakespeare', and for long wrongly associated with the Russian literary critic Dmitry Pisarev

Fedor Dostoevsky 1821–81: in *Epokha* 1864

Barbara Pym 1913–80

1 What is the future of my kind of writing? . . . Perhaps in retirement . . . a quieter, narrower kind of life can be worked out and adopted. Bounded by English literature and the Anglican Church and small pleasures like sewing and choosing dress material for this uncertain summer.
on having a novel rejected

Barbara Pym 1913–80: diary, 6 March 1972

Jean Racine 1639–99

2 Racine will go out of style like coffee.

Marie de Sévigné 1626–96: attributed

Jean Rhys *c.*1890–1979

3 A doormat in a world of boots.
of herself

Jean Rhys *c.*1890–1979: in *Guardian* 6 December 1990

Samuel Richardson 1689–1761 see also 298:2

4 I look upon this [*Clarissa*] and *Pamela* to be two books that will do more general mischief than the works of Lord Rochester.

Lady Mary Wortley Montagu 1689–1762: letter to Lady Bute, 1 March 1752

5 Why, Sir, if you were to read Richardson for the story, your impatience would be so much fretted that you would hang yourself.

Samuel Johnson 1709–84: James Boswell *Life of Samuel Johnson* (1791) 6 April 1772

6 Oh Richardson! thou singular genius.

Denis Diderot 1713–84: Isaac D'Israeli *Curiosities of Literature* (1849 ed.)

7 There is more knowledge of the heart in one letter of Richardson's than in all *Tom Jones*.

Samuel Johnson 1709–84: James Boswell *Life of Samuel Johnson* (1791)

8 Richardson was well qualified to be the discoverer of a new style of writing, for he was a cautious, deep, and minute examiner of the human heart, and . . . left neither head, bay nor inlet behind him, until he had traced its soundings, and laid it down in his chart, with all its minute sinuosities, its depths, and its shallows.

Sir Walter Scott 1771–1832: *Lives of the Poets* (1827) 'Samuel Richardson'

9 The censure which the Shakespeare of novelists has incurred for the tedious procrastination and the minute details of his fable; his slow unfolding characters, and the slightest gesture of his personages, is extremely unjust; for is it not evident that we could not have his peculiar excellences without these accompanying defects.

Isaac D'Israeli 1766–1848: *Curiosities of Literature* (1849 ed.)

Salman Rushdie 1947–

1 Frankly I wish I had written a more critical book.
after The Satanic Verses *had provoked the fatwa invoked against him by Ayatollah Khomeini*

Salman Rushdie 1947– : in *Weekend Guardian* 18 February 1989; cf. **35:14**

John Ruskin 1819–1900

2 In face, in manner, in talk, in mind, he is weakness pure and simple. I use the word, not invidiously, but scientifically. He has the beauties of his defects; but to see him only confirms the impression given by his writing, that he has been scared back by the grim face of reality into the world of unreason and illusion, and that he wanders there without a compass and a guide—or any light save the fitful flashes of his beautiful genius.

Henry James 1843–1916: letter, 20 March 1869

3 I am, and my father was before me, a violent Tory of the old school; Walter Scott's school, that is to say, and Homer's.

John Ruskin 1819–1900: *Praeterita* (1885)

George Sand 1804–76

4 Thou large-brained woman and large-hearted man.

Elizabeth Barrett Browning 1806–61: 'To George Sand—A Desire' (1844)

Sappho late 7th century BC

5 Dark Sappho! could not verse immortal save
That breast imbued with such immortal fire?
Could she not live who life eternal gave?

Lord Byron 1788–1824: *Childe Harold's Pilgrimage* (1812–18)

6 The isles of Greece, the isles of Greece!
Where burning Sappho loved and sung.

Lord Byron 1788–1824: *Don Juan* (1819–24)

Siegfried Sassoon 1886–1967

7 It is realism of the right, of the poetic kind.
reviewing Siegfried Sassoon's war poems 1917

Virginia Woolf 1882–1941: in *Times Literary Supplement* 31 May 1917

8 A booby-trapped idealist.
on himself

Siegfried Sassoon 1886–1967: *Siegfried's Journey* (1945)

Richard Savage *c.*1697–1743

1 Those are no proper judges of his conduct, who have slumbered away their time on the down of plenty; nor will any wise man presume to say, 'Had I been in Savage's condition I should have lived or written better than Savage'.

Samuel Johnson 1709–84: *Life of Savage* (1744)

Dorothy L. Sayers 1893–1957

2 We conversed until 2.15 a.m. I liked the old dear but found her heavy going.

Charles Williams 1886–1945: Humphrey Carpenter *The Inklings* (1978)

Sir Walter Scott 1771–1832 see also 18:2

3 Walter Scott has no business to write novels, especially good ones—It is not fair.—He has fame and profit enough as a poet, and should not be taking the bread out of other people's mouths.—I do not like him, and do not mean to like *Waverley* if I can help it—but fear I must.

Jane Austen 1775–1817: letter to Anna Austen, 28 September 1814

4 Full many a gallant man lies slain
On Waterloo's ensanguined plain,
But none by bullet or by shot
Fell half so flat as Walter Scott.
comment on Scott's poem 'The Field of Waterloo' (1815)

Anonymous: sometimes attributed to Thomas Erskine; Una Pope-Hennessy *The Laird of Abbotsford* (1932)

5 His works (taken together) are almost like a new edition of human nature. This is indeed to be an author!

William Hazlitt 1778–1830: *The Spirit of the Age* (1825)

Seneca ('the Younger') *c.*4 BC–AD 65

6 Seneca writes as a boar does piss, *scilicet* by jerks.

Ralph Kettell 1563–1643: John Aubrey *Brief Lives* 'Ralph Kettell'

Thomas Shadwell 1642–92

7 The rest to some faint meaning make pretence,
But Shadwell never deviates into sense.
Some beams of wit on other souls may fall,
Strike through and make a lucid interval;
But Shadwell's genuine night admits no ray,
His rising fogs prevail upon the day.

John Dryden 1631–1700: *MacFlecknoe* (1682)

Shakespeare 1564–1616

1 Soul of the Age!
The applause, delight, the wonder of our stage!

Ben Jonson *c.*1573–1637: 'To the Memory of My Beloved, the Author, Mr William Shakespeare' (1623)

2 He was not of an age, but for all time!

Ben Jonson *c.*1573–1637: 'To the Memory of My Beloved, the Author, Mr William Shakespeare' (1623)

3 Sweet Swan of Avon!

Ben Jonson *c.*1573–1637: 'To the Memory of My Beloved, the Author, Mr William Shakespeare' (1623)

4 Thou hadst small Latin, and less Greek.

Ben Jonson *c.*1573–1637: 'To the Memory of My Beloved, the Author, Mr William Shakespeare' (1623)

5 Who, as he was a happy imitator of Nature, was a most gentle expresser of it. His mind and hand went together: And what he thought, he uttered with that easiness, that we have scarce received from him a blot.

John Heming 1556–1630 and **Henry Condell** d. 1627: First Folio Shakespeare (1623) preface

6 What needs my Shakespeare for his honoured bones,
The labour of an age in pilèd stones,
Or that his hallowed relics should be hid
Under a star-ypointing pyramid?

John Milton 1608–74: 'On Shakespeare' (1632)

7 The players have often mentioned it as an honour to Shakespeare that in his writing, whatsoever he penned, he never blotted out a line. My answer hath been 'Would he had blotted a thousand' . . . But he redeemed his vices with his virtues. There was ever more in him to be praised than to be pardoned.

Ben Jonson *c.*1573–1637: *Timber, or Discoveries made upon Men and Matter* (1641) 'De Shakespeare Nostrati'

8 He was the man who of all modern, and perhaps ancient poets, had the largest and most comprehensive soul . . . He was naturally learn'd; he needed not the spectacles of books to read Nature: he looked inwards, and found her there . . . He is many times flat, insipid; his comic wit degenerating into clenches, his serious swelling into bombast. But he is always great.

John Dryden 1631–1700: *An Essay of Dramatic Poesy* (1668)

9 [Shakespeare] is the very Janus of poets; he wears almost everywhere two faces; and you have scarce begun to admire the one, ere you despise the other.

John Dryden 1631–1700: *Essay on the Dramatic Poetry of the Last Age* (1672)

10 He was a handsome, well-shaped man: very good company, and of a very ready and pleasant smooth wit.

John Aubrey 1626–97: *Brief Lives* 'William Shakespeare'

11 One of the greatest geniuses that ever existed, Shakespeare, undoubtedly wanted taste.

Horace Walpole 1717–97: letter to Christopher Wren, 9 August 1764

1 Shakespeare has united the powers of exciting laughter and sorrow not only in one mind but in one composition . . . That this is a practice contrary to the rules of criticism will be readily allowed; but there is always an appeal open from criticism to nature.

Samuel Johnson 1709–84: *Plays of William Shakespeare . . .* (1765) preface

2 A quibble is to Shakespeare, what luminous vapours are to the traveller; he follows it at all adventures, it is sure to lead him out of his way and sure to engulf him in the mire.

Samuel Johnson 1709–84: *Plays of William Shakespeare . . .* (1765)

3 Corneille is to Shakespeare . . . as a clipped hedge is to a forest.

Samuel Johnson 1709–84: Hester Lynch Piozzi *Anecdotes of . . . Johnson* (1786)

4 Was there ever such stuff as great part of Shakespeare? Only one must not say so! But what think you?—what?—Is there not sad stuff? what?—what?

George III 1738–1820: to Fanny Burney; Fanny Burney, diary, 19 December 1785

5 Shakespeare one gets acquainted with without knowing how. It is part of an Englishman's constitution. His thoughts and beauties are so spread abroad that one touches them everywhere, one is intimate with him by instinct.

Jane Austen 1775–1817: *Mansfield Park* (1814)

6 Our *myriad-minded* Shakespeare.

Samuel Taylor Coleridge 1772–1834: *Biographia Literaria* (1817)

7 Shakespeare . . . is of no age—nor of any religion, or party or profession. The body and substance of his works came out of the unfathomable depths of his own oceanic mind.

Samuel Taylor Coleridge 1772–1834: *Table Talk* (1835) 15 March 1834

8 Others abide our question. Thou art free.
We ask and ask: Thou smilest and art still,
Out-topping knowledge.

Matthew Arnold 1822–88: 'Shakespeare' (1849)

9 He was not a man, he was a continent; he contained whole crowds of great men, entire landscapes.

Gustave Flaubert 1821–80: letter, 19 September 1852

10 'With this same key
Shakespeare unlocked his heart,' once more!
Did Shakespeare? If so, the less Shakespeare he!

Robert Browning 1812–89: 'House' (1876); cf. **174:1**

11 With the single exception of Homer, there is no eminent writer, not even Sir Walter Scott, whom I can despise so entirely as I despise Shakespeare when I measure my mind against his. The intensity of my impatience with him occasionally reaches such a pitch, that it would positively be a relief to me to dig him up and throw stones at him, knowing as I do how incapable he and his worshippers are of understanding any less obvious form of indignity.

George Bernard Shaw 1856–1950: in *Saturday Review* 26 September 1896

12 When I read Shakespeare I am struck with wonder
That such trivial people should muse and thunder
In such lovely language.

D. H. Lawrence 1885–1930: 'When I Read Shakespeare' (1929)

1 Brush up your Shakespeare,
Start quoting him now.
Brush up your Shakespeare
And the women you will wow . . .
If she says your behaviour is heinous
Kick her right in the 'Coriolanus'.
Brush up your Shakespeare
And they'll all kowtow.

Cole Porter 1891–1964: 'Brush Up your Shakespeare' (1948 song)

2 Shakespeare is so tiring. You never get a chance to sit down unless you're a king.

Josephine Hull ?1886–1957: in *Time* 16 November 1953

3 Shaw is like a train. One just speaks the words and sits in one's place. But Shakespeare is like bathing in the sea—one swims where one wants.

Vivien Leigh 1913–67: letter from Harold Nicolson to Vita Sackville-West, 1 February 1956

4 The remarkable thing about Shakespeare is that he is really very good—in spite of all the people who say he is very good.

Robert Graves 1895–1985: attributed, 1964

5 Shakespeare—the nearest thing in incarnation to the eye of God.

Laurence Olivier 1907–89: in *Kenneth Harris Talking To* (1971) 'Sir Laurence Olivier'

6 Shakespeare is the Canon. He sets the standards and the limits of literature.

Harold Bloom 1930– : *The Western Canon* (1995)

George Bernard Shaw 1856–1950 see also 93:3

7 He [Bernard Shaw] hasn't an enemy in the world, and none of his friends like him.

Oscar Wilde 1854–1900: Bernard Shaw *Sixteen Self Sketches* (1949)

8 Mr Shaw is (I suspect) the only man on earth who has never written any poetry.

G. K. Chesterton 1874–1936: *Orthodoxy* (1908)

9 A good man fallen among Fabians.

Lenin 1870–1924: Arthur Ransome *Six Weeks in Russia in 1919* (1919) 'Notes of Conversations with Lenin'

10 Shaw's plays are the price we pay for Shaw's prefaces.

James Agate 1877–1947: diary, 10 March 1933

11 It seemed to me inorganic, logical straightness and not the crooked road of life.
of Arms and the Man

W. B. Yeats 1865–1939: *Autobiographies* (1955)

12 I do not think that Shaw will be a great literary figure in 2000 AD. He is an amazingly brilliant contemporary; but not in the Hardy class.

Harold Nicolson 1886–1968: diary, 11 December 1950

13 Shaw's judgements were often scatterbrained, but at least he had brains to scatter.

Max Beerbohm 1872–1956: in 1954; S. N. Behrman *Conversations with Max* (1960)

14 The magic of Shaw's words may still bewitch posterity . . . but it will find that he has nothing to say.

A. J. P. Taylor 1906–90: in *Observer* 22 July 1956

Mary Shelley 1797–1851 see also **112:8**

1 [*Frankenstein* is] a book about what happens when a man tries to have a baby without a woman.

Anne K. Mellor 1941– : in *Sunday Correspondent* 8 April 1990

Percy Bysshe Shelley 1792–1822

2 You I am sure will forgive me for sincerely remarking that you might curb your magnanimity and be more of an artist, and 'load every rift' of your subject with ore.

echoing Edmund ***Spenser*** The Faerie Queene *(1596): 'And with rich metal loaded every rift'*

John Keats 1795–1821: letter to Shelley, August 1820

3 Shelley is truth itself—and honour itself—notwithstanding his out-of-the-way notions about religion.

Lord Byron 1788–1824: letter to Douglas Kinnaird, 2 June 1821

4 The author of the *Prometheus Unbound* has a fire in his eye, a fever in his blood, a maggot in his brain, a hectic flutter in his speech, which mark out the philosophic fanatic.

William Hazlitt 1778–1830: *Table Talk* (1821–2) 'On Paradox and Common-Place'

5 In poetry, no less than in life, he is 'a beautiful and ineffectual angel, beating in the void his luminous wings in vain'.

Matthew Arnold 1822–88: *Essays in Criticism* Second Series (1888) 'Shelley' (quoting from his own essay on Byron in the same work)

6 I made my then famous declaration (among 100 people) 'I am a Socialist, an Atheist and a Vegetarian' (ergo, a true Shelleyan), whereupon two ladies who had been palpitating with enthusiasm for Shelley under the impression that he was a devout Anglican, resigned on the spot.

George Bernard Shaw 1856–1950: letter, 1 March 1908

Philip Sidney 1554–86

7 Will you have all in all for prose and verse? Take the miracle of our age, Sir Philip Sidney.

Richard Carew 1555–1620: William Camden *Remains concerning Britain* (1614) 'The Excellency of the English Tongue'

Edith Sitwell 1887–1964

8 A high altar on the move.

Elizabeth Bowen 1899–1973: V. Glendinning *Edith Sitwell* (1981)

John Skelton *c.*1460–1529

9 The work of the 16th-century poet John Skelton because I don't like his rhythms.

asked what he would like to see blown up

Peter Ackroyd 1949– : in *Daily Telegraph* 7 January 1995

Christopher Smart 1722–71

1 For in my nature I quested for beauty, but God, God hath sent me to sea for pearls.

Christopher Smart 1722–71: *Jubilate Agno* (*c.*1758–63)

2 His infirmities were not noxious to society. He insisted upon people praying with him, and I'd as lief pray with Kit Smart as with anyone else.

Samuel Johnson 1709–84: James Boswell *Life of Samuel Johnson* (1791)

C. P. Snow 1905–80

3 A man who so much resembled a Baked Alaska—sweet, warm and gungy on the outside, hard and cold within.

Francis King 1923– : *Yesterday Came Suddenly* (1993)

Alexander Solzhenitsyn 1918–

4 A bearer of light!
on meeting Solzhenitsyn, summer 1962

Anna Akhmatova 1889–1966: Robert Reeder *Anna Akhmatova* (1995)

Sophocles *c.*496–406 BC

5 But he was contented there, is contented here.
there *on earth;* here *in Hades*

Aristophanes *c.*450–*c.*385 BC: *The Frogs* (405 BC)

6 Who saw life steadily, and saw it whole:
The mellow glory of the Attic stage;
Singer of sweet Colonus, and its child.

Matthew Arnold 1822–88: 'To a Friend' (1849)

Muriel Spark 1918–

7 Glimpses that seem like a microcosm of reality.
of her own novels

Muriel Spark 1918– : in *Sunday Times* 1962

8 I think I am still a poet. I think my novels are the novels of a poet. I think like a poet and react like one.

Muriel Spark 1918– : in *Listener* 1970

Stephen Spender 1909–95

9 To see him fumbling with our rich and delicate language is to experience all the horror of seeing a Sèvres vase in the hands of a chimpanzee.

Evelyn Waugh 1903–66: in *The Tablet* 5 May 1951

Edmund Spenser *c.*1552–99

1 Thee gentle Spenser fondly led;
But me he mostly sent to bed.

Walter Savage Landor 1775–1864: 'To Wordsworth: Those Who Have Laid the Harp Aside' (1846)

2 When Spenser wrote of Ireland he wrote as an official, and out of the thoughts and emotions that had been organized by the state. He was the first of many Englishmen to see nothing but what he was desired to see.

W. B. Yeats 1865–1939: 'Edmund Spenser' (1902)

3 The quotation of two or three lines of a stanza from Spenser's *Faerie Queene* is probably as good an all-round silencer as anything.

Stephen Potter 1900–69: *Lifemanship* (1950)

4 First I thought Troilus and Criseyde was the most *boring* poem in English. Then I thought Beowulf was. Then I thought Paradise Lost was. Now I *know* The Faerie Queene is the *dullest thing out. Blast* it.
written in pencil in St John's College library copy of The Faerie Queene, *c.*1941

Philip Larkin 1922–85: Kingsley Amis *Memoirs* (1992)

Madame de Staël 1766–1817

5 Mme de Staël has succeeded in disguising us *both* as women.
on her novel Delphine *(1802)*

Charles-Maurice de Talleyrand 1754–1838: Evangeline Bruce *Napoleon and Josephine* (1995)

Richard Steele 1672–1729

6 A rake among scholars, and a scholar among rakes.

Lord Macaulay 1800–59: *Essays Contributed to the Edinburgh Review* (1850) 'The Life and Writings of Addison'

Gertrude Stein 1874–1946

7 Gertrude Stein's prose-song is a cold, black suet-pudding. We can represent it as a cold suet-roll of fabulously-reptilian length. Cut it at any point, it is the same thing; the same heavy, sticky, opaque mass all through, and all along. It is weighted, projected, with a sibylline urge. It is mournful and monstrous, composed of dead and inanimate material. It is all fat, without nerve. Or the evident vitality that informs it is vegetable rather than animal. Its life is a low-grade, if tenacious one; of the sausage, by-the-yard, variety.
of Three Lives *(1909)*

Wyndham Lewis 1882–1957: *Time and Western Man* (1927)

8 Gertrude Stein and me are just like brothers.

Ernest Hemingway 1899–1961: John Malcolm Brinnin *The Third Rose* (1960)

1 The mama of dada.

Clifton Fadiman 1904– : *Party of One* (1955)

2 Miss Stein was a past master in making nothing happen slowly.

Clifton Fadiman 1904– : *Appreciations* (1955)

Laurence Sterne 1713–68

3 At present, nothing is talked of, nothing admired, but what I cannot help calling a very insipid and tedious performance: it is a kind of novel, called *The Life and Opinions of Tristram Shandy*; the great humour of which consists in the whole narration always going backwards.

Horace Walpole 1717–97: letter to David Dalrymple, 4 April 1760

4 The Scotsman is wanton, transparent and artless, haunted by the fear of the Presbyterian devil, whereas we can be sure that the devil himself was afraid that the half-Irish Sterne would drag him into bad company.
comparing ***Boswell*** *and Sterne*

V. S. Pritchett 1900– : Noel Annan *Our Age* (1990)

Robert Louis Stevenson 1850–94

5 This be the verse you grave for me:
'Here he lies where he longed to be;
Home is the sailor, home from sea,
And the hunter home from the hill.'

Robert Louis Stevenson 1850–94: 'Requiem' (1887)

6 Valiant in velvet, light in ragged luck,
Most vain, most generous, sternly critical,
Buffoon and poet, lover and sensualist;
A deal of Ariel, just a streak of Puck,
Much Antony, of Hamlet most of all,
And something of the Shorter-Catechist.

W. E. Henley 1849–1903: 'In Hospital' (1888); cf. **285:6**

7 I am an Epick writer with a k to it, but without the necessary genius.

Robert Louis Stevenson 1850–94: letter to Henry James, 5 December 1892

8 Stevenson seemed to pick the right word up on the point of his pen, like a man playing spillikins.

G. K. Chesterton 1874–1936: *The Victorian Age in Literature* (1912)

9 He worked at his style like a diamond-cutter, and responded to sensations with the delicacy of a poetical geiger counter.

John Carey 1934– : in *Sunday Times* 9 May 1993

Lytton Strachey 1880–1932

10 He was, for all his brilliance, glitter, irony and wit, an unsound biographer: he was concerned with effect rather than truth.

Robert Blake 1916– : 'The Art of Biography' (1988)

Johan August Strindberg 1849–1912

1 Strindberg was the precursor of all modernity in our present theatre . . . the most modern of moderns.

Eugene O'Neill 1888–1953: in 1924; Malcolm Bradbury and James McFarlane (eds.) *Modernism* (1991)

Jonathan Swift 1667–1745

2 Yet malice never was his aim;
He lashed the vice, but spared the name;
No individual could resent,
Where thousands equally were meant.

Jonathan Swift 1667–1745: 'Verses on the Death of Dr Swift' (1731)

3 Where fierce indignation can no longer tear his heart.
Swift's epitaph

Jonathan Swift 1667–1745: S. Leslie *The Skull of Swift* (1928)

4 Cousin Swift, you will never be a poet.

John Dryden 1631–1700: Samuel Johnson *Lives of the English Poets* (1779–81) 'Dryden'

5 Swift was *anima Rabelaisii habitans in sicco*—the soul of Rabelais dwelling in a dry place.

Samuel Taylor Coleridge 1772–1834: *Table Talk* (1835) 15 June 1830

6 To read Swift is like being locked up on a desert island with Napoleon in the capacity of secretary. There is no prospect of relief.

Harold Laski 1893–1950: letter to Oliver Wendell Holmes, 12 January 1919

7 Swift has sailed into his rest;
Savage indignation there
Cannot lacerate his breast.
Imitate him if you dare,
World-besotted traveller; he
Served human liberty.

W. B. Yeats 1865–1939: 'Swift's Epitaph' (1933); cf. **332:3**

John Millington Synge 1871–1909

8 He loves all that has edge, all that is salt in the mouth, all that is rough to the hand, all that heightens the emotions by contest, all that strings into life the strength of tragedy.

W. B. Yeats 1865–1939: 'J. M. Synge and the Ireland of his Time' (1910)

Alfred, Lord Tennyson 1809–92

9 Out-babying Wordsworth and out-glittering Keats.

Edward George Bulwer-Lytton 1803–73: *The New Timon* (1846)

10 It is beautiful; it is mournful; it is monotonous.
of In Memoriam

Charlotte Brontë 1816–55: letter to Mrs Gaskell, 27 August 1850

1 I thought nothing could be grander than the first poem till I came to the third; but when I had read the last, it seemed to be absolutely unapproached and unapproachable.
of Idylls of the King

Charles Dickens 1812–70: letter to John Forster, 25 August 1859

2 Whenever I feel disposed to reflect that Tennyson is not personally Tennysonian, I summon up the image of Browning, and this has the effect of making me check my complaints.

Henry James 1843–1916: letter, 17 November 1878

3 It is the height of luxury to sit in a hot bath and read about little birds.
having had running hot water installed in his new house at Aldworth

Alfred, Lord Tennyson 1809–92: Hallam Tennyson *Tennyson and his Friends* (1911); cf. **334:3**

4 Brahms is just like Tennyson, an extraordinary musician, with the brains of a third rate village policeman.

George Bernard Shaw 1856–1950: letter to Pakenham Beatty, 4 April 1893

5 Tennyson had the British Empire for God, and Queen Victoria for Virgin Mary.

Lady Gregory 1852–1932: W. B. Yeats diary, 17 March 1909

6 The great length of his mild fluency: the yards of linen-drapery for the delight of women.

George Meredith 1828–1909: Frank Harris *My Life and Loves* (1922–7)

7 He could not think up to the height of his own towering style.

G. K. Chesterton 1874–1936: *The Victorian Age in Literature* (1912)

William Makepeace Thackeray 1811–63

see also **116:1**

8 They say he is like Fielding; they talk of his wit, humour, comic powers. He resembles Fielding as an eagle does a vulture: Fielding could stoop on carrion, but Thackeray never does.

Charlotte Brontë 1816–55: *Jane Eyre* (2nd ed., 1848) preface; cf. **298:4**

9 Thackeray is unique. I *can* say no more, I *will* say no less.

Charlotte Brontë 1816–55: letter to W. S. Williams, 29 March 1848

10 Papa, why do you not write books like Nicholas Nickleby?

Harriet Thackeray 1840–75: Anne Thackeray Ritchie *Records of Tennyson, Ruskin, and Robert and Elizabeth Browning* (1892)

11 Thackeray is like the edited and illustrated edition of a great dinner.

Walter Bagehot 1826–77: in *Spectator* 9 August 1862

12 Thackeray settled like a meat-fly on whatever one had got for dinner, and made one sick of it.

John Ruskin 1819–1900: *Fors Clavigera* (1871–84) Letter 31, 1 July 1873

Dylan Thomas 1914–53

1 I am in the path of Blake, but so far behind him that only the wings of his heels are in sight.

Dylan Thomas 1914–53: letter to Pamela Hansford Johnson, undated, probably September 1933

2 I'm a freak user of words, not a poet. That's really the truth.

Dylan Thomas 1914–53: letter, 9 May 1934

3 Poetry is not the most important thing in life . . . I'd much rather lie in a hot bath reading Agatha Christie and sucking sweets.

Dylan Thomas 1914–53: Joan Wyndham *Love is Blue* (1986) 6 July 1943; cf. **333:3**

4 Thomas's poetry is so narrow—just a straight conduit between birth and death, I suppose—with not much space for living along the way.

Elizabeth Bishop 1911–79: letter to Ilse and Kit Barker, 23 November 1953

5 The only honest way of doing it is to attack it . . . *Someone* ought to give Dylan a bouquet of old bogwort before long.
on a planned review of Dylan Thomas's prose pieces for the Spectator

Kingsley Amis 1922–95: letter to Robert Conquest, 1955

6 He was one of the great ones, there can be no doubt of that. And he drank his own blood, ate of his own marrow, to get at some of that material.

Theodore Roethke 1908–63: E. W. Tedlock (ed.) *Dylan Thomas: The Legend and the Poet* (1960)

7 He's exactly what I would have been if I had not been a Catholic.

Evelyn Waugh 1903–66: Noel Annan *Our Age* (1990); attributed

8 He was a detestable man. Men pressed money on him, and women their bodies. Dylan took both with equal contempt. His great pleasure was to humiliate people.

A. J. P. Taylor 1906–90: *A Personal History* (1983)

J. R. R. Tolkien 1892–1973 see also 68:5, 86:1

9 A real taste for fairy-stories was wakened by philology on the threshold of manhood, and quickened to full life by war.

J. R. R. Tolkien 1892–1973: *Tree and Leaf* (1964) 'On Fairy-Stories'

Leo Tolstoy 1828–1910 see also 116:3

10 A queer combination of the brain of an English chemist with the soul of an Indian Buddhist.

E. M. de Vogüé 1848–1910: *The Russian Novel* (1886)

11 When literature has a Tolstoy, it is easy and gratifying to be a writer.

Anton Chekhov 1860–1904: letter, 28 January 1900

12 It is hopeless to grapple with Tolstoy. The man is like yesterday's east wind, which brought tears when you faced it and numbed you meanwhile.

T. E. Lawrence 1888–1935: letter to E. M. ***Forster***, 20 February 1924

13 With God he maintains very suspicious relations. They are like two bears in one den.

Maxim Gorky 1868–1936: Conor Cruise O'Brien *The Great Melody* (1993)

1 I know as well as others that no man is more worthy than he of the name of genius; more complicated, contradictory, and great in everything—yes, yes, in everything. Great—in some curious sense, wide, indefinable by words—there is something in him which made me desire to cry aloud to everyone: 'Look what a wonderful man is living on earth.'

Maxim Gorky 1868–1936: *Reminiscences of Tolstoy* (1934)

2 As I reread *Hadji-Murad* again, I thought: this is the man one should learn from. Here the electric charge went from the earth, through the hands, straight to the paper, with no insulation at all, quite mercilessly stripping off all the outer layers with a sense of truth—a truth, furthermore, which was clothed in dress both transparent and beautiful.

Isaac Babel 1894–1940: interview, Union of Soviet Writers, 28 September 1937

William Trevor 1928–

3 I'm a short-story writer, really, who happens to write novels. Not the other way round.

William Trevor 1928– : in *Paris Review* 1989

Anthony Trollope 1815–82

4 Amid a little knot of Parliamentary swells conversed chiefly with Anthony Trollope—'all gobble and glare', as he was described by someone who heard him make a speech.

Henry James 1843–1916: letter, 28 February 1877

5 He never leaves off . . . and he always has two packages of manuscript in his desk, besides the one he's working on, and the one that's being published.
on her husband

Rose Trollope 1820–1917: Julian Hawthorne *Shapes that Pass: Memories of Old Days* (1928)

6 I have read Trollope's autobiography and regard it as one of the most curious and amazing books in all literature, for its density, blockishness and general thickness and soddenness.

Henry James 1843–1916: letter, 25 November 1883

7 His first, his inestimable merit was a complete appreciation of the usual.

Henry James 1843–1916: *Partial Portraits* (1888)

8 A big, red-faced, rather underbred Englishman of the bald with spectacles type. A good roaring positive fellow who deafened me (sitting on his right) till I thought of Dante's Cerberus.

James Russell Lowell 1819–91: H. S. Scudder *James Russell Lowell* (1901)

9 Even the crowd seems to have been offended (consciously or not) by revelation of mechanism. Of course all artistic work is done, to a great extent, mechanically. Trollope merely talked about it in a wrong and vulgar tone.
of public reaction to Trollope's Autobiograpy

George Gissing 1857–1903: *Commonplace Book* (1962)

10 The whole of Barsetshire . . . seems to be mapped out in dear old Trollope's countenance.
on Julia Cameron's photograph of Trollope

Max Beerbohm 1872–1956: letter, 6 October 1954

Frances Trollope 1780–1863

1 She was in no sense a *poseuse*, but just a vulgar, brisk, and good-natured kind of well-bred hen wife, fond of a joke and not troubled with squeamishness.

Mrs Lynn Lynton 1822–98: *My Literary Life* (1899)

Ivan Turgenev 1818–83

2 Curiosity will never impel you to look at the last page of one of his books, and you reach it without regret. To read him is like travelling by river, a calm and steady transit without adventure or emotion.

W. Somerset Maugham 1874–1965: *A Writer's Notebook* (1949) written in 1917

Mark Twain 1835–1910

3 Sole, incomparable, the Lincoln of our literature.

William Dean Howells 1837–1920: *My Mark Twain* (1910)

4 The true father of our national literature, the first genuinely American artist of the blood royal.

H. L. Mencken 1880–1956: in *Smart Set* February 1913

5 A hack writer who would not have been considered fourth rate in Europe, who tricked out a few of the old proven 'sure fire' literary skeletons with sufficient local colour to intrigue the superficial and the lazy.

William Faulkner 1897–1962: in *The Mississippian* 24 March 1922

6 All modern American literature comes from one book by Mark Twain called *Huckleberry Finn*.

Ernest Hemingway 1899–1961: *Green Hills of Africa* (1935)

Kenneth Tynan 1927–80

7 Isis named me on its list of Oxford's six leading personalities: 'Oxford's best journalist, objectionable Kenneth Tynan'. I am well content.

Kenneth Tynan 1927–80: letter to Hugh Manning, 20 June 1946

Gore Vidal 1925–

8 Just the sight of Gore had the effect of instantly cleansing my palate—like some tart lemon sorbet.

Elaine Dundy 1927– : Gore Vidal *Palimpsest* (1995)

François Villon fl. *c.*1460

9 Villon, our sad bad glad mad brother's name.

Algernon Charles Swinburne 1837–1909: 'Ballad of François Villon' (1878)

Virgil 70–19 BC see also **52:10**

1 *Cedite Romani scriptores, cedite Grai!*
Nescioquid maius nascitur Iliade.

Make way, you Roman writers, make way, Greeks!
Something greater than the Iliad is born.
of Virgil's Aeneid

Propertius *c.*50–after 16 BC: *Elegies*

2 *Animae dimidium meae.*

Half my own soul.

Horace 65–8 BC: *Odes*

3 *Vergilium vidi tantum.*

I have just seen Virgil.

Ovid 43 BC–AD *c.*17: *Tristia*

4 The shepherd in Virgil grew at last acquainted with Love, and found him a native of the rocks.

Samuel Johnson 1709–84: letter to Lord Chesterfield, 7 February 1755

5 Roman Virgil, thou that singest
Ilion's lofty temples robed in fire,
Ilion falling, Rome arising,
wars, and filial faith, and Dido's pyre.

Alfred, Lord Tennyson 1809–92: 'To Virgil' (1882)

6 I salute thee, Mantovano,
I that loved thee since my day began,
Wielder of the stateliest measure
ever moulded by the lips of man.

Alfred, Lord Tennyson 1809–92: 'To Virgil' (1882)

Mrs Humphrey Ward 1851–1920

7 Mrs Ward is dead; poor Mrs Humphrey Ward; it appears that she was merely a woman of straw after all—shovelled into the grave and already forgotten.

Virginia Woolf 1882–1941: diary, 10 April 1920

Sylvia Townsend Warner 1893–1978

8 She has the spiritual digestion of a goat.

John Updike 1932– : C. Harman *Sylvia Townsend Warner* (1989)

Evelyn Waugh 1903–66

9 I regard writing not an as investigation of character but as an exercise in the use of language, and with this I am obsessed. I have no technical psychological interest; it is drama, speech and events that interest me.

Evelyn Waugh 1903–66: in *Paris Review* 1962

10 You have no idea how much nastier I would be if I was not a Catholic. Without supernatural aid I would hardly be a human being.
replying to Nancy Mitford who rebuked him for cruelty

Evelyn Waugh 1903–66: Noel Annan *Our Age* (1990)

1 Despite all Waugh's efforts to appear to be an irascible, deaf old curmudgeon, a sort of inner saintliness kept breaking through.

Malcolm Muggeridge 1903–90: Miriam Gross *The World of George Orwell* (1971)

2 There was always in Evelyn a conflict between the satirist and the romantic.

Graham Greene 1904–91: *Ways of Escape* (1980)

3 Whereas most great writers are richer in imaginative resource than normal men or women, Waugh's distinction lay in being poorer. The acid refinement of his style required a certain part of his brain to remain dead. His blanket denunciations of fellow humans would have been impossible for a fully-formed intelligence.

John Carey 1934– : in *Sunday Times* 19 April 1992

4 He had the sharp eye of a Hogarth alternating with that of the Ancient Mariner.

Harold Acton 1904–94: attributed

John Webster *c.*1580–*c.*1625

5 A play of Webster's is full of the feverish and ghastly turmoil of a nest of maggots.

Rupert Brooke 1887–1915: *John Webster and the Elizabethan Drama* (1916)

6 Webster was much possessed by death
And saw the skull beneath the skin.

T. S. Eliot 1888–1965: 'Whispers of Immortality' (1919); cf. **53:4**

7 Webster is not concerned with humanity. He is the poet of bile and brainstorm, the sweet singer of apoplexy; ideally, one feels, he would have had all his characters drowned in a sea of cold sweat. His muse drew nourishment from Bedlam, and might, a few centuries later, have done the same from Belsen.

Kenneth Tynan 1927–80: in *Observer* 18 December 1960

Frank Wedekind 1864–1918

8 With Tolstoy and Strindberg one of the great educators of the new Europe.

Bertolt Brecht 1898–1956: in 1918; Malcolm Bradbury and James McFarlane (eds.) *Modernism* (1991)

H. G. Wells 1866–1946 see also 4:2, 4:3

9 He is the old maid among novelists; even the sex obsession that lay clotted on *Ann Veronica* and *The New Machiavelli* like cold white sauce was old maid's mania.

Rebecca West 1892–1983: in *Freewoman Review* September 1912

10 What a little bourgeois! What a philistine!
after a 'barney' with H. G. Wells in the Kremlin

Lenin 1870–1924: Michael Foot *The History of Mr Wells* (1995)

11 It scarcely needs criticism to bring home to me that much of my work has been slovenly, haggard and irritated, most of it hurriedly and inadequately revised, and some of it as white and pasty in its texture as a starch-fed nun.

H. G. Wells 1866–1946: *Experiment in Autobiography* (1934)

1 Wells, in part of Europe and in the United States, will for some years have wielded an intellectual dominion comparable to that won and held by Voltaire in the eighteenth century.

André Maurois 1885–1967: André Maurois *Poets and Prophets* (1936)

2 He's the Shakespeare of science fiction.

Brian Aldiss 1925– : on *Bookmark* (BBC2) 24 August 1996

Rebecca West 1892–1983

3 I would not call Miss West a feminist because this suggests—and is meant to—an aggrieved and strident person. I would say she is on the side of women.

Stevie Smith 1902–71: in *World Review* 1950s; Jack Barbera and William McBrien *Stevie* (1985)

4 She regarded me as a piece of fiction—like one of her novels—that she could edit and improve.
a son's view of his mother, 10 June 1984

Anthony West 1914–87: attributed, 1984

Edith Wharton 1862–1937

5 Mrs Wharton at her best was an analyst of the paralysis that attends success. Hers was not a world where romance was apt to flourish.

Louis Auchincloss 1917– : Irving Howe (ed.) *Edith Wharton* (1962)

Patrick White 1912–90

6 Patrick White is a dead loss to libraries, a great asset to English literature.

John Betjeman 1906–84: review of *The Aunt's Story* in 1948; attributed

7 If I am anything of a writer it is through my homosexuality, which has given me additional insights, and through a *very strong vein of vulgarity*.

Patrick White 1912–90: letter to Geoffrey Dutton, 17 September 1980

Walt Whitman 1819–92

8 The effort of an essentially prosaic mind to lift itself, by a prolonged muscular strain, into poetry.
on Whitman's 'Drum-Taps'

Henry James 1843–1916: 'Mr Walt Whitman' (1865)

9 This awful Whitman. This post-mortem poet. This poet with the private soul leaking out of him all the time. All his privacy leaking out in a sort of dribble, oozing into the universe.

D. H. Lawrence 1885–1930: *Studies in Classic American Literature* (1924)

10 Walt Whitman who laid end to end words never seen in each other's company before outside of a dictionary.

David Lodge 1935– : *Changing Places* (1975)

Oscar Wilde 1854–1900

in his viva at Oxford Wilde was required to translate a passage from the Greek version of the New Testament. Having acquitted himself well, he was stopped:

1 Oh, do let me go on, I want to see how it ends.

Oscar Wilde 1854–1900: James Sutherland (ed.) *The Oxford Book of Literary Anecdotes* (1975)

2 That sovereign of insufferables.

Ambrose Bierce 1842–*c.*1914: in *Wasp*, San Francisco, 1882

3 What has Oscar in common with Art? except that he dines at our tables and picks from our platter the plums for the puddings he peddles in the provinces.

James McNeill Whistler 1834–1903: in *World* November 1886

4 The doddering rococo and oh so flat 'fizz' . . . of *Lady Windermere's Fan.*

Henry James 1843–1916: letter, 25 October 1911

5 He seemed at ease and to have the look of the last gentleman in Europe.

Ada Leverson 1865–1936: *Letters to the Sphinx* (1930)

6 If, with the literate, I am
Impelled to try an epigram,
I never seek to take the credit;
We all assume that Oscar said it.

Dorothy Parker 1893–1967: 'A Pig's-Eye View of Literature' (1937)

7 From the beginning Wilde performed his life and continued to do so even after fate had taken the plot out of his hands.

W. H. Auden 1907–73: in *New Yorker* 9 March 1963

Tennessee Williams 1911–83

8 Williams recognized that great theatre begins with great talkers, and that great talkers obey two rules: they never sound like anyone else and they never say anything directly.

Edmund White 1940– : in *New Republic* 13 May 1985

Angus Wilson 1913–91

9 A colourful bird, in a vast circular cage, bowtied, blue-rinsed, chattering loudly.
as deputy superintendent of the British Library reading room, sitting on his dais

Anonymous: in *Independent on Sunday* 28 May 1995

Edmund Wilson 1895–1973

10 Hell with compensations.
of life with her husband Edmund Wilson

Elena Wilson 1906–79: Jeffrey Meyers *Edmund Wilson* (1995)

11 Wilson is not like other critics; some critics are boring even when they are original; he fascinates even when he is wrong.

Alfred Kazin 1915– : Max J. Herzberg (ed.) *The Reader's Encyclopedia of American Literature* (1963)

P. G. Wodehouse 1881–1975

1 English literature's performing flea.

Sean O'Casey 1880–1964: P. G. Wodehouse *Performing Flea* (1953)

2 I wrote from the age of five. Before that, I suppose I loafed.

P. G. Wodehouse 1881–1975: attributed

Tom Wolfe 1931–

3 A pretentious fad-chaser . . . the pom-pom girl of American letters.

Edward Abbey 1927–89: attributed

Virginia Woolf 1882–1941

4 Your novels beat me—black and blue. I retire howling, aching, sore; full, moreover, of an acute sense of disgrace. I return later, I re-submit myself to your discipline. No use: I am carried out half-dead. Of course I admire your creative work immensely—but only in a bemused and miserable manner.

Max Beerbohm 1872–1956: letter to Virginia Woolf, 30 December 1927; cf. **341:5**

5 Can I put up any defence? . . . I'm afraid it's not a good one; it is simply that I can't write other than I do. I admit that when I spoke to the undergraduates I made up a plausible theory about the spirit of the age; but these theories are made after the art is done: I say to myself (as I might say about anybody's book) what made the poor woman write like that? And then I sit down and concoct something about life and literature, whereas the truth is I write these books which bruise you black and blue—you won't believe it, but so it is—simply to amuse myself.

Virginia Woolf 1882–1941: letter to Max Beerbohm, 29 January 1928; cf. **341:4**

6 It was like watching someone organize her own immortality. Every phrase and gesture was studied. Now and again, when she said something a little out of the ordinary, she wrote it down herself in a notebook.

Harold Laski 1893–1950: letter to Oliver Wendell Holmes, 30 November 1930

7 I enjoyed talking to her, but thought *nothing* of her writing. I considered her 'a beautiful little knitter'.

Edith Sitwell 1887–1964: letter to Geoffrey Singleton, 11 July 1955

8 She was a bit malicious, you know—she'd say the most dreadful things about people. Of course, one does oneself. But one doesn't expect it of Virginia Woolf.

Ivy Compton-Burnett 1884–1969: Hilary Spurling *Secrets of a Woman's Heart: the Later Life of Ivy Compton-Burnett* (1984)

William Wordsworth 1770–1850 see also **71:9**

1 Who, both by precept and example, shows
That prose is verse, and verse is merely prose,
Convincing all by demonstration plain,
Poetic souls delight in prose insane;
And Christmas stories tortured into rhyme,
Contain the essence of the true sublime.

Lord Byron 1788–1824: *English Bards and Scotch Reviewers* (1809)

2 This will never do.
on The Excursion *(1814)*

Francis, Lord Jeffrey 1773–1850: in *Edinburgh Review* November 1814

3 Wordsworth—stupendous genius! damned fool! These poets run about their ponds though they cannot fish.

Lord Byron 1788–1824: fragment of a letter to James Hogg, recorded in the diary of Henry Crabb Robinson, 1 December 1816

4 For the sake of a few fine imaginative or domestic passages, are we to be bullied into a certain philosophy engendered in the whims of an egotist?
on the overbearing influence of Wordsworth upon his contemporaries

John Keats 1795–1821: letter to J. H. Reynolds, 3 February 1818

5 A drowsy frowzy poem, called the 'Excursion',
Writ in a manner which is my aversion.

Lord Byron 1788–1824: *Don Juan* (1819–24)

6 We learn from Horace, Homer sometimes sleeps;
We feel without him: Wordsworth sometimes wakes.

Lord Byron 1788–1824: *Don Juan* (1819–24); cf. **304:6**

7 Just for a handful of silver he left us,
Just for a riband to stick in his coat.
of Wordsworth's implied abandonment of radical principles by his acceptance of the Laureateship

Robert Browning 1812–89: 'The Lost Leader' (1845)

8 He was . . . a man of an immense head and great jaws like a crocodile's, cast in a mould designed for prodigious work.

Thomas Carlyle 1795–1881: in conversation, *c.*1849; Charles Gavan Duffy *Conversations with Thomas Carlyle* (1892)

9 He spoke, and loosed our heart in tears.
He laid us as we lay at birth
On the cool flowery lap of earth.

Matthew Arnold 1822–88: 'Memorial Verses, April 1850' (1852)

10 Wordsworth went to the lakes, but he was never a lake poet. He found in stones the sermons he had already hidden there.

Oscar Wilde 1854–1900: *Intentions* (1891) 'The Decay of Lying'; cf. **155:4**

11 How thankful we ought to be that Wordsworth was only a poet and not a musician. Fancy a symphony by Wordsworth! Fancy having to sit it out! And fancy what it would have been if he had written fugues!

Samuel Butler 1835–1902: *Notebooks* (1912)

12 What a gross absurdity is the moral lesson of Wordsworth's 'Resolution and Independence'! How can a man strengthen himself by the example of another whose needs and capacities have nothing in common with his own? How can a fiery-hearted youth see an example to be

George Gissing 1857–1903: *Commonplace Book* (1962)

imitated in a bloodless old fellow bent double with infirmities?
on the example offered by the leech-gatherer of the poem

1 Mr Wordsworth, a stupid man, with a decided gift for portraying nature in vignettes, never yet ruined anyone's morals, unless, perhaps, he has driven some susceptible persons to crime in a very fury of boredom.

Ezra Pound 1885–1972: in *Future* September 1913

2 Snowdrifts of Wordsworth.
a reviser's comment on the content of previous editions of ODQ

Anonymous: introduction to *Oxford Dictionary of Quotations* (ed. 3, 1979)

3 Wordsworth was nearly the price of me once. I was driving down the M1 on a Saturday morning: they had this poetry slot on the radio . . . and someone suddenly started reading the Immortality ode, and I couldn't see for tears. And when you're driving down the middle lane at seventy miles an hour . . .

Philip Larkin 1922–85: *Required Writing* (1983)

W. B. Yeats 1865–1939

4 I, the poet William Yeats,
With old mill boards and sea-green slates,
And smithy work from the Gort forge,
Restored this tower for my wife George;
And may these characters remain
When all is ruin once again.

W. B. Yeats 1865–1939: 'To be Carved on a Stone at Thoor Ballylee' (1918)

5 I declare this tower is my symbol; I declare
This winding, gyring, spiring treadmill of a stair is my ancestral stair;
That Goldsmith and the Dean, Berkeley and Burke have travelled there.

W. B. Yeats 1865–1939: 'Blood and the Moon' (1927)

6 Wherever one cut him, with a little question, he poured, spurted fountains of ideas.

Virginia Woolf 1882–1941: diary, 8 November 1930

7 Scoffed at fairies, but they made his living.

Anonymous: obituary of Yeats in *Daily Express* 30 January 1939; in *Quote Unquote Newsletter* October 1995 vol. 4 no. 4

8 You were silly like us; your gift survived it all:
The parish of rich women, physical decay,
Yourself. Mad Ireland hurt you into poetry.

W. H. Auden 1907–73: 'In Memory of W. B. Yeats' (1940)

Author Index

Doctorow, E. L. (1931–)
90:14
Donaldson, Stephen (1947–)
85:11
Donatus, Aelius (fl. 4th century AD)
195:12
Donne, John (1572–1631)
30:2, 51:4, 51:5, 128:5, 142:8
Dos Passos, John (1896–1970)
210:9, 227:2
Dostoevsky, Fedor (1821–81)
321:10
Douglas, O. (1877–1948)
129:6, 197:2, 242:10
Douglas, William O. (1898–1980)
35:2
Dowson, Ernest (1867–1900)
30:3
Doyle, Arthur Conan (1859–1930)
44:1, 94:11, 110:4, 131:4
Dozois, Gardner (1947–)
202:2
Drabble, Margaret (1939–)
31:1
Dryden, John (1631–1700)
41:10, 46:6, 46:7, 97:1, 109:4, 112:2, 169:2, 172:6, 179:9, 191:9, 204:12, 211:8, 232:10, 256:6, 257:13, 261:14, 289:5, 308:9, 319:2, 324:7, 325:8, 325:9, 332:4
Du Maurier, Daphne (1907–89)
164:15
Dunant, Sarah (1950–)
190:15
Dundy, Elaine (1927–)
336:8
Dunmore, Helen (1952–)
147:9
Duppa, Richard (1770–1831)
99:6
Duras, Marguerite (1914–)
66:11, 260:6
Durrell, Gerald (1925–95)
296:5
Durrell, Lawrence (1912–90)
296:4
Dworkin, Andrea (1946–)
260:7

Eagleton, Terry (1943–)
137:3, 137:5, 256:1
Eco, Umberto (1932–)
28:8, 115:11
Edelman, Maurice (1911–75)
35:9
Edwards, Graham (1965–)
86:5
Edwards, Ruth Dudley (1944–)
25:4
Eliot, George (1819–80)
7:7, 16:7, 16:9, 23:2, 82:1, 82:2, 99:7, 110:3, 129:1, 134:3, 148:3, 185:5, 218:10, 218:11, 247:11, 250:8, 271:13
Eliot, T. S. (1888–1965)
5:8, 21:9, 53:4, 53:10, 68:13, 71:8, 87:12, 88:1, 88:10, 122:7, 131:10, 145:5, 149:12, 152:1, 156:2, 157:3, 157:7, 164:16, 168:5, 175:5, 175:6, 176:4, 189:11, 193:4, 200:11, 204:3, 246:5, 259:3, 264:8, 264:9, 272:10, 295:2, 297:3, 297:4, 297:5, 317:6, 338:6
Elizabeth I (1533–1603)
20:3
Elkin, Susan
194:8
Ellman, Richard (1918–87)
154:6
Elytēs, Odysseus (1911–96)
125:8
Emerson, Ralph Waldo (1803–82)
7:8, 57:11, 60:8, 97:7, 104:3, 121:12, 146:9, 165:15, 187:1, 196:8, 196:10, 199:12, 245:11, 246:1, 249:2
Empson, William (1906–84)
62:4, 125:2, 139:15
Eno, Brian (1948–)
222:1
Enright, D. J. (1920–)
92:2, 309:10
Evelyn, John (1620–1706)
62:11
Ewart, Gavin (1916–95)
54:10, 298:1

Fadiman, Clifton (1904–)
222:3, 331:1, 331:2
Farquhar, George (1678–1707)
172:7, 262:3
Farrell, Randall
48:9
Faulkner, William (1897–1962)
13:9, 30:10, 66:5, 82:10, 114:10, 243:7, 267:5, 267:10, 336:5
Fenton, James (1949–)
33:4
Ferber, Edna (1887–1968)
74:10
Fielding, Henry (1707–54)
95:8, 158:7, 238:1

James, William (1842–1910)
151:9
Jay, Antony (1930–)
197:16
Jefferson, Thomas (1743–1826)
34:3
Jeffrey, Francis, Lord (1773–1850)
87:3, 342:2
Jennings, Paul (1918–89)
257:8
Jenyns, Soame (1704–87)
308:5
Jerome, Jerome K. (1859–1927)
95:11, 107:12
Jerome, St (*c.* AD 342–420)
20:1, 41:7
Johnson, Samuel (1709–84)
3:11, 22:3, 22:4, 22:5, 22:6, 27:4, 32:1, 32:2, 39:6, 39:7, 41:13, 46:11, 46:12, 47:1, 51:11, 56:3, 57:8, 59:13, 60:1, 60:2, 60:3, 60:5, 64:12, 67:1, 67:3, 70:2, 72:9, 73:1, 79:3, 86:10, 93:11, 99:4, 103:7, 103:8, 116:9, 117:4, 121:7, 124:1, 128:9, 130:7, 151:1, 172:8, 172:9, 196:3, 199:3, 199:4, 199:5, 205:2, 209:7, 217:11, 217:13, 217:14, 251:10, 253:10, 262:6, 269:1, 271:6, 271:10, 276:1, 282:2, 286:2, 300:5, 300:6, 302:5, 316:7, 316:8, 320:10, 322:5, 322:7, 324:1, 326:1, 326:2, 326:3, 329:2, 337:4
Johnston, Jennifer (1930–)
72:4
Jones, James (1921–77)
66:6
Jong, Erica (1942–)
216:5
Jonson, Ben (*c.*1573–1637)
3:9, 46:3, 57:5, 57:6, 64:8, 78:13, 83:11, 96:12, 107:4, 144:1, 150:9, 217:2, 231:4, 245:4, 245:5, 279:2, 294:9, 312:3, 315:5, 325:1, 325:2, 325:3, 325:4, 325:7
Joseph, Keith (1918–94)
158:3
Joseph, Michael (1897–1958)
193:3, 193:5
Jowett, Benjamin (1817–93)
266:4
Joyce, James (1882–1941)
11:3, 11:6, 11:8, 37:12, 48:1, 74:8, 94:13, 157:6, 164:13, 192:12, 202:11, 219:11, 229:4, 236:6, 239:6, 249:12, 263:13, 269:9, 272:8, 273:3, 279:7, 289:6, 309:1, 309:9
Jung Chang (1952–)
165:7
'Junius'
156:5
Juvenal (AD *c.*60–*c.*130)
106:4, 128:4, 149:3, 231:2, 237:6, 265:6

Kafka, Franz (1883–1924)
164:12, 266:9
Kaufman, George S. (1889–1961)
210:6, 319:8
Kazin, Alfred (1915–)
68:12, 340:11
Keane, Molly (1904–96)
282:7, 310:1
Keats, John (1795–1821)
7:4, 31:2, 43:8, 52:3, 52:4, 52:5, 52:6, 65:3, 65:4, 65:5, 81:8, 81:9, 83:14, 91:10, 97:3, 109:9, 112:7, 119:16, 127:1, 133:8, 142:14, 153:10, 163:13, 163:14, 163:15, 172:15, 173:4, 173:6, 173:7, 173:8, 173:9, 173:10, 181:9, 199:9, 205:5, 251:11, 265:12, 291:3, 304:11, 310:4, 310:5, 317:2, 328:2, 342:4
Keeshig-Tobias, Lenore
36:3
Keillor, Garrison (1942–)
253:5
Kennedy, John F. (1917–63)
183:10, 183:11
Kerouac, Jack (1922–69)
53:14
Kerr, Katharine (1944–)
85:12
Kettell, Ralph (1563–1643)
324:6
Keynes, John Maynard (1883–1946)
299:8
Khomeini, Ruhollah (1900–89)
35:14
Khrushchev, Nikita (1894–1971)
183:12
Kilmer, Joyce (1886–1918)
155:10
King, Francis (1923–)
329:3
King, Stephen (1947–)
106:1
Kingsley, Charles (1819–75)
21:3
Kipling, Rudyard (1865–1936)
7:14, 24:5, 24:6, 30:6, 30:8, 40:1, 80:1, 90:7, 114:2, 114:3, 138:8, 157:2, 159:11, 168:3, 189:7, 196:11, 208:2, 210:1, 210:2, 219:7, 219:10, 239:1, 263:5, 264:1, 285:8, 305:3

Petronius (d. AD 65)
305:2
Petroski, Henry (1942–)
244:10
Phillips, Tom
293:8
Pilger, John (1939–)
119:4
Pilley, W. Charles
313:1
Pinker, Steven (1954–)
58:7, 101:9, 123:7, 123:8
Pinter, Harold (1930–)
18:10, 89:1, 182:7, 319:10, 320:2
Pirandello, Luigi (1867–1936)
37:7, 37:8
Plath, Sylvia (1932–63)
54:2, 127:12
Pliny the Elder (AD 23–79)
167:6
Pliny the Younger (AD c.61–c.112)
96:11, 128:3
Plomer, William (1903–73)
259:10
Poe, Edgar Allan (1809–49)
87:2, 212:4
Pohl, Frederik (1919–)
223:3
Pollitt, Harry (1890–1960)
255:1
Pope, Alexander (1688–1744)
31:4, 31:13, 41:11, 46:9, 49:7, 62:13, 62:14, 72:8, 97:2, 142:12, 144:3, 179:11, 186:9, 198:14, 211:9, 211:10, 256:7, 265:7, 265:8, 268:14, 271:4, 293:5, 295:9
Porter, Cole (1891–1964)
327:1
Potter, Dennis (1935–94)
29:2, 55:2, 64:3, 127:13, 204:9
Potter, Stephen (1900–69)
50:4, 330:3
Pound, Ezra (1885–1972)
42:8, 68:4, 77:10, 104:10, 139:1, 139:3, 145:2, 145:4, 151:12, 166:9, 181:2, 204:7, 212:8, 267:8, 281:6, 290:2, 311:6, 321:6, 343:1
Powell, Anthony (1905–)
28:6, 162:5, 273:10, 292:1
Powell, Enoch (1912–98)
59:9, 126:6, 126:7, 220:4, 287:8
Power, Eileen (1889–1940)
19:5
Pratchett, Terry (1948–)
86:1, 86:3, 133:1
Preston, Keith (1884–1927)
157:5
Priestland, Gerald (1927–91)
119:5
Priestley, J. B. (1894–1984)
63:13, 190:1
Prince, J. C.
242:5
Prior, Matthew (1664–1721)
142:11, 196:1, 262:4
Pritchett, V. S. (1900–97)
19:9, 44:5, 76:7, 147:6, 170:13, 228:8, 244:14, 289:10, 289:12, 294:3, 331:4
Propertius (c.50–after 16 BC)
237:5, 337:1
Proust, Marcel (1871–1922)
30:7, 34:9, 113:11, 134:13, 143:4, 200:8
Pullman, Philip (1946–)
41:4, 171:3
Pulteney William, Lord Bath (1684–1764)
33:10
Punch (1841–1992)
246:3
Pushkin, Alexander (1799–1837)
55:9
Puzo, Mario (1920–)
19:13
Pym, Barbara (1913–80)
66:1, 203:1, 203:3, 241:3, 322:1

Quarles, Francis (1592–1644)
106:5, 133:3, 198:9
Quasimodo, Salvatore (1901–68)
178:4
Quennell, Peter (1905–93)
6:4, 301:2
Quiller-Couch, Arthur (1863–1944)
97:9
Quine, W. V. (1908–)
122:12
Quintilian (AD c.35–c.96)
140:6

Raban, Jonathan (1942–)
251:4, 312:8
Rae, John (1931–)
255:5
Raine, Craig (1944–)
71:13, 167:2, 276:9, 308:12
Ralegh, Walter (c.1552–1618)
103:3, 103:4
Raleigh, Walter (1861–1922)
23:8, 197:1

Keyword Index

ban If faced with a b., he can decline 24:12
banal fiction often takes the b. 91:1
banality manufacture of b. 2:5
bandage wound, not the b. 204:9
banker b. has no business 297:1
bankers threat to literature is b. 69:2
bankruptcy intellectual b. 166:2
banks Letters of thanks, letters from b. 129:8
banned that any book should be b. 34:11
bar b. exercises 59:10
When I have crossed the b. 53:1
Barabbas B. was a much misunderstood 194:1
B. was a publisher 192:4
barbarisms clear it from colloquial b. 99:4
barbarous b. phrase hath often made 96:12
invention of a b. age 211:6
barbarousness confess mine own b. 14:8
barber going to the tailor or b. 72:5
barbers rank, roughly speaking, of b. 118:12
bard b. in an oral culture 69:3
Poor starving b., how small thy gains 66:14
bards As much the worst of b. confessed 288:6
barkeeper feel like a b. 278:6
barking b. up the wrong tree 50:7
barmie My b. noddle's working prime 112:4
barometer may be used as the b. 177:6
barrel In our language rhyme is a b. 212:7
just polished off a b. 134:5
barren b. superfluity of words 262:2
Close up these b. leaves 218:2
inch or two upon very b. rock 315:4
barrenness In b., at any rate 269:11
barricade kick at the b. 162:12
Barsetshire whole of B. . . . seems to be 335:10
Basingstoke hidden meaning—like B. 263:1
basset low-swung b. 208:4
bastard behave like a b. 95:6
bath in a hot b. reading Agatha Christie 334:3
sit in a hot b. and read 333:3
bathtub in the b., think of me 155:2
Batman B. comics 256:4
battle language and sent it into b. 231:10
Baudelaire that of B. 279:12
be should not mean But b. 176:1
beadle b. on boxin' day 174:5
beadroll On Fame's eternal b. 289:4
beanbag make dance the dullest b. 232:2
bear as she [a b.] doth her young ones 209:3
I am a B. of Very Little Brain 264:4
lest you wake a sleeping b. 308:5
bearer b. of light 329:4
bears like two b. in one den 334:13
tap crude rhythms for b. to dance to 121:13
beating b. myself for spite 268:12
Beatles B.' first LP 227:4
beauties concealed b. of a writer 46:10
beautiful b. and ineffectual angel 328:5
important or profoundly b. 234:6
It is b.; it is mournful 332:10
moved by the presence of b. objects 49:14
poet produces something b. 176:3
beauty b. lives though lilies die 175:4
b. of inflections 144:14
B. plus pity 9:7
Keats had B. 297:8
loved the principle of b. 205:5
more b. in the works of 93:8
quested for b. 329:1
What is b. saith my sufferings 111:5
Beckett Samuel B. 38:1
become what man can b. 301:6
bed combination of b. and book 202:7
getting in b. with women 255:4
in b. with my catamite 165:6
I write in b. 244:9
me he mostly sent to b. 330:1
need to get out of b. for it 54:6
read me in b. 155:2
Who goes to b. with whom 148:9
Bedford tinker out of B. 285:8
Bedlam B. vision 109:10
muse drew nourishment from B. 338:7
beds rather Make odes than b. 259:7
bee as brisk as a b. in conversation 269:1
beef roast b. of old England 93:1
beer helping himself to a b. 168:12
bees you b. make honey 167:3
Beethoven find out about a B. symphony 78:7
before that's not been said b. 165:9
begetter To the onlie b. of these 55:7
beggar as a b. would enfold 196:11
beggary knew luxury; they knew b. 67:7
begged HOMER b. his bread 304:9
begin B. at the beginning 16:10
My way is to b. with the beginning 16:2
To b. at the beginning 165:2
beginning b., a middle, and an end 232:9
b., a muddle, and an end 233:7
b. of a book holds more 17:10
chunks, the b., the middle 114:8
Each venture Is a new b. 88:10
end badly from the b. 17:3
good b. means a good book 18:1
Great is the art of b. 16:12
I began *again* at the b. 146:1
In my b. is my end 164:16
There is no difficulty in b. 17:2
To begin at the b.: It is spring 165:2
beginnings B. are always troublesome 16:9
behind In a moment it will be b. me 207:7
being just coming into b. 201:13

concordance my Bible and my C. 20:7
Concorde put at the controls of C. 244:8
concubine c. of a warlord general 165:7
condensed lucid and c. narrative 235:1
conduit c. between birth and death 334:4
confederacy dunces are all in c. 93:7
confessional c. passage 224:11
confidence I don't lack c. 224:15
confirmed just going to be c. 204:1
conglomerates My souls are c. 37:4
conjecture not beyond all c. 217:7
conjugation finishes the c. with 226:9
connect Only c.! . . . Only connect 143:3
Conrad Henry James, C. 246:7
conscience daily examination of c. 274:7
general c. of mankind 34:10
principal voice of the c. 148:5
Wherein I'll catch the c. of the king 62:9
consciousness c. has been modified 48:10
only genuine c.-expanding drug 223:4
our sympathetic c. 160:5
stream of thought, of c. 151:9
consecutive no six c. words 269:12
conservative fear it would make me c. 183:4
consider but to weigh and c. 198:6
When I c. how my light is spent 133:5
constable as if it was a c.'s handbook 21:3
constellations little c. of language 100:14
those stars joined in c. 103:5
constitution Englishman's c. 326:5
constructional drama—in the c. part 169:9
consume haven't yet learnt to c. 178:5
contemplation this perfect c. 125:12
contemporary amazingly brilliant c. 327:12
contempt of the moderns without c. 245:10
content new problems of Form and C. 5:14
contented But he was c. there 329:5
context that had no place in the c. 235:8
word changes according to its c. 100:14
continent not a man, he was a c. 326:9
continentals these serious C. 141:13
continuity C. . . . it is that which 135:7
contract sort of literary c. 188:6
contradict Read not to c. and confute 198:6
contradictory more complicated, c. 335:1
contrariness c. and courage 153:6
contrary On the c. 127:6
contribution I've made a small c. 206:5
make so full a c. 190:2
control have c. of your stories 36:3
his novel is taking c. 75:11
provided it's kept rigidly under c. 35:6
conversation brisk as a bee in c. 269:1
but a different name for c. 271:8
C. is a game of circles 57:11
C. is imperative 58:5
Free verse is ultimately allied to c. 212:14
from an author's books to his c. 57:8
half-gathered, c.-scraps 57:10
silence, that make his c. 314:4
stick on c.'s burrs 230:11
tell by his c. which volume 306:6
what ordinary c. looks like 58:7
conversations without pictures or c. 27:13
convict like taking a c. out of his cell 118:5
conviviality Chesterton's resolute c. 290:3
cook closer to the Chinese c. 161:5
cookery GARDENING and the c. 226:6
cooking better than a smell of c. 279:6
cooks He liked those literary c. 196:4
like short-order c. 12:1
made still plainer by plain c. 236:9
please my guests, not fellow c. 213:3
cool c. web of language 122:6
writer is perfectly c. and detached 87:12
cooled hath been C. a long age 65:5
iron which has c. to burn a hole 112:9
copied outside model that can be c. 299:7
copies disposed but of two c. 225:11
few originals and many c. 104:4
sold twenty thousand c. 19:5
copy number of c.-books 243:1
writers of smaller gifts c. 168:4
copyright £140 besides the c. 67:6
any sense in any c. law 192:7
copyrights from English authors their c. 67:11
Corelli reading Marie C. 152:6
cork pulls the c. out of the bottle 66:12
Corneille C. is to Shakespeare 326:3
corner some c. of a foreign field 164:11
correct C. English is the slang 99:7
corrected c. into illegibility 209:11
correctness political c. 36:5
correspondences C. are like 128:13
correspondent special c. for posterity 293:10
corroborative Merely c. detail 56:7
corsets Heine so loosened the c. 125:3
Cortez like stout C. 304:11
cosmopolitan become c. in the end 8:2
costermonger sound-headed c. 207:6
couch broken spring in the c. of fate 299:2
countenance bright c. of truth 251:8
in dear old Trollope's c. 335:10
counters Words are wise men's c. 261:12
countess hear what the c. is saying 307:7
country from the right part of the c. 100:11
I come from a sad c. 282:1
My c. house is full of people 289:7
past is a foreign c. 165:1
Poetic Genius of my C. found me 286:7
countrywoman She was a proper c. 282:7
couplet When Rogers produces a c. 73:6
courage contrariness and c. 153:6

critics (*cont.*)
C. are like eunuchs in a harem 50:9
C. search for ages for the wrong word 50:12
failed; therefore they turn c. 206:7
favourable nor the unfavourable c. 48:11
I didn't think about the c. 190:12
I wish c. would judge me 258:8
lot of c. is to be remembered 50:2
most severe of c., but—a perfect wife 83:15
own generation, the c. of the next 11:4
playwright how he felt about c. 50:14
punch-up between two British c. 281:7
some c. are boring 340:11
Turn c. out of mere revenge 46:6
Turned c. next, and proved plain fools 49:7
under my skin are the academic c. 208:9
You know who the c. are 49:12
critique Your servant the c. 207:5
crocodile great jaws like a c.'s 342:8
Cromwell Just as Oliver C. aimed 286:1
Roundhead? I'd have been C. 313:9
Cromwellian C. Directors laid down 181:13
crooked I strive to set the c. straight 187:5
not the c. road of life 327:11
cross adjective 'c.' as a description 42:9
crossness make c. and dirt succeed 309:5
crow We had the old c. over at Hull 305:9
crowd Far from the madding c. 30:1
hardly a c.-puller 241:6
crowding come c. in so fast 112:2
crucible cast a violet into a c. 248:11
talent in the sacred c. 95:4
cruel c. playful mind 309:4
cruelty deny Latin is c. to children 126:7
crusade Booker Prize is half a c. 190:5
crush c. the columns together 207:8
crushes c. the entire century 3:14
crust beneath the c. of their age 152:8
crustacean some kind of sensitive c. 154:3
crutches upstairs backwards on c. 319:9
cry Make-'em-laugh, make-'em-c. 169:7
cryptogram charm of a c. 13:8
cucumbers c. and the castration 35:7
cudgel c. of the people's war 254:2
cultivate C. simplicity, Coleridge 290:11
cultural chapter in c. history 260:3
culture literature in ordinary c. 139:13
mass c. of this one 106:3
More than half of modern c. 200:2
Western c. was a grand ancestral 255:11
What other c. could have produced 303:7
cultures C. of East and West 132:6
Two C. 221:5
curate I feel like a shabby c. 221:6
curb use the snaffle and the c. all right 235:10
curds you can still clot the c. a little more 33:2
cure Amis, and there's no known c. 276:4
curiosa *Horatii c. felicitas* 305:2
curiosity childish c. that keeps me going 150:4
C. will never impel you 336:2
lost all c. about the future 13:10
Love, c., freckles, and doubt 319:7
tasks for the educated man of c. 132:5
curious c. talent 307:10
curmudgeon irascible, deaf old c. 338:1
current what a strong c. ideas are 73:7
curse Artistry's haunting c. 73:9
greatest c. of modern times 242:8
launching a c. not less explicit 23:9
paper in the typewriter and c. a bit 244:5
curtain I'm very fond of c. lines 18:10
putteth aside the c., that we may look 248:6
curtains it must draw its c. round us 79:4
customs on manners, c., usages 246:2
cut artistry which would let me c. out 235:8
efforts to c. out 50,000 words 209:15
Shakespeare's c. and thrust 295:3
Wherever one c. him 343:6
You can c., or you can drug 187:7
cutlet enough if he eats a c. 56:12
cuts his tragedies were large c. 165:8
cut-throat their c. behaviour 214:11
cutting c. down of 30 pages 70:5
none of your damned c. and slashing 70:3
pleasure Of c. all the pictures out 28:2
cuttlefish like a c. squirting out ink 122:9
cynicism when it comes to c. 134:5

dada mama of d. 331:1
daemon D. lives in their pen 114:2
my d. doesn't suggest 68:11
My D. was with me 114:3
daffodils what d. were for Wordsworth 115:8
dainties not fed of the d. 198:4
daintily d. dressed Walt Whitman 316:3
daisies d. growing over me 52:6
daisy it's always d.-time 216:1
damage d. suffered in learning 140:1
damaged Archangel a little d. 290:13
damaging when it comes to d. others 148:12
damn with faint praises one another d. 49:6
damnations Twenty-nine distinct d. 20:11
damned better to have written a d. play 63:3
Publish and be d. 192:3
damning by d. another 49:2
dance d. attention upon my old age 5:10
engage with the d. of the spirit 222:2
You should be able to d. it 179:3
dancing as d. is to walking 181:5
danger d. that overtops all others 156:11
dangerous d. as an author 265:13
literature is that it is d. 139:14

dignity maintained the d. of history 103:6
Tragedy is tender to man's d. 108:8
digressions D. are the sunshine 169:3
digs d. my grave at each remove 51:7
dinner illustrated edition of a great d. 333:11
on whatever one had got for d. 333:12
ruin your lunch but not your d. 208:10
dinners from Homer's mighty d. 165:8
Diogenes I have espied land, as D. said 15:6
diplomats D. lie to journalists 254:4
direction to some particular d. 93:11
dirt blood, d. and sucked sugar stick 319:5
I know d. when I smell it 313:1
make crossness and d. succeed 309:5
to insult sex, to do d. on it 78:2
dirtiest d. man I have ever liked 277:7
dirty scorched foretop, the d. hands 308:8
dirty-mindedness journalistic d. 309:8
disagree if they d., they are pernicious 203:5
disagreeable most d.-looking child 164:9
no person so perfectly d. 265:13
disagreeables making all d. evaporate 7:4
disapprove I d. of what you say 34:1
disbelief willing suspension of d. 173:2
disciples Every great man has his d. 23:4
discipline I re-submit myself to your d. 341:4
discomforts d. that will accompany 43:7
discovered d. the nature of DNA 221:10
discoveries consequence of d. 241:9
discovery portals of d. 94:13
Why is there not a d. in life 135:2
discreet more dull than a d. diary 59:3
discretion D. is not the better part 23:11
discrimination art being all d. 134:11
disease Biographers are generally a d. 23:2
d. called friendship 129:13
d. of admiration 3:12
incurable d. of writing 265:6
progress of his d. 76:4
disenchanting proper effect, in fact, is d. 8:12
disestablishment sense of d. 106:1
disguising d. us *both* as women 330:5
disgust began to d. this refined age 62:11
disgusting description, it is always d. 56:4
dishabille d. of the male 77:6
disinterested criticism: *a d. endeavour* 47:4
dislike d. every thing that is writ 257:14
I do not much d. the matter 233:13
I, too, d. it: there are things 176:8
only equalled by his d. of the places 313:6
dismantling Deconstruction is not a d. 136:12
disobedience Of man's first d. 163:10
disown making statements I can d. 90:11
dispiriting this cannot but be d. 115:2
disreputable put me in a d. genre 102:7
dissatisfied want to leave everybody d. 16:4
dissect We murder to d. 218:2
dissecting I've been d. for forty years 5:6
dissection biography should be a d. 24:2
dissident Every journalist should be a d. 119:4
dissimilitude d. in similitude 147:11
dissociation d. of sensibility 152:1
distance power of action at a d. 317:7
through the d. of time 116:5
distant view from a d. star 223:3
distinction great d. of our nature 109:5
distinguished call upon the d. dead 197:16
here it is at last, the d. thing 53:3
they want us to be d., to be good 205:13
distraction excellent for *d.* 60:6
seek d. in the artist's work 200:5
distress in the height of a present d. 86:8
distribution d. at the last of prizes 16:15
distrust d. the feminine in literature 259:3
disturb Art is meant to d. 221:4
divided d. by a common language 125:7
divineness some participation of d. 171:12
divorce because he has a d. to pay for 70:1
DNA not discovered the nature of D. 221:10
do confidence in what I can d. 224:15
difficult to know what to d. otherwise 273:10
I don't d. it at all 269:14
Listen, I can d. it! Look how well 76:2
realize that this will d. 18:12
doctors D. in verse Being scarce 178:2
doctrine winds of d. were let loose 251:9
doctrines not to preach d. 160:2
documents historian wants more d. 104:8
world is too full of such d. 219:1
dog as d. is to lamppost 118:9
black d. I hope always to resist 86:10
fox jumps over the lazy d. 243:3
not unblack d. was chasing 100:5
ties a kettle to a d.'s tail 295:4
topography of its blots, and d.'s ears 27:5
wild d. that has praised his fleas 214:4
doggedly if he will set himself d. to it 72:9
dogs d. being prose, the cat poetry 302:2
d. of war 29:8
lamppost how it felt about d. 50:14
dollars though I had a million d. 69:8
dolour d. of pad and paper-weight 243:5
domestic d. obsessions 191:1
dominion wielded an intellectual d. 339:1
don Remote and ineffectual D. 290:1
done 30—and I have d. nothing yet 283:5
doing what has been d. before 166:5
so well d., I feel very good 98:15
what has not yet been d., and to do it 167:2
What I have d. is yours 55:6
Donne D.'s thin, cerebral laughter 295:3
donnée his subject, his idea, his *d.* 47:5
Don Quixote theme of *D.* 160:13
door come through the d. with a gun 170:4

generation is knocking at the d. 280:4
opening and closing of a d. 175:10
doormat d. in a world of boots 322:3
doors d. of perception were cleansed 119:14
Shut not your d. to me proud libraries 238:8
dossier d. of human imbecility 138:11
dotage Pedantry is the d. of knowledge 219:9
doubt I d. everything, even my doubt 298:7
Love, curiosity, freckles, and d. 319:7
Our d. is our passion 266:5
when in d., strike it out 56:10
doubtful edgy, d. sort of way 225:4
doubting d. and inquiring minds 141:9
doubts d. about the Booker 191:2
draft passion to alter someone else's d. 71:3
drafts First d. are for learning 210:10
hundred sheets of paper with d. 210:3
intact through all the following d. 18:8
dragged d. out, by tongs, a bloody mess 75:4
dragon could not say 'a green great d.' 100:8
man whose father was a d. 85:8
traditional d. stories 86:5
dragons keen on d. and magic 40:11
dram Tuppenny d.-shops 131:12
drama D. criticism 48:10
D. criticism is a verbal reflexion 48:6
D. is akin to other inventions 64:5
D. is life with the dull bits left out 64:1
Film is d. at its most impatient 3:7
Thro' all the d. 142:13
whole secret of fiction and the d. 169:9
dramatic injurious for a d. work 63:4
true storyteller is always d. 170:12
dramatist always congenial to the d. 312:4
d. wants more liberties 104:8
novelist, or poet, or d., requires 73:10
Shake was a d. of note 196:12
would have been a d. indeed 296:2
dramatize murmur, 'D. it, d. it' 63:8
draw it must d. its curtains 79:4
drawer occupant of a file d. 222:7
drawers open everybody's d. and see 150:4
drawing no d. back 22:13
drayman d., in a passion, calls out 116:11
dream d. of the soft look 5:5
Let me d. a little in my waning 5:6
represent the d. we are waking from 120:3
Where is it now, the glory and the d. 109:7
dreamer artist is a d. consenting 266:7
D. of dreams, born out of my due 187:5
poet and the d. are distinct 173:10
dreamers d., rebels and sceptics 183:2
dreams All books are either d. or swords 187:7
as we see it in our d. 63:6
awoke one morning from uneasy d. 164:12
d. of a poet doomed at last 60:2
Only d. enable me to fight 270:4
pain of living and the drug of d. 200:11
dreamt d. I went to Manderley again 164:15
drench strong horse d. 291:2
dress Language is the d. of thought 121:7
Style is the d. of thought 234:2
dressing d. old words new 167:9
dribble On paper I did d. it daintily 112:1
drink D. heightens feeling 66:3
quite a lot to d. 281:8
Some writers take to d. 268:4
terminate in d. or worse 66:7
drinker first great nonstop literary d. 320:9
drinkers My generation are d. 66:10
drinking as inveterate as d. 266:1
drinks man you don't like who d. 66:4
drive knows the way but can't d. 50:10
driving d. down the middle lane 343:3
droghte d. of March hath perced 163:5
dromedary whose muse on d. trots 295:1
drudge of dictionaries, a harmless d. 59:13
drudges score of lucid and laborious d. 219:10
drug consciousness-expanding d. 223:4
I assure you, sir: literature is a d. 138:3
most powerful d. used by mankind 264:1
often a form of the d. habit 200:13
Poetry's a mere d., Sir 172:7
Really, I can't imagine the d. scene 66:10
you can d., with words 187:7
drum still the most effective d. 254:10
drunk It has seen Wordsworth d. 65:12
I've been d. for about a week now 131:11
drunken d. played-out fool 282:6
dry old man in a d. month 5:8
Rabelais dwelling in a d. place 332:5
result of so d. a view of life 306:7
Dryden Milton and D. 152:1
poetry of D., Pope, and all their school 175:2
Dubliners read the manuscript of *D.* 202:11
Dubuque not for the old lady in D. 157:8
duchess like being married to a d. 193:6
ducklings ugly d. 170:11
ducks turning into confident d. 170:11
dud Rudyard the d. yard 311:6
dude d. Who lets the girl down 185:9
duels handsome highwaymen, d. 216:7
dukedom library Was d. large enough 130:5
dukes drawing room full of d. 221:6
dulce old Lie: D. et decorum est 254:7
dull Drama is life with the d. bits left out 64:1
man ought to be d. sometimes 9:14
Most of life is so d. 134:14
To make dictionaries is d. work 60:1
when any part of this paper appears d. 156:4
who can be d. in Fleet Street 117:6
duller Truth is always d. than fiction 253:4

eggs lay solid gold e. at night 224:5
ego between reality and the e. 110:13
not betraying this *e.* 37:2
egoism do with any amount of e. 225:2
If you do not want to explore an e. 13:3
egotism height of e. 14:1
egotist whims of an e. 342:4
egotistical e. sublime 173:8
elbow Forethought is the e.-grease 73:10
electric e. charge went from the earth 335:2
E. typewriters 244:13
to buy an e. typewriter 244:8
electricity like the introduction of e. 153:5
some kind of e. will occur 114:5
electronic kind of e. machine 110:12
elegance final e., not to console 236:7
elegant e. and pregnant texture 235:2
elegy nearly the whole of Gray's E. 302:3
elephant biggest thing you can say is 'e.' 2:8
e.'s trunk is different 123:7
like getting an e. into a suitcase 3:8
male, female, or an e. 193:11
very amusing pantomime e. 280:7
elephants take the shape of identical e. 122:12
Eliot E.'s mother-in-law 281:2
even the E. voice 305:10
greats like Yeats, E. and Lawrence 230:1
How unpleasant to meet Mr E. 297:3
Jane Austen, George E., Henry James 246:7
'Mr E.' was a fictional character 297:6
sex life of George E. 194:9
Eliots would-be George E. 171:3
elite internet is an e. organisation 245:1
memoranda for the e. 158:4
Elizabethans doing what the E. did 264:3
eloquence Continual e. is tedious 231:5
embellisher of ornate e. in our English 289:3
Talking and e. are not the same 231:4
eloquent indulge in e. soliloquy 313:5
elvish *e.* to *elfish* 232:7
Elysium What E. have ye known 65:3
emasculate certain sort of e. twaddle 97:8
emendation suspected the e. wrong 217:13
Emily of all, least sought for: E., hear 294:8
emolument considerable e. 218:9
emotion degree of my aesthetic e. 47:10
e. recollected in a highly emotional 89:7
e. recollected in tranquillity 87:1
If you want to express e., scream 178:12
not a turning loose of e., but an escape 88:1
Poetry attaches its e. to the idea 203:12
What in the world is this e. 89:4
emotional e. content 152:11
Poetry is so e. and very tiring 178:1
Sentimentality is the e. promiscuity 89:2
emotions grounds for the noble e. 174:10
ways of tapping their own e. 89:6
emphasis unpleasant e. on the *palate* 310:10
empire founded the British E. 286:1
Tennyson had the British E. for God 333:5
we've got an E. and it stretches 153:9
empirically finding the right road e. 95:3
enchantment like some victim of e. 307:8
encouragement without whose e. 55:12
Encyclopedia Britannica Behind the *E.* 200:11
which volume of the E. 306:6
encyclopedias E., centuries, dynasties 132:6
end beginning, a middle, and an e. 232:9
beginning, a muddle, and an e. 233:7
do not very much care, how it is to e. 16:14
e. badly from the beginning 17:3
forthwith put an e. to the chapter 15:8
In my beginning is my e. 164:16
in the end, there was no e. 43:14
just as well that it came to an e. 17:1
lest he should make an e. 279:2
till you come to the e.: then stop 16:10
endeavour criticism: *a disinterested e.* 47:4
ended e. with the word *mayonnaise* 18:4
ending bread-sauce of the happy e. 17:5
for the novelist than the e. 17:10
greater the art is of e. 16:12
endings By e. as by hunger 233:9
I *do* incline to melancholy e. 16:11
Nothing so simple as 'happy e.' 9:10
ends E. always give me trouble 17:13
having similar sounds at their e. 212:13
want to see how it e. 340:1
endure will e. forever 314:9
enduring E. fame is promised only 82:3
Endymion In E., I leaped headlong 310:4
enemies fast as my e. could wish 52:1
no time for making new e. 126:12
turning one's e. into money 119:7
enemy book of my e. 215:5
hasn't an e. in the world 327:7
energy I have exhausted my fiction e. 18:5
enfin *E. Malherbe vint* 315:1
enforce not attempts to e. a poor idea 197:14
enforced e. orthodoxy 34:14
engine like an e. starting up 38:12
engineering electricity into e. 153:5
engineers age of the e. 187:8
Artists are not e. of the soul 183:10
e. of the soul 183:3
England being vomited forth in E. 141:3
belief in the future of E. 157:4
difference in E. is that they want us 205:13
E. and America are two countries 125:7
E. hath need of thee 317:1
foreign field That is for ever E. 164:11

England (*cont.*)
In E. . . . each man works by himself 141:4
roast beef of old E. 93:1
English abused the E. 309:7
always very good at E. at school 291:10
as penetrating as an E. fog 3:13
blackguardism of an E. sporting paper 157:1
brain of an E. chemist 334:10
can't think of the E. for a thing 124:9
Certain men the E. shot 187:9
Dan Chaucer, well of E. undefiled 289:4
day-by-day life of an E. gamekeeper 207:10
difficulty in writing E. 125:4
[E. departments where] Batman 256:4
E. is the great vacuum cleaner 126:10
E. is the language of the world 124:7
E. reading public 11:3
failure of E. masters, at all the schools 195:7
five or six E.-speaking people 95:11
French criticism of E. work 47:8
his E. sweete upon his tonge 230:9
in E. the undergrowth is part 125:2
in favour of boys learning E. 125:1
in reality E. is about as pure as 126:3
Larkin was so E. 312:9
licence that E. people give themselves 235:7
made our E. tongue a gallimaufry 123:11
mobilized the E. language 231:10
most accomplished pronouncer of E. 230:13
most beautiful words in E. 263:12
no E. poet unless he has completed 196:5
No one has written worse E. 302:11
No one working in the E. language 225:6
not be too severe on E. novels 159:4
Obsessive denigration of E. fiction 142:2
Of all E. writers Chaucer is the clearest 289:6
oppression of the E. language 126:8
Others may speak and read E. 126:6
sort of E. up with which I will not put 100:7
speaking E. as to the manner born 101:4
sucking the blood of E. novelists 159:8
Take away from E. authors 67:11
teachers of E. literature 230:1
There is no contemporary E. writer 293:9
thew and sinew of the E. language 296:1
thought of E. literature as the richest 141:11
To speak E., one must place 123:14
twentieth century E. verse 152:11
virtue of its not being E. 250:4
we E., never lost our civil war 255:6
Whoever wishes to attain an E. style 276:1
Written E. is now inert and inorganic 124:15
Englishman E.'s constitution 326:5
religious rights of an E. 156:5
What most offends an E. 141:8
Englishmen first of many E. 330:2
sheer, inveterate E. 101:11
enigmas I've put in so many e. 219:11
enjoy I shan't be here to e. them 53:13
literature except how to e. it 139:10
Poets have got to e. themselves 92:1
We do not e. poetry unless 174:9
enjoying who judges while e. 199:10
enlightenment e. driven away 104:11
ennui feeling of vagueness and e. 268:7
Only sheer e. sometimes 200:5
entente e. is al, and nat the lettres 31:12
entertain Tickle and e. us, or we die 10:1
entertained e. on one another's remains 23:8
go to the theatre to be e. 63:11
entertainment how a particular e. 48:6
enthusiasm E. is taken through 88:6
in the height of e. I have been cheated 310:5
enumeration Realism is indefinite e. 33:1
envelopes On backs of tattered e. 178:8
envious Hot, e., noisy, proud 213:7
envy e. of the successful 215:9
E.'s a sharper spur than pay 213:6
mutual e. of the living 3:10
sulphur of e. 215:11
Toil, e., want, the patron 217:11
épater *Il faut é. le bourgeois* 229:1
epic e. in the prose and poetry 141:10
novel is a subjective e. 158:11
only surviving Old English e. 256:2
we are in our ballad or e. age 141:5
write a romance than an e. poem 101:10
epick I am an E. writer with a k 331:7
epigram all existence in an e. 32:9
day of the jewelled e. is passed 236:12
Impelled to try an e. 340:6
until it purrs like an e. 118:2
What is an E.? a dwarfish whole 256:11
epigrams his neat And witty e. 223:9
epilogue three more chapters and an e. 17:8
epiphany By an e. he meant 273:3
episodic e. are the worst 168:13
epistolary e. form is an antiquated 159:3
e. style is the most proper 158:7
epitaph And were an e. to be my story 127:10
epithets Such e., like pepper 56:6
erotica in the e. business 78:8
error as an e. of judgement 302:8
nothing but the possibility of e. 136:8
truth is machine-like, e. is alive 253:3
errors His e. are volitional 94:13
imitation of the common e. of our life 107:2
eruption small e. of a disease 129:13
escape e. from emotion 88:1
forced into effort as an e. 75:12
He needed me to e. from being fifty 6:1
What's writing? A way of e. 150:3
you shall not e. my iambics 171:7

Esperanto unless the poet writes in E. 47:12
essay *E.* A loose sally of the mind 79:3
e. defies strict definition 79:6
e. is just a grown-up version 79:7
e. must have this permanent quality 79:4
e. on the life-history of insects 239:2
essayist e. . . . can pull on any sort 79:5
essayists Mere e. 78:13
essays E. The word is late 79:1
go by the name of e. 79:2
essence e. of a human soul 27:8
essential e. part of all my education 21:6
establishment humanist literary E. 239:11
estate writer of real e. advertisements 13:15
eternities e. inside a manufacturer 283:6
eternity in the e. of print 97:14
My eyes are on e. 280:8
Silence is deep as E. 121:11
etherealizes Flaubert e. all 279:6
etherized patient e. upon a table 92:3
ethical great e. importance 252:7
ethics they drew a system of e. 287:6
étonne *É.-moi* 166:6
etymology their e. being buried 155:1
Euclid fifth proposition of E. 44:1
eulogist foggy e. 48:4
eulogy improvise a e. 69:3
eunuch Time's e. 269:6
eunuchs Critics are like e. in a harem 50:9
Europe E. made his woe her own 287:7
look of the last gentleman in E. 340:5
European E. moderns are all *trying* 152:3
E. view of a poet 47:12
history of the E. novel 142:1
Eurotrash House organ of the E. 158:6
evening see if e.—any evening 92:3
evenings long winter e. 150:1
event always hurries to the main e. 15:3
events ordinary train of human e. 158:9
turn e. into ideas 139:7
everyday e. language 180:11
poetry of our e. life 314:8
everything as Tom Macaulay is of e. 314:3
E. mankind does, their hope, fear 237:6
novel tends to tell us e. 228:8
evidence state that e. exists 24:12
evil e. religious in its intensity 149:9
Inventing really e. people is great fun 39:1
Money doesn't mind if we say it's e. 147:8
witness to man's knowledge of e. 253:1
evils necessary e. 217:14
exaggerate obliged to e. 134:14
example fiery-hearted youth see an e. 342:12
examples History is philosophy from e. 102:9
excavate e. the experience of the people 273:6
excellence never a judge of e. 48:4
excellencies dwell rather upon e. 46:10
excellent e. lies before us 97:4
who did not think himself super-e. 223:6
excess blasted with e. of light 316:6
should surprise by a fine e. 173:4
excitement e. and the revelation 40:3
exclamation Cut out all these e. points 195:4
exclude e. from this publication 77:3
Letters . . . e. not only the reader 130:2
excluded utterly defeated and e. 18:11
excrescence morbid e. 214:2
excursion frowzy poem, called the 'E.' 342:5
excuse No plagiarist can e. the wrong 168:8
execute zealous Muslims to e. them 35:14
exercise e. in the use of language 337:9
violent e. he got with his knife 277:6
what e. is to the body 198:13
exhausted I have e. my fiction energy 18:5
exhausting Writing fiction is e. 76:6
exile Ovid remained classical even in e. 319:4
exist that didn't e. 115:6
existence single e. is itself an illusion 161:7
exists fact that it e. 132:7
expels science arrives it e. literature 221:2
expense at very small e. 46:11
expenses facts are on e. 119:1
experience All e. is good for writers 268:8
all your e. of the world 201:15
balloon of e. is in fact tied to 110:7
excavate the e. of the people 273:6
flower of any kind of e. 174:4
imposing of a pattern on e. 8:13
keep parts of the human e. alive 179:4
more acute the e., the less articulate 89:1
province of art is all e. 7:11
publish books on their e. in public life 183:5
restricted to the heights of e. 315:3
thought to Donne was an e. 295:2
writes truthfully out of individual e. 106:12
experiences mind of the poet these e. 175:6
experimental e. verification 138:1
experiments simply a set of e. in life 271:13
explain e. his explanation 291:6
You e. nothing, O poet 175:3
explainer village e. 321:4
explainers sciences yielded great e. 222:1
explicable all things become e. 175:3
exploiter post-mortem e. 23:9
explore do not want to e. an egoism 13:3
explosion It *should* be an e. of truth 228:4
express desire you have to e. yourself 34:6
not so much to e. our wants 121:6
expressed ne'er so well e. 256:7
expression e. he's spent a long time hunting 234:1
express what sometimes resists e. 76:3
in the wide waters of e. 292:7

expression (*cont.*)
less articulate its e. 89:1
looking for the unique e. 181:8
loss of e. 263:10
undervalued as a means of e. 265:4
What is freedom of e. 36:2
expurgated E. by learned men 77:4
not sufficiently 'e.' 34:5
external by means of certain e. signs 8:1
extinct Seek younger friends; I am e. 5:12
extinction some threat of e. 78:6
extracting Life is a means of e. fiction 135:11
extraordinary this is an e. man 286:2
would not appear so e. 308:3
write about the e. 239:6
extreme all *trying* to be e. 152:3
eye *Cast a cold e.* 127:9
comparative e. of God 50:3
composes 'with his e. on the object' 249:1
harvest of a quiet e. 172:11
if you have the e. 197:3
nearest thing to the e. of God 327:5
eyes Closed his e. in endless night 316:6
From women's e. this doctrine I derive 142:4
good Lord made your e. 168:9
its feathers are all e. 241:10
My e. are on eternity 280:8
reader could read with his e. alone 139:6
soft look Your e. had once 5:5
So my e. get tired 38:2
visions of the e. and the spirit 123:4

Faber labour for F. and Faber 194:7
Fabians good man fallen among F. 327:9
fable Read my little f. 10:7
that thai be nocht bot f. 89:9
fables Refuse old wives' f. 89:8
face blind man feeling the f. 172:12
downright repulsive f. of a poet 279:12
draw a full f. 256:6
everybody's f. but their own 256:8
mask that eats into the f. 83:7
My f. looks like a wedding-cake 277:9
take off his f. and reveal his mask 280:5
faces wears almost everywhere two f. 325:9
fact always be some foundation of f. 89:12
give us the creative f. 24:9
idea *is* the f. 203:12
judges of f., tho' not judges of laws 33:10
faction pride and impudence in f. knit 150:9
factories years spent in the f. 162:1
facts Collect all the f. 23:5
Comment is free but f. are on expenses 119:1
Comment is free, but f. are sacred 118:1
curse of f. and the blessing of illusions 106:9
f. of life are to the biographer 26:1
have to be accurate and keep to f. 22:14
no such things as f. 252:6
not to deny the f. 80:3
scrape together a few f. 23:1
shilling life will give you all the f. 24:3
those who gather long-forgotten f. 219:3
fad-chaser pretentious f. 341:3
faded make sure that the ink had not f. 192:10
Faerie Queene F. is the *dullest thing out* 330:4
Spenser's *The F.* 310:3
stanza from Spenser's *F.* 330:3
while reading *The F.* 91:10
failed his life f. to be disagreeable 316:4
I have been idle. I have *f.* 269:13
men who have f. in literature 49:12
most editors are f. writers 71:8
failure audience was a total f. 63:5
final accolade of f. 203:3
step between success and f. 96:6
success and f. are usually crippling 202:13
failures another of those numerous f. 204:7
faint with f. praises one another damn 49:6
fairies I had never heard of f. 39:9
I saw nothing about f. 27:11
Rewards and f. 30:8
Scoffed at f., but they made his living 343:7
fairy designated as 'f. money' 72:4
f. kind of writing 109:4
F. stories are about one king 80:9
f.-tale of olden times 79:8
F. tales, unlike any other sort 80:7
folk tale or the f. tale 80:2
I left f. stories lying on the floor 79:10
I was ten, I read f. tales in secret 80:4
modern f. tales 44:6
myth is, of course, not a f. story 80:3
read some things, especially f.-stories 40:5
real taste for f.-stories was wakened 334:9
value of f.-stories 80:5
What's more moral than a f. tale 149:2
fairyland not in some f. 237:8
fait *un seul f. accompli* 62:12
faith to hem yive I f. and ful credence 198:2
faithful seldom strictly f. 250:1
fall Did he f. or was he pushed 45:9
f. guy and a father figure 71:12
fallen good man f. among Fabians 327:9
false Rudyard the f. measure 311:6
falsehoods f. which interest dictates 253:10
fame achieved f. by literary merits 296:9
also call the Temple of F. 117:5
best fame is a writer's f. 83:9
dead is my f. 205:4
defending himself against f. 83:6
Enduring f. is promised only 82:3

establishment of my f. 15:9
F. is the spur 29:9
F. often makes a writer vain 82:11
For having granted me the f. 81:2
For me I never cared for f. 68:6
Literary f. is the only fame 81:11
love of f. is the last thing 81:3
On F.'s eternal beadroll 289:4
only f. I care for 196:9
Poets' food is love and f. 173:11
share of the artist's f. 47:14
families 3 or 4 f. in a country village 238:5
All happy f. resemble one another 164:6
family about a man that left his f. 285:7
character of a f. 83:12
read *Bleak House* to the f. any more 202:5
famous by that time I was too f. 82:8
I wrote about someone f. 25:4
Not a f.-last-words Peaceful 54:3
one morning and found myself f. 81:10
fan Thank you, earnest f. 81:2
fanatic mark out the philosophic f. 328:4
fancied He didn't love God, just f. him 277:12
fancy makes f. lame 10:1
odoriferous flowers of f. 319:1
polar star of poetry, as f. is the sails 172:15
Tell me where is f. bred 109:3
fantasies fed the heart on f. 110:9
fantasy F. deals with things 85:9
F. is the oldest form of literature 85:12
F. literature, in its broadest definition 86:2
I prefer to see f. written in a purer way 86:5
I regard f., as distinct from SF 86:4
Most modern f. just rearranges 86:1
people think the boundaries of f. lie 86:3
present spate of so-called heroic f. 85:10
ruling f. which drove him to write 149:9
far F. from the madding crowd 30:1
just too f. away for him to hear 307:7
Faraday choose to be F. 221:1
Farewell to Arms Hemingway's *A F.* 43:5
farrago *f. libelli est* 237:6
farts smell of their own f. 224:13
fascinates he f. even when he is wrong 340:11
fascinating find it f. 50:11
fascination f. of what's difficult 74:4
fascism form of linguistic f. 36:5
fashion Language is more f. 101:8
so far out of the literary f. 316:4
fashions latest literary f. 153:7
fastidious duty not to be f. 294:4
lover of literature is never f. 138:2
fat enjoys supper—to that extent of f. 317:10
f. of others' works 167:10
It is all f., without nerve 330:7
fate Art is a revolt against f. 9:3
In case it tempted F. 54:7
reader's fancy makes the f. of books 9:13
father fall guy and a f. figure 71:12
F. of the Novel 285:8
If you are a single f. 84:11
man whose f. was a dragon 85:8
my f. was before me 323:3
worshipful f. and first founder 289:3
fathered f. the Modern Movement 152:10
fathom For thou canst not f. it 174:3
Faulkner know all about F.'s 25:13
fault artist is his own f. 267:2
fall into the abominable f. 234:9
faultless If she had been f. 36:11
faults blind to all his f. 295:10
many f. have escaped 145:9
whole training is to detect f. 208:9
Faust author as Christ or F. 37:6
favourites Lady Mary's chief f. 184:5
fear by means of pity and f. 247:8
I f. those big words, Stephen said 263:13
those with an irrational f. of life 193:2
You need not f. to be a poet 177:14
fears our f. gather 96:5
When I have f. that I may cease 52:3
feather f. to tickle the intellect 256:12
feather-footed F. through the plashy fen 236:3
feathers few remaining f. 286:6
its f. are all eyes 241:10
feebly His words came f. 231:7
feed We f. on the ancients 245:7
feel f. anything and everything 88:11
tragedy to those that f. 133:6
who would make us f., must feel 86:9
feeling Art is the objectification of f. 9:5
display taste and f. 220:11
Drink heightens f. 66:3
for people of f. 134:2
general mess of imprecision of f. 88:10
Lessons in f. 318:9
not observation—it is f. 89:3
revelation of a f. 178:4
style overflowing with f. 294:7
waves of f. that wash over adolescents 40:10
what the other side must be f. 159:1
feelings f. he has lived through 8:1
hard for a woman to define her f. 258:14
other people's f. 87:12
very f. which ought to taste it 173:1
feels One only f. as one should 87:9
feet take more care of their f. 217:8
felicities f. of Solomon 20:4
felicity all hastening together to perfect f. 16:1
Horace's careful f. 305:2
Felix killed the Bishop and F. 53:2
fell F. half so flat as Walter Scott 324:4
fellows For these f. of infinite tongue 142:5

genius (*cont.*)
Oh Richardson! thou singular g. 322:6
Poetic G. of my Country found me 286:7
raised to the power of g. 289:11
secret casket of his g. 292:8
Since when was g. found respectable 94:6
solitary g. in the garret 260:11
takes a lot of time to be a g. 94:15
talent instantly recognizes g. 94:11
true g. is a mind of large powers 93:11
True G., like Armida's wand 93:10
Unless one is a g., it is best to aim 94:9
What a commonplace g. he has 302:10
what a g. I had when I wrote 93:9
What is g.—but the power 94:4
What Romantic terminology called g. 95:3
When a true g. appears in the world 93:7
without the necessary g. 331:7
Wordsworth—stupendous g. 342:3
works of a great g. who is ignorant 93:8
works of g. are watered with its tears 94:3
geniuses all of his characters into g. 279:9
considering their literary g. 94:14
G. are the luckiest of mortals 95:2
those of the great g. are wine 185:6
genre put me in a disreputable g. 102:7
genteel marks of the beast to the truly g. 42:2
gentle Do not go g. into that good night 53:12
gentleman as an educated g. 124:12
I'm a g. 13:2
look of the last g. in Europe 340:5
misfortune not to be a g. 282:4
gentlewomen all Turgenev's g. 37:5
genuine g. poetry is conceived 175:2
place for the g. 176:8
geography G. is about Maps 23:7
geometry subject as precise as g. 174:8
George *Madness of G. III* 241:5
Georgians successor to the G. 153:7
German corsets of the G. language 125:3
language of his poems is G. 229:9
one G. adjective 124:10
Waiting for the G. verb 125:10
Germans G. can understand 287:4
germs recognizing on the spot as 'g.' 113:10
gerund Save the g. and screw the whale 101:6
gesture Morality's a g. 148:10
ghost G. stories . . . tell us about things 96:8
Hamlet without mentioning the g. 65:9
no longer get a good g. story 95:9
Shakespeare's g. 219:6
than g. stories are written for ghosts 222:4
We will each write a g. story 112:8
writer of g. stories must freeze 96:4
ghostly Dad was my g. sub-editor 85:2
ghosts be allowed to us moderns, are g. 95:8
by our lack of g. we're haunted 255:6
place to get our g. from 95:10
wonder what g. will be left 263:10
giant g.'s wings prevent him 174:12
giants like to be told of g. and castles 39:6
Gibbon scribble! Eh! Mr G. 32:4
gift your g. survived it all 343:8
gifts imagination conjures g. 111:3
gigantic g. body, the huge massy face 308:8
gilding amusement is the g. 271:5
gin G.-and-water is the source 65:6
spiritual g. 185:5
gives writing g. you up 274:6
giveth author g. and the author taketh 210:6
gladiatorship its cruelty, its g. 47:6
gladly And g. wolde he lerne 216:11
gladness in our youth begin in g. 172:13
Gladstone Mr G. read Homer for fun 305:1
glamour word *g.* comes from 101:9
glare Trollope—'all gobble and g.' 335:4
glass g. I drink from is not large 168:1
his own face in the g. 151:10
No g. renders a man's form 57:6
Satire is a sort of g. 256:8
Glaswegian monologue of G. low life 311:1
glimpses G. that seem like a microcosm 329:7
gloomy that far more g. character 306:4
glory ardent for some desperate g. 254:7
mellow g. of the Attic stage 329:6
School for Scandal in its g. 5:1
There's g. for you 144:10
Where is it now, the g. and the dream 109:7
gloves War is capitalism with the g. off 255:7
glue wide sea of g. 308:10
glutton g. of wordes 261:6
gluttons Young people are g. for detail 39:11
go G., litel bok, go, litel myn tragedye 55:4
I think you couldn't g. on 54:4
someone to tell you to g. on 150:2
goat spiritual digestion of a g. 337:8
gobbets gulp the stuff down in g. 294:4
gobble Trollope—'all g. and glare' 335:4
God agree with the book of G. 203:5
artist, like the G. of the creation 272:8
be in his work as G. is in creation 271:12
British Empire for G. 333:5
But only G. can make a tree 155:10
comparative eye of G. 50:3
declaration of the skill of G. 135:9
G. and I both knew what it meant 144:5
G. and Robert Browning knew 285:1
G. has written all the books 21:7
G. help the Minister that meddles 183:1
G. is the perfect poet 203:8
He didn't love G., just fancied him 277:12
here is G.'s plenty 289:5
he wrote of Angels and G. 316:9

tragedy with a h. ending 63:7
Well, I've had a h. life 127:2
hard he gathered only h. words 234:7
unable to be h. on himself 210:8
hardback modern h. writer 83:8
hardening h. of the paragraphs 5:13
hardest h. thing in all literature 166:1
Hardy as it was upon Thomas H. 155:11
H. and *Thomas* and *Frost* 246:10
not in the H. class 327:12
Rereading H., I was struck 240:11
harem like eunuchs in a h. 50:9
harm may do you extreme h. 139:14
harmonies inventor of h. 317:3
harmony give them the other h. 112:2
harp And his wild h. slung behind him 254:1
Harrods as she moves out of H. 38:4
harrow Would h. up thy soul 105:5
Harvard my Yale College and my H. 218:6
harvest h. of a quiet eye 172:11
haste Journalism encourages h. 119:11
hastening h. together to perfect felicity 16:1
hate I h. the common herd 223:8
such a thing as creative h. 87:11
to h. your neighbour 287:6
hated I thought I h. everybody 84:10
Kipling is intensely loved and h. 312:1
loved well because he h. 293:7
read them as if he h. them 284:8
hatred Regulated h. 278:8
haunt certain to h. her 83:13
haunted grimacing, h. creature 295:7
Hawthorne Poe is a kind of H. 320:5
hay Antic h. 28:13
haze looking through a luminous h. 301:1
head h. so high it'll strike the stars 223:7
more care of their feet than their h. 217:8
ominous thing put out its h. 96:2
Or in the heart or in the h. 109:3
unfavourable critics move into your h. 48:11
What though his h. be empty 58:9
headlines papers get their scare h. 157:6
heads over the h. of your readers 10:6
within the secrecy of our own h. 140:4
health classical is h. 151:4
regaining my h. through reading 74:5
hear written word, to make you h. 272:4
hearers h. like my books 213:5
heart As my poor h. doth think 142:6
bitter insights of the h. 55:9
foul rag and bone shop of the h. 88:9
from my own h. to the h. of others 19:2
gives you a clutch at the h. 43:4
grass grow and the squirrel's h. beat 134:3
h. is a lonely hunter 30:5
h.'s invisible furies 277:11
h. speaks to heart, whereas language 121:1
h. was piercèd through the ear 261:9
He spoke, and loosed our h. in tears 342:9
he tears out the h. of it 49:9
his h. is in the right place 182:7
holiness of the h.'s affections 251:11
hopeless h. of man 292:12
I found not my h. moved 14:8
indignation can no longer tear his h. 332:3
into the h. of an immense darkness 164:8
It came from mine own h. 112:1
look in thy h. and write 268:12
minute examiner of the human h. 322:8
more knowledge of the h. 322:7
My h. did do it 142:7
natural language of the h. 121:5
One must have a h. of stone 87:10
Only an aching h. 88:4
Or in the h. or in the head 109:3
passions of the human h. 317:5
poets bicycle-pump the human h. 143:5
sealing up of a nation's h. 35:8
Shakespeare unlocked his h. 326:10
somehow the h. seems squeezed out 320:6
stab the h. with such force 195:2
that which everyone knows by h. 131:9
thou hast my h. 142:11
We had fed the h. on fantasies 110:9
heartbreak moment of purest h. 108:12
heartbreaking inept title to h. bosh 240:7
heartlessness H. masked 294:7
Heart of Darkness Joseph Conrad's *H.* 292:10
heat body h. of a healthy Anglican life 303:8
Write while the h. is in you 112:9
heathen any example in any h. author 20:5
heaven entering the kingdom of h. 278:6
how deep is Hell, and H. how high 281:9
Is it any better in H., my friend Ford 299:5
things are the sons of h. 262:6
heavy What a h. thing is a pen 73:12
hedge as a clipped h. is to a forest 326:3
heels wings of his h. are in sight 334:1
heights restricted to the h. of experience 315:3
Heine H. so loosened the corsets 125:3
heir first h. of my invention 55:5
heirs crew of missing h. 159:11
Helicon watered our houses in H. 172:2
hell Blake knew how deep is H. 281:9
has been in h. and seen there 295:5
h. of a profession to be a writer 149:8
H. with compensations 340:10
printing house in H. 241:11
help They look on and h. 53:5
trying to get out and wants h. 115:3
helpless passionless, h. creatures 258:13
Hemingway admirable profile of H. 288:9

Hemingway (*cont.*)
produced someone like H. 303:7
soft-boiled sub-H. prose 45:7
hen well-bred h. wife, fond of a joke 336:1
hens fate of literary h. 224:5
Henty for boys, G. A. H. 102:2
herbs goodly green h. of sentences 20:3
heresy No h. can excite the horror 52:9
heritage boring part of one's h. 256:2
hermit rake turned h. 184:8
hero don't want to be a h. 255:7
h. has to spear it 86:5
h. of my tale 251:13
he who aspires to be a h. 64:12
In every first novel the h. is the author 37:6
left your h. and heroine tied up 78:1
Show me a h. and I will write you 248:1
tells us the truth about its h. 159:12
heroes Children should acquire their h. 40:8
h. of French fiction 141:8
h. were good through and through 37:9
heroic h. poem of its sort 22:11
present spate of so-called h. fantasy 85:10
work of an h. mind 309:6
heroine could not have been the h. 36:11
going to take a h. whom no-one 36:7
O Lord, Sir—when a h. goes mad 63:2
herself there was a 'not h.' 296:10
HIBK detective story writers of the 'H.' 44:3
hidden lie h. within all of us 96:8
hide my dear Lucy, h. these books 184:7
hiding not because you're h. something 14:7
highbrow opinions as to what a h. is 120:8
What is a h.? He is a man who 120:5
higher find my own the h. 208:5
'H. Cannibalism' in biography 24:6
I am capable of h. things 224:9
Highland Walter Scott gave H. legends 141:7
highway mirror which passes over a h. 158:10
highwaymen give them handsome h. 216:7
hill coal-cart down an icy h. 273:4
hunter home from the h. 331:5
when you're half-way down a h. 48:12
hills Blue remembered h. 29:2
hippopotamus painful h. 307:4
hiss dismal universal h. 46:5
hissed audience . . . that h. yesterday 35:2
historian H.—An unsuccessful novelist 104:13
h., essentially, wants more documents 104:8
h. to rise each morning saying 105:3
life of the h. must be short 103:10
not requisite for an h. 103:7
historians alter the past, h. can 104:6
H. desiring to write the actions 103:4
h. left blanks in their writings 104:10
H. repeat each other 104:9
historical any h. romance 55:8
h. novel *Salammbô* 102:4
put the h. novel in a category apart 102:3
This Uriah Heep of h. writing 285:5
histories studied h. 103:5
those who left no h. behind them 36:11
history absence of romance in my h. 102:8
Anybody can make h. 104:5
can't get at the truth by writing h. 105:4
contribution to the h. of my time 206:5
funeral oration rather than a h. 22:6
He took all h. for his province 102:2
H. gets thicker as it approaches 105:2
H. is a gallery of pictures 104:4
h. is a rest 104:7
H. . . . is, indeed, little more than 103:9
H. is philosophy from examples 102:9
H. is the essence of innumerable 104:2
h. of art is the history of revivals 166:3
h. openly subjective, and 'feigned' 104:14
If h. record good things 102:10
'make h.' at the National Theatre 318:7
of the same stuff as h. itself 102:3
poets make . . . h. 166:12
Read no h.: nothing but biography 104:1
seven thousand years of human h. 245:6
shame the pride of documentary h. 160:1
takes a great deal of h. 138:5
There is properly no h. 104:3
Whosoever, in writing a modern h. 103:3
worthy of serious attention than h. 171:6
history-making Man is a h. creature 105:1
hoarse pack has yelled itself h. 4:1
hobbit in the ground there lived a h. 164:14
hobby Poetry? It's a h. 69:7
whatever his *h.* may be 297:1
Hobson H. barking up the wrong tree 50:7
hodgepodge English tongue a h. 123:11
Hogarth sharp eye of a H. 338:4
hogwash great ideas are h. 233:6
hold h. readily in your hand 27:4
secret is to try to h. you there 202:3
hold-all deep old desk, or capacious h. 59:1
hole h.-in-the-wall fringe literature 223:2
In a h. in the ground there lived 164:14
holiness h. of the heart's affections 251:11
Hollywood not have been invited to H. 288:8
holy between-The-sheets, h.-water death 54:3
h. simplicity 41:7
We dropped the word 'H.' 21:13
Holy Ghost pencil of the H. 20:4
home Censorship should begin at h. 35:10
For a writer, going back h. means 75:10
granted me a sort of h. 202:7
H. is the sailor, home from sea 331:5
name of his or her h. river 154:6
there's nobody at h. 268:14
Homer from H.'s mighty dinners 165:8

literary (*cont.*)
l. world is not conducted 166:10
more than most l. forms, the essay 79:6
Of all the l. scenes 157:5
only connection with the l. world 281:2
parole of l. men 196:3
Real l. creation uses . . . reality 135:6
Shaw will be a great l. figure 327:12
so far out of the l. fashion 316:4
stupid axiom of l. criticism 284:2
uncorrupted with l. prejudices 47:1
literature All l. is autobiographical 138:13
All modern American l. comes from 336:6
American professors like their l. 138:14
as for l. It gives no man 68:4
bad l. gets written 97:15
Bad l. of the sort called amusing 185:5
before it qualifies as a subject for l. 143:8
can only be a newspaper l. 183:2
canon of English and American l. 255:12
can't stamp out l. in the country 34:12
central function of imaginative l. 139:15
Cham of l., Samuel Johnson 308:1
character of American l. 140:8
doomed to a life of l. 266:8
English l. and the Anglican Church 322:1
English l.'s performing flea 341:1
escaped teachers of English l. 230:1
events into ideas is the function of l. 139:7
foundation and condition of all *l.* 139:6
generally a disease of English l. 23:2
give prizes for l. 190:3
great asset to English l. 339:6
greatest masterpiece in l. 61:9
greatest threat to l. 69:2
Great l. cannot grow from a neglected 247:1
Great l. is simply language charged 139:1
great l. is thus chiefly the product 141:9
great work of l. 309:6
Ideas are to l. what light is to painting 138:7
I don't think l. is ever finished 190:9
If God exists, why write l. 204:4
image of l. to be found 139:13
in our l. to render them helpless 258:13
it becomes l. 302:11
itch of l. comes over a man 265:14
judged in isolation as a piece of l. 63:4
knew everything about l. except 139:10
know about success in l. 214:1
limits of l. 327:6
Lincoln of our l. 336:3
l. appear a morbid excrescence 214:2
L. cannot be the business 258:5
L. flourishes best 138:12
l. goes as freight 139:12
l. has no relation with 134:13
l., is a dossier of human imbecility 138:11
l. is a drug 138:3
L. is a luxury 90:3
L. is a method of arrangement 138:10
L. is a splendid mistress 138:8
l. is formal 139:9
L. is mostly about having sex 139:11
l. is my mistress 67:12
L. is news that STAYS news 139:3
L. is strewn with the wreckage 224:6
L. is the art of writing 139:4
L. is the orchestration of platitudes 139:8
l. is the principal voice 148:5
l. is without gender 261:1
L., like property, is theft 168:10
L. nowadays is a trade 67:13
l. of women would be different 260:2
l. seeks to communicate power 186:11
l. that has absorbed the taste 140:3
l., though the grandest occupation 138:4
louse in the locks of l. 205:7
machine-minders of l. 152:7
made by l. something near £70,000 67:10
make l. one's only means of support 68:1
My theories and views of l. vary 139:5
nation whose l. is cut short 35:8
newest works; in l., the oldest 220:8
no ideas of their own about l. 192:6
no l. can outdo real life 134:5
object of a student of l. 219:12
of history to produce a little l. 138:5
Oh l., oh the glorious Art 138:9
on the edge of the chair of L. 107:13
Our l. is a substitute for religion 204:3
Poetry is simply l. reduced 176:5
relationship between l. and science 221:7
Remarks are not l. 139:2
Roman l. is Greek literature 141:6
Russian l. saved my soul 230:3
Science fiction is the l. of *might be* 222:14
secondly, the l. of *power* 187:3
sensation of looking down on l. 50:3
small proportion of l. does more 140:1
standard l. of Canada 140:9
study of Greek l. 218:9
task of every piece of l. is to move 187:6
This ain't your silly English L. 219:7
to l. what brandy is to beverage 117:7
To me l. is forever blowing a horn 140:5
virtue of much l. 139:14
wash l. off ourselves 106:11
What l. can and should do 230:7
When l. has a Tolstoy 334:11
When science arrives it expels l. 221:2
why l. should be any different 9:6
Your true lover of l. is never fastidious 138:2
littérature *Et tout le reste est l.* 138:6

little Go, l. bok, go, litel myn tragedye 55:4
l. may be diffused 58:10
l. people take revenge 26:4
L. subject, little wit 211:11
say much in l. and then take half 2:3
use big words for l. matters 41:13
littleness his incredible l. 321:7
long l. of life 284:1
liturgical as l. objects to a priest 242:6
live enough into the world to l. a novel 158:13
not l. who life eternal gave 323:5
one wouldn't *l.* under Niagara 314:2
Read in order to l. 199:14
Who l. under the shadow 254:9
write too much, and l. too long 4:12
lived I should have l. or written better 324:1
l. in social intercourse 22:4
something that I have l. through 238:9
liver l.-wing of a fowl 189:6
livers grave L. do in Scotland use 231:7
lives could not write their own l. 24:1
determined to live their own l. 267:3
not how a man dies, but how he l. 51:11
where so many l. come and go 134:12
living beyond the language of the l. 53:10
could make a decent l. 149:10
I want to go on l. even after death 53:11
makes a reasonable l. 69:11
much of it leads to l. for one's diary 59:5
must earn a l. some other way 68:13
mutual envy of the l. 3:10
need to earn a l. and my need to write 69:9
novel is a l. thing 159:7
pain of l. and the drug of dreams 200:11
there are no l. people in it 63:6
they made his l. 343:7
Who, l., had no roof 304:8
write because they are not l. properly 274:9
writing books about l. men 24:4
load 'l. every rift' of your subject 328:2
loafed Before that, I suppose I l. 341:2
loathe C— taught me to l. Horace 305:3
loathsome more l. age 150:9
local l., but prized elsewhere 83:3
l. habitation and a name 109:2
Locke L. and Bacon 245:11
locked spacious l. cellar 266:9
locks louse in the l. of literature 205:7
logic this danger does lie in l. 110:6
logical exchange life for a l. process 272:6
logo bears its manufacturer's l. 276:8
loitering Alone and palely l. 163:14
Lolita L., light of my life 165:3
London art, in L. only is a trade 172:6
He describes L. 293:10
like driving to Edinburgh (from L.) 274:5
L. Library, for a private library 131:10
will soon come out in L. 105:7
loneliness deep well of l. 150:8
essential l. of my life 149:7
lonely heart is a l. hunter 30:5
needs a mentor, otherwise it's very l. 150:2
long foolish thing to make a l. prologue 31:10
foot and a half l. 261:4
L. books, when read 33:3
l. poem is a test of invention 172:15
Not that the story need be l. 209:9
shall be witty and it sha'n't be l. 256:9
So l. as men can breathe 186:7
longer wished l. by its readers 32:2
Longford Lord L. is against us reading 227:3
longhand to the press in l. 243:6
longitude l. with no platitude 166:8
look sensitive to the way things l. 162:3
They l. on and help 53:5
looking in my nicely polished l.-glass 309:1
loop l. the l. on a commonplace 166:7
loosed He spoke, and l. our heart 342:9
lopped would be a limb l. off 282:2
lord consists in saying 'L. Jones Dead' 117:11
let a L. once own 97:2
lose Winsome, l. some 281:1
loss Patrick White is a dead l. 339:6
lost [I have] l. (or won if you like) 283:5
l. valleys of the imagination 251:3
Poetry is what is l. in translation 48:7
louse l. in the locks of literature 205:7
love After a man has done making l. 73:14
can do you blood and l. 63:12
comely in nothing but in l. 91:8
grew at last acquainted with L. 337:4
half in l. with easeful Death 52:4
He didn't l. God, just fancied him 277:12
I dared to l. 276:10
If music be the food of l., play on 163:8
I l. thee in prose 142:11
I'm tired of L.: I'm still more tired 146:10
In our culture, l. needs a mixer 143:8
L., curiosity, freckles, and doubt 319:7
L. gilds the scene 142:13
l. him for the rest of my days 305:3
L. made me poet 142:7
l. that moves the sun 43:6
l. your neighbour's wife 287:6
Man's l. is of man's life a thing 143:5
morbid marriage of l. and death 153:4
more than the usual number to l. 85:6
No one would ever have fallen in l. 142:10
Only l. can apprehend and hold them 47:7
Ovid, the soft philosopher of l. 319:2
Poets' food is l. and fame 173:11
reading a very sensual l.-scene 77:6

love (*cont.*)
someone doesn't l. you any more 203:1
They l. indeed who quake to say 142:3
truth about his or her l. affairs 24:11
two people who go into l. step for step 143:2
We men have got l. well weighed up 143:6
loved Dante, who l. well 293:7
Kipling is intensely l. and hated 312:1
They have l. reading 200:14
lovely how l. it must be to write 75:4
lover I had a l.'s quarrel with the world 127:10
love-story as if you worked a l. into 44:1
loving For l., and for saying so 142:8
low man who has a l. opinion of himself 224:3
what is l. raise and support 203:7
LSD L.? Nothing much happened 66:8
PC is the L. of the 90s 244:11
luck I had the freak of l. to start high 214:10
luckiest Geniuses are the l. of mortals 95:2
lucky sometimes l. on Sundays 60:13
Lucky Jim *L.* is a remarkable novel 276:2
L. is Just William, bigger 276:3
lucubrations your agglomerated l. 4:3
lumber loads of learned l. in his head 198:14
l. room of his library 131:4
luminous his l. wings 328:5
L.! oh, I meant—voluminous 300:7
lunatic ideally, be a dedicated semi-l. 40:9
lunch he was always having l. 281:8
ruin your l. but not your dinner 208:10
luncheon read a novel before l. 160:12
lunches great, ordinary hunting l. 282:7
lurk l. outside all around us 96:8
lust l. and rage 5:10
luxuriant L. song 310:8
luxury ancient languages is mainly a l. 124:11
It is the height of l. 333:3
Literature is a l. 90:3
They knew l. 67:7
lynching l. mobs 44:7
lyre 'Omer smote 'is bloomin' l. 168:3
lyric include me among the l. poets 223:7
now it's l. verse 197:10
lyrical purely l., poetical ones 304:2
so remorseless and yet so l. 15:2
lyrics Fourteen hundred l. 304:3

Macaulay M.'s few pages of introduction 16:9
Macbeth How many children had Lady M. 47:16
Little Nell and Lady M. 319:6
machine I'm a sausage m. 290:8
I remember a m. 76:8
m.-minders of literature 152:7
truth is m.-like, error is alive 253:3
mad All poets are m. 172:3
All Rome is m. about my book 18:13
great ones are thought m. 265:7
M., bad, and dangerous to know 287:3
m. . . . proceed by punning 265:3
Poets do not go m. 110:6
sad bad glad m. brother's name 336:9
when a heroine goes m. 63:2
you will surely go m. 195:9
madding Far from the m. crowd 30:1
made She was a m. woman 296:11
Thank you, I've already m. it 318:7
madman think he is a m. 282:4
Victor Hugo was a m. 306:2
madmen m., heretics, dreamers 183:2
madness despondency and m. 172:13
m. is terrific 113:13
M. of George III 241:5
Now Ireland has her m. 229:7
rest is the m. of art 266:5
Maecenas Death is the great M. 54:9
time M. found for Horace 72:6
magazine inexhaustible m. 238:12
themselves and the m. 158:5
magazines graves of little m. 157:5
writing for the m. 68:9
maggots turmoil of a nest of m. 338:5
magic Art is not M. 8:12
keen on dragons and m. 40:11
knowledge that words are m. 232:2
m. of Shaw's words 327:14
technology is replaced by m. 85:10
We need metaphors of m. 85:11
magical m. quality in names 154:9
something m. about rhythm 212:2
magistrate that shocks the m. 77:9
magnificence m. of a Russian noble 295:11
magnifies Opium m. 65:8
maid old m. among novelists 338:9
main always hurries to the m. event 15:3
majesty Why is there not a M.'s library 131:1
make lest he should m. an end 279:2
M. IT NEW 166:9
wish I knew how to m. £200 a year 68:3
maker meet my M. brow to brow 208:5
makers doom of the M. 114:2
male as much as possible in m. hands 259:3
describes the dishabille of the m. 77:6
genius in the garret is a m. myth 260:11
kind of m. turkeycocking 276:6
sensibility of a m. adolescent 305:6
Malherbe At last came M. 315:1
What M. writes will endure forever 314:9
malice m. towards none 215:9
Much m. mingled with a little wit 46:7
Yet m. never was his aim 332:2
malicious She was a bit m., you know 341:8
malt m. does more than Milton can 65:10

OED (*cont.*)
for inspiration I read the O. 115:13
unconscious of the race is the O. 62:2
Oedipus If *Hamlet* and O. were published 19:3
offend Without the freedom to o. 36:2
offended easy not to be o. by a book 36:4
offer I would refuse this o. 189:3
offering o. of my thoughts 55:10
officers writers were o. 254:12
officials not by trustworthy o. 183:2
offspring books should be the o. 113:11
oft What o. was thought, but ne'er 256:7
oil as providers they're o. wells 216:4
consumed the midnight o. 119:12
his words were smoother than o. 261:3
Pour o. into their ears 57:5
to me it's the o. of life 178:13
old cheerful and robust in my o. age 87:8
dance attendance upon my o. age 5:10
dressing o. words new 167:9
edited for the o. lady in Dubuque 157:8
I cannot read the o. books 246:3
if it had been called *The O. Sailor* 240:6
less fond of poems about o. age 6:3
lived to be a florid o. gentleman 5:7
make me conservative when o. 183:4
new stories are born from o. 247:2
o. age, it is the last gap but one 58:5
O. age should burn and rave 53:12
o. maid among novelists 338:9
o. man dies, a library burns 120:14
o. man in a dry month 5:8
o. men from the chimney corner 168:14
perfection of the o. 287:2
Say I'm growing o., but add 287:9
violent Tory of the o. school 323:3
when one is middle-aged or o. 134:6
When you are o. and grey 5:5
worth any number of o. ladies 267:10
writer's o. age can be very strange 6:2
Old English only surviving O. epic 256:2
older As I grow o. and older 148:9
olla putrida what a clumsy *o.* 309:8
Omar diver O. plucked them 249:4
omelette What a fuss about an o. 34:2
ominous o. thing put out its head 96:2
omit o. that part of poem 146:5
omnis *Non o. moriar* 51:1
once old way, 'O. upon a time' 169:5
O. upon a time 163:6
O. upon a time and a very good time 164:13
preamble, 'O. upon a time' 39:9
one number o. book of the ages 21:11
square root of minus o. 54:13
only O. connect 143:3
To the o. begetter 55:7
oozes as a gum, which o. 111:8
open mind which keeps o. house 291:7
opening dreaded essential o. sentences 17:11
only too easy to write o. chapters 17:9
opera galleries of grand o. 279:6
kind of o. in prose 299:1
No o. plot can be sensible 170:5
operation performing a major o. 301:7
opiate use books as an o. 201:8
opinion Nobody holds a good o. 224:3
opinions minded the o. of others 224:6
not wise to solicit the o. of publishers 194:5
reject a play because of its o. 181:13
very teeth of all o. and prejudices 81:7
opium Coleridge without the o. 65:9
constable's handbook—an o.-dose 21:3
oh just, subtle, and mighty o. 65:7
O. magnifies things 65:8
o. that numbs the soul 87:5
produced by raw pork and o. 109:10
opposites must very often proceed by o. 56:11
sin and sanctity are o. only 135:5
opprobrious any of those o. terms 256:6
optical almost an o. one 3:6
optimism advocate a policy of o. 157:4
oral bard in an o. culture 69:3
orating lonely, foreign midget o. up there 82:9
oration funeral o. rather than a history 22:6
not studied as an o. 128:7
orators one of those o. of whom 231:8
Our swords shall play the o. for us 253:9
order all in silence, all in o. stand 130:10
best words in the best o. 180:2
not murder but the restoration of o. 45:2
o. of the phrases 99:8
poetry can't be written to o. 115:9
Yet each in solemn o. followed each 231:7
orderly our instinct to be o. 61:11
ordinary going about their o. business 96:2
lives quite o. people lead 291:11
made an o. one seem original 41:6
uncommon and the o. 272:2
ore 'load every rift' with o. 328:2
organ God-gifted o.-voice of England 317:3
organism like any other o. 159:7
organize o. her own immortality 341:6
original authors of o. talent 157:7
every great and o. writer 165:13
I fear I have nothing o. in me 165:14
irresistible desire for the o. 248:12
it saves o. thinking 197:6
made an ordinary one seem o. 41:6
o. is unfaithful to the translation 250:5
o. writer is not he who refrains 165:12
shockingly o. with your first novel 239:11
when once an o. line has been 166:1
originality pen or chisel to seek o. 166:4

I live by my p. as they say 235:9
long lonely scratch of his p. 112:10
man who takes up p. or chisel 166:4
No p., no ink, no table 269:9
peaceful, the pure, the victorious P. 242:5
p. accomplishes a lot more 150:5
p. and tablet clutched 282:6
p. can draw blood 188:5
p. has been in their hands 258:3
p. is mightier than the sword 186:12
p. is mightier than the wrist 97:12
p. is preferable to the sword 186:5
poet's p., all scorn 257:10
power of the p. 188:10
prevents his holding a p. 73:5
right word on the point of his p. 331:8
scratching of a p. 265:14
sight of an inkwell and of a p. 242:7
sit with book and p. 270:9
spark-gap is mightier than the p. 187:8
squat p. rests. I'll dig with it 243:12
take a p. in his hand 269:1
that man's knowledge in p.-craft 15:8
their Daemon lives in their p. 114:2
Then to my p., from whence 112:1
These stores supply the female p. 184:8
What a heavy oar the p. is 73:7
woman's p. presents you with a play 257:11
woman that attempts the p. 258:1
pencil be a writer with a p. 244:1
goes missing in Nature is a p. 243:2
only if I have a p. and I can write 244:7
p. of the Holy Ghost 20:4
writing a history of the p. 244:10
pencils inexorable sadness of p. 243:5
Pendennis Mrs P.'s treatment of Fanny 229:3
Penguin I applaud the P. Books 193:1
penis more brain or more p. 227:8
pens assortment of rotting p. 244:14
If all the p. that ever poets held 111:5
Let other p. dwell on guilt and misery 238:4
pension made his p. jingle in his pockets 308:4
wild as p. plans 179:2
people country house is full of p. 289:7
He is too many p. 24:8
Most p. ignore most poetry 178:7
P. are not ships 91:12
p. planets of its own 109:8
still a poetry of the p. in the main 141:5
peopled then the world is p. for me 239:9
peotry P. is sissy stuff 177:10
pepper Such epithets, like p. 56:6
perception doors of p. were cleansed 119:14
perfect but—a p. wife 83:15
make one's name by a p. work 204:11
pismire is equally p. 155:6
perfected woman is p. 127:12
perfection Art finds her own p. within 7:13
closer a work of art is to p. 188:3
P. of the life, or of the work 135:3
p. of the old achieving the shock 287:2
performance like giving a p. on the page 76:6
very insipid and tedious p. 331:3
performed Wilde p. his life 340:7
periodical exhalation of p. trash 140:8
periphery on the p. of things 312:6
periphrastic p. study 145:5
perish p. in a foreign tongue 249:11
perjury witness can be guilty is p. 253:1
Persian pearls of thought in P. gulfs 249:4
person I long for the P. from Porlock 114:11
p. on business from Porlock 112:6
personal believes to be interior and p. 178:4
My p. animosity against a writer 214:8
Titles are so very p., one hesitates 241:2
personality escape from p. 88:1
publication has to have a p. 158:5
she felt her own p. to be merely 296:10
perverse transform real life in some p. 108:13
perversion universal p. 255:5
pessimist call Mr Aldous Huxley a p. 306:4
petal like dropping a rose p. down 176:11
Petrarch if Laura had been P.'s wife 142:15
petrifactions p. of a plodding brain 119:15
petrol not a necessity like p. 178:13
petticoat never keep down a single p. 147:12
phantoms becomes a band of p. 17:4
Pharisee from the face of the P. 148:1
philistine little bourgeois! What a p. 338:10
philistines Though the P. may jostle 151:8
philistinism horns in the fog of p. 229:5
our yawning P. 44:5
philologists P., who chase 124:2
philology wakened by p. 334:9
philosopher Ovid, the soft p. of love 319:2
philosophic p. fanatic 328:4
philosophical something more p. 171:6
philosophy bullied into a certain p. 342:4
History is p. from examples 102:9
linguistic p., which cares only 122:10
no role to play except beyond p. 175:12
religion and p. will be replaced 175:1
should study at least enough p. 226:8
to the devil with your p. 169:6
phone call him up on the p. 201:6
never even made a p. call 245:1
photographed minor ones may be p. 38:9
photographer glibly despises the p. 230:5
p.'s eye 57:3
photographs not as handsome as his p. 277:2
phrase barbarous p. 96:12
I like that ancient Saxon p. 124:4

phrase (*cont.*)
minute a p. becomes current 42:7
p. . . . a clutch of words 43:4
p. is born into the world 42:11
summed up all systems in a p. 32:9
phrases nervous force into p. 292:6
not to believe in well-turned p. 234:13
order of the p. makes No difference 99:8
prefabricated p. 183:6
physical memorable p. characteristic 39:2
p. appetite 315:7
physicists p. sometimes think 317:7
piano playing the p. with lead balls 298:8
picked moment I p. up your book 207:9
picklocks all the p. of biographers 24:10
Pickwick P., the Owl, and the Waverley 242:5
picture both a p. and an idea 238:13
from the p. to the diagram 218:10
obliged to draw a p. of the result 92:7
One p. is worth ten thousand words 264:5
speaking p., with this end 171:11
pictures cutting all the p. out 28:2
like apples of gold in p. of silver 41:5
without p. or conversations 27:13
piece irregular indigested p. 79:3
pig as soon kill a p. as write a letter 129:2
looked from p. to man 43:13
reconstruct the p. 48:2
sort of p. in clover 281:4
pilgrimage with songs beguile your p. 175:4
Pilgrim's Progress 'P.', about a man 285:7
pill Instruction, Madam, is the p. 271:5
pillars seven p. of wisdom 30:9
pilot I hope to see my p. face to face 53:1
pimples scratching of p. 309:3
pimps Translators are like busy p. 248:12
pin I never p. up my hair with prose 179:10
more wounded by a p.-prick 299:2
pinheads only the history of p. 131:6
Pinteresque Oh, this dread word P. 320:2
pioneer P. of the bizarre 308:12
pipe he wished might be through a p. 52:8
p. a simple song for thinking hearts 238:3
p. for the hour of work 65:11
pirate he did not p. 168:8
when one's a p. at heart 266:8
pirates never about p. 39:9
pismire And the p. is equally perfect 155:6
piss Johnny Keats's p.-a-bed poetry 310:6
writes as a boar does p. 324:6
pistol like a p.-shot 182:9
[pun] is a p. let off at the ear 256:12
pit many-headed monster of the p. 62:14
pith all the p. is in the postscript 312:5
pitiable punctuation is p. 195:5
pity *Beauty plus p.*—that is the closest 9:7
by means of p. and fear 247:8
honest men do p. 39:3
p. for the poor fellow 303:1
Poetry is in the p. 254:6
place all in one p., all in one day 62:12
from out our bourne of time and p. 53:1
full stop put just at the right p. 195:2
having found a p. in poetry 314:8
namely, of Time, P., and Action 232:10
places Proper words in proper p. 234:3
plagiarism steal from one author, it's p. 168:7
plagiarist No p. can excuse the wrong 168:8
situation of the p. 168:1
plagiarize P.! Let no one else's work 168:9
plague They were not such a p. 5:10
plain made still plainer by p. cooks 236:9
plain man in his p. meaning 143:10
plainness *Iliad* itself, perfect p. of speech 21:1
plait that p. down her back 39:2
plan for want of a p., a method 258:4
uncertainty of being able to p. ahead 84:12
planet landed from another p. 290:6
When a new p. swims into his ken 304:11
plangently reiterated his message so p. 305:8
plashy through the p. fen 236:3
plastic by-products of a p. factory 118:10
plates can think of no suggestions for p. 27:15
platitude longitude with no p. 166:8
stroke a p. until it purrs 118:2
platitudes orchestration of p. 139:8
play better to have written a damned p. 63:3
Did that p. of mine send out 187:9
For what's a p. without a woman in it 62:7
House Beautiful is p. lousy 208:3
If any p. has been produced only twice 63:10
impossible to write a film p. without 2:10
know what to say about a p. 47:11
last act crowns the p. 133:3
Let a p. have five acts 62:6
never accept or reject a p. because 181:13
novelist, you're writing a p. 162:6
p., I think, ought to make sense 64:5
p.'s the thing 62:9
p. was a great success 63:5
p. was consumed in wholesome fashion 11:7
structure of a p. is always the story 170:3
what p. is to the child 90:1
which is what one does in a p. 228:3
woman's pen presents you with a p. 257:11
writing a good p. is difficult 63:13
Writing is *p.* 274:1
Your p.'s hard to act 63:6
play-bills no time to read p. 63:1
players perhaps twenty p. 38:1
playful cruel p. mind 309:4
playrooms by temporary custom p. 80:5
plays did one of my p. at A-level 220:6

poets (*cont.*)
at first for wits, then p. passed 49:7
but why don't p. tell 239:1
Good p. have a weakness for bad puns 98:6
greatest p. need something to cling to 297:8
he the worst of p. ranks 288:6
Horses and p. should be fed 92:10
Immature p. imitate; mature p. steal 168:5
impossible to hold the p. back 254:10
Irish p., learn your trade 239:5
I used to think all p. were Byronic 179:2
list of available p. 225:7
may be termed the metaphysical p. 151:1
most indigestible p. 304:2
most masculine of our p. 296:1
most p. Are their own patients 178:2
none but pikes and p. prey 213:10
Painters and p. alike 33:5
please the touchy breed of p. 213:2
P. are the policemen of language 263:2
P. are the unacknowledged 173:13
P. arguing about modern poetry 214:7
P. belong to the language 250:6
p. bicycle-pump the human heart 143:5
P. do not go mad; but chess-players 110:6
P.' food is love and fame 173:11
P. have got to enjoy themselves 92:1
P. in our civilization 175:5
p. only deliver a golden 155:3
P. or artists are sometimes married 115:5
P. that lasting marble seek 123:13
p. themselves could not write 24:1
P. . . . though liars by profession 89:11
poor in novelists but rich in p. 141:12
put up with p. being second-rate 96:10
room for p. in this world 174:11
something similar in us p. 113:3
Souls of p. dead and gone 65:3
strongest slang of all is the slang of p. 99:7
Strong p. make . . . history 166:12
struggling p. drink Camp coffee 66:1
Tenderest of Roman p. 288:7
To judge of p. is only the faculty 46:3
very Janus of p. 325:9
way p. were neglected 69:6
We p. in our youth begin 172:13
We p. keep our mouths shut 254:8
We p. of the proud old lineage 175:4
what would be theft in other p. 308:9
When amatory p. sing their loves 143:1
Which only p. know 73:2
While pensive p. painful vigils keep 72:8
who wants p. at all in lean years 67:8
Your praise for p. in the grave 51:2
poignant Be p., man, be poignant 88:3
point There is no p. to life 136:2
points Cut out all these exclamation p. 195:4
poise full of p. 297:2
poison only a cover for p. 93:1
poisoning I felt like p. a monk 115:11
p. of Bovary made me throw up 87:6
poked fire that has been p. 210:2
poker p. of whom everyone is afraid 278:2
pokers iron p. into true-love knots 295:1
polar p. star of poetry 172:15
poles literary work has two p. 136:9
police encourage among p. officers 201:10
policeman third rate village p. 333:4
policemen Poets are the p. of language 263:2
Polish P. nobleman, cased in British tar 292:5
political I believe that p. correctness 36:5
P. history is far too criminal 40:8
P. language . . . is designed 183:7
p. poem that's accomplished 188:8
slightest economic or p. importance 179:4
politically as a poet exerts himself p. 182:10
politician Journalist is to p. as dog is 118:9
politicians Top p. 14:6
politics p. and poetry have in common 183:13
P. in the middle of things 182:9
pome while I pen a p. 61:6
pom-pom p. girl of American letters 341:3
pomposity p. and intricacy of style 321:8
pooh 'p.-poohing' something 262:14
poor All the Protestants were p. 310:1
poorer sympathy with the p. classes 294:1
pop make them p. like chestnuts 187:2
Pope poetry of Dryden, P. 175:2
P. composes with his eye on style 249:1
P. took money 267:4
popes quarrels of p. and kings 103:11
popular If they have a p. thought 158:1
p. imagination that is fiery 113:8
should so much have loved to be p. 11:2
popularity source of my p. 89:5
popularize attempt to p. art 204:7
pork produced by raw p. and opium 109:10
Porlock by a person on business from P. 112:6
I long for the Person from P. 114:11
received the Person from P. 270:1
pornography P. is rather like trying 78:7
P. is the attempt to insult sex 78:2
sex is a substitute for p. 78:12
war stories, the p. of war 255:5
What p. is really about 78:5
widespread taste for p. 78:6
porpentine Like quills upon the fretful p. 105:5
Porson Wordsworth drunk and P. sober 65:12
port just as grocer's p. is preferable 236:11
liquor for boys; p., for men 64:12
p. from which I set out 149:7

said *(cont.)*
Everything has been s. 245:6
Everything I've ever s. 319:8
he would like to have s. 119:8
How I wish I had s. that 196:13
knew nobody had s. it before 196:16
not been s. before 165:9
said at all can be s. clearly 122:5
s. our remarks before us 195:12
Whatever is well s. by another 167:5
sailor Home is the s., home from sea 331:5
saintliness sort of inner s. 338:1
Saintsbury principal thrill of reading S. 50:3
sake never to write for the s. of writing 112:7
salary receipts for your s. 130:11
salesmen little s. can fondle her breasts 125:3
Salieri S. of letters 292:13
sally loose s. of the mind 79:3
salt all that is s. in the mouth 332:8
little grain of s. 116:10
sugar of literature and adverbs the s. 100:2
salute I s. thee, Mantovano 337:6
salvation Outside prose, no s. 180:9
Sam think of me as 'S.' 155:2
sampler as a girl shows her s. 42:5
sands Footprints on the s. of time 22:9
sandstorms gyrating s. 295:8
sandwich-board s. man 319:5
Sangreal endeth the story of the S. 15:5
sanity He was s. raised to the power 289:11
sap dried the s. out of my veins 74:4
Sappho Where burning S. loved 323:6
sashes Prizes are like s. 190:13
sat when they have s. down 231:8
Satanic Verses book entitled *The S.* 35:14
satin she always goes into white s. 63:2
satire let s. be my song 192:1
S. is a sort of glass 256:8
S. is dependent on strong beliefs 257:7
S. is simply humour in uniform 257:8
s. out of time 112:3
s., when you make fun 257:5
Verse s. indeed is entirely our own 140:6
satirical certain sign of a s. wit 230:10
s. benevolence towards manners 278:10
satirist between the s. and the romantic 338:2
I shouldn't call myself a s. 257:6
Reality goes bounding past the s. 257:2
satisfaction there's s. then in toil 72:6
with a degree of s. 271:7
Saturn golden days of S.'s reign 237:3
sauce like cold white s. 338:9
sausage hold on s. and haddock 93:5
I'm a s. machine 290:8
sausages start with a string of s. 48:2
saving It [poetry] is capable of s. us 176:2
Saxon I like that ancient S. phrase 124:4
say because you've got something to s. 149:1
Have something to s. 235:
he has nothing to s. 327:1
I had a great deal of s. 3:
know what I think till I see what I s. 145:
manage to s. what we meant 123:
not know what they are going to s. 231:
one must have something to s. 180:
one would s. to the same person 128:1
she'd s. the most dreadful things 341:
something to s. that you think 150:
Then you should s. what you mean 144:
There's not much to s. 291:1
what a poet does not s. is as important 145:
writer who has nothing to s. 235:
saying For loving, and for s. so 142:
never finished s. what it has to say 246:1
standing on a platform s. things 63:1
sayings s. are like women's letters 312:
says not what he s. 97:1
scale puts his thumb in the s. 148:
scarlet His sins were s. 205.
scatterbrained often s. 327:1
scene by s.-painting 314:
every day Speaks a new s. 133:
I can't rewrite a s. 211:
scenery spoke of s. 56:
scepticism S. the tonic of minds 252:
Scheherazade line of Aesop and S. 153:
schmucks S. with Underwoods 2:
scholar But I'm such a bad s. 120:1
Christian and a s.—but a brute 308:
learns more from a good s. in a rage 219:1
mark what ills the s.'s life assail 217:1
s. all Earth's volumes carry 217:
s. among rakes 330:
Why is it that the s. is the only 220:1
scholars S. manage to evade 220:
well-meaning s. tend to repeat 253:
scholarship combines s. and art 104:1
school few s. stories in foreign languages 40:
very good at English at s. 291:1
schoolboy I see a s. when I think of him 310:
schoolboys to delight s. 231:
School for Scandal to have seen the *S.* 5:
schoolman knew no s.'s subtle art 142:1
schoolmaster s. friend reads it 195
schoolmasters Let s. puzzle their brain 64:1
schools at all the s. I attended 195.
hundred s. of thought 183
science Art is myself; s. is ourselves 220.
cold-blooded demon called S. 95:
Enough of s. and of art 218.
fatal process of applied s. 222:
In s., read, by preference, the newest 220
labours of the men of s. 220:
Language is more fashion than s. 101:

short (*cont.*)
S. dictionaries should be improved 62:4
solitary, poor, nasty, brutish, and s. 133:4
take a long while to make it s. 209:9
shorter had the time to make it s. 209:4
shortlist getting on to the s. 191:3
short stories compact as all s. ought 181:12
short story I'm a s. writer 335:3
key to a s. is tension 228:5
s. is an Impressionist 228:4
s. tells us only one thing 228:8
shot Certain men the English s. 187:9
deliberately stand up and be s. at 207:3
he once s. a bookseller 192:2
Hungarian writers had been s. 183:12
novels that began with 'A s. rang out' 46:1
shoulder someone looking over my s. 211:1
shoures Aprill with his s. soote 163:5
show How can I s. him 71:7
I'm going to s. them 225:3
showing without s. off 208:6
shrapnel picking s. out of your head 190:6
shrew Journalism's a s. and scold 118:4
shrimp I shall be but a s. of an author 302:4
shrined bower we s. to Tennyson 82:5
shuffle All s. there 219:2
shut sound of books slapping s. 18:2
You just have to s. it 36:4
shyness without s. 236:1
Sicilian S. storytellers 233:8
sick like emerging from a s. room 298:2
sickness romantic s. 151:4
sighs S. are the natural language 121:5
sight make the not-seen accessible to s. 136:5
signature one's style is one's s. always 235:4
significant Art is s. deformity 8:10
choose words that are, first, s. 43:1
signified signifier and the s. 121:16
signifier s. and the signified 121:16
signs pages of s. 123:4
silence bound the common of s. 57:11
idea of pronouncing the word 's.' 259:11
left a stain upon the s. 280:3
Lo! all in s., all in order stand 130:10
[Macaulay] has occasional flashes of s. 314:4
offspring of darkness and s. 113:11
on the other side of s. 134:3
private s. in which we live 289:10
S. is deep as Eternity 121:11
small change of s. 121:14
two minutes' s. 320:1
who shall s. all the airs 33:9
silencer as good an all-round s. 330:3
silent S. as the sleeve-worn stone 175:13
S., upon a peak in Darien 304:11
thereof one must be s. 122:5
silk he was shot s. 279:3
s., too often hides eczema 236:10
silly He wrote some s. poems 298:1
You were s. like us 343:8
silver apples of gold in pictures of s. 41:5
Just for a handful of s. he left us 342:7
similes exaggerated s. 92:5
Frank Wilstach's book of s. 61:5
similitude dissimilitude in s. 147:11
simple cannot be too *clear*, too s. 234:8
rarely pure, and never s. 252:5
simplest s. and most natural one 234:1
simplicity Cultivate s., Coleridge 290:11
not crude verbosity, but holy s. 41:7
simplify frittered away by detail . . . S. 134:1
simply say it as s. as possible 234:6
sin Excepting Original S. 165:14
My s., my soul 165:3
Would you like to s. 301:3
sincerely s. from the author's soul 97:16
sincerity proof of their s. 228:11
Sometimes even s. should be edited 71:13
sinecure gives no man a s. 68:4
sinew s. of the English language 296:1
sing s. to find your hearts 175:4
S. whatever is well made 239:5
singer Lulled by the s. of an empty day 187:5
S. of sweet Colonus 329:6
single devoted year after year to s. lines 73:8
If you are a s. father, it's lucky 84:11
s. completed action 62:12
s. man in possession 163:12
singular Oh Richardson! thou s. genius 322:6
write out some very s. books 5:11
singularity not by s. 173:4
sinkholes clear water over granite, no s. 43:5
sins His s. were scarlet 205:8
sirens Blest pair of S. 172:4
sissy Peotry is s. stuff that rhymes 177:10
sister Fiction is Truth's elder s. 90:7
sisters Sphere-born harmonious s. 172:4
sit I now s. down on my botom 128:11
I s. down for eight hours 269:8
never get a chance to s. down 327:2
six When I was six he was s. 6:1
sixpence appeal at s. to the masses 185:7
sixty past S. it's the young 5:14
s. for the last 25 years 312:10
skeletons 'sure fire' literary s. 336:5
skies like some watcher of the s. 304:11
skiing technique of s. 48:12
skilled S. or unskilled, we all scribble 171:8
skin locked within a piece of s. 26:10
my s. bristles 88:7
saw the skull beneath the s. 53:4
s. of an innocent lamb 241:8

skip Let's s. sex 227:6
S. when my book becomes obscene 77:1
skull major operation on my own s. 301:7
saw the s. beneath the skin 53:4
slag body like a s. heap 290:6
slang All s. is metaphor 91:11
Correct English is the s. of prigs 99:7
S. is a language that rolls up its 122:11
S. is, at least, vigorous 264:2
slashing your damned cutting and s. 70:3
slate write his thoughts upon a s. 174:6
slave I am a galley s. to pen and ink 73:4
slavish O imitators, you s. herd 167:4
sleep old and grey and full of s. 5:5
sleepers s. in that quiet earth 43:9
sleepless S. themselves 72:8
sleeps Homer sometimes s. 342:6
sleeves language that rolls up its s. 122:11
slip Under the tension, s., slide, perish 264:9
slipper Channel is a s. bath of irony 141:13
slippers *OED* in carpet s. 277:13
slips *two* rejection s. 202:12
sloth If I were to paint S. 225:8
overcome by my own amazing s. 269:14
slovenly His mind was of a s. character 295:11
slower practice only make *me* write s. 73:16
slum swear-word in a rustic s. 263:9
sluttish s. magnificence 295:11
small lot of them were s. 304:3
Thou hadst s. Latin, and less Greek 325:4
too s. for his boots 50:6
small-clothes like s. 128:13
smaller s. fleas that on him prey 167:11
smallest about the s. in the world 280:6
Boswell was one of the s. men 22:8
I am sitting in the s. room 207:7
small-talk Town s. 57:10
small-talking Where in this s. world 166:8
smart as lief pray with Kit S. 329:2
s. for so moving a book 241:1
smile rare occasions for a s. 61:3
s. of accomplishment 127:12
There *Dryden* sits with modest s. 296:3
vain tribute of a s. 224:2
smilest Thou s. and art still 326:8
smoke watching people s. in old films 78:10
words curling like rings of s. 264:7
smokers drinkers and s. 66:10
Smollett Fielding and S. 153:5
smoother his words were s. than oil 261:3
smut S. detected in it 77:5
snail like the s. in the problem 209:12
snake conceals his s.-in-the-grass 158:12
like a wounded s. 211:10
snakes no s. to be met with 238:2
snakeskin s.-titles of mining-claims 154:2
sneaky have a little, snouty, s. mind 59:6
sneer cultivated to perfection the s. 313:10
sneeze like having a good s. 312:11
sneezed L. 400 a-year is not to be s. at 189:3
sniffs s. I get from the ink 259:6
snobbery born in response to s. 160:13
school of S. with Violence 44:8
snobs effete corps of impudent s. 120:11
Nearly all bookish people are s. 19:4
snow like footprints left in the s. 171:2
they have no word for s. 264:14
snowdrifts S. of Wordsworth 343:2
snuffed let itself be s. out 206:9
sober I thought it might s. me up 131:11
much too s. to be a champ 288:9
seen Wordsworth drunk and Porson s. 65:12
social Art has its roots in s. realities 9:6
first s. regenerator of the day 228:12
I'm not a s. punster 257:9
quality of his s. admirations 321:7
s., political, or personal moral values 230:6
socialist called s. realism 153:1
flourishing s. culture 183:8
S., an Atheist and a Vegetarian 328:6
socially often s. impressive 197:13
society economic basis of s. 278:7
midwife to s. 8:11
no importance whatever to s. 11:11
novel reflects s. 230:2
product of our s. 268:3
sock If Jonson's learnèd s. be on 62:10
Socrates Christ nor Buddha nor S. 272:6
sodomy artists who spend on s. 239:4
soft Ovid, the s. philosopher of love 319:2
s. as the dawn 216:3
soil cannot grow from a neglected s. 247:1
mind is a very thin s. 315:4
when you idealize the s. 155:11
sold book which somehow s. well 19:10
every copy of *Sense and Sensibility* is s. 67:6
soldier s. details his wounds 237:5
soldiers With twenty-six lead s. 242:4
solemn confounded with a s. writer 266:12
solicitor one's agent, and one's s. 69:4
solid all that is s. has melted 91:3
soliloquy indulge in eloquent s. 313:5
solitariness of an infinite s. 47:7
solitude by the resonance of his s. 88:12
enables us to endure our own s. 289:10
Solomon felicities of S. 20:4
solutions inevitable, s. are not 222:9
solved not a single problem is s. 272:3
solvency S. was my only aim 68:6
something you've got s. to say 149:11
song let satire be my s. 192:1
Luxuriant s. 310:8
needless Alexandrine ends the s. 211:10

song (*cont.*)
poetry is ultimately allied to s. 212:14
s. is considered a perfect gem 144:9
s. would come in the right rhythms 211:3
spur me into s. 5:10
Unlike my subject will I frame my s. 256:9
What! all this for a s. 146:6
What s. the Syrens sang 217:7
what they teach in s. 173:5
Whenever I remake a s. 209:14
songs harsh after the s. of Apollo 261:8
I sing s. never heard before 223:8
with s. beguile your pilgrimage 175:4
sonnet Scorn not the S. 174:1
s. is a moment's monument 174:14
true s. goes eight lines 177:11
write a good iambic pentameter s. 181:4
sonneter I shall turn s. 111:6
sonnets He would have written s. 142:15
write ten passably effective s. 97:13
sons God's s. are things 262:5
soothing Irish for s. and quieting 124:13
sorbet like some tart lemon s. 336:8
sorriness show the s. underlying 238:10
sorrow And so beguile thy s. 130:4
paying interest and fines on s. 229:5
powers of exciting laughter and s. 326:1
soul accomplishes more than his s. 150:5
body and the s. 144:1
conceived and composed in the s. 175:2
engineers of the s. 183:3
feed his s. on such raw material 303:1
furnished with a Russian s. 313:11
half conceal the S. within 262:9
Half my own s. 337:2
largest and most comprehensive s. 325:8
Lord take my s. 128:1
Memorial from the S.'s eternity 174:14
opium that numbs the s. 87:5
poet with the private s. leaking out 339:9
purest essence of a human s. 27:8
relates the adventures of his s. 50:1
Russian literature saved my s. 230:3
s. of Rabelais 332:5
S. of the Age 325:1
stuff of the s. 295:8
tender, unique, and coruscating s. 295:6
terrible venture of a man's s. 129:4
they are the life, the s. of reading 169:3
To wake the s. by tender strokes of art 62:13
When the s. of a man is born 229:4
souls more than kisses, letters mingle s. 128:5
S. of poets dead and gone 65:3
s. (or characters) are conglomerates 37:4
sound s. and the fury 30:10
s. must seem an echo to the sense 41:11
s. of the living voice 125:4
thought is the front and s. the back 122:3
soundbite wants to say—unlike a s. 197:15
sounds become mere s. 155:1
having similar s. at their ends 212:13
s. will take care of themselves 121:15
soup learnt to consume like s. 178:5
like a cake of portable s. 58:10
must be satisfied with the s. 79:9
sovereign That s. of insufferables 340:2
spade I call a s. a spade 41:8
spades shows us the ace of s. face up 290:9
Spain Go to S. and get killed 255:1
Spanish I must learn S. 124:5
spark Gie me ae s. o' Nature's fire 218:1
s. of inextinguishable thought 262:8
spark-gap s. is mightier than the pen 187:8
sparkle S. for ever 218:5
Spartans learn to take like S. 203:4
speak And did you s. to him again 81:12
If I am to s. for ten minutes 231:9
s. as the common people do 271:1
s. before you think 48:5
s. ill of everybody except oneself 13:6
S. the speech, I pray you 231:3
to speak, and to s. well 231:4
whereof one cannot s. 122:5
speaking s. picture, with this end 171:11
speaks If she s. of a chair 317:9
specialized s. entertainment 202:4
species belongs to the s. 15:1
not an individual, but a s. 238:1
not the individual, but the s. 56:3
spectacles he needed not the s. of books 325:8
of the bald with s. type 335:8
speculations Not wrung from s. 165:11
speech aspersion upon my parts of s. 99:5
extensive transcripts of real-life s. 58:7
history of human s. 61:1
Human s. is like a cracked kettle 121:13
Iliad itself, perfect plainness of s. 21:1
imitates not life but s. 169:8
in forme of s. is chaunge 123:10
making an after-dinner s. 197:10
manner of his s. 233:13
our concern was s. 122:7
rule of s. 99:1
so close to modern educated s. 306:9
so true as his s. 57:6
Speak the s., I pray you 231:3
s. attempted 129:7
s. created thought 121:8
s. is shallow as Time 121:11
S. is the small change 121:14
stately s. 231:7

untrue man who's u. to his wife 120:7
Myth does not mean something u. 80:8
untrustworthy publishers are u. 192:5
unusual things u. to things eternal 169:9
upright that is, u. 267:7
upstairs u. backwards on crutches 319:9
urban u. poetry of modern life 308:12
urge procreant u. of the world 113:1
Uriah This U. Heep of historical writing 285:5
urinal mistake the drawer for a u. 222:7
urn storied u. or animated bust 51:10
urs those dreadful *u.* 230:11
Uruguay how big she is in U. 278:11
usage will drop out, if u. so choose 99:1
use We must u. words as they are used 43:3
useful u. like Latin or Greek 125:9
useless u. and need not be preserved 203:5
user I'm a freak u. of words, not a poet 334:2
usual complete appreciation of the u. 335:7
utopia we'd have a u. in this country 229:12

vacancy another v. very soon 190:1
vacuum English is the great v. cleaner 126:10
'Waiting for Godot' is a dramatic v. 280:2
vaginas Who says v. can't have teeth 260:1
vague *vago* (v.) also means 'lovely' 126:4
vagueness v. and ennui 268:7
vain Fame often makes a writer v. 82:11
Most people are v. 225:5
valium We're better than v. 216:6
valleys lost v. of the imagination 251:3
value destroys the v. of the book 226:5
dies unsure of one's own v. 52:10
Its v. depends on what is there 145:4
values as moneys are for v. 261:10
of more importance than v. 120:12
our newspapers have high moral v. 158:2
social, political, or personal moral v. 230:6
v. I would like passed on 140:3
vanity v. of human hopes 130:7
vapour v. rather than a jewel 292:8
vase Sèvres v. 329:9
vegetarian Atheist and a V. 328:6
veil She is a v., rather than a mirror 7:13
velvet hand of steel in a v. glove 319:6
Valiant in v., light in ragged luck 331:6
veracity he heard and saw with v. 271:9
verb first tense of the v. 'aimer' 226:9
v. chasing its own tail 101:7
vile new v. 262:14
Waiting for the German v. 125:10
word is the V., and the Verb is God 203:10
verbal v. art like poetry is reflective 177:8
verbiage torrent of v. 252:4
verboojuice Sesquippledan v. 263:7
verbosity not crude v. 41:7
verbs v.: they're the proudest 262:12
verify v. your references, sir 218:7
vers *sentir dans les v. une juste cadence* 315:1
verse all that is not v. is prose 179:8
as soon write free v. 212:10
blank v. has suffered not only arrest 317:6
denied the faculty of v. 288:2
Doctors in v. 178:2
Every educated man should write v. 268:2
false hair become a v. 251:7
Free v. is allied to conversation 212:14
give up v., my boy 68:4
have all in all for prose and v. 328:7
hoarse, rough v. 211:9
I court others in v. 142:11
indignation makes me write v. 149:3
I wasn't pleased with Browning's v. 207:5
learn from them the art of his v. 23:5
Let the v. the subject fit 211:11
Not v. now, only prose 180:7
No v. can give pleasure for long 64:6
Only with those in v., Mr Witwoud 179:10
Prose is for ideas, v. for visions 180:10
prose is v., and v. is merely prose 342:1
Regular v. is, so to speak, portable 212:11
run them into v. 112:2
Sappho! could not v. immortal save 323:5
scarcely written a single v. 180:11
sisters, Voice, and V. 172:4
tempt me from this craft of v. 269:10
This be the v. you grave for me 331:5
this unpolished rugged v. I chose 179:9
twentieth century English v. 152:11
v. may find him, who a sermon flies 203:6
Who died to make v. free 157:5
why writing v. should terminate 66:7
work to construct a single v. 210:3
verses can still make v. and rhymes 180:4
One day I will write v. about him 85:4
poverty drove me to writing v. 66:13
rhyme the rudder is of v. 211:5
Tear him for his bad v. 46:2
version v. of his own poem 71:9
versions more v. you see 210:11
vespers barefoot friars were singing v. 112:5
vex V. not thou the poet's mind 174:1
vexes other v. it 173:10
vice Art is v. 8:
He lashed the v., but spared the name 332:
most hopeless form of intellectual v. 256:1
Reading, that unpunished v. 200:
vices he may keep v. out of sight 22:
he redeemed his v. with his virtues 325:
paint the v. and follies 107:
vicious We didn't know what v. was 184:
victim poet, is a v.: a man given over 114:

walk (*cont.*)
no possibility of taking a w. that day 164:1
when people don't w. out of my plays 318:6
walked As I w. through the wilderness 163:11
walking close relatives of the w. dead 132:9
Poetry is to prose as dancing is to w. 181:5
prevent him from w. 174:12
walks Gibbon levelled w. 300:8
wall beat upon the w. 281:10
Chinese W. of Milton 317:6
waning dream a little in my w. days 5:6
wanted she w. nothing but death 52:2
war As soon as w. is declared 254:10
because it deals with w. 239:3
book that made this great w. 187:4
cudgel of the people's w. was lifted 254:2
dogs of w. 29:8
Forth from the w. emerging 238:8
gone wrong since the W. 265:1
In a time of w. 117:4
like w. and fornication 251:2
Minstrel Boy to the w. is gone 254:1
My subject is W., and the pity of War 254:6
no interest in a w. that drags on 255:2
poems written in the Great W. 254:12
quickened to full life by w. 334:9
real w. will never get in the books 254:3
think of his poetry as a great w. 277:4
under the shadow of a w. 254:9
w. has used up words 263:10
W. is capitalism with the gloves off 255:7
W. is the universal perversion 255:5
'w.' poet is not one who chooses 255:8
w. wasn't fought that way 255:4
When w. is declared 253:10
warbler ev'ry w. has his tune by heart 320:11
wardrobe w. lady and the tea boy 2:11
warlord concubine of a w. general 165:7
warmth what *he* wanted was more w. 301:4
warn All a poet can do today is w. 254:5
wartime this w. atmosphere 90:6
wash w. literature off ourselves 106:11
washing line to hang the w. on 170:6
wastebasket good stuff into the w. 98:8
waste-paper in the w. basket 210:1
'Recessional' into the w. basket 311:5
w. basket is the writer's best friend 210:12
watch much easier to w. something 202:5
w. my characters crossing the room 38:2
watcher felt I like some w. of the skies 304:11
posted presence of the w. 90:5
watches Dictionaries are like w. 60:5
water In diction clear as w. 253:6
My books are w. 185:6
name was writ in w. 127:1
when you've got all the w. out of them 33:2
written by drinkers of w. 64:6
watered w. our houses in Helicon 172:2
Watergate W. tapes 58:7
Waterloo On W.'s ensanguined plain 324:4
waters why his w. never run dry 234:10
wide w. of expression 292:7
waterspouts w. which hiss and boil 295:8
Waugh Evelyn W.'s to the highly born 315:7
W., who made such fun 6:2
wave grasped w. functions 221:9
Waverley do not mean to like *W.* 324:3
Pickwick, the Owl, and the W. pen 242:5
wax night-light, suffocated in its own w. 54:5
way Let Shakespeare do it his w. 215:4
That was a w. of putting it 145:5
ways justify the w. of God to men 203:7
vindicate the w. of God to man 271:4
we right to use the editorial 'w.' 99:13
weak Conclusions are the w. point 16:7
I have a w. voice 58:1
Where is human nature so w. 226:1
wealth Mere w., I am above it 83:4
weapon art is not a w. 183:10
only honourable w. 257:3
weapons books are w. 187:10
wearied flesh, alas, is w. 200:1
weariness w. of the flesh 216:8
wears Comedy naturally w. itself out 107:8
weasel If you use a 'w. word' 263:11
w. under the cocktail cabinet 319:10
weather has her madness and her w. 229:7
he is also part of the w. 177:6
w.-beaten old military man 298:9
web cool w. of language 122:6
fiction is like a spider's w. 90:8
w., then, or the pattern 235:2
Webster W. in modern idiom 224:8
W. was much possessed by death 53:4
wedding-cake My face looks like a w. 277:9
weed Call it but a w. 10:2
weeds bred among the w. and tares 165:1
garden with pedantic w. O'erspread 294:1
week need a w. for preparation 231:
weep W. not for little Léonie 219:
weighs it w. sixty pounds 206:1
weird women were w. 321:
well as w. as can be expected 73:
because I want to do something w. 269:1
Faith, that's as w. said, as if 224:
totally pessimistic, but so w. done 98:1
Wells W. and I, contemplating 280:
W., George Bernard Shaw 152:
W. thought that the creative urge 227:1
well-spent almost as rare as a w. one 22:1
well-turned w. phrases 234:1
well-written w. Life is almost as rare 22:1
Welsh W. language has survived 126:

Every educated man should w. verse 268:2
firm restraint with which they w. 235:10
how lovely it must be to w. 75:4
how to think—worse! how to w. 74:1
I don't see how to w. them better 209:10
I don't write books; I w. writers 72:3
I just don't w. badly very often 3:4
I like to w. when I feel spiteful 312:11
I love to w. to the moment 265:9
It is very difficult to w. 75:7
I w. like a distinguished author 318:3
I w. of melancholy, by being busy 86:7
journalism is people who can't w. 119:3
Learn to w. well, or not to write 271:3
look in thy heart and w. 268:12
make *me* w. slower and slower 73:16
man may w. at any time 72:9
maybe one couldn't w. any more 227:10
men had ceased to w. for students 151:6
Men like women who w. 260:6
much more easy to w. on money 146:7
much more important to w. 83:5
my need to w. 69:9
never to w. for the sake of writing 112:7
Nobody can w. the life of a man 22:4
not enough for me to w. 142:6
Nothing we w., if we hope 98:14
Novelists do not w. as birds sing 75:8
Only a great man can w. it 104:5
only w. when one has 234:6
people that read, people that w. 106:6
People who w. obscurely 221:8
people w. because they are not living 274:9
rough and ready man who w. apace 119:17
see His brother w. as well as he 213:8
shame to women so to w. 185:1
spent in reading, in order to w. 271:10
such as cannot w., translate 248:7
There is nothing to w. about, you say 128:3
They who w. ill 46:6
They w. about it 143:6
those who cannot w. 265:8
Though an angel should w. 242:2
To make me w. too much 4:12
to teach other people to w. 98:7
To w.: that is to sit in judgement 55:11
tried to w. straight from my own heart 19:2
unless he w. it for himself first 39:10
want to read a novel, I w. one 159:2
What we w. pleases us 149:6
When men w. for profit 67:4
when people w. every other day 129:6
with sex so much harder to w. about 78:9
w. as though I had a million dollars 69:8
w. because you've got something 149:11
w. for the fire as well as for the press 209:2
W. to amuse 150:7
W. what will sell 225:10
w., who had any thing better 265:10
You don't w. to support yourself 68:12
you have to w. very, very badly 3:1

writer anything worse for a w. 206:2
asked how he became a w. 149:13
basket is the w.'s best friend 210:12
be a reader or a w. 273:12
be a woman and a w. 259:7
being a w. here means nothing 190:8
best answer I got was from a w. 137:4
best fame is a w.'s fame 83:9
Beware the w. who puts forward 182:7
could be a w. with a pencil 244:1
dangerous in a critic than in a w. 98:10
essential gift for a good w. 268:1
every great and original w. 165:13
Everything is useful to a w. 267:6
far more damaging to a w. 101:2
good w. knows how to listen 98:12
good w. often finds 234:1
gratifying to be a w. 334:11
great w. creates a world of his own 98:1
hand in hand with being a w. 66:6
hell of a profession to be a w. 149:8
How can I help this w. to say it better 71:7
I am grown up, they call me a w. 268:6
identify a woman w. by her style 259:8
if a w. needs a dictionary 61:8
If you're a w., a real writer 170:10
incinerator is a w.'s best friend 210:7
in my capacity as w. 193:1
kind of w. that people think 318:4
life of the modern hardback w. 83:8
loose, plain, rude w. 41:8
lucky you're a w. 84:11
master? The w. or the reader 199:7
more interested in the w. 26:2
most significant thing a w. does 26:5
My personal animosity against a w. 214:8
No tears in the w. 88:8
No w. is really part of a group 153:3
only function of a w. 98:3
only kind of power a w. is entitled to 274:4
original w. is not he who refrains 165:12
people who suffer from w.'s block 270:7
read twenty or thirty pages by a w. 18:9
reviewer then tells the w. 208:8
serious w. is not to be confounded 266:12
spent years as a professional w. 208:11
still want to be a w. 267:4
three reasons for becoming a w. 150:1
Until you understand a w.'s ignorance 10:3
what one w. can make in the solitude 245:2
whether the w. of it be a black 199:1
w., in the eyes of many film producers 2:11
w. is unfair to himself 210:8

Oxford
Paperback
Reference

OXFORD PAPERBACK REFERENCE

From *Art and Artists* to *Zoology*, the Oxford Paperback Reference series offers the very best subject reference books at the most affordable prices.

Authoritative, accessible, and up to date, the series features dictionaries in key student areas, as well as a range of fascinating books for a general readership. Included are such well-established titles as Fowler's *Modern English Usage*, Margaret Drabble's *Concise Companion to English Literature*, and the bestselling science and medical dictionaries.

The series has now been relaunched in handsome new covers. Highlights include new editions of some of the most popular titles, as well as brand new paperback reference books on *Politics*, *Philosophy*, and *Twentieth-Century Poetry*.

With new titles being constantly added, and existing titles regularly updated, Oxford Paperback Reference is unrivalled in its breadth of coverage and expansive publishing programme. New dictionaries of *Film*, *Economics*, *Linguistics*, *Architecture*, *Archaeology*, *Astronomy*, and *The Bible* are just a few of those coming in the future.

Oxford
Paperback
Reference

THE CONCISE OXFORD COMPANION TO ENGLISH LITERATURE

Edited by Margaret Drabble and Jenny Stringer

Derived from the acclaimed *Oxford Companion to English Literature*, the concise maintains the wide coverage of its parent volume. It is an indispensable, compact guide to all aspects of English literature. For this revised edition, existing entries have been fully updated and revised with 60 new entries added on contemporary writers.

- **Over 5,000 entries on the lives and works of authors, poets and playwrights**
- **The most comprehensive and authoritative paperback guide to English literature**
- **New entries include Peter Ackroyd, Martin Amis, Toni Morrison, and Jeanette Winterson**
- **New appendices list major literary prize-winners**

From the reviews of its parent volume:

'It earns its place at the head of the best sellers: every home should have one'
Sunday Times

WORLD'S CLASSICS SHAKESPEARE

'not simply a better text but a new conception of Shakespeare. This is a major achievement of twentieth-century scholarship.' Times Literary Supplement

Hamlet
Macbeth
The Merchant of Venice
As You Like It
Henry IV Part I
Henry V
Measure for Measure
The Tempest
Much Ado About Nothing
All's Well that Ends Well
Love's Labours Lost
The Merry Wives of Windsor
The Taming of the Shrew
Titus Andronicus
Troilus & Cressida
The Two Noble Kinsmen
King John
Julius Caesar
Coriolanus
Anthony & Cleopatra